P9-BTM-300

POLICY ANALYSIS IN CANADA
THE STATE OF THE ART

The growth of what some academics refer to as 'the policy analysis movement' represents an effort to reform certain aspects of government behaviour. The policy analysis movement is the result of efforts made by actors inside and outside formal political decision-making processes to improve policy outcomes by applying systematic evaluative rationality to the development and implementation of policy options. This volume offers a comprehensive overview of the ways in which policy analysis has been conducted and to what effect by Canadian governments and – for the first time – by business associations, labour unions, universities, and other non-governmental organizations.

Editors Laurent Dobuzinskis, Michael Howlett, and David Laycock have brought together a wide range of contributors to address important questions: What do policy analysts do? What techniques and approaches do they use? What is their influence on policy-making in Canada? Is there a policy analysis deficit? What norms and values guide the work done by policy analysts working in different institutional settings? Contributors focus on the sociology of policy analysis, demonstrating how analysts working in different organizations tend to have different interests and utilize different techniques. They compare and analyse the significance of these different styles and approaches and speculate about their impact on the policy process.

LAURENT DOBUZINSKIS is an associate professor in the Department of Political Science at Simon Fraser University.

MICHAEL HOWLETT is a professor in the Department of Political Science at Simon Fraser University.

DAVID LAYCOCK is a professor and chair of the Department of Political Science at Simon Fraser University.

IPAC **IAPC**
The Institute of
Public Administration of Canada

L'Institut d'administration
publique du Canada

**The Institute of Public Administration of Canada series
in Public Management and Governance**

Editor: Donald Savoie

This series is sponsored by the Institute of Public Administration of
Canada as part of its commitment to encourage research on issue in
Canadian Public Administration, public sector management, and public policy. It also seeks to foster wider knowledge and understanding
among practitioners, academics, and the general public.

For a list of books published in the series, see page 605

Policy Analysis in Canada

The State of the Art

EDITED BY

LAURENT DOBUZINSKIS
MICHAEL HOWLETT
DAVID LAYCOCK

IPAC

The Institute of
Public Administration of Canada

IAPC

L'Institut d'administration
publique du Canada

UNIVERSITY OF TORONTO PRESS
Toronto Buffalo London

© University of Toronto Press Incorporated 2007
Toronto Buffalo London
Printed in Canada

ISBN 978-0-8020-8004-2 (cloth)

ISBN 978-0-8020-3787-9 (paper)

Printed on acid-free paper

Library and Archives Canada Cataloguing in Publication

Policy analysis in Canada : the state of the art / edited by Laurent
Dobuzinskis, Michael Howlett, David Laycock.

(Institute of Public Administration of Canada series in public management
and governance)
Includes bibliographical references and index.
ISBN 978-0-8020-8004-2 (bound)
ISBN 978-0-8020-3787-9 (pbk.)

1. Political planning – Canada – Textbooks.   2. Policy sciences – Textbooks.
I. Dobuzinskis, Laurent, 1947–   II. Laycock, David H. (David Howard),
      1954–   III. Howlett, Michael, 1955–   IV. Series

JL75.P436 2007   320.60971   C2007-900195-5

University of Toronto Press acknowledges the financial assistance
to its publishing program of the Canada Council for the Arts and the
Ontario Arts Council.

University of Toronto Press acknowledges the financial support for
its publishing activities of the Government of Canada through the
Book Publishing Industry Development Program (BPIDP).

Contents

Tables

Figures

POLICY ANALYSIS IN CANADA

1 Policy Analysis in Canada: The State of the Art

LAURENT DOBUZINSKIS, MICHAEL HOWLETT,
AND DAVID LAYCOCK

Introduction

In this volume we hope to help lay the foundations for a more systematic understanding of policy analysis in Canada, and thereby contribute to the enhanced practice and utilization of analytical work undertaken within both governments and those organizations that wish to influence public policy. Before moving to the various contributions made to this project by the individual chapter authors, we will attempt to briefly clarify what policy analysis is, and how its practice has been broadly construed by academic researchers over the past several generations, and to identify several general research questions that provide a framework for ongoing research into policy analysis in Canada.

Knowledge Utilization and Policy Analysis

Over the past generation, academic literature has often distinguished between policy study and policy analysis. The former term is sometimes used to refer to the study *of* policy and the latter to study *for* policy. Policy studies, the subject of an earlier volume by the editors (Dobuzinskis, Howlett, and Laycock 1996), is conducted mainly by academics, and relates to 'meta-policy' or the overall nature of the activities of the state. It is generally concerned with understanding the development, logic, and implications of overall state policy processes and the models used by investigators to analyse those processes. 'Policy analysis,' in comparison, refers to applied social and scientific research – but also involves more implicit forms of practical knowledge – pursued by government officials and non-governmental organizations usually directed at designing, implementing and evaluating existing policies, programmes and other courses of action adopted or contemplated by states. In a general sense, it is 'the discipline's application of intellect to public problems' (Pal 2006, 14). This book combines the two approaches, providing a study of the nature of policy analysis conducted in Canada, with the aim of identifying, describing and evaluating the different kinds of analysis carried out in this country by actors both inside and outside government.

Policy analysis in the sense employed in this volume has relatively recent origins in the wartime planning activities and 'scientific management' thinking of the mid-twentieth century. It was then more widely applied in the 1960s and 1970s to large-scale social and economic planning processes in areas such as defence, urban redevelopment and budgeting – especially as a result of the implementation of the Planning Programming Budgeting System (PPBS) in the United States, Canada and other countries (Heineman et al. 1990; Garson 1986; see also Lindblom 1958; Dobuzinskis 1977; Wildavsky 1979; Starling 1979). Since then, 'policy analysis' has spread around the world, with the development of professional associations and dedicated schools and teaching programs. At the same time, movement towards the application of scientific precepts to policy questions continues to be moderated by adherence to older, more partisan political modes of decision making and program planning (Webber 1986a), and despite a discernable trend toward professionalization, a variety of actors continues to contribute diverse ideas to policy debates. It may well be, in fact, that the quality of democratic deliberation hinges on the preservation of this diversity, in the sense that not all interests can be granted fair treatment by professional experts whose theoretical knowledge does not always adequately relate to the circumstances experienced by particular groups or individuals. Openness towards a diversity of approaches can prepare the ground for democratic deliberation and the active search for untapped sources of more or less implicit knowledge.

The growth of what some academics refer to as 'the policy analysis movement' represents an effort to reform certain aspects of government behaviour. In this sense it is similar to earlier movements that attempted to root out corruption and partisan patronage in government appointments and tendering, or to improve the sociological representativeness of civil servants and officials. The policy analysis movement represents the efforts of actors inside and outside formal political decision-making processes to improve policy outcomes by applying systematic evaluative rationality to the development and implementation of policy options (Meltsner 1976). However, as this volume makes clear, this movement has not become nearly as strong or widespread in Canada, or outside the United States generally, as it has, arguably, in the United States.

As Lindquist (1990) and others have noted, policy actors generally are arrayed in three general 'sets' or 'communities.' The first set is composed of the 'proximate decision makers' themselves – that is, those with actual authority to make policy decisions, including cabinets and executives as well as parliaments, legislatures, and congresses, and senior administrators and officials delegated decision-making powers by those other bodies. The second set is composed of those 'knowledge generators' located in academia and research institutes who provide the basic scientific, economic and social scientific data upon which analyses are often based and decisions made. The third set is composed of those 'knowledge brokers' who serve as intermediaries between the knowledge generators and proximate decision makers, repackaging data and information into usable form. These include, among others, permanent specialized research staff inside government as well as their temporary equivalents in commissions and task forces, and a large group of non-governmental specialists associated with think tanks and interest groups.

While the existence of all of these actors preceded the recent trend toward more systematic policy analysis, they have come to share a common interest in ensuring that policies reflect the latest knowledge, and a common desire to improve policy making through better and more systematic analysis of policy options and outcomes. That having been said, however, these interested parties differ in several important ways, based on the roles each has vis-à-vis the knowledge utilization process – as producer, broker, and consumer – and upon the interests each represents or promotes.

Policy Analysis in Different Guises

Governments have always been involved in the analysis of public policies, both their own and those of other countries, and those government officials who carry out analyses remain at the core of the knowledge brokering that occurs in government. However, in recent years much public policy analysis has also been increasingly generated by analysts working for temporary or arm's-length agencies of government, or for nongovernmental organizations. Some of these analysts work for re-search councils, royal commissions, task forces, and other investigative bodies established by governments. Others work directly for groups affected by public policies, such as trade unions, corporations, and business associations, or for private think tanks and research institutes, some of which have close ties to government agencies and pressure groups, or for political parties. Finally, some of these analysts, most of them associated with the university system, work independently, while others earn a living as consultants employed by the growing number of private firms which provide information and advice to governments. The former set of analysts, working for temporary government agen-cies, can be thought of as existing inside government, along with 'core' actors, while the latter group of private and university sector employ-ees usually operate outside both the core and government itself and inside it. But these groups and divisons are complex and policy analysts within them are often connected in complex networks through which paradigmatic ideas and ways of posing policy problems are exchanged across organizational and professional boundaries.

Generally speaking, however, analysts do differ depending on the organization they work for. As Lindquist has suggested, important differences in the roles and techniques of policy analysis employed by different policy actors are linked to the positions they hold within government and outside the authoritative arms of the state, and to their sources of funding in the private and public sector. Many analysts working for governments and for groups and corporations affected by public policies, for example, tend to focus their research on policy outcomes. They often have a direct interest in condemning or condon-ing specific policies on the basis of projected or actual impact on their client organization. Private think tanks and research institutes usually enjoy somewhat more autonomy from political, governmental, and economic interests, though some may be influenced in a general sense by the preferences of their funding organizations. Nevertheless, they remain interested in the 'practical' side of policy issues and also tend to concentrate either on policy outcomes or on the instruments and tech-niques that generate those outcomes. Academics, on the other hand, have a great deal of independence and usually have no direct personal stake in the outcome of specific policies. They can therefore examine public policies much more abstractly than can members of the other two groups and, as such, tend to grapple with the theoretical, concep-tual, and methodological issues surrounding the making of public policy.

Some academics, however, especially economists, also enjoy lucrative side careers as consultants and experts on Commissions of Inquiry and are thus sometimes more engaged in practical policy work than are their less disinterested counterparts.

Ongoing Research Questions in the Study of Canadian Policy Analysis

Policy analysis texts usually describe a range of qualitative and quantitative techniques that analysts are expected to learn and apply in specific circumstances, providing advice to decision makers about optimal strategies and outcomes to pursue in the resolution of public problems (MacRae and Wilde 1976; Patton and Sawicki 1993; Weimer and Vining 1999; Irwin 2003). This positivist or modern approach to policy analysis has dominated the field for decades (Radin 2000).

More and more, however, this understanding of policy analysis as 'speaking truth to power' has been challenged. Critics have focused attention on the practical difficulties associated with the application of formal analytical techniques, such as cost-benefit analysis, to policy problems, looking especially at the extent to which uncertainty and ambiguity in problem definition and evaluation have been ignored or downplayed by proponents of such techniques (Morgan and Henrion 1990; Dunn 2004; Yanow 1992). They have also pointed out how analyses can be consciously or unconsciously biased towards promotion of certain implicit or explicit goals (Hahn and Dudley 2004). Other critics have ventured meta-critiques, arguing that the techniques themselves embody philosophical and epistemological biases towards particularly instrumental conceptions of public policy problems and solutions, thereby ruling out by fiat or definition alternative conceptions and courses of action (Carrier and Wallace 1990; Dixon and Dogan 2004).

This meta-critique of the traditional techniques of modern policy analysis has led to several developments. Most noticeably, it spawned the emergence of a newer 'postpositivist' or 'postmodern' form of analysis focused much less on quantitative analytical techniques for analysis and much more on process-related techniques for affecting policy discourses, ideas and arguments (Radin 2000; Kirp 1992; Fischer 2003; Hajer and Wagenaar 2003; see also Woodside-Jiron 2004; Muntigle 2002).

However, these critiques of the rational biases of the policy sciences are not new (Tribe 1972; Nelson 1977; Banfield 1980) and the epistemological challenges posed to the traditional formal techniques used in the discipline are not devastating (Lynn 1999). A 'third way' exists between the 'modern' and 'postmodern' approaches that utilizes the critiques and self-reflections of both approaches to contribute towards improved empirical efforts to understand existing patterns of policy analysis and influence, and how they differ across organizations and jurisdictions. Sympathetic to the basic postulates and aims of the modern policy analysis movement, some observers advocate a middle position between it and the post-modern approach. They argue that (a) different styles of policy analysis can be found in different organizations and jurisdictions (Mayer et al. 2004; Jenkins-Smith 1982), and (b) that these styles are not random or completely manipulable by policy actors but are linked to larger patterns of political behaviour and culture that are, in a sense, quasi-permanent features of the policy analysis landscape (Geva-May 2002a, 2002b; Hajer 2003).

This volume falls squarely into this third category in its approach to understanding and studying policy analysis. Following this third way, several key dimensions of current empirical research into policy analysis stand out for those interested in evaluating the state of the art of policy analysis in Canada, and inform the studies of particular actors developed in each chapter:

1 There is a clear need for better empirical research into the sociology of policy analysis. Who is doing what in government and outside of it? Where are they trained? What techniques do they bring to the analysis? How dominant is the position held by economists and lawyers, for example (Cravens 2004; Markoff and Montecinos 1993; see also Bobrow 1977; Aaron 1992; Gardner 2002)? What does it means to be a policy 'professional' (Parsons 2001; Abbott 1988), and to what extent is policy analysis also practised by actors who are not professionals in the usual sense of the term? How has the rise of consultants affected policy making and outcomes (Lapsley and Oldfield 2001)? Studies in Canada are limited (Prince 1979; Prince and Chenier 1980; Hollander and Prince 1993), but those undertaken in other countries such as the Netherlands, France, the UK and New Zealand emphasize the significance of training and overall approach to assessing the impact of policy analyses on policy outcomes (Don 2004; Smith 1999; Bhatta 2002; Young et al. 2002; on Canada, see Cohn 2004; Pal 1985).

2 How is policy analysis influential? How are the results of analysis transmitted to policy makers, if at all? What is their impact? The

literature on the utilization of knowledge by governments was pioneered by Carole Weiss and William Dunn, but has not moved very far beyond the 'two communities' and 'enlightenment' metaphors of the early 1980s (Weiss 1977; Dunn 1980, 1983; Webber 1983, 1986b). Work by Whiteman (1985) and Webber (1992) was helpful in pointing out the significance of context to knowledge use, but recent work by Lester and Wilds (1990) and Parsons (2004) on the contexts of policy analysis and the need to address issues of the capacity of governments both to generate and to absorb knowledge, however, point to additional factors remaining to be examined in this area (Adams 2004). Pathbreaking research by Landry and colleagues (2001, 2003) provides some indication of the situation in Canada, but more can be done in this area.

3 Attention has been specifically focused on how an earlier exclusive emphasis on the analysis of alternative substantive outcomes has been replaced by a focus on realizing those outcomes through modifications in the design of institutions and processes. Such modifications are intended to reflect the increased 'networkization' of society and of policy processes (de Bruijn and Porter 2004; de Bruijn and ten Heuvelhof 2002; Bolong 2003; Qureshi 2004; Brandl 1988; Walters 2000). How Canada has fared in this regard is virtually unknown.

4 There remains a need to develop clearer evaluation criteria for policy analysis. Evaluation of public policy analysis in Canada lags behind that in Europe and the United States. Studies in those countries have moved some distance towards the assessment of the requirements for good policy analysis (Thissen and Twaalfhoven 2001; Sanderson 2002a and 2002b) and the integration of those results into the design of educational and training programs for professional policy analysts (Shulock 1999; Radin 2000; see also contributions from Bobrow, deLeon and Longobardi, Dryzek, Ostrom, Pickus and Dostert, Smith and Ingram, and Weimer (2002), to a symposium organized by the Committee on the Political Economy of a Good Society). Canadian studies on such topics have been very limited but many authors in this volume go some considerable distance towards closing that gap.

5 Finally, what are the pedagogical implications of these findings? Do our schools of public policy provide appropriate training for future policy analysts (Fleishman 1990)? Again, Canada lags behind in evalu-

ating its current training regimes, and in terms of implementing reforms that will enhance policy analysis in its varied practical contexts (Light 1999; Gow and Sutherland 2004).

The Origins and Purposes of the Book

This book presents the results of a broad and deep examination of policy analysis activities, at all levels of Canadian governments, as well as in the seldom studied nongovernmental sector. The questions that the contributors address include: What are the defining characteristics of sophisticated yet useful policy analysis? Which institutional constraints influence the outcomes or styles of analysis in Canada? How does policy analysis contribute to democratic debates? And are there lessons to be learned from the variations in policy analysis accross different countries, and within Canada?

The book brings together a team of researchers to examine policy analysis in government and in nongovernmental organizations. Each author has published extensively in his or her area of expertise. These contributors examine policy analysis in interest groups, think tanks, federal government departments, provincial governments, royal commissions, legislatures, local governments, trade unions, and business associations. Most of these investigators took part in one or both of two research workshops, one in Winnipeg in June 2004 and the second in Vancouver in September 2004. The workshops developed linkages between the participants' areas of expertise and helped to build an enhanced understanding of the state of the art of policy analysis in Canada. These workshops were carried out in conjunction with the Canadian Political Science Association and the new Centre for Public Policy Research at Simon Fraser University (Harbour Centre).

Section by Section Summary

The book is organized into six parts. The first part provides an overview of the styles and methods of policy analysis, with special emphasis on the ways it is practised in Canada, and offers an overview of trends in the field over the past quarter-century. Topics addressed by Stephen Brooks, Aidan Vining and Anthony Boardman, Michael Howlett and Evert Lindquist, and Lindquist and James Desveaux include the nature of formal policy analysis techniques, the various roles policy analysts play in the policy process as well as the institutional constraints they face.

The second part provides three chapters by Michael Mintrom, Michael Prince, and Iris Geva-May and Allan Maslove. These chapters approach some of the same themes developed in the previous part but from a more historical and comparative perspective.

The third part considers the issues of concern to policy analysts occupying key positions within Canadian governments. The situations of the federal, provincial and municipal governments are examined and developments (and continuing weaknesses) in general policy analytic style and capacity are described and assessed by, respectively, Jean-Pierre Voyer, Doug McArthur, and Patrick J. Smith and Kennedy Stewart.

The fourth part looks at public sector policy analysis 'insiders,' those analysts who are 'in' but not 'of' governments. Chapters by Liora Salter, Laurent Dobuzinskis, and Josie Schofield and Jonathan Fershau assess the capacity, limits and influence of policy analysis carried out at arm's length from government in quasi-independent but still formally authoritative institutions such as public inquiries, royal commissions and task forces, government policy research councils and legislative committees. Attention is also paid by François Pétry and Kimberly Speers to the role of public opinion surveys and consultants as means by which outside values and knowledge are transmitted to government decision makers.

The fifth and sixth parts deals with policy analysis by outsiders in political parties and interest groups, that is, analysis conducted outside the formal halls of government and aimed at promoting partisan or socio-economic interests. In Part V, chapters by William Cross, Andrew Stritch, Andrew Jackson and Bob Baldwin, and Susan Phillips examine, respectively, the kinds of analyses undertaken by political parties, business associations, trade unions, and the voluntary sector.

The sixth part focuses on organizations and analysts who typically claim to be objective critics of government policy or other policy-relevant developments but whose views are, nevertheless, and probably inevitably, skewed towards certain identifiable perspectives. The point here is not that their views are narrowly tied to specific societal interests, but rather that they reflect in varying degrees ideological commitments or disciplinary biases that need to be carefully examined. In their discussions, Catherine Murray looks at how information is mediated by journalists and media organizations, Donald Abelson looks at how think tanks disseminate their ideas, and Dan Cohn argues that academic research is influenced by disciplinary and other biases that can, under certain circumstances, be mobilized to support specific policy priorities.

In sum, contributors to this volume have explored the variety of perspectives, analytical techniques, institutional locales and processes, and broad socio-political environments through which modern policy analysis is conducted in Canada. We trust that readers will find their results and observations stimulating, useful, and conducive to much-needed academic and broader public discussion on the nature, purposes, and value of policy analysis in this country and elsewhere.

REFERENCES

Aaron, Henry J. 1992. 'Symposium on Economists as Policy Advocates.' *The Journal of Economic Perspectives* 6(3), 59–60.
Abbott, Andrew. 1988. *The System of Professions: An Essay on the Division of Expert Labor.* Chicago: University of Chicago Press.
Adams, David. 2004. 'Usable Knowledge in Public Policy.' *Australian Journal of Public Administration* 63(1), 29–42.
Banfield, Edward. 1980. 'Policy Science as Metaphysical Madness.' In R.A. Goldwin, ed., *Bureaucrats, Policy Analysts, Statesmen: Who Leads?* Washington, DC: American Enterprise Institute for Public Policy Research.
Bhatta, Gambhir. 2002. 'Evidence-Based Analysis and the Work of Policy Shops.' *Australian Journal of Public Administration* 61(3), 98–105.
Bobrow, David B. 1977. 'Beyond Markets and Lawyers.' *American Journal of Political Science* 21(2), 415–33.
– 2002. 'Knights, Dragons and the Holy Grail.' *The Good Society* 11(1), 26–31.
Bolong, Liu. 2003. 'Improving the Quality of Public Policy-Making in China: Problems and Prospects.' *Public Administration Quarterly* 27(1/2), 125–41.
Brandl, John. 1988. 'On Politics and Policy Analysis as the Design and Assessment of Institutions.' *Journal of Policy Analysis and Management* 7(3), 419–24.
Carrier, Harold D., and William A. Wallace. 1990. 'A Philosophical Comparison of Decision Aid Techniques for the Policy Analyst.' *Evaluation and Program Planning* 13, 293–301.
Cohn, Daniel. 2004. 'The Best of Intentions, Potentially Harmful Policies: A Comparative Study of Scholarly Complexity and Failure.' *Journal of Comparative Policy Analysis* 6(1), 39–56.

Cravens, Hamilton. 2004. *The Social Sciences Go to Washington: The Politics of Knowledge in the Postmodern Age.* New Brunswick: New Jersey.

de Bruijn, Hans, and Ernst ten Heuvelhof. 2002. 'Policy Analysis and Decision-Making in a Network: How to Improve the Quality of Analysis and the Impact on Decision Making.' *Impact Assessment and Project Appraisal* 20(4), 232–42.

de Bruijn, Hans and Alan L. Porter. 2004. 'The Education of a Technology Policy Analyst – to Process Management.' *Technology Analysis & Strategic Management* 16(2), 261–74.

deLeon, Peter, and Ralph C. Longobardi. 2002. 'Policy Analysis in the Good Society.' *The Good Society* 11(1), 37–41.

Dixon, John, and Rhys Dogan. 2004. 'The Conduct of Policy Analysis: Philosophical Points of Reference.' *Review of Policy Research* 21(4), 559–79.

Dobuzinskis, Laurent. 1977. 'Rational Government: Policy, Politics and Political Science.' In T.A. Hockin, ed., *Apex of Power: The Prime Minister and Political Leadership in Canada,* 2nd ed. Scarborough, ON: Prentice-Hall.

Dobuzinskis, Laurent, Michael Howlett, and David Laycock, eds. 1996. *Policy Studies in Canada: The State of the Art.* Toronto: University of Toronto Press.

Don, E.J.H. 2004. 'How Econometric Models Help Policy Makers: Theory and Practice.' *de economist* 152(2), 177–95.

Dryzek, John S. 2002. 'A Post-Positivist Policy-Analytic Travelogue.' *The Good Society* 11(1), 32–6.

Dunn, William N. 1980. 'The Two-Communities Metaphor and Models of Knowledge Use.' *Knowledge: Creation, Diffusion, Utilization* 1(4), 515–53.

– 1983. 'Measuring Knowledge Use.' *Knowledge: Creation, Diffusion, Utilization* 5(1), 120–33.

– 2004. *Public Policy Analysis: An Introduction.* Upper Saddle River, NJ: Pearson/Prentice-Hall.

Fischer, Frank. 2003. *Reframing Public Policy: Discursive Politics and Deliberative Practices.* Oxford: Oxford University Press.

Fleishman, Joel L. 1990. 'A New Framework for Integration: Policy Analysis and Public Management.' *American Behavioural Scientist* 33(6), 733–54.

Gardner, Bruce. 2002. 'Economists and the 2002 Farm Bill: What is the Value Added of Policy Analysis.' *Agricultural and Resource Economics Review* 3(1/2), 139–46.

Garson, G. David. 1986. 'From Policy Science to Policy Analysis: A Quarter Century of Progress.' In W.N. Dunn, ed., *Policy Analysis: Perspectives, Concepts, and Methods,* 3–22. Greenwich, CT: JAI Press.

Geva-May, Iris. 2002a. 'From Theory to Practice: Policy Analysis, Cultural Bias and Organizational Arrangements.' *Public Management Review* 4(4), 581–91.

– 2002b. 'Cultural Theory: The Neglected Variable in the Craft of Policy Analysis.' *Journal of Comparative Policy Analysis* 4(3), 243–66.

Gow, J.I., and S.L. Sutherland. 2004. *Comparison of Canadian Masters Programs in Public Administration, Public Management and Public Policy.* Toronto: Canadian Association of Schools of Public Policy and Administration.

Hahn, Robert W., and Patrick Dudley. 2004. *How Well Does the Government Do Cost-Benefit Analysis.* Washington, DC: AEI-Brookings Joint Centre for Regulatory Studies Working Paper.

Hajer, Maarten. 2003. 'Policy without Polity? Policy Analysis and the Institutional Void.' *Policy Sciences* 36, 175–95.

Hajer, Maarten, and Hendrik Wagenaar, eds. 2003. *Deliberative Policy Analysis: Understanding Governance in the Network Society.* London: Cambridge University Press.

Heineman, Robert A., William T. Bluhm, Steven A. Peterson, and Edward N. Kearny. 1990. *The World of the Policy Analyst: Rationality, Values and Politics.* Chatham, NJ: Chatham House.

Hollander, Marcus J., and Michael J. Prince. 1993. 'Analytical Units in Federal and Provincial Governments: Origins, Functions and Suggestions for Effectiveness.' *Canadian Public Administration*, 36(2), 190–224.

Irwin, Lewis G. 2003. *The Policy Analysts Handbook: Rational Problem Solving in a Political World.* Armonk, NY: M.E. Sharpe.

Jenkins-Smith, Hank C. 1982. 'Professional Roles for Policy Analysts: A Critical Assessment.' *Journal of Policy Analysis and Management* 2(1), 88–100.

Kirp, David L. 1992. 'The End of Policy Analysis.' *Journal of Policy Analysis and Management* 11(4), 693–6.

Landry, Réjean, Nabil Amara, and Moktar Lamari. 2001. 'Utilization of Social Science Research Knowledge in Canada.' *Research Policy* 30(2), 333–49.

Landry, Réjean, Moktar Lamari and Nabil Amara. 2003. 'The Extent and Determinants of the Utilization of University Research in Government Agencies.' *Public Administration Review* 63(2), 192–205.

Lapsley, Irvine, and Rosie Oldfield. 2001. 'Transforming the Public Sector: Management Consultants as Agents of Change.' *The European Accounting Review* 10(3), 523–43.

Lester, James P., and Leah J. Wilds. 1990. 'The Utilization of Public Policy Analysis: A Conceptual Framework.' *Evaluation and Program Planning* 13, 313–19.

Light, Paul C. 1999. *The New Public Service.* Washington, DC: Brookings Institute.

Lindblom, Charles E. 1958. 'Policy Analysis.' *American Economic Review* 48(3), 298–312.

Lindquist, Evert A. 1990. 'The Third Community, Policy Inquiry and Social Scientists.' In S. Brooks and A.C. Gagnon, eds., *Social Scientists. Policy and the State,* 21–52. New York: Praeger.

Lynn, Laurence E. 1999. 'A Place at the Table: Policy Analysis, Its Postpositive Critics, and the Future of Practice.' *Journal of Policy Analysis and Management* 18(3), 411–24.

MacRae, Duncan, Jr, and James A. Wilde. 1976. *Policy Analysis for Public Decisions.* North Scituate, MA: Duxbury Press.

Markoff, John, and Veronica Montecinos. 1993. 'The Ubiquitous Rise of Economists.' *Journal of Public Policy* 13(1), 37–68.

Mayer, I.P. Bots, and E. van Daalen. 2004. 'Perspectives on Policy Analysis: A Framework for Understanding and Design.' *International Journal of Technology, Policy and Management* 4(1), 169–91.

Meltsner, Arnold J. 1976. *Policy Analysts in the Bureaucracy.* Berkeley: University of California Press.

Morgan, M. Granger, and Max Henrion. 1990. *Uncertainty: A Guide to Dealing with Uncertainty in Quantitative Risk and Policy Analysis.* Cambridge: Cambridge University Press.

Muntigle, Peter. 2002. 'Policy, Politics and Social Control: A Systemic Functional Linguistic Analysis of EU Employment Policy.' *Text* 22(3), 393–441.

Nelson, Richard. 1977. *The Moon and the Ghetto: An Essay on Public Policy Analysis.* Chicago: Norton.

Ostrom, Elinor. 2002. 'Policy Analysis in the Future of Good Society.' *The Good Society* 11(1), 42–48.

Pal, Leslie A. 1985. 'Consulting Critics: A New Role for Academic Policy Analysts.' *Policy Sciences* 18, 357–69.

– 2006. *Beyond Policy Analysis: Public Issue Management in Turbulent Times.* 3rd ed. Scarborough, ON: Nelson Thompson Learning.

Parsons, Wayne. 2001. 'Modernising Policy-Making for the Twenty First Century: The Professional Model.' *Public Policy and Administration* 16(3), 93–110.

– 2004. 'Not Just Steering But Weaving: Relevant Knowledge and the Craft of Building Policy Capacity and Coherence.' *Australian Journal of Public Administration* 63(1), 43–57.

Patton, Carl V., and David S. Sawicki. 1993. *Basic Methods of Policy Analysis and Planning.* Englewood Cliffs, NJ: Prentice-Hall.

Pickus, Noah M.J., and Troy Dostert. 2002. 'Ethics, Civic Life and the Education of Policymakers.' *The Good Society* 11(1), 49–54.

Prince, Michael J. 1979. 'Policy Advisory Groups in Government Departments.' In G.B. Doern and P. Aucoin, eds., *Public Policy in Canada: Organization, Process, Management*, 275–300. Toronto: Gage.

Prince, Michael J., and John Chenier. 1980. 'The Rise and Fall of Policy Planning and Research Units.' *Canadian Public Administration* 22(4), 536–550.

Qureshi, Hazel. 2004. 'Evidence in Policy and Practice: What Kinds of Research Designs?' *Journal of Social Work* 4(1), 7–23.

Radin, Beryl A. 2000. *Beyond Machiavelli: Policy Analysis Comes of Age*. Washington, DC: Georgetown University Press.

Sanderson, Ian. 2002a. 'Evaluation, Policy Learning and Evidence-Based Policy-making.' *Public Administration* 80(1), 1–22.

– 2002b. 'Making Sense of What Works: Evidence Based Policy-making as Instrumental Rationality?' *Public Policy and Administration* 17(3), 61–75.

Shulock, Nancy. 1999. 'The Paradox of Policy Analysis: If It Is Not Used, Why Do We Produce So Much Of It?' *Journal of Policy Analysis and Management* 18(2), 226–44.

Smith, Andy. 1999. 'Public Policy Analysis in Contemporary France: Academic Approaches, Questions and Debates.' *Public Administration* 77(1), 111–31.

Smith, Steven Rathgeb, and Helen Ingram. 2002. 'Rethinking Policy Analysis: Citizens, Community and the Restructuring of Public Services.' *The Good Society* 11(1), 55–60.

Starling, Grover. 1979. *The Politics and Economics of Public Policy: An Introductory Analysis with Cases*. Homewood, IL: Dorsey Press.

Thissen, W.A.H., and Patricia G.J. Twaalfhoven. 2001. 'Toward a Conceptual Structure for Evaluating Policy Analytic Activities.' *European Journal of Operational Research* 129, 627–49.

Tribe, Laurence H. 1972. 'Policy Science: Analysis or Ideology?' *Philosophy and Public Affairs* 2(1), 66–110.

Walters, Lawrence C., James Aydelotte, and Jessica Miller. 2000. 'Putting More Public in Policy Analysis.' *Public Administration Review* 60(4), 349–59.

Webber, David J. 1983. 'Obstacles to the Utilization of Systematic Policy Analysis: Conflicting World Views and Competing Disciplinary Markets.' *Knowledge, Creation, Diffusion, Utilization* 4(4), 534–60.

– 1986a. 'Analyzing Political Feasibility: Political Scientists' Unique Contribution to Policy Analysis.' *Policy Studies Journal* 14(4), 545–54.

– 1986b. 'Explaining Policymaker's Use of Policy Information: The Relative

Importance of the Two-Community Theory versus Decision-Maker Orientation.' *Knowledge, Creation, Diffusion, Utilization* 7(3), 249–90.

– 1992. 'The Distribution and Use of Policy Knowledge in the Policy Process.' In W.N. Dunn and R.M. Kelly, eds., *Advances in Policy Studies Since 1950*, 383–418. New Brunswick, NJ: Transaction.

Weimer, David L. 2002. 'Enriching Public Discourse: Policy Analysis in Representative Democracies.' *The Good Society* 11(1), 61–65.

Weimer, David L., and Aidan R. Vining. 1999. *Policy Analysis: Concepts and Practice.* Englewood Cliffs, NJ: Prentice-Hall.

Weiss, Carol H. 1977. 'Research for Policy's Sake: The Enlightenment Function of Social Science Research.' *Policy Analysis* 3(4), 531–45.

– 1990. 'The Uneasy Partnership Endures: Social Science and Government.' In S. Brooks and A.G. Gagnon, eds., *Social Scientists, Policy, and the State*, 97–111. New York: Praeger.

Whiteman, David. 1985. 'The Fate of Policy Analysis in Congressional Decision Making: Three Types of Use in Committees.' *Western Political Quarterly* 38(2), 294–311.

Wildavsky, Aaron B. 1979. *Speaking Truth to Power: The Art and Craft of Policy Analysis.* Boston: Little, Brown.

Woodside-Jiron, Haley. 2004. 'Language, Power, and Participation: Using Critical Discourse Analysis to Make Sense of Public Policy.' In R. Rogers, ed., *An Introduction to Critical Discourse Analysis in Education*, 173–205. London: Lawrence Erlbaum Associates.

Yanow, Dvora. 1992. 'Silences in Public Policy Discourse: Organizational and Policy Myths.' *Journal of Public Administration Research and Theory* 2(4), 399–423.

Young, Ken, et al. 2002. 'Social Science and the Evidence-Based Policy Movement.' *Social Policy and Society* 1(3), 215–24.

PART I

The Styles and Methods of Public Policy Analysis in Canada

Modern policy analysis in Canada is a professional activity, carried out by a corps of specially trained individuals. Their emergence, and the training, administrative, and research institutes in which they work, has been frequently called 'the policy analysis movement,' and has been a characteristic development of governments and governance in the late twentieth century.

The extent to which different countries have been influenced by this movement, however, has been little studied outside the United States, its archetypal case. In this section of the book, the basic activities and types of policy analysis are set out, establishing the foundation for the study of the contours of the policy analysis movement, and its reception in Canada, in Part II.

In chapter 2, Stephen Brooks reflects upon how policy analysts in Canada can be considered a professional corps, and traces their origins and emergence in Canadian governments in the last half of the twentieth century. He notes the continued increase in the autonomy and capacity of civil servants in Canada throughout this period, and the gradual augmentation of their capacity to carry out policy analyses and 'speak truth to power.' Brooks recounts the gradual emergence of a professional ethos and its impact on the training, recruitment, and hiring of policy analysts in Canadian governments and, ultimately, nongovernmental organizations.

In chapter 3, Aidan Vining and Anthony Boardman set out the basic tools utilized by 'traditional' policy analysts in Canada and elsewhere. They discuss the different formal methods, such as cost-benefit analysis, at the core of the profession and note some of the difficulties that analysts face in identifying and applying these methods to specific

analytical circumstances. The difficulties of 'meta-analysis,' or the identification of the appropriate analytical technique, they argue, require
careful thought and experience on the part of the analyst, skills only
possessed by members of an identifiable professional group.

In chapter 4, Michael Howlett and Evert Lindquist detail other types
of skills and analytical activities undertaken by policy analysts beyond
those identified by Vining and Boardman. Drawing on the work of
Mayer, van Daalen, and Bots, they identify a range of other tasks and
duties – including policy process design and network management –
which contemporary policy professionals are called upon to conduct
and implement. They argue that these other, less formal, analytical
tasks have grown substantially in recent years, both in Canada and
elsewhere, as policy analysts have adapted to contemporary governance challenges.

Finally, in chapter 5, Evert Lindquist and James Desveaux examine
and critically assess policy analytical mechanisms brought to bear on
problems faced within contemporary governments. Identifying options
such as in-house systems, internal think tanks, and the use of consultants, they assess their merits and demerits as a means of augmenting
existing policy analytical capacity in Canadian governments.

2 The Policy Analysis Profession in Canada

STEPHEN BROOKS

Introduction

On the face of it, the question of how a given number of dollars can be used to achieve the best health care outcomes for a population might appear to be a matter on which experts should be able to agree. Answering this question should be facilitated, one might also think, by the fact that there exists today more data on more aspects of the health care system – both resources and outcomes – than at any point in Canadian history. Moreover, there are more health care experts, including economists, public health researchers, sociologists, health administration experts, and health policy analysts, than ever before. There is no significant corner of the health care map that has not been subjected to intensive scrutiny by Canada's small army of health care experts. Agreement among them on what needs to be done to make the system work better is, however, nowhere in sight.

This may seem paradoxical. More information and more expertise should, one might assume, lead to a clearer picture of how to get from point A to point B more effectively and efficiently. If two experts agree on the destination, then it would seem reasonable that they should be able to agree on the roadmap to get there. Recent history shows, however, that this is far from the case. The commission on the Future of Health Care in Canada (2000–2002) drew on the expertise of dozens of researchers and received testimony from hundreds more in producing a report whose major recommendations were that significantly more resources needed to be spent by governments in Canada to produce acceptable levels of health care, and that Ottawa's funding role should be placed on a firmer basis and its monitoring role institutionalized

(Canada 2002a). At about the same time, a Senate committee studying health care, which also received input from hundreds of health care interests and experts, arrived at a fairly similar diagnosis, but made rather different recommendations, including a steeply progressive dedicated health tax on personal income and more competition between health care providers within the system (Canada 2002b).

Meanwhile, the Fraser Institute, a conservative think tank, continued to publish studies purporting to show that the health care system could best be improved, from the standpoint of health outcomes, by allowing more competition between health care providers, more choice for health care consumers, and more transparency in the performance of hospitals, clinics, and practitioners within the system (Esmail, Walker, and Yeudall 2004). The left-wing Canadian Centre for Policy Alternatives took exactly the opposite position. Its experts argued that more competition, which would be achieved through the privatization of certain parts of the health care services, would actually produce a more expensive system and one that would deliver significantly worse outcomes for all but the wealthy (Schafer 2002; Yalmzyan 2004).

We have grown used to the spectacle of sparring experts, locked in disagreement over their understanding of a problem and what should be done. More knowledge and more experts have not meant greater consensus on either the problems that face us as a society or how to deal with them. At the same time, however, that knowledge and those experts have become indispensable to the policy-making process. Policy analysis is firmly embedded in modern governance, both within the state and in society.

In this chapter I examine the development of the policy analysis profession in Canada. I argue that the *professionalization* of policy analysis should be viewed as a cultural phenomenon that encompasses not only the expert's relationship to the state and to various groups in society, but also the impact of policy experts on the popular consciousness and the general discourse within which more specialized policy discourses are situated. Viewed from this wider angle, the influence of policy analysts and their specialized knowledge has never been greater, not even during the heyday of the mandarinate on the Rideau.

The policy analysis community in Canada has, of course, grown enormously. However, the true measure of its significance is not its size, but rather its contribution at all stages of the policy-making process, from shaping the policy agenda, through the formulation and implementation of policies, to policy analysts' impact on popular reception to government policies. In tracing the professionalization of policy analysis, I am concerned chiefly with how analysts and their craft have become embedded in our culture and governance, in the widest sense. One of the themes that runs through this volume is the putative shift from the rational-hierarchal model of policy analysis that dominated thinking about the policy analyst's craft and role throughout most of the twentieth century, to a more nuanced and variegated conceptualization of the functions and styles of policy analysis (Mayer, van Daalen, and Bots 2001; Radin 2000). The traditional characterization of the policy analyst's role was 'speaking truth to power.' While this remains an important part of the self-image that many in the policy analysis community have of what they do and what they should do, the contemporary reality of policy analysis is much more complex than the profession's founding ethos can capture. The professionalization of policy analysis has produced a larger community of analysts whose activities and influence are more securely embedded in the processes and culture of governance in Canada. But it has also produced a more diverse analysis community than existed in the past, in terms of where, how and why analysis-related activities are undertaken.

Perspectives on the Policy Analysis Profession

The policy analysis profession may be viewed from three perspectives: the technical, political, and cultural. The first draws its inspiration from Max Weber's work on modern bureaucracy and the ascendance of rationally based authority. The second perspective achieved prominence as a result of the Dreyfus Affair in *fin de siècle* France, which triggered the twentieth-century debate on the political role of intellectuals, particularly their relationship to the powerful and their societal obligations. The third perspective can be traced to various sources, among whom Michel Foucault, Pierre Bourdieu, and Neil Postman are probably the best known. It focuses attention on the symbolic meaning of the expert and expertise. This may be the least developed of the three perspectives on the professionalization of policy analysis. I believe, however, that it also may be the most important.

From the Weberian perspective, professionalization is a process of acquiring authority based on recognized expert credentials that may include formal training, degrees, certification, and particular types of experience. One's status as a member of a profession depends on the possession of these credentials, and the profession's collective authority rests on the willingness of others to acknowledge the special skills, knowledge, and function of its membership. Economics is an obvious and important example of a field that has undergone professionalization during the twentieth century. But social workers, criminologists, urban planners, ethicists, pollsters, and a host of other groups have experienced a similar development.

Professionalization in the Weberian sense is inextricably tied to the dynamic of modernization, a dynamic that is characterized by increasing levels of specialization and the displacement of traditional forms of authority by rational ones. Rational authority rests upon the cardinal importance of rules, not persons. Under a rational system of domination, acts are legitimate or not depending on their correspondence to impersonal rules that exist apart from those who administer them. It is a social order under which bureaucrats and experts – elites whose judgements are, in Weber's famous words, 'without prejudice or passion' – occupy a dominant place.

The modern state is a rational state. It has generated a need for experts whose special knowledge is indispensable to the activities of the state. The policy analysis profession is, from this perspective, an offshoot of the rationalization and bureaucratization of social relations, and the needs of the administrative state. It is not, however, exclusively the handmaiden of the state. Policy analysts are found in non-governmental organizations as well, which is natural enough given that the administrative state and the administrative society are complementary aspects of the same historical process.

The second perspective on the development of the policy analysis profession focuses on its relationship to power. Whose side are they on? Are they wittingly or otherwise defenders of the status quo, and therefore of the powerful, or are they critics, agents of social change and a tick in the hide of the Establishment? To the extent that the policy analysis profession has developed largely within the state and in response to its needs, one would expect it to play an essentially conservative role in politics. Likewise, where powerful private interests finance the activities of policy analysts and shape the agenda of their research, this will perforce mould the profession, or at least part of it, in a politically conservative direction.

The policy analysis community that exists today is diverse in its ideological tendencies and social affiliations. Nevertheless, a large part of it is directly or indirectly tied to either the state or powerful corporate interests. This segment of the profession exists not merely to meet the needs of state agencies, corporations, and business associations for information and expert analysis, but also to legitimize the interests and actions of their employers/benefactors in ways ranging from the production and dissemination of studies to interviews with the media.

Left-wing social critics have long argued that the overwhelming preponderance of what the policy analysis community does buttresses the status quo. They view professionalization as a response to the needs of the corporate elites and the capitalist state. While there is much in this view that should be taken seriously, it also understates the significance of non-mainstream elements in the policy analysis community and the impact of social institutions other than the state and corporations on the development of the profession.

The third perspective on professionalization emphasizes the symbolic and cultural impacts of policy analysts' activities. The policy expert – the university professor commenting on the ethical implications of an assisted suicide law, the think tank economist interviewed for her views on a government budget, or the criminologist talking about the experience of the victims of crime – has become a routine and even necessary part of popular political discourse. Experts have moved from the shadows (where they have long been influential) into the sunlight of public debate on policy. In doing so, the 'expert' has become an icon in a society whose consciousness and values are powerfully affected by his or her activities. The rise of expert authority does not eliminate the influence of other individuals and groups whose political leverage and social status may rest on the size or attributes of the interests they represent, the position they occupy in the policy-making system, their access to or influence on public opinion, or some other factor that is not associated with technical expertise. However, in the age of the expert, most groups and individuals will realize the importance of expressing their views using the word concepts that are associated with experts and their specialized knowledge, and which have become the lingua franca of policy discourse.

What I am calling the cultural perspective views policy analysis and analysts as having meaning in themselves, apart from whatever ideas and information are associated with them. A researcher commenting on claims about exposure to second-hand smoke and cancer signifies the relevance of scientific expertise to public discourse and policy making. The same is true of the criminologist interviewed on the evening news for her views on gun control, or the economist whose assessment of the government's interest rate policy is in the newspaper. Indeed, it cannot have escaped any reflective person's notice that most of the 'soundbites' and printed quotations that experts contribute to the news are either statements of the obvious, things that have been said many times before or, when not mere platitudes, claims or ideas that require supporting arguments and information that are not, however, provided. In these circumstances, expertise and the expert are used in magical ways. Far from promoting rational policy debate, experts offer, and their use itself can act as, incantations that cast a spell of scientific authority over the viewpoints they support.

This may sound too cynical and certainly is not intended to dismiss the relevance of expert knowledge nor diminish the enlightenment that experts can bring to bear on an issue. I merely wish to make the point – one that has been made more ably by others – that the medium is indeed the message. Just as film footage or photographs of Parliament Hill, the White House, or scenes of violence in the Middle East trigger certain associations in the minds of viewers, the 'expert' also produces associations regardless of the content of his or her remarks. Words like 'study,' 'institute,' 'findings,' 'relationship,' and 'specialist' let us know that we are in the realm of scientific reason. A backdrop of books and the expert's institutional affiliation signify the weightiness and scientific respectability of the person being interviewed. The expert becomes not merely a medium for the expression of certain thoughts, but a message herself. The message is that expert knowledge is an indispensable part of policy discourse.

Policy analysis in Canada has undergone professionalization in all three senses in which I have used the term. In the remainder of this chapter I will explore the development of the policy analysis profession, using these three perspectives as my guideposts. I will argue that the influence of policy analysts and their craft rests on their technical skills and expert knowledge in our administrative society (perspective no. 1), their relationship to powerful groups in society (perspective no. 2), and their role in shaping public consciousness in the age of electronic mass media (perspective no. 3). This third basis of their influence is, I would argue, not sufficiently appreciated.

The Formative Period 1913–45

It is difficult to pinpoint the moment when the policy analysis profession emerged in Canada, but the early years of this century is probably a fair starting point for several reasons. My choice of 1913 is not entirely arbitrary (though non-political scientists may find it to be shamelessly self-congratulatory). The Canadian Political Science Association (CPSA) was founded in that year, under the leadership of some of the country's leading social scientists, public servants, and reformers. They included people like Adam Shortt, a Queen's political economist and member of the Civil Service Commission (1908–1917), O.D. Skelton, likewise a Queen's political economist who become under-secretary of state for External Affairs in 1925, Herbert Ames (1897), a reform-minded businessman whose social scientific credentials were established by his study of working-class Montreal, and Quebec political economist Édouard Montpetit.

The philosophy of the CPSA was summed up in the words of Shortt, its first president, who viewed it as an agent for generating solutions to social problems. Shortt and most of the other leading figures in the fledgling CPSA were solidly in the progressive movement that had emerged in the United States during the late 1800s. This movement was dedicated to closer ties between government and academe, based on the belief that rational inquiry by experts could produce solutions to social and economic problems.[1] Its adherents believed that social service, not the advancement of knowledge for knowledge's sake, ought to be their foremost goal. As was true of the progressive reform movement as a whole, the inspiration for social service was diverse. Some were motivated by religious conviction and a belief that the New Jerusalem was within man's power to achieve (Allen 1971). Others were inspired by a more secular faith in reform, in some cases based on socialist principles. These and other differences aside, the original members of the CPSA constituted Canada's first self-conscious coterie of policy analysts, committed to using public policy to remedy the social and economic ills of the country.

The outbreak of World War I brought an early end to the activities of the CPSA. But although it was not reconstituted until 1929, the founding of the organization had signalled the emergence of policy analysis on the Canadian scene. The CPSA crystallized various intellectual tendencies current at the time, giving them an institutional voice.

One of these tendencies was the movement for civil service reform. Not until 1918 were competitive examinations and other requirements of the merit system established parts of federal hiring procedures. Although it applied to only a minority of civil service positions, the merit system represented an important change in the idea and practice of governance, away from amateur administration toward the Weberian ideal of rational bureaucracy. Although few of those appointed under the early merit system could be described as policy analysts, the technical professionalization of the bureaucracy would eventually generate many such positions, beginning most significantly in the Department of Finance.

Positions at the top of the bureaucratic hierarchy continued to be staffed at the prime minister's discretion. But the idea of merit quickly became entrenched at this level too. The 1925 appointment of O.D. Skelton as under-secretary of state for External Affairs was certainly not the first case of a formally trained expert being appointed to a top bureaucratic job. Skelton's boss, Prime Minister Mackenzie King, had been appointed deputy minister of the newly created Department of Labour in 1900. Mackenzie King had studied economics at Harvard and Chicago, and was perhaps the Canadian prototype of the expert-turned-administrator. Nonetheless, Skelton's influence on policy during his 16 years at External Affairs (1925–41) was probably unsurpassed by any previous bureaucrat.

Doug Owram (1986) argues that the major turning point in the influence of non-political experts occurred in 1932, when Prime Minister R.B. Bennett was preparing for trade negotiations that took place at the Imperial Economic Conference. Bennett solicited the advice of several professional economists, including Clifford Clark, whom he would appoint as deputy minister of finance within the year. Clark was the first professionally trained economist to hold the position, and built Finance into the unrivalled centre of economic policy analysis within the Canadian state. 'Dr Clark's boys,' as the economists under his direction came to be known, were among the best and the brightest in Ottawa, and included his eventual successors R.B. Bryce and John Deutsch. What Skelton was to foreign policy, Clark was to domestic policy. Indeed, his personal influence extended far beyond economic matters to include issues of social policy with which the Liberal government was grappling in the 1940s (Porter 1965, 425–8).

The Canadian state was transformed during the 1930s and 1940s, and a key feature of this transformation involved the increasingly influential role of non-political experts within the Ottawa bureaucracy. The 'Ottawa men,' as Jack Granatstein (1982) calls them, were both a response to the changing demands on government but also architects of its evolution. They established the policy analysis profession at the heart of the state, a development that most social scientists welcomed as the triumph of reason.

The growing prominence of economists and other social scientists was not merely state-driven. Intellectual developments in Canada had a major impact on the activities and goals of the fledgling policy analysis profession. The social activism that had been advocated by Adam Shortt and the founders of the CPSA gained renewed vigour among intellectuals as Canada slid deeper into the Depression. The League for Social Reconstruction (LSR) was the most obvious sign of this intellectual activism, attracting the energies mainly of left-leaning intellectuals like Frank Underhill, F.R. Scott, Irene Bliss, Eugene Forsey, and Graham Spry. Underhill's vision of the LSR was of a Canadian version of the British Fabian Society, generating ideas that would spur public debate and influence the policies of political parties. The League's ideological affinity to the newly created Cooperative Commonwealth Federation (CCF) prevented it from attracting those intellectuals who did not share its predominantly class-based view of society and who were not willing to write off the traditional parties as agents of reform. Nonetheless, the idea championed by the LSR, namely that the 'intelligent use of the expert to plan the pragmatic intervention of the state to meet social and economic needs' (Owram 1976, 177), was one shared by most intellectuals of this generation, and provided common ground for individuals as ideologically different as Underhill and Clark.

Faith in technocracy was a distinguishing feature of this first generation of policy analysts. Indeed, technocracy was believed by many to be the solvent of ideological differences. Economist W.A. Mackintosh (1937) spoke for most social scientists when he said, 'Our philosophy should always be ready to retreat before science.' Those who went to work for the Canadian state shared a technocratic liberalism: interventionist, confident in the ability of government to manage social and economic problems, but also fundamentally supportive of capitalism and hostile to the idea of a class-based redistribution of wealth. Their credo was the 1945 White Paper on Employment and Income, which laid the basis for the Keynesian welfare state in Canada. Some of those who remained outside the state, and whose intellectual links were with the LSR and/or the CCF, were technocratic socialists – in favour of large-scale economic planning and social entitlements, and mistrustful of capitalism and capitalists. Their philosophy and aspirations were embodied in the 1933 *Regina Manifesto*, which set forth the principles and policies of the CCF, and in the LSR's *Social Planning for Canada* (1935).

The economic crisis of the 1930s gave rise in Canada to what Neil Bradford (1998) characterizes as two quite different groups of policy-oriented intellectuals. The 'socialist partisans,' as he calls them, included historians, economists and other social scientists – the disciplinary lines between the social sciences were much less rigid than they would become – who developed a critical analysis of capitalist democracy and proposed sweeping and concrete changes to both the economic and political systems. Frank Underhill, F.R. Scott, and other intellectuals who came together through the League for Social Reconstruction were at the forefront of this group.

The second group of policy intellectuals that Bradford identifies are those he calls the 'liberal technocrats.' This group included academics like W.A. Mackintosh, B.S. Kierstead, and the economists and other social scientists who worked for the Royal Commission on Dominion-Provincial Relations (1937–1940). Referred to disparagingly by Frank Underhill as the 'garage mechanics of capitalism,' these university-trained intellectuals, the most prominent of whom were economists, would become the prototype of the policy analyst in Canada. 'The liberal technocrats,' writes Bradford, 'offered their expertise to the state in the expectation that such policy knowledge would increase economic efficiency and stabilize the incomes of individuals ... The bureaucracy and (royal commissions) were focal points for liberal technocratic engagement' (1998, 32).

The Department of Finance, the Department of Labour, the Dominion Bureau of Statistics, and the Bank of Canada became major points of contact between the state and academe, through the recruitment of liberal technocrats from the universities but also through the importation into the structures and policy-making processes of the state of the applied policy analysis model. A state-managed capitalist economy along the lines that John Maynard Keynes and his intellectual followers proposed, and which was officially adopted by the Government of Canada in the 1945 White Paper on Employment and Income, requires a sophisticated apparatus to collect information and monitor trends in economic activity, and ultimately experts to interpret this data and make policy recommendations. The state's need for the analysts who are indispensable to the Keynesian welfare state that emerged after World War II influenced the nature of academic economics. As Harry Johnson observes, 'the presence of a large-scale government demand for the product (of university economics departments) cannot help but bias the tone or ethos of the subject toward conservatism ... The presence of an assured market for economists in government service, in contrast to the position confronting students in the other social sciences

... accounts for the universally contrasting behaviour of students and faculties in economics and the other social sciences during the "student troubles" of the 1960's' (1974, 102).

Johnson's observations on the greater conservatism of academic economics, due, he argues, to its integration into the structures and policy-making processes of the state, point to a rift in academic policy analysis that goes back to the 'socialist partisan' versus 'liberal technocrat' dichotomy identified by Bradford, and which widened during the 1960s and persists today. This rift continues to pit critical analysts, those whose analysis of policy and recommendations for change are generated from an intellectual perspective that fundamentally rejects major features of the economic, social, cultural, or political status quo, against technocratic analysts. The difference between these groups is less one of analytical methods than of their respective self-images in relationship to power and society. The former see themselves in an adversarial relationship to established systems of power and view their proper function as that of *l'intellectual engagé*, advocates supporting the causes and advancing the interests of the oppressed and disadvantaged. They are, perforce, supportive of sweeping policy change. Much, indeed probably most, policy analysis carried out by university-based experts continues to conform more closely, however, to the liberal technocratic model.

In summary, the formative era in the development of the policy analysis profession was characterized by a changing conception of the state and a growing belief in the utility of the analyst's craft for policy making. The positive state required technical expertise, particularly in areas of economic management but increasingly in areas of social and, eventually, cultural policy. To a large degree, therefore, the early professionalization of policy analysis was externally driven, shaped by changes in the state and society. But it was also influenced by internal factors, notably the reformist impulses of many social scientists and the Keynesian philosophy that was rapidly becoming *de rigeur* among economists. Neither those who went to work for the state nor those who sniped at it from the LSR, the CCF, and the pages of the *Canadian Forum* believed that the sidelines were the appropriate place for a social scientist. Assessments of this early period in the development of policy analysis generally conclude that the profession constituted what T.S. Eliot called a 'clerisy,' that is, intellectual defenders of the status quo and thus the servants, wittingly or not, of the powerful (Porter 1965). This is not entirely fair, unless we restrict use of the term policy analyst to those who actually worked for the state. If, however, the term is understood more broadly to include politically involved experts wherever they are located – in political parties, the media, academe, or organizations like the LSR – it is clear that the early profession contained a significant number of critics of the establishment. That they constituted a minority voice within the profession is, however, undeniable.

At the same time it must be acknowledged that the dominant self-image that emerged in the fledgling policy analysis profession during this period was very much in the 'speaking truth to power' mould. Of the six distinct policy styles that Mayer, van Daalen, and Bots identify (see the list in Howlett and Lindquist's chapter, p. 90), the *rational* category was clearly the dominant one, with the argumentative policy analysis style a minor, although not politically insignificant alternative on the left. But even among the CCF and LSR types, the goal was to eventually control the levers of state power and therefore move their expertise from the margins into the structures of governance. In other words, their conception of the analyst's role was not so different from that of those experts who had already been recruited by the state, but their politics was.

Consolidating Its Influence, 1945–68

The pattern that was set by the end of World War II continued afterward. The machinery of government had become dependent on the technical knowledge of formally trained experts, particularly within key agencies like the Department of Finance, the Bank of Canada, and the Department of External Affairs. But in other parts of the state and in other policy domains, the growing importance of non-political experts was also evident. Porter's observation that 'the upper levels [of the federal bureaucracy] constitute what is probably the most highly trained group of people to be found anywhere in Canada' (1965, 433) was doubtlessly correct. He found that in 1953, just under 80 per cent of senior officials were university graduates, with the figure close to 90 percent among deputy ministers. Lest it be thought that their degrees were mainly in law or some traditional area of the humanities, Porter notes that about one-quarter were in science or engineering and about an equal share in the social sciences (1965, 43–4).

Likewise, the precedent of expert research for royal commissions, established by the Royal Commission on Dominion-Provincial Relations (1937–40), continued during the postwar era. The Royal Commission on National Development in the Arts, Letters and Sciences (1949–51) commissioned 51 special studies in disciplines ranging from chemistry to sociology. The Royal Commission on Canada's Economic Prospects (1955–56) was supported by 33 studies, all in economics and many by professional economists. The Royal Commission on Health Services (1961–65) commissioned 20 studies, carried out by economists and sociologists. The Royal Commissions on Banking and Finance (1964) and Taxation (1962–66) produced 12 and 26 special studies respectively, most by trained economists. Finally, the 'mother' of royal commissions, the Royal Commission on Bilingualism and Biculturalism (1963–69), commissioned 124 special studies and employed the services of many of the country's most respected historians, political scientists, and sociologists.

The status of the policy analyst had never been greater. At the pinnacle of the profession were the Ottawa 'mandarins,' as they came to be called. These were the key deputy ministers and certain other top-level bureaucrats like the Governor of the Bank of Canada, whose influence on policy during the roughly two decades following World War II was profound. Twenty-two unbroken years of Liberal government led to, not surprisingly, doubts about the political impartiality of these experts at the top. But as Reg Whitaker observes, the question of whether the bureaucrats had become Liberals might well be turned around to ask whether the Liberals had become bureaucrats (1977, 167).

The end of Liberal rule in 1957 may indeed have signalled the beginning of the end for the Ottawa mandarinate, as J.L. Granatstein argues. But its decline was not accompanied by a diminished role for expert policy analysis within the state. Despite John Diefenbaker's prairie populism rhetoric, no significant restructuring of the machinery of governance took place during his tenure as prime minister. The size of the bureaucracy continued to grow under the Conservatives, although less rapidly than in the early 1950s. More importantly, the idea of policy making as an enterprise requiring the knowledge and participation of specially trained experts was not seriously challenged. Despite the frostier relationship between the civil service and the Conservatives, and the palpable relief of many top bureaucrats when the Liberals were returned to power in 1963, the administrative state that had put down roots in the 1930s continued to grow.

Although the policy analysis profession was firmly entrenched in the postwar Keynesian welfare state, its status and influence in society were considerably less secure. For example, very few interest groups employed people whose job could be described as that of policy analyst and whose training was in the social sciences. Likewise, the mass media rarely called upon social scientists for their analysis of contemporary events. Few journalists had any specialized training in economics, sociology, international affairs, etc., and the academic community that might have contributed this expertise was, with few exceptions, largely disengaged from day-to-day politics. The university community was still relatively small and the private-sector think tanks that today are important contributors to policy discourse – the C.D. Howe Institute, the Fraser Institute, Canadian Centre for Policy Alternatives, the Vanier Institute on the Family, and the Institute for Research on Public Policy, to mention a few – did not yet exist.

In these respects, Canada's policy analysis profession lagged far behind its counterpart in the United States. There, the Ford and Rockefeller foundations were already major private sources of funding for social scientific research, and the prototypes of the policy think tanks, like the Rand Institute and Brookings Institution, originated in the United States. The explosion in the demand for university education began earlier in the United States, producing both an enormous increase in the number of social science professors and a sharp rise in the share of the population exposed to their ideas, further embedding the idea of the relevance of social science expertise. Magazines like the *Atlantic Monthly, Harper's,* and the *New Yorker,* as well as America's newspaper of record, the *New York Times,* regularly featured articles by social scientific experts. But perhaps the single most important development contributing to the consolidation of the policy analysis profession in the United States was the growth of attitudinal surveys and their rapid acceptance by the mass media, public officials, and the general population as scientific and therefore worthy of serious public consideration. By the 1950s surveys, and those who implemented and interpreted them, already had this stature.

In Canada, the turning point in the consolidation of the policy analysis profession occurred in the mid-1960s. No single development was responsible; rather, a combination of factors elevated the social profile of the analyst's craft. One of these was that old Canadian favourite, the royal commission. The Royal Commission on Bilingualism and Biculturalism (B & B) (1963–69) was assigned the largest research budget and the most ambitious research agenda of any royal commission before or, at least in regard to its scope, since that time. Its 124 special studies sucked into the commission's vortex the energies of most of the country's most prominent social scientists. The impact of their work on the commission's recommendations and on policy provides an instructive lesson in the functions of a mature policy analysis profession.

One of those functions – according to Ira Horowitz (1970), the *key* function – of the policy analysis profession is to provide a 'political formula' that justifies the preferences of the powerful. Whereas the legitimizing rhetoric of previous eras drew upon religion, political ideology and philosophy, that of post-industrial society borrows heavily from the social sciences. No less than previous political formulas, however, the rhetoric of the social sciences is easily enlisted in the service of those who rule.

Gertrude Laing, a B & B commissioner and former head of the Canada Council, agrees. She notes that 'the policy-makers did what people generally do, who commission research – they used the B & B report in accordance with their predetermined priorities' (1979, 171). In other words, the chief, if unacknowledged, role of the legions of policy analysts who worked for the commission was to provide a 'political formula' that would justify policies shaped by other forces. This does not imply that there was a consensus among the researchers who worked for the commission. The 'political formula' they provided consisted of the specialized language of the social sciences and the very fact that social science research was a highly visible part of the policy-making process.

Other factors contributing to the consolidation of the policy analysis profession's stature included rapid expansion of the university system, the growth in state funding of social science research, the media's increasing use of social science experts, and the 1963 creation of the Economic Council of Canada and the Science Council of Canada in 1966. The era of the mandarin expert was definitely being eclipsed by the institutional expert, but one whose social authority rested largely on his or her affiliation to an organization with a research/analysis role. These experts were found mainly in universities, think tanks and state agencies. On the other hand, the linkages between policy analysts and political parties remained fairly tenuous, except in the case of the New Democratic Party (NDP). Nationalist academics and left-leaning social scientists were important figures in the councils of the NDP. The nationalist Committee for an Independent Canada provided another channel for social and economic criticism by policy experts.

At the same time as the policy analysis profession was becoming more securely embedded in the state and society, it was becoming more specialized and fragmented in its internal structures. After enduring years of an increasingly uneasy relationship, political science and economics formally separated in 1967. Branches within policy-related academic disciplines became increasingly specialized during the 1960s and have since continued to diverge. This specialization has been reflected in both a proliferation of technical journals and a widening gap of incomprehension between what previously were closely allied fields.

Fragmentation advanced on the linguistic front as well. Influenced by the strong currents of nationalism in Quebec during the 1960s, the rift between anglophone and francophone social scientists grew ever larger. In 1964 the Société canadienne de science politique was established as the breakaway francophone, and mainly Québécois, counterpart of the Canadian Political Science Association (in 1979 it would change its name to the Société québécoise de science politique). It was following the lead of the Association canadienne des sociologues, which had split from the Canadian Association of Sociologists and Anthropologists in 1961. The energies of Quebec's francophone social scientists were increasingly channelled through a separate network of organizations, conferences, and journals, the latter of which included *Recherches sociographiques* (1961) and *Sociologie et sociétés* (1961). These would be followed by *Les Cahiers du socialisme* (1978) and *Politique* (1982).

The nationalization of the Quebec-centred francophone social science community was abetted by the actions of the Quebec state. It created several funding agencies and research centres during the 1960s, promoting both the natural and social sciences. By decade's end, the Quebec state was the principal source of funding for social scientific research in Quebec, a role held by the Canada Council in the other provinces. The nationalist impetus behind the Quebec government's support for scientific research was reflected in the considerably greater share of provincial than federal money devoted to the social sciences. Whereas only about 10 to 15 per cent of federal money went to the social sciences, the rest going to the natural and applied sciences, about 40 per cent of Quebec funding was earmarked for the social sciences in the late 1960s and early 1970s.

Despite individual social scientists who straddled the line dividing the two linguistic communities, and occasional efforts at cooperation between organizations representing the two groups, the rupture within the profession was deep and permanent. Many francophone economists and other policy analysts continued to work for the Canadian state, but the centre of gravity for their linguistic wing of the profession had moved decisively to Quebec. Perhaps the most obvious and, for those laypersons who naively imagine that professional social scientists of all backgrounds are single-mindedly devoted to discovery of the 'truth,' the most disturbing indication of this rift, involved the ongoing battle of the balance sheets between separatists and federalists. It pits many Québécois economists (led by onetime Parti Québécois leader Jacques Parizeau) who maintain that Quebec has been bled economically by its membership in Canada, against those members of the profession whose calculations show that Quebec has profited considerably.

In summary, this second era in the development of the policy analysis profession was marked by consolidation of its role within the state and an increase in the profession's social stature in both French-speaking Quebec and in the rest of Canada. The era of the Ottawa mandarins, the first generation of expert bureaucrats, was fading from the scene, only to be replaced by a new generation of specialist administrators whose influence was less personal, more diffuse and embedded in the very nature of the administrative state that the first generation had helped build. Indeed, the post-mandarin generation conformed more closely to Weber's ideal type of the expert administrator. The influence of the first generation had depended too much on the fact that they constituted a personal elite whom circumstances had given the opportunity to exercise an exceptional influence on public affairs. By the time the Diefenbaker Conservatives came to power the influence of the policy specialist-administrator was securely entrenched in Canada's Keynesian welfare state.

Outside the state, the policy analysis profession grew slowly, until the 1960s, when it expanded rapidly on the coattails of growth in the university system and increased state funding for the social sciences. At the same time, the profession became increasingly fragmented, both in terms of the orientation and technical language of the various policy-related disciplines, and along linguistic lines. The consolidation of the profession in French-speaking Quebec was powerfully influenced by Quebec nationalism and the dense network of ties that arose with the provincial state. In English Canada, however, the period of consolidation took place under the aegis of federal policies and institutions, and this linguistic wing of the profession maintained a much more Canadian outlook than its nationalist Québécois counterpart.

In political terms, the profession continued to play the predominantly conservative role that John Porter attributed to it. A policy analysis community whose growth, prospects, and prestige are tied to state funding, royal commissions, and the universities is unlikely to do otherwise. Pockets of criticism existed within the profession, clustered around the NDP, the Committee for an Independent Canada, and, in Quebec, the emerging separatist movement. Their influence on the development of the profession and on Canadian politics was, however, marginal. The B&B commission and the Economic Council of Canada were the defining events for this generation of policy analysts, consolidating the policy-making beachhead that had been won by the earlier generation of reform-minded experts and Keynesian welfare state managers.

In terms of the styles that characterized this second period in the professionalization of policy analysis, the rational style occupied centre stage. The creation and early prestige of the Economic Council of Canada and the Science Council of Canada, and the analysis vortex created by the B&B commission, showed very clearly that the 'speaking truth to power' conceptualization of the analyst's role continued to dominate. However, the argumentative policy style continued to be a viable alternative stance and the incipient signs of other policy styles can be traced back to this period. They would not fully emerge, however, until the processes of governance and Canada's political culture changed in ways that created new opportunities and roles for policy analysts. These changes were already taking place during the first Trudeau government and have accelerated since the 1980s.

Policy Analysis in the Age of Scientism: 1968 Onward

The early years of Pierre Trudeau's prime ministership appeared to usher in a new golden era for the policy analysis profession. In place of the bureaucratic mandarins whom Trudeau mistrusted, however, the distinguishing characteristic of this new era would be the policy analysis unit. Trudeau's sometimes gushing enthusiasm for rationality in policy making contributed to the proliferation of such units throughout government. His well-known rhapsody to planning at the Liberals' 1969 Harrison Hot Springs conference was music to many a technocrat's ear: 'We are aware that the many techniques of cybernetics, by transforming the control function and the manipulation of information, will transform our whole society. With this knowledge we are wide awake, alert, capable of action; no longer are we blind, inert pawns of fate' (quoted in Doern 1971, 65).

Trudeau's philosophy of governance helped elevate the status of the policy analysis profession, but the prime minister's contribution was more a nudge toward a destination where the profession was already heading than a decisive push. Other factors were also at work. One of these involved reform of the budgetary process during the 1960s, including the introduction of Planning, Programming, Budgeting (PPB). PPB and its successors require much more information and evaluation than traditional budget making. The decision to separate the Treasury Board from the Department of Finance in 1964, and the growth in Treasury Board Secretariat personnel that followed, were signs of the analysis-oriented budgeting approach that was pioneered in the United States and imported into Canada. PPB has come and gone, followed by various incarnations that retain its rational-analytical spirit. Perhaps its most important legacy has been a large bureaucratic apparatus whose central purposes involve preparing information in the forms required by rational budgeting systems, and evaluating this information. Hardly any disinterested party would claim that these reforms have produced greater efficiency in government, or prevented the possibility for major miscalculations, like the enormous cost overruns associated with the federal gun registry.

The creation of several new bureaucratic agencies and departments was another factor that elevated the status of policy analysts and their craft. They included the Science Council of Canada (1966), the Department of Regional Economic Expansion (1969), the Department of the Environment (1970), the Ministry of State for Urban Affairs (1971), and the Ministry of Science and Technology (1971). Only a few of these organizations have survived the various bureaucratic reorganizations that have occurred over the last two decades, the others having been disbanded or absorbed into other parts of the machinery of state. But the spirit that spawned this cluster of policy-oriented agencies has persisted within departments and agencies throughout government.

Although it is impossible to get a precise fix on the number of bureaucrats whose jobs involve policy analysis, there is no doubt that they number in the thousands. The Department of the Environment is probably typical. It includes more than two dozen units, scattered across its various directorates, whose functions relate exclusively or chiefly to program and policy analysis, planning, and coordination. A sprawling ministry like Health and Welfare includes hundreds of bureaucrats designated 'policy/programme analysts,' 'policy advisers,' 'researchers,' 'consultants,' 'systems analysts,' and 'evaluators.'

Analysis, in its various guises, is very much embedded in the structure of the state and the processes of governance. Its ubiquity should not be confused, however, with influence. Those who have carefully studied policy analysis units and policy analysts agree that their impact is generally small and their numbers far out of proportion to their real influence (Porter 1965, 433–4). Nevertheless, along with royal commissions, task forces and other special studies that review policy and make recommendations, expert analysis performed within government is assumed to be a necessary part of the policy-making process even if, in the priceless words of one analyst, it involves 'turning cranks not connected to anything' (Savoie 1990, 213–16).

Outside the state, the growth of the policy analysis profession has been even more explosive. The publications and conferences offered by think tanks like the Fraser Institute, the C.D. Howe Institute, the Institute for Research on Public Policy, the Canadian Centre for Policy Alternatives, and the Caledon Institute of Social Policy contribute to the contours of elite discourse on policy issues. Other organizations, like the Canadian Council on Social Development, the Centre for Social Justice, the Vanier Institute of the Family, the Canadian Council of Chief Executives, the Canadian Environmental Law Association, and the Canadian Labour Congress, also draw on the services of social scientists in producing studies, submissions to government bodies, and information intended for the public. Large interest groups and professional lobbying firms provide employment opportunities for policy analysts. The mass media, both print and electronic, have specialized journalists for subjects like science, the environment, economics, native affairs, defence, health care, and education. Some of these journalists, through their impact on the policy agenda and on the terms of debate surrounding particular issues, and in combination with other actors and forces, occasionally are able to have a significant influence on policy.

The policy analysis community is much less exclusive than once was the case. Before the Second World War, it was entirely reasonable to speak of fewer than one hundred persons belonging to the fledging profession, mainly public servants and university professors, but including some journalists and individuals from the private sector (Owram 1986). Today that number is in the thousands. The highly elitist and personal character of the profession has disappeared, replaced by a more institutional quality that would not have surprised Max Weber. Indeed, the transition from an elite whose influence was based largely on personal attributes and group characteristics to a profession whose role and influence depend mainly on characteristics of the state and society is precisely what one expects to happen as a result of modernization in the Weberian sense.

Canada's policy analysis profession has always been a net importer of ideas, practices and practitioners. For much of the twentieth century it was common for those who ascended to the top of the policy analysis community, both within the state and in academe, to have received their graduate training outside Canada. The United Kingdom and the United States were particularly important training grounds for these policy analysts. With the growth of Canadian universities and graduate programs since the 1960s, the number and proportion of Canadian-trained analysts have increased. Education abroad continues, however, to be an important channel through which Canada's policy analysis community is open to international influences, as is immigration to Canada of highly trained policy experts.

The national origins of policy analysts and where they were educated are today probably less important than in the past. This is because of the globalization that has taken place in knowledge and policy discourses, such that it has become more difficult – and in some cases nonsensical – to speak of a national tradition or national differences in particular policy analysis domains. The policy conversation among experts on, for example, global warming cuts across national lines, as is also true of human rights, trade and many other issue domains. Canadians have been very active participants in these global policy communities, and indeed the 'soft power' of ideas and advocacy is seen by many opinion leaders in Canada as a way in which their country can exercise some influence on the global stage and, at the same time, maintain some degrees of separation from American interests and policies.

Politically, the question remains whether the policy analysis profession – diverse in terms of the specialized training of its members and their institutional affiliations – can reasonably be summed up using a single label. I would argue that while the profession's political centre of gravity is not fundamentally critical of the social or economic status quo, reformist elements on both the left and right of the ideological spectrum are politically influential. On the right, that part of the policy analysis community whose voice is heard through organizations like the Fraser Institute, the C.D. Howe Institute, the Canadian Council of Chief Executives, the Canadian Taxpayers Federation, and the *Financial Post*, and whose chief academic standard bearers are economists, clearly believes that reform of the status quo is necessary. Those on the left, including most policy analysts with ties to the environmental and feminist movements, and to the NDP, believe just as strongly that reforms are needed. Their diagnosis of what is wrong and prescriptions for change are, of course, very different from those of their right-wing counterparts. Both reform-minded wings of the profession are vocal and successful in capturing media attention for their ideas. In recent years the issues of taxation and health care reform have emerged as the chief lightning rods attracting their energies and crystallizing their differences.

But what is most significant about this third phase in the development of the policy analysis profession is how analysis and the policy analyst have become integral parts of public life, contributing to the conversations surrounding policy issues, and helping to shape both the thinking of policy makers and the contours of public opinion. This leads me to *scientism*, the label used by Neil Postman to describe a culture in which social science has assumed the role of touchstone for knowing moral truths. Postman provides a vivid illustration of scientism in action:

> I have been in the presence of a group of United States congressmen who were gathered to discuss, over a period of two days, what might be done to make the future of America more survivable and, if possible, more humane. Ten consultants were called upon to offer perspectives and advice. Eight of them were pollsters. They spoke of the 'trends' their polling uncovered; for example, that people were no longer interested in the women's movement, did not regard environmental issues as of paramount importance, did not think the 'drug problem' was getting worse, and so on. It was apparent, at once, that these polling results would become the basis of how the congressmen thought the future should be managed. The ideas the congressmen had (all men, by the way) receded to the background. Their own perceptions, instincts, insights, and experience paled into irrelevance. Confronted by 'social scientists,' they were inclined to do what the 'trends' suggested would satisfy the populace. (1993, 133)

There is nothing particularly wrong, of course, and much that is commendable, in paying serious attention to public opinion. But what the behaviour of these politicians confronted with the 'data' of pollsters and the interpretations of consultants illustrates is the more general phenomenon of modern society's faith in the techniques and authority of the social sciences. Statements like, 'Recent survey data indicate,' '80 per cent of Canadians believe,' and 'recent polling information demonstrates' are so commonly used in the media that one hardly notices the assumptions regarding knowledge, truth, and the best ways of ascertaining these that underlie them. Today, no one can seriously claim to know the will or mood of the populace without a survey that conforms to the methodological canons of the pollster's trade. This ensures, of course, a central role for the social scientist, both as technician and diviner of public opinion. Inevitably, the expert is looked to for answers to the question 'What should we do?' and not just 'How should we do it?'

Measured against the enormous expectations held for policy analysis and its practitioners as recently as the 1960s – namely, to *solve* problems whose roots lie in either structural circumstances or human behaviour, or both – the actual accomplishments of policy analysis have been relatively modest. Nevertheless, the fundamental premise that trained experts can generate knowledge and insights that should form the basis for better public policies, and thereby advance the general good, is widely accepted. There are, however, at least three reasons to be sceptical about the applied social science model.

First, experts often disagree profoundly in their diagnosis of a problem and their recommendations for action. To give but one example, research on the family in Western societies is roughly polarized into two camps, one of which concludes that heterosexual two-parent intact families are more likely than other family configurations to produce emotionally stable children who finish school and get good jobs. The other camp argues that family configuration does not matter and that whatever advantages this heterosexual two-parent family may appear to have are due largely to the typically higher incomes of these families compared to single-parent ones. Despite the hundreds of studies into the relationship between family configuration and the behaviour and adult lives of children, researchers remain far apart in their interpretations of cause and effect.

Second, experts and their research may be hijacked by powerful interests. For decades the tobacco industry managed to find scientists who were willing to declare that no conclusive link had been established by researchers between tobacco consumption and either respiratory disorders or cancer, despite an enormous accumulation of studies that concluded just the opposite. Researchers, like other mortals, may occasionally be willing to sell their souls for a research grant, a prestigious position, or some other enticement. The corruption of analysis by money and power usually operates in more subtle ways. One of the most important of these is the impact that the priorities of granting agencies, public and private, have on the subjects that researchers examine and the questions they pose. Another is the pervasive use of techniques developed in the social sciences and the employment of social scientists in the arts of manipulation. Marketing, public relations, advertising, lobbying, and government communications with the public all rely on methods generated in the social sciences.

Finally, the recommendations of policy analysts may be ignored for political or other reasons. Politicians are elected to govern, not to conduct a sort of academic seminar on public affairs. Most of them are not trained experts in the often highly technical policy matters they are called upon to decide. The political advisers and bureaucrats to whom they turn for advice are as likely as they are to view policy through the distorting prism of interests, public opinion, bureaucratic preferences and sensitivities, and other factors that, in an ideal world that does not exist, would not cloud the lens of the policy analyst.

Today, policy analysis is a firmly established part of the process by which public issues are framed and debated and by which public policies are judged. But despite its pervasiveness, it has failed to live up to the lofty expectations of those who pioneered policy analysis, for whom applied social research held the promise of eradicating the major problems facing mankind and of substituting scientific consensus for political squabbling. This has not happened. On the contrary, studies and recommendations are regularly judged and either approved or rejected on an *ad hominem* basis, the assumption being that the credibility and quality of the analysis can be determined by who produced it.

The shortcomings of policy analysis are many. Analysis may be ideologically biased, methodologically flawed or simply ignored when its conclusions are found to be inconvenient or contrary to the preferences of policy makers. But even with its limitations, few among us would prefer that policy issues be discussed and resolved without the involvement of experts, the commissioning of studies, the contributions of think tanks and the steady diet of information, ideas, and recommendations they generate.

The proliferation of policy experts and of sites within and outside the state, from which their contributions to the framing and making of policy are made, has been accompanied by a decline in the dominance of the rational-hierarchical policy analysis style. While 'speaking truth to power' is a characterization that many policy analysts, particularly within the state, would continue to embrace, 'upsetting the apple cart,' 'struggling for social justice,' and 'providing value to my client' are alternative self-images that many would find a better fit. As Michael Prince points out in his chapter, the ways in which policy analysts/ advisors in the state think of their roles and do their jobs have changed significantly (see table 1 in chapter 7). But in the broader analysis profession, change is no less apparent. The *client advice, participative*, and *argumentative* policy analysis styles have all become more prominent during the last few decades. Those who provide analysis to a client for a price and those whose policy analysis activities – choice of issues, methodology, and interpretive framework – are guided by social justice concerns share one important trait: neither conforms to the traditional 'speaking truth to power' model. Indeed, to a generation trained to believe that policy agendas and the conversations and conceptualizations associated with issues are inevitably constructed, and that one of the important functions of analysis is to deconstruct the accepted narratives of the powerful, the slogan 'speaking truth to power' probably sounds hopelessly quaint (and surely ideological!). Ironically, perhaps, the age of scientism is also an era when – at least in the human sciences – the proposition that knowledge will lead to the discovery of truths that can, in turn, guide policy choice seems very distant.

Conclusion

The policy analysis profession has undergone enormous changes since its inception almost a century ago. From a small, reform-minded elite, it achieved a secure status within the postwar Keynesian welfare state, and more recently has assumed an influential role in society through its impact on public consciousness and the terms of policy debate. The highly personal influence of the fledgling profession's leading members – individuals like Adam Shortt, W.A. Mackintosh, and Clifford Clark – has been replaced by a more collective influence that is based on the popular authority of social scientific knowledge in the modern age. Every age requires its priests, shamans, or elders: some group whose role it is to make sense of life and explain its truths to others. Ours turns to policy experts, social scientists, and pollsters, giving the policy analysis profession an influence that is profound, if diffuse and indirect, in the age of scientism.

NOTE

1 For a discussion of the ideas underlying the progressive movement, see
  Hawkins 1976.

REFERENCES

Allen, Richard. 1971. *The Social Passion: Religion and Social Reform in Canada,
  1914–1928.* Toronto: University of Toronto Press.
Ames, Herbert. 1897. *The City Below the Hill.* Montreal.
Bradford, Neil. 1998. *Commissioning Ideas.* Toronto: Oxford University Press.
Brooks, S., and A.G. Gagnon. 1988. *Social Scientists and Politics in Canada:
  Between Clerisy and Vanguard.* Kingston and Montreal: McGill-Queen's
  University Press.
Canada. 2002a. Commission on the Future of Health Care in Canada. *Final
  Report.* November.
– 2002b. Standing Senate Committee on Social Affairs, Science and Technol-
  ogy. *The Health of Canadians: The Federal Role.* October.
Doern, G. Bruce, and Peter Aucoin, eds. 1971. *The Structures of Policy-Making
  in Canada.* Toronto: Macmillan.
Esmail, Nadeem, and Michael Walker with Sabrina Yeudall. 2004. *How Good is
  Canadian Health Care? 2004 Report.* Vancouver: Fraser Institute.
Granatstein, J.L. 1982. *The Ottawa Men: The Civil Service Mandarins, 1935–1957.*
  Toronto: Oxford University Press.
Hawkins, Hugh. 1976. 'The Ideal of Objectivity Among American Social
  Scientists in the Era of Professionalization, 1876–1916.' In C. Frankel, ed.,
  Controversies and Decisions. New York: Russell Sage Foundation.
Horowitz, Ira. 1970. 'Social Science Mandarins: Policymaking as a Political
  Formula.' *Policy Sciences* 1(3), 339–60.
Johnson, Harry G. 1974. 'The Current and Prospective State of Economics in
  Canada.' In T.N. Guinsberg and G.L. Reuber, eds., *Perspectives on the Social
  Sciences in Canada.* Toronto: University of Toronto Press.
Laing, Gertrude. 1979. 'The Contributions of Social Scientists to Policy-
  making – The B&B Experience.' In A.W. Rasporich, ed., *The Social Sciences
  and Public Policy in Canada.* Calgary: University of Calgary Press.
Mackintosh, W.A. 1937. 'An Economist Looks at Economics.' *Canadian Journal
  of Economics and Political Science* 3(3), 311–457.
Owram, Doug. 1986. *The Government Generation: Canadian Intellectuals and the
  State, 1900–1945.* Toronto: University of Toronto Press.

Porter, John. 1965. *The Vertical Mosaic*. Toronto: University of Toronto Press.

Postman, Neil. 1993. *Technopoly: The Surrender of Culture to Technology*. New York: Vintage Books.

Savoie, Donald J. 1990. *The Politics of Public Spending in Canada*. Toronto: University of Toronto Press.

Schafer, Arthur. 2002. *'Waiting for Romanow': Canada's Health Care Values Under Fire*. Toronto: Canadian Centre for Policy Alternatives.

Yalmzyan, Armine. 2003. *Paying for Keeps: Securing the Future of Public Health Care in Canada*. Toronto: Canadian Centre for Policy Alternatives.

Whitaker, Reginald. 1977. *The Government Party: Organizing and Financing the Liberal Party of Canada, 1930–58*. Toronto: University of Toronto Press.

3 The Choice of Formal Policy Analysis Methods in Canada

AIDAN R. VINING AND ANTHONY E. BOARDMAN

Introduction: The Problem of Policy Choice[1]

One of the primary purposes of applied policy analysis is to assist public policy decision makers in comparing and evaluating policy alternatives.[2] However, there is considerable evidence from all levels of government in Canada, as well as from other countries, that policy analysts, as well as their political and bureaucratic clients, have considerable difficulty at this stage of the policy analysis process (Mayne 1994; Muller-Clemm and Barnes 1997; Greene 2002). Although a major purpose of *ex ante* analysis, also sometimes referred to as policy or project appraisal, is to assist decision making, the Treasury Board Secretariat (TBS) notes 'its actual use has often proved to be limited, especially in relation to policy decisions and budget allocations' (TBS n.d., 2).[3] The evidence is broadly similar in the United States (Hahn 2000).

A number of governmental institutions in Canada are leading the push for better and more transparent analysis. At the federal level, the auditor general has been the most consistent voice over the last decade in the call for better and more transparent analysis and evaluation (Auditor General of Canada 1996, 1997, 2000, 2003). It has not, however, been the only federal agency to do so. The Government of Canada's recent Regulatory Policy, for example, now requires cost-benefit analysis of regulatory changes (Privy Council Office 1999). Many other federal agencies now routinely require 'economic evaluations.' Sport Canada, for example, in its funding requirements for hosting international sports events, requires an assessment of both economic benefits and economic impacts. In addition, Sports Canada suggests applicants consider both 'social benefits' (such as the impact on Canadian identity, youth involvement, and gender equity) and 'cultural benefits' (such as exposure of Canadian culture to tourists and the involvement of cultural organizations). Similarly, the National Crime Prevention Strategy requires that applications for crime prevention funds adopt a cost-benefit approach based on the Treasury Board's Benefit-Cost Analysis Guide (1976, 1998) and Program Evaluation Methods (1997). Provincial governments also require ministries and other agencies to provide *ex ante* evaluations of new programs, policies and regulations.

Even though a variety of guidelines now suggest or require some type of formal analysis, including the explicit comparison of alternatives, none that we are aware of specify in detail what this means. For example, while federal Regulatory Impact Analysis Statements (RIAS) require an assessment of costs and benefits, there is no elaboration on the meaning of these terms. As a result, the requirements are quite permissive in terms of analytic method and depth of analysis – as can be seen by a quick perusal of agency RIAS submissions published in the *Canadian Gazette*. At the same time, some agencies, as illustrated by the Sports Canada example, are demanding cost-benefit analysis *and more*. Adding to the high methodological degrees of freedom is the fact that many managers and analysts misunderstand the meaning of the terms 'costs' and 'benefits,' as well as of other relevant analytic terminology (Boardman, Vining, and Waters 1993).

There are many reasons for poor or superficial analysis by government agencies. Lack of methodical sophistication is only one of them. In some cases political clients foresee that they will dislike the recommendations of good analysis and deliberately discourage it. Other politicians simply prefer more informal decision aids, including discussion papers and (relatively) unstructured briefing papers. But at least some of the deficiency in the supply of good analysis stems from lack of knowledge, or confusion, about appropriate methods. To actually conduct effective formal analysis, analysts and decision makers must first decide *how* to analyse the problem and compare policy alternatives; that is, they must choose the choice method – in short, they must make a metachoice. In practice, however, metachoice decisions are frequently made without explicit consideration or thought, and are often totally implicit. This is an issue not only in Canada; it has been noted across the OECD countries generally (OECD 1995) and has been well documented in the United States (GAO 1998; Hahn et al. 2000). Currently, the United

Kingdom government is making the most effort to specify permissible analytic methods and their usage, and to assist agencies in these respects (HM Treasury 1997; Dodgson et al. 2001).

Confusion on metachoice decisions is perhaps not surprising given that there has been relatively little guidance on the topic (but see Moore 1995; Pearce 1998; and Dodgson et al. 2001 for some discussion of these issues). We have already noted that Canadian governments are increasingly calling for analysis, but are sometimes reluctant to describe in detail what specific analytic methodologies would be appropriate. Given this, the purpose of this chapter is to present a metachoice framework. The following section posits four *choice method classes*. Within some of these classes, there are a variety of different *analytic choice methods*. The following section of the chapter discusses each of the four choice methods and provides examples of their uses in Canada.

A Metachoice Framework

Our metachoice framework has both descriptive and normative purposes. The descriptive purpose is to document the various analytical methods that are mandated for or used by government *analysts* in Canada. This is not a claim that *clients* (even if they formally require such analyses) necessarily use them to make their own agency decisions (Boardman, Vining, and Waters 1993; Radin 2002; Vining and Weimer 2001). The normative purpose is to assist policy analysts and interested public decision makers more clearly understand the fundamental differences between the different choice methods and when each should be used.

The *ex ante* evaluation phase of policy analysis requires five steps: (1) generating a set of mutually exclusive policy alternatives; (2) selecting a goal, or set of goals, against which to evaluate the policy alternatives; (3) predicting, or forecasting, the impact of the policy alternatives in terms of the selected goal or goals; (4) valuing the predicted impacts in terms of the goal or goals (or in terms of a set of performance criteria that are proxies for the goal or goals) over the complete set of policy alternatives; and (5) evaluating the set of policy alternatives against the set of goals. As will become clearer later, metachoice issues arise at each of the steps, except alternatives generation (step 1). Metachoice directly and explicitly concerns goal selection (step 2) and valuation method (step 4). But metachoice also pertains to the prediction of impacts (step 3) because willingness to engage in monetization, in practice, often depends on the nature of predicted impacts. Metachoice also affects

Table 3.1 Metachoice Framework and Choice Method Classes

	Single goal of efficiency	Multiple goals including efficiency
Comprehensive monetization of all efficiency impacts	Cost-benefit analysis	Embedded cost-benefit analysis
Less-than-comprehensive monetization of efficiency impacts	Efficiency analysis	Multi-goal analysis

evaluation (step 5), as this step is necessarily dependent on goal selection (step 2), prediction (step 3), and valuation (step 4).

The fundamental metachoice decision depends on two factors: (1) goal orientation and breadth, and (2) willingness to monetize impacts. Put simply, in deciding among different potential choice methods, policy analysts face two important questions. The first question is: What are the policy goals? The second question is: Is the analyst willing and able to monetize all of the *efficiency* impacts of all alternatives? Reponses to the first question can be dichotomized into the 'Goal of Efficiency' or 'Multiple Goals Including Efficiency.' For reasons explained below, we posit that efficiency should always be a goal in public policy analysis. Responses to the second question can be dichotomized into 'Comprehensive Monetization of all efficiency impacts' or 'Less-than-Comprehensive Monetization.' Dichotomization of each of these two factors results in four policy choice method classes: (comprehensive) cost-benefit analysis, efficiency analysis, embedded cost-benefit analysis, and multi-goal analysis (see table 3.1). As we describe later, there are a number of specific methods within each method class. The purpose of the paper is *not* to normatively rank these method classes, but rather to clarify the main normative and practical issues that arise in choosing a class in a particular context. We also briefly discuss some of the methodological issues and implications relating to the use of specific choice methods (techniques) within each method class.

Goals

Goal selection is obviously a difficult normative exercise in public policy. The ultimate purpose of public policy is to increase the welfare of society. Consequently, theorists usually posit a social welfare function that is a function of the utilities of all members of society (Bergson

1938). The issue then becomes what form the welfare function should take in a public policy context (Mueller 1989, 373–441). Obviously, this can be a source of considerable controversy. However, there is generally agreement in principle that the allocation of resources should be efficient. (The formal requirements for *ex ante* evaluation cited in the introduction of this paper clearly mandate an important, often dominant or exclusive, role for efficiency as a goal.) There is also general agreement that equity is a desirable goal in specific policy contexts.

However, under reasonable assumptions, there is a fundamental trade-off between allocative efficiency and equity. This trade-off is represented diagrammatically in figure 3.1, where allocative efficiency is on the vertical axis and equity is on the horizontal axis. The goal possibility frontier (GPF) is analogous to a production possibility frontier, but the output variables are goals (allocative efficiency and equity), rather than traditional 'goods.' In figure 3.1, the GPF represents the 'goal efficient' combinations of allocative efficiency and equity. Its shape reflects the inherent trade-off between allocative efficiency and equity. As Okun (1975, 88) points out, 'in places ... some equality will be sacrificed for the sake of efficiency, and some efficiency for the sake of equality.'[4]

This trade-off arises largely due to incentive effects. If, for example, it is agreed that everyone should have the same income, there would be little incentive for anyone to work and output would be low or possibly zero, as at point T. As society moves from point T to point S on the GPF frontier, allocative efficiency increases, but this is only likely to happen if some people have an incentive to do better than others, i.e., only at the expense of equity.

It is possible that society is at an interior point, such as Z. For example, it may transfer resources to poorer members of society in an inefficient way – in effect, using a 'leaky bucket.' Increasing efficiency by using a less leaky bucket, for example, would necessarily increase allocative efficiency and could also improve equity. This would move society from Z toward X or Y or some other point on the GPF above and possibly to the right of Z.

Through appropriate taxes and transfers, it is possible to obtain any point on the GPF. The unresolved question is where on the frontier society should be. To answer this, we need to know the social welfare function. Figure 3.1 also shows a set of social indifference curves (SICs) where each curve represents a combination of allocative efficiency and equity that provide society with equal levels of welfare or utility. For

Figure 3.1 The Efficiency/Equity Trade-Off

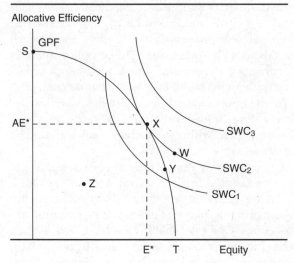

example, society is indifferent between points X and W on SIC_2. The negative slopes of these SICs imply that society is willing to give up some allocative efficiency in order to increase equity. Society would, of course, wish to reach the highest possible indifference curve. Given the SICs and the GPF shown in figure 3.1, society would maximize social welfare at X on SIC_2. At this point, the GPF curve and SIC_2 are tangential to each other.

An allocatively efficient policy is one that achieves the maximum difference between the social benefits and social costs relative to the alternatives, including the status quo. Even if society mostly cared about redistributing resources to poorer members of society, few would argue that this should be done with leaky buckets if it could be avoided. Improving allocative efficiency increases the resources available for distribution (to anyone): it, therefore, facilitates redistribution. Thus, allocative efficiency should always be a goal of policy analysis.

A key question is whether policy analysts should treat allocative efficiency as the *only* goal against which to analyse policy alternatives. Weimer and Vining (2005) argue that allocative efficiency should often be the only relevant goal in some policy analyses, but that for many other policy problems, multiple goals are relevant. Okun (1975) argues that the efficiency-equity trade-off is the 'big one.' Many other commentators have implicitly or explicitly made similar arguments (Reinke 1999; Whitehead and Avison 1999; Myers 2002). Kaplow and Shavell (2002, 2005), however, advance the thesis that public policy analysis should not consider 'fairness' as a separate goal. Nussbaum (2000) argues that basic social entitlements should act as a separate goal, or at least as a constraint.[5] As the Sports Canada example described earlier demonstrates, Canadian federal agencies often mention the relevance of distributional analysis, but often without specifying how it should be incorporated into an analysis.

The net government revenue of a policy may also be a legitimate public policy goal. Both the United States General Accounting Office (GAO 1998) and the Congressional Budget Office (CBO 1992) explicitly posit three goals in many of their analyses: efficiency, equity, and impact on government revenues. One rationale for the latter goal is that, although government has the power to increase revenues through taxes, subprovincial governments are not permitted to run deficits. Thus, increases in government revenues or reductions in expenditures are often relevant impacts in terms of this goal. In practice, governments and agencies often have a more or less fixed budget when considering alternative policies. More usually, therefore, the impact on net government revenue flows enters the analysis as a constraint, rather than as a goal.

Ethical behaviour is nearly always an implicit goal or constraint. Maximizing allocative efficiency alone *in specific contexts* may be morally objectionable (Adler and Posner 2000). Where ethics is a potential concern (for example, in some developing country projects), it is useful to explicitly identify ethical behaviour as a goal.

Political feasibility is often an appropriate goal of analysts (Webber 1986). All major decisions require cooperation or approval by political actors (Rich 1989). Analysts may well wish to take this reality explicitly into account in choosing between policy alternatives. On the other hand, many clients prefer political feasibility to be implicit even when all other goals are treated explicitly.

There may be other goals in addition to the ones described above.[6] In practice, analysts and decision makers almost always know intuitively whether they wish to pursue only the one goal of efficiency or multiple goals. Formally, there are effectively multiple goals when a marginal increment of efficiency (one goal) is not perfectly correlated with marginal increments of any other goal.

Monetization

Monetization means attaching a monetary value (e.g., dollars) to each efficiency impact. It goes beyond quantification (where each impact is typically measured in quantitative but disparate units) as all predicted impacts are measured using the same metric. For example, quantitative measures of impacts, such as the number of lives saved by a highway improvement project or the number of hours of commuting time saved, may be monetized by multiplying them by the value of a life saved and the value of an hour of commuting time saved, respectively. Monetization makes impacts commensurable so that they can be added or subtracted (Adler 1998). Monetization also means that analysts can compute the social costs and benefits (and the net social benefits) of each alternative. Although it is not a necessary requirement that the common metric be money, this is the most natural measure as many impacts of public policies are most appropriately valued using actual costs or prices or through shadow prices.

We distinguish between comprehensive monetization and less-than-comprehensive (or partial) monetization. Comprehensive monetization requires the analyst to attach monetary values to *all* efficiency impacts. Sometimes, however, public decision makers, academic commentators or policy analysts are unwilling to explicitly monetize the full range of efficiency impacts, even when the only goal is efficiency. There are at least four reasons for this reluctance. First, many senior decision makers and analysts resist quantification, and particularly monetization, for psychological reasons. This tendency increases with uncertainty concerning the predicted outcomes. Second, resistance can stem from the difficulty of determining appropriate monetary values for every impact. Monetization can be difficult and costly, especially in the absence of appropriate 'plug-in' values (Boardman et al. 1997). Third, analysts and managers may have ideological, political, or strategic reasons for avoiding monetization and even quantification (Adams 1992; Rees 1998; Flyvbjerg, Holm, and Buhl 2002). Fourth, some believe that from a normative perspective, monetization of some impacts is inherently wrong. For example, Ackerman and Heinzerling (2002, 1562) argue 'the translation of all good things into dollars and the devaluation of the future are inconsistent with the way many people view the world. Most of us believe that money doesn't buy happiness. Most religions tell us that every human life is sacred.' (For the argument in favour of monetization, see Vining and Weimer 1992.) Of the method classes described below, only cost-benefit analysis requires comprehensive monetization, while embedded cost-benefit analysis requires monetization of only the efficiency impacts. In multi-goal analysis there may be no monetization at all.

The Four Choice Method Classes

Putting the two dimensions together results in four classes of choice method. We describe them as 'classes' because there are many variations within some classes. We now discuss each of the four method classes in turn.

(Comprehensive) Cost-Benefit Analysis

Cost-benefit analysis is conceptually straightforward (Boardman et al. 2006). It requires both prediction *and* valuation of all efficiency impacts using actual prices or shadow prices. All impacts, and therefore all policy alternatives, are made *explicitly* commensurate through monetization. Future impacts are weighted less than current impacts by the use of a positive social discount rate in the net present value (NPV) formula.

Some analysts base decisions on the benefit-cost ratio or the internal rate of return (IRR). The benefit-cost ratio provides a measure of efficiency – in effect, the best 'bang for the buck.' However, it more accurately measures technical (managerial) efficiency than allocative efficiency. The project with the largest benefit-cost ratio is not necessarily the most allocatively efficient project. This outcome can arise when projects are of different scales (sizes). The IRR can be used for selecting projects when there is only one alternative to the status quo. However, there are a number of potential problems. The IRR may not be unique and, because it is a ratio, it also suffers from problems due to different scaled projects.

As Green (2002) points out, 'cost-benefit analysis appears to be experiencing a revival of its credibility'. While it has always played a role in infrastructure areas such as transportation (e.g., Martin 2001; HLB Decision Economics 2002), it now plays an important role in a range of policy areas where it traditionally had little influence on public policy making, such as environmental policy (e.g., Hrudey et al. 2001) and welfare policy (e.g., Richards et al. 1995; Friedlander, Greenberg, and Robins 1997). Scholars are also paying more attention to cost-benefit analysis's philosophical underpinnings (e.g., Adler and Posner 2000).

Cost-benefit analysis has a number of practical limitations (Boardman, Mallery and Vining 1994). First, it may not include relevant efficiency impacts (omission errors), because the analysts failed to discern them. For example, offsetting impacts of programs are often difficult to foresee – enhanced safety features on automobiles may induce faster driving that injures more pedestrians. Second, precise monetization is not always possible (valuation errors). There is, for example, considerable disagreement about the value of a statistical life. Third, there may be errors in prediction (forecasting errors), especially for unique projects and policies with long time frames. Fourth, there may be errors in measurement (measurement errors). Fifth, the fact that cost-benefit analysis requires explicitness and comprehensiveness means that it is usually more expensive than alternative methods (Moore 1995). While these limitations may appear to reduce the practicality of cost-benefit analysis, it is important to emphasize that other choice methods do not avoid the first four limitations; these limitations are just more implicit.

The major value of cost-benefit analysis, as Hahn and Sunstein (2002, 1491) emphasize, is that it can move society toward more efficient resource allocation decisions. It provides information on which policy alternatives are in 'the right ballpark.' An additional important value is that it is more explicit about the predictions and valuations. This, of course, permits critics to more cogently dispute these predictions and valuations. This form of criticism is more difficult to do when policy proposals do not explicitly lay out the basis of predictions or valuations. Of necessity, however, these predictions and valuations are there.

An example of government using cost-benefit analysis is a report prepared by the BC Ministry of Industry and Small Business Development on the northeast coal development project (Bowden and Malkinson 1982). A summary of the results of an *ex ante* analysis is shown in table 3.2. Because the coal was exported, the benefits are in the form of increased profits (producer surplus) to industry and increased taxes to government. There was no direct benefit (consumer surplus) to Canadian consumers. It was a well-conducted study that included sensitivity analysis with respect to both the real price of coal and the market

Table 3.2 Benefit-Cost Analysis of the Northeast Coal Project

	Benefits	Costs	Net benefits
Mining sector	3316	3260	56
Transport sector			
Trucking	33	33	0
Canadian National Railway	504	358	146
BC Railway	216	202	14
Port Terminal	135	150	−15
Analysis & survey	11	11	0
British Columbia			
Royalties & taxes	231		231
Infrastructure	0	88	−88
Tumbler Ridge Branchline	91	267	−176
Canada			
Corporate taxes	134	0	134
Highways, port navigation	0	26	−26
Total	4671	4395	276

Source: Bowden and Malkinson (1982, 108). All figures are present values in 1980 dollars, using a 10 per cent discount rate and assuming no terminal value in 2003, the end of the discounting period.

prospects for coal. A subsequent re-analysis by Waters (undated) produced similar results. Waters suggested the net benefits were slightly higher than the ministry's study due to the appropriate inclusion of $50 million benefits accruing to labour (producer surplus) and $5 million net environmental benefits. Despite the quality of the report, actual outcomes were considerably different from those predicted, largely due to much higher mine costs and the decline in the world price of coal.

As emphasized earlier, many regulations at both the federal and provincial levels mandate some form of evaluation of costs and benefits, although it is not clear that all of these mandates require cost-benefit analysis, rigorously defined. For example, the Government of Canada Regulatory Policy simply requires that 'the benefits outweigh the costs to Canadians, their government and businesses' (Privy Council Office 1999, 1). While cost-benefit analysis would clearly suffice to demonstrate that a proposed policy met these conditions, it is unclear that this type of analysis *per se* is required: some more limited consideration of efficiency might also suffice (Moore 1995). Such forms, which do not comprehensively monetize impacts, are considered next.

Efficiency Analysis

Here, the analyst accepts the legitimacy of allocative efficiency as the sole goal, but is not willing (or able) to monetize all of the impacts. Efficiency analysis can take on a wide variety of forms, depending on the degree to which analysts include efficiency impacts that extend beyond the client agency, bureau or organization and on the willingness to monetize these impacts (Moore 1995). Table 3.3 contains different forms of efficiency analysis and illustrates how they vary depending on how costs and benefits are included and monetized. In this table, costs and benefits are generally measured more comprehensively as one reads from the top-left corner to the bottom-right. The measurement of costs and benefits can be categorized into five levels of inclusiveness and monetization: (1) costs or benefits are not included at all; (2) only the agency's costs or benefits are included; (3) some non-agency costs or benefits are included;[7] (4) all social costs or benefits are included, but not all of them are monetized; and (5) all social costs or benefits are included and monetized.

In the top left-hand cell, there is obviously no efficiency analysis, as neither costs nor benefits are included. In these situations, efficiency is not considered and analysis is based on other goals, such as political goals. In the bottom right-hand cell, *all* efficiency impacts are included and monetized. This cell corresponds to cost-benefit analysis and the analysis is equivalent to the top-left quadrant of table 3.1 (it is also included in table 3.3 for comparison purposes).

Table 3.3 identifies eight main efficiency analysis methodologies (apart from cost-benefit analysis): cost analysis, social costing, revenue analysis, effectiveness analysis, economic impact analysis, revenue-expenditure analysis, cost-effectiveness analysis, monetized net benefits analysis and qualitative cost-benefit analysis. Each of these methods measures efficiency (broadly defined) to some degree. They differ depending on the manner in which 'costs' and 'benefits' are included and valued.

Cost analysis (CA) measures the monetary cost to the agency of a policy or project. CA is used in virtually every agency to some extent. This methodology is simple in principle. The performance of an agency on a project can be assessed by comparing the agency's costs to those in other jurisdictions or by examining changes in costs over time. Obviously, a major potential problem is that outputs may change over time or vary across jurisdictions. A more conceptual problem is that analysts often measure the average cost of a project, rather than its marginal (incremental) cost because it is more readily available and more 'objec-

Table 3.3 Typology of Efficiency Analysis Methodologies

'Costs' inclusion and monetization	'Benefits' inclusion and monetization				
	No 'benefits' included	Agency revenue only	Some non-agency benefits included also	All social benefits included, but not all monetized	All social benefits included and monetized
No 'costs' included	No efficiency analysis	Revenue analysis	Effectiveness analysis; economic impact analysis	Effectiveness analysis	Effectiveness analysis
Agency costs only	Cost analysis	Revenue-expenditure analysis	Cost-effectiveness analysis, MNBA, IQCBA	IQCBA, MNBA	IQCBA, MNBA
Some non-agency costs also included	Incomplete social costing	IQCBA, MNBA	Cost-effectiveness analysis, MNBA, IQCBA	IQCBA, MNBA	IQCBA, MNBA
All social costs included, but not all monetized	Incomplete social costing	IQCBA, MNBA	Cost-effectiveness analysis, MNBA, IQCBA	Qualitative CBA/ MNBA+	Qualitative CBA, MNBA+
All social costs included and monetized	Complete social costing	IQCBA, MNBA	Cost-effectiveness analysis, MNBA, IQCBA	Qualitative CBA/ MNBA+	CBA

tive.' But, marginal cost is usually the appropriate cost measure for public policy analysis purposes. Another fundamental problem with using CA is that, even for government impacts, it may not reflect the opportunity cost of a resource. For example, the cost of a piece of land used in a project may not be included if it is government-owned. The land is treated as if it has a zero opportunity cost when, in fact, the opportunity cost may be very high.

Social costing (SC) includes at least some non-agency costs in addition to agency costs. SC may include and quantify all social costs or be incomplete (either it does not include, or does not monetize, some social cost). It is almost always useful to know the cost of a policy or the social cost of a problem (e.g., Anderson 1999). Of course, similar to CA, SC suffers from the problem that it does do not take into account the benefits of a program.

Revenue analysis (RA) simply measures the monetary benefits to the agency of a policy or project. While we know of no agency that explicitly advocates this as an exclusive approach to public sector valuation, it can implicitly become an important criterion. It is well known that revenues *per se* are never a good measure of the social value of the good that the agency would produce (willingness-to-pay is always a superior measure of value).

Effectiveness analysis (EA) includes benefits to other members of society, usually the public or taxpayers. It focuses on quantified measures of the outcomes of projects or policies: for example, the effectiveness of garbage collection might be measured by the number of tons of garbage collected or the effectiveness of a safety regulation by the number of lives saved. The performance of agencies can be assessed by analysis of changes in effectiveness over time or by comparison to comparable activities in other regions. Sometimes, agencies or programs are evaluated on the basis of the extent to which they attain their effectiveness goals.

EA has two major weaknesses. First, there may be other impacts that are not measured; for example, a project whose primary purpose is to save lives may also reduce injuries. Second, no consideration is given to the cost of the inputs used to generate the outputs. Thus, EA is a very limited form of efficiency analysis.

Economic impact analysis (EIA) generally produces a quantitative measure of the economic effect of an intervention. In practice, through income-expenditure analysis (not revenue-expenditure analysis, which we discuss later) or input-output analysis, it inevitably involves the use of multipliers – the overall impact is a multiple of the initial impact. It is important to note that EIA studies may ignore costs completely and do not specifically measure the value of a project. As Davis (1990, 6) stresses, 'such (impact) studies say nothing about the social *valuation* of the results (of a project or stimulus).' Further, he points out, 'the information produced by an impact analysis is at most a subset of that required by an evaluation analysis ... evaluation analysis necessitates information regarding the project's associated costs' (7). Despite these fatal normative weaknesses, governments probably use EIA analysis more than any other method.[8]

Revenue-expenditure analysis (REA) measures both agency benefits (revenues) and costs and takes the difference between them to compute the net agency revenue or net agency cost of a project. Sometimes, REA is called 'net budget impact analysis.' REA is the bread and butter of bureaucrats whose job it is to 'guard' overall budget integrity (Boardman, Vining, et al. 1993). Although it is very different from cost-benefit analysis, policy makers quite often slide into treating the two methods as equivalent. This is perhaps not surprising because agencies often have an incentive to conflate the two methods. Additionally, agencies are increasingly encouraged to adopt a strategic or 'business case' approach to analysis, which encourages a revenue-expenditure orientation (Phillips and Phillips 2004). Unfortunately, some scholars also conflate the two methods. Ackerman and Heinzerling (2002, 1554), for example, clearly do not understand the distinction between allocative efficiency and net government revenues.

REA is a more useful efficiency analysis method than those described above because it includes *some measures of both costs and benefits.* However, it suffers from many of the same problems as the methods discussed earlier in this section. For example, this method commonly omits important social impacts (e.g., customer waiting time); it measures budgetary costs rather than opportunity costs; it measures revenues rather than willingness-to-pay, and it excludes non-agency costs. REA and cost-benefit analysis often generate quite different appraisals of the net 'benefits' of a program; Boardman, Vining, and Waters (1993) describe these differences in detail.

Cost-effectiveness analysis (CEA) computes the ratio of costs-to-effectiveness. In standard CEA, there is a single non-agency benefit (or effectiveness) impact category, such as lives saved, and only agency costs are included in terms of costs. CEA computes the ratio of costs-to-effectiveness to obtain, for example, a measure of the average cost per life saved. It recommends the alternative with the smallest ratio. CEA is useful where there is only one major benefit category and the analyst is only prepared to quantify, rather than to monetize, that impact category, such as lives saved. On the cost side, it is common to include only agency budgetary costs (or net budgetary costs) and to ignore social costs and opportunity costs. Sometimes, non-agency costs are included, such as patient travel time or waiting time. It is possible that all social costs are included and monetized. CEA may occur in the four cells shown in table 3.3. Obviously, as the range and importance of omitted costs or benefits increase, the usefulness of CEA as an evaluative mechanism decreases (Dolan and Edlin 2002).[9]

Monetized net benefits analysis (MNBA) computes the NPV of those efficiency aspects that can be monetized easily. In many practical policy contexts, some efficiency impacts can be monetized relatively easily, while others are more difficult. In these situations, it often makes sense to compute the NPV of the efficiency aspects that can be easily monetized. MNBA pertains to all cells to the right of or below the cell pertaining to revenue-expenditure analysis. If all impacts were monetized then MNBA would be the same as CBA.

Qualitative cost-benefit analysis (MNBA+) entails consideration of all of the efficiency impacts of each alternative, but the analyst is not willing or able to monetize all of the impacts. As all efficiency impacts are included, qualitative CBA applies to the three cells near the bottom right-hand corner of table 3.3. At one extreme, this might look like a 'back of the envelope' analysis, where no entries are monetized and the cell entries are simply '+'s or '−'s. At the other extreme, it might look like a fairly comprehensive MNBA and also include the non-monetized intangible impacts. We refer to this type of qualitative CBA as MNBA+, where the + reflects the inclusion of all efficiency impacts in the analysis. This type of analysis is very similar to CBA.

Often, however, even in qualitative CBA, one or more efficiency impacts are omitted. This type of analysis is best described as *Incomplete Qualitative Cost-Benefit Analysis* (IQCBA). A great deal of economic policy analysis is of this type or is qualitative CBA, as analysts often fail to monetize all efficiency impacts.

Arrow et al. (1996) are probably arguing for MNBA+ analysis when they posit that analysts should 'give due consideration to factors that defy quantification but are thought to be important.' The Clinton administration also moved explicitly in this direction: 'the Clinton Executive Order allowed that: (1) not all regulatory costs and benefits can be monetized; and non-monetary consequences should be influential in regulatory analysis' (Cavanagh, Hahn, and Stavins 2001, 6).

An example of MNBA is provided by Health Canada's (2004) analysis of a regulation concerning the ignition propensity of cigarettes. Analysts expected that cigarette manufacturers would modify their paper technology. The cost of compliance includes new equipment purchases, changes in production, and undertaking quality assurance checks. Estimates of these costs varied between $0.126 per carton (according to the analysts) and $0.257 per carton (according to the industry) (all figures in 2002 dollars). The largest benefit category was the reduction in fatalities. Under one scenario (67 per cent reduction in fires), the regulations would save an average of 36 fatalities a year, while a second scenario (34 per cent reduction in fires) suggests that the regulations would save 18 fatalities per year. Assuming the value of a statistical life (VSL) equals $5.8 million, the value of the annual reduction in fatalities would range from $104 million to $209 million. To value injuries, analysts used the health care cost approach rather than willingness-to-pay. The estimated cost is $1,679 for a non-fatal injury to a firefighter. For others, analysts used estimates of $161 for any type of injury, but $78,738 for a serious burn that requires hospitalization. Assuming that these benefits and costs would accrue in perpetuity and using a discount rate of 3 per cent, the present values of the benefits and costs are presented in table 3.4.

This well-conducted study uses reasonable estimates of the VSL and the social discount rate. The perpetuity assumption could be questioned, but is not unreasonable. Another questionable assumption is that there is no change in prices and no change in demand, although the report does discuss the issue. However, even this is not a (comprehensive) cost-benefit analysis, because of some of the simplifying assumptions and because some impacts are not quantified. For example, as the authors note, the cost estimates did not include the cost of administering or enforcing the new policy, transitional costs (such as changes in employment) or social surplus losses due to higher prices. Also, the injury cost savings are underestimated because they are based on health care costs, rather than willingness-to-pay estimates.

A hypothetical example of the results of a MNBA+ analysis is provided in table 3.5. Here, all efficiency impacts are monetized, except some dimensions of environmental protection. The layout of information in this manner helps to clarify the decision problem. The decision maker may be able to decide immediately which option she prefers. Clearly, alternative B can be dropped, as it is dominated by alternative

Table 3.4 Monetized Net Benefit Analysis of Proposed Ignition Propensity Standard

	Analyst's estimates		Industry's estimates	
	Scenario 1	Scenario 2	Scenario 1	Scenario 2
Benefits:				
Reduced fatalities	6960	3480	6960	3480
Reduced injuries	7	3	7	3
Reduced property damage	637	320	637	320
Costs:				
Compliance	867	867	1766	1766
Net benefits	6737	2936	5837	2036

Source: Derived from Health Canada (2004). All figures are present values in 2002 $CDN millions, assuming impacts occur in perpetuity and a 3 per cent discount rate.

Table 3.5 A Hypothetical Example of MNBA+ Analysis

	Policy alternatives		
Goals/impacts	Alternative A	Alternative B	Alternative C
NPV of monetized efficiency impacts	$105 M	$78 M	$96 M
Environmental protection	Low	Medium	High

C. The choice depends on her preferences for alternatives A and C. In effect, she has to ask herself whether it is worth paying $9 million (or more) for the environmental protection benefits of alternative C than for the environmental protection benefits of alternative A. Answering this question may be easier (psychologically less painful) than giving a specific monetized value to the non-monetized impact, which would be required for cost-benefit analysis. Note, however, that some form of monetization cannot be completely avoided.[10]

When there are *multiple* non-monetized efficiency impacts, decision making is more complex. Nijkamp (1997, 147) suggests 'the only reasonable way to take account of intangibles in the traditional cost-benefit analysis seems to be the use of a balance with a debit and credit side in which all intangible project effects (both positive and negative) are represented in their own (qualitative or quantitative) dimensions.' Explicitly or implicitly, decision makers have to weight the different efficiency impacts. We discuss this further in multi-goal analysis.
Embedded Cost-Benefit Analysis

Embedded cost-benefit analysis is appropriate where there are other goals in addition to efficiency. As its title suggests, embedded cost-benefit analysis is a hybrid method. *All* aspects of efficiency are monetized. Therefore, the analyst performs a (comprehensive) cost-benefit analysis that includes the NPV of the social benefits and costs. But, in addition, at least one other goal is important – typically equity or the impact on government revenues. The non-efficiency goal or goals may be assessed using either a quantitative measure (e.g., '10% increase in equity') or a qualitative measure (e.g., 'politically infeasible'). Sometimes more than one non-efficiency goal is included, but for descriptive simplicity in this section we will refer only to the singular case.[11]

In practice, many government agencies in Canada use this general approach. The 1998 edition of the Treasury Board Benefit-Cost Guide goes further than the original 1976 version and declares 'Distributional issues are important to the Government of Canada and should be considered in-depth in each benefit-cost analysis' (TBS 1998, 82). The New Brunswick government and Human Resources Development Canada use this approach to evaluate the New Brunswick Job Corps, embedding a cost-benefit analysis (and a cost-effectiveness analysis) within a broader evaluation. In the United States, Hahn and Sunstein (2002, 6) point out, 'there may also be cases in which an agency believes that it is worthwhile to proceed even though the quantifiable benefits do not exceed the quantifiable costs.'[12] This implies that they are using embedded cost-benefit analysis or MNBA+.

Table 3.6 shows a simple example of Embedded Cost-Benefit Analysis, illustrating the trade-off between efficiency and equity. This trade-off can be clarified by returning to figure 3.1. Alternative B, which is technically inefficient, is equivalent to a point in the interior such as Z. Alternative A is equivalent to point X and alternative C is equivalent to point Y. Both of these latter points are on the GPF. The specific numbers in table 3.6 indicate the slope of the GPF – the dollar amount of efficiency that has to be foregone to obtain an increment in equity. If the decision maker has the indifference curves as shown, she would prefer A. Put another way, she feels that increasing equity from a medium rating to a high rating is not worth $9 million.[13]

The methods shown in tables 3.5 and 3.6 have some similarities. In table 3.5, the decision maker makes a trade-off between the NPV of the monetized net benefits and the additional, intangible efficiency impact. In table 3.6, the decision maker makes a trade-off between the NPV of

Table 3.6 An Example of Embedded NPV Analysis

Goals	Policy alternatives		
	Alternative A	Alternative B	Alternative C
Efficiency (NPV of all efficiency impacts)	$55 M	$28 M	$46 M
Equity	Medium	Low	High

all the efficiency impacts and equity, a different goal. In practice, it does not make much difference whether the problem involves an efficiency impact that is difficult to monetize or a non-efficiency goal (in addition to an NPV). However, this is an important conceptual distinction. If the analyst thinks it is the former, the analytic technique is in the bottom-left cell of table 3.3, while if the latter, the applicable technique is in the top-right cell. There are two other common forms of embedded cost-benefit analysis.

Distributionally Weighted Cost-Benefit Analysis (DW-CBA) is common in policy areas where the distributional impact on target populations is important as well as the aggregate efficiency impact on society (Harberger 1978; Boardman et al. 2006). While some scholars argue that its use should be limited (Birch and Donaldson 2003), others argue for much greater use (Hurley 1998; Buss and Yancer 1999), sometimes based on citizen opinions (Nord et al. 1995).[14] More rigorous statistical techniques that produce empirically robust estimates of the distributional consequences of programs now make the estimation more feasible (e.g., DiNardo and Tobias 2001; Heckman 2001). The use of DW-CBA is quite common in health policy (Birch and Donaldson 2003) and employment training policy generally, but especially in welfare-to-work policy (Greenberg 1992; LaLonde 1997) and educational policy (Currie 2001). One version of DW-CBA simply reports costs, benefits, and net benefits for 'participants' and 'non-participants' (the rest of society) in addition to the aggregate NPV (e.g., Long, Mallar, and Thornton 1981; Friedlander, Greenberg, and Robins 1997). In practice, the implications of using DW-CBA will differ from those of using CBA when a policy either (1) passes the efficiency test (i.e., has a positive NPV), but renders disadvantaged people worse off or (2) fails the efficiency test (i.e., has a negative NPV), but renders disadvantaged individuals better off.

An example of a DW-CBA is shown in table 3.7. KPMG (1996) prepared this report on treaty settlements for the Ministry of Aboriginal Affairs in BC. It delineates the benefits to First Nations and the costs to other British Columbians. The report focuses on the immediate cash receipts or payments, but makes no assumptions about how First Nations recipients would use the cash or other resources they receive. In this context it is reasonable to equate revenues with benefits. The benefit-to-cost ratio is about three. The main reason why the benefits exceed the costs is large transfers (approximately $5 billion) from the federal government. However, there is little explanation in the report about how either benefits or costs are calculated. It posits some intangible benefits, such as increased employment and greater self-reliance among First Nations, but does not attempt to quantify such impacts.

Budget-constrained cost-benefit analysis (BC-CBA) is based on the premise that most agencies and governments face explicit budget constraints. BC-CBA can be used to choose between alternative projects when efficiency is the main goal and there is a budget constraint. When the alternatives have a similar major purpose, the analyst simply selects the project with the largest NPV (efficiency) that satisfies the budget constraint. BC-CBA can also be used where the alternatives have different purposes or come from different agencies. In such circumstances, the analyst computes the ratio of the net social benefits (i.e., the NPV) to the net budget cost for each project. Projects should be ranked in terms of this ratio, which is equivalent to ranking them in the order of their benefit-cost ratios. Projects are selected until the budget constraint becomes binding. In practice, BC-CBA is used frequently, but somewhat less formally than described here. For example, analysts simply exclude alternatives that require large government expenditures. Published examples of formal BC-CBA are rare.

Multi-Goal Analysis

In multi-goal analysis there are multiple goals and not all elements of efficiency are monetized. In Canada, it is sometimes called 'socio-economic analysis.'[15] Many versions of multi-goal analysis (MGA) involve quantitative impacts. Some labels for this type of analysis include multiple criteria weighting (Easton 1973), multi-attribute decision making (Edwards and Newman 1982), multiple objectives' analysis (Keeney and Raiffa 1976), multi-criteria decision analysis (Joubert et al. 1997), and multi-criteria analysis (Dodgson et al. 2001). Other versions of MGA are primarily qualitative. Public sector versions of the Balanced

Table 3.7 Total Net Financial Benefits to British Columbia of Treaty Settlements

	Scenario 1	Scenario 2
	($5 millions, 1995 constant dollars)	($5 millions, 1995 constant dollars)
First Nations		
• Cash, resource revenues, and cash equivalents	$5,300	$6,000
• Tenures from third parties	380	160
• Interest-free loans and grants	90	90
• Funding of First Nations' core institutions	250	380
Total Financial Benefits to First Nations	$6,020	$6,630
Costs to other British Columbians		
A. Provincial government costs		
• Provincial share of cash, cash equivalent, and resource revenues to First Nations	$640	$1,330
• Pre-treaty costs	780	750
• Implementation costs	1,040	980
• Costs to third parties for purchase of tenures	190	80
• Reduction in provincial program costs	(740)	(1,710)
	$1,910	$1,430
B. Other costs for British Columbians		
• Provincial taxpayers' share of net federal costs	200	(60)
Total financial costs to other British Columbians	$2,110	$1,370
Total net financial benefit to British Columbia	$3,910	$5,260

Scorecard illustrate this form of evaluation (Kaplan and Norton 1996). Herfindahl and Kneese (1974, 223) make the case that a qualitative analysis is the only feasible approach in some circumstances: 'a final approach is that of viewing the various possible objectives of public policy as being substantially incommensurable on any simple scale and therefore necessitating the generation of various kinds of information, not summable into a single number, as the basis for political decision.'

Hrudey et al. (2001) usefully describe the various ways multi-attribute decision-making versions can be actually used. Formal MGA generally has three characteristics. First, there is a clear distinction between alternatives and goals. This is not necessarily easy to accomplish. Second, it clarifies the distinction between prediction and valuation.[16] This is particularly useful whenever there is disagreement between decision makers about either prediction or valuation, or the relationship between the two – in other words, almost always! Third, analysis is both explicit and comprehensive; thus, it involves the prediction and valuation of the impacts of each and every alternative on each goal.

One tool that forces comprehensiveness in MGA is a goals-by-alternatives matrix. Table 3.8 shows an example from Schwindt, Vining, and Weimer (2003). The distinction between goals and alternatives is clear. The cells contain the predicted impacts and valuation of each alternative on each goal.

The Health Canada (2004) study that we discussed earlier contains a monetized net benefits analysis, but it also incorporates other efficiency impacts and goals. Thus, it is in effect a multi-goal analysis. An efficiency impact that was not monetized was the loss of consumer surplus due to higher prices. Non-efficiency goals reflected the distributional impacts on consumers and the industry, and on different provinces' tax revenues. The study also considered the potential differential impact on Canadian and non-Canadian manufacturers. Some of these impacts were quantified, such as the estimated reduction in provincial tax revenues of $4.1 million to $8.2 million; others were not.

In BC, the Crown Corporation Secretariat (1993) prepared a set of multiple account evaluation (MAE) guidelines. The five goals are net government revenues (including those accruing to Crown corporations), customer service (e.g., consumer surplus), environmental costs, economic development (incremental income and employment), and social implications (e.g., impacts on Aboriginal community values). Net government revenues are usually measured in monetary terms, customer service and environmental costs may be qualitative or quantitative, and social impacts are usually qualitative. The first four 'accounts' in aggregate might produce a result similar to a cost-benefit analysis. In addition, the MAE format makes the distributional implications explicit, as does distributionally weighted cost-benefit analysis. However, the explicit inclusion of 'government net revenues' and 'social implications' indicate that MAE is really a form of multi-goal analysis.

A recent example of the use of MAE is shown in table 3.9. This table presents a summary evaluation of five alternative road routes from Vancouver to Squamish, BC (Ministry of Transportation 2001). Note

Table 3.8 An Example of a Multi-Goal Analysis: BC Salmon Fishery

Goals	Criteria	Alternative policies			
		Current policy: continued implementation of the Mifflin Plan	Harvesting royalties and license auction (Pearse Plan)	River-specific exclusive ownership rights	Individual transferable quotas to current license holders
Efficient resource use	Impact on rent dissipation	Poor – large negative net present value	Good – considerable improvement over status quo	Very good – major improvement over status quo, lowest cost technology	Good – considerable improvement over status quo
Protection	Impact on the number of viable runs	Poor – high risk	Poor – continued risk for vulnerable runs	Good – very good except possibly for Fraser River	Reasonable (provided 'share' quotas used)
Equitable distribution	Fairness to current license holders	Good	Good	Depends upon compensation for licenses	Very good
	Fairness to native fishers	Neutral, good for incumbents	Neutral, good for incumbents	Good	Neutral, very good for incumbents
	Fairness to taxpayers	Poor, large net costs	Excellent after phase-in	Excellent	Poor, but depends on fees

Source: Schwindt, Vining, and Weimer (2003)

that equal weight is implicitly given to each impact factor so that, in effect, customer service is weighted 6/24, the financial account (construction cost), the environment and social impacts are equally weighted at 5/24 each, and economic development is weighted 3/24. This is somewhat surprising given that the costs of the Vancouver to Squamish route alternatives range from $1.3 to $3.9 billion. This report contains fairly detailed costings and a discussion of various engineering issues. However, the assumptions behind the consumer impacts, such as the values of a life and of time, are not specified.

There are numerous valuation rules (Dyer et al. 1992; Easton 1973, 183–219); for some simple public policy examples, see Dodgson et al. 2001). Some decision makers do not like to reveal their valuation rules: they may make their predictions explicit and will make a recommendation, but are reluctant to explicitly articulate their valuation procedure. Where valuation is explicit, quantitative rules can be classified in terms of three criteria: first, the willingness of decision makers to structure the metric level of attribute attractiveness (ordinal, interval, ratio); second, the willingness to lexicographically order attributes (good, better, best); and third, the willingness to impose commensurability across attributes (Svenson 1979).

Most explicit multi-goal valuation methods apply linear, commensurable ('compensatory') schemes to attribute scores (Davey, Olson, and Wallenius 1994). Most non-compensatory rules are not useful for evaluating policy alternatives, as they do not result in a single superior alternative. Commensurability rules enable a higher score on one goal to compensate for a lower score on another goal. Probably the most commonly used rule is simple 'additive utility,' where the decision is based on a summation of the utilities of each impact for each alternative policy. The policy alternative with the highest total score is selected (Svenson 1979). Another rule computes the product of the utilities of each impact for each alternative.

A multi-goal valuation matrix example is shown in table 3.10. This table contains quantified efficiency impacts (measured by MNBA), non-monetized efficiency impacts (pollution reduction and impact on employees), revenue-expenditure impacts, and equity impacts. Each impact for each alternative is assigned a number on a scale of 1 to 10 depending on the magnitude of the impact. For example, alternative C, with a monetized net benefit of $60 million is assigned a higher score (8) than alternative A, with a monetized net benefit of $30m (3). Using equal

Table 3.9 Multi-Goal Analysis of Alternative Routes Between Vancouver and Squamish

Cost and impact factors 1 = least preferable to 5 = most preferable	Route options				
	Highway 99 North upgrade	Capilano River	Seymour River	Indian Arm/ Indian River	Hybrid Seymour/ Indian River
Financial account					
• Capital cost					
– route cost	5	3	1	1	2
– link to provincial network	5	3	3	1	3
– network upgrade cost	4	4	4	2	4
• Added operating/					
maintenance cost	5	4	3	1	4
• Traffic disruption cost	1	4	5	4	5
Customer service account					
• User travel time reduction	3	5	5	2	5
• System integration	3	3	3	5	3
• Mode shift potential	5	3	3	1	3
• Timing of benefits	5	1	1	1	1
• Vehicle operating cost					
reduction	5	4	3	3	3
• Accident cost reduction	5	5	5	5	5
Economic development account					
• developable land accessed	5	3	1	1	1
• interior interaction	2	2	2	2	2
• generated travel	3	3	3	5	3
Social account					
• urban land-use impact	3	3	3	2	3
• park/recreation impact	4	4	3	1	3
• First Nations impact	4	4	3	1	3
• consistency with regional					
growth plans	5	3	3	1	3
• emergency route	1	2	3	5	4
Environmental account					
• watershed impact	5	1	1	3	3
• geotechnical concern	3	5	1	1	1
• physical env. impact	3	2	2	1	2
• avalanche concern	5	4	2	1	1
• archaeology	5	3	2	1	2
Total	94	78	65	51	69

Source: Ministry of Transportation (2001, 12).

Table 3.10 A Hypothetical Example of a Multi-Goal Valuation Matrix

Goals	Policy alternatives		
	Alternative A	Alternative B	Alternative C
Efficiency(MNBA)	$30M	$43M	$60M
	3	5	8
Revenue-expenditure impact	−$100M	−$100M	−$200M
	8	8	3
Equity	Medium	Low	High
	5	2	7
Pollution reduced	3.0%	2.6%	2.4%
	7	4	3
Impact on employees	No change	10% layoff	Increased
	8	3	workloads,
			no layoffs
			5
Sum of equally weighted scores	31	22	26

weights of utility for each impact results in a total weighted score of 31, 22 and 26 for alternatives A, B, and C, respectively. Thus, alternative A is the preferred alternative. If, however, the quantified efficiency impacts were assigned a weight of 0.5 and each of the other goals was assigned a weight of 0.125, then alternative C would be the preferred alternative.

Some decision makers argue that multi-goal matrix valuation is overly mechanistic and simplistic. However, in discussion it frequently emerges that their concerns are not so much with the decision rule as a desire to add new goals (or criteria) or to add more complex policy alternatives. Prediction, valuation, and evaluation then form part of an iterative policy choice process.

An advantage of the multi-goal framework is that it generates discussion among decision makers. Decision makers can engage in active debate about the impacts of each alternative and the weights that should be attached to each goal. Through this experience, the multi-goal framework informs the dialogue about alternative selection.

Conclusion

Table 3.11 summarizes the specific methods that fall within the four choice method classes. It provides a detailed elucidation of table 3.1.

The four method classes can be summarized as follows:

- Cost-benefit analysis: efficiency is the only goal and all dimensions of efficiency are monetized. It is equivalent to a multi-goal analysis with a single row in which all cell entries are monetized.
- Efficiency analysis: efficiency is the only goal, but not all dimensions of efficiency are monetized. Other dimensions of efficiency may be quantified and some may be expressed in qualitative terms.
- Embedded cost-benefit analysis: all efficiency impacts are monetized. Thus, there is an embedded NPV component. Other goals, such as equity or impact on government revenue are also included.
- Multi-goal analysis: there are multiple goals, including efficiency. Not all dimensions of efficiency are monetized. Other goals are expressed quantitatively or qualitatively.

In practice, cost-benefit analysis and embedded cost-benefit analysis are of most value for significant public investments. While they are certainly conceptually appropriate for major social programs, decision makers in Canada appear most comfortable with these method classes as decision aids for physical infrastructure projects, such as major highways, dams, bridges, and water projects (McArthur in this volume). Cost-effectiveness analysis is used extensively by Health Canada and provincial governments to decide funding of new drugs and for other health care decisions. Revenue-expenditure analysis is frequently used by 'guardians' in financial or treasury positions at any level of government (Boardman, Vining, and Waters 1993). The other various forms of efficiency analysis are more frequently used by regional and municipal government for infrastructure projects and other capital investments. Multi-goal analysis probably occurs more frequently than the other types of analysis in practice. Its application varies enormously from being formal, such as explicit use of MAE, to being highly informal and implicit. Decision makers may use multi-goal analysis without being particularly aware that they are doing it, and without knowledge or consideration of alternative choice methods. As mentioned earlier, such concerns provide the major motivation for this chapter.

A clearer understanding of metachoice issues is a useful step in improving Canadian public sector policy analysis. The empirical evidence as well as experience working with analysts from several levels of Canadian government suggests that there is a lack of understanding about the differences between the various analytical methods and

Table 3.11 Choice Methods within Each Choice Method Class

	Single goal of efficiency	Multiple goals (including efficiency)
	CBA analysis	**Embedded CBA analysis**
Comprehensive monetization of efficiency impacts	NPV	NPV + other goals (equity, human dignity, net revenues)
	Benefit-cost ratio	
	IRR	Distributionally weighted CBA
	Payback period	Budget constrained CBA
	Efficiency analysis	**Multi-goal analysis**
Less-than-comprehensive monetization of efficiency impacts	Cost analysis	Additive utility rule
	Social costing	Product of utility rule
	Revenue analysis	
	Effectiveness analysis	Qualitative assessment
	Revenue-expenditure analysis	Satisfycing
	Economic impact analysis	Lexicographic ordering
	Cost-Effectiveness Analysis	
	Qualitative CBA	
	MNBA	
	MNBA+ (MBA plus intangible impacts)	

whether they are appropriate in specific circumstances. Some of this stems from the lack of a metachoice framework. The increasing requirement for the formal consideration of costs and benefits, in spite of the lack of preciseness as to their meanings, will force analysts to confront this issue. Of course, metachoice clarity is by no means a panacea. Offsetting this progress is the continued prominence of economic impact analysis. EIA is like Count Dracula – no matter how many times a wooden stake is driven through his heart you know he will be back for the sequel. Furthermore, even with a transparent metachoice framework, policy actors can and will engage in strategic behaviour (De Alessi 1996; Flyvbjerg, Holm, and Buhl 2002; Sanders 2002), ignore analysis (Radin 2002), or deliberately use idiosyncratic definitions of benefits and costs (Boardman, Vining, and Waters 1993).

NOTES

1 The authors would like to thank Diane Forbes for finding many excellent examples. This chapter builds upon, and discusses in a Canadian context, Vining and Boardman (2006).
2 This is to not to argue that this is the only kind of policy analysis nor that other forms of policy analysis are not valuable. Mayer et al. (2004), for example, argue there are six kinds ('activities') of policy analysis: (1) research and analysis, (2) design and recommend, (3) provide strategic advice, (4) clarify arguments and values, (5) democratize, and (6) mediate. Our concern overlaps largely only with their categories of 'design and recommend,' and 'provide strategic advice.'
3 In practice, there is considerable confusion on the distinction between *ex ante* evaluation and *ex post* evaluation. Many of the techniques described in this chapter can also be used in *ex post* analysis, but the major focus of this paper is on *ex ante* analysis (see Boardman, Mallery, and Vining 1994; Boardman et al. 2006, 2–5; and Howlett and Lindquist in this volume).
4 The concave shape of the GPF indicates that society has to give up greater amounts of allocative efficiency to increase equity as the level of equity increases.
5 A goal can always be reformulated as a constraint.
6 It is important not to confuse goals in the sense used here with implementation 'goals,' which are actually statements of intended policies or specific impact categories that are used to measure achievement of goals; see Weimer and Vining (2005, 343–56, 363–79).
7 Agency costs may or may not be included.
8 For relatively recent examples from BC, see Levelton, Kershaw, and Reid (1966) on fuel cells, and Gray (2002) and Inter*VISTAS* Consulting Inc. (2002) concerning the 2010 Winter Olympic and Paralympics Games.
9 CEA is actually a special case of productivity analysis where the inputs are monetized. In productivity analysis either the inputs are not weighted or some non-monetary weight, such as factor proportions, is used. If inputs are not weighted, the result is a simple average productivity measure, such as tons of garbage per employee. If they are weighted, the result is

total factor productivity.

10 After a decision has been made, partial (range) monetization can be inferred. If the analyst/decision maker prefers C to A, then she values the intangible environmental protection impact of alternative C, $9 million, more than under alternative A.

11 Where there is more than one additional goal, most of the operational heuristics relating to Multi-Goal Analysis (see below) apply.

12 In this case they are clearly referring to Multi-Goal Analysis rather than simply an unwillingness to monetize efficiency impacts.

13 Sometimes equity is expressed as a constraint.

14 Harberger (1997) argues against distributional weights and in favour of 'basic needs externalities.' As this adjustment is based on 'donor' valuations, it can be thought of as Cost-Benefit Analysis.

15 For an example of a socio-economic analysis, see ARA Consulting Group (1995). This report was prepared for the British Columbia Ministry of Forests. It included an economic impact analysis that focused on employment and employment income, provincial government revenue-expenditure analysis, and other impacts including regional job gains or losses, First Nations impacts and environmental impacts. Also see Marvin Shaffer & Associates Ltd (1992) for a comprehensive socio-economic analysis of the Kispiox Timber Supply Area.

16 The distinction between prediction and valuation tends to be obscured in CBA by the fact that prediction and valuation stages are often combined, or at least not discussed separately.

REFERENCES

Ackerman, Frank, and Lisa Heinzerling. 2002. 'Pricing the Priceless: Cost-Benefit Analysis of Environmental Protection.' *University of Pennsylvania Law Review* 150(5), 1553–84.

Adams, J. 1992. 'Horse and Rabbit Stew.' In A. Coker and C. Richards, eds., *Valuing the Environment: Economic Approaches to Environmental Evaluation*, 65–73. New York: John Wiley & Sons.

Adler, Matthew D. 1998. 'Incommensurability and Cost-Benefit Analysis.' *University of Pennsylvania Law Review* 146(5), 1371–1419.

Adler, Matthew D., and Eric A. Posner. 2000. 'Implementing Cost-Benefit Analysis When Preferences Are Distorted.' *Journal of Legal Studies* 29(2), 1105–47.

Anderson, David A. 1999. 'The Aggregate Burden of Crime.' *Journal of Law and*

Economics 42(2), 611–42.

ARA Consulting Group. 1995. 'Prince George Timber Supply Area Socio-Economic Analysis.' Victoria: The Queen's Printer.

Arrow, Kenneth J., Maureen L. Cropper, George C. Eads, Robert W. Hahn, Lester B. Lave, Roger C. Noll, Paul R. Portney, Milton Russell, Richard Schmalensee, Kerry V. Smith, and Robert N. Stavins. 1996. 'Benefit-Cost Analysis in Environmental, Health and Safety Regulation: A Statement of Principles.' Washington DC: American Enterprise Institute for Public Policy Research.

Auditor General of Canada. 1996. *Report of the Auditor General of Canada 1996.* 'Evaluation in the Federal Government' (chapter 3, May), 'The Canada Infrastructure Works Program: Lessons Learned' (chapter 26, November). Ottawa: Ministry of Supply and Services.

– 1997. *Report of the Auditor General of Canada 1997.* 'Reporting Performance in the Expenditure Management System' (chapter 5, April), 'Moving Toward Managing for Results' (chapter 11, April). Ottawa: Ministry of Supply and Services.

– 2000. *Report of the Auditor General of Canada 2000.* 'Reporting Performance to Parliament – Progress too Slow' (chapter 19, December), 'Managing Departments for Results' (chapter 20, December). Ottawa: Ministry of Supply and Services.

– 2003. *Report of the Auditor General of Canada 2000.* 'Rating Departmental Performance Reports' (chapter 1). Ottawa: Ministry of Supply and Services

Bergson, Abram. 1938. 'A Reformulation of Certain Aspects cf Welfare Economics.' *Quarterly Journal of Economics* 52, 314–44.

Birch, Stephen, and Cam Donaldson. 2003.'Valuing the Benefits and Costs of Health Care Programmes: Where's the "Extra" in Extra-Welfarism?' *Social Science & Medicine* 56(5), 1121–33.

Boardman, Anthony E., David H. Greenberg, Aidan R. Vining, and David L. Weimer. 1997. 'Plug-In Shadow Price Estimates for Policy Analysis.' *Annals of Regional Science* 31(4), 299–324.

– 2006. *Cost-Benefit Analysis: Concepts and Practice.* 3rd ed. Upper Saddle River, NJ: Prentice-Hall.

Boardman, Anthony E., Wendy L. Mallery, and Aidan R. Vining. 1994. 'Learning from *Ex Ante/Ex Post* Cost-Benefit Comparisons: The Coquihalla Highway Example.' *Socio-Economic Planning Sciences* 28(2), 69–84.

Boardman, Anthony E., Aidan R. Vining, and William Waters III. 1993. 'Costs and Benefits through Bureaucratic Lenses: Example of a Highway Project.' *Journal of Policy Analysis and Management* 12(3), 532–55.

Bowden, Gary K., and Wally H. Malkinson. 1982. 'Benefit-Cost Analysis of the

North East Coal Development.' Victoria, BC: Ministry of Industry and Small Business Development.

Buss, Terry F., and Laura C. Yancer. 1999. 'Cost-Benefit Analysis: A Normative Perspective.' *Economic Development Quarterly* 13(1), 29–37.

Cavanagh, Sheila M., Robert W. Hahn, and Robert N. Stavins. 2001. 'National Environmental Policy During the Clinton Years.' Washington, DC: AEI-Brookings Joint Center Working Paper no. 01–09.

Congressional Budget Office (CBO). 1992. *Auctioning Radio Spectrum Licenses.* Washington, DC, March.

Crown Corporations Secretariat. 1993. *Multiple Account Evaluation Guidelines.* Victoria, BC: Province of British Columbia.

Currie, Janet. 2001. 'Early Childhood Education Programs.' *Journal of Economic Perspectives* 15(2), 213–238.

Davey, Anne, David Olson, and Jyrki Wallenius. 1994. 'The Process of Multiattribute Decision Making: A Case Study of Selecting Applicants for a Ph. D. Program.' *European Journal of Operational Research* 72(3), 469–85.

Davis, H. Craig. 1990. *Regional Economic Impact Analysis and Project Evaluation,* Vancouver, BC: University of British Columbia Press.

De Alessi, Louis. 1996. 'Error and Bias in Benefit-Cost Analysis: HUD's Case for the Wind Rule.' *Cato Journal* 16(1), 129–147.

DiNardo, John, and Justin L. Tobias. 2001. 'Nonparametric Density and Regression Estimation.' *Journal of Economic Perspectives* 15(4), 11–28.

Dodgson, John, Michael Spackman, Alan Pearman, and Lawrence Phillips. 2001. *Multi-Criteria Analysis: A Manual.* Department of the Environment, Transport and the Regions. London: Office of the Deputy Prime Minister (ODPM).

Dolan, Paul, and Richard Edlin. 2002. 'Is It Really Possible to Build a Bridge Between Cost-Benefit Analysis and Cost-Effectiveness Analysis?' *Journal of Health Economics* 21(5), 827–843.

Dyer, James S., Peter C. Fishburn, Ralph E. Steuer, Jyrki Wallenius, and Stanley Zionts. 1992. 'Multiple Criteria Decision Making, Multiattribute Utility Theory: The Next Ten Years.' *Management Science* 38(5), 645–54.

Easton, Allan. 1973. *Complex Managerial Decisions Involving Multiple Objectives.* New York: Wiley.

Edwards, Ward, and J. Robert Newman (with the collaboration of Kurt Sapper and David Server). 1982. *Multiattribute Evaluation.* Beverly Hills, CA: Sage Publications.

Flyvbjerg, Bent, Mette S. Holm and Soren Buhl. 2002. 'Underestimating Costs in Public Works Projects.' *Journal of the American Planning Association* 68(3), 279–95.

Friedlander, David, David H. Greenberg, and Philip K. Robins. 1997. 'Evaluating Government Training Programs for the Economically Disadvantaged.' *Journal of Economic Literature* 35(4), 1809–55.

General Accounting Office (GAO). 1998. 'Regulatory Reform: Agencies Could Improve Development, Documentation, and Clarity of Regulatory Economic Analyses.' Report to the Committee on Governmental Affairs, US Senate, GAO/RCED-98-142, May.

Gray, John B. 2002. 'The Economic Impact of the Winter Olympic & Paralympics Games.' Report prepared by the Capital Projects Branch, Ministry of Competition, Science and Enterprise, British Columbia.

Greenberg, David H. 1992. 'Conceptual Issues in Cost-Benefit Analysis of Welfare-to-Work Programs.' *Contemporary Policy Issues* 10(4), 51–63.

Greene, Ian. 2002. 'Lessons Learned from Two Decades of Program Evaluation in Canada.' In Deitmar Braunig and Peter Eichorn, eds., *Evaluation and Accounting Standards in Public Management*, 44–53. Baden-Baden: Nomos Verlagsgesellschaft.

Hahn, Robert W. 2000. 'State and Federal Regulatory Reform: A Comparative Analysis.' *Journal of Legal Studies* 29(2), 873–912.

Hahn, Robert W., Jason K. Burnett, Yee-Ho I. Chan, Elizabeth A. Mader, and Petrea R. Moyle. 2000. 'Assessing Regulatory Impact Analyses: The Failure of Agencies to Comply with Executive Order 12,866.' *Harvard Journal of Law & Public Policy* 23(3), 859–85.

Hahn, Robert W., and Cass R. Sunstein. 2002. 'A New Executive Order for Improving Federal Regulation? Deeper and Wider Cost-Benefit Analysis.' *University of Pennsylvania Law Review* 150(5), 1489–1552.

Harberger, Arnold C. 1978. 'On the Use of Distributional Weights in Social Cost-Benefit Analysis.' *Journal of Political Economy* 86(2), S87–120.

– 1997. 'Economic Project Evaluation, Part 1: Some Lessons for the 1990s.' *Canadian Journal of Program Evaluation* Special Issue, 5–46.

Health Canada. 2004. 'Economic Evaluation of Health Canada's Regulatory Proposal for Reducing Fire Risks from Cigarettes.' Ottawa, ON: Health Canada.

Heckman James, L. 2001. 'Micro Data, Heterogeneity, and the Evaluation of Public Policy: Nobel Lecture.' *Journal of Political Economy* 109(4), 673–748.

Herfindahl, Orris C., and Allan V. Kneese. 1974. *Economic Theory of Natural Resources*. Columbus, OH: Charles Merrill.

HLB Decision Economics (in association with ICF Consulting and PB Consult). 2002. *Cost-Benefit Framework and Model for the Evaluation of Transit and Highway Investments: Final Report*. Ottawa, 23 January.

HM Treasury. 1997. *Appraisal and Valuation in Central Government: Treasury Guidance*. 'The Green Book.' London, UK: The Stationary Office.

Hrudey, Steve E. (chair), Vic Adamowicz, Alan Krupnick, John McConnell,

Paolo Renzi, Robert Dales, Morton Lippmann, and Beverley Hale. 2001. *Report of an Expert Panel to Review the Socio-Economic Models and Related Components Supporting the Development of Canada-Wide Standards for Particulate Matter and Ozone to the Royal Society of Canada*, RSC EPR 01–2. Ottawa, ON: Royal Society of Canada.

Hurley, J. 1998. 'Welfarism, Extra-Welfarism and Evaluative Economic Analysis in the Health Sector.' In Morris Barer, T. Getzen, and G.L. Stoddard, eds., *Health, Health Care and Health Economics: Perspectives on Distribution*, 373–95. Chichester, UK: John Wiley.

Inter*VISTAS* Consulting Inc. 2002. 'The Economic Impact of the 2010 Winter Olympic and Paralympics Games.' Prepared for the Honourable Ted Nebbeling, minister of state for Community Charter and the 2010 Olympic Bid. Victoria.

Joubert, Alison R., Anthony Leiman, Helen M. de Klerk, Stephen Katua, and J. Coenrad Aggenbach. 1997. 'Fynbos (Fine Bush) Vegetation and the Supply of Water: A Comparison of Multi-Criteria Decision Analysis and Cost-Benefit Analysis.' *Ecological Economics* 22(2), 123–140.

Kaplan, Robert S., and David P. Norton. 1996. 'Linking the Balanced Scorecard to Strategy.' *California Management Review* 39(1), 53–79.

Kaplow, Louis, and Steven Shavell. 2002. *Fairness versus Welfare*. Cambridge, MA: Harvard University Press.

– 2005. 'Fairness versus Welfare: Notes on the Pareto Principle, Preferences and Distributive Justice.' *Journal of Legal Studies* 32(1), 331–62.

Keeney, Ralph L., and Howard Raiffa. 1976. *Decisions with Multiple Objectives: Preferences and Value Trade-offs*. NY: John Wiley & Sons.

KPMG. 1996. 'Benefits and Costs of Treaty Settlements in British Columbia – A Financial and Economic Perspective.' Victoria, BC: Queen's Printer.

LaLonde, Robert J. 1997. 'The Promise of Public Sector-Sponsored Training Programs.' *Journal of Economic Perspectives* 9(2), 149–68.

Levelton, Paul, Lisa Kershaw, and William Reid. 1966. 'Estimating Economic Impacts and Market Potential Associated with the Development and Production of Fuel Cells in British Columbia.' KPMG report prepared for the Ministry of Environment, Lands and Parks, 60058/WPL/br. Victoria, BC.

Long, David, Charles D. Mallar, and Craig V. Thornton. 1981. 'Evaluating the Benefits and Costs of the Jobs Corps.' *Journal of Policy Analysis and Management* 1(1), 55–76.

Martin, Fernand. 2001. 'Evaluating a Large-Scale Infrastructure Project: A High-Speed Railway Along the Quebec City to Windsor Corridor.' In Aidan R. Vining and John Richards, eds., *Building the Future: Issues in Public Infra-*

structure in Canada, 195–213. Toronto, ON: C.D. Howe Institute.

Marvin Shaffer & Associates Ltd. 1992. 'Kispiox Resource Management Plan Socio-Economic Impact Assessment.' Final report, submitted to Economic and Trade Branch, Ministry of Forests. British Columbia.

Mayer, Igor S., C. Els van Daalen, and Peter W.G. Bots. 2004. 'Perspectives on Policy Analyses: A Framework for Understanding and Design.' *International Journal of Technology Policy and Management* 4(2), 169–91.

Mayne, John. 1994. 'Utilizing Evaluation in Organizations: The Balancing Act.' In Frans L. Leeuw, Ray C. Rist, and Richard C. Sonnichsen, eds., *Can Governments Learn?* 17–44. New Brunswick, NJ: Transaction Publishers.

Ministry of Transportation. 2001. *Highway 99 Alternative Routes Analysis Vancouver to Squamish and Corridor Improvement Analysis Squamish to Cache Creek*, draft. Vancouver, BC: Ministry of Transportation, June.

Moore, John L. 1995. 'Cost-Benefit Analysis: Issues in its Use in Regulation.' *Congressional Research Service Report for Congress*. Washington, DC: The Committee for the National Institute for the Environment, June.

Mueller, Dennis C. 1989. *Public Choice II*. Cambridge: Cambridge University Press.

Muller-Clemm, Werner J., and Maria P. Barnes. 1997. 'A Historical Perspective on Federal Program Evaluation in Canada.' *Canadian Journal of Program Evaluation* 12(1), 47–70.

Myers, Samuel L. 2002. 'Presidential Address – Analysis of Race as Policy Analysis.' *Journal of Policy Analysis and Management* 21(2), 169–90.

Nijkamp, Peter P. 1997. *Theory and Application of Environmental Economics*. Amsterdam: North-Holland.

Nord, Erik, Jeff Richardson, Andrew Street, Hega Kuhse, and Peter Singer. 1995. 'Maximizing Health Benefits vs. Egalitarianism: An Australian Survey of Health Issues.' *Social Science & Medicine* 41(10), 1429–37.

Nussbaum, Martha C. 2000. 'The Costs of Tragedy: Some Moral Limits of Cost-Benefit Analysis.' *Journal of Legal Studies* 29(2), 1005–36.

OECD. 1995. *Recommendation on Improving the Quality of Government Regulation*. Paris. OECD.

Okun, Arthur M. 1975. *Equality and Efficiency: The Big Trade-off*. Washington, DC: The Brookings Institution.

Pearce, David. 1998. 'Cost-Benefit Analysis and Environmental Policy.' *Oxford Review of Economic Policy* 14(4), 84–100.

Phillips, Patti P., and Jack J. Phillips. 2004. 'ROI in the Public Sector: Myths and Realities.' *Public Personnel Management* 33(2), 139–49.

Privy Council Office. 1999. *Government of Canada Regulatory Policy*. Ottawa, ON.

Radin, Beverly. 2002. 'The Government Performance and Results Act and the

Tradition of Federal Management Reform: Square Pegs in Round Holes?'
Journal of Public Administration Research and Theory 10(1), 111–35.

Rees, William E. 1998. 'How Should a Parasite Value Its Host?' *Ecological Economics* 25(1), 49–52.

Reinke, William A. 1999. 'A Multi-Dimensional Program Evaluation Model: Considerations of Cost-Effectiveness, Equity, Quality, and Sustainability.' *Canadian Journal of Program Evaluation* 14(2), 145–60.

Rich, M.J. 1989. 'Distributive Politics and the Allocation of Federal Grants.' *American Political Science Review* 83(1), 193–213.

Richards, John, Aidan Vining, D. Brown, M. Krashinsky, W. Milne, E. Lightman, and S. Hoy. 1995. *Helping the Poor: A Qualified Case for 'Workfare.'* Toronto, ON: C.D. Howe Institute.

Sanders, Heywood T. 2002. 'Convention Myths and Markets: A Critical Review of Convention Center Feasibility Studies.' *Economic Development Quarterly* 16(3), 195–210.

Schwindt, Richard, Aidan R. Vining, and David Weimer. 2003. 'A Policy Analysis of the BC Salmon Fishery.' *Canadian Public Policy* 29(1), 73–93.

Svenson, Ola. 1979. 'Process Description of Decision Making.' *Organizational Behavior and Human Performance* 23(1), 89–92.

Treasury Board of Canada Secretariat (TBS). 1976. *Benefit-Cost Analysis Guide.* Ottawa, ON: Treasury Board of Canada Secretariat.

– 1997. *Program Evaluation Methods.* 3rd ed. Ottawa, ON: Treasury Board of Canada Secretariat.

– 1998. *Benefit-Cost Analysis Guide.* Ottawa, ON: Treasury Board of Canada Secretariat.

– no date. *Study of the Evaluation Function in the Federal Government.* Available online at http://www.tbs-sct.gc.ca/eval/stud_etud/func-fonc-01_e.asp (26 April 2006).

Vining, Aidan R., and Anthony E. Boardman. 2006. 'Metachoice in Policy Analysis.' *Journal of Comparative Policy Analysis* 8(1), 77–87.

Vining, Aidan R., and David L. Weimer. 1992. 'Welfare Economics as the Foundation for Public Policy Analysis: Incomplete and Flawed But Nevertheless Desirable.' *Journal of Socio-Economics* 21(1), 532–55.

– 2001. 'Criteria for Infrastructure Investment: Normative, Positive, and Prudential Perspectives.' In Aidan R. Vining and John Richards, eds., *Building the Future: Issues in Public Infrastructure in Canada*, 131–165. Toronto: C.D. Howe Institute.

Waters II, W.W. Not dated. 'A Reanalysis of the North East Coal Development.' University of British Columbia, Vancouver, BC, mimeo.

Webber, David J. 1986. 'Analyzing Political Feasibility: Political Scientists'

Unique Contribution to Policy Analysis.' *Policy Studies Journal* 14(4), 545–64.

Weimer, David L., and Aidan R. Vining. 2005. *Policy Analysis: Concepts and Practice*. 4th ed. Upper Saddle River, NJ: Pearson Prentice-Hall.

Whitehead, Paul C., and William R. Avison. 1999. 'Comprehensive Evaluation: The Intersection of Impact Evaluation and Social Accounting.' *Canadian Journal of Program Evaluation* 14(1), 65–83.

4 Beyond Formal Policy Analysis: Governance Context, Analytical Styles, and the Policy Analysis Movement in Canada

MICHAEL HOWLETT AND EVERT LINDQUIST

Introduction

Seen as an intellectual movement in government, as Michael Mintrom describes it in chapter 6 in this volume, policy analysis represents the efforts of actors inside and outside formal political decision-making processes to improve policy outcomes by applying systematic evaluative rationality (Heineman et al. 2002). Policy analysis, in this sense, is a relatively recent phenomenon, dating back to the 1960s and the U.S. experience with formalized large-scale planning processes and statistical analyses in areas such as defence, urban redevelopment, and budgeting (Lindblom 1958; Wildavsky 1969; MacRae and Wilde 1985; Garson 1986). While there have been debates about whether policy analysis has improved on the outcomes associated with earlier, less instrumental processes such as bargaining, compromise, negotiation, and log-rolling (Tribe 1972; Fischer and Forester 1993; Majone 1989), there has been no fundamental challenge to the raison d'être of policy analysis, which remains to improve policy outcomes by applying systematic analytic methodologies to policy problems (Meltsner 1972; Webber 1986; Fox 1990).

There has always been a range of methodologies used in policy analysis, from formal techniques such as cost-benefit analysis to the less formal emphasis of techniques of argument and persuasion. However, the policy analysis movement has come to be closely associated with the idea that a generic formal analytic toolkit (stemming from and involving law, political science, public administration, economics, quantitative methods, organizational analysis, budgeting, etc.) could be productively applied to a wide range of substantive problems by astute policy analysts inside and outside government (House and Shull 1991).[1] Education and training has for many years therefore been largely a matter of familiarizing students with generic formal analytical tools, along with presenting and studying cases, workshops, simulations, or real-world projects designed to illustrate their use in specific circumstances. The idea was to show students that the art and craft of policy analysis owed much to deductive reasoning: matching tools and context, and producing time-sensitive advice that policy makers could absorb (Wildavsky 1979; Vining and Weimer 2002; Guess and Franham 1989; Weimer 1992; Bardach 2000; Geva-May 1997).

Many countries, however, were less influenced by the policy analysis movement than was the United States, the archetypal case of the rise of policy analysis in government. Some countries, including many in Western Europe, had traditions of legal oversight of government or centralized top-down public administration that placed the evaluative and analytical tasks of government within the judicial or financial branches of the civil service and delayed the arrival of problem-oriented policy analysis (Bekke and van der Meer 2000). Other countries, such as those in eastern Europe under socialist regimes, featured large-scale planning bureaus that analysed problems but in a much different context from that of the policy analysis movement in the United States (Verheijen 1999). Many other countries in the developing world until very recently lacked the internal capacity and external autonomy required to conduct the independent analytical tasks required of U.S.-style policy analysis (Burns and Bowornwathana, 2001). In Canada, as Prince and Brooks show in their chapters, efforts have certainly been made over the years to bring knowledge to policy making, but many of the techniques used for so doing – such as royal commissions and the use of program reviews and central agencies – have been somewhat idiosyncratic and have lacked in support from universities, think tanks, NGOs, and other branches of government, as is characteristic of the U.S. movement.

These national differences in the pattern in which the techniques and structures of policy analysis have been adopted has turned scholarly attention to both evaluating the influence and effectiveness of policy analysis (Thissen and Twaalfhoven 2001) and to the empirical study of how policy research and analysis is actually generated, interpreted and utilized in different governments and agencies (in this regard see the range of subjects discussed in newer journals such as the *Journal of Comparative Policy Analysis* and *Evidence & Policy*, as well as the older tradition of studies on knowledge utilization in government). These studies have consistently shown how policy analytical processes are affected by a large range of factors such as the needs and beliefs of ultimate users, the delicacy of the political relations, coalitions and conflicts among decision makers, the history of previous policy reform efforts, individual personalities and agendas, organizational structures and routines, and other factors (Weiss 1977a, 1977b; Jenkins-Smith 1982; Sabatier 1987; Shulock 1999; Hird 2005; Weimer 2005). In short, these studies have shown that, methodologically speaking, 'one size does not fit all.' That is, analytic opportunities are not ontologically idiosyncratic and methodologically generic, but, rather, require the careful matching of analytical technique and governance context. Hence, while still sympathetic to the basic postulate and aim of the policy analysis movement to enhance the 'rationality quotient' of public policy making, these studies belie the idea that a single set of generic analytical tools can be used in every circumstance and thus undermine many of the suppositions that underlie the 'classical' policy analysis movement.

Rather, they suggest that (a) different 'styles' of policy analysis can be found in different organizations and jurisdictions (Peled 2002), and (b) these can be linked to larger patterns of political behaviour and structures whose condition is not completely manipulable by policy actors (Bevir and Rhodes 2001; Bevir, Rhodes, and Weller 2003a, 2003b). This, in turn, suggests that the nature of policy analysis, and the effectiveness of the analysts' repertoire of techniques and capabilities, depends on how congruent they are with governance and administrative contexts (Peled 2002; Howlett 2004; Christensen, Laegreid, and Wise 2003). Continuing with the toolbox metaphor, this implies that rather than simply adapting a generic tool for the job, analysts must carefully choose different tools for different jobs, with the key criterion of effectiveness being the matching of analytical technique to governance context.

This chapter taps into 'post-modern' frameworks that have broadened our conception of the methods of policy analysis and our notions of the hegemony of a single policy analysis movement. The chapter contributes to the growing interest in matching the observed use of analytical techniques, tools, repertoires and capabilities to governance contexts; one which presumes that very different patterns or styles and 'movements' of policy analysis can exist in different jurisdictions, policy sectors, and organizational contexts. These styles can include a penchant for the use of traditional 'generic' tools such as cost-benefit analysis, but can also, legitimately, include propensities for the use of alternate or complementary analytical techniques such as consultation and public or stakeholder participation, or long-standing preferences for the use of specific types of 'substantive' policy instruments or governance arrangements, such as regulation or public enterprises or the use of advisory commissions or judicial review, in order to solve policy problems (Richardson, Gustafsson, and Jordan 1982; Van Waarden 1995; Howlett 2000).

We argue that successful modes of policy analysis are not simply a matter of the choice and skill of policy analysts and managers in adapting formal techniques to analytical opportunities, but that the choice of techniques itself is conditioned by contextual elements which favour particular analytical types or 'analytical styles' (Shulock 1999; Radin 2000). Whether these larger contextual elements are cultural, institutional, or derive from other aspects of the policy-making context is an empirical question to be resolved in each case, but it is the combination of these forces that constrains or creates opportunities for different policy analysis activities and produces discernable policy analytic styles and movements in different countries and contexts.

This chapter explores how policy analysis has developed in Canada by way of an examination of the linkages between analytical style and analytical context. We begin by identifying ways in which policy analysis can be differentiated, and then review three different governance contexts – national, policy sector, and organization – and consider their implications for the type of policy analysis required in each setting. We use the case of Canada to identify distinctive policy styles, and to consider the implications of this argument for governments seeking to build policy capacity and, ultimately, for university programs that seek to train policy analysts.

Parsing Out Policy Analysis

If we are to explore whether policy analysis might vary in different governance contexts, then we must be clear about the sources and dimensions of variation. In this section we identify several contextual aspects that affect how policy analysis is conducted: the role of the analyst vis-à-vis politicians and others, sources of expertise, analytical capacity, and the relative autonomy of analysts compared to those commissioning policy analysis or standing as its intended audience.

Modes of Policy Analysis

Recent empirical work has identified several of the basic parameters of the analytical styles found in different locales. Drawing on U.S. experience, Beryl Radin (2000) identifies two ideal types: the rational, 'modern' analyst of the 1960s and 1970s, focused on the quantification of economic costs and benefits, and the 'post-modern' analyst of the 1980s and 1990s, concerned with the social construction of policy problems, policy discourses, and the politics of the policy process.

Drawing on European experience, Mayer, van Daalen, and Bots (2004) have provided a finer-grained dissection of the policy analysis function. They argue that policy analysis embraces very distinct tasks – research, clarification, design, advice, mediation, and democratization – and use pairs of these activities to produce six distinct, though not mutually exclusive, styles of policy analysis.

The six different styles identified by Mayer et al. (2004) are:

- *rational*, referring to the traditional neo-positivistic style in which researchers apply mainly economic and other empirical methods to specific cases and the generation of new knowledge is the main task of the analyst;
- *client advice*, where the analyst provides political and strategic advice to clients;
- *argumentative*, where the analyst is actively involved in debate and policy discourse as a distinct, independent actor, both within and outside governments;
- *interactive*, where the analyst serves as a facilitator in consultations in which key players and participants define their preferred outcome;
- *participative*, where the researcher/analyst is an advocate, aggregating and articulating the interests of silent players in the policy process: the poor, the general interest, or any other actor not represented in the policy process; and
- *process*, where the analyst acts a 'network manager,' steering the policy process towards a preferred outcome defined as part of the analytic task.

Mayer et al.'s framework embraces Radin's two archetypes of policy analysis, and provides additional roles to consider when thinking about different styles of policy analysis. Each style, of course, involves the use of specific analytical techniques and skills, ranging from traditional quantitative data analysis to much more qualitative political judgments concerning the feasibility of specific policy options.

Differential Policy Skills and Analytical Capacities

With respect to the skills required of policy analysts in each circumstance, Mayer et al.'s framework can be elaborated on in a manner similar to Quinn's (1988) 'competing values' framework, which identifies eight broad competencies (and specific skills within each area) needed by managers dealing with organizational challenges and their complexities. While this framework could be interpreted to argue for grooming the 'complete' policy analyst, the reality is that individuals come to their analytic roles with different strengths and weaknesses, depending on training and work experience. Following Quinn's thinking, 'analysing,' just like 'managing,' is a balancing act, requiring analysts to rely on different skills to address different challenges at different points in time. Moreover, as we discuss later, organizations also have recruitment systems, incentive structures, or cultures that cultivate different mixes of analytic skills.

Invoking specific skills and competencies as a way to comprehend different types of policy analytic activity naturally disposes us to think in terms of individuals. But we know that policy analysis is usually an organized activity in two senses (Lindquist and Desveaux, this volume): first, it is often done *for* organizations of some sort and, second, it is usually produced *by* teams of analysts or researchers, however tightly or loosely coupled (even single-authored notes and studies are vetted, reviewed, and often commissioned by other actors). Here we see another aspect of policy analytical style: how expertise is secured and managed by key actors.

When an organization seeks to address a policy issue, it should have a good sense of the skills required to do a credible job. However, those skills – whether indicating a generalist or specialist in the areas we noted earlier – may or may not reside with the organization in question. Organization leaders or project managers make choices in the short term and the longer term about the kind of competencies that they keep on staff on a full-time basis, and what they might secure from internal (rotational or temporary assignment from elsewhere in a larger organization) or external markets on a contract basis (Lindquist and Desveaux, 1998; this volume). Some organizations may prefer a relatively small core staff and tap into other sources of expertise as required, and others may retain far more staff with a mix of generalists and specialists, which may be buttressed by different recruitment systems and ways to identify and develop talent. This also suggests that, depending on the mix of expertise, policy organizations may have distinct ways or repertoires for approaching policy work (March and Simon 1958).

A final consideration involves assessing the capabilities mobilized, and the actual demands of the policy challenge in question. Whether the challenge is a thorny issue or a rival analysis with competing values and evidence, one has to determine if existing analytic capacities can meaningfully address the challenge; one could have the right mix of skills and expertise, but in insufficient amounts to produce a credible response within an allotted time frame.

Differential Values and Politics

In addition to considerations of the differential sets of skills and capacities for analysis contained by individuals and organizations, analyses also vary according to the nature of the values and politics brought to the analytical table. All policy analysis seeks, as Aaron Wildavsky famously put it, to 'speak truth to power' at some level, and is informed by the values of the analyst and audience in so doing (Wildavsky 1979; Sabatier 1988). Here we simply want to acknowledge that, beyond specific skill sets and capacities, policy analysis will vary according to underlying values, aspirations of immediate relevance, and the extent to which analysis seeks to challenge or reinforce existing policy and administrative regimes. Whatever its specific nature, policy analysis is undertaken to, and has the effect of, furthering, supporting, challenging, or testing certain values.

In recent years, increasingly sophisticated models of policy-making processes have shown how analysis and research support actors inside and outside the state as well as prevailing policy orthodoxies (Sabatier 1987; Kingdon 1984). The extent to which policy analysis challenges or reinforces those in power (or whoever commissioned it) affects both the conduct of policy analysis and its reception. Competing perspectives from inside and outside governments on policy questions driven by differing values, methodologies and political aspirations is a fact of policy analytical life (Allison 1971; Atkinson and Coleman 1989). Policy analysis and research is often produced with very different time horizons (short term or long term) and impact pathways (direct or indirect) in mind, and sometimes the intention is to play a brokering role between competing values and political orientations (Sabatier 1987).

Scepticism with respect to the aims and ambitions of those who commission policy research is an important function of policy analysis, in order to ensure that such analysis, of whatever kind, won't degenerate into communications or public relations. The relative autonomy of policy analysis vis-à-vis the government in power or the funders of analytical activity, then, is an important element affecting a policy style. This independence should be evident whether the case in question represents an individual, team, professional, or even networked activity.

Differential Governance Contexts: National, Sectoral, and Agency Variations

This discussion shows that policy analysis is a highly variegated activity. We have outlined several dimensions (see figure 4.1) along which it might vary, including: different roles and techniques to inform policy making; different ways to mobilize expertise; different degrees of analytical capacity; different types of relationships with policy actors; and different aspirations of relevance and immediacy of impact. We also argue that, even when policy analysis is undertaken for specific clients, it necessarily challenges how people conceive of, and approach the solving of, policy problems, thereby creating a tension even when analysis is 'aligned' with its intended audience. Although this variegation suggests a very large range of possible analytical types, a focus on common governance contexts allows a smaller number of 'typical' types to be identified.

The above discussion strongly suggests that patterns of policy analysis are intimately linked with governance context and analytical culture. A full discussion of the impact of analytical culture is beyond the scope of this article (Peters 1990). However, in modern polities in which recruitment is standardized and credentials are required from professional policy, public administration, management, or law schools, the variation in this variable is much muted from times past (Wise 2002; Considine and Lewis 2003). Distinct governance contexts for policy making, however, have been identified at different levels of analysis (Howlett 2002c). Here we identify these common structural factors and their implications for policy analysis.

National governance traditions. National policy systems can be seen as the offshoots of larger national governance and administrative traditions or cultures (Dwivedi and Gow 1999; Bevir and Rhodes 2001), such as parliamentary or republican forms of government, and federal or unitary states. This leads to different concentrations of power in the central institutions of government, degrees of openness and access to information, and reliance on certain governing instruments.[2] Civil service organizations have rules and structures that govern policy and administrative behaviour, such as the constitutional order establishing and empowering administrators, and that affect patterns and methods of recruiting civil servants and how they interact with each other and the public (Bekke, Perry, and Toonen 1993). Accordingly, the policy analysis function is influenced by the precepts of the governance and administrative model constituting its operating environment (Castles 1990; Kagan 1991, 1996; Vogel 1986; Eisner 1993, 1994; Harris and Milkis 1989). For example, if the top priority of a national government is debt reduction or increasing internal security, then the scope for other new policy initiatives will be reduced, and there may be more of a focus on review, control and accountability. Or if a country has a more inclusive governance tradition, or if an elected government aims to make this a hallmark of its mandate, then a greater premium will be placed on consultation and facilitation. Similarly, countries with weaker central institutions of government will likely provide more scope to departments and agencies in developing new policy ideas, while stronger, more autonomous representative legislatures will create additional demand for policy analysis, which can challenge bureaucratic policy expertise. And, if civil service institutions centrally control recruitment and seek 'generalists,' and place limits on contracting, this may constrain policy units that would otherwise seek specialists to deal with emerging issues.

Policy sectors. Vogel and others have argued that policy makers work within specific national policy or regulatory contexts. Many policy studies, however, have suggested that distinct contexts can be discerned not only at the national level but also at the sectoral level, and are linked to common approaches taken towards problems such as health, education and forestry (Lowi 1972; Salamon 1981; Freeman 1985; Burstein 1991; Howlett 2001). Freeman, for example, has observed that 'each sector poses its own problems, sets its own constraints, and generates its own brand of conflict' (1985, 468). Moreover, the authority and capability for making and influencing policy may vary considerably across sectors. Like Allison (1971), Smith, Marsh, and Richards have argued that the 'central state is not a unified actor but a range of institutions and actors with disparate interests and varying resources' (1993, 594), and therefore not only may there be different degrees of coherence within the state, but also different cultures of decision making and inclusion of outside actors with respect to policy development (collaboration, unilateral, reactive) in different sectors.

In each sector, different configurations of societal actors – such as business, labour and special interest groups, as well as think-tanks and university centres – exist, with different analytical capabilities and policy expertise, different degrees of independence with respect to funding, and different relationships with state actors. For example, in some sectors, policy expertise might be located with non-state actors and governments might tap into it regularly. Different policy sectors may have higher priority for governments, depending on their policy ambitions and circumstances, or the regime may be contested to a greater degree, which may affect not only the appetite for change but also for policy analysis and research (Lindquist 1988). Some policy sectors, broadly speaking, may be anticipatory or reactive on how to deal with challenges confronting the entire sector, and therefore will differ in their support for analysis and research that challenges existing regimes (Atkinson and Coleman 1989). Finally, some sectors might only have 'thin' policy expertise, more conductive to partisan or ideological positioning, as opposed to more extensive talent and forums for debating policy issues in the context of research-based findings (Sabatier 1987; Lindquist 1992).

Agency-level organizational factors. Policy analysis is also shaped by the nature and priorities of public-sector departments and agencies (Wilson 1989; Richardson, Jordan, and Kimber 1978; Jordan 2003), which have distinct organizational mandates, histories, cultures, program delivery and front-line challenges (Lipsky 1980; Hawkins and Thomas 1989; Quinn 1988; Scholz 1984, 1991). Organizations and leaders might attach different value to policy analysis in light of managerial and budgetary priorities; have different views on how inclusive to be when developing policy with inside and outside actors; demand certain types of policy analysis; have different degrees of comfort with challenges from policy analysis of current policy and program regimes; and have different models of accessing and dispersing policy capabilities across the organization (for example, whether there is a single corporate policy unit, or others attached to program areas). This may lead to certain repertoires for policy analysis and types of recruitment for policy expertise. The more operational a department or unit, the more likely it is that its policy style will be rational. The more involved a department is in a major policy initiative, boundary-spanning activity, or liaising with central agencies, the more likely it is that its policy style will be participatory and facilitative. If a policy shop is a corporate entity, as opposed to directly supporting a specific program, it is more likely that its policy style will emphasize client advising and interaction. Finally, the more involved in regulatory activity and enforcement, the more likely an agency will have an interactive or process style (Jordan 2003).

Figure 4.1 summarizes these three levels of governance contexts as well as the constraints and opportunities they present for policy analysis. While policy analysis encompasses a diverse range of activities and techniques, different governance contexts can lead to 'grooved' patterns or distinct 'bundles' or 'styles' of policy analysis (including skill mix, capabilities and value congruence) that may reinforce each other, creating a distinct and enduring policy analytical style. However, the contexts can also create cross-currents that make the patterns more precarious and highly dependent on what government is in power and who leads key departments in policy networks. Generally, we believe that the concept of policy analytical style should be reserved for aggregate assessment. Teasing through and assessing the extent of influence of these factors on patterns of policy analysis augers strongly for systematic comparative analysis (Freeman 1985; Smith, Marsh, and Rhodes 1993).

Patterns and Trends in Canadian Policy Analytic Styles

We have argued that fully exploring how different governance contexts affect policy analysis will require systematic comparative research. In what follows we elaborate on some of these concepts by reviewing at a broad level Canada's evolving governing contexts – national, policy sector, and departments and agencies – and explore the implications of these changes for the demand and conduct of policy analysis.

National Level: Westminster Traditions, Competitive Federalism

The critical factor conditioning policy advising found inside and outside the Canadian state is the predominance of British Westminster

Figure 4.1 Governance Context and Institutional Focal Points

Level	Structural vantage point	Dimensions to consider
National governance traditions	National and subnational governments	Governance system Civil service traditions Government priorities Strong or weak centres Strong or weak legislatures Recruitment systems
Policy sectors	Policy networks and communities	Distribution of power Distribution of expertise Depth of expertise Dynamics of dominant and other advocacy coalitions Priority of government Moment of crisis
Departments, agencies	Organizational culture, repertoires, capacities	Organization culture policy, service delivery, control Types of policy capability Distribution of internal policy expertise Critical challenges Priorities of the centre Disposition towards inclusion and engagement External networks for policy expertise

parliamentary institutions and relationships at the federal and provincial levels. The result is executive-dominated government without the checks and balances associated with the U.S. style of government, which established competing branches of government, or with European and other systems, where legislatures enjoy relative autonomy due to proportional representation or upper-house elections (Savoie 1999a, 1999b). Despite the vigorous efforts of reformers, particularly from the Western provinces, national governments have steadfastly resisted ideas to convert the Canadian Senate into an elected institution and to adopt forms of proportional representation into either the House of Commons (elected) or the Senate (appointed). The adoption of UK-style institutions also meant that Canadian governments did not have to contend with strong judicial review for many decades (Thomas 1997; Franks 1987; Dunn 1995; Manfredi 1997; Manfredi and Maioni 2002).

This has several implications for the conduct and training of policy analysts. First, non-partisan and professional public service institutions generally serve governing parties and their executives (Lindquist 2000). The unwillingness of prime ministers and premiers to grant autonomy and to fund competing advice in legislatures meant that, for many years, governments and their public service institutions had analytic capabilities rivalled only by the largest business firms and associations and, to a lesser extent, labour organizations. This led to patterns of closed sectoral bargaining relationships between major government, business and labour actors, not subject to great public scrutiny (Montpetit 2002; Pross 1992; Atkinson and Coleman 1989; Lascher 1999). The British influence also resulted in a preference for quasi-legal regulation, with more emphasis on education and negotiation than on litigation, although U.S. influences and the arrival of the Charter of Rights and Freedoms in 1982 has steadily shifted this emphasis (Howlett 2002a, 2002b; Kagan 1991).

Federalism is the second distinctive feature of Canada's governance landscape. Despite the efforts of the country's founders to allocate residual powers to the federal government, the unanticipated changes in the challenges confronting the country, as well as key court decisions, ensured that the provinces steadily accrued increasingly more responsibility throughout the twentieth century for delivering and designing programs for citizens, including shared jurisdiction with the federal government in almost every policy domain (Smiley 1964; Banting 1982). Many policy initiatives proceed in the context of 'peak bargaining' between and among federal, provincial, and territorial governments (Tuohy 1992; Atkinson and Coleman 1989), conditioned, of course, by the stricture of parliamentary systems. Aside from political debates over policy directions in different domains, this resulted in a steadily increasing frequency of federal-provincial-territorial committee meetings for premiers and the prime minister and their ministers in specific policy domains (health, labour market, transportation, education, finance, and many others), and myriad working committees and subcommittees of officials (Simeon 1980). It is difficult to overstate the complexity of Canadian federalism and its supporting policy institutions in such a huge, regionally and linguistically diverse country, with provinces and territories of starkly different fiscal, population, and land bases (Howlett 1999; McRoberts 1993).

Ministerial and official intergovernmental committees are instruments of the executive branches of each government, and usually work *in camera* without the direct scrutiny of legislatures and the public (Doer 1981; Radin and Boase 2000). Citizens are typically only engaged if certain governments are attempting to build public support for positions, usually at the agenda-setting stage of the policy process, or if statements or decisions are communicated. Intergovernmental officials – who may be located in cabinet agencies or line departments depending on the size of government – function like central officials, as either primarily process facilitators or actively championing positions and values on behalf of the government. Although some units and individuals might develop considerable substantive expertise, they typically do not rival that of policy units in line departments or in finance or treasury departments.

Discerning Canada's policy analytical style through the lens of federalism does not produce an image of orderly, productive and co-operative processes. Rather, it is one of increasing distrust and rivalry between different orders of government, particularly since the federal government steadily reduced the real value of transfer payments to provincial governments and the tradition of supporting shared-cost programs in many different policy sectors since the 1960s. Provinces and territories attempt to create a united front against the federal government, but this papers over fundamental regional differences on transfer payment and financial regimes, as well as other policy, regulatory, and representational issues. For these arenas, policy analysis is rational and argumentative, intended to support government positions.

Policy Sectors: Dispersed Expertise, Selective Consultation, Power Asymmetries

The emergence of an 'attentive public' that monitors the 'subgovernment' of principal state and non-state actors actively shaping public policy and existing programs has been a key characteristic of the development of the governance context of Canadian policy making in the past two decades. This context has a significant impact upon the types of policy analytical styles present in the country. The growth of policy-relevant expertise residing with interest groups, think-tanks and universities has also significantly expanded the range of actors present in the networks associated with policy sectors.

Think tanks, for example, began proliferating in the early 1970s, although by U.S. standards Canada still lacks a significant, well-resourced cadre of such organizations. This is due, partly, to insufficient sustained demand for policy research and analysis from actors other than government departments and, partly, to the lack of a strong philanthropic tradition in Canada (Sharpe 2001; Lindquist 2006b). Thus, while think tanks have greatly expanded in number and diversity, their policy expertise typically does not rival that of federal and provincial governments (Abelson 2002; Dobuzinskis 1996a; Lindquist 1989, 2004). The same holds for academics at universities; while institutes have expanded tremendously over the last few years, often serving as home bases for world-renowned specialists in certain fields, they tend to lack the data and specialized expertise required to challenge governments in the policy analytic process. Generally, think tanks, institutes, and public academics monitor and provide commentary on government actions, and may try to influence agenda setting through framing, critical evaluations, and other techniques, but rarely do they have a strong impact on decision and design (Abelson 2002; Lindquist 1989; Soroka 2002).

The attentive public also includes citizens and interest groups, and the literature points to the enduring challenge for governments regarding how to engage them on specific issues (Lenihan and Alcock 2000). Canadian governments are often accused of not undertaking enough consultation with citizens and groups. On the other hand, some government departments do regularly consult, and leaders inside and outside government often worry about 'consultation fatigue' of key stakeholders (Howlett and Rayner 2004; Lindquist 2005, 2006a). The federal Privy Council Office has a small unit that monitors and coordinates consultation activities across the government, and serves as a node for a functional community of consultation specialists across the public service. The federal government experimented by creating councils in the 1960s with representatives from different sectors and regularly relied on royal commissions to tackle big policy questions by commissioning research and holding public hearings over several years (Bradford 1999–2000). During the late 1980s and early 1990s it also launched mega-consultation processes for the Green Plan, the Charlottetown Accord, budget making, and the Social Security Review, including, among other initiatives, public conferences, and workshops co-hosted with independent think tanks and other organizations, which received exposure as media events (Lindquist 1994, 1996b, 2005).

Current Canadian governments are more likely to opt for the somewhat less public, but perhaps less expensive and more effective, selective and low-key consultations, working with representatives of interests from specific sectors and constituencies (Atkinson and Pervin 1998). There has been interest in and flirtation with e-consultation as a new means of engaging citizens, but this has not substantially modified policy making, though it has increased efficiencies in distributing information and receiving views from groups and citizens (Alexander and Pal 1998). Think tanks and consultants have been engaged to manage citizen 'dialogues' on issues, but this has not supplanted more traditional decision making (Lindquist, 2004).

Other orders of government and sectors are increasingly important policy actors. The courts have repeatedly affirmed that major urban municipalities are creatures of provincial governments, but the federal government views them as important drivers of economic growth, anchors for regions and rural communities, and deserving of federal assistance. Such awareness leads to both vertical and horizontal interventions spanning the traditional boundaries of departments and governments, despite federal and provincial rivalries, and has been best illustrated with the new jointly funded Infrastructure Works program. Aboriginal communities increasingly seek resolution of land claims, closure on treaty negotiations, and self-government, including, at the very least, co-management of natural resources (Notzke 1994). These matters, as well as the stark health and social issues confronting their communities, require working across the traditional boundaries of government to better align policy initiatives and dispersed expertise. Progress on land claims and treaties has been mixed, but prodded by impatient courts, governments are exploring new ways of sharing power. Recently, the federal government has sought to increase transparency and accountability for management of the funds received by bands. The federal government also launched the Voluntary Sector Initiative, designed to build capacity to better deliver public goods in communities in exchange for better governance and accountability. This was a clear reversal from the early 1990s when, labelled as 'special interest groups,' many voluntary and nonprofit organizations lost sustaining funding as part of the Program Review exercise and its precursors (Philips 2001), even if the tax status of charitable organizations constrained the amount of policy advocacy they could undertake.

Canada's policy analytical context has steadily evolved. In the 1960s and 1970s, the introduction of formal policy analysis by central agencies and lead departments in support of new cabinet and expenditure management systems adopted by federal and provincial governments was very much the rational type identified by Mayer et al. (Prince 1979; French 1980). By the early 1980s, it was apparent that purely rational analysis had not fulfilled its promise in complex political and bureaucratic environments (Hartle 1978; Dobell and Zussman 1980). Additional changes in policy communities, such as the rise of special interest groups, think tanks, citizens, and international actors, further complicated agenda setting and policy making, and created alternative sources of policy analysis, research, and data (Pross 1986; Atkinson and Coleman 1989; Coleman and Skogstad 1990).

The Agency Level: Analytic Capacity Varies by Jurisdiction and Sector

Departments, ministries, and agencies vary significantly with respect to the size and scope of responsibilities but are key suppliers and demanders of policy analysis. They have different institutional histories, styles of executive leadership, and patterns of recruitment that flow from their core tasks and missions (Wilson 1989). Within Canadian governments, the policy analysis capacity of departments and ministries varies widely, and derives largely from the size of the government. Smaller provinces may have less capacity than the largest municipalities, and some of the largest provinces have capabilities rivalling other national jurisdictions (Ontario and Quebec, respectively, have populations of 11 and 7.4 million citizens, comparable to the populations of New Zealand and Sweden).

The principles and practices of parliamentary governance ensure that central agencies in each jurisdiction regulate policy development and oversee the activities of departments or ministries, even if they are not as operationally well informed as the policy analysis and research units of those same departments and ministries (Savoie 1999a and 1999b). In some cases, departments will have corporate policy shops and others attached to specific program areas, and even the smallest departments may have dedicated policy research capabilities (Hollander and Prince 1993). However, since all ministers and deputy ministers are appointed directly by the prime minister and premiers (in some provinces, they also appoint assistant deputy ministers), policy analysis in Canadian governments, no matter how professional and non-partisan the public service in question, tends to lack independence. In some cases, efforts to seriously study new or daunting challenges can only be addressed by creating temporary administrative advocacies to tap into technical expertise, coordinate across departments and agencies, consult with outside groups, and deal with central authorities (Desveaux, Lindquist, and Toner 1993). If time is not of the essence, then governments can appoint independent inquires, task forces or royal commissions to ensure that research and analysis are at arm's length from the normal pressures on departments by ministers (Salter 1990; Salter and Slaco 1981; Sheriff 1983; Peters and Parker 1993).

During the 1980s and the early 1990s, executives in the Canadian public service did not rise to the top by stewarding policy initiatives but rather by handling transition and restructuring departments and programs, better managing resources, and helping the government and ministers deal with difficult political files such as federalism, Quebec and the sovereignty movement, and free trade with the United States. While the policy function did not disappear, governments focused less on thinking broadly about problems and more on achieving focus and specific results, and more resources were allocated to sophisticated polling and communications organizations inside and outside the government (Bakvis 2000). Following the June 1993 restructuring of the public service and the 1994–95 Program Review decisions, which resulted in budget cuts, consolidations, and lay-offs, it was generally acknowledged that the policy capacity of the public service had atrophied, in part because deputy ministers allocated scarce resources to deal with pressing challenges and because demand for new policies lessened. The extent to which the policy functions of departments declined, if at all, varied across the public service, yet probably remained considerably greater than those of provincial, territorial and municipal governments. One result of tighter budgets in the early 1990s was that departments often became more creative in managing policy analysis and research, an approach that was accelerated by the Policy Research Initiative. They worked with other departments, relied on external consultants to deal with specific demands if internal expertise was insufficient, and cultivated networks of researchers in universities and think-tanks. Moreover, beginning in the late 1990s federal governments have made it clear to the public service that they are seeking long-term policy thinking. However, it is an open question as to whether the incentives for producing high-quality policy advice, and perhaps building long-term internal capacity, outweigh the demand to improve service delivery of existing programs while lowering costs, to ensure that programs are prudently and tightly managed from the standpoint of financial control, and to measure and report on performance.

Concluding Remarks: Canada's Policy Analytic Style

Our high-level review of different governance trends affecting policy function in Canada has shown that parliamentary traditions in a federal context have a defining influence on where policy analytical capacity is concentrated and ensure that, despite the proliferation of many more policy-capable players in each policy sector – interest groups, think-tanks, Aboriginal communities, NGOs, and international organizations – the fulcrum of power among major actors inside and outside government has not changed. However, in a post-deficit and newly security-conscious environment, the national government has more actively demanded policy advice, which has led to departments seeking creative ways to tap into expertise within and across governments, and with analysts and researchers in consulting firms, universities, think tanks, and associations. It is a far more complicated policy-making environment for government leaders to navigate, and this requires that policy analysts have more process-related skills. Figure 4.2 summarizes our arguments and suggests that the country's policy analytic style has shifted from an emphasis on rationalism, client advice and argumentative skills, to encompass those relating to process management, inter-activity and participation.

We can also characterize this shift by applying Radin's two ideal types of modern and post-modern analyst to national policy styles that encompass 'bundles' of the skills identified by Mayer et al. at different levels of the policy-making context. The 'modern' bundle of analytical styles was appropriate to Canada's governance context in the 1960s, with relatively top-down centralized national control of policy making, simple bi-lateral or trilateral subgovernment structures and managerial agency activity. This bundle was rational at the level of national systems, client-oriented at the level of the subgovernment or policy community and, at the department level, provided argumentative advice. However, it was less well suited to the post-1990 context of a fiscally strapped central government, stronger provincial governments, and more complex policy communities and 'intelligent' agencies in an international context. A post-modern bundle of policy capabilities has thus emerged alongside the more traditional orientations, and features Mayer et al.'s other three analytical styles: process management, interactivity, and participatory analysis. Prima facie, similar patterns in governance and policy analysis appear to exist in other jurisdictions, such as the Netherlands and the UK (Kickert 2003; Considine and Lewis 2003).

Figure 4.2 Governance Contexts and Elements of Canada's Policy Style

Level	Focal point	Old context 1960–1980	Old analytic style	New context 1980–2000	New analytic style
National governance systems	National and subnational governments	Top-down, centralized parliamentary federalism	Rationalism	Fiscal austerity and decentralization	Process
Policy sectors	Policy communities	Bi-partite and tri-partite business/ labour peak associations	Client advice	More challenge from diverse communities	Interactive
Departments and agencies	Organizational culture, repertoires, capacities	Managerialism	Argumentative	Balance tipping away from management back to policy creativity	Participatory

Even though our primary focus has been theoretical in nature, with the ambition to encourage more systematic comparative empirical research, we believe there are implications for pedagogical practices in professional schools of policy analysis, administration, and management. The Mayer et al. framework, and the other features of policy analysis that we identified, gives us a better sense of the range of roles and skills potentially required of policy analysis in support of clients and communities. The skills, knowledge, and dispositions required to perform those functions at a high level of competency go beyond the traditional skill-set or bundle typically taught in professional schools (Gow and Sutherland 2004a, 2004b; but see Lindquist 1993 about how many schools have gone beyond the traditional skill-set, albeit in a quiet manner). Schools of public policy should systematically expose students to a broader range of techniques and skills along with instruction on the nature of Canada's policy style and its evolution so that students will be able to match policy and analytic style to the context in which they work.

Most of our professional programs are currently dedicated to producing generalists to perform the traditional analytic roles, but our analysis suggests the importance of redesigning or supplementing curricula to deepen knowledge and skill in facilitation, negotiation, or advocacy, and of finding ways to ensure that our students and graduates can see the value of these approaches and understand how to work productively with specialists in those areas (Mintrom 2003). More generally, our framework might also help graduates better determine how they might begin and build their careers.

NOTES

1 Policy analysis texts usually describe a range of qualitative and quantitative techniques that analysts are expected to learn and apply in specific circumstances, providing advice to decision makers about optimal strategies and outcomes to pursue in the resolution of public problems (Elmore 1991; Weimer and Vining 1999; Patton and Sawicki, 1993).
2 A parallel argument can be found in the field of regulation. Knill (1998) has stated that regulatory styles are defined by 'the mode of state intervention' (hierarchical versus self-regulation, as well as uniform and detailed requirements versus open regulation allowing for administrative flexibility and discretion) and the mode of 'administrative interest intermediation' (formal versus informal, legalistic versus pragmatic, and open versus closed relationships). Franz van Waarden argues that 'National regulatory styles are formally rooted in nationally specific legal, political and administrative institutions and cultures. This foundation in a variety of state institutions should make regulatory styles resistant to change and hence, from this perspective one would expect differences in regulatory styles to persist, possibly even under the impact of economic and political internationalization' (1995).

REFERENCES

Abelson, Donald E. 2002. *Do Think Tanks Matter? Assessing the Impact of Public Policy Institutes*. Montreal and Kingston: McGill-Queen's University Press.
Aberbach, J.D., and B.A. Rockman. 1987. 'Comparative Administration: Methods, Muddles and Models.' *Administration and Society* 18, 473–506.
Anderson, George. 1996. 'The New Focus on the Policy Capacity of the Federal Government.' *Canadian Public Administration* 39(4), 469–99.
Armit, Amelita, and Jacques Bourgualt, eds. 1996. *Hard Choices or No Choices: Assessing Program Review*. Toronto: Institute of Public Administration of Canada.
Armstrong, Jim, Nick Mulder, and Russ Robinson. 2002. *Strengthening Policy*

Capacity: Report on Interviews with Senior Managers, February-March 2002.
Ottawa: The Governance Network.

Alexander, Cynthia J., and Leslie A. Pal, eds. 1998. *Digital Democracy: Policy and Politics in the Wired World.* Toronto: Oxford University Press.

Association of Public Service Financial Administrators. 2003. *Checks and Balances: Rebalancing the Service and Control Features of the Government of Canada (GOC) Financial Control Framework.* Ottawa: Association of Public Service Financial Administrators, December.

Atkinson, Michael, and William D. Coleman. 1989. *Business, the State, and Industrial Change.* Toronto: University of Toronto Press.

Atkinson, Michael M., and Cassandra W. Pervin. 1998. 'Sector Councils and Sectoral Corporatism: Viable? Desirable?' In M. Gunderson and A. Sharpe, eds., *Forging Business-Labour Partnerships: The Emergence of Sector Councils in Canada,* 271–94. Toronto: University of Toronto Press.

Bakvis, Herman. 2000. 'Rebuilding Policy Capacity in the Era of the Fiscal Dividend: A Report from Canada.' *Governance* 13(1), 71–103.

Banting, Keith G. 1982. *The Welfare State and Canadian Federalism.* Kingston: Queen's University Institute of Intergovernmental Relations.

Bardach, Eugene. 2000. *A Practical Guide for Policy Analysis: The Eightfold Path to More Effective Problem Solving.* New York: Chatham House Publishers.

Bekke, Hans, James L. Perry, and Theo Toonen. 1993. 'Comparing Civil Service Systems.' *Research in Public Administration* 2, 191–212.

Bekke, Hans, and Frits M. van der Meer, eds. 2000. *Civil Service Systems in Western Europe.* Cheltenham: Edward Elgar.

Bevir, Mark, and R.A.W. Rhodes. 2001. 'Decentering Tradition: Interpreting British Government.' *Administration & Society* 33(2), 107–32.

Bevir, Mark, R.A.W. Rhodes, and Patrick Weller. 2003a. 'Traditions of Governance: Interpreting the Changing Role of the Public Sector.' *Public Administration* 81(1), 1–17.

– 2003b. 'Comparative Governance: Prospects and Lessons.' *Public Administration* 81(1), 191–210.

Bradford, Neil. 1999–2000. 'Writing Public Philosophy: Canada's Royal Commissions on Everything.' *Journal of Canadian Studies* 34(4), 136–67.

Burns, John P., and Bidhya Bowornwathana, eds. *Civil Service Systems in Asia.* Cheltenham: Edward Elgar, 2001.

Burstein, Paul. 1991. 'Policy Domains: Organization, Culture and Policy Outcomes.' *Annual Review of Sociology* 17, 327–50.

Castles, Francis G. 1990. 'The Dynamics of Policy Change: What Happened to the English-Speaking Nations in the 1980s.' *European Journal of Political Research* 18(5), 491–513.

Christensen, Tom, Per Laegreid, and Lois R. Wise. 2003. 'Evaluating Public Management Reforms in Central Government: Norway, Sweden and the United States of America.' In H. Wollman, ed., *Evaluation in Public Sector Reform: Concepts and Practice in International Perspective*, 56–79. Cheltenham: Edward Elgar.

Coleman, William D., and Grace Skogstad, eds. 1990. *Policy Communities and Public Policy in Canada: A Structuralist Approach.* Toronto: Copp Clark Pitman.

Considine, Mark, and Jenny M. Lewis. 2003. 'Bureaucracy, Network, or Enterprise? Comparing Models of Governance in Australia, Britain, the Netherlands, and New Zealand.' *Public Administration Review* 63(2), 131–40.

Desveaux, James A., Evert A. Lindquist, and Glen Toner. 1994. 'Organizing for Policy Innovation in Public Bureaucracy: AIDS, Energy, and Environmental Policy in Canada.' *Canadian Journal of Political Science* 27(3), 493–528.

Dobuzinskis, Laurent. 1996. 'Trends and Fashions in the Marketplace of Ideas.' In Laurent Dobuzinskis, Michael Howlett, and David Laycock, eds., *Policy Studies in Canada: The State of the Art*, 91–124. Toronto: University of Toronto Press.

Dobell, Rodney, and David Zussman. 1981. 'An Evaluation System for Government: If Politics is Theatre, then Evaluation is (mostly) Art.' *Canadian Public Administration* 24(3), 404–27.

Doerr, Audrey D. 1981. *The Machinery of Government in Canada.* Toronto: Methuen.

Dunn, Christopher. 1995. *The Institutionalized Cabinet: Governing the Western Provinces.* Kingston and Montreal: McGill-Queen's University Press.

Dwivedi, O.P., and James Iain Gow. 1999. *From Bureaucracy to Public Management: The Administrative Culture of the Government of Canada.* Toronto: IPAC.

Eisner, Marc Allen. 1993. *Regulatory Politics in Transition.* Baltimore: Johns Hopkins University Press.

– 1994. 'Discovering Patterns in Regulatory History: Continuity, Change and Regulatory Regimes.' *Journal of Policy History* 6(2), 157–87.

Elmore, Richard E. 1991. 'Teaching, Learning and Education for the Public Service.' *Journal of Policy Analysis and Management* 10(2), 167–80.

Fischer, Frank, and John Forester, eds. 1993. *The Argumentative Turn in Policy Analysis and Planning.* Durham, NC: Duke University Press.

Fox, Charles J. 1990. 'Implementation Research: Why and How to Transcend Positivist Methodology.' In Dennis J. Palumbo and D.J. Calisto, eds., *Implementation and the Policy Process: Opening up the Black Box*, 199–212. New York: Greenwood Press.

Franks, C.E.S. 1987. *The Parliament of Canada*. Toronto: University of Toronto Press.

Freeman, Gary P. 1985. 'National Styles and Policy Sectors: Explaining Structured Variation.' *Journal of Public Policy* 5(4), 467–96.

French, Richard. 1980. *How Ottawa Decides: Planning and Industrial Policy-Making 1968–1980*. Toronto: Lorimer.

Garson, G. David. 1986. 'From Policy Science to Policy Analysis: A Quarter Century of Progress.' In William N. Dunn, ed., *Policy Analysis: Perspectives, Concepts, and Methods*, 3–22. Greenwich, CT: JAI Press.

Geva-May, Iris, and Aaron Wildavsky. 1987. *An Operational Approach to Policy Analysis: the Craft - Prescriptions for Better Analysis*. Boston: Kluwer.

Golob, Stephanie R. 2003. 'Beyond the Policy Frontier: Canada, Mexico, and the Ideological Origins of NAFTA.' *World Politics* 55, 361–98.

Gow, J.I., and S.L. Sutherland. 2004a. *Comparison of Canadian Masters Programs in Public Administration, Public Management and Public Policy*. Toronto: Canadian Association of Schools of Public Policy and Administration.

– 2004b. 'Comparison of Canadian Masters Programs in Public Administration, Public Management and Public Policy.' *Canadian Public Administration* 47(3), 379–405.

Guess, George M., and Paul G. Farnham. 1989. *Cases in Public Policy Analysis*. New York: Longman.

Harris, Richard, and Sidney Milkis. 1989. *The Politics of Regulatory Change*. New York: Oxford University Press.

Hartle, Douglas G. 1978. *The Expenditure Budget Process in the Government of Canada*. Canada: Canadian Tax Foundation.

Hawkins, Keith, and John M. Thomas. 1989. 'Making Policy in Regulatory Bureaucracies.' In K. Hawkins and J. M. Thomas, eds., *Making Regulatory Policy*, 3–30. Pittsburgh: University of Pittsburgh Press.

Heineman, Robert, et al. 2002. *The World of the Policy Analyst*. New York: Chatham House Publishers.

Hird, John A. 2005. 'Policy Analysis for What? The Effectiveness of Nonpartisan Policy Research Organizations.' *Policy Studies Journal* 33(1), 83–105.

Hollander, Marcus J., and Michael J. Prince. 1993. 'Analytical Units in Federal and Provincial Governments: Origins, Functions and Suggestions for Effectiveness.' *Canadian Public Administration* 36(2), 190–224.

House, Peter W., and Roger D. Shull. 1991. *The Practice of Policy Analysis: Forty Years of Art & Technology*. Washington, DC: The Compass Press.

Howlett, Michael. 1999. 'Federalism and Public Policy.' In James Bickerton and Alain Gagnon, eds., *Canadian Politics*, 3rd ed., 523–39. Peterborough, ON: Broadview Press.

- 2000. 'Beyond Legalism? Policy Ideas, Implementation Styles and Emula-
  tion-Based Convergence in Canadian and US Environmental Policy.' *Journal
  of Public Policy* 20(3), 305–29.
- ed. 2001. *Canadian Forest Policy: Adapting to Change.* Toronto: University of
  Toronto Press.
- 2002a. 'Policy Development.' In Chris Dunn, ed., *The Oxford Handbook of
  Canadian Public Administration.* Toronto: Oxford University Press.
- 2002b. 'Policy Instruments and Implementation Styles: The Evolution of
  Instrument Choice in Canadian Environmental Policy.' In Debora L. Van
  Nijnatten and Robert Boardman, eds., *Canadian Environmental Policy: Con-
  text and Cases*, 25–45. Toronto: Oxford University Press.
- 2002c. 'Understanding National Administrative Cultures and Their Impact
  Upon Administrative Reform: A Neo-Institutional Model and Analysis.'
  Policy, Organization & Society 21(1), 1–24.
- 2004. 'Administrative Styles and the Limits of Administrative Reform:
  A Neo-Institutional Analysis of Administrative Culture.' *Canadian Public
  Administration* 46(4), 471–94.
Howlett, Michael, and Jeremy Rayner. 2004. '(Not so) "Smart Regulation"?
  Canadian Shellfish Aquaculture Policy and the Evolution of Instrument
  Choice for Industrial Development.' *Marine Policy* 28(2), 171–84.
Jenkins-Smith, Hank C. 1982. 'Professional Roles for Policy Analysts: A
  Critical Assessment.' *Journal of Policy Analysis and Management* 2(1),
  88–100.
Jordan, Andrew. 2003. 'The Europeanization of National Government and
  Policy: A Departmental Perspective.' *British Journal of Political Science* 33(1),
  261–282.
Kagan, Robert A. 1991. 'Adversarial Legalism and American Government.'
  Journal of Policy Analysis and Management 10(3), 369–406.
- 1996. 'The Political Consequences of American Adversarial Legalism.' In
  A. Ranney, ed., *Courts and the Political Process.* Berkeley: Institute of Govern-
  mental Studies Press.
Kickert, Walter J.M. 2003. 'Beneath Consensual Corporatism: Tradition of
  Governance in the Netherlands.' *Public Administration* 81(1), 119–140.
Knill, Christoph. 1998. 'European Policies: The Impact of National Adminis-
  trative Traditions.' *Journal of Public Policy* 18(1), 1–28.
Lascher, Edward L. 1999. *The Politics of Automobile Insurance Reform: Ideas,
  Institutions and Public Policy in North America.* Washington, DC: Georgetown
  University Press.
Lenihan, Donald G.. and Reg Alcock. 2000. *Collaborative Government in the
  Post-Industrial Age: Five Discussion Pieces – Changing Government.* Volume I.
  Ottawa: Centre for Collaborative Government.

Lindblom, Charles E. 1958. 'Policy Analysis.' *American Economic Review* 48(3), 298–312.

Lindquist, Evert A. 1989. 'Behind the Myth of Think Tanks: The Organization and Relevance of Canadian Policy Institutes.' PhD dissertation, Graduate School of Public Policy, University of California, Berkeley.

– 1993. 'Postmodern Politics and Policy Sciences.' *Optimum* 24(1), 42–50.

– 1994. 'Citizens, Experts, and Budgets.' In Susan D. Phillips, ed., *How Ottawa Spends 1994–95: Making Change.* Ottawa: Carleton University Press.

– 1996a. 'New Agendas for Research on Policy Communities: Policy Analysis, Administration, and Governance.' In L. Dobuzinskis, M. Howlett, and D. Laycock, eds., *Policy Studies in Canada: The State of the Art,* 219–41. Toronto: University of Toronto Press.

– 1996b. 'Reshaping Governments and Communities: Must Program Reviews Remain Unilateral, Executive Processes?' In Amelita Armit and Jacques Bourgualt, eds., *Hard Choices or No Choices: Assessing Program Review,* 137–46. Toronto: Institute of Public Administration of Canada.

– 2001. 'How Ottawa Plans: The Evolution of Strategic Planning.' In Leslie A. Pal, ed., *How Ottawa Spends 2001–02: Power in Transition,* 61–93. Toronto: Oxford University Press.

– 2004. 'Three Decades of Canadian Think Tanks: Evolving Institutions, Conditions and Strategies.' In Diane Stone and Andrew Denham, eds., *Think Tank Traditions: Policy Research and the Politics of Ideas,* 264–80. Manchester: Manchester University Press.

– 2005 'Organizing for Mega-Consultation: HRDC and the Social Security Review.' *Canadian Public Administration* 48(3), 348–85.

– 2006a. *A Critical Moment: Capturing and Conveying the Evolution of the Canadian Public Service.* Ottawa: Canada School of Public Service.

– 2006b *Think Tanks, Foundations and Policy Discourse: Ebbs and Flows, Investments and Responsibilites.* Ottawa: Canadian Policy Research Networks.

– ed. 2000. *Government Restructuring and Career Public Service in Canada.* Toronto: Institute of Public Administration of Canada.

Lindquist, Evert, and James Desveaux. 1998. *Recruitment and Policy Capacity in Government.* Ottawa: Public Policy Forum.

Lipsky, Michael. 1980. *Street-Level Bureaucracy: Dilemmas of the Individual in Public Services.* New York: Russell Sage Foundation.

Lowi, Theodore J. 1972. 'Four Systems of Policy, Politics and Choice.' *Public Administration Review* 32(4), 298–310.

MacRae, Duncan, Jr, and James A. Wilde. 1985. *Policy Analysis for Public Decisions.* Lanham, MD: University Press of America.

Majone, Giandomenico. 1989. *Evidence, Argument, and Persuasion in the Policy Process:* New Haven, CT: Yale University Press.

Manfredi, Christopher. 1997. 'The Judicialization of Politics; Rights and Public Policy in Canada and the United States.' In Keith Banting, George Hoberg, and Richard Simeon, eds., *Degrees of Freedom; Canada and the United States in a Changing World*. Kingston and Montreal: McGill-Queen's University Press.

Manfredi, Christopher P., and Antonia Maioni. 2002. 'Courts and Health Policy: Judicial Policy-making and Publicly Funded Health Care in Canada.' *Journal of Health Politics, Policy and Law* 27(2), 213–240.

Mayer, I.S., C.E. Van Daalen, and P.W.G. Bots. 2004. 'Perspectives on Policy Analysis: A Framework for Understanding and Design.' *International Journal of Technology, Policy and Management* 4(2), 169–91.

McRoberts, Kenneth. 1993. 'Federal Structures and the Policy Process.' In M. Michael Atkinson, ed., *Governing Canada: Institutions and Public Policy*. Toronto: Harcourt Brace Jovanovich.

Meltsner, Arnold J. 1972. 'Political Feasibility and Policy Analysis.' *Public Administration Review* 32, 859–67.

Mintrom, Michael. 2003. *People Skills for Policy Analysts*. Washington, DC: Georgetown University Press.

Montpetit, Eric. 2002. 'Policy Networks, Federal Arrangements, and the Development of Environmental Regulations: A Comparison of the Canadian and American Agricultural Sectors.' *Governance* 15(1), 1–20.

Notzke, Claudia. 1994. *Aboriginal Peoples and Natural Resources in Canada*. Toronto: Captus Press.

Patton, Carl V., and David S. Sawicki. 1993. *Basic Methods of Policy Analysis and Planning*. Englewood Cliffs, NJ: Prentice-Hall.

Peled, Alan. 2002. 'Why Style Matters: A Comparison of Two Administrative Reform Initiatives in the Israeli Public Sector, 1989–1998.' *Journal of Public Administration Research and Theory* 12(2), 217–40.

Peters, B. Guy. 1990. 'Administrative Culture and Analysis of Public Organizations.' *Indian Journal of Public Administration* 36, 420–8.

Peters, B. Guy, and Anthony Parker, eds. 1993. *Advising West European Governments: Inquiries, Expertise and Public Policy*. Edinburgh: Edinburgh University Press.

Phillips, Susan D. 2001. 'From Charity to Clarity: Reinventing Federal Government-Voluntary Sector Relationships.' In L.A. Pal, ed., *How Ottawa Spends 2001–2002: Power in Transition*, 145–76. Toronto: Oxford University Press.

Prince, Michael J. 1979. 'Policy Advisory Groups in Government Departments.' In G.B. Doern and Peter Aucoin, eds., *Public Policy in Canada: Organization, Process, Management*, 275–300. Toronto: Gage.

Pross, A. Paul. 1992. *Group Politics and Public Policy*. 2nd ed. Toronto: Oxford University Press.

Quinn, Robert E. 1988. *Beyond Rational Management: Mastering the Paradoxes and Competing Demands of High Performance*. San Francisco: Jossey-Bass.

Radin, Beryl A. 2000. *Beyond Machiavelli: Policy Analysis Comes of Age*. Washington, DC: Georgetown University Press.

Radin, Beryl A., and Joan Price Boase. 2000. 'Federalism, Political Structure, and Public Policy in the United States and Canada.' *Journal of Comparative Policy Analysis* 2(1), 65–90.

Richardson, J.J., A.G. Jordan, and R.H. Kimber. 1978. 'Lobbying, Administrative Reform and Policy Styles: The Case of Land Drainage.' *Political Studies* 26(1), 47–64.

Richardson, Jeremy, Gunnel Gustafsson, and Grant Jordan. 1982. 'The Concept of Policy Style.' In J.J. Richardson, ed., *Policy Styles in Western Europe*, 1–16. London: George Allen and Unwin.

Sabatier, Paul A. 1987. 'Knowledge, Policy-Oriented Learning, and Policy Change.' *Knowledge: Creation, Diffusion, Utilization* 8(4), 649–92.

Salamon, Lester M. 1981. 'Rethinking Public Management: Third-Party Government and the Changing Forms of Government Action.' *Public Policy* 29(3), 255–75.

Salter, Liora. 1990. 'The Two Contradiction in Public Inquiries.' In A. Paul Pross, Innis Christie, and John A. Yogis, eds., *Commissions of Inquiry*, 175–95. Toronto: Carswell.

Salter, Liora, and Debra Slaco. 1981. *Public Inquiries in Canada*. Ottawa: Science Council of Canada.

Savoie, Donald J. 1999a. 'The Rise of Court Government in Canada.' *Canadian Journal of Political Science* 32(4), 635–64.

– 1999b. *Governing from the Centre: The Concentration of Power in Canadian Politics*. Toronto: University of Toronto Press.

Scholz, John T. 1984. 'Cooperation, Deterrence, and the Ecology of Regulatory Enforcement.' *Law and Society Review* 18(2), 179–224.

– 1991. 'Cooperative Regulatory Enforcement and the Politics of Administrative Effectiveness.' *American Political Science Review* 85(1), 115–36.

Sharpe, David. 2001. 'The Canadian Charitable Sector: An Overview.' In J. Phillips, B. Chapman, and D. Stevens, eds., *Between State and Market: Essays on Charities Law and Policy in Canada*. Toronto: University of Toronto Press.

Sheriff, Peta E. 1983. 'State Theory, Social Science, and Governmental Commissions.' *American Behavioural Scientist* 26(5), 669–80.

Shulock, Nancy. 1999. 'The Paradox of Policy Analysis: If It Is Not Used, Why

Do We Produce So Much Of It?' *Journal of Policy Analysis and Management* 18(2), 226–44.

Simeon, Richard. 1980. 'Intergovernmental Relations and the Challenges to Canadian Federalism.' *Canadian Public Administration* 23(1), 14–32.

Smiley, Donald. 1964. 'Public Administration and Canadian Federalism.' *Canadian Public Administration* 7(3), 371–88.

– 1987. *The Federal Condition in Canada.* Toronto: McGraw-Hill Ryerson.

Smith, Martin J., David Marsh, and David Richards. 1993. 'Central Government Departments and the Policy Process.' *Public Administration* 71, 567–94.

Soroka, Stuart N. 2002. *Agenda-Setting Dynamics in Canada.* Vancouver: UBC Press.

Thissen, W.A.H., and Patricia G.J. Twaalfhoven. 2001. 'Toward a Conceptual Structure for Evaluating Policy Analytic Activities.' *European Journal of Operational Research* 129, 627–49.

Thomas, Paul G. 'Ministerial Responsibility and Administrative Accountability.' In Mohamed Charih and Arthur Daniels, eds., *New Public Management and Public Administration in Canada,* 143–63. Toronto: IPAC.

Tribe, Laurence H. 1972. 'Policy Science: Analysis or Ideology?' *Philosophy and Public Affairs* 2(1), 66–110.

Tuohy, Carolyn J. 1992. *Policy and Politics in Canada: Institutionalized Ambivalence.* Philadelphia, PA: Temple University Press.

van Waarden, Frans. 1995. 'Persistence of National Policy Styles: A Study of Their Institutional Foundations.' In Brigitte Unger and Frans van Waarden, eds., *Convergence or Diversity? Internationalization and Economic Policy Response,* 333–72. Aldershot, UK: Avebury.

Verheijen, Tony, ed. 1999. *Civil Service Systems in Central and Eastern Europe.* Cheltenham: Edward Elgar.

Vining, Aidan R., and David L. Weimer. 2002. 'Introducing Policy Analysis Craft: The Sheltered Workshop.' *Journal of Policy Analysis and Management* 21(4), 683–95.

Vogel, David. 1986. *National Styles of Regulation: Environmental Policy in Great Britain and the United States.* Ithaca, NY: Cornell University Press.

Webber, David J. 1986. 'Analyzing Political Feasibility: Political Scientists' Unique Contribution to Policy Analysis.' *Policy Studies Journal* 14(4), 545–54.

Weimer, David L. 1992. 'The Craft of Policy Design: Can It Be More Than Art?' *Policy Studies Review* 11(3/4), 370–88.

– 2005. 'Institutionalizing Neutrally Competent Policy Analysis: Resources for Promoting Objectivity and Balance in Consolidating Democracies.' *Policy Studies Journal* 33(2), 131–46.

Weimer, David L., and Aidan R. Vining. 1999. *Policy Analysis: Concepts and Practice*. Englewood Cliffs, NJ: Prentice-Hall.

Weiss, Carol H. 1977a. 'Research for Policy's Sake: The Enlightenment Function of Social Science Research.' *Policy Analysis* 3(4), 531–54.

– 1977b. *Using Social Research in Public Policy Making*. Lexington, MA: Lexington Books.

Wildavsky, Aaron B. 1969. 'Rescuing Policy Analysis from PPBS.' *Public Administration Review* March-April, 189–202.

– 1979. *Speaking Truth to Power: The Art and Craft of Policy Analysis*. Boston: Little, Brown.

Wilson, James Q. 1989. *Bureaucracy: What Government Agencies Do and Why They Do It*. New York: Free Press.

Wise, Lois Recascino. 2002. 'Public Management Reform: Competing Drivers of Change.' *Public Administration Review* 62(5), 555–67.

5 Policy Analysis and Bureaucratic Capacity: Context, Competencies, and Strategies

EVERT LINDQUIST AND JAMES DESVEAUX

Introduction

The policy literature has done a good job of delineating the full array of possibilities for where policy-related work can be undertaken inside and outside public sector bureaucracies. Marcus Hollander and Michael Prince (1993) have shown that many kinds of analytic work are pursued in different parts of public service bureaucracies, in addition to the work of policy units: research, policy, planning, evaluation, auditing, operational reviews, quality assurance, financial analysis, management consulting, and information systems. John Halligan (1996) reviewed the many different sources of policy advice from inside and outside government, which include internal expertise, other government departments, other governments, consultants, interest groups, think tanks, and universities. Jonathan Boston (1994) explored issues in 'purchasing' policy advice, evaluating whether internal and external markets could be created to compete for the policy work of departments. As Jon Pierre (1996) observed, there has emerged a 'public market' for the provision of policy advice.

In delineating these possibilities, however, too much emphasis has been placed on the options available to policy managers and too little on evaluating the advantages, disadvantages and fit of strategies for mobilizing capacity needed to properly direct and staff policy units in government agencies. Casting the policy advice function as a spot market, where analysis is 'purchased' on demand, risks ignoring the critical issue of whether public service institutions adopt the best strategies for securing policy analysis to achieve both the short-term objectives of advising governments and the robust longer-term advisory capabilities of the public service.

This chapter sets out a conceptual framework for evaluating different approaches to mobilizing policy expertise. We begin by identifying the different locations where policy analysis is conducted in the public service institutions and where policy expertise is sought from inside and outside government. We delineate the objectives that might inform the recruitment of expertise in policy units, making a broad distinction between the knowledge required to inform policy analysis and the qualities managers need to ensure that policy 'teams' reach full potential. We identify three recruitment strategies available to departments and policy units:

- *in-house systems* that rely on attracting talent from outside the public service at the early stage of careers or from other parts of a department, and then developing and promoting that talent over time;
- *internal policy think tank systems* that are premised on lateral movement for developing the skills of policy analysts and rely on regular rotation of staff at all levels of the policy unit, drawing on expertise from other parts of the public service; and
- *consulting strategies* that rely heavily on a small core of staff to serve as brokers of the work of external free agents, which includes analysts working for consulting firms, think tanks, universities, or as independent contractors.

Each strategy has its own benefits, costs, and risks. No strategy is superior to the others in all circumstances; the effectiveness of a recruitment strategy is highly contingent on the workflow patterns of policy units and the required mix of generalist and specialist expertise, and on the political and policy challenges confronting a department or program area. Each strategy has differing capabilities for responding to error or evolving political demands, and for promoting creativity and knowledge capture. Managers and observers should carefully evaluate the costs of adopting one strategy at the expense of others, but each strategy requires astute management and the retention of 'rare talent' if it is to succeed.

We conclude by identifying general lessons and probe the implications for improving the policy function at the system level. First, leaders may want to establish a centre of excellence dedicated to developing and deploying specialized and rare talent within the system. Second, rare talent must be retained within the public service in order to build trust, deepen linkages, and make them sufficiently interesting to warrant the participation of the best experts at think tanks, universities, and consulting firms. Third, we warn that attempts by governments to shift responsibilities for the conduct of policy analysis outside the public service are not likely to succeed if the primary rationale is to lower costs. Finally, we suggest a program of research that should yield useful results for practitioners and academic observers alike.

The Institutional Setting for Policy Analysis

Policy-oriented units are distributed across public service institutions, which are complex bureaucratic systems serving duly elected governments. Before considering what types and sources of expertise are sought out to undertake policy analysis and related activities (supply), we need to understand the diverse locations and general rationale for acquiring it (demand).

The Demand for Policy Expertise

Policy analysis proceeds at several levels inside a public service, even if the ultimate consumers are deputy ministers seeking to best serve ministers as individuals and as a collectivity. The immediate demand for policy expertise will emanate from the following locations:

- *Corporate policy units.* These units are usually headed by an assistant deputy minister, and report directly to the deputy minister. Their work typically spans not only the full range of department programs but also the range of issues encompassed by the ministerial portfolio. Due to their proximity to the minister's office and the deputy minister's office, these units are often involved with communications, consultation, and intergovernmental matters, but should not be confused with corporate services divisions.
- *Sectoral policy units.* Attached to program sectors in operating departments, these units are usually led by directors or director generals. Their expertise is closely aligned with the programs encompassed by the sector. They are more likely to conduct detailed policy analyses and program evaluations, and maintain pertinent data streams. Accordingly, they tend to have more technical knowledge than corporate policy units, although sectoral units do prepare strategic plans, cabinet documents, and communications materials.
- *Central agency bureaus.* Cabinet offices, as well as finance departments and management boards, have teams of analysts responsible

for monitoring and liaising with operating departments on policy and other matters, and sometimes take on design responsibilities. Ordinarily, they challenge, facilitate, and coordinate department proposals, in preparation for consideration by ministers and cabinet committees.

• *Functional policy community.* The horizontal nature of many issues means that public service leaders increasingly view policy analysts and their managers as a corporate resource and functional community (Canada 1995). In other words, they are less inclined to see either new or established policy analysts as the 'property' of a given policy unit and more disposed to see them as a system resource.

The list of locations in which 'policy work' gets conducted could be expanded, but for the purpose of exploring the costs and benefits of different recruitment strategies, it is sufficient to deal with those listed above. Each location (see figure 5.1) presents a different level of analysis and vantage point for considering what skills and knowledge need to be emphasized for undertaking policy analysis in a public service, and each has different recruitment needs and opportunities.

The Supply of Policy Expertise

If corporate policy units, program policy units, central bureaus, and the functional policy community comprise the 'demand side,' where do governments obtain policy expertise? Here, we consider where policy managers in all of those locations might seek pertinent expertise, in addition to staff already in place, to deal with short-term and longer-term needs. They include:

• *Operations divisions.* Many policy analysts begin their public service careers by working in operational units delivering or supporting programs for departments. They may have been scientists, engineers, IT specialists or clerks – to name just a few possibilities. Such individuals are valuable to policy units precisely because they are familiar with how programs are delivered and have an acute sense of how policies get translated into services. They may upgrade key policy skills, either through government training opportunities or their own initiative, but this can also transpire 'on the job.'
• *Sectoral policy units.* Many operating departments have several sectoral or program-based policy units, depending on a

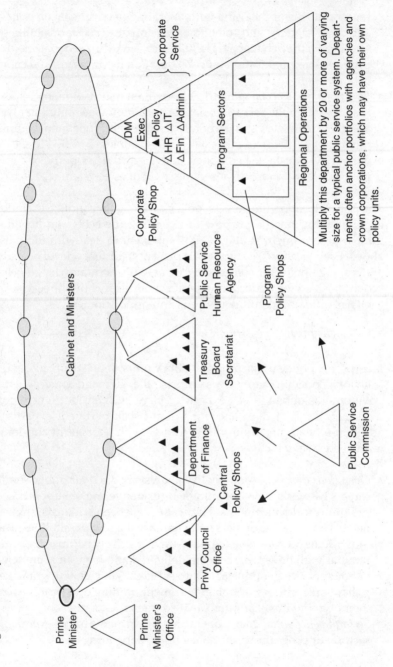

Figure 5.1 Policy Units and Talent Distributed across the Public Service

department's size and the number of programs it administers. While senior analysts are not responsible for developing a corporate view on policy matters, they often directly brief deputy ministers and ministers because they know the most about certain programs. These analysts are strong candidates to become program or portfolio analysts in central agencies, and very promising analysts may move to a department's corporate policy shop, since such units should have expertise spanning the programs comprising the ministerial portfolio.

- *Corporate policy units.* The responsibilities and depth of expertise housed in corporate policy units will vary according to how the deputy minister structures a department. Some corporate units are analytic powerhouses, containing the most talented policy experts in the department for all program areas. At the other extreme, corporate units may oversee, liaise, and coordinate the work of sectoral policy units, even if the 'experts' are in the latter locations. In all instances, though, corporate policy units should have a department-wide and a portfolio-wide view of priorities and issues, and the capacity to respond to the immediate needs of the minister and the deputy minister, and to monitor and move forward issues throughout the system (which includes working with other departments and central agencies, and supporting cabinet decision making). Experienced analysts in these units are attractive to departments grappling with similar challenges, or to central agencies seeking talent to manage interdepartmental issues across portfolios.

- *Central agency bureaus.* Policy analysts in central agencies may not possess the detailed knowledge of programs as analysts working in departments, but they should have a broad understanding of the operational and strategic challenges of departments. They have a good sense of how the cabinet decision-making system works and a corporate view of how policy matters are handled across departments and central agencies. Thus, it is this system expertise, as well as a central agency perspective on a department or particular program, that may be highly valued by corporate and sectoral policy shops in operating departments and by other central agencies.

- *Outside experts.* Analytic expertise can be recruited from consulting firms (boutique or integrated), independent consultants or academics. Individuals or teams can be hired by the government for specific projects, or they may work on retainer, a longer-term contractual arrangement. There are three reasons for hiring outsiders for policy work: 1) to handle tasks for the department or on an overload basis; 2) to tap into expertise that is either not available inside the public service or not available on a full-time basis; and 3) to undertake tasks the government believes should be fully contracted out.

• *Specialist recruitment programs.* Some governments sponsor public-service-wide or department-specific 'fast-track' programs to attract talent for policy and management positions. Assignments often involve policy analysis responsibilities, and many of the candidates aspire to policy as opposed to purely management careers. The assignments are negotiated by the candidate, central agencies, and departments, and at the end of the program, they must compete for more permanent positions.[1]

A final source of expertise cuts across those previously mentioned: many public service institutions support exchanges (e.g., Interchange Canada). Staff can take positions in the private sector or with other governments on a temporary basis. Sometimes these arrangements involve a 'swap,' with staff from participating organizations exchanging positions. In other cases it might involve only one person. Furthermore, this approach can be used within the public service to move staff across departmental or functional divides to broaden horizons and develop skills.

Competencies for Well-Performing Policy Units

Policy analysis is often thought of as a generic activity, but addressing complex issues in large public sector bureaucratic systems requires assembling a multitude of skills and expertise (Mayer et al. 2004), and the right coordinating capabilities. Moreover, although it is tempting to see the mobilization of expertise as tapping into a 'spot market,' it is intimately connected to recruitment dedicated to building short-term and longer-term capabilities. In what follows we identify the kinds of skills and competencies that policy managers need to assemble in their units in varying degrees.

Identifying the institutional bases for the supply and the demand of policy expertise is one matter, but it is equally important to understand the features of well-performing policy organizations in a public service context. Several features have to do with the expertise, information, and norms that ought to be on tap in the policy unit. They include:

- *Specialized policy knowledge.* Policy units should have on tap sufficient expertise on the specific technical issues pertinent to its domain of responsibility (Desveaux 1995). The goal here would be to ensure that the unit cannot be challenged on technical details. This imperative will vary according to whether the policy shop is located in a departmental program sector, at the departmental corporate level, or in a central agency.
- *Access to data streams.* The quality of policy analysis is significantly affected by the quality of data available to analysts (Lindquist 1988). Policy units need to either generate their own streams of data or gain access to needed data. To the extent that a policy unit has a monopoly over pertinent streams of data, it has a competitive advantage over other units in the system.
- *Generalized policy knowledge.* Specialized expertise and access to good data streams are necessary but not sufficient conditions. Capabilities must exist to develop broader views on policy issues, to identify horizontal linkages across issues, and sometimes to develop more comprehensive as opposed to selective policy initiatives. This requires the capacity to coordinate the work of more specialized analysts and producers of data (Desveaux 1995).
- *System knowledge.* Policy units may have specialized and generalist policy expertise, which is complemented by good data flows, but they must also have the capacity to work with other units and other departments, and to move ideas and conclusions through the larger public service and cabinet decision-making system. This requires employing officials who can be effective boundary-spanners, who can 'work the system' inside and outside departments (Desveaux, Lindquist, and Toner 1993).
- *Process skills.* Policy units not only design policy, they also have to manage consultations with citizens, handle communications and convey information to the public, and oversee negotiations with other departments, governments, and sectors. The ability to anticipate and deal with process issues is increasingly important in modern policy environments (Meyer, Van Daalen, and Bots 2004; Howlett and Lindquist 2004).
- *Public service norms.* Cutting across these desired competencies is a more fundamental requirement, one that is often taken for granted inside central agencies and departments, and that is the need to protect and preserve public service norms such as probity, loyalty, cabinet confidences, discretion, anonymity, and the like.

Figure 5.2 Three Kinds of Policy Expertise

- *Generalist expertise*: people with skills, competencies, and learning capabilities who can take up new tasks within a reasonably short period of time.

- *Specialist expertise*: people with a reasonably deep understanding of a field or mastery of a set of technical skills; requires a longer-term investment in training.

- *Rare talent*: people who are acknowledged experts and at the top of their fields.

The balance struck among these different competencies will vary according to where a policy unit is located in the public service. For example, as we move from a sector policy unit to a department's corporate policy shop to a central agency unit, the balance between technical expertise/data flows and system knowledge should shift accordingly, and the need for generalized policy knowledge is probably higher in the leadership of sector units, among all staff in corporate units, and certainly among central agency analysts.

Some additional distinctions are in order. In thinking about the kinds of skills and knowledge demanded by organizations and supplied by individuals, we find it useful to think in terms of three kinds of expertise: generalist, specialist, and rare talent. By generalist expertise, we mean people with skills, competencies, and learning capabilities who can take up new tasks within a reasonably short period of time. By specialist expertise, we mean people who have a reasonably deep understanding of a field or mastery of a set of technical skills, which requires a longer-term investment in training. By 'rare talent' we mean people who are the acknowledged experts in the field, and at the top of their fields.[2] All three kinds of expertise (see Figure 5.2) can be found inside and outside the public service.

As the manager of any sports team will tell you, it is one thing to assemble the requisite talent to field a competitive team, but quite another to ensure that the talent is sufficiently motivated and coordinated so as to meet maximum potential (see Figure 5.3). The best teams or work units must also have a degree of resilience, and sufficient adaptability to recognize and to adjust in response to error or inadequate strategies adopted. These additional competencies include:

- *Timeliness.* This is the imperative associated with policy work from the standpoint of elected leaders and senior officials. If not available when needed, even the best policy analysis or research is irrelevant. Obviously, some types of policy work necessarily have longer time

Figure 5.3 Recruitment Objectives for Policy Analysis Units

Competencies and capacities	Team competencies
• Specialized policy knowledge	• Timeliness
• Access to data streams	• Quality control
• Generalized policy knowledge	• Flexibility
• System knowledge	• Sustainability
• Public service norms	• Loyalty

horizons, but this suggests the need for ways to tap into the work-in-progress.

- *Quality control.* The managers of the policy function must be attentive to quality, if the policy unit and the larger department are to retain the confidence of the minister and deputy minister. Policy managers need to monitor and assess the quality of work undertaken by subordinates and outsiders, and to ensure that resources are deployed in the most efficient and effective manner. Oversight of quality also pertains to communicating analysis since even the best work, if not put in digestible form for ministers and deputy ministers, could be ignored.
- *Flexibility.* Even though specialized expertise can be an important asset, so too is versatility and flexibility. Hiring and then developing a team so that individuals and groups can respond to new demands, entertain new perspectives and approaches, or assist colleagues with overload situations is a critical capacity. This capability also encompasses the need on specific projects to work with colleagues in other parts of a department, other departments, and outsiders.
- *Sustainability.* More generally, all policy work is conducted in the context of limited resources, and therefore an additional management consideration is whether the talent acquired inside or outside the unit will be available for the longer term, and whether those arrangements are cost-effective. This, of course, relates to whether the challenges confronting a policy unit are of the long-term variety, or if there are one or more significant projects with time horizons of a few months or, say, two years.
- *Loyalty.* This criterion goes beyond the manifold concept of public service norms. From a managerial perspective, it matters considerably whether members of a team owe loyalty to the unit itself, so its deliberations and strategies can be kept confidential as needed, and extra effort can be called upon as needed by managers.

The balance between all of these competencies, whether related to specific policy capabilities or the management of the function, are contingent on the challenges confronting a department and a policy shop, and on the broader strategies utilized for acquiring and mobilizing that expertise.

Mobilizing Policy Expertise: Three Modal Strategies

Organizations can build capacity in different ways. Before delving into examples of strategies for doing so, we need to introduce some concepts from the world of sports, since professional and amateur sports organizations exert considerable effort to develop the best teams. We can then apply these concepts to the world of bureaucratic policy analysis.

Sports organizations generally rely on two strategies to develop teams. The first is a combination of 'draft systems' to attract or assign promising players to different teams, and 'farm systems' to develop, socialize, and monitor the progress of those players until they take on 'first string' positions; where public service bureaucracy is concerned, we refer to this strategy as 'in-house recruitment.'[3] A second strategy involves 'free agents,' experienced players purchased from the open market, which corresponds in government to experts brought in from outside a policy unit to take on certain tasks – such talent has not been groomed or socialized inside the unit. There are two kinds of free agents that can be recruited to policy units:

- *External free agents.* These consist of policy experts from consulting firms, think-tanks, other governments, or universities from *outside* the public service. These experts provide a range of policy-related tasks, and may be former public servants.
- *Internal free agents.* This category consists of experts from elsewhere in the public service. These are typically officials either sought by departments, or parachuted in by central agencies, to trouble-shoot or offer skills and perspectives in short supply.

Both kinds of free agents can perform very different tasks for policy units,[4] and do so for very short or longer periods of time. The tasks may range from conducting selective policy analyses or think pieces, to undertaking policy research projects or managing significant policy projects, including managing the work of internal and external analysts.

We could delineate many different strategies, but for the purposes of teasing out important analytic issues we think it best to identify three modal strategies. They include:

- *In-house recruitment.* This strategy relies heavily on identifying and grooming talent from within the department, and presumes that analysts must have a thorough grounding in the work of the department. The great majority of senior policy analysts begin their policy careers in entry-level positions. These recruits are drafted either from university drafts, management trainee programs, or from operational divisions. Depending on the critical challenges confronting the department, which may require manifestly different expertise or liaising capabilities, senior analysts may be hired on term contracts from other departments or central agencies. External free agents may also be retained, but this is done more to cope with overload – the work typically involves speechwriting, and narrow and selective analytic or research tasks. In short, the full-time policy staff retains primarily responsibility for thinking and analysis.
- *Internal think tank.* This strategy emphasizes the importance of bringing in fresh ideas and alternative perspectives into the department or sector, though not at the expense of dealing with the transactional imperatives of the policy unit. Many junior analysts are recruited from within the department, but they are encouraged to work elsewhere in the federal public service as part of their career development. Likewise, senior analysts are regularly brought in from other departments, and sometimes from outside the public service. The goal is to generate new ideas, to take advantage of the latest thinking and techniques, and to challenge program sectors in the department. Under this recruitment strategy, generalists with experience outside the departments are balanced equally with technical, specialized expertise groomed from within the department. Again, external free agents are used more to deal with overload.
- *Contracting out.* This strategy presumes that the best way to gain access to the best possible expertise inside and outside the public service is through markets and contracts. Significant chunks of analysis, research, and sometimes data generation are contracted to consultants in the private and nonprofit sector. Sometimes the contracts include project management. The recruitment of consultants is driven by a strong view as to the specific products required by the department. A strong, experienced core of in-house staff –

sensitive to political and operational needs – is groomed in order to manage, interpret, and challenge the work conducted by the free agents. In this strategy, draft choices are more likely to enter into the picture as junior consultants who, once they have proven their skills, may receive more substantial assignments. On the other hand, critical in-house recruitment decisions must be made so as to ensure continuity as senior policy staff retire or leave for new positions inside or outside the public service.

These 'modal' recruitment strategies have been delineated for analytic purposes; real-world strategies employed by policy units may not be so stark. Indeed, typically policy units use a mixture of recruiting devices, which together implicitly or explicitly constitute a strategy, and which may evolve over time. Moreover, in big policy advisory units, different sections may be characterized by different strategies. Nevertheless, the work of policy units can be achieved in very different ways, and are closely linked to recruitment patterns. They provide a useful point of departure for exploring the effects and risks of different recruitment strategies and, as we discuss in the conclusion, for conducting empirical research.

Policy managers and the public service traditionally relied on in-house strategies: recruits start in entry-level positions and, depending on capability and circumstance, rise in the hierarchy. However, in recent years, this environment has changed in two ways. First, the incentive system for employers and employees has grown more complex: the advent of more flexible budgetary regimes, new technologies, and increasing competition from outside contractors means policy units are increasingly open to influences from the private sector. Second, in the context of government restructuring and downsizing, public service leaders must consider what kinds of expertise the government should retain, and how such expertise should be supported. Together, these developments have potential not only to affect the size and scope of bureaus, but also to influence the choice-sets of potential recruits and current employees alike.

Evaluating Strategies for Mobilizing Policy Capacity

This section sets out a framework for comparing the advantages and disadvantages for the in-house, internal think tank, and contracting-out strategies. It begins by briefly introducing the many issues that should be considered under the following headings: workflow and uncertainty; loyalty, security, and norms; management capacity; adaptability; and gossip and knowledge capture. Then we review each mobilization strategy on its own terms, considering its benefits, risks, and the contexts for which it would be most appropriate.

Workflow and uncertainty. Efforts to mobilize policy expertise are best understood against the backdrop of multiple demands, uncertainty, and resource constraints. Here we begin with workload patterns: the three critical dimensions are the *flow, content*, and *predictability* of policy work. The aggregate flow of work can be even or it can be uneven, thus leading to peak and non-peak periods of work. But the content of work may also change – while the aggregate flow of work remains even, the tasks may vary during peak and non-peak periods. A final source of variation derives from the reality that policy managers often cannot anticipate what sort of demands they will have to contend with, nor how long they may have to contend with them.

If the work or portfolio of work demanded in different periods varies significantly, then the larger the difference, the more likely completely different skills will be required of staff or contractors.[5] On the other hand, how long such shifts will persist, how often the shifts might occur, and whether they are predictable are critical questions. Predictability in tasks would permit senior managers to hire and contract for the right mix of talent with considerable confidence. If the work is uneven, but there is a predictable workflow, and it consists of relatively similar tasks, it can be handled by ensuring there is a sufficient number of generalists and by rescheduling staff workloads, and by contracting to external free agents as required. However, if the tasks and skills required vary significantly, internal and external free agents can handle specialized work that is not an ongoing core responsibility. If the workflow is more or less even, but its content is unpredictable, this suggests a somewhat larger core of generalists and a smaller budget for free agents. If the workflow is uneven *and* unpredictable, this may point to a situation of overload and possibly turbulence (Emery and Trist 1965). This may constitute a 'turn-around' situation for the government and the policy unit in question, requiring 'fixers' from elsewhere in the system or from outside the public service.

Decisions about how to mobilize expertise should be driven not only by a good sense of the matches between work demands and available skill sets but also by financial outlays and the transaction costs of hiring staff and letting out contracts.[6] On the other hand, there are overhead costs and risks associated with grooming internal expertise.

Loyalty, security, and norms. Through socialization and monitoring, bureaucratic hierarchies are often believed to encourage a higher degree of loyalty on the part of employees and offer a higher level of security when giving advice and implementing decisions (Boston 1994). However, external free agents can provide considerable loyalty and security under contractual arrangements because they must also cultivate reputations for reliability and discretion.

Norms inform and guide the work of policy analysts, encompassing perceptions about the critical tasks confronting public sector organizations, notions of the public interest and which groups are relevant stakeholders, planning horizons and the depth of information gathering to inform analysis, and the criteria for addressing alternatives. Norms develop at several levels: specific programs; departments or agencies; the entire public service; and the private sector. To be sure, shared norms can ensure high organizational performance, but the question is whether they are congruent with critical tasks and future challenges. The norms of a policy unit can be either seen as an asset or a liability, depending on future needs and priorities. Different mobilization strategies can challenge, supplement, or reinforce critical values and skill-sets.

Management capacity. Policy managers must be able to forecast short-term and long-term priorities, determine what essential capacities are needed to meet those priorities, and ensure that policy work is timely and of high quality. This implies leaders with considerable experience in policy analysis, facility in handling both political and bureaucratic politics, and knowledge of the pertinent policy domains. As policy units draw more heavily on advice from outside the public service, this should increase their internal and external coordination costs for 'purchasing' (Boston 1994). Moreover, heavier reliance on internal free agents or outside contractors to manage or conduct critical policy work suggests that in-house managerial capacity will be thinner, concentrated in the hands of fewer permanent public servants, and more vulnerable if 'rare talent' leaves.

Public servants do 'come and go,' but the question is whether policy units can offer sufficient inducements to attract replacements of a similar calibre, since highly talented individuals are crucial to ensuring that internal think tank and consulting organization models work. In-house strategies reduce, but do not eliminate, this exposure. If a unit's management is weak or if recent recruits are of a lower calibre than in the past, this is a recipe for policy units of declining quality.

Adaptability. No matter how carefully chosen, strategies could prove inadequate for several reasons: the policy environment may have shifted significantly due to new political dynamics or the emergence of different policy problems; the assembled policy expertise may have been unable to deliver promised outputs; or new problems and challenges may have risen which make the department appear unresponsive. Strategies for mobilizing expertise should be evaluated according to how well they can adapt or be reversed in response to new external demands.

Critical questions might include whether given strategies can be adjusted sufficiently in order to send the right signals or produce desired effects quickly enough to satisfy political masters and top officials. Another question concerns whether the pace of rotation and grooming of experts can be accelerated sufficiently to remedy a serious performance gap, whether the desired skills are indeed available in the system or the market, or whether employees or contractors can be terminated for poor performance for reasonable costs and new contractors hired. Finally, remedial adjustment can proceed at an entirely different level. Rather than evaluate how policy managers can redress performance problems *within* a given strategy, another question concerns the start-up and closure costs if managers want to *switch over* to an alternative strategy.

Gossip and knowledge capture. Too often we evaluate policy analysis in purely instrumental terms; that is, with respect only to its relevance to the specific choices that decision makers and organizations must make. March and Sevon (1988) have argued that 'gossip' and the non-decision-specific trading of information are important development activities for organizations: they are means for conducting surveillance, testing ideas, providing a shared sense of context, maintaining channels of communication, and developing trust. It is hallway conversations and chance encounters that often lead to new ideas and to knowledge capture for any organization (Barnard 1938).

So, as policy units increasingly rely on external free agents to manage or conduct analysis, they may forsake less tangible but no less important aspects of analytic activity crucial to developing well-performing organizations. Contracting out may reduce the opportunities for such serendipity and capturing promising ideas stimulated through exchanges between the policy unit and the consultant. This logic also applies to cultivating networks extending outside policy units that include consultants, academics and analysts in other parts of the department and the public service. For external networks to function productively requires regular interaction, rich and commonly shared information, and a high degree of trust.

Policy Mobilization Strategies in Perspective

Having reviewed the many different issues that have to be addressed when undertaking policy analysis and managing policy expertise, we review each strategy on its own terms.

In-house recruitment. This approach works best in stable policy and political environments that, in turn, produce predictable work patterns. In-house recruitment can handle modest undulations in workload by means of levelling techniques and, if required, additional work can be performed without incurring overtime costs. Analysts selected through draft choices and farm systems will usually have norms consistent with the prevailing culture of the department, and tend to be more loyal and knowledgeable about departmental operations and policies. In-house systems are also notable because they capture informal discussions and idea generation. Skilful recruitment from different sectors or professional groups, though, can lead to modest changes in the culture of policy units over time, and lead to the hiring of analysts with necessary generalist and specialist skills. On the other hand, it is more difficult to deal with poorly performing staff; significant and rapid change in the skill-mix can only proceed with wholesale restructuring that respects the rights of employees.

Farm systems work best when the closed 'biosphere' of the department is sufficient for replenishing the pool from talent that is selected and groomed to meet new needs. Moreover, if the environment evolves modestly, training, development, and selective recruitment can be used in an anticipatory manner to upgrade skills and competencies. However, if the environment changes rapidly, the skills of the policy unit could be quickly outstripped by new political demands and problems – policy managers could tap into internal and external free agents as necessary, without giving up farm and draft systems, but this may not lead to deep cultural change unless recruitment priorities are altered. Generally, policy units that rely on in-house systems should be less exposed when rare talent and specialized expertise departs because hierarchies contain a larger group of managers and analysts. However, if public/private salary differentials continue to increase, and if the best talent continues to depart, it is not clear that good farm and draft systems can fill the gap.

Internal think tanks. This approach is defined by greater rotation of analysts from other parts of the public service, and thus relies more heavily on 'internal free agents.' From the perspective of resource allocation, this approach should not cost more than in-house recruitment systems since external recruits should receive similar compensation. Regular rotation of analysts creates more opportunities to attract new recruits with different expertise and normative frameworks. However, this presumes, first, that the desired skills are indeed available elsewhere in the public service and, second, that the rotation is sufficiently deep so as to affect the pool of talent and its value-sets. The strategy lends itself to knowledge capture and organizational development because outsiders work for the policy unit for a certain period of time on a full-time basis and, over time, this leads to an expanding network of contacts throughout the public service. Regular rotation offers a useful means for dealing with low performers, and also provides leaders with a tool for dealing with 'turnaround' situations, such as when a department wants to convey to political and public service leaders that more responsive policy managers are in place.

There are several risks. First, recruits confront a steep learning curve concerning how the department and its programs work, which may be a key constraint if there is limited time to work miracles. Second, while internal free agents should understand well the larger public service system and its norms, and while they have incentive to perform well on the assignment, they will not necessarily be loyal to the traditional culture and programs of the department. Third, reliance on top-flight internal free agents could make a policy unit vulnerable since there might not be a stable, deep, and experienced core of managers and analysts when they leave. Finally, there is the question of reversability: the pace of rotation can be reduced if more traditional patterns in recruitment are desired (i.e., longer tenure in positions), perhaps requesting rotations only in certain areas, or ensuring that assignments are also open to external free agents.

Contracting out. Policy units can be managed as if they are brokers. The advantage is the ability to acquire precisely the expertise required to deal with particular problems and only for the time required. This is particularly important if desired expertise is not available inside the public service.[7] Loyalty and security should not loom large as issues when hiring external free agents, since they need to cultivate reputations for integrity and a large proportion of consultants have significant public sector experience. External free agents will not have the same allegiance to departmental norms and practices, but they can perform difficult tasks and leave. Moreover, they can be hired into leadership positions, deal with turnaround situations, and serve to signal a responsiveness to emerging political demands. If the work is of low quality or controversial, the contractor can be released, thus giving the policy unit and the department some buffer.

However, reliance on external free agents is more expensive since consulting overhead must be covered – the meter is always running if additional work needs to be done. Permanent staff lose access to 'gossip' and resulting knowledge capture, and promising ideas are less likely to be generated since external free agents are commissioned to work on specific projects and typically do not share office space during 'down time.' Unless experienced, external free agents will have a very steep learning curve, and there are costs attached to properly letting and monitoring contracts, though stable policy areas lend themselves to contracting out due to predictability in work patterns, and even more so if performance can be easily monitored. Indeed, releasing contractors may be an expensive proposition due to potential litigation costs and the fact that replacement expertise may not be available in a tight market. Reliance on external free agents may greatly expose the policy unit, particularly if the most senior managers or experts leave, and will cause in-house recruitment systems to atrophy, which may require substantial investment and risk to rebuild.

By way of conclusion, we want to emphasize that high-quality management and policy expertise aligned to the tasks at hand, as well as access to reliable streams of data, are essential preconditions if *any* strategy is to succeed. What makes this analysis very interesting and somewhat inconclusive is that many governments do not currently have a shortage in the supply of external free agents who share normative frameworks with public servants. Downsizing of core public services and early retirements created a large cadre of talented former public servants with experience and expertise. Thus, departments can obtain outside expertise steeped in public service norms and familiar with department policy issues, operations, and culture. An interesting question to ask is, will the pool of external expertise be replenished at the same rate and will the skills be relevant for future policy work? Conversely, outsiders can be brought in to effect transitory change, but deep change in expertise and values must be supported by parallel and sustained patterns in recruitment, because most of the 'work' continues to be undertaken by staff inculcated with certain values and possessing certain skill-sets.

Conclusion: Implications for Management, Reform and Research

This chapter introduced a conceptual framework to help practitioners and academics alike better analyse recruitment issues connected to improving policy capacity of government agencies. We identified the various kinds of policy units inside and outside the public service and the criteria for expertise to best serve the needs of ministers and departments. We developed three models of how policy units could recruit policy expertise – in-house recruitment, internal policy think tank, and consulting organization – and probed the advantages and disadvantages of each with respect to workflow patterns, institutional values, management, and oversight, responding to error or new demands, and developing the informal organization. In what follows, this conceptual analysis helps to identify important lessons for the managers of policy units, point to ideas for institutional reform, and suggest a useful research agenda.

Lessons for Management

Managers must closely review different strategies for mobilizing expertise and recruitment systems, no matter how well they have served a department, because they may be securing competencies and norms out of synch with the challenges confronting a government. The advantage of recruiting from within, or drafting from past suppliers of recruits, is that skill levels and potential are more predictable. However, this may be an asset or liability depending on whether or not the ethos of a department, a sector or policy unit needs to be altered. The choice of strategies should address not only skills and competencies, but also values and norms – short-term hiring and contracting decisions shape organizational character in the longer term.

Many policy tasks can be contracted out, but striking an optimal balance not only between general and specialist expertise, but also between internal and external expertise, is highly contingent on current workflows and predictions about how those workflow patterns might change. The costs of 'un-strategic' recruitment, particularly in a fluid policy and political environment, can be quite high. Moreover, the costs of forsaking an 'in-house' recruitment system, without considering the cost of re-investment should expectations not be met, can be significant and take time to remedy.

Each model requires strong leaders with considerable experience in policy analysis, facility in handling both political and bureaucratic politics, and knowledge of pertinent policy domains. There must also be sufficient managerial capacity to assign, monitor, and utilize policy work, whether conducted inside or outside the policy unit. This is why the public service must strive to recruit, groom, and retain its *rare talent*, not only to best utilize generalist and specialist expertise inside and outside government, but also to challenge similar talent located outside government.

The leaders of departments and of policy units should partly evaluate recruitment strategies according to how well they can deal with error or new external demands. Appointing outsiders can send strong signals in the short term, but the ability to produce high-quality analysis on a sustained basis may be a medium- to long-term proposition. If a department relies heavily on internal free agents or outside contractors to manage or conduct critical policy work, it follows that its managerial capacity is thinner and concentrated in the hands of a few permanent public servants. Outsiders can be brought in to effect transitory change, but deep change in expertise and values must be supported by parallel and sustained patterns in recruitment.

Finally, downsizing of public services and early retirement has led to a large pool of former public servants and to a lowered intake of younger recruits inside public service bureaucracies. Departments can access talented free agents with policy expertise steeped in public service norms and familiar with policy issues and government operations and culture. There are, however, two nagging problems. First, as policy units increasingly rely on external free agents, they may forsake less tangible benefits of informal organization and serendipity. Second, it is not clear that the current pool of external expertise can be replenished at the same rate by the future career public service, nor that their skills will be relevant for future policy work.

Implications for Institutional Design

Our analysis was focused on those who manage or oversee policy units. However, we think that our analysis has implications for the management of functional policy communities within a public service or of external networks of expertise outside the public service.

Institutionalize internal free agents. Policy analysts are now viewed as a functional community that requires specific training, development and systematic recruiting. However, conceiving of the policy analysis community as a corporate resource to be nurtured does not deal with the need to coordinate and deploy talent where needed in the system. Indeed, our analysis points to the important role of 'internal free agents' and thought should be given to establishing an institute or centre of excellence *within* the public service to deploy rare and specialized talent on a contractual basis to policy units in departments and to conduct research and professional development. This might serve to attract and retain the very best policy experts in the public service and could compete with the private sector to supply services to departments.

Better manage networks. Tapping into the expertise of consultants, think-tanks and universities will continue to be an important facet of managing the policy function of departments. However, such networks are typically loosely organized, with departments or policy units often functioning as the nodes of those networks. To the extent that more policy work is contracted out, our analysis suggests that such arrangements do not lend themselves well to creativity and knowledge capture and, given demographic trends, they are not well positioned to replace institutional memory. If they are to supplement smaller bureaucratic hierarchies, networks must be seen as entities of value beyond contracts, so as to increase capture of insights. This requires continuous interaction and fostering a high degree of trust in order to nurture a better informal organization and better communication links throughout the network. Policy units must have high quality leaders and senior analysts in order to challenge and extract the most from the networks, and to make them attractive entities for outside experts to participate in and work with. And the public service needs to reward rare talent so as to make private sector opportunities less attractive, and to make it easier to recruit new leaders of the same calibre.

Implications for resource allocation. Given the directions governance will take in the next decade – increased reliance on alternative service delivery, contractual arrangements and performance regimes – public sector bureaucracies will have to significantly improve capacities for policy design, monitoring, and evaluation. This suggests a front-end investment in new talent and infrastructure inside and outside the public service, and implies that policy units should be grown at a higher rate than other functions. This should be particularly so if public service leaders and departments want to achieve a good balance between turnover versus renewal.[8] However, public service leaders may see external experts and networks simply as lower-cost alternatives to in-house capacities, which, incidentally, may not be the sort of work that outsiders can do well. In short, although seeking efficiency and value for tax dollars expended on policy work should be high priorities, this should not preclude making the necessary investments for improving internal and external capacities to obtain high-quality policy work.

A New Research Agenda

All of these issues deserve deeper analysis and lend themselves to empirical research since context is crucial as a point of departure for designing, monitoring and evaluating different strategies of specific policy units and departments. Possible research projects include:

- Tracking how resource allocation to policy units has evolved since 1990 in operating departments and central agencies, the evolving mix of in-house and free agents, and compare with the trajectories of outlays for programs or other functions (on the latter, see Perl and White 2002).
- Examining the spending patterns of policy units during the last decade, including envelopes for contracts issued to external free agents for policy analysis, to determine if there has been a shift in recruitment strategies utilized by departments and policy units.
- Conducting simulations examining the pools of policy analysts inside and outside the public service based on different relative pay scales, quality of recruitment, retention rates, and flow from internal to external pools.

Such research is worth pursuing because, if policy work becomes a larger proportion of a smaller public service in an era of alternative service delivery and decentralized arrangements, then the issues surrounding policy capacity are fundamentally related to the future character of public service. Different strategies for mobilizing policy expertise contain implicit recruitment strategies, and are therefore connected to a larger goal of attracting and retaining the best possible talent for public service work. The research is important because the public service should have sustainable policy capacities that are resilient and adaptable to evolving political demands and policy problems, and able to fruitfully tap into external networks of expertise, offer good value for taxpayers and provide the best possible advice for ministers and citizens.

NOTES

1 Consider two examples from the Canadian public service. The Management Trainee Program (MTP) takes in as many as 100 people each year, and consists of a series of rotational assignments with operating departments and central agencies, and courses at the Canada School of Public Service. The Accelerated Economist Training Program (ATEP) is a similar, but smaller and more narrowly focused initiative. Its aim is to hire and groom policy economists. Several departments have their own recruitment programs.

2 Rare talent can also be understood through the language of transaction cost economics which has, as one of its concerns, the importance of 'asset specific' human capital, in this case policy expertise (Desveaux 1995; Williamson 1995; Boston 1994). Boston notes there can be variation in the amount of asset specificity or the distribution of generalist, specialist, and rare talent across policy domains. Here, we focus more on the implications of uncertainties in workflow, but neither approach is inconsistent with the other.

3 There may be considerable variation in what constitutes the farm system. Those entering the farm system may be: (1) junior analysts selected from internal 'public service drafts' of the 'graduates' from a management trainee program, a specialized training program, or even a surplus pool; (2) junior analysts may be selected by means of 'external drafts' from university academic and professional programs, and must demonstrate their capabilities over several years to receive promotions and larger responsibilities; and (3) analysts, whether junior or senior, may come from operational, corporate, and evaluation and audit units elsewhere in the

department, and there may be internal 'departmental drafts' to select the best candidates. The concept of *free agents* is borrowed from the world of sports. For more detail on recruitment systems in professional sports and the similarities and differences with public service recruitment strategies, see Desveaux (1989) and Lindquist and Desveaux (1998).

4 A very useful description and analysis of these possibilities was presented by Jim Mitchell to Evert Lindquist's course on 'Rethinking Government in Canada' at the University of Toronto on 30 January 1997. See 'Soliciting Advice: Inside or Outside,' speaking notes, mimeo.

5 Hannan and Freeman (1977) model how organizations deal with changing environments, although they ask very different questions from ours. They were more concerned about the match between organizational competencies and those required to exploit particular niches. Hannan and Freeman (1989) also make a useful distinction between fine-grained and coarse-grained environments.

6 Our analysis is made difficult by the awareness that deputy ministers, at any given time, can liberate resources in order to enable a policy unit to anticipate new challenges or cope with ministerial demands. However, there are limits to the number of times that deputy ministers can 'go to the well' for special requests, since all units must be treated fairly. Accordingly, it seems reasonable to presume that departments and policy units do have constrained resources. This suggests that, unless an abundance of slack resources are at the disposal of policy managers, they must make crucial choices and trade-offs when recruiting new expertise from different sources.

7 We would expect proponents for increased use of outside contractors to be sanguine about the severity of this problem. Advocates would be willing to substitute the relative stability and certainty of an integrated hierarchy, where most of the work is designed and administered in-house, with the flexibility provided by the market system for analysis. They would maintain that technology and competition would encourage a surfeit of competent outside contractors, and that the costs of inevitable adjustment problems are manageable.

8 March (1991) offers an interesting discussion of optimal turnover, particularly with respect to maintaining fidelity to the 'organizational code' while encouraging experimentation and adaptation.

REFERENCES

Barnard, Chester. 1938. *The Functions of the Executive*. Cambridge, MA: Harvard University Press.

Boston, Jonathan. 1994. 'Purchasing Policy Advice: The Limits to Contracting Out.' *Governance* 7(1) (January), 1–30.

Canada. 1995. Task Force on Strengthening the Policy Capacity of the Federal Government. *Strengthening Our Policy Capacity.* 3 April.

Desveaux, James A. 'Farm Systems, Draft Choices, and Free Agents: Patterns of Leadership Recruitment and Institutionalization.' Paper delivered at the Annual Meetings of the American Political Science Association, Atlanta, Georgia, September 1989.

– 1995. *Designing Bureaucracies: Institutional Capacity and Large-Scale Problem Solving.* Stanford: Stanford University Press.

Desveaux, James A., Evert A. Lindquist, and Glen Toner. 1994. 'Organizing for Policy Innovation in Public Bureaucracy: AIDS, Energy, and Environmental Policy in Canada.' *Canadian Journal of Political Science* 27(3) (September), 493–538.

Emery, Fred E., and E.L. Trist. 1965. 'The Causal Texture of Organizational Environments.' *Human Relations* 18, 21–32.

Halligan, John. 1996. 'Policy Advice and the Public Service.' In B. Guy Peters and Donald J. Savoie, eds., *Governance in a Changing Environment*, 138–72. Ottawa and Montreal: Canadian Centre for Management Development and McGill-Queen's University Press.

Hannan, Michael T., and John Freeman. 1977. 'The Population Ecology of Organizations.' *American Journal of Sociology* 82, 929–64.

– 1989. *Organizational Ecology.* Cambridge, MA: Harvard University Press.

Hollander, Marcus J., and Michael J. Prince. 1993. 'Analytical Units in Federal and Provincial Governments: Origins, Functions and Suggestions for Effectiveness.' *Canadian Public Administration* 36(2) (summer), 190–224.

Howlett, Michael, and Evert Lindquist. 2004. 'Policy Analysis and Governance: Analytical and Policy Styles in Canada.' *Journal of Comparative Policy Analysis* 6(3) (December), 225–49.

Lindquist, Evert A. 1988. 'What Do Decision Models Tell Us about Information Use.' *Knowledge in Society* 1(2) (summer), 86–111.

– 1992. 'Public Managers and Policy Communities: Learning to Meet New Challenges.' *Canadian Public Administration* 35(2) (summer), 127–59.

– 1996. 'New Agendas for Research on Policy Communities: Policy Analysis, Management, and Governance.' In Laurent Dobuzinskis, Michael Howlett, and David Laycock, eds., *Policy Studies in Canada: The State of the Art*, 219–41. Toronto: University of Toronto Press.

Lindquist, Evert A., and James A. Desveaux. 1998. *Recruitment and Policy Capacity in Government.* Ottawa: Public Policy Forum, June.

March, James G. 1991. 'Exploration and Exploitation as Organizational Learning.' *Organization Science* 2, 71–87.

March, James G., and Guje Sevon. 1988. 'Gossip, Information and Decision-Making.' In James G. March, ed., *Decisions and Organizations*, 429–42. New York: Basil Blackwell.

Mayer, I.S., C.E. Van Daalen, and P.W.G. Bots. 2004. 'Perspectives on Policy Analysis: A Framework for Understanding and Design.' *International Journal of Technology, Policy and Management*. 4(2), 169–91.

Perl, Anthony, and Donald J. White. 2002. 'The Changing Role of Consultants in Canadian Policy Analysis.' *Policy, Organization & Society* 21(1) (June), 49–73.

Pierre, Jon. 1996. 'The Marketization of the State: Citizens, Consumers, and the Emergence of the Public Market.' In B. Guy Peters and Donald J. Savoie, eds., *Governance in a Changing Environment*, 55–81. Ottawa and Montreal: Canadian Centre for Management Development and McGill-Queen's University Press.

Williamson, Oliver E. 1995. *The Economic Institutions of Capitalism*. New York: Free Press.

PART II

Public Policy Analysis in Canada: Historical and Comparative Context

The rise of policy analysis and analysts in government, and later in the nongovernmental sector, is often portrayed as the backbone of a more general 'policy analysis movement.' This movement is alleged to have aimed to 'rationalize' politics by bringing reason and evidence to bear on political decision making.

Although it is frequently assumed that this general movement has been a characteristic development of governments and governance in the late twentieth century, its impact on different countries has been little studied. In this section of the book, the contours of the policy analysis movement and its reception in Canada are set out, with particular attention to government hiring and structure and teaching, training, and pedagogy.

In chapter 6, Michael Mintrom describes the general characteristics of the policy analysis movement as it emerged in the United States over the second half of the twentieth century. He sets out its general principles, aims, and philosophy and the impact it had both on policy-making discourses as well as on policy practices in government and elsewhere.

This analysis is followed in chapter 7 by Michael Prince's careful description of the actual analytical practices and techniques utilized in Canada over the last quarter of the twentieth century. Prince's retrospective on developments in policy analysis and advice in Canadian governments over the past generation also offers a look at the present situation in the federal government and considers the future of policy advice in this country. He concludes that in contrast with the early years of the movement in Canada, we now see a plurality of advisory sources, with an array of actors inside and outside government offering various

kinds of policy advice and analysis to decision makers. He argues that
this pluralistic policy advice environment within government has implications for the roles and relations of government analysts to governing politicians and their staffs, and to non-state actors in think tanks,
lobby associations, and polling and consulting firms. This raises many
issues related to the capacity and influence of civil society organizations
and clientele groups on Canadian governments and policy analysis.
Public service policy advice in Canada, he argues, has moved away
from 'speaking truth to power' toward what we may now describe
more accurately as 'sharing truths with multiple actors.'

Finally, Iris Geva-May and Allan Maslove discuss the training received by professional policy analysts in Canada, and ask whether this
training matches the needs of the 'new' policy analysis identified by
Prince. In their comparative examination of Canadian practice, they
discuss the characteristics and training needs of policy analysis, and the
development of the field to date. They examine how orientations arising from conceptual and historical developments in Canada, the United
States, and Europe have shaped the particular public policy programs,
curriculum orientations and practices found in those countries and,
finally, they look at the implications of and lessons drawn from these
studies for the future training of Canadian policy analysts.

6 The Policy Analysis Movement

MICHAEL MINTROM

Since the mid-1960s, an increasingly large number of people have come to devote their professional lives to producing policy analysis. This is a global phenomenon, although the intensification of activities associated with policy analysis has been most pronounced in the United States. Here, I term this amassing of personnel and resources *the policy analysis movement*. Use of the term is intended to imply a deliberate effort on the part of many people to reconceive the role of government in society and renegotiate aspects of the relationships that exist between individuals, collectivities, and governments. However, the term should not be taken to imply either consistency of purpose or a deliberate striving for coordination among producers of policy analysis. While not directly comparable in a political sense with other social movements, the policy analysis movement has been highly influential. It has served to transform the advice-giving systems of governments and, as a consequence, challenged informal yet long-established advising practices through which power and influence flow. The profundity of this transformation has often eluded the attention of social and political commentators. That is because the relevant changes have caused few immediate or obvious ruptures in the processes and administrative structures typically associated with government or, more broadly speaking, public governance.

Early representations tended to cast policy analysis as a subset of policy advising. As such, policy analysis was seen primarily as an activity conducted inside government agencies with the purpose of informing the choices of a few key people, principally elected decision makers (Lindblom 1968; Wildavsky 1979). Today, the potential purposes of policy analysis are understood to be much broader. Many more audiences are seen as holding interests in policy and as being open to –

indeed, demanding of – appropriately presented analytical work (Radin 2000). Beyond people in government, people in business, members of nonprofit organizations, and informed citizens all constitute audiences for policy analysis. While policy analysts were once thought to be mainly located within government agencies, today they can also be found in most organizations that have direct dealings with governments, and in many organizations where government actions significantly influence the operating environment. In addition, many university-based researchers, who tend to treat their peers and their students as their primary audience, conduct studies that ask questions about government policies and that answer them using forms of policy analysis. Given this, an appropriately encompassing definition of contemporary policy analysis needs to recognize the range of topics and issue areas policy analysts work on, the range of analytical and research strategies they employ, and the range of audiences they seek to address. In recognizing the contemporary breadth of applications and styles of policy analysis, it becomes clear that effective policy analysis calls for not only the application of sound technical skills, but also deep substantive knowledge, political perceptiveness, and well-developed interpersonal skills (Mintrom 2003). Although producing high-quality, reliable advice remains a core expectation for many policy analysts, advising now appears as a subset of the broader policy analysis category. The transition from policy analysis as a subset of advising to advising as a subset of analysis represents a significant shift in orientation and priorities from earlier times. In what follows, I first review the sources of increasing demand for policy analysis. I then review the growth and adaptation in the supply of policy analysis that have occurred in response to this demand. I conclude by discussing the current state of the policy analysis movement and its likely future trajectory.

The Evolving Demand for Policy Analysis

Demand for policy analysis has been driven mostly by the emergence of problems and by political conditions that have made those problems salient. Early in the development of policy analysis techniques, the people who identified the problems that needed to be addressed tended to be government officials. They turned to academics for help. Frequently, those academics deemed to be most useful, given the problems at hand, were economists with strong technical skills who had the ability to estimate the magnitude of problems, undertake statistical analyses, and determine the costs of various government actions. During the twentieth century, as transportation, electrification, and telecommunications opened up new opportunities for market exchange, problems associated with decentralized decision making became more apparent (McCraw 1984). Meanwhile, as awareness grew of the causes of many natural and social phenomena, calls emerged for governments to establish mechanisms that might effectively manage various natural and social processes. Many matters once treated as social conditions, or facts of life to be suffered, were transformed into policy problems (Cobb and Elder 1983). Together, the increasing scope of the marketplace, the increasing complexity of social interactions, and expanding knowledge of social conditions created pressures from a variety of quarters for governments to take the lead in structuring and regulating individual and collective action. Tools of policy analysis, such as the analysis of market failures and the identification of feasible government responses, were developed to guide this expanding scope of government. Yet as the reach of policy analysis grew, questions were raised about the biases inherent in some of the analytical tools being applied. In response, new efforts were made to account for the effects of policy changes, and new voices began to contribute in significant ways to policy development. To explore the factors prompting demand for policy analysis, it is useful to work with a model of the policy-making process. A number of conceptions of policy making have been developed in recent decades. Here, I apply the 'stages model,' where five stages are typically posited: problem definition, agenda setting, policy adoption, implementation, and evaluation (Eyestone 1978).

Initial demands for policy analysis were prompted by a growing awareness of problems that government could potentially address. Questions inevitably arose concerning the appropriateness of alternative policy solutions. Thus, in the United States in the 1930s, as the federal government took on major new roles in the areas of regulation, redistribution, and the financing of infrastructural development, the need arose for high-quality policy analysis. With respect to regulatory policy, concerns about the threat to the railroads of the emerging trucking industry prompted the expansion of the Interstate Commerce Commission (Eisner 1993). This body employed lawyers and economists who helped to devise an expanding set of regulations that eventually covered many industries. Although the American welfare state has always been limited compared with the welfare state elsewhere, especially European welfare states, its development still required concerted policy analysis and development work on the part of a cadre of bureaucrats (Derthick 1979). Initially, much of the talent needed to fill these positions was drawn from states like Wisconsin, where welfare policies had been pioneered by Robert LaFollette. As the role of the United States government in redistribution expanded, policy analysts swelled the ranks of career bureaucrats in the Treasury, the Office of Management and Budget, and the Department of Health and Human Services. Meanwhile, benefit-cost analysis, a cornerstone of modern policy analysis and a core component of public economics, was developed to help in the planning of dam construction in the Tennessee Valley in the 1930s. Politicians at the time worried that some dams were being built mainly to perpetuate the flow of cash to construction companies rather than to meet growing demand for electricity and flood control (Eckstein 1958). The broad applicability of the technique soon became clear and its use has continually expanded. At the same time, efforts to improve the sophistication of the technique, and to develop variations on it that are best suited to different sets of circumstances have also continued to occur (see Vining and Boardman in this volume).

Several features of policy development, the politics of agenda setting, and the policy-making process have served over time to increase demand for policy analysts. The dynamics at work have been similar to those through which an arms race generates on-going and often expanding demand for military procurements. In Washington, DC, the growing population of policy analysts employed in the federal government bureaucracy led to demand elsewhere for policy analysts who could verify or contest the analysis and advice emanating from government agencies. A classic example is given by the creation of the Congressional Budget Office (CBO). This office was established as an independent resource for Congress that would generate analysis and advice as a check on the veracity of the analyses prepared and disseminated by the executive-controlled Office of Management and Budget (Wildavsky 1992). The General Accounting Office was also developed to provide independent advice for Congress. In the latter case, the scope of the analysis has always been broader than that of the Congressional Budget Office.

As the analytical capabilities available to elected politicians grew, groups of people outside of government but with significant interests in the direction of government policy began devoting resources to the production of high-quality, independent advice. Think tanks like the Brookings Institution and the American Enterprise Institute, established in 1920s and 1940s, respectively, and both still going strong, represent archetypes of many independent policy shops now located in Washington, DC (Smith 1991). These organizations engage in original research and policy analysis, the synthesis of findings from prior studies, and the marketing of policy ideas, all in the service of more informed policy debate. Among government agencies, the growing quality of the technical advice generated by some has typically promoted renewed effort on the part of others to build their analytical and advice-giving capabilities. When agencies must compete among themselves for funding of new programs, or for ongoing funding of core functions, a degree of learning occurs, so that incremental improvements are observed in the overall quality of analysis and advice being produced.

Although policy analysis is often understood as work that occurs before a new policy or program is adopted, demand for policy analysis has also been driven by interest in the effectiveness of government programs. The question of what happens once a policy idea has been adopted and passed into law could be construed as too operational to deserve the attention of policy analysts. Yet, during the past few decades, elements of implementation have become recognized as vital for study by policy analysts (Bardach 1977; Lipsky 1984; Pressman and Wildavsky 1973). In part, this has been led by results of program evaluations, which have often found policies not producing their intended outcomes, or worse, creating whole sets of unintended and negative consequences. One important strain of the work devoted to assessing implementation has contributed to what is now known as the 'government failure' literature (Niskanen 1971; Weimer and Vining 2005; Wolf 1979). The possibility that public policies designed to address market failures might themselves create problems led to a greater respect for market processes and a degree of skepticism on the part of policy analysts towards the remedial abilities of government (Rhoads 1985). In turn, this required policy analysts to develop more nuanced understandings of the workings of particular markets. The government failure literature has led to greater interest in government efforts to simulate market processes, or to reform government and contract out aspects of government supply that could be taken up by private firms operating in the competitive marketplace (Osborne and Gaebler 1993). Where efforts to reform government have been thorough, an interesting dynamic has developed. As the core public sector has shrunk in size, the number of policy analysts employed in the sector has increased, both in relative and in absolute terms. This dynamic is indicative of governments developing their capacities in the management of contracts rather than in the management of services (Savas 1987). In these new environments, people exhibiting skills in mechanism design and benefit-cost analysis have been in demand. Therefore, employment opportunities for policy analysts have tended to expand, even as the scope of government has been curtailed. Fiscal conservatism, which has been a hallmark of governments in many jurisdictions over recent decades, has added to this trend (Yergin and Stanislaw 1998; Williamson 1993). When budgets are squeezed, it becomes critical for all possible efficiency gains to be realized. More than any other trained professionals, policy analysts working in government are well placed to undertake the kind of analytical work needed to identify cost-saving measures and to persuade elected decision makers to adopt them.

Early discussions of the role of policy analysts in society often portrayed them as 'whiz kids' or 'econocrats' on a quest to imbue public decision making with high degrees of rigour and rationality (Self 1977; Stevens 1993). Certainly, proponents of benefit-cost analysis considered themselves to have a technique for assessing the relative merits of alternative policy proposals that, on theoretical grounds, trumped any others on offer. Likewise, proponents of program evaluation employing quasi-experimental research designs considered their approach to be superior to other approaches that might be used to determine program effectiveness (Cook and Campbell 1979). That the application of both benefit-cost analysis and quantitative evaluation techniques has continued unabated for several decades speaks to their perceived value for generating useable knowledge. However, the limitations of such techniques have not been lost on critics. In the case of benefit-cost analysis, features of the technique that make it so appealing – such as the reduction of all impacts to a common metric and the calculation of net social benefits – have also attracted criticism. In response, alternative methods for assessing the impacts of new policies, such as environmental impact assessments, social impact assessments, and health impact assessments, have gained currency (Barrow 2000; Lock 2000; Wood 1995). Similarly, widespread efforts have been made to promote the integration of gender and race analysis into policy development (Myers 2002; True and Mintrom 2001). In the case of evaluation studies, fundamental and drawn-out debates have occurred covering the validity of various research methods and the appropriate scope and purpose of evaluation efforts. Significantly for the present discussion, these debates have actually served to expand demand for policy analysis. Indeed, government agencies designed especially to audit the impacts of policies on the family, children, women, and racial minorities have now been established in many jurisdictions. Further, evaluation of organizational processes, which often scrutinize the nature of the interactions between organizations and their clients, are now accorded equivalent status among evaluators as more traditional efforts to measure program outcomes (Patton 1997; Weiss 1998). Yet these process evaluations are motivated by very different questions and draw upon very different methodologies than traditional evaluation studies that assessed program impacts narrowly.

This review of the evolving demand for policy analysis has identified several trends that have served both to embed policy analysts at the core of government operations and to expand demand for policy analysts both inside and outside of government. These trends have much to do with the growing complexity of economic and social relations and knowledge generation. Yet there is also a sense in which policy analysis itself generates demand for more policy analysis. While these trends have been most observable in national capitals, where a large amount of policy development occurs, they have played out in related ways in other venues as well. For instance, in federal systems, expanding cadres of well-trained policy analysts have become engaged in sophisticated, evidence-based policy debates in state and provincial capitals. Cities, too, are increasingly making extensive use of policy analysts in their strategy and planning departments. At the global level, key coordinating organizations, such as the World Bank, the International Monetary Fund, the World Trade Organization, and the Organization for Economic Cooperation and Development, have made extensive use of the skills of policy analysts to monitor various transnational developments and national-level activities of particular relevance and interest.

Today, the demand for policy analysis is considerable, and it comes both from inside and outside of governments. This demand is likely to keep growing as calls emerge for governments to tackle emerging, unfamiliar problems. On the one hand, we should expect to see ongoing efforts to harness technical procedures drawn from the social sciences and natural sciences for the purposes of improving the quality of policy analysis. On the other hand, more people are likely to apply these techniques, reinvent them, or develop whole new approaches to counteract them, all with the purpose of gaining greater voice in policy making at all levels of government, from the local to the global.

The Evolving Supply of Policy Analysis

To meet the growing demand for policy analysis, since the mid-1960s supply has greatly expanded. But this expansion has been accompanied, at least around the edges of the enterprise, by a transformation in the very nature of the products on offer. Consequently, it is now commonplace to find politically motivated policy analysts who question the central motivating questions of the past, or who seek to satisfy intellectual curiosity rather than offer solutions to immediate problems. Thus, the apparently straightforward question of what constitutes policy analysis cannot be addressed in a straightforward manner. Answers given will be highly contingent on context. For example, an answer offered in the mid-1970s would be narrower in scope than an answer offered now. Likewise, the question of who produces policy analysis is also contingent. Economists have always been well represented in the ranks of policy analysts. People from other disciplines have also contributed to policy analysis, although there has often been a sense that other disciplines have less to contribute to policy design and the weighing of alternatives. Today, practitioners and scholars hailing from an array of disciplines are engaged in this kind of work, and the relevance of disciplines other than economics is well understood. In this review of the evolving supply of policy analysis, I consider both the development of a mainstream and the growing diversity of work that now constitutes policy analysis.

There has always been a mainstream style of conducting policy analysis. That style is more prevalent today than it has ever been. The style is portrayed by practitioners and critics alike as the application of a basic, yet continually expanding, set of technical practices (Stokey and Zeckhauser 1978). Most of those practices derive from microeconomic analysis. They include the analysis of individual choice and trade-offs, the analysis of markets and market failure, and the application of benefit-cost analysis. Contemporary policy analysis textbooks tend to build on this notion of policy analysis as a technical exercise (Bardach 2000; MacRae and Whittington 1997; Munger 2000; Weimer and Vining 2005). For example, in his practical guide to policy analysis, Eugene Bardach (2000) contends that a basic, 'eightfold' approach can be applied to analyzing most policy problems. The approach requires us to define the problem, assemble some evidence, construct the alternatives, select the criteria, project the outcomes, confront the tradeoffs, decide, and tell our story. As with Stokey and Zeckhauser's approach, Bardach's approach clearly derives from microeconomic analysis, and benefit-cost analysis in particular. None of this should surprise us since, to the extent that a discipline called policy analysis exists at all, it is a discipline that grew directly out of microeconomic analysis. That disciplinary linkage remains strong. Economists comprise the majority of members of the United States-based Association for Public Policy Analysis and Management (APPAM), the largest such association in the world. Likewise, contributions to the association's *Journal of Policy Analysis and Management* are authored predominantly, although certainly not exclusively, by economists.

Viewed positively, we might note that the basic approach to policy analysis derived from microeconomics is extremely serviceable. As scholars have continued to apply and expand this style of analysis, a rich body of technical practices has been created. Extensive efforts have been made to ensure that university students interested in careers in policy analysis gain appropriate exposure to these approaches and receive opportunities to apply them. Most master's degree programs in public policy analysis or public administration require students to take a core set of courses that expose them to microeconomic analysis, public economics, benefit-cost analysis, descriptive and inferential statistics, and evaluation methods. Sometimes the core is augmented by courses on topics such as strategic decision making, the nature of the policy process, and organizational behaviour. Students are usually also given the opportunity to supplement their core course selections with a range of elective courses from several disciplines. Without doubt, graduates of these programs emerge well equipped to immediately begin contributing in useful ways to the development of public policy. Over recent decades, many universities in the United States have introduced master's programs designed to train policy analysts along the lines suggested here. More recently, similar programs have been established in many other countries around the globe. Those establishing them know there is strong demand for the kind of training they seek to provide. These professional courses create opportunities for people who have already been trained in other disciplines to acquire valuable skills for supporting the development of policy analyses. Graduates end up being placed in many organizations in the public, private, and nonprofit sectors.

Viewed more negatively, the mainstream approach to teaching and practicing policy analysis can be critiqued for its narrowness and the privileging of techniques derived from economic theory over analytical approaches that draw upon political and social theory. Suppose we again describe the policy-making process as a series of stages: Problem definition, agenda setting, policy adoption, implementation, and evaluation. The mainstream approach to policy analysis has little to contribute to our understanding of agenda setting, or the politics of policy adoption, implementation, and evaluation. Steeped as it is in the rational choice or utilitarian perspective, mainstream policy analysis is poorly suited to help us understand why particular problems might manifest themselves at given times, why some policy alternatives might appear politically palatable while others will not, and why adopted policies often go through significant transformations during the implementation stage. In addition, technical approaches to program evaluation, while obviously necessary for guiding the measurement of program effectiveness, typically prescribe narrow data collection procedures that can leave highly relevant information unexamined. Studies that dwell on assessing program outcomes are unlikely to reveal the multiple, and perhaps conflicting, ways that program personnel and program participants often make sense of programs. In turn, this might cause analysts to misinterpret the motivations that lead program personnel and participants to redefine program goals from those originally intended by policy makers. Problems of program design or program theory might end up being ignored in favour of interpretations that place the blame on faulty implementation (Chen 1990). More generally, mainstream approaches to policy analysis can encourage practitioners to hold tightly to assumptions about individual and collective behaviour that are contradicted by the evidence. In the worst cases, this can lead to inappropriate specification of proposals for policy change.

The foregoing observations might cause us to worry that mainstream training in policy analysis does not sufficiently equip junior analysts to become reflective practitioners, ones who listen closely to the voices of people who are most likely to be affected by policy change (Forrester 1999; Schön 1983). Certainly, strong critiques of mainstream analytical approaches have led to some rethinking of the questions that policy analysts should ask when working on policy problems (Stone 2002). Yet it is a fact that many people who have gone on to become excellent policy managers and leaders of government agencies began their careers as junior policy analysts fresh out of mainstream policy programs. This suggests that, within professional settings, heavy reliance is placed on mechanisms of tacit knowledge transfer, whereby narrowly trained junior analysts come to acquire skills and insight that serve them well as policy managers. My sense is that the key components of this professional socialization can be codified and are teachable (Mintrom 2003). But much of what it takes to be an effective policy analyst is not captured in the curricula of the many university programs that now exist to train future practitioners.

Beyond mainstream efforts to expand the supply of policy analysts, all of which place heavy emphasis on the development of technical skills informed primarily by microeconomic theory, other disciplines also contribute in significant ways to the preparation of people who eventually become engaged in policy analysis. In these cases, the pathway from formal study to the practice of policy analysis is often circuitous. People with substantive training in law, engineering, natural sciences, and the liberal arts might begin their careers in closely related fields, only to migrate into policy work later. For example, individuals trained initially as sociologists might gain professional qualifications as social workers and, after years in the field, assume managerial roles that require them to devote most of their energies to policy development. People pursuing these alternative professional routes towards working as policy analysts can bring rich experiences and diverse insights to policy discussions. The resulting multidisciplinary contributions to policy discussions have been known to generate their share of intractable policy controversies (Schön and Rein 1994). Yet, when disagreements that emerge from differences in training and analytical perspectives are well managed, these multidisciplinary forums can produce effective policy design. Indeed, increasing efforts are now being made to address significant problems through 'joined-up government' initiatives (6 2004). Through these, individuals with diverse professional backgrounds who are known to have been working on similar problems are brought together to work out cohesive policy strategies to address those problems. For example, pediatricians, police officers, social workers, and educators might be asked to work together to devise policies for effective detection and prevention of child abuse.

Two somewhat contradictory trends in the evolving supply of policy analysis have been noted here. On the one hand, the growth of university-based professional programs designed to train policy analysts has contributed to a significant degree of analytical isomorphism. No matter the university or the country in which such programs are based, the students are required to study much the same set of topics and to read from a growing canon of articles and books covering aspects of policy analysis. These programs promote ways of thinking about public policy that owe heavy debts to the discipline of economics. On the other hand, researchers and practitioners working out of other disciplines have increasingly become involved in the production of policy analysis. These contributions from outside the mainstream have tended to promote analytical diversity. Taken together, these contradictory trends define the contemporary field of policy analysis. Often, the differences are downplayed. For example, while the *Journal of Policy Analysis and Management* publishes research articles and shorter pieces on teaching practice, all of which can be informed by a variety of disciplinary perspectives, the overall impression given is that of a journal devoted to the furtherance of mainstream methods of policy analysis. In contrast, controversies in the interdisciplinary field of evaluation studies have left a distinctly different impression. As a result, courses on policy evaluation, when taught in professional public policy programs, can introduce perspectives that sit uncomfortably with those taught in other core courses. Similarly, the eclecticism of contributions to organizational studies can transform otherwise staid courses on public management and administration into eye-opening explorations of organizational behaviour that present perspectives and analyses differing starkly from mainstream economic interpretations.

The evolving supply of policy analysis is likely to continue to be defined by a mixture of mainstream and alternative analytical perspectives. New policy problems generated by changing social conditions, technologies, and political agendas cannot be expected to readily lend themselves to mainstream policy analysis. Indeed, although policy analysis textbooks present specific forms of market failure or government failure as defensible rationales for policy action, many contemporary problems defy such categorization. For example, changing understandings of morally appropriate behaviour (Mooney 2000) and differing perspectives on the degree to which parents and the state should be trusted to act in the best interests of children (Nelson 1984; Shapiro 1999) have provided impetus for a range of recent policy disputes. Mainstream approaches to policy analysis are not well suited to assessing the relative merits of competing arguments and perspectives in these areas. This suggests that, for any headway to be made in addressing disputes of this sort, the comparative strengths of alternative disciplinary perspectives must be drawn upon to guide policy analysis. The frontiers of policy analysis are also being advanced by a growing awareness of the degree to which national policies hold implications for international relations, transnational norms, and global trade or environmental concerns (Sandler 2004; Tabb 2004). These developments will require further innovation in the design and application of policy analysis techniques. In many instances, the mainstream perspective will need to be augmented by alternative perspectives that offer sound analytical traction on otherwise difficult conceptual and practical problems. Thus, definitions of policy analysis are likely to keep expanding and the set of actors that have relevant and important contributions to make will remain dynamic.

Prospects for the Policy Analysis Movement

The policy analysis movement began to emerge in the mid-1960s. Today, it is large, diverse, and global. The phenomenon of many people generating policy analysis for consumption by an array of audiences can be claimed to be a movement for several reasons. First, policy analysts, no matter where they are located within society, all focus their energies in one way or another on identifying, understanding, and confronting public problems. As techniques of policy analysis have been more routinely applied to investigating public problems, new problems and new approaches to addressing them have been revealed. While a finite set of known policy problems might exist at any given time, that set is continually being revised, as particular problems are resolved and as others become salient. Second, while people engaged in policy analysis work out of a variety of perspectives and often make contradictory and conflicting arguments, there is a widely shared recognition that knowledge of public problems and how they can best be addressed requires thorough, theory-driven, and evidence-based investigation. This is highly significant, because changing perceptions of what kind of claims should guide public deliberations have made it harder for long-entrenched groups to use their informal, quiet power to influence government actions. Third, the increasing reliance placed on this style of policy analysis has required a core of people to routinely apply a well-established set of analytical and research methods. The result has been the clear definition of a mainstream of policy analysis, and many university programs have been established to professionalize budding analysts. Fourth, the development of policy analysis has not been restricted to those people applying mainstream techniques. Indeed, there has been a level of openness to people from various disciplines offering alternative theoretical and empirical arguments concerning particular policy matters. Critique of mainstream methods has often resulted in significant efforts to improve the analytical approaches employed. Finally, people engaged in policy analysis, regardless of their substantive interests or their immediate purposes, have shared an understanding that they are engaged in important, socially relevant work. They share a common understanding that, at base, public policy involves systematic efforts to change social institutions. The seriousness of this work helps explain why policy disputes are often prolonged and heated. Taken together, these various features of contemporary policy work clearly represent markers of a policy analysis movement. Those associated with it are, in their many particular ways, contributing to the ongoing task of defining the appropriate role of government in society, and how governments can best mediate social and economic relations.

What are the future prospects of this movement? How might it continue to evolve? Internal and external dynamics are likely to ensure further expansion of the movement. With respect to internal dynamics, a clear lesson of the foregoing discussion is that good policy analysis creates its own demand. This happens because, in competitive settings like debates over policy choices, opposing parties face strong incentives to find ways to outsmart their opponents. If one party's arguments are consistently supported by strong policy analysis and this appears to give them an edge in debate, then other parties will soon see the merit in upping their own game. This can involve emulating, revising, or critiquing the methods of opponents. But, no matter what, the result is further production of policy analysis. Aside from this, careful policy studies, especially evaluations of existing programs, often reveal aspects of policy design or implementation that require further attention. When we are forced to return to the drawing board, further policy analysis occurs. The lesson that good policy analysis creates its own demand suggests that the currently observed momentum and vibrancy of that movement will continue.

The external dynamics that drive expansion of the policy analysis movement derive from changing social, economic, and political conditions. In the future, the increasing integration of economies and societies, referred to generally as globalization, can be expected to generate new sets of policy problems. In this regard, the changes associated with globalization echo the dynamics that were observed from the late nineteenth century well into the twentieth century in federal systems. During that period, increasing commerce across state and provincial borders, and the emergence of intensive inter-jurisdictional competition, prompted new considerations of the role of government in society. Extensive effort also went into determining what levels of government were best suited to performing different functions. New times introduce new problems and questions. Drawing lessons from the past, it seems clear that many new policy problems will arise on government agendas in the coming decades. While globalizing forces will be responsible for generating many of these challenges, the challenges themselves will be manifest at all levels of government, from the local upwards. As in the past, people both inside and outside of government can be expected to show intense interest in these policy challenges, and they will call for further supply of innovative and high-quality policy analysis.

Strong grounds exist for believing that the policy analysis movement is here to stay. While a mainstream core will continue to evolve, the range of issues and concerns that are likely to arise in the future will offer many opportunities for practitioners and academics working from outside the mainstream to make important contributions to the core. Some of these contributions may well be paradigm shifting. That is an exciting prospect indeed.

REFERENCES

Bardach, Eugene. 1977. *The Implementation Game: What Happens After a Bill Becomes a Law.* Cambridge, MA: MIT Press.
– 2000. *A Practical Guide for Policy Analysis: The Eightfold Path to More Effective Problem Solving.* New York: Seven Bridges Press/Chatham House.
Barrow, C.J. 2000. *Social Impact Assessment: An Introduction.* New York: Oxford University Press.
Chen, Huey-Tsyh. 1990. *Theory-Driven Evaluations.* Newbury Park, CA: Sage Publications.
Cobb, Roger W., and Charles W. Elder. 1983. *Participation in American Politics: The Dynamics of Agenda-Building.* 2nd ed. Boston, MA: Allyn and Bacon.
Cook, Thomas D., and Donald T. Campbell. 1979. *Quasi-Experimentation: Design and Analysis Issues for Field Settings.* Boston, MA: Houghton Mifflin.
Dahl, Robert A. 1998. *On Democracy.* New Haven, CT: Yale University Press.
Derthick, Martha. 1979. *Policymaking for Social Security.* Washington, DC: Brookings Institution.
Eckstein, Otto. 1958. *Water Resource Development.* Cambridge, MA: Harvard University Press.
Eisner, Marc Allen. 1993. *Regulatory Politics in Transition.* Baltimore, MD: Johns Hopkins University Press.
Eyestone, Robert. 1978. *From Social Issues to Public Policy.* New York: John Wiley.
Forester, John. 1999. *The Deliberative Practitioner: Encouraging Participatory Planning Processes.* Cambridge, MA: MIT Press.

Lindblom, Charles E. 1968. *The Policymaking Process*. Englewood Cliffs, NJ: Prentice-Hall.

Lipsky, Michael. 1980. *Street-Level Bureaucracy: The Dilemmas of the Individual in Public Services*. New York: Russell Sage Foundation.

Lock, Karen. 2000. 'Health Impact Assessment.' *British Medical Journal* 320, 1395–1398.

MacRae, Duncan, Jr., and Dale Whittington. 1997. *Expert Advice for Policy Choice*. Washington, DC: Georgetown University Press.

McCraw, Thomas K. 1984. *Prophets of Regulation*. Cambridge, MA: Belknap Press.

Mintrom, Michael. 2003. *People Skills for Policy Analysts*. Washington, DC: Georgetown University Press.

Mintrom, Michael, and Sandra Vergari. 1996. 'Advocacy Coalitions, Policy Entrepreneurs, and Policy Change.' *Policy Studies Journal* 24, 420–35.

Mooney, Christopher Z., ed. 2000. *The Public Clash of Private Values: The Politics of Morality Policy*. New York: Chatham House Publishers of Seven Bridges Press.

Munger, Michael C. 2000. *Analyzing Policy: Choices, Conflicts, and Practices*. New York: Norton.

Myers, Samuel L., Jr. 2002. 'Presidential Address – Analysis of Race as Policy Analysis.' *Journal of Policy Analysis and Management* 21, 169–90.

Nelson, Barbara. 1984. *Making an Issue of Child Abuse*. Chicago: University of Chicago Press.

Niskanen, William A., Jr. 1971. *Bureaucracy and Representative Government*. Chicago, IL: Aldine-Atherton.

Osborne, David, and Ted Gaebler. 1993. *Reinventing Government: How the Entrepreneurial Spirit is Transforming the Public Sector*. New York: Penguin Books.

Patton, Michael Quinn. 1997. *Utilization-Focused Evaluation: The New Century Text*. Thousand Oaks, CA: Sage Publications.

Pressman, Jeffrey L., and Aaron Wildavsky. 1973. *Implementation*. Berkeley, CA: University of California Press.

Radin, Beryl A. 2000. *Beyond Machiavelli: Policy Analysis Comes of Age*. Washington, DC: Georgetown University Press.

Rhoads, Steven E. 1985. *The Economist's View of the World: Government, Markets, and Public Policy*. New York: Cambridge University Press.

Rochefort, David A., and Roger W. Cobb, eds. 1994. *The Politics of Problem Definition: Shaping the Policy Agenda*. Lawrence, KS: University Press of Kansas.

Sabatier, Paul A. 1988. 'An Advocacy Coalition Framework of Policy Change and the Role of Policy-Oriented Learning Therein.' *Policy Sciences* 21, 129–68.

Sandler, Todd. 2004. *Global Collective Action*. New York: Cambridge University Press.

Savas, E.S. 1987. *Privatization: The Key to Better Government*. Chatham, NJ: Chatham House.

Schön, Donald A. 1983. *The Reflective Practitioner: How Professionals Think in Action*. New York: Basic Books.

Schön, Donald A., and Martin Rein. 1994. *Frame Reflection: Toward the Resolution of Intractable Policy Controversies*. New York: Basic Books.

Self, Peter. 1977. *Econocrats and the Policy Process: The Politics and Philosophy of Cost-Benefit Analysis*. Boulder, CO: Westview Press.

Shapiro, Ian. 1999. *Democratic Justice*. New Haven, CT: Yale University Press.

6, Perri. 2004. 'Joined-up Government in the Western World in Comparative Perspective: A Preliminary Literature Review and Exploration.' *Journal of Public Administration Research and Theory* 14, 103–38.

Smith, James A. 1991. *The Idea Brokers: Think Tanks and the Rise of the New Policy Elite*. New York: Free Press.

Stevens, Joe B. 1993. *The Economics of Collective Choice*. Boulder, CO: Westview.

Stokey, Edith, and Richard Zeckhauser. 1978. *A Primer for Policy Analysis*. New York: Norton.

Stone, Deborah. 2002. *Policy Paradox: The Art of Political Decision Making*. Revised ed. New York: Norton.

Tabb, William K. 2004. *Economic Governance in the Age of Globalization*. New York, NY: Columbia University Press.

True, Jacqui, and Michael Mintrom. 2001. 'Transnational Networks and Policy Diffusion: The Case of Gender Mainstreaming.' *International Studies Quarterly* 45, 27–57.

Weimer, David L., and Aidan R. Vining. 2005. *Policy Analysis: Concepts and Practice*. 4th ed. Upper Saddle River, NJ: Prentice-Hall.

Weiss, Carol H. 1998. *Evaluation*. 2nd ed. Upper Saddle River, NJ: Prentice-Hall.

Wildavsky, Aaron. 1979. *Speaking Truth to Power: The Art and Craft of Policy Analysis*. Boston, MA: Little, Brown.

– 1992. *The New Politics of the Budgetary Process*. 2nd ed. New York: HarperCollins.

Williamson, John, ed. 1994. *The Political Economy of Policy Reform*. Washington, DC: Institute for International Economics.

Wolf, Charles, Jr. 1979. 'A Theory of Nonmarket Failures.' *Journal of Law and Economics* 22, 107–39.

Wood, Christopher. 1995. *Environmental Impact Assessment: A Comparative Review*. Harlow, UK: Longman Scientific & Technical.

Yergin, Daniel, and Joseph Stanislaw. 1998. *The Commanding Heights: The Battle Between Government and the Marketplace That Is Remaking the Modern World*. New York: Touchstone.

7 Soft Craft, Hard Choices, Altered Context: Reflections on Twenty-Five Years of Policy Advice in Canada

MICHAEL J. PRINCE

This chapter offers a retrospective view on developments in policy analysis and advice in Canadian governments over the past generation. I also look at the present situation in the federal government and consider the future of policy advice. These reflections come from my own academic research on policy advice and consulting work with governments, the writings of other colleagues on policy analysis, and from change in the politics, policy making, and governance of Canada since the late 1970s. I am interested in reflecting on policy analysis and advice as public service work in Canadian governments and, at the same time, reflecting on some key concepts and premises we commonly find in the literature in thinking about and assessing the state of the art of public policy analysis.

A quarter-century ago, Aaron Wildavsky dubbed policy analysis the art and craft of 'speaking truth to power' (1979), an expression widely adopted in the Canadian public administration and policy studies literature (Doern and Phidd 1992; Good 2003; Savoie 2003). A central argument I wish to present is that the concepts of truth and power in relation to policy advice, as well as ideas such as policy capacity, have changed over time and their meanings need investigating in the contemporary context. I question the notion of policy advice and policy capacity as part of a larger rationality project (Rasmussen 1999), in favour of the view that nothing is more political, organizational, and relational than doing policy work in and for the state.

Much of my own work since the late 1970s on this topic has been an interrogation of the rationalist themes and proverbs associated with public policy analysis in federal and provincial government departments (Prince 1979, 1983, 1986, 1999, 2002; Prince and Chenier 1980;

Russell and Prince 1992; Hollander and Prince 1993). Of course, rationality is important in policy development and decision making (Doern
and Phidd 1992; Pal 2001). However, my research, buttressed by a range
of consulting experiences, underscores the hard choices of how policy
advice as a subtle craft actually emerges and operates in public service
settings typically characterized by ambiguous goals, multiple roles and
structures, resource constraints, uncertain outcomes, and competing
interests, ideas, and policy agendas. As a former senior public servant
says of management in Canadian government, 'there are such fundamental and inherent contradictions in public administration that hard
trade-offs are required and one value must be explicitly sacrificed in
order to achieve others' (Good 2003, 184).

The milieu in which the art and craft of policy advice is done has
changed significantly in a number of respects over the last few decades
in Canada, as elsewhere. I will review these changes and discuss their
repercussions for policy advice as public service work. Under the speak-
ing-truth-to-power model, policy advice is, largely, a bipartite relationship involving public servants and executive politicians, with career
officials offering advice to cabinet ministers. For a number of years now,
however, it is clear that a plurality of advisory sources exist, with an
array of actors both inside and outside government offering various
kinds of policy advice and analysis in various forms to decision makers.
This pluralism of policy advice has implications for the roles and relations of government analysts to governing politicians and their staffs, to
non-state actors in think tanks, lobby associations, polling and consulting firms and, alongside these actors, raises disquieting issues of the
capacity and influence of civil society organizations and clientele groups.

To the point, changes over the last 25 years in both the context and
content of Canadian politics and government have produced a shift in
the approach to policy analysis: public service policy advice has moved
away from 'speaking truth to power' toward what we may describe as
'sharing truths with multiple actors.'

Policy Advice as Public Sector Work: The Soft Craft of Hard Choices

In referring to policy advice as a *soft* craft, I wish to convey the politic
nature of this work; that is to say, that policy advice occurs in and
around the state and the wider political setting, and pertains to developing and promoting certain ideas and directions for a government and

economy and society. I am not suggesting that policy work is a weak and feeble activity of the Canadian state or that policy advice is woolly-headed and unsystematic. On the contrary, doing policy analysis and giving advice to politicians is not for the faint of heart. It requires enthusiasm, conviction, and instincts for survival (Prince 1983). As a soft craft, the activity of policy advising is variable, adapting to the specific and often changing organizational and temporal contexts in which it occurs. Policy advising is about human relations and social psychology as much as it is about hard data and statistical packages. As the author of a practical guide to policy analysis states: 'Policy analysis is more art than science. It draws on intuition as much as method' (Bardarch 2000, xiv). Thus, effective policy advising is astute, shrewd, and subtle.

As a *craft*, the giving of policy advice is an art, to be sure, as well as a job, a set of tasks and activities, shaped by certain skills and talents for this line of work. The giving of policy advice, when done well, exemplifies skill, tact, creativity, sagacity, and ingenuity, among other attributes. It is, after all, a political endeavour in disciplined thinking and interacting; an exercise in intellectual cogitation plus social interaction (Wildavsky 1979). Practitioners and researchers describe the craft of policy analysis as creating political arguments (Stone 2002); giving reasoned advice on solving or at least mitigating public problems (Bardach 2000); producing inquiry and recommendations for decision makers (Anderson 1996); giving counsel to leaders on choices of issues, goals and resources (Axworthy 1988); and offering ideas, knowledge, and solutions to executive politicians (Kroeger 1996; Rasmussen 1999). The craft side of this entails knowing your audience and their environment; picking your time in making certain proposals; presenting each option fairly; being aware of the history of the issue and policy field; knowing the impacts of options for specific key groups; knowing how your jurisdiction compares with others in the country or internationally; and keeping your sense of humour.

A wide assortment of occupations represents the policy advisory activities of government in Canada. Included are researchers, evaluators, planners, consultants, internal auditors, financial analysts, policy analysts, quality assurance experts, executive assistants, program development staff, public affairs or communications staff, social projects staff, operational review staff, and discipline-specific staff such as agrologists, economists, epidemiologists, lawyers, sociologists, and psychologists, among others. Regardless of titles, the range of analytical activities provided by these staff include scientific and social scientific research, policy work, planning on the scale of communities, programs or projects, evaluations of various sorts (e.g., formative or process, summative, outcome or impact, and meta-evaluation), and audits and reviews of various sorts (internal, financial, management, operational, composite, and comprehensive).

Policy work, more specifically, encompasses whatever policy analysts and policy units choose to do or in response to requests by senior officials. An overview of such activities is as follows:

- policy development in defining government goals and objectives, and conducting priority reviews;
- program design work of designing courses of action or programs to achieve policy objectives;
- program evaluation to examine proposed or actual programs to determine if they will achieve, or have achieved, their objectives;
- policy firefighting work such as doing rush assignments, crisis management, work under pressure, and studies of 'hot' issues of the moment demanding a 'quick and (perhaps) dirty look';
- coordinating of strategic outlooks, operational and long-term plans, or the programs of various branches in a department, and providing liaison with other departmental groups and other departments and central agencies, other governments, and outside stakeholder groups;
- socio-economic research projects and forecasting activities, perhaps including scenario writing;
- scanning of the external environment to identify threats and opportunities, and conducting inquiries into the nature, causes, and possible solutions of new and existing policy issues;
- stakeholder analysis and development of consultation and engagement strategies;
- strategic communications planning and development and possibly implementation of public communication plans;
- needs assessment to determine the need for new or revised policies, programs, and services;
- budget analyses and planning designed to determine what to cut, terminate, maintain, and increase under various resource scenarios;
- legislative support by providing advice on legislation, and assisting program staff to work with legislative counsel to draft new legislation or regulations and/or amendments to existing legislation and regulations;

- executive assistant support by preparing speeches for the minister and senior officials, preparing correspondence, hosting visitors, compiling data from line divisions, and arranging meetings, workshops, and conferences; and,
- policy advice work in preparing policy papers, having input into priority setting, and assisting in defining overall objectives and strategic plans (Hollander and Prince 1993, 205).

With this tremendous assortment of activities that typify the soft craft of policy work, invariably comes a series of tensions and trade-offs – the *hard choices* intrinsic to the world of public administration and policy making. According to one observer, the hardest part of policy analysis is 'getting organizations to act' (Wildavsky 1979, 6), because of established interests and ideas vested in organizations, and their tendency to resist change, including evaluation-induced reform, driven by a bureaucratic need for internal loyalty and external support to survive and flourish. He adds: 'If policy problems arise from tensions, policy solutions are the temporary and partial reduction of tension. Solutions are temporary in that the conditions producing the initial dislocation change in time, creating different tensions' (Wildavsky 1979, 390).

The phenomenon of 'policy capacity,' much explored of late in the policy and management literatures (Bakvis 2000; Canada 1995), is not some universal or singular activity or straightforward process animated by an ethos of rationality. Anderson (1996) and Rasmussen (1999) have outlined policy capacity in terms of the ability to do several functions: advising ministers and other politicians, thinking longer-term and focusing on strategic issues and priorities of government, dealing with issues of a horizontal or interdepartmental nature across government, and working with external groups in the relevant policy community to obtain important input on issues and feedback on programs.

This range of work, Anderson and Rasmussen both suggest, requires policy generalists and policy specialists and, we can add, policy managers (Prince 1986) at senior and operational program levels in government departments. This work also requires a *demand* for policy analysis, along with *supply* (now commonly called capacity). If analysis is not used, the position and influence of policy analysts and analytical units declines, and they are at risk of disappearing altogether (Prince and Chenier 1980). Thus, advisors continuously active in policy processes deliberately engage in shaping agendas by suggesting ideas, identifying opportunities, building support, and bargaining with interests and institutional leaders (Prince 1983; Maley 2000).

Of course, beyond departmental portfolios, variations of policy capacity are essential for prime ministers and premiers, central agencies, cabinet committees, parliamentary committees and officers as well as in tribunals, courts, think tanks, and research institutes, and civil society groups and social movement organizations. This tells us that policy capacity, writ large, is shaped and defined by a number of organizational and individual relationships inside government, across governments, and outside with societal groups, as explored in chapters 4, 5, 9 and 20. More readily, policy capacity and thus the craft of policy work is the result of the material nature of power dynamics operating on individuals, groups and organizations in specific policy sectors and time periods. Policy analysis and advice giving are an amalgam of relations of authority and influence marked by alliances and struggles, information and uncertainties, effects and counter-effects.

Viewed in this perspective, policy capacity and policy advising are negotiated practices. They also are complex and contested processes featuring numerous tensions and trade-offs. 'What every government has to undertake in its time is to seek such balance as may be possible among the complicated and diverse factors that bear upon decision-making,' notes a veteran senior public servant (Kroeger 1996, 468). In a parliamentary system of cabinet government, a fundamental task concerns managing the interplay between overall government priorities and central direction on one side, and the disparate multiplicity of departmental interests, ministerial autonomy, and ambitions on the other (Doern and Phidd 1992). In a cabinet of 30 to 40 members, there are numerous ministers with strong views about policy that 'are often diametrically opposed. A prime minister must balance the opposing views while keeping the proponents within the nest' (Axworthy 1988, 255). Another balance to be struck concerns maintaining a line, while drawing on both, between two kinds of staff and policy advice, namely, partisan personal staff and the neutral public service. As Axworthy sketches the differences: 'Partisans bring creativity; public servants provide perspective. The political arm makes things move; bureaucratic routines prevent errors' (1988, 248). Additional tensions Axworthy mentions deal with working to prevent the pressures of the urgent from overwhelming the plans of the important, and 'knowing when to proceed and when to delay, sensing when to be bold and when to be prudent' (1988, 252).

Still other trade-offs and tensions intrude on doing policy analysis and giving policy advice to governments. A study by federal officials in the mid-1990s identified some well-known and traditional strains and conflicts, including that between 'line' and 'staff' relations generally, in work cultures and relations between communication roles and policy analyst roles, between research scientists and policy advisors, between program managers and program evaluators on the value of formal evaluations, between departments with dissimilar mandates and worldviews sharing a policy area, between government officials and external groups differing over the purpose and intended outcome of consultations (Anderson 1996). In a similar manner, a study on policy capacity that focused on experienced senior public servants in the Saskatchewan government found tensions between the centre (central agencies and cabinet committees) and departments; departmental policy units 'guilty of excluding operational considerations from their deliberations'; trade-offs between community input and the need for timely government action; and frustrations in working horizontally on issues due to the existence of strong 'departmental loyalties' (Rasmussen 1996, 341 and 344).

On this last issue, I noted years ago that some policy advisory groups in the federal bureaucracy arose not simply to rationalize the government's policy process, but so that departments could better integrate their internal activities and protect their 'turf' from encroaches by central agencies and cabinet (Prince 1979, 291–2).

As a consequence, such tensions hinder departmental and government-wide policy development and program implementation, frustrate and discourage staff and publics, strain inter-organizational relations, and unfortunately also create or perpetuate stereotypes of government staff, community groups and agency types. If these tensions and challenges to 'speaking truth to power' were not enough, the context of public service policy advising has changed dramatically in the last few decades.

A Changing Context of Policy Advice in Canada

Changes in the context and content of Canadian politics and government through the 1980s and 1990s have shifted public service policy advice from speaking truth to power toward what we may describe as many actors sharing many truths. I examine each of these approaches in turn, describing them and offering some criticisms, as well as noting trends in Canada that relate to this altered context of policy advising.

Speaking Truth to Power as a Model of Policy Advising

Speaking truth to power, as already noted, is a widely held view in the literature of what policy analysis is as art and craft. This conception of policy advice highlights the relation between, and respective roles of, policy advisors and elected officials in government. In the words of Wildavsky, who popularized the phrase and the model of policy advice implicitly linked with it, 'speaking truth to power remains the ideal of analysts who hope they have the truth, but realize they have not (and, in a democracy, should not have) power' (1979, 12). So, while Wildavsky held that facts and values are inseparable in analysis and action, he did posit a separation between the knowledge of the advisor and the authority of the elected decision maker. A contrasting view, expressed by Michel Foucault among others, is that truth and power intertwine. Truth is not outside power or lacking in power itself. Policy advising lies within relations of power (Foucault 1980). We also know that the power of cabinet ministers can be fluid and changing, due to cabinet shuffles, elections, shifting government priorities, scandals, crises, and other unanticipated challenges.

At times, policy analysts, like tattlers and busybodies, speak things that are not welcome. The truth that Wildavsky foresaw is, in large part, negative knowledge; information that 'tells us what we cannot do, where we cannot go, wherein we have been wrong' (1979, 401). Axworthy makes the point as follows: 'Often the greatest service rendered to a leader is to force him to face unpalatable realities' (1988, 257). Speaking truth to power involves public servants tendering professional, non-partisan advice to a leader, minister, or government of the day, advice that may well be critical of government thinking but which, nonetheless, public servants offer in a forthright and fearless manner (Good 2003; Savoie 2003). For Wildavsky, the truth spoken to politicians stressed resource constraints, laws to follow, pitfalls to avoid, and risks to heed. Thus, the danger advisors face is carrying negative or uninspiring messages to ambitious political leaders. Yet, the truth or advice policy analysts communicate can be positive, identifying new opportunities, promising courses of action, and suggesting innovative reforms. We need, therefore, to avoid simple notions of understanding speaking truth to power as necessarily and exclusively a negative and constraining relationship.

Foreshadowing a post-modern view of policy analysis, Wildavsky did not embrace uncritically a positivist notion of the truth. For him, there was no objective, observable, and verifiable reality existing 'out there' in the economy, society, or international arena, waiting to be discovered by research done in a detached manner, completely immune from values, biases, and interests. In this model of policy advising, truth is incomplete, variable, and socially constituted. On truth as incomplete: 'In an aspiring democracy, the truth we speak is partial. There is always more than one version of the truth and we can be most certain that the latest statement isn't it' (1979, 404). On truth as variable: 'The truth that analysts claim today is not always the same truth they will claim tomorrow. There are tides in the affairs of analysts ... There are fashions too' (1979, 402). On the policy analysts' truth as socially created and authoritatively sanctioned: 'For the truth they have to tell is not necessarily in them, nor in their clients, but in ... their give and take with others whose consent they require ... over and over again' (1979, 405). When he wrote of speaking truth to power, this is the truth Wildavsky envisaged. The production of policy knowledge may be systematic and scientific, yet the message, and in the context it is conveyed, are inherently political in nature.

A notable feature of this conception of policy analysis is recognition of different truths or ways of knowing: truth in belief and morality, truth in the professional expertise of analysts, and truth as the politically negotiated consensus of what is acceptable and possible in policy terms. An alternative view on truth, again one clearly expressed by Foucault, is that truth is more established, stable, and prevailing than Wildavsky implies. While also noting the social construction of truth, Foucault stresses a structure to truth: 'Truth is a thing of this world: it is produced only by virtue of multiple forms of constraint. And it induces regular effects of power. Each society has its regime of truth, its 'general politics' of truth: that is, the types of discourse which it accepts and makes function as true' (1980, 131). For Foucault, then, policy work operates in a 'political economy of truth,' with people occupying specific positions in government and society. Indeed, some truths may only be spoken openly after a change in political regime has taken place; and even then, special procedures may need to be created to enable the voicing of past 'unspeakable truths' (Haynes 2002).

At the national level in Canada, the speaking truth to power model of policy development operated at its fullest during the 'golden age' of the civil service, from approximately the 1940s to the early 1970s (Bryden 1997; Granatstein 1982; Kent 1988; Porter 1965). Key elements of the model in action were an anonymous, neutral, and merit-based civil service as the sole or primary source for providing sound and non-partisan policy advice, in a candid and up-front manner, to senior officials, ministers, and cabinet for approval. The civil servants' advisory role was both legitimate and invaluable to governing politicians, and officials made important contributions to the policy formation of Canada's economic development, foreign affairs, and the national network of social security. This model of governance reflects closely what Stefan Dupré (1985) calls the 'departmentalized cabinet,' in which strong ministers with strong portfolio loyalty, aided by departmental officials and an underdeveloped set of central agencies, dominated policy advice and policy development at the federal level.

As Savoie (2003, 62) explains this working model: 'Ministers knew that they were in charge, and they welcomed the advice of the senior mandarins. Senior officials, meanwhile, sought to serve their ministers well and did not hesitate to be forthright in their advice, even if the advice was not always welcomed.' The truth or truths officials spoke to ministers came from their own professional expertise and career experience that included a rich organizational memory and policy history. 'Career stability meant that civil servants remember a long line of past policies and their fates. The system also allowed them to offer unwelcome advice to decision makers. Their tenure and the respect that they enjoyed permitted them to advise a minister that he or she was heading in the wrong direction. That advice was not always heeded, but it was very probably given' (Savoie 2003, 68). In sum, these were the elements constituting the 'traditional bargain' or understanding between executive politicians and career public servants on their respective roles and responsibilities in policy development.

A New Model of Policy Advising: Many Actors Sharing Many Truths

Since the 1970s, the environment of public policy making and, therefore, policy analysis and advising, have changed substantially. Many commentators (Anderson 1996; Canada 1995; Hajer 2003; Kroeger 1996; Pal 2001; Rice and Prince 2000; Savoie 2003) have detailed how and why the context and methods of governing have altered in modern democracies and welfare states. There is broad agreement that the golden age of the mandarins has passed and that events also have overtaken the historic relationship between civil servants and cabinet ministers of speaking truth to power.[1]

Linked to political decision making, policy analysis both reflects and creates different preferences and worldviews (Stone 2002) concerning claims for core ideas and interests regarding efficiency, community, personal liberty and responsibility, and social justice (Doern and Phidd 1992). As a 'truth-game,' policy advising is about persuasive presentations and explanations of what is good for an individual, group or system, as shaped through discourses and relations of power (Foucault 1997).

Significant trends pertinent to policy development can be briefly enumerated here: the further globalization of the economy and pluralization of Canadian society (Rice and Prince 2000); the growing contestation and thus politicization of various forms of expert knowledge (food safety, medical, environmental, natural sciences) in society; shifting boundaries between governments and other institutions, captured by the shift in terminology from government to governance, with associated concepts and practices of alternative service delivery, public-private partnerships, and a mix of new organizational forms; shifts in policy instruments related to the fiscal (mis)fortunes and (in)capacities of governments; the constitutional entrenchment of the *Canadian Charter of Rights and Freedoms* and attendant rights discourse expressed in an 'identity politics' articulated by social movements for women, persons with disabilities, and other disadvantaged groups; Aboriginal activism manifested in a heightened profile, land claims, and treaty negotiations; and deregulation and trade liberalization measures linked with international trade agreements.

To these, we can add other factors that are transforming the way Canadian governments develop policy and make decisions: a more aggressive and critical mass media, increased scrutiny of the public service by the auditor general and other newer parliamentary watch-dogs, access to information legislation, expanding complexity and interconnectedness of most policy issues today, growing public cynicism and loss of confidence toward politicians, bureaucrats, and even scientists in government, the rise of a policy analysis movement and industry in Canada, and political leaders themselves engaging, at times, in 'bureaucrat bashing,' and gazing beyond the career public service for policy advice (Canada 1995; Doern and Phidd 1992; Good 2003; Savoie 2003).

Developments within the federal government and bureaucracy, as well, directly contributed to undermining the traditional speaking truth to power model of policy advising. A series of resources cuts to departmental budgets and operations over many years, sometimes more than once a year and at times announced quite abruptly, led to a turbulent environment, making policy and program planning not just difficult but often seemingly pointless. Downsizing of the public service naturally led to demands by governments for advice from outside the bureaucracy. Managerial reforms encouraged the frequent shuffling of senior officials around departments and from department to central agencies or Crown corporations, all with a view to creating a cadre of generalist senior executives to manage the federal public service. Coupled with retirements and the politicization of some segments of the upper echelons of the public service with partisan staffers, these management reforms eroded the organizational memory, the policy and scientific-based expertise, and the morale of many senior officials (Splane 1987).

From the mid-1980s onwards, the federal social policy sector exhibited a style called policy change by stealth (Prince 1999, 158). Championed by Department of Finance officials, instrument preferences involved cutting social expenditures on benefits to persons and transfers to other governments, plus raising tax revenues through surcharges and limiting the indexation of tax brackets. Changes by stealth typically come through the closed process of budgets, in arcane and technical language involving amendments to obscure legislation or regulations. The policy process is largely a closed and monopolistic process. Social policy departments and Parliament play little if any meaningful role in policy reforms by stealth.

Through the 1980s and 1990s, in a climate heavily shaped by government restraint, analytical activities shifted from needs assessment, policy planning and new program design toward an increased emphasis on the analysis of ongoing operational activities and on matters related to efficiency and effectiveness. Environmental scanning activities by policy units in government also appeared to increase in response to the growing use of the media by lobby groups and by others involved in collective action, to advance and market their points of view. Alternatively, communications and public affairs units in government assumed enhanced mandates in this area. Some policy analysts in Ottawa became 'slide-deckers,' offering visual summaries of the research or advice of other people or organizations.

Another trend is that in-house research activities declined, owing to government downsizing measures and perhaps a shrinking of the credibility of this kind of analysis among the public and interest groups. As Laurent Dobuzinskis discusses in chapter 13, the federal advisory councils for economic and scientific matters disappeared in the early 1990s. Acceptance of analysis by in-house units is not automatic, particularly if the results of their analysis run counter to what individuals or groups outside of government wish to hear or believe to be true. One response to the need for high-quality, longer-term studies of importance to governments has been the establishment of university-based centres of excellence in applied, or policy-related, research (Hollander and Prince 1993, 196–97).

Given this altered state of affairs, what does it mean for public policy analysis? What, today, do public service advisors' relationships with government politicians look like? Savoie's answer to these questions is multifaceted and enlightening. First, Savoie notes: 'Politics enters the policy process much earlier than in the past and career officials now share the policy-making space with a variety of actors. Indeed, the consent, if not the direct participation, of stakeholders is now required even at the data-gathering stage' (Savoie 2003, 116). Gone with the old world of policy development work is the relative privacy and shelter of policy advisors in government departments. Second, today, 'Ministers prefer a deputy minister who has intimate knowledge of the system, can work well with the centre of government, and has the ability to get proposals through the consultative decision-making process over one with sectoral expertise or who knows intimately the department, its policies, and its history' (Savoie 2003, 254). In other terms, the old forms of knowledge and truth that officials spoke to ministers is no longer valued as highly, with other forms of wisdom or shrewdness prized in the relationship. Third, Savoie reports a decline in the willingness of officials to give, and the interest of ministers to receive, fearless and forthright policy advice. The premium today, it seems, is on avoiding errors and steering clear of blame for any possible mistakes. A hidden risk to this approach, however, is that there is an increased likelihood of 'groupthink' (Janis 1982) or excessive deference and acquiescence to leaders, with a decline in critical thought and reality checks, leading to policy fiascos. Speaking truth to power suggests challenging groupthink. Sharing truths with many actors suggests that groupthink may well become part of the policy process.[2]

Together, these changes are creating a public policy process that is more complex and fragmented, more open in some respects with external consultative exercises now almost *de rigueur*, and more competitive because of the diverse number of ideas and information, amplified by the Internet and information technologies, coming from other governments, think tanks, policy research institutes, interest groups and associations, public affairs consultants, lobbyists, and pollsters (Pal 2001). In this context, Hajer (2003, 182) points out, 'When Wildavsky coined the phrase "speaking truth to power," he knew whom to address. The power was the state and the state was therefore the addressee of policy analysis. Yet this is now less obvious. We might want to speak truth to power but whom do we speak to if political power is dispersed?' Some leading academic analysts in Canada concur with this interpretation, suggesting that the Canadian political system now appears to have 'multiple centres of influence rather than of power' (Savoie 2003, 267) and that 'government is a player and an occasional leader but more rarely the dominant actor' (Pal 2001, 325). Under our executive style of parliamentary government, while formal power remains largely concentrated, in recent decades general socio-political influence has dispersed, state-society relations have fragmented, and governments have become embedded in overlapping networks (Cairns 1986).

To this, we can add the point that *who* is doing the speaking has likewise greatly multiplied into numerous voices that may be in harmony or discord, communicating assorted truths. A noteworthy feature of contemporary Canada is the deconstruction of dominant ideas and conventional wisdoms and theories. The values and beliefs of Canadians resemble an attitudinal mosaic of diverse life priorities and choices. As it pertains to policy development, the pluralization of Canadian values and beliefs involves questioning, critically, and perhaps ultimately rejecting, taken-for-granted assumptions of such key concepts as citizenship, family, the public interest, and work. It also involves the assertion that alternative perspectives and social relationships are valid and legitimate. Today, in various policy sectors, groups consider truth as scientific rationality, as contestable and controversial knowledge. In this standpoint, claims of impartiality and universality of policies and practices are fiction. In their place is the idea of the diverse society, emphasizing the particularities of ethnicity, race, gender, culture, age, religion, sexual orientation, ability, social class, and geography (Rice and Prince 2000, 29).

In the emerging model of policy advising, senior public servants inhabit a less anonymous and not so career-oriented setting, offering advice, as one source among several others inside and outside government, to their ministers as well as to other federal departments and central agencies and perhaps to various external stakeholders. The advice senior officials give is generally palatable and responsive to their

superiors' wishes and commitments. Press clippings, focus group results, web-based chat rooms, issue management, and polling results are
as much the stuff of speaking truth to power today as are social analysis, economic forecasting, program histories, and policy research.

Concluding Reflections

For public service officials, the multiple changes over the past 25 years
in the public policy context and the policy development processes
means that these officials are sharing the advisory craft of grappling
with hard social choices with many more actors inside and outside
government.

In the new and still emerging environment in which Canadian politics and policy making take place, sharing policy advisory space also
entails sharing truths and thus sharing influence. The art and craft of
policy analysis has gone from speaking truth to the power of cabinet
ministers, toward sharing truths with multiple actors. Power was never
unidirectional or one-dimensional in government or in the policy-ad-
vising relationship. It was not solely a formal thing, such as a mandate,
that one set of actors (ministers) possessed and another set of actors
(career public servants) did not. The notion of power preferred here is
that power operates within countless sites and relations among people
and societal institutions. What I am suggesting, and others too of course
(Hajer 2003; Pal 2001; Rice and Prince 2000; Savoie 2003) is that power is
now more diffused, complex, and nuanced inside and outside the state
than a generation or more ago. Governments are not impotent, but
certainly, they need to work with networks of governance to create
new approaches and responses to the hard choices of economic, environmental, and social issues found in the new context playing out in
political communities.

If the world of public-service-based policy advice has changed and is
moving toward the second approach, this has implications for which
research paradigms students of public policy and administration should
consider using. Certainly the literature has moved some distance from
the positivist legacy of rationalist analysis to post-positivist perspectives on how we understand and research policy processes and systems
(Lindquist 1993; Radin 2000; Stone 2002). To the extent that policy
advice increasingly involves sharing and shaping truths with many
actors and groups, then social constructivist and interpretive approaches,
if taken up explicitly and thoroughly in policy studies, will yield impor-

tant insights on the nature and role of knowledge, values and voices, and relations of power.

Table 7.1 summarizes the differences between the two approaches to policy advising in and for Canadian governments examined in this chapter. The approaches are best thought of as analytical constructs rather than definitive descriptions of practice in specific organizational contexts. As abstractions of realities and projections of trends, the models overstate the elements of each approach and underestimate the blurring and blending between the approaches. Actual practices in policy analysis and advice constitute a mixture of elements outlined here and most likely other factors. These models might be helpful in identifying the combination of features in working contexts of policy advice, promoting inquiry into differences between concrete settings and the models, and interpreting and better understanding existent activities. In any event, we should not take for granted what doing policy analysis or giving policy advice to those in government means.

So what does the altered context of governing mean for policy advising? Many policy analysts still see themselves and conduct their work as researchers striving to create as objective data as possible given the obvious limitations of time, resources, information availability, and political concerns. Gathering data on public issues, client needs, and program impacts remains critical work in the craft of policy analysis. In recent decades, additional qualitative research, designed to develop accounts of issues and public needs, joins this data gathering. As well as confidants to politicians, the role of senior policy advisors encompasses that of connectors to groups, associations, and possibly coalitions in their respective policy fields.

Skills and competencies in networking, building capacity and strategic alliances, and teamwork are at a premium in the new policy world of sharing truths with multiple actors. So too is the ability to participate in and lead policy planning activities in collaborative and, at times, competitive environments, with intricate issues and divergent interests. A revived recognition of the importance of policy development work is detectable, I believe, in some quarters of government in Canada and elsewhere. In some matters, the roles policy advisors perform in the new political context are not that different. Collecting information, communicating confidential strategic counsel effectively and persuasively, managing interdepartmental relations, consulting with other orders of governments, and meeting with key program constituencies are all familiar aspects of Canadian policy making. Activities that have

Table 7.1 Two Idealized Models of Policy Advising in Canadian Government

Elements	Speaking truth to power of Ministers	Sharing truths with multiple actors of influence
Focus of policy making	Departmental hierarchy and vertical portfolios	Interdepartmental and horizontal management of issues with external networks and policy communities
Background of senior career officials	Knowledgeable executives with policy-sector expertise and history	Generalist managers with expertise in decision processes and systems
Locus of policy processes	Relatively self-contained within government, supplemented with advisory councils and Royal commissions	Open to outside groups, research institutes, think-tanks, consultants, pollsters, and virtual centres
Minister/deputy minister relations	Strong partnership in preparing proposals with ministers, trusting and taking policy advice largely from officials	Shared partnership with ministers drawing ideas from officials, aides, consultants, lobbyists, think-tanks, media
Nature of policy advice	Candid and confident advice to ministers given in a neutral and detached manner. Neutral competence	Relatively more guarded advice given to ministers by officials in a more compliant or preordained fashion. Responsive competence
Public profile of officials	Generally anonymous	More visibility to groups, parliamentarians, and media
Roles of officials in policy processes	Confidential advisors inside government and neutral observers outside government. Offering guidance to government decision makers	Active participants in policy discussions inside and outside government. Managing policy networks and perhaps building capacity of client groups

Source: Adapted from Hajer 2003; Pal 2001; Savoie 2003; Wildavsky 1979.

taken on greater importance for policy staff include managing external consultations, responding to policy announcements of the prime minister (Savoie 1999), rebuilding rapport after years of cutbacks and building the capacity of groups and associations in policy communities (Pal 2001; Rice and Prince 2000), dealing with the media and seeking consensus among different actors and perspectives on policy options and priorities (Savoie 2003).

There are some challenging constants in this new policy advisory context for practitioners and students of public policy and administration to think about. Here are a handful of ongoing issues and questions for apprentices, admirers and aficionados in policy analysis to ponder.

1 Even with greater consultations with outside groups, Savoie (2003, 271) rightly argues, in my view, that the federal government's consultative processes remain largely 'Ottawa-based and elitist,' with policy making the preserve of 'a relatively small circle' of actors proximate to the national capital region. Savoie has in mind the regions across the country, although the concern he raises also relates to other interests, such as social movements and vulnerable client groups. The issue arises: How do you create a more inclusive and participatory process, especially for groups at the margins of the political system and the economy and community? If parliamentary committees, among other bodies, become more involved in policy and take to the road, then a larger regional and societal voice in consultations can be expected. Chapters 10, 12, 14, and 20 in this volume address these matters of consultation and citizen engagement more fully.
2 While there are more policy voices, there also seems to be more concentration of advice around the prime minister and the PMO. The literature and recent experience in Canadian politics suggest that governmental power at the federal level remains concentrated in and around the Office of the Prime Minister, despite a change in leaders and recent rhetoric about addressing the democratic deficit and reforming federal mechanisms of decision making (Martin 2003; Savoie 1999; Simpson 2001). A question here is: Can Parliament's role vis-à-vis the policy process materially expand so as to enhance the accountability and legitimacy of government decisions?
3 At the same time, though, despite recent emphasis given to horizontal management of issues in Ottawa and provincial governments, the vertical perspective of departments persists as a strong factor in shaping policy development and cabinet decision making, with a horizontal approach to issues occurring only episodically, when triggered (usually) by the prime minister's intervention (Doern and Phidd 1992; Rasmussen 1999; Pal 2001; Savoie 2003).[3] Can the horizontal management of policy issues occur as general practice in government policy processes? And can we achieve horizontality

without sacrificing public accountability, ministerial leadership, or policy creativity? The search for balance between vertical or departmental (for which there is a time and place) and horizontal development will be ongoing. Openness may decrease the internal autonomy of departments but, at the same time, it also provides them with more advantage and increases their power in relation to the centre by building coalitions and mobilizing consent around issues.[4]

4 What is the skill-set and knowledge base required for the demands of relatively more open, contested, and inclusive policy development practices? Beside cabinet ministers and public bureaucrats, the participation of others raises numerous challenges as well as opportunities, to be sure, and calls for new and modified skills in doing policy analysis and giving advice. One challenge, not entirely new of course, is managing expectations in more open and candid processes of discussing and developing policies and programs.

5 'Generally speaking,' wrote the classic scholar of modern organizations, Max Weber, 'the trained permanent official is more likely to get his way in the long run than his nominal superior, the cabinet Minister, who is not a specialist' (1947, 338). For Weber, the superior influence of bureaucratic administration lay in the technical knowledge, reinforced over time by experience, of the permanent officials. In the altered context of sharing and shaping truths, how apt is Weber's analysis today for Canadian public policy and administration? If the traditional influence and power of the federal bureaucracy in policy relied on a relatively autonomous base of knowledge (Porter 1965), and that knowledge is now more contested and challenged by other sources and forms of knowing and advising, what does this mean for the place of governmental officials and agencies in the power structure of Canadian politics and governance? In short, what are the repercussions for the roles and relations of the public service, non-state bureaucracies and interests, and liberal democracy in the early stages of the twenty-first century?

Now 25 years ago, I concluded an essay on public policy analysis noting, 'Disagreements over the appropriate way to conduct a policy or program analysis and review are considerable and inevitable. Organizing and conducting policy advice in government departments is bound to be a political activity' (Prince 1979, 296). I continue to believe this and, indeed, conjecture that policy advice is even more political today than it was then, certainly more discursive, and also possibly a bit more democratic.

NOTES

I wish to thank several colleagues and friends for helpful comments and constructive suggestions on the original version of this chapter: John Chenier, Bruce Doern, David Good, M. Ramesh, and Donald Savoie.

1 It is ironic that the 'golden age' in Canadian government, when officials were said to speak truth to power, coincides with a time when we had no cabinet committees, no formally defined policy roles or units, and ministers had no independent sources of advice and little or no political staff to speak of. This time also corresponded to a period when the power of mandarins (and departments) in Ottawa was said to be at its peak. At least one reviewer for this chapter, former public servant and long-time observer of Ottawa politics and administration, John Chenier, suggests there is too much of a tendency for the decision-making process to bask in the glory of those days. In a similar fashion, John Porter (1965, 3) warned that so-called 'golden ages' are held up as models long after the historical period 'has been transformed into something else.'

2 The search nowadays for 'responsive competence' in policy advice rather than 'neutral competence' (Rourke 1992; Ponder 2000) opens the door to groupthink. Groupthink can happen when policy advisors face pressures of conformity and loyalty to current political leaders and their ideas, under circumstances of tight time constraints, partisanship, and high personal stress. In these conditions, the research and analysis phase may be hurried and shortened, doubts and other viewpoints suppressed, and perhaps most crucially, a critical analysis is not done or published on the costs and benefits of the leader's desired policy option. The fact that governments in Ottawa seem increasingly to seek out broad policy experience rather than sectoral expertise to lead both departments and policy units further opens the door to groupthink.

3 Of course, a focus by Canadian governments on horizontal policy issues, and how best to address these issues, is not new, as evident by the innovations in the 1970s with ministries of state and priority exercises and, in the 1980s and early 1990s, with super-departments such as Human Resources

Development Canada and the Department of Foreign Affairs, Industry and Trade.

4 I wish to thank John Chenier for this point and others on horizontal versus vertical policy development.

REFERENCES

Anderson, George. 1996. 'The New Focus on the Policy Capacity of the Federal Government.' *Canadian Public Administration* 39(4), 469–88.

Axworthy, Thomas S. 1988. 'Of Secretaries to Princes.' *Canadian Public Administration* 31(2), 247–64.

Bakvis, Herman, 2000. 'Country Report: Rebuilding Policy Capacity in the Era of the Fiscal Dividend: A Report from Canada.' *Governance* 13, 71–103.

Bardach, Eugene. 2000. *A Practical Guide for Policy Analysis: The Eightfold Path to More Effective Problem Solving.* New York: Chatham.

Bryden, P.E. 1997. *Planners and Politicians: Liberal Politics and Social Policy, 1957–1968.* Montreal and Kingston: McGill-Queen's University Press.

Cairns, Alan. 1986. 'The Embedded State: State-Society Relations in Canada.' In Keith Banting, ed., *State and Society*, 53–86. Toronto: University of Toronto Press.

Canada. 1995. Task Force on Strengthening the Policy Capacity of the Federal Government. *Strengthening our Policy Capacity.* Ottawa, April.

Doern, G. Bruce, and Richard W. Phidd. 1992. *Canadian Public Policy: Ideas, Structure, Process.* 2nd ed. Toronto: Nelson.

Dupré, J. Stefan. 1985. 'Reflections on the Workability of Executive Federalism.' In R. Simeon, ed., *Intergovernmental Relations*, 1–32. Toronto: University of Toronto Press.

Foucault, Michel. 1980. *Power/Knowledge.* Ed. Colin Gordon. New York: Pantheon.

– 1997. *The Politics of Truth.* Ed. S. Lotringer and L. Hochroth. Boston: MIT Press.

Good, David A. 2003. *The Politics of Public Management: The HRDC Audit of Grants and Contributions.* Toronto: University of Toronto Press.

Granatstein, Jack L. 1982. *The Ottawa Men: The Civil Service Mandarins, 1935–1957.* Toronto: Oxford University Press.

Hajer, Maarten. 2003. 'Policy Without Polity? Policy Analysis and the Institutional Void.' *Policy Sciences* 36(2), 175–95.

Haynes, Priscilla B. 2002. *Unspeakable Truths: Facing the Challenge of Truth Commissions.* London: Routledge.

Hollander, Marcus J., and Michael J. Prince. 1993. 'Analytical Units in Federal and Provincial Governments: Origins, Functions and Suggestions for Effectiveness.' *Canadian Public Administration* 36(2), 190–224.

Kent, Tom. 1988. *A Public Purpose: An Experience of Liberal Opposition and Canadian Government.* Montreal and Kingston: McGill-Queen's University Press.

Kroeger, Arthur. 1996. 'A Retrospective on Policy Development in Ottawa.' *Canadian Public Administration* 39(4), 457–68.

Lindquist, Evert A. 1993. 'Postmodern Politics and Policy Sciences.' *Optimum: The Journal of Public Sector Management* 23, 42–50.

Maley, Maria. 2000. '"Conceptualising Advisers" Policy Work: The Distinctive Policy Roles of Ministerial Advisers In the Keating Government, 1991–96.' *Australian Journal of Political Science* 35(3), 449–70.

Martin, Paul. 2003. *Making History: The Politics of Achievement.* Ottawa, 15 November.

Pal, Leslie A. 2001. *Beyond Policy Analysis: Public Issue Management in Turbulent Times.* Toronto: Nelson.

Ponder, Daniel E. 2000. *Good Advice: Information and Policy-making in the White House.* College Station, TX: Texas A&M Press.

Porter, John. 1965. *The Vertical Mosaic: An Analysis of Social Class and Power in Canada.* Toronto: University of Toronto Press.

Prince, Michael J. 1979. 'Policy Advisory Groups in Government Departments.' In G. Bruce Doern and Peter Aucoin, eds., *Public Policy in Canada.* Toronto: Macmillan.

– 1983. *Policy Advice and Organizational Survival.* Aldershot, England: Gower Press.

– 1986. 'The Management of Policy Advice and Policy Advisors in Government.' In O.P. Dwivedi, ed., *Public Policy and Administrative Studies,* vol. 3, 34–43. Guelph: University of Guelph.

– 1999. 'From Health and Welfare to Stealth and Farewell: Federal Social Policy, 1980–2000.' In Leslie A. Pal, ed., *How Ottawa Spends 1999–2000, Shape Shifting: Canadian Governance Toward the 21st Century.* Toronto: Oxford University Press.

– 2002. 'The Return of Directed Incrementalism: Innovating Social Policy the Canadian Way.' In G. Bruce Doern, ed., *How Ottawa Spends 2002–2003, The Security Aftermath and National Priorities.* Toronto: Oxford University Press.

Prince, Michael J., and John A. Chenier. 1980. 'The Rise and Fall of Policy Planning and Research Units.' *Canadian Public Administration* 22(4), 519–41.

Radin, Beryl A. 2000. *Beyond Machiavelli: Policy Analysis Comes of Age.* Washington, DC: Georgetown University Press.

Rasmussen, Ken. 1999. 'Policy Capacity in Saskatchewan: Strengthening the Equilibrium.' *Canadian Public Administration* 42(3), 331–48.

Rice, James J., and Michael J. Prince. 2000. *Changing Politics of Canadian Social Policy.* Toronto: University of Toronto Press.

Rourke, Francis. 1992. 'Responsiveness and Neutral Competence in American Bureaucracy.' *Public Administration Review* 52 (November/December), 539–46.

Russell, Sharon, and Michael J. Prince. 1992. 'Environmental Scanning for Social Services.' *Long Range Planning* 25(5), 106–13.

Savoie, Donald J. 1999. *Governing from the Centre: The Concentration of Power in Canadian Politics.* Toronto: University of Toronto Press.

– 2003. *Breaking the Bargain: Public Servants, Ministers, and Parliament.* Toronto: University of Toronto Press.

Simpson, Jeffrey. 2001. *The Friendly Dictatorship.* Toronto: McClelland and Stewart.

Splane, Richard B. 1987. 'Social Policy-Making in the Government of Canada: Further Reflections: 1975–1986.' In Shankar Yelaja, ed., *Canadian Social Policy.* Revised ed. Waterloo, ON: Wilfred Laurier University Press.

Stone, Deborah. 2002. *Policy Paradox: The Art of Political Decision Making.* Revised ed. New York: Norton.

Weber, Max. 1947. *The Theory of Social and Economic Organizations.* Trans. and ed. by A.M. Henderson and T. Parsons. New York: Free Press.

Wildavsky, Aaron. 1979. *Speaking Truth to Power: The Art and Craft of Policy Analysis.* Boston: Little, Brown.

8 In Between Trends: Developments of Public Policy Analysis and Policy Analysis Instruction in Canada, the United States, and the European Union

IRIS GEVA-MAY AND ALLAN M. MASLOVE

Introduction

This chapter seeks to place academic Canadian public policy programs in a comparative context and provide an overview that identifies the status of policy analysis/policy studies instruction in light of domestic and global developments.[1]

In this comparative examination we will primarily discuss: a) the characteristics and training needs of policy analysis by tracking the needs of the profession; b) the development of the field to date; c) orientations arising from conceptual and historical developments in Canada, the United States, and Europe, shaping particular public policy programs, curriculum orientations and practices; and d) implications of and lessons drawn from the various contexts in comparison to Canada. Throughout the paper we use the terms 'policy analysis' and 'policy studies' interchangeably because in the various traditions highlighted in this paper, programs of policy studies, rather than policy analysis, are prevalent. Policy analysis skills are promoted, albeit with various degrees of emphasis, within these programs.

The Policy Analysis Profession: Characteristics and Needs

Public policy is, as Wildavsky coined it, an 'art and craft' (1979) or, rather, both an academic and professional field. While in business, management and public administration programs, the concept of practice is tied to behaviours and attitudes, in policy analysis skill and reasoning are tied to diagnostic processes, which require both innate knowledge and practice. In other professions such as medicine, psychology, law, economics or management,[2] the concept of practical application dovetails with instructional methods within specialized programs designed to develop, enhance, and reinforce reasoning skills and embodied knowledge within the profession. As in these other diagnostic/clinical professions (Geva-May 2005), for policy analysis this means learning a wide range of theories, but mainly being able to synthesize and to apply theory in problem-solving settings, and using acquired experiential knowledge for future expert terms of reference. Furthermore, more than in any other discipline, policy analysis and decision making regarding policies take place within contexts affected by competing political and economic considerations, differing agendas, and multiple actors and stakeholders representing a variety of interests. Book-derived medical or legal knowledge is insufficient to treat patients or represent clients in court; similarly, only exposure to real policy problems can provide toolboxes for future professional points of reference for policy analysts (Geva-May 2005).

Most policy analysis programs in the United States, for instance, recognize the value of introducing learners to professional (as opposed to purely academic) reasoning, and assisting students in acquiring at least entry-level practical skills. To supplement studies of theory, students in most public policy programs analyse case studies, undertake real policy analysis projects, serve internships, and acquire supervised professional field experience. Programs sometimes require completion of a 'capstone project' as opposed to, or in addition to, the more academically based traditional 'thesis.'

Traditional modes of instruction, which see students as passive recipients of knowledge imparted by instructors, or which rely on purely theoretical academic curricula – based on the premise that this is the learners' only opportunity to be exposed to scholarly work – run contrary to current knowledge of pedagogy (Bruner 1963; Dewey 1933, 1938; Lewin 1938; Piaget 1953, 1977, 1985). Policy studies/policy analysis instruction within theoretically oriented departments of political science, for instance, usually does not provide students with sufficient exposure and opportunity to acquire practical analytical skills. 'Thinking like a policy analyst' requires the acquisition of tacit knowledge common to the members of the professional community (Polanyi 1966; Gigerenzer 1999; Reiner and Gilbert 2000; Sternberg et al. 2000; Collins 2001; Geva-May 2005), based on strategies and procedural tools influenced by the context of the problem (March and Simon 1956), or 'decision frames' leading to mastery (Tversky and Kahneman 1981). These 'toolboxes' (Gigerenzer 1999) distinguish the future skilled technician or expert from the impostor (Meltsner 1976).[3] They lead to a higher level of knowledge acquisition, which can subsequently be adapted to individual styles and a variety of future contexts (Anis, Armstrong, and Zhu 2004; Geva-May 2005).

The shared goal of policy programs in Canada, the United States, and Europe is to provide knowledge, skills and understanding of the craft of policy analysis, and facilitate expert status in the profession. Nevertheless, approaches to policy studies and policy analysis in Canada, the United States, and Europe (and within Europe) differ. The need to comprehend local and global trends affecting policy analysis as a profession is at the forefront of this study. The development of programs of policy analysis studies in Canada, the United States, and Europe is highly dependent on the regional governance context and prevailing regional analytical culture. In turn, developments in these regions relate to the historical and political events which shaped those contexts – institutional traditions inherited within national governments (Bevir and Rhodes 2003; Hajnal 2003), regulatory bodies (Vogel 1986) or public agencies (Wilson 1989; Jordan 2003. See also Peters 1990; Geva-May 2000; Hoppe 2000; Howlett and Linquist's chapter in this book).

Recruitment patterns for policy analysts prior to the emergence of separate policy analysis/studies programs and institutions saw graduates drawn from schools of law, economics, business, management, and public administration. This orientation shaped policy making as well as the characteristics of emerging policy programs (Kagan 1991, 1996; Hajnal 2003). Later in this chapter we will address the different contextual triggers that shaped the emergence of policy studies in Canada, the United States, and Europe (Western and Central/Eastern Europe).

How can knowledge and mastery of policy analysis best be acquired? Which institutions provide fluent practitioners? These questions constantly re-emerge in policy analysis and policy studies dialogues. Michael Luger (2005) recounts that scholars of public policy and public administration have frequently questioned whether member schools of the Association for Public Policy and Management (APPAM) are keeping up with changes in the profession. Don Stokes (1996) in his APPAM presidential address reflects on 'successive waves of educational innovation,' and tracks changes in curricula over five waves of instruction for public service, dating back to the post-WWII period. Don Kettl (1997) and Larry Lynn (1998, 1999), among others, write about the 'revolution' in public management and implications for curricula. Ed Lawler (1994) and Larry Walters and Ray Sudweeks (1996) shed light on changes in the theory and practice of policy analysis, with related consequences for curriculum development.

In the 1980s, APPAM leaders met in South Carolina to discuss and compare curricula (Luger 2005). A recent book by Geva-May (2005) features a number of distinguished scholars sharing their views on policy analysis instruction. European public administration and public affairs scholars met for seven consecutive years beginning in 1997 in various European cities to share similar concerns. The result of their deliberations was the foundation of the European Association for Public Administration Accreditation (EAPAA), following the model of the U.S. National Association of Schools of Public Affairs and Administration (NASPAA). The purpose of the EAPAA was to promote and coordinate public administration programs and their modes of instruction in Europe (EAPAA 2003)

The European Group of Public Affairs (EGPA) and the Canadian Association of Programs of Public Administration and Public Affairs Education and Research (CAPPA) focus primarily on promoting public administration and public affairs education and research. Neither body, however, acts as an oversight organization, in Europe or Canada respectively, to coordinate or regulate the nature and quality of public policy programs. Neither do they act as research associations of scholars devoted to policy analysis in the manner of the American Association of Public Policy Analysis and Management (APPAM). APPAM, nevertheless, is not an accreditation association. It is NASPAA in the United States, like the newly established EAPAA in Europe, which offers accreditation for public administration and public affairs. Note that these organizations do not represent public policy studies or policy analysis programs, although 'public affairs' programs are included in their mission statement. Unlike professional programs in other disciplines, which expressly prepare students for careers (operate on norms and conventions, with clear guidelines, standardized requirements and measurable competencies for licensing practitioners), policy analysis lacks such professional accreditation guidelines. This is the case at both the level of accreditation of policy analysis/policy studies instructional programs or at the level of specialized accreditation to practitioners.

Institutional Developments in Canada, the United States, and Europe

Policy Analysis in Canadian Universities

While policy analysis in Canada was influenced by developments elsewhere, especially the United States (e.g., the advent of Planning Programming Budgeting Systems), it was also strongly affected by the particular context of Canadian parliamentary government and federalism, and the highly heterogeneous nature of the country (linguistically, culturally, and economically regionalized) (Howlett and Lindquist 2005). In fact, one could speculate that despite the geopolitical proximity to the United States, this may be the reason why it took so long (a lag time of almost 40 years between U.S. and Canadian sectors) for the policy analysis field and policy studies to develop within Canadian higher education institutions. The shift towards adopting policy analytic methods in curriculum has only started to be increasingly visible in recent years mainly, for instance, with changes of perspective adopted by Carleton University in the early 2000s and Simon Fraser's distinctive Program of Public Policy in 2003 and even more recent initatives at the University of Toronto and York University.

A first major impetus for policy analysis training in Canada came in the late 1960s, when Pierre Trudeau became the prime minister and expressed dissatisfaction with the process of policy formation in Ottawa. He was determined to make policy formation in the federal government more analysis-driven, more scientific, and more rational.[4]

The demands of the federal government and, later on, of provincial and municipal governments, spurred the universities to become more involved with both policy analysis teaching and research. Trudeau's demands created a market for more analytically trained civil servants to staff the new branches of policy analysis and program evaluation that were established in virtually every government department and agency, led by the Treasury Board. Nevertheless, the earliest cohorts of staff and consultants were drawn primarily from university economics departments, and it is still the case today that economics methodology plays a major role in policy analysis (reflected in a continuing high demand for people with economics training and the strong representation of microeconomics in public policy programs). But a demand was also created for graduates who possessed a broader background than the economists typically offered (especially as many economics departments became increasingly more mathematical and theoretical). This was another key impetus for the new public policy programs and for the older, traditional public administration programs to become more policy analysis oriented.

In Canada, the training of policy analysts occurs mostly in graduate and undergraduate university programs with labels such as 'Public Policy,' 'Public Administration,' and 'Policy Studies.' In the last five years some Canadian institutions have developed programs in public policy and have added the 'label' of policy studies to their existing programs. One example is the School of Public Policy and Administration at Carleton University ('public policy' added in 2001). Simon Fraser University initiated a Public Policy Program in 2003. The Guelph-McMaster and Regina programs combine Public Administration or Management with Public Policy. Concordia includes Public Policy in its Political Science Department. The Political Science Department and the Sauder School of Business share the University of British Columbia's policy group.

Generally speaking, there are three types of programs. In the first group are those programs that are wholly or largely within departments of political science (Concordia, Manitoba/Winnipeg, Guelph/McMaster, Laval). This is the oldest model, though there are such programs in some universities that are relatively recent. In this model, public administration is regarded as one of the subfields of the discipline. The study of public administration – what governments do, and how they make and carry out their decisions – is deemed an inherent part of political science. These programs are essentially uni-disciplinary, though some, especially new or newly revised ones, draw on other fields to a limited extent. These programs are sometimes offered alongside programs in international studies or international relations, being identified, in effect, as two professionally oriented subfields of the discipline.

Such programs tend to study the institutions and processes of governing and decision making, intra- and inter-organization relations, values and ethics, the history of policy fields, and politics. Increasingly these programs have come to include analytical methods courses such as quantitative and qualitative analysis and survey techniques.

The second model is the (small) group of programs (Regina, York) that are located within schools or faculties of business. While the discipline of political science dominates the first group, it is all but absent in the second. These programs tend to reflect the perspective that management is generic, and that all organizations – public and private – undertake similar activities such as financial management, human resource management, planning, and budgeting. These programs tend to share a common core with the Master of Business Administration programs that dominate these schools in terms of enrolments and curricular design. It is usually only in the latter part of these programs that the 'public sector' is explicitly introduced through specialized and/or elective courses for students in that particular stream of management studies.

The third model, and the one that constitutes the mainstream approach, is the group of stand-alone schools of public administration or public policy (Carleton, Dalhousie, ENAP-Quebec, Moncton, Queen's, Simon Fraser, Victoria). These schools, for the most part, offer comprehensive programs. All offer degrees at the master's level and some at the doctoral level. These programs are all based on a view that public policy analysis must necessarily draw on methodologies and techniques from several of the traditional disciplines, with economics and political science being the core foundation disciplines, but with significant contributions from at least some or all of law, sociology/organization studies, accounting and finance, and quantitative analysis. Ideally these programs are *inter-disciplinary*, in that students are taught in a way that more or less simultaneously integrates the insights and techniques of the underlying disciplines. In practice, some turn out to be *multi-disciplinary*, teaching the disciplinary contributions separately and leaving it to the students to discover the integration themselves. Some allow for 'practice'-oriented activities, although exposure to real-life experiences within internships or capstones, as compared to U.S. program requirements, is rather limited.

Gow and Sutherland (2004) note that Canadian programs of public administration tend to include more on public policy than do public administration programs in the United States, and are lighter on management material than their NASPAA-accredited counterparts. We note that Canadian programs are also much more likely to include a course on the theory of public policy and/or public administration, and in recent years, similar to trends in Europe, on comparative policy studies.[5]

While some of the Canadian institutions (especially those with doctoral programs) interpret their missions, at least in part, as educating future academic researchers and teachers, it is fair to say that the schools and programs attending to policy studies view themselves primarily as professional programs, preparing the great majority of their graduates for careers in government or other organizations that participate in some fashion in the public policy arena. This orientation is perhaps best expressed by certain properties that are often (though not universally) associated with these programs.

First, these programs are likely to include a co-op or internship placement component (e.g., Carleton, Dalhousie, Queen's, Simon Fraser, Victoria), which is highly recommended or required of all students, with the exception of those who already have professional experience.

Second, many of these programs have executive programs alongside their regular master's degrees. In some cases these are executive degree programs, while in other cases they are specialized certificate or diploma programs. These programs are designed to accommodate 'mid-career' public servants or others who view the programs as vehicles to hone their policy analysis skills and, relatedly, to enhance their prospects for promotion or other employment opportunities. The executive and certificate programs, in recognition of the constraints under which their clients take these programs, are often offered in various non-standard timetables and formats (e.g., intensive weekends once per month, summer sessions, evening classes, and online teaching or distance education).

A current issue for professional training is the accreditation of schools and programs (Gow and Sutherland 2004). The public administration and public affairs schools in the United States have established the NASPAA as a national accreditation program, but exclusively policy analysis programs do not fall under NASPAA jurisdiction. In Canada the Canadian Association of Programs in Public Administration (CAPPA) is currently implementing an accreditation system, albeit a looser one than in the United States.[6]

The Canadian model does not define a standard core curriculum to which accredited institutions must adhere. Rather, each institution will be assessed against the goals and standards it sets for itself. This looser model reflects a number of Canadian particularities including language differences and the regional identifications of Canadian universities.

In addition to their teaching programs, some universities also house units that conduct policy analyses. They are often structured as research units with links to their respective academic programs in policy analysis (e.g., the Centre for Policy and Program Assessment at Carleton, the Centre of Public Policy Research at Simon Fraser, the Local Government Institute at Victoria). They undertake and publish research on a wide range of public policy issues, depending on their respective mandates, and host or participate in seminars, conferences, public consultations, and public forums. Such units function, in part, like think tanks, insofar as they undertake and publish self-initiated research, and partly as consulting firms when they undertake research on a contract basis for governments or other clients. Some are quite broad in the range of issues they investigate; others specialize in a particular policy area or sector. The activities of these units constitute another avenue of university participation in the policy analysis community, usually in the public domain. Canadian university research units also provide a laboratory for the institutions' students of policy analysis, providing them with direct participation in policy analysis activities.[7] In this way universities provide a bridge between the academic training of future analysts and the 'real-world' analysis that occurs in governments and elsewhere among policy communities.[8]

Policy Analysis in American Universities

In the United States, the development of instructional programs of public policy coincided with developments in the field, beginning with the initial definition of policy studies by Lasswell in 1951.[9] The American pragmatic tradition[10] provided a fertile soil for development of the field of policy studies and related policy analysis instruction, because it promoted the following social and democratic goals: improving efficiency in the way that resources were allocated; increasing the use of knowledge and information in the actual making of decisions; and allowing for control by top agency officials over fragmented and diffuse organizational and program units (Radin 1996). Clients provided the perspective, values, and agenda for the analytic activity, while policy analysis contributed to the improvement of effective, scientifically assessed, and transparent decision making (Dror 1971; Meltsner 1976; and Wildavsky 1979).

The first programs that addressed issues of public policy were started in departments of political science and in public administration schools by the middle of the twentieth century. They traditionally focused on training students on how to administer and implement government decisions, rather than training them to analyse policy problems, develop alternatives, and advise decision makers.

During the 1960s and 1970s in the United States, policy analysis took a major leap forward.[11] Developments throughout the 1960s promoted the creation of public affairs programs that focused on policy problems and best alternatives. These were spearheaded by economists and political scientists who worked to refine the methods used to promote optimal choices made by governments.[12] The U.S. federal government increasingly utilized these services, and the demand for experts in analysis methods increased.

As the market for trained policy analysts expanded, public policy programs proliferated. Some U.S. schools of public administration or public affairs converted into public policy programs; other public policy programs were created from the ground up. Still others kept their public administration or public affairs titles and focus, but expanded their curriculum to include public policy analysis. During the 1970s, growing interest in implementation led public management programs in business schools to develop either distinct public policy programs or public policy and policy analysis curricula for inclusion in existing programs.

The key directional shift in the field of policy studies and policy analysis took place in the United States starting in the 1980s, and accelerated throughout the 1990s. It was influenced by the widespread development of policy analysis units, both within the government and on the periphery (within think tanks, policy analysis centres, non-governmental organizations, interest groups, and so forth). The proliferated but diffused influence held by analysts led to the realization that policy analysts were no longer able to speak truth close to power (Rivlin 1984; Lynn 1989; Radin 1996). At the methodological level, they gradually realized that there were other factors beyond objective, systematic analysis – like that performed by economists, for instance – affecting recommendations (Radin 1996).

When comparing the policy analysis activity in Canadian and American universities, one is immediately struck by the differences in size and breadth between the two systems. Even accounting for population size differences, both the number of policy analysis schools and variety of specialized programs in the United States is far greater than in Canada. In addition, the American universities have addressed and resolved several issues with which Canadian institutions still grapple (particularly accreditation).

As is often the case, with a larger scale comes more specialization. As in Canada, there are also American programs grounded in political science and programs that are structured to be inter-disciplinary. There is also considerable specialization by policy field and sector. In addition to general programs in policy analysis and public administration, the American schools offer a variety of specialized programs in areas such as health policy/administration, education, urban government, and the nonprofit sector. These specialized programs, while often carrying their own distinct degree designations, are usually offered by more broadly focused public policy units and share common characteristics of a core program. The Goldman School of Public Policy at Berkeley, for instance, offers a program in housing and urban policy (one of several specializations). The Harris Graduate School of Public Policy Studies at the University of Chicago offers a specialization in environmental science and policy, among others. The Kennedy School at Harvard offers numerous specialization opportunities, including a program in technology and economic policy. Many schools, certainly the larger ones, offer degree programs at all three levels (undergraduate, master's, and doctoral) as well as a range of specialized certificate and executive programs. While one can also see evidence of this variety in Canada, even taking into account the population size difference, the United States has a much more extensive range of offerings.

American schools of public policy are often located in private universities and are thus more connected to private support and less dependent on government funding than is the case in Canada or Europe. At the same time, they appear often to be more closely linked to governments in terms of the two-way flow of expertise. It is quite common for faculty members to work for a time in government, and for people who have held senior government positions (both appointed and elected) to move to academia. Such cross-fertilization occurs in Canada as well, but to a lesser extent than in the United States. In part, this may be the consequence of the American political system, where senior bureaucrats come and go with presidents and governors. In part, it is also the result of a more open and welcoming environment in U.S. universities towards individuals who do not regard academia as their lifetime vocation.

How might this difference impact the nature of policy analysis training? One area of difference might be in the formal curricula and in styles of teaching and training. American schools tend to put somewhat more emphasis on management and analytical techniques, while Canadian programs tend to contain more theory, and are perhaps more abstract. While programs in both countries offer internship terms, these placements tend to be emphasized somewhat more in the American context. For example, New York University's Wagner School offers an imaginative capstone program in which teams of students undertake policy analysis projects for client organizations; the same is the case at the Goldman School of Public Policy. The Public Policy Program at the University of North Carolina, Chapel Hill sends students to Washington, DC, on a regular basis for internships, as do the large majority of U.S. policy studies programs.

Probably the major difference in policy analysis education between Canada and the United States is the system of accreditation in the

United States. This occurs through a voluntary association of American schools and programs called the National Association of Schools of Public Affairs and Administration (NASPAA), referred to earlier in this chapter. The NASPAA, which welcomes memberships from institutions (whether accredited or not), also represents a large majority of the U.S. institutions that offer public affairs, administration, and policy programs. It accepts affiliate memberships from non-American universities as well. Program accreditation standards and procedures were developed initially for public affairs and public administration programs. They do not particularly focus on policy analysis, but were subsequently broadened to include public policy programs as well.

The NASPAA accreditation process (see www.naspaa.org), which dates from the mid-1970s, has settled debates in the United States that are still ongoing in Canada. European programs appear to fall somewhere between Canada and the United States, but are moving towards an accreditation system at least partly patterned on NASPAA (see section on 'Policy Analysis in European Universities' below). There are benefits flowing from a formal accreditation process: appearance to the external world as a 'profession' that, like most professions, establishes standards for training and admission. For an individual member institution, the system offers recognition and a seal of approval; in the first instance, these benefit the graduates of the program, but ultimately serve to enhance the reputation of the institution and its faculty. A potential disadvantage is diminished institutional autonomy and potential infringement of the right of each university to determine what its faculty collectively decides is an appropriate curriculum and standard of performance. The latter argument is predominantly heard when the issue of accreditation for programs of policy analysis is raised in the United States. We note that several of the leading U.S. public policy schools have not sought NASPAA accreditation (e.g., the Harris School at the University of Chicago, and Woodrow Wilson at Princeton University).

Many American schools opted for the enhanced professionalism associated with program accreditation, though the regime employed does not prevent a school from designing a diverse set of offerings. Master's programs, which are seen as the 'professional degree,' were accredited against a set of standards that largely focused on defining a core. Guidelines were also developed for undergraduate programs, but doctoral programs – where the arguments for academic independence and unconstrained inquiry are strongest – have been left unregulated.

The NASPAA move to accreditation was influenced by the much larger community of business schools and their system of accreditation for Master of Business Administration (MBA) programs. On the one hand, the NASPAA initiative confronted a movement by the business schools to extend their reach to the public affairs and public administration programs. As was noted with respect to the Canadian scene, there is a view that 'management is management,' that is, the skills, techniques, issues and sensitivities are essentially the same across the two broad sectors. A separate and independent accreditation system was, in part, intended to ensure that a distinction between these two sectors was maintained. At the same time, there was a desire to gain a professional status similar to that afforded the MBA degree; it was at least a tacit goal to create a public perception of 'professional training' comparable to that of the MBA for the Master of Policy Analysis (MPA) and similar designations.

Finally, also consistent with the move towards professional education, the NASPAA engages in the range of other activities one would expect in a professional association. For example, it offers an annual conference and publishes the *Journal of Public Affairs Education* (J-PAE). It also includes an active international program that helps to 'export' the American model of public affairs/policy analysis education to other countries.

In general, American universities actively engage in *doing* as well as *teaching* policy analysis through research centres attached to their policy analysis schools. Virtually every U.S. program of policy analysis has a research centre attached to it and, in most cases, there are several. These centres cover a wide range of specialties, focusing on federal, state, and local government in one dimension, and on an array of policy fields (defence and national security, health, education, government/business relations, environment, poverty, and others). At least in some cases, these institutes have a higher public profile than their Canadian counterparts, and actively participate in American public policy debates through their publications, conferences, media contributions, and so forth. They are comparable to the university-based centres in Canada in their contribution to policy analysis and in providing policy analysis laboratories for students in training. Nevertheless, U.S. policy analysis research centres are significantly more widespread at the federal, state, and NGO level than is the case in Canada. To enumerate only a few of the many such organizations, which also serve as internship venues, we could mention the Urban Institute, Mathematica, the Brookings Institute, the RAND Corporation, and the American Enterprise Institute.

Policy Analysis in European Universities

The field of policy analysis in Europe (and elsewhere) has been heavily influenced by developments in the United States. Indeed, when we compare the development of the field of policy studies and policy analysis in various countries, we detect attempts to adopt 'normative' policy analysis as developed in the United States, or to use normative American policy analysis methods as benchmarks for systematic policy analysis. The increased adoption of this systematic approach to policy making in Europe is driven by a move to accountability, transparency, proof of efficiency, harmonization, and corruption deterrence. In the last decade, systematic approaches to policy analysis studies have been embraced even more aggressively in Central and Eastern European countries than in Western Europe. So have discussions about accreditation in the public policy profession.[13] In the European context, Hoppe points to the increasing belief in the importance of acquiring maximum rational judgment and of producing viable policy recommendations (1999, 201). But in the same breath he also points to studies showing great pluralism in the way policy analytical aspects are handled among the EU states (see also Beck 1992; Van Gunstreren 1998; Hoppe 1999; Hoppe and Grin 2000). He advises that the challenge in the EU in this regard is to 'cope intelligently and creatively with pluralism and diversity' (2002, 235).

With the unification of Europe, we note that the main challenge has been to move from largely diverse, culturally driven analytic traditions to a more uniform, common method of policy analytic work. Since the mid-1990s, this new vision has brought significant changes to the way policy analysis infiltrates European bureaucracy. As a result, similar to developments that took place in the 1980s in the United States, the demand for public administration and public policy training programs with common core curricula in policy studies and policy analysis has been steadily increasing.[14] A comparison between the American and the EU policy venues and modes of instruction is rather striking. Indeed, many of the policy-oriented courses in the European programs are comparative in nature, especially among the Erasmus intra-university coordinated programs) (see the EAPAA at www.eapaa.org.), but most focus on comparisons *between* countries *within* fields of public policy.

Most of the programs do not overtly train students in applied public policy analysis practice, and internships are less widespread than in the United States. In contrast to U.S. standard practice in policy studies, which promotes capstone projects, internships, and reflective thinking courses (de Leon 2005; Smith 2005), European practice features final dissertations based on social science inquiry methods applied to public administration or public policy, and does not necessarily feature internships (as defined, for instance, by the EAPAA). Policy analysis seems to feature more prominently in programs offered in the new Central and Eastern European programs of public administration (see the NISPAcee website at www.nispa.sk; Hanjal 2003).

It is difficult to highlight a unified 'European approach' to policy analysis, and therefore we will note some variations between EU countries. Notably, only a handful of European institutions offer explicit policy analysis or policy studies programs, although a current shift towards the establishment of schools of public policy can be observed in the UK and Germany. Similar to the developments of the policy analysis field in the United States and the prominent models of instruction during the 1970s and 1980s, most public policy instruction in Europe is undertaken in schools of public administration, business, economics, or political science. Within these programs we note social science-oriented curricula such as welfare economics, public choice, social structure, political/legal philosophy, systematic programming, and comparative European policies.

Our study shows that the main venues for instruction of policy studies and policy analysis in various European countries fall into four categories: 1) public management departments within business schools, 2) schools of economics, 3) departments of political science and 4) schools of public administration. This is consistent with Hajnal's (2003) study, although his categories and sample countries are somewhat different.

We found policy studies curricula offered (1) in public management departments within business schools, among others, in the UK universities of Aston, Glasgow, Sussex, and Manchester, and at Bocconi University Center for Applied Social Studies of Management, Italy; (2) in schools of economics: for instance at the Erasmus University, Rotterdam, with its School of Economics and Management; and at the University of Minho, Portugal, within the School of Economics; (3) in departments of political science (London School of Economics, UK, and in six institutes of political sciences in France and political science departments in Switzerland; and (4) in schools of public administration: ENA, Ecole Nationale d'Administration, France; the Department of Public Administration at the University of Leiden, Belgium, and eight Erasmus universities throughout Europe (EMPA).

Hajnal's (2003) comprehensive statistical comparative study of public administration education programs identifies three orientation clusters of reference: *legal*, including Greece, Hungary, Italy, Moldova, Poland, Portugal, Romania, and Yugoslavia; *public management*, including Belgium, France, Spain, and Sweden; and *corporate*, comprised of schools in Armenia, Bulgaria, Czech Republic, Denmark, Estonia, Ireland, Latvia, Lithuania, the Netherlands, Slovakia, and Ukraine. [15]

Like those in the United States, and unlike those in Canada, policy-oriented programs in Europe offer a wide range of policy specializations. For instance, the London School of Economics' Department of Social Policy offers 18 different specialties, ranging from criminal justice policy, gender and social policy, health and international health policy, social policy, social policy and planning in developing countries, to youth policy and education policy. Many institutions offer policy studies with an orientation towards science and technology: the University of Namur, Belgium; Maastricht, the Netherlands; East London; Louis Pasteur, Strasbourg, France; Universidad del Pais Vasco/Euskal Herrico Unibersitatea, Bilbao, Spain; University of Madrid; University of Lisbon; and the University of Oslo. In France, policy studies are also often offered within faculties of law.

An additional orientation in some European institutions is towards urban planning. We note that the Ecole Polytechnique Fédérale de Lausanne in Switzerland, Lund University in Sweden, and the Erasmus University in Rotterdam, the Netherlands, all offer a joint program with the Institute of Housing and Urban Development (IHS) in Rotterdam.

In most EU institutions policy analysis is not offered as a particular core course, but rather as 'policy studies' with a strong penchant towards European governance, organization, management, and administration. Recently, the EMPA,[16] which is part of an intra-university joint enterprise headed by the Katholieke Universiteit Leuven, Belgium, includes a series of core courses in comparative European policy studies.[17] A common core degree program, Master of European Politics and Policies, was initiated by Twente University and the EGPA (European Group of Public Affairs) and involves several EU institutions that offer policy-oriented courses dealing with decision making in Europe; comparative federalism; public policy and public management; comparative public administration; and aspects of European integration. The University of Nottingham offers a public policy program, and the National University of Ireland offers policy analysis in the context of European integration. The only school of public policy in Switzerland is the IDHEAP, the Swiss Graduate School of Public Administration, in Lausanne. It offers explicit policy analysis courses. The University of Oslo's Master's Program in European Social Policy Analysis has an overt orientation towards policy analysis as well. Several German universities offer clearly stated policy certificates: the Erfurt School of Public Policy has a Master's in Public Policy; the University of Potsdam has a Master's of Global Public Policy (Faculty of Economics and Social Sciences); University of Konstanz has Public Policy and Management, and Public Policy and Evaluation (Department of Politics and Management); and the Austrian Institute for International Affairs (OIIP) has a Master's in Public Policy, Public Administration and International Development. Among the more interesting developments in Germany is the privately funded school (the Hertie School of Governance) that is aggressively recruiting and planning curricula to start public policy programs within a year.

Central and Eastern Europe offer a particularly interesting intellectual arena for policy analysis because of the challenge presented in the last decade to transform perceived obsolete government, public administration, and policy-making practices, and to fill in a perceived void in systematic, analytical policy development. As in Western Europe, the challenge was intensified by the fact that Eastern Europe includes different regional histories and variations of organizational autonomy. Nevertheless, unlike Western Europe, most of the countries lacked a critical mass of experts in public policy administration and management. This fuelled the need for a new orientation, programs, curricula in teaching and training public administration, and for recruiting. For instance, Budapest University of Economic Sciences (formerly Karl Marx University) initiated a Centre for Public Affairs Studies in 1991, and finally merged with the College of Public Administration. Now called Budapest University of Economic Sciences and Public Administration, it offers public affairs degrees. The National Academy of Public Administration in Kyiv, Ukraine, is sponsored by the president of the Ukraine, and is the first Eastern European institute to be accredited by the EAPAA. The Central European University (CEU) recently initiated a public policy postgraduate degree. George Soros' Open Society Institute has been instrumental in providing both financial and intellectual support to CEU and for the diffusion of policy studies in the post-communist countries (Straussman 2005).

Sponsorship and technical assistance also influences the academic and professional orientation taken by the various schools in Central and Eastern Europe. According to Hajnal (2003), the perspective of the United States and the Scandinavian countries is dominant because they are key advisors and donors to schools of public administration and public policy in the region. Further, he asserts that countries that already had sovereign statehood prior to their respective transition, belong to the legal orientation cluster, while countries that gained independence only through the transition process have a business/corporate orientation (Hajnal 2003, 252).

Inspired mainly by the APPAM and the NASPAA, several Western, Central, and Eastern European associations are actively coordinating and promoting public administration, policy studies, and policy analysis in the EU and soon-to-be member states. The EAPAA and the NISPAcee deserve special attention. Akin to its American counterpart, the APPAM, the EGPA, which is the professional association (group) of public administration, does not accredit programs. Inspired by the NASPAA, the EAPAA is, among others, trying to organize Europe-wide accreditation.[18] While some European programs have been nationally accredited in the past by national standards (for instance in Germany and the Netherlands), until recently there have not been common standards for accreditation of schools in Europe. Common EU accreditation is a rather new but promising concept. The first EAPAA-accredited program was the Erasmus Public Administration Program in the Netherlands (previously already accredited by NASPAA), followed by others. In all cases, the European accreditation recognizes that programs have different missions and approaches, and that they stem from different educational systems. A balance is expected between each institution's unique mission and substantial conformance with commonly agreed-upon standards. This will be a critical consideration if any form of accreditation is considered for Canada.

In Eastern Europe, the NISPAcee, the Network of Institutes and Schools of Public Administration in Central and East Europe, is an organization of institutes and universities whose main role is to promote education in public affairs through the exchange of ideas, skills, and relevant information among institutions. It advocates raising the quality of public administration and developing the civil service in the region. It promotes faculty training, curricula development, development of graduate programs, conferences, and research in order to advance and spread the practices 'of good professional public management, public policy and governance' (see www.nispa.sk, 10). The NISPAcee also offers consultancy and is a nexus between Western European and U.S. consultants and the CEE countries.

Policy analysis is practised in Western Europe through a myriad of think tanks and research-oriented centres and institutes. The UK is home to a particularly large number. Listing them is not the purpose of this paper, but it is important to observe that they all contribute to the comparative policy database within the EU, mainly in fields such as economics, migration, welfare, and security. Some of the think tanks are funded and supported by governments fostering inter-nations collaboration within the EU.[19] Others are funded by parties or by NGOs.[20]

Conclusions: Canada in a Comparative Context

The central aim of this paper has been to identify the state of Canadian public policy analysis and public policy programs, and to place Canadian public policy programs in a comparative holistic perspective. To achieve this perspective, we carried out a comparative study of developments in the field of policy studies and policy analysis in the United States, Western and Eastern Europe, and Canada. We hope that the findings presented may help provide an understanding of the needs of the public policy field in Canada, and assist higher education institutional planners in preparing students for their immersion in the policy analysis profession.

The development of the field of policy analysis coincided with the emergence of performance-oriented efficient governments, faith in rational decision making, objectivity, and systematic policy analysis and with 'speaking truth to power' – the understanding that policy analysts can affect policy making (Radin 1996, 2000). Initially, the notion of policy analysis was that it was 'craft driven,' stemming from both positivist social science and normative economic models, with the economic models providing the clearest and most powerful basis for improvement and change orientation (Aaron 1989, Radin 1996).[21]

Significant increased demand for policy analysis experts due to developments in Canada and Europe has been the driver for public administration, political science, and business schools to change their orientation and, increasingly, to include public policy studies and policy analysis in their curriculum offerings. As previously noted, some have created, or are in the process of creating, discrete public policy programs. Nevertheless, including policy studies in business schools is still a trend in the UK today.

In Canada and Europe (mainly Germany and the UK), instructional programs are slowly moving away from affiliations with political science and public administration departments, and institutions are establishing discrete public policy programs.[22] In Canada, the shift towards adopting policy analytic methods in curriculum is increasingly visible in recent years. Canada's geopolitical proximity to the United States makes this development understandable. The Commonwealth/Westminster administrative tradition and its implications for policy analysis as a Canadian profession seem to place developments in Canada somewhere between the U.S. and the European approaches to policy studies and policy analysis instruction. This is particularly true in the case of the 'practicum,' which is a key requirement in programs of policy analysis in the United States, but still thesis-oriented in Europe, and the initiation of positions and courses in comparative policy studies.

We have noticed that a key trend across policy analysis programs in all these regions is the movement towards a more professional orientation and a determination to be perceived as more professional. There are differences in the expression of this increased professionalism in the three study regions, reflecting differences in both the academic environments and in governance traditions and histories.

Clearly, there is a longer history of formal public policy studies, public affairs, and policy analysis in the United States. Reflecting the American pragmatic tradition of systematic policy making, efficiency, and effectiveness, American schools have developed a common core policy analysis methodology, and the United States has produced a large volume of public policy analysis tools. Thus, prevalent policy analysis materials utilized internationally are influenced by U.S. methodology and materials. The export of U.S. influence is also due, in part, to the large number of consultants and advisors from American institutions of public policy, who promote and influence the profession worldwide, but primarily in Central and Eastern Europe and Southeast Asia.

The unification of Europe and the need for common policy analytical tools has led to the cognizant adoption of policy studies and policy analysis as systematic decision-making tools. In most cases this has translated into comparative European policy studies in schools of public administration or political science. With the exception of the UK and Germany, there are very few schools that actually offer policy analysis courses per se. Nevertheless, policy analysis is increasingly taught in Central and Eastern Europe, with the aggressive establishment of schools of public administration and public policy in response to the void created after the fall of the communist bureaucracies. In both Europe and Canada, public policy is usually offered in faculties other than public policy or public affairs (for example, within departments or schools of political science, economics, management, business, administration, law, or urban studies).

Since its beginnings in the late 1960s, with Prime Minister Trudeau's discontent regarding the mechanisms of federal decision making, the shift towards a more comprehensive approach to policy analysis as a profession has been relatively slow in Canada. Global changes in orientation towards a more systematic approach to policy making, as increasingly adopted throughout the EU and Eastern European countries, are gradually infiltrating Canada. The primary question we should pose at this juncture is: What are the most suitable Canadian policy analysis instruction venues and curricula, given the country's unique national characteristics and its role on the international stage? A first major attempt at answering this question was made by Gow and Sutherland (2004) in their study sponsored by the CAPPA.

The most striking manifestation of this movement toward a more systematic approach within training institutions is the practice of accreditation of programs, albeit under the 'public administration' umbrella of the NASPAA and the EAPAA. The EU and Canada have been influenced by the focused orientation towards policy studies promoted in the United States (for instance, by the Kennedy School or UC Berkeley's Goldman School of Public Policy), and by developments outside the academic world. In the EU and Canada, the legal, political, and social context has been as influential as the export of ideas from the U.S. experience. Note, however, that in Europe the move to accreditation seems to be following the American example fairly closely, with the EAPAA pursuing a similar accreditation system to the NASPAA, and with the Eastern and Central European countries receiving counsel or sponsorship from U.S. universities. In this regard Canada stands quite clearly apart from the other two regions. While the desire for professional acceptance and recognition certainly exists in Canada, thus far, tension exists between opposing forces seeking to preserve academic autonomy and regional identities. This tension has limited the 'template' that schools are willing to utilize in a formal, national accreditation regime.

Accreditation is seen to advance the goal of being perceived as professional, especially among the 'clients' of the programs – governments, non-academic think tanks, interest groups, and, ultimately, prospective faculty and students. The development of think tanks *within* universities also contributes to this goal. The output of studies and advice that emerges from these institutes helps to create a perception of schools that are engaged and relevant, offering contributions that advance the policy process. Again, while we recognize that these developments proceed in different ways and at different paces in the three study regions, the broad trends are consistent across all three.

We note that, unlike in the fields of law, medicine, or psychology, the existent accreditation processes for policy analysis are limited to the programs that choose to be included in the accreditation process of the NASPAA or the EAPAA. There are no licensing requirements for practitioners of public administration or policy analysis. While this is not an issue for the schools per se, or for the training of policy analysts, it remains an important distinction between policy analysis and other professions.

Common trends notwithstanding, ultimately, policy analysis is craft and art rather than a precise science. It is characterized by scholarly and theoretical grounding and offers commonly accepted methodologies, but it is heavily influenced by many political realities inherent in policy formation. These political practicalities, along with different traditions and approaches to governance – *within* each of the three regions, as well as *across* them – imply that the differences we observe between programs that produce policy analysts are firmly rooted in place, and are contextually necessary.

This underscores the relevance of behaviours and attitudes as central to effective professional practice, and supports the view that early, classical policy analysis, featuring scientific reasoning and systematic problem solving, has to be adapted to social and political realities. In Canada, such influencing factors include the Westminster parliamentary governance model, federalism, and a highly diverse population, all of which are reflected in the evolution of Canadian policy analysis studies.

Comparing developments in Canada, the United States, and the EU allows us to locate Canada on the map of recent shifts of perspective in public policy analysis and analytic policy instruction. Moreover, the main benefit of this study is that it has raised a number of questions directly pertaining to Canada: Given, for instance, the comparative adaptation felt to be needed in Europe, what should be the content orientation of programs of public policy specific to Canada? What should be the best institutional arrangements providing policy analysis practice? Because of their major importance for the field of policy analysis and for the nature of Canadian policy making, these and other related questions should be brought forward on the research agenda.

NOTES

1 For a good definition and comparison of the two terms see Howlett and Ramesh (2003). According to them, policy studies are conducted mainly by academics, relate to 'meta-policy' or the overall nature of the activities of the state, and are generally concerned with understanding the development, logic, and implications of overall state policy processes and the models used by investigators to analyse those processes. In comparison, policy analysis refers to applied social and scientific research pursued by government officials and non-governmental organizations, and usually directed at designing, implementing, and evaluating existing policies, programs, and other specific courses of action adopted or contemplated by states. A third discipline, public administration, is regarded as more management-oriented, having to do with the administration of public programs in accordance with given legal and financial norms and established management principles. (See also Weimer and Vining 1999, chapter 2, figure 1, comparing the fields of policy analysis, policy studies, and public administration.)

2 For detailed discussions on policy analysis, public management, and other fields as clinical professions requiring awareness of reasoning processes acquired through practice, see I. Geva-May, chapter 1, in *Thinking Like a Policy Analyst*, 2005.

3 Meltsner's work describes four types of policy analysts and their characteristics.

4 Brooks' chapter in this volume provides a historical overview of the policy analysis profession in Canada, which he dates from the early years of the previous century. Brooks also notes the beginning of the Trudeau years as one of the watersheds in this history. Similarly, McArthur's contribution in this volume draws attention to the Trudeau period.

5 We note, for instance, the new Canada Research Chair in Comparative Public Policy at Concordia University, Montreal (2003), and a new position at the University of Toronto in 2005.

6 It is important to note that, at this stage, the CAPPA is a much looser and less established body (for example, the CAPPA has no secretariat) than its American counterpart.

7 As do a number of policy research centres, such as the C.D. Howe Institute, the Institute for Research on Public Policy, the Fraser Institute, the Canadian Centre for Policy Alternatives, and the Caledon Institute.

8 The chapters in this volume by Abelson and Dobuzinskis provide a wider perspective on the work of think tanks and research centres and their contribution to policy analysis in Canada.

9 Studies by Gow and Sutherland (2004) in Canada, and Cleary (1990), Henry (1995), and Breaux et al. (2003) in the United States, present an in-depth account of the development of public policy. DeLeon's stages (1989) and, a decade later, Beryl Radin's presidential address (1996) and her *Beyond Machiavelli* (2000) provide a comprehensive account of shifts in the development of the field of policy studies and policy analysis. So does the more finessed account of policy analysis frameworks by Mayer, Van Daalen, and Bots (2004).

10 This tradition was defined by John Dewey and presented a belief in objectivity and the scientific study of social problems.

11 The period was marked by wartime policy issues, large-scale social and welfare initiatives, national defence concerns, new economic and budget planning processes, and a reliance on the 'scientific management'-style of thinking prevalent in the mid-twentieth century.

12 An important stepping-stone was the initiation of the Planning Programming Budgeting System (PPBS) in the United States and similar developments in Canada and other countries (Heineman et al. 1990; Garson 1986; Lind-bloom 1958; Dobuzinskis 1977; Wildavsky 1979; Starling 1979; Radin 2000; Howlett and Lindquist 2006; Mintrom 2003).

13 There is no major comparative study of programs of public policy in Europe, although the European Public Administration Network (EPAN) and the Network of Institutes and Schools of Public Administration in Central and Eastern Europe (NISPAcee) have been producing valuable information. At the 2003 Swiss Political Science annual conference, the working group on public policy chose the topic of comparing the state of the art in public policy analysis across Switzerland, Germany, and France. Hajnal (2003) has published an important statistical analysis of programs in Western and Eastern Europe. Additional data has been collected from the websites of various schools and programs in the EU. We thank Geert Bouchaert, Bruno Dente, Stephen Osborne, Salvador Parrado Diez, Christine Rothmayr, Monika Steffen, Colin Talbot, Frans van Nispen, Jann Werner, and others for their invaluable comments and explanations.

14 Historical and political factors have increasingly impacted the development of the public policy and policy analysis field in Europe in the last
decade. The challenge has been to promote harmonization and unification
within the EU. This has brought about the need for a common denominator in policy making. In recent years the traditional schools of political
science, public management and administration have gradually started to
provide programs in mainly comparative policy studies, policy analysis,
or common core curricula in public administration and public policy.

15 It should be noted that for statistical significance reasons key countries
such as the UK and Germany have not been included in this study. A
comprehensive discussion regarding developments in Central and Eastern
European countries is provided separately in this section.

16 The EMPA (European Masters in Public Administration) is a consortium
consisting of eight Erasmus universities.

17 Including Leiden University, Erasmus University Rotterdam (the Netherlands), Hochschule für Verwaltungswissenschaften (Speyer, Germany),
and the University of Economic Sciences (Budapest, Hungary).

18 The EAPAA is viewed as the new European consortium for public administration accreditation and is presently based at the University of Leuven,
Belgium. Its aim is to contribute to quality improvement and assurance of
academic excellence in public administration programs throughout the
Council of Europe states. The institutions already accredited include the
School of Public Administration (NSOB) in The Hague; Erasmus University, Rotterdam; Goteborg University, Goteborg; the Kyiv National Academy of Public Administration; the Business School at Aston; and the
School of Public Administration, Erasmus, Rotterdam, Warwick and
Copenhagen. To offer another common denominator, the language of
accreditation is English.

19 The following are only some of the many think tanks and research centres
in the EU countries and they were chosen to reflect intra-EU interests and
concerns. Country-specific centres can be found in almost every European
country and seem to be part of a long-established tradition. These include
the Centre for the Study of Public Policy, at the University of Strathclyde,
Glasgow, Scotland; and the Centre for Economic Policy Research, based at
the University of Essex. The European Policy Centre (EPC) is an example
of such an independent not-for-profit think tank. Its *Journal of European
Public Affairs* promotes debates on European integration. The Institute for
European Studies based in Brussels takes part in many research programs
funded by the European Union, international organizations, and regional
Belgian authorities. They publish the journal of *European Integration* and a

series, *Études europeennes*. The Franco-Austrian Centre for Economic Convergence (CFA) is another example of an intergovernmental organization created in 1978 by Jacques Chirac and Chancellor Bruno Kreisky and fin-anced by the European Commission. The Centre for International Studies and Research (CRI) has developed policy partnerships. The European Research Centre of Migration and Ethnic Relation, University of Utrecht; the Geneva Centre for Security Policy (GCSP), an international foundation under the framework of Swiss participation in the Partnership for Peace (1995); the Stockholm International Research Institute, established in 1996, financed by the Swedish government and providing support for studies on arms control, disarmament, conflict management, security building, etc., have also done so.

20 For instance, in the UK, the Centre of Policy Studies, founded by Margaret Thatcher and Keith Joseph in 1974; and, on the other hand, the IPPR (Institute for Public Policy Research in London), which is described as 'left to centre society, an independent charity based on donations.'

21 Policy analysts were typically short-term experts contracted from universities or research centres, usually with a background of expertise in economics or operations research. This remains the case today in many European countries.

22 In Europe, for instance, public policy is part of public management programs in business schools, political science departments, and public administration schools, with only a relative few providing core courses in policy analysis. The United States, on the other hand, is swinging slightly toward re-examination of a more holistic approach, which recognizes the symbiosis between the fields of management, public administration and policy analysis (see the mission statement of the APPAM research conference, October 2005). See Howlett and Ramesh (2003) for insightful definitions distinguishing between public management, public administration and public policy.

REFERENCES

Aaron, A.J. 1989. *Politics and the Professors: The Great Society in Perspective.* Washington, DC: The Brookings Institution.

Anis, M., S. Armstrong, and Z. Zhu. 2004. 'The Influence of Learning Styles on Knowledge Acquisition in Public Sector Management.' *Educational Psychology* 24(4), 549–71.

Beck, Ulrich. 1992. *Risk Society.* London: Sage.

Bevir, M., and R.A.W. Rhodes. 2001. 'Decentering Tradition: Interpreting British Government.' *Administration and Society* 33(2), 107–32.

Bevir, M., R.A.W. Rhodes, and P. Weller. 2003. 'Traditions of Governance: Interpreting the Changing Role of the Public Sector.' *Public Administration* 81(1), 1–17.

Bobrow, D.B., and J.S. Dryzek. 1989. *Policy Analysis by Design.* Pittsburgh, PA: Pittsburgh University Press.

Breaux, D.A., E.J. Clynch, and J.C. Morris. 2003. 'The Core Curriculum Content of NASPAA-Accredited Programs: Alike or Different?' *Journal of Public Affairs Education* 9(4), 260.

Bruner, J.S. 1963. *The Process of Education.* New York: Vintage Books.

Cleary, R.E. 1990. 'What do Public Administration Masters Programs Look Like? Do They do What is Needed?' *Public Administration Review* 50(6), 663–73.

Collins, H. 2001. 'Tacit Knowledge, Trust, and the Q of Sapphire.' *Social Studies of Science* 31, 71–85.

DeLeon, P. 1989. 'The Stages Approach to the Policy Process. What Has It Done? Where Is It Going?' In S. Coda, ed., *The New State,* 19–31. London: Lynn Rainer Pal.

DeLeon, P., and Spiros Protopsaltis. 2005. 'Preparing for the Craft of Policy Analysis: The Capstone Experience.' In I. Geva-May, ed., *Thinking Like a Policy Analyst: Policy Analysis as a Clinical Profession,* 171–186. New York: Palgrave Macmillan.

Dewey, J. 1933. *How We Think: A Restatement of the Relationship of Reflective Thinking to Educative Process.* Boston: Heath.

– 1938. *Logic and the Theory of Inquiry.* New York: Holt, Rinehart & Winston.

Dobuzinskis, L. 1977. 'Rational Government: Policy, Politics and Political Science.' In T.A. Hockin, ed., *Apex of Power: The Prime Minister and Political Leadership in Canada.* 2nd ed. Scarborough, ON: Prentice-Hall.

Dobuzinskis, L., M. Howlett, and D. Laycock, eds. 1996. *Policy Studies in Canada: The State of the Art.* Toronto: University of Toronto Press.

Dror, Y. 1971. *Designs of Policy Sciences.* New York: Elsevier.

EAPAA Accreditation Criteria. June 2003, p. 2. Leuven: European Association for Public Administration Accreditation (http://www.eapaa.org/eapaa/).

Garson, D. 1986. 'From Policy Science to Policy Analysis: A Quarter Century of Progress.' In William N. Dunn, ed., *Policy Analysis: Perspectives, Concepts, and Methods,* 3–22. Greenwich, CT: JAI Press.

Geva-May, I. 2002. 'Cultural Theory: The Neglected Variable in the Craft of Policy Analysis.' In Robert Hoppe, ed., *Journal of Comparative Policy Analysis, Special Issue: Policy and Culture* 4(3), 243–65.

– ed. 2005. *Thinking Like a Policy Analyst: Policy Analysis as a Clinical Profession.* New York: Palgrave Macmillan.

Geva-May, I., with A. Wildavsky. 1997. *An Operational Approach to Policy Analysis: The Craft. Prescriptions for Better Analysis.* Boston: Kluwer.

Gigerenzer, G. 1999. 'The Adaptive Toolbox.' In G. Gigerenzer and R. Selten, eds., *Bounded Rationality: The Adaptive Toolbox.* Cambridge, MA: MIT Press.

Gow, J.I., and S.L. Sutherland. 2004. *Comparison of Canadian Masters Programs in Public Administration, Public Management and Public Policy.* Toronto: Canadian Association of Schools of Public Policy and Administration.

Hajnal, G. 2003. 'Diversity and Convergence: A Quantitative Analysis of European Public Administration Education Programs.' *Journal of Public Affairs Education* 9(4), 245–58.

Heineman, R.A., et al. 1990. *The World of the Policy Analyst: Rationality, Values and Politics.* Chatham, NJ: Chatham House.

Henry, L.L. 1995. 'Early NASPAA History.' Available at the NASPAA website, at http://naspaa.org/about_naspaa/about/history.asp.

Hood, C. 1998. *The Art of the State.* Oxford: Oxford University Press.

Hoppe, R. 1999. 'Policy Analysis, Science and Politics: From "Speaking Truth to Power" to Making Sense Together.' *Science and Public Policy* 26(3), 201–10.

– 2002. 'Cultural Theory and Its Contribution to Policy Analysis.' *Journal of Comparative Policy Analysis,* Special Issue, 4(3), 235–41.

Hoppe, R., and J. Grin. 2000. 'Traffic Problems go Through the Technology Assessment Machine: A Cultural Comparison.' In N. Vig and H. Paschen, eds., *Parliament and Technology: The Development of Technology Assessment in Europe,* 273–324. Albany, NY: SUNY Press.

Howlett, M., and E. Lindquist. 2007. 'Beyond Formal Policy Analysis: Governance Context, Analytical Styles, and the Policy Analysis Movement in Canada.' In M. Howlett, L. Dobuzinskis, and D. Laycock, eds., *Policy Analysis in Canada: The State of the Art.* Toronto: University of Toronto Press.

Jordan, A. 2003. 'The Europeanization of National Government and Policy: A Departmental Perspective.' *British Journal of Political Science* 33(1), 261–82.

Kagan, R.A. 1991. 'Adversarial Legalism and American Government.' *Journal of Policy Analysis and Management* 10 (3), 369–406.

– 1996. 'The Political Consequences of American Adversarial Legalism.' In A. Ranney, ed., *Courts and the Political Process.* Berkeley: Institute of Governmental Studies Press.

Kettl, D. 1997. 'The Global Revolution in the Public Management: Driving Themes, Missing Links.' *Journal of Policy Analysis and Management* 16(3), 346–50.

Lasswell, H.D. 1950. *The World Revolution of our Time. A Framework for Basic Policy Research.* Stanford, CA: Stanford University Press.

Lawler, E.F. 1994. 'Reconciling Policy Analysis, Theory and Policy.' Paper presented at the APPAM research conference, Chicago, IL, November.

Lerner, D., and H.D. Lasswell, eds. 1951. *The Policy Sciences.* Palo Alto, CA: Stanford University Press.

Lewin, K. 1938. *The Conceptual Representations and the Measurement of Psychological Forces.* Durham, NC: Duke University Press.

Lindblom, C.E. 1958. 'Policy Analysis.' *American Economic Review* 48(3), 298–312.

Lynn, L.E. 1987. *Managing Public Policy.* Boston: Little, Brown.

– 1998. 'The New Public Management: How to Transform the Theme into Legacy.' *Public Administration Review* 58(3), 231–37.

– 1999. 'Public Management in North America.' Working paper series 993. Chicago, IL: Graduate School of Policy Studies.

Luger, M. 2005. 'Balancing Pedagogy.' In I. Geva-May, ed., *Thinking Like a Policy Analyst: Policy Analysis as a Clinical Profession.* New York: Palgrave Macmillan.

March, J., and H. Simon. 1985. *Organizations.* New York: John Wiley.

Mayer, I., P. Bots, and E. van Daalen. 2004. 'Perspectives on Policy Analysis: A Framework for Understanding and Design.' *International Journal of Technology, Policy and Management* 4(1), 169–91.

Meltsner, A.J. 1972. 'Political Feasibility and Policy Analysis.' *Public Administration Review* 32, 858–67.

– 1976. *Policy Analysts in the Bureaucracy.* Berkeley: University of California Press.

Mintrom, M. 2003 *People Skills for Policy Analysts.* Washington, DC: Georgetown University Press.

Peters, B.G. 1990. 'Administrative Culture and Analysis of Public Organizations.' *Indian Journal of Public Administration* 36, 420–28.

Piaget, J. 1953. *Logic and Psychology.* Manchester, UK: Manchester University Press.

– 1977. *The Development of Thought.* New York: Viking Press.

– 1985. *The Equilibrium of Cognitive Structures: The Central Problem of Intellectual Development.* Chicago: University of Chicago Press.

Polanyi, M. 1966. *The Tacit Dimension.* London: Routledge & Keegan Paul.

Radin, B. 1996. 'The Evolution of Policy Analysis Field: From Conversation to Conversations.' Presidential Address, the Association for Public Policy Anlaysis and Management. Washington, DC.

– 2000. *Beyond Machiavelli: Policy Analysis Comes of Age*. Washington, DC: Georgetown University Press.

Reiner, M. 1998. 'Thought Experiments and Collaborative Learning in Physics.' *International Journal of Science Education* 20, 1043–58.

Reiner, M., and J. Gilbert. 2000. 'Epistemological Resources for Thought Experimentation in Science Learning.' *International Journal of Science Education* 22(5), 489–506.

Rivlin, A. 1984. 'A Public Policy Paradox.' *Journal of Policy Analysis and Management* 4(1), 17–22.

Smith, D. 2005. 'The Wagner Program.' In I. Geva-May, ed., *Thinking Like a Policy Analyst: Policy Analysis as a Clinical Profession*. New York: Palgrave Macmillan.

Starling, G. 1979. *The Politics and Economics of Public Policy: An Introductory Analysis with Cases*. Homewood, IL: Dorsey.

Sternberg, R. 1985. *Beyond IQ: A Triarchic Theory of Human Intelligence*. New York: Cambridge University Press.

Sternberg, R., G. Foersythe, J. Hedlund, R. Wagner, and W. Williams. 2000. *Practical Intelligence in Everyday Life*. New York: Cambridge University Press.

Stokes, D. 1996. 'Presidential Address: The Changing Environment of Education for Public Service.' *Journal of Policy Analysis and Management* 15(2), 158–70.

Tversky, A., and D. Kahneman. 1981. 'Judgment Under Uncertainty: Heuristics and Biases.' *Science* 185, 1124–31.

Van Gunsteren, H.R. 1998. *A Theory of Citizenship Organizing*, Boulder, CO: Westview Press.

Vogel, D. 1986. *National Styles of Regulation: Environmental Policy in Great Britain and the United States*. Ithaca, NY: Cornell University Press.

Walters, L., and R. Sudweeks. 1996. 'Public Policy Analysis: The Next Generation of Theory.' *Journal of Socio-Economics* 25(4), 425–52.

Weimer, D.L., and A.R. Vining. 1999. *Policy Analysis: Concepts and Practice*. Englewood Cliffs, NJ: Prentice-Hall.

Wildavsky, A. 1979. *Speaking Truth to Power: The Art and Craft of Policy Analysis*. Boston: Little, Brown.

Wilson, J.Q. 1989. *Bureaucracy*. New York: Free Press.

PART III

Policy Analysis by Governments

Many players contribute to the policy process, but none more directly than elected and appointed government officials. Not surprisingly, therefore, policy analysts working within government departments and agencies occupy a strategic position: the advice these analysts provide is usually viewed by political or administrative decision makers as being immediately relevant to their concerns. This is not to say, however, that policy makers always get the information they expect, nor to suggest that 'in-house' policy analysts have access to all the resources they need to carry out their research.

Budgetary priorities led all levels of government to make more or less deep cuts in the resources devoted to policy analysis in recent decades. Jean-Pierre Voyer argues, however, that since the mid-1990s the federal government has taken a series of measures to address a weakened policy analysis capacity in many of its departments, especially with respect to issues that cut across several policy fields and extend beyond short-term considerations. The Policy Research Initiative (PRI) is one of the best examples of that renewed effort to commit resources and talents to policy analysis.

Doug McArthur, on the other hand, relies on his experience in the provincial arena to recommend new directions in thinking about policy analysis. It is unfortunate that the literature tends to neglect what is going on at that level because this is actually where 'the action' is in many fields directly relevant to the concerns of Canadian citizens: the provinces now provide almost two-thirds of government services in Canada. Precisely because of the often controversial nature of social policy problems, McArthur argues that policy analysts need not only to pay attention to the technical aspects of policy development – aspects that have so far been at the centre of a long series of administrative reforms, if not fads – but even more so to the processes of deliberation that shape policy options. He observes, however, that 'the state of theory' with respect to negotiations and deliberation is 'underdeveloped.'

Sounding a far more pessimistic note, Kennedy Stewart and Patrick Smith argue that elected officials in most Canadian cities do not get the kind of in-depth policy information and advice they would need to effectively play their part in the democratic process. As a result, it would seem that in most municipalities, 'un- or under-supervised civil servants drive and dominate the policy process.'

9 Policy Analysis in the Federal Government: Building the Forward-Looking Policy Research Capacity

JEAN-PIERRE VOYER[1]

Introduction

A decade ago, senior managers within the federal public service had a collective *prise de conscience* with regard to the need to reinvest in the federal government's policy capacity. A special Deputy Minister Task Force on Strengthening our Policy Capacity was established in 1995, and it subsequently issued what is commonly referred to as the Fellegi Report. This report presented a key examination of the state of policy capacity across the federal government, and laid out a roadmap for future reinvestment in this capacity. Almost ten years after the Fellegi Report, what has happened?

Studies of policy analysis in government often emphasize different elements of what they understand analysis to be. A not atypical recent definition broadly describes policy analysis as the activity of thinking systematically or scientifically about policy problems, the goal of which is policy prescription (Brooks 2002, 192). Such systematic thinking is the lifeblood of the policy development process in government: from issue identification and agenda setting, through policy research and policy development, to decision making and implementation, and finally evaluation and adjustment, policy analysis is a core activity.

Rarely, of course, does the development of policy occur in the linear, rationalistic fashion suggested by this typology. While policy analysts in the federal government strive to be as professional, systematic, and scientific as possible in offering their research and advice, they must have the flexibility to respond to the needs of their ministers in circumstances that may be less than ideal. Indeed, the environment in which policy development and analysis occurs is becoming increasingly complex. As Donald Savoie (2004) has recently noted, the policy-making process is opened to an ever-wider array of stakeholders and faced with multifaceted and interconnected issues that cut across ministerial lines of responsibility.

This said, the Fellegi Report a decade ago, as well as more recent interviews with senior government managers (Armstrong et al. 2002) suggest that most departments in the federal government are fairly strong in the provision of short-term advice and analysis. The larger area of concern, both then and now, has been with regard to the capacity within the federal government to undertake policy analysis work focused on the medium to longer term, i.e., the capacity to conduct policy research. The focus of this paper will be, therefore, on those elements of the federal government dedicated to undertaking medium- to longer-term analytical policy research work, where that analysis can be more systematic and rigorous, as it is freer from the immediate day-to-day pressures of government operations.

I begin by reviewing the concerns about federal policy capacity that led to the Deputy Minister Task Force and the diagnostic offered in their report, with its call for more forward-looking policy capacity. This chapter then touches on key areas of progress over the past decade, including the establishment of the Policy Research Initiative, new initiatives to build connections to the extra-governmental research community, improvements in the medium-term policy research capacity of departments, and the development of new tools for research. The conclusion offers a look at what lies ahead in terms of further progress.

The Fellegi Report

By now, the story of the initial investment and enthusiasm in policy analysis within the federal government, followed by a subsequent long period of retrenchment, has become a familiar one (Pal 2001, 24; Hollander and Prince 1993; see also Brooks in this volume). With the rapid expansion and institutionalization of policy analysis capacity, beginning in the sixties and carrying on into the seventies, the federal government took a lead role in the development of policy research and analysis in Canada. It was a time of increasing investment in research and a strong faith in the power of rational, systematic analysis to make a difference. The government also invested in a number of mechanisms to harvest research from the wider policy analysis community, such as the Economic and Science Councils of Canada, various Royal Commissions, and a variety of granting mechanisms. Beginning in the mid-1980s, however, there was a shift in emphasis and resources from policy analysis to program implementation. The preoccupations with (new) public management concerns, combined with fiscal restraint, meant that the medium-term analysis in many policy areas was sidelined, and the in-house capacity of a number of departments declined. By the mid-1990s, following more than a decade of diminishing capacity and the recent loss of the Economic Council of Canada (a major source of medium and longer-term research for the federal government, see Dobuzinskis in this volume) and other advisory councils, concerns over the state of the federal government's policy capacity led the then Clerk of the Privy Council, Jocelyne Bourgon, to launch a Deputy Minister Task Force on Strengthening our Policy Capacity. Chaired by the Government of Canada's chief statistician, Ivan Fellegi, the task force produced a milestone diagnostic of the state of the federal government's policy capacity.

The Fellegi Report stressed the continued need for a high-quality policy capacity to address key challenges faced by the federal government. It suggested that, in this regard, a most notable weakness centred on the capacity to undertake rigorous, longer-term strategic and horizontal analytical work. The task force found that most, though not all, departments were doing little work in this area owing to a range of factors including a shortage of resources, urgent day-to-day requirements, a perceived lack of demand from senior managers and officials, and a weak example from key central agencies. While longer-term planning may be difficult in an increasingly complex environment, the report affirmed that positioning the government to deal with longer-term issues in a coherent fashion was the central strategic issue for the government (Canada 1996, 20). It noted that such work was more likely to occur where there were dedicated internal resources (distinct from day-to-day operations), supportive external resources, useful techniques and methodologies, and where there was a strong demand for such work from senior management. The report concluded that while the bulk of such strategic work must take place within departments, the central agencies and the Privy Council Office (PCO), in particular, have a vital role to play in increasing the focus on strategic and major horizontal issues. Yet there is no fully effective central function that helps to define issues of strategic importance, to guide the process for developing longer-term and horizontal policies, and to promote interdepartmental networks (Canada 1996, 39).

Canada was not the only country in the 1990s to express concerns about the state of policy capacity within government. Similar questions were being raised in other Western democracies that also experienced a significant period of fiscal pressure and emphasis on new public management (Curtain 2000). For example, in the United Kingdom, Tony Blair's Labour government released a white paper on modernizing government, which suggested that previous emphasis on management reform had paid insufficient attention to policy capacity. Policies too often take the form of incremental change to existing systems, rather than new ideas that take the long-term view and cut across organizational boundaries to get at the root of the problem (United Kingdom 1999, 16). The UK government committed itself to improved horizontal and strategic policy development. Recent years have seen the establishment of a number of key new policy analysis units in that government, most notably the Prime Minister's Strategy Unit.[2]

The Policy Research Initiative

Perhaps the most important development since the Fellegi Report, in terms of addressing the federal government's capacity to undertake medium-term, horizontal policy analysis, has been the establishment of the Policy Research Initiative (PRI). The PRI was launched in 1996 by the Clerk of the Privy Council and the community of deputy ministers as a corporate effort aimed at rebuilding policy capacity. The PRI first began as an interdepartmental committee of assistant deputy ministers from over 30 federal departments and agencies that were asked to engage in a medium-term scanning exercise to identify future policy challenges faced by Canada. The committee prepared a report, titled 'Growth, Human Development, Social Cohesion,' on the key pressure points likely to arise in Canadian society by the year 2005 as a result of shifting socio-economic trends, and identified research gaps that needed to be addressed to position the government to deal with those challenges.

The experience was highly successful in many ways. Not only did it produce a report that demonstrated how policy research focused on the medium term had much to contribute to the formulation of the policy agenda, but it also confirmed the benefits of interdepartmental collaboration in policy research. The exercise revealed the horizontal nature of many key policy challenges and the need to confront various perspectives and analysis in order to establish a common diagnosis on socio-economic trends and developments facing the country. In the process of drafting the joint report, much was learned on the relative policy research capacity strengths of the various federal departments. A policy research community started to emerge, as many government policy researchers, contrary to their colleagues working on policy design or policy implementation, had seldom encountered real opportunities to work with their counterparts from other departments.

Following these first steps, a permanent secretariat, the Policy Research Secretariat (PRS), was established as a more formal institutionalized entity within the Government of Canada, with the mandate to support a newly formed interdepartmental research networks of analysts, and to reach out to the wider policy research community of think-tanks and university academics. From 1997 to 2002, the PRS was particularly active in establishing these linkages through major forums such as high-profile national policy conferences involving hundreds of government and non-government researchers and through the management of publications, such as ISUMA and TRENDS,[3] which aimed to tap the contributions of scholars and other external experts on medium-term policy issues of relevance to the federal government. However, over this period, the PRS, which was renamed the PRI in 2000, was never able to reproduce the scale and climate of interdepartmental collaboration that characterized the early days of the initiative, with the result that most of the research work emerging from the PRI during this period was from external sources to the federal government, through initiatives such as the Trends Project Series. The interdepartmental networks did not generate much new research work, with the exception perhaps of a pilot project on the Knowledge-Based Economy/Society, which was led by HRDC, Industry Canada, Canadian Heritage, and the Canadian International Development Agency. The KBE/S project produced three major conferences in 1998 and 1999, with a corresponding number of volumes of proceedings, and was by and large managed by the departments directly involved, with little or no direct contribution from the PRI secretariat.[4]

The fact that the interdepartmental networks generated little new work is hardly surprising. Department researchers had been asked to conduct interdepartmental research work in addition to their regular departmental responsibilities and activities. No additional resources had been assigned to the research program of the interdepartmental networks, except for a small staff at the PRI that was mostly involved in coordinating activities and publications. For the departments involved, the horizontal work around the first report might have been exciting but proved difficult to sustain. The creation of interdepartmental research networks was a necessary, but not sufficient, condition for the strengthening of the federal government's capacity to undertake medium-term, horizontal policy analysis. New departmental resources had to be devoted to policy research activities.

In late 2002, the Policy Research Initiative entered a third phase, characterized by a deepened internal research capacity and increased emphasis on generating in-house knowledge products. Attached to the PCO, with oversight from the Deputy Secretary for Plans and Consultation, the PRI's core mandate today is to advance research on emerging horizontal issues that are highly relevant to the federal government's medium-term policy agenda, and to ensure the effective transfer of this knowledge to policy makers.[5] The PRI leads research projects, rather than primarily coordinating department-based efforts. A team of approximately 25 policy research analysts, from diverse academic backgrounds, works on several research projects in partnership with participating federal departments. Projects in early 2005 centred on issues related to population aging and increased life-course flexibility, new approaches to address poverty and exclusion, the role of social capital as a policy tool, the social economy, the management of fresh water in Canada, the emergence of Canada-U.S. cross-border regions, the need for increased Canada-U.S. regulatory cooperation, and the costs and benefits of a customs union with the United States.

While the PRI is now more focused on meeting the needs of the internal federal community, it still undertakes extensive work to build linkages between federal analysts and extra-governmental researchers. Through a partnership with the Social Sciences and Humanities Research Council (SSHRC), the two organizations have hosted more than a dozen research roundtables in 2003 and 2004, bringing together leading Canadian scholars with senior federal officials to address specific, targeted issues relating to the PRI horizontal projects.

Since its creation, the PRI has used different means to promote horizontal collaboration and to foster a sense of community among federal researchers. Beyond its crosscutting research projects and its publication *Horizons*, the PRI's contribution to supporting horizontal research collaboration extends to its leadership of the Policy Research Data Group (PRDG). The PRDG is an interdepartmental committee formed in 1998 to address data gaps that link to medium- to longer-term policy priorities. Composed of senior managers from departments with identifiable research functions, together with officials from Statistics Canada and the central government agencies, the PRDG manages a fund of $20 million per year allocated for the development of data needed to carry out horizontal research. Priority data projects are identified by the group and the data is then developed by Statistics Canada, primarily through surveys (such as the General Social Survey, the Longitudinal Survey of Immigrants to Canada, the Workplace and Employee Survey, the Post-secondary Transition Survey, and the International Adult Literacy and Lifeskills Survey, amongst several others). The PRDG holds regular workshops on data-related issues, where departments and external researchers can present proposals for new surveys or other data developments. The PRI chairs the PRDG and provides the group with the necessary support and coordination.

Reaching Out to the External Policy Analysis Community

One of the principal areas of progress with regard to the policy capacity of the federal government since the Fellegi Report has been in the variety of new partnerships with extra-departmental researchers. Interviews with senior managers in 2002 (Armstrong et al. 2002) demonstrated a consensus that building such connections is no longer viewed as a problem that needs to be addressed. The Policy Research Initiative has played a key role in building these links, but several other initiatives have played a similar role in reaching out to the wider analysis community.

The Metropolis Project represents one creative new partnership model. Launched in 1996 at Citizenship and Immigration Canada (CIC), this project sought to develop the government's analytic capacity to manage immigration and diversity by actively developing linkages to the academic community through institutionally coordinated grant-funded research. Funded by a consortium of federal departments and agencies, including the CIC and SSHRC, the project provides core funds to five university-based Centres of Excellence in Montreal, Toronto, Edmonton, Vancouver, and Atlantic Canada, with which over 200 Canadian researchers are affiliated. In addition, the Metropolis Project has an international arm that involves partnerships with policy makers and researchers from over 20 countries, including the United States, most of Western Europe, Israel, Argentina, and from the Asia-Pacific region. Knowledge generated is transferred to federal officials through annual national and international conferences, and frequent workshops and seminars. The project has been successful in building links between academics and government policy researchers, and mid-level federal managers.

Another important development in recent years has been the introduction of the Research Data Centres program. In 1998, a national task force, the Canadian Initiative on Social Statistics, recommended the creation of research facilities to give academic researchers improved access to Statistics Canada's microdata files to allow researchers in the social sciences to build expertise in quantitative methodology and analysis and improve the availability of rigorous, policy-relevant research. In partnership with SSHRC and a number of universities, Statistics Canada has developed 12 Research Data Centres (RDCs) located across the country. RDCs provide researchers with access, in a secure university setting, to microdata from population and household surveys. The centres are operated under the provisions of the Statistics Act in accordance with all the confidentiality rules and are accessible only to researchers with approved projects who have been sworn in under the Statistics Act as 'deemed employees.'

The issue of knowledge transfer and building stronger bridges between government officials and researchers undertaking policy-relevant work has become a central concern for the three major federal granting agencies, including SSHRC, the Natural Sciences and Engineering Research Council (NSERC) and the Canadian Institutes of Health Research (CIHR). For example, the CIHR had a knowledge translation requirement built into its founding act in 2000. More recently SSHRC, Canada's primary research funding agency in the social sciences and humanities, has embarked on a process of transformation, from a granting council to a knowledge council. That is, although SSHRC continues to deliver grants awarded through peer review, it will increase its support for transfers of research knowledge to analysts and decision makers in government, as well as other mediators and knowledge users. Some of SSHRC's programs have already begun to stress this knowledge transfer capacity. For example, the Community-University Research Alliances (CURA) program connects the knowledge produced with community-based user needs. Similarly, SSHRC has recently partnered with the PRI to organize a series of important policy-relevant roundtables, bringing together academics and federal policy officials. The council recently launched the Strategic Research Clusters Design Grants program, which is advertised as the first concrete step towards its transformation as a knowledge council. The strategic clusters are national research networks, each focused on a particular theme, that enable researchers to interact on an ongoing basis with each other and with research users and other stakeholders.

Although predating the Fellegi Report, the Canadian Employment Research Forum (CERF), established in 1991, remains a reference point when looking at ways to connect the federal policy research community with the external community. The forum is a nonprofit corporation, governed by a board of directors of both government officials and university-based academics, that was set up at the invitation, and with the financial support, of Employment and Immigration Canada. It has successfully brought labour market researchers together at a series of conferences and workshops, enabling academic researchers to better identify the policy needs of government officials, and for government officials to be better informed of the latest relevant academic research. The forum has grown to be a robust bridge between university researchers and policy researchers from the federal government. However, the initiative has lost some momentum in more recent years, and activities have been limited as the federal government core funding was replaced with irregular event-based financial support.

Departmental Policy Research Capacity

Although these represent important initiatives, the Fellegi Report was particularly insistent on the importance of investing in the policy capacity within departments. What has happened to departmental capacity since Fellegi?

Concerns remain that the medium- to longer-term capacity in many departments is still weak, and that the tyranny of the urgent still predominates, with far too much analysis being simply reactive and overly superficial (Armstrong et al. 2002, 6–8). That said, there are clearly some departments that have made strong investments in medium-term research work over the past decade.

The Leaders

The Department of Finance is probably where policy analysis in the federal government has been the most stable, as the department was largely unaffected by program reviews and spending cuts. In addition to providing ongoing policy analysis in its various areas of responsibilities, Finance has always maintained a capacity to carry rigorous policy research on medium-term issues. The Economic Studies and Policy

Analysis Division is the focal point of that research, with working papers being published regularly on a wide range of issues.

The Bank of Canada is also staffed with a load of policy analysts, mostly economists, devoted to financial market analysis, banking issues, macroeconomics and monetary policy. The Research Department alone, where most of the work falls into the mid-term research category, is staffed with more than 60 researchers.

Over the last decade, Statistics Canada has considerably increased the quantity of analytical products coming from their data collection activities. Four groups are responsible for the bulk of the department's research publications: Business and Labour Market Analysis, Family and Labour Studies, Health Analysis, and Measurement and Micro-Economic Analysis. Staffed with some 50 social scientists and a few affiliated researchers from academia, these groups conduct research on various labour market topics, productivity, technology and innovation, family outcomes, and health topics. Statistics Canada researchers benefit from direct and unrestricted access to the rich data sets collected by the organization.

While commenting on the recent deterioration of policy capacity across the federal government, the Fellegi Report noted that Human Resources Development Canada was an exception, with its investment in forward-looking planning and research. The Applied Research Branch, created in 1994, conducted policy research covering labour market, human capital development, income security, social development, labour adjustment and workplace innovation issues and for several years had the largest social policy research capacity in Canada. The ARB built on the significant investments made by Employment and Immigration Canada in the area of surveys, social experiments and program evaluation well before the creation of HRDC. The ARB proposed a new model for managing mid-term policy research, by getting actively engaged not only in the interpretation of data, but also in the planning of surveys and other data collected through social experiments. External experts would be invited to collaborate with the ARB's research staff and the organizations responsible for the data collection in developing research hypotheses, planning the survey or the experiments in accordance with these hypotheses and then harvesting the information and conducting primary research as various waves of data became available. The branch lost some momentum when HRDC got caught in the middle of a highly publicized and quite overblown scandal over data holdings and data linkages. As part of an internal reorganization plan, the research branch was partly dismantled in the early 2000s and the remaining research group was further split when HRDC resources were reallocated in December 2003 into two new departments, Social Development and Human Resources and Skills Development.

The Micro-Economic Policy Analysis (MEPA) branch of Industry Canada also ranks among the large research units of the federal public service. The branch emerged in the early 1990s as a central point of policy research expertise on a wide range of issues related to the knowl-edge-based economy and the need to improve Canada's innovation performance. The 40 or so economists who work in the branch divide their time between the management of research contracts, their own research work and the articulation of key messages to policy makers. The MEPA has been particularly successful in the past ten years in attracting contributions from top North American scholars to their re-search agenda and in transferring the results of this research to policy makers, thanks to a special talent at translating research findings into decks, which have become the standard way of communication with senior officials and decision makers.

Strategic analytical efforts at Health Canada were at one time quite diffuse throughout the department. In recent years the department has moved to a hybrid model with the creation of a core corporate applied research group, the Applied Research and Analysis Directorate, com-bined with a number of smaller units distributed through its various branches. The core function of the directorate is to develop and imple-ment a strategic policy research agenda for medium- and long-term issues, helping co-ordinate Health Canada's internal and external policy research activities, and funding extramural research under the Health Policy Research Program.[6] The directorate, with over 50 researchers, now compares very well with the research capacity of other line depart-ments like Industry, HRSD, and SD, and engages in research partner-ships, modelling and data collection activities, as well as program evaluation.

Why do these high-capacity departments stand out? It is often thanks to the leadership of particular senior managers who, even in a period of downsizing, insisted on the importance of investment in medium-term strategic research capacity. Despite fiscal restraint and a focus on pro-gram management, these managers continued to ask questions that demanded analytical, evidence-based responses, and made sure that some resources were made available to provide those answers (Riddell 1998, 5). As well, these departments did not hesitate to regroup their research resources to create critical masses that could be identified with a mid- to long-term focus, and remained somewhat remote and protected from the daily demands and crises faced by most policy shops.

The B Pool

Other departments have made notable attempts to build up their mid-term research capacity in response to the Fellegi Report. Indian and Northern Affairs Canada, Heritage Canada and Citizenship and Immigration fall into this category. Indian and Northern Affairs Canada established a Strategic Research and Analysis Directorate in 1993, with a mandate to pursue a program of policy research, analysis and advice to support the federal government's policy making regarding the changing relationship between the federal government and First Nations, Inuit and northern peoples of Canada. The directorate has a small staff that manages research from external experts and participates directly with products of their own as well. In November 2002, INAC and the University of Western Ontario organized the first Aboriginal Policy Research Conference. The nearly 700 delegates came from the federal government and universities and Aboriginal organizations to spend three days discussing research and policy.

Heritage Canada invested in building some mid-term policy research capacity in the second half of the 1990s with the creation of the Strategic Policy and Research Branch, which provides a corporate research function to support the long-term strategic direction of the department and contributes to the overall government research agenda in areas which affect the mandate of Canadian Heritage. International Trade Canada has a small unit devoted to trade policy research and since 2001 it has produced an annual compendium of trade-related research work and analysis undertaken within and on behalf of the department.

In addition to supporting the Metropolis project as one of the key funding partners, Citizenship and Immigration Canada maintains an internal research program mainly oriented towards the exploitation of the information provided by the Longitudinal Immigration Database and by surveys dealing with the labour market performance of immigrants. Agriculture Canada's Research and Analysis Directorate relies on large-scale computer models and other sectoral models to measure how changes in market conditions or policies affect the agricultural sector. Canada Mortgage and Housing Corporation conducts mid-term research to help address national housing issues and has a large grants and awards program to foster innovation and the development of the external housing research community. Infrastructure Canada is the new kid on the block with substantial investment in research since its creation in 2003. A small research unit, the Research and Analysis Division, manages a series of research priorities on public infrastructure issues in collaboration with other federal governments, and devotes a significant amount of resources to external research contracts.

Status of Women Canada has a handful of researchers who have managed, since 1996, to support independent, forward-thinking policy research on gender equality issues. Over 40 projects have been funded since the first call for proposals was issued in 1997. The Law Commission of Canada was, from 1997 to 2006, an independent federal law reform agency that advised Parliament on how to improve and modernize Canada's law. The commission managed research projects, mostly commissioned to external experts, on various themes.[7] The Canada Rural Partnership supports research and analysis that provides socioeconomic information and analysis on rural Canada and matters of interest to rural Canada.

The Canada School of Public Service has a vice-president heading a unit named Research and University Relations, which seeks to provide relevant, accessible and leading-edge research in governance and public management for federal public servants. The unit is relatively small, with less than a dozen staff, but it also draws on external experts and works with many Canadian universities to carry out its research workplan. The RCMP's Strategic Direction Sector incorporates policy development and research capacity to provide advice and support to senior management in setting the strategic direction of the organization. The sector is mainly known outside of the RCMP for its thorough environmental scan of the socio-economic, technological, legal, and political environment, both at the domestic and international levels.

The above does not represent a comprehensive review of all policy research capacity across federal departments. Our brief overview nevertheless suggests that the amount of resources engaged in medium-term policy analysis and research across the federal government is not negligible. Of course, the number of issues calling for in-depth analysis, and of particular relevance to the federal government, is also far from negligible.

Has progress been made since the Fellegi Report? Overall progress in some of the departments may have offset some setbacks in other departments. Also, the distribution of research capacity remains highly unequal from one department to another. What the above description does not reflect is the impact of recent budgetary measures calling for spending cuts and reallocation across all departments. For several departments, these pressures just add to previous department-specific reallocation exercises and have led to a gradual erosion of departmental research and data development budgets. While researchers' jobs may not have been cut, there are clear indications that the branch budgets devoted to non-salary items, contracts, conferences, data development, or other operational items have clearly suffered.

Analytic Tools and Methods

Over the past decade, the federal government has invested in a number of new tools and methodologies to improve its medium- to longer-term policy research capacity. For example, Statistics Canada, in partnership with a number of departments such as HRDC and CIC, and with the guidance and support of the Policy Research Data Group, has introduced a number of important new longitudinal surveys that, while costly and time-consuming to produce, have significant advantages over cross-sectional data. Examples include the National Longitudinal Survey of Children and Youth, the Longitudinal Survey of Immigrants to Canada, the National Graduate Surveys, and follow-up surveys: the School Leavers Surveys and the Workplace and Employees Survey. These surveys provide federal government analysts with the capacity to much better identify the key trends and challenges in several strategic policy areas, including early childhood development, labour market transitions, and immigrant integration.

Federal departments have also continued to invest in modelling techniques, which have improved their capacity to undertake medium- and longer-term analysis. Macroeconomic models, introduced in the seventies, remain a key tool for any research or analysis involving macroeconomic forecasting or macro policy analysis. The Department of Finance and the Bank of Canada have traditionally been the most intensive users, but other departments use them as well. For instance, occupational projections introduced at Employment and Immigration in the early eighties are produced regularly with the help of such macroeconomic models and their derivatives. General equilibrium models were instrumental in assessing the merits of introducing key policy reforms, such as the GST or the Free Trade Agreement. They are still used today by departments like Finance, Industry Canada, International Trade, and Agriculture Canada to assess the economic efficiency gains and potential increases in GDP per capita that could result from major policy changes.

Microsimulation models, such as Statistics Canada's Social Policy Simulation Database and Model (SPSD/M), have been handling the distributional impact of proposed policy options for the last two decades. More recently, Statistics Canada introduced a new model, the LifePaths microsimulation model of individuals and families. The model allows for a better appreciation of how various policies designed to impact decisions at different points in the life course interact to affect the outcomes of individual trajectories. The LifePaths model creates data about an artificial population that mirrors the characteristics of Canadian society. As Rowe notes, this represents a radical addition to the analytic tool kit, and offers the prospect for improved public policy investments to support Canadians in all the diversity of their life courses (2003, 8). Health Canada also developed its own microsimulation models. The Pharmasim model quantifies the impact of changes to provincial pharmacare programs on households and government expenditures. The Health-Tax Microsimulation Model (HTSIM) enables analysts to quantify the impact of changes to tax measures.

Through HRDC, the federal government also made substantial investments in social experimentation in the 1980s. A yearly budget approximating $20 million supported several large field experiments and demonstration projects in various locations during most of the 1990s. Projects such as the Self-sufficiency Project, based in BC and New Brunswick, the Community Employment Innovation Project, taking place in Cape Breton, Nova Scotia, and the Learn$ave Project, implemented in 10 sites across Canada, involved thousands of participants and used rigorous quantitative analysis, in the form of random-assignment evaluation design, to test and evaluate proposals for new programs and policy initiatives. However, HRDC (and now HRSD) investments in social experimentation are unique, as other departments have not yet devoted any resources to this powerful analytical tool for better policy design. HRDC has also been innovating by making use of laboratory experiments, or experimental economics, to inform policy design. In 2002, the Canada Student Loans Program commissioned the Social Research and Demonstration Corporation (SRDC) to conduct an economic experiment to test the response of program recipients to the provision of various forms of short-term/part-time student financial assistance.

Environmental scanning is a technique that has gained in popularity with several federal departments. Generally a typical scan is a report capturing a view of the socio-cultural, economic, technological, environmental and even political trends and circumstances around the organization (Howe 2004, 81). Efforts are currently being made to better integrate the various departmental scans currently underway, but for now, this activity is only carried out on a small scale and remains highly decentralized.

Does All This Make a Difference?

One might question the need to be concerned about the federal government's policy research capacity, given the assertions that such policy analysis work has little impact on either day-to-day government operations or longer-term policy directions (Pal 2001, 23; Brooks 1996, 85). Yet the work of such units, with a medium- to long-term focus, can and does often make an important difference to the development of government policy. Often this influence is only indirect, introducing concepts, insights, and alternatives that may only gradually, depending upon the right circumstances, resonate with decision makers and take hold in the policy development process. At other times, such work may have a much more direct impact. For example, in the late 1990s, the deputy minister of Industry made 10 presentations in 12 months of the work of the department's Micro-Economic Policy Branch (Riddell 1998, 7), work that very directly informed the government's innovation agenda. Picot (2003) also offers several examples where the quantitative analysis of Statistics Canada has played a substantial role in informing many key policy areas over the past decade, including the reform of Employment Insurance, child poverty efforts, promotion of research and development, immigrant integration, and issues of access to post-secondary education. Similarly, the work of the Applied Research Branch of HRDC during the 1990s contributed to inspire various government initiatives in the area of adult education, child development, youth employment, and parental benefits. It also prevented the government from reacting to alarmist diagnoses, like the claim regarding the end of work in the mid-1990s, by producing thorough analysis of labour market trends.

Conclusion: Looking Ahead

Policy research capacity within the federal government is healthy and compares well with the capacity observed in other OECD governments. Recent analysis points to a problem of demand as opposed to a problem of supply (Armstrong 2002). Decision makers and senior government officials are overloaded with information and are captive to the crisis or issues of the day. They rarely find the time to give proper consideration to research findings. This demand deficiency makes the supply more vulnerable. If policy researchers fail to create opportunities to present the results of their work, they may not survive the recurrent waves of resource reallocation, departmental reorganizations and spending cuts that have characterized the lives of all levels of governments, as well as private sector businesses, since the last recession. More emphasis has to be put on knowledge transfers and finding appropriate mechanisms to package and convey the results of the policy research to senior officials and ministers. The role of the knowledge broker is bound to increase in future years, especially in large organizations. It is therefore imperative that the federal government preserves a solid internal policy research capacity that has the ability to speak the language of policy as well as the language of research. Canada can afford more think tanks and scholars devoted to the analysis of policy issues. In that regard we may be lagging other countries, such as the United States or the UK. But without a strong internal capacity to produce, process, and synthesize research information, and to translate and communicate it, new investments in research capacity external to governments may not do much to improve the quality of policy making.

NOTES

1 I would like to thank Robert Judge, from the Policy Research Initiative, for his assistance in writing this paper.
2 As part of its commitment to improved horizontal and strategic policy development, in 1998 the UK government established the Performance and Innovation Unit (PIU) in the Cabinet Office, reporting directly to the prime minister through the cabinet secretary. The PIU was designed to report on select issues crossing departmental boundaries and to propose policy innovations to improve the delivery of government objectives. In 2001, a

second unit, the Prime Minister's Forward Strategy Unit, was established to provide the prime minister and other cabinet ministers with strategic, private thinking. A year later the two units were merged to form the Prime Minister's Strategy Unit. The Strategy Unit is located in the Cabinet Office and reports directly to the prime minister.

3 Under the Trend Project, the PRI, in cooperation with the Social Sciences and Humanities Research Council of Canada, developed six books, in which a team of academics examined different forces that are driving change in Canada and identified the potential implications for policy.

4 The proceedings of these conferences were published under the following titles: *Transition to the Knowledge of Society: Policies and Strategies for Individual Participation and Learning,* ed. Kjell Rubenson and Hans G. Schuetze (Vancouver, BC: UBC Institute for European Studies, 2000); *Doing Business in the Knowledge-Based Economy: Facts and Policy Challenges,* ed. Louis A. Lefebvre, Elisabeth Lefebvre, and Pierre Mohnen (Boston: Kluwer Academic Publishers, 2001); and *Citizenship and Participation in the Information Age,* ed. Manjunath Pendakur and Roma Harris (Aurora, ON: Garamond Press, 2002).

5 In the summer of 2006, the PRI was placed under the responsibility of the Deputy Minister of Human Resources and Social Development Canada. While PRI's horizontal mandate has not changed, some of its activites are under review.

6 The Health Policy Research Program was discontinued a part of the spending reduction announced by the federal government on 25 September 2006.

7 The Law Commision ceased operation as a result of the spending reduction announced by the federal government on 25 September 2006.

REFERENCES

Armstrong, Jim, et al. 2002. 'Strengthening Policy Capacity: Report on Interviews with Senior Managers.' Ottawa: The Governance Network (February-March).

Brooks, Stephen. 1996. 'The Policy Analysis Profession in Canada.' In Laurent Dobuzinskis et al., eds., *Policy Studies in Canada.* Toronto: University of Toronto Press.

– 2002. 'Policy Analysis in Canada.' In Christopher Dunn, ed., *The Handbook of Canadian Public Administration.* Don Mills, ON: Oxford University Press.

Canada. 1996. 'Strengthening Our Policy Capacity. Report of the Task Force on Strengthening the Policy Capacity of the Federal Government' (The Fellegi Report). Ottawa.

Curtain, Richard. 2000. 'Good Public Policy-Making: How Australia Fares. Agenda: A.' *Journal of Policy Analysis and Reform* 8(1), 33–46.

Hollander, Marcus J., and Michael J. Prince. 1996. 'Analytical Units in the Federal and Provincial Governments: Origins, Functions and Suggestions for Effectiveness.' *Canadian Public Administration* 36(2), 190–224.

Howe, Valerie. 2004. 'Environmental Scan Initiative.' *Horizons* 7(1), 81–2.

Pal, Leslie. 2001. *Beyond Policy Analysis: Public Issue Management in Turbulent Times*. Scarborough, ON: Nelson Thompson.

Picot, Garnett. 2003. 'Does Statistical Analysis Matter?' *Horizons* 6(1), 6–10.

Riddell, Norman. 1998. *Policy Research Capacity in the Federal Government*. A report prepared for the Policy Research Initiative, Ottawa.

Rowe, Geoff. 2003. 'Fragments of Lives: Enabling New Policy Directions through Integrated Life-Course Data.' *Horizons* 6(2), 7–11.

Savoie, Donald J. 2004. 'Searching for Accountability in a Government Without Boundaries.' *Canadian Public Administration* 47(2), 1–26.

United Kingdom, Cabinet Office. 1999. *The Modernising Government White Paper*. London.

Voyer, Jean-Pierre, 2003. 'Les techniques expérimentales au service de la politique sociale.' *Sociologie et sociétés* 35(1), 257–74.

10 Policy Analysis in Provincial Governments in Canada: From PPBS to Network Management

DOUG MCARTHUR

Introduction

There is a relative paucity of scholarly work on provincial governments and their workings with respect to policy making (Imbeau and Lachapelle 1996). This is somewhat odd, given that the provincial government sector now provides almost two-thirds of the services of the government sector in Canada. Further, a very large part of federal activity is made up of passive transfers to individuals, requiring minimal policy and management attention, compared to the dynamic, ever-shifting environment within which provincial governments work. The simple fact is that in substantive terms, the largest proportion of policy development, adaptation, and change is concentrated in the provincial sector (Boychuk 1998; Dyck 1997).

Part of the reason for the relative neglect of the provinces is arguably the limited amount of information available about the workings of provincial governments. The internal workings of provincial governments are not widely observed, and it is difficult to systematically gather information on 10 separate entities, each of which may differ in important respects.[1] It also appears that provincial governments are not particularly introspective or self-conscious, adding to the paucity of reliable information. Provincial governments produce relatively few reports on their workings, and those that are produced are not readily accessible. In part, this seems to indicate a less reflective pre-disposition. Provincial government officials are arguably sceptical about theory and the study of how government works, and see the management of government as a very practical matter. Incremental change, and change driven by experience and practice, are favoured over 'big ideas,' complex study, and theory-driven innovation (Brownsey and Howlett 1992).

Two other factors appear to contribute to the lesser importance placed on the study and observation of provincial governments. The first is that a substantial amount of work on the science and practice of government is undertaken by international organizations. Government reform has been a favoured topic of organizations such as the Organization for Economic Cooperation and Development (OECD), the World Bank, and other respected groups. The OECD, for instance, has devoted a great deal of attention to government processes in member countries, including Canada. However, little of this work addresses provincial governments. Second, provincial governments are generally of less interest to the academic community. Provincial governments are most commonly seen as junior players, less important as objects of study than the federal government, with the majority of works being single case studies.[2]

Policy Analysis and Provincial Politics

The particular focus in this paper is the role of analysis in policy making within provincial governments. Analysis involves techniques and procedures rooted in an objective/procedural view of the policy process. It challenges politics and interest group competition for legitimacy in the policy process, and is procedurally different from voting, interest reconciliation, and the negotiating and bargaining that dominate elections, legislatures, party processes, lobbying, and networks of interests. The normative case for analysis is linked to rationality and an underlying belief in utilitarianism in agenda setting, policy formulation, and decision making (MacRae and Wilde 1985).

No discussion of the role of analysis can proceed without acknowledging the special role of professional public servants and professional advisers. These actors occupy a privileged role in analysis. The professionalization of policy making is necessarily linked to analysis in government processes, but this has in itself been a source of a certain amount of tension. Analysis is not always seen as fully compatible with the idea that policy is the prerogative of elected politicians (see Brooks, Mintrom in this volume).

At one level, it is hard to see how information, knowledge, and analysis can be faulted, steeped as we are in a belief in the merits of making rational choices. But it is sometimes claimed that analysis often preempts politics and, more importantly, the legitimate role of political actors. Some fear that the professionally oriented policy process is largely a system that serves the interests of public servants and professionals, rather than that of the larger society. The challenge is one of how to relate professionalism to policy, or put another way, how to relate analysis to decision making in inherently political environments.

Policy encompasses the things governments do intentionally in order to achieve change in the larger society. Policy is purposeful and planned, setting out intended actions under given sets of conditions. Purposeful and planned action entails objectives and intended results. In an ever more complicated world, with larger and more complex government organizations, more specialized skills and competencies in assembling and processing information and knowledge take on increasing value in planning and articulating government intentions. This in turn means that professional, merit-based public services themselves assume greater value.

The inevitable result has been a growing importance placed on public administration based on professional qualifications and merit. The Canadian provinces have not been immune to this trend. Saskatchewan was the first to commit to a professional public service, with legislation passed in 1945 (Johnson 2004). Most of the other provinces followed in the 1950s and 1960s, although in some cases purely operational low-skill jobs remained outside the merit system until quite recently (Bourgeault, Demers, and Williams 1997; Lindquist 2000). Associated with this trend to professionalization was the development of procedures that supported or encouraged analysis as a distinct part of policy making.

But these developments also generated the potential for a clash between elected and appointed officials. Two aspects of the provincial political scene account for this. First, policy analysis and knowledge is not understood generally by the political executive to be a form of expertise to the same degree as in the federal system. Policy advice is still often treated by provincial elected officials as being no more objective than their own sources of information. Second, policy making is generally based on a higher degree of personal engagement between the political executive and those with policy knowledge. As a result, the degree of conflict between politics and policy making, and between politicians and public servants, is more evident at the provincial level than at the federal level.

In part this is a result of the relative size of the bureaucracy, and the smaller numbers of public servants in the typical provincial government who will have knowledge and understanding of a policy matter. The engagement between the elected executive and officials is less formalized and more intense. Typically management and policy officials will engage more frequently with their political masters, and the engagements will be characterized by more give and take, debate and argument.

Policy analysts, for instance, usually interact directly with the deputy minister and typically are involved in a number of files simultaneously. Many program managers also provide analysis and advice on policy issues because there are no specialized policy analysts dedicated to the issue in question. The result is that those with policy knowledge are known by the minister to be working on particular issues, are called upon frequently to provide information and advice, and have relatively frequent contact with the minister. Relationships between the political executive and public servants with policy knowledge and analytical skills are thus not nearly as hierarchical, structured, and formalized as in larger systems of government.

This interaction leads to a higher degree of familiarity between those with policy knowledge and the political executive. Ministers also have a much more intense relationship with the public impacted by policy. The processes that engage policy advisors, ministers, and the affected public are thus much more likely to be based on shared information in forums in which there is a lesser degree of differentiation of these key actors in terms of policy knowledge and understanding.

The clashes have not been limited to any political party or set of beliefs, nor were they limited to the early period of professionalization. By way of example, they were most prominently held by the Conservative Devine government when elected in Saskatchewan, but also by the NDP Rae government when elected in Ontario, and the Liberal Campbell government when elected in British Columbia (Michelmann and Steeves 1985; Biggs and Stobbe 1991; Walkom 1994).

The approach to the policy process in these circumstances is almost always the same. Various attempts are made to shift the focus of the process from the bureaucracy to the political offices of government. Professional analysis as it applies to agenda setting, articulating problems, and identifying and assessing alternatives is blamed for past policy failures or misdirections. Senior political appointments are typically made in ministers' and premiers' offices, with the claim that in the future policy will be the responsibility of the elected members of the executive. The 'modern' trend toward relying heavily on professional analysis is discounted because of its bias against the direction of the newly elected government (Bernier, Brownsey, and Howlett 2005).

It is common to consider the results of these efforts to 'politicize' policy making misguided, and to suggest that policy making under such circumstances becomes error-ridden and ineffective. Politics dominates, but at the expense of the effective participation of professionals, and effective policy making breaks down because of the absence of effective policy analysis. The underlying argument is that workable and effective policy processes require, in today's complex world, the engagement of professionals and the results of good analysis.

Why is professional analysis assumed to be so important to good policy? The issue is clouded by the claims made about the dangers of politicizing policy making. There are some difficult-to-answer questions about the relationship between the political process and a workable policy process. The politicians suspicious of professional policy analysts are not entirely misguided. Clear definitions about the appropriate separation of the political process from the policy process, and of the appropriate linkages between the two are not as readily available as one might think. And to some considerable degree this is because the relationship is a complex one that is not often adequately addressed by proponents of professional analysis. Indeed, we can learn a great deal from the struggle that has gone on for some years in the provinces over these questions.

Arguably, it is at the provincial level of government in Canada that the complexities and even contradictions involved in policy analysis are most intensively played out. The smaller size, the tendency for governments to change frequently and for the changes to involve significant ideological shifts, and the absence of a prevailing elite view about the proper place of government in society, such as has existed for so long in Ottawa, all make the provincial level the most instructive for observing the complexities of the relationship between analysis and politics (White 2005).

Organizing Policy Deliberations in Provincial Governments

One way of better understanding what provincial governments do when they make policy is to consider how they organize decision making in terms of the higher-level policies in which political actors play an important role. An obvious place to look is at provincial cabinets and the processes that most directly relate to them: what cabinets do when they make policy, how they are organized to make policy, and how linkages are made between the professional public service and the elected office. This permits a focus on how the elected people themselves approach policy making, and what they consider important in structuring that part of their work.

Historical Background

An explicit commitment to planning in Canada first found expression in the structure of the cabinet system within a provincial government, namely, Saskatchewan, not in the federal government as one might expect. Analysis as a required activity certainly played a role. However, the initial undertaking was not directly rooted in the concerns and ideas advanced by the early advocates of the policy sciences, active at about the same time, with their interest in objectivity, technique, and professional capacity (Lerner and Lasswell 1951).

The central idea focused on how to bring professional knowledge and ability of a particular sort into the making of policy. When planning first explicitly appears in Saskatchewan, after the election of the Co-operative Commonwealth Federation (CCF) in 1944, it was associated with ideological concerns that differed considerably from the objective/instrumental view of the newly developing policy sciences. Along with establishing the merit system for hiring public servants, the government established a Planning Board, with a staff and other resources, which operated as a subsidiary body to cabinet (Johnson 2004). It was mandated to address the shortcomings of capitalism, which emphasized production for profit rather than human needs, and failed to coordinate the use of productive resources to achieve sustained development, full employment, and investment for the public good. The ideas behind this innovation were essentially rooted in a belief that socialism was needed to rescue the economy, and that socialism required the coordination and control associated with central planning.

The idea of the centrally planned economy was integral to all socialist thought of the time (Lipset 1959).

This first experiment in central planning was accompanied by no shortage of ambitious intentions. The language in support of it was redolent with the standard appeals of the socialist rhetoric of the day. George Cadbury spurned the family chocolate empire, and assumed the responsibility for making socialism work in one small corner of the empire, certain that the principles of rational planning could be applied to the greater good by working for the people (Richards and Pratt 1977). As things turned out, the undertaking proved to be more difficult than even the most optimistic advocates anticipated. Arguably, not enough tools were available to restructure capitalism in one small province. Or perhaps the analysis required to plan the solutions was simply too difficult.

As time passed, the Planning Board found that a more manageable task was to support government policy making in a less ambitious way. The board came to operate more and more as a committee of cabinet responsible for ensuring that policy was developed in a deliberate and carefully considered manner. Rules and procedures were established, setting out how ministers were to prepare proposals to cabinet. Guidance was developed for departments in an effort to ensure that proposals were carefully researched and analysed, alternatives developed, implications considered and recommendations formulated. The developing professional public service was called upon to become part of the policy process in a new way, largely free of partisan considerations. The committee, which soon included only members of cabinet, took on responsibility for undertaking strategic planning, policy due diligence and policy coordination functions, in support of and on behalf of cabinet. The committee evolved into a policy deliberation body. A secretariat oversaw and coordinated the work of the committee and soon assumed a role of reviewing and commenting on the work brought forward by departments. A central agency responsible for the policy process began to emerge and assumed a powerful place within the machinery of government, becoming a more or less permanent force to be reckoned with (Johnson 2004).

The Planning Board remained a key feature of the machinery of government for the whole of the 20 years of the CCF administration, from 1944 to 1964. Over time, as it assumed the role of policy oversight and management, it became the prototype for an approach to organizing government policy making that remained popular for half a century and which to this day has considerable influence. In the 1960s the Manitoba government of Conservative Premier Duff Roblin drew upon the experience of Saskatchewan to form a committee of cabinet with very similar features. Other provinces followed suit, most notably New Brunswick, Quebec, and, later, British Columbia (Dunn 1995 and 1996).[3]

Contemporary Policy-Making Machinery in the Provinces

Today, all provincial governments have in place cabinet committee processes to ensure effective policy deliberations (Bernier, Brownsey and Howlett 2005). The most recent comparative information on the 'state of the art' in cabinet-related policy decision making at the provincial level can be found in the results of a cooperative survey, undertaken jointly in 1998 by provincial deputy ministers to the premier/cabinet secretaries, in association with the clerk of the Privy Council Office (Privy Council Office 1998). This survey reports that all provinces have in place central policy committees of cabinet, staffed with and supported by a well-developed system of policy analysis. In all cases, the mandates of these committees included the review of major policy matters, and the making of recommendations to cabinet (Dunn 2002).

While the cabinet committee structure has been adopted over the years by both the federal government and the provinces, there are some noticeable differences between the two levels. All provincial governments depend extensively on two types of committees, one on policy and priority and the other on treasury board or financial management. The use of more complex policy envelope committees, common at the federal level, is not nearly so prevalent at the provincial level. The process for providing information and analysis for these provincial committees is also generally much less complex and less overwhelmed by paperwork than is the case at the federal level. In part this is a reflection of size, but it is perhaps more importantly also a reflection of the differing styles of policy decision making. The less hierarchical, more open and less differentiated roles played by the elected officials and public servants means that, more so than at the federal level, the advice sought by elected officials in committee deliberations in the provincial system is less about diagnosis and abstract analysis, and more about practical considerations regarding impacts and options.

Functional policy cabinet committees work because they provide a mechanism for quality review, debate, and deliberation. There has been growing acceptance that a model for formulating policy that leaves the work largely to individual departments does not effectively serve the process of policy formulation. While departments have, as the merit system developed, become relatively well staffed with professional experts, major policy deliberations have shifted over time to cabinets and their committees.

The ability of departments in the provinces to undertake policy analysis was not at issue. Policy analysis was something that departments did relatively well. Science and analytical techniques became ever more sophisticated. Yet there was a growing consensus among provincial executives that policy making needed to be more centralized in government. Over time, the trend was toward central policy committees, where analysis played a prominent role in assisting deliberations (Dunn 1996; White 2001). And while in some cases headstrong premiers have considered such committees to be a hindrance to the exercise of their own will over an agenda, the committees have become the rule rather than the exception.

The central role played by committees is also reflected in the shifting role of the senior deputy ministers, reporting to their premiers and acting as heads of the public service and chief policy advisors to cabinet and the premier. For many years, these officials played a powerful yet limited and relatively unobtrusive role in the operations of their respective governments. They coordinated the flow of documents to and from cabinet, maintained a general record of cabinet decisions, and acted as the eyes and ears of the premier with respect to the functioning of government in a general sense. Over the past few years, however, the role of these officials has expanded across all provinces. Today, the modern cabinet secretary/head of the public service/deputy minister to the premier extends his or her power and influence in ways unheard of 15 or more years ago. Now most often referred to as the deputy minister to the premier, this position is key to ensuring that analysis is undertaken to support the deliberations of cabinet and its policy committees. Line department deputy ministers and agency heads are generally brought together weekly to review the analytical work that has been undertaken on major questions to be reviewed by the cabinet committees (Balls 1976; Bourgault and Dion 1989; Savoie 2003).

A further activity routinely undertaken under the direction of the central policy group surrounding the cabinet and its committees is that of strategic planning. Virtually all provincial governments now set priorities through a strategic plan. The work in developing the annual strategic plan is now part of the routine work of the policy analysts deployed at the centre. Strategic planning and policy analysis are now widely accepted as inextricably linked activities essential to good governance (Alberta 2004).

Most readers will be familiar with the literature on the centralization of control in the federal government and in national governments more generally (Savoie 1990, 1999a, 1999b). Defenders of such centralization say that it has been necessary to manage priorities, make departments more responsible in terms of program reviews and expenditure management, improve the quality of appointments, and better manage an integrated and coordinated policy agenda. Others would say it is an inevitable consequence of a system of government that concentrates as much power in the hands of a premier as he or she wishes to assume. And even others would say that in the face of a continuing decline in policy capacity due to globalization, the existence of immense corporate power on an international scale, and various structural factors, it is essential that the policy capacity of government be buttressed through centralization to provide coherent and effective policy responses.

You can hear these kinds of arguments being expressed among advocates for centralization in equal measure both at the provincial and the federal level, and they appear to be winning. The trend toward centralization of policy processes at the provincial level over the past few years has been almost as pronounced as at the federal level. The presence and power of central cabinet policy committees, carefully controlled and directed by premiers, is one indicator of this. While there has been some variation in this pattern arising from particular circumstances, the overall direction is clear (Bernier, Brownsey, and Howlett 2005). Perhaps the most interesting dimension of this centralization is these committees' growing capacity to oversee and undertake policy analysis.

Accompanying this centralization of policy making has been a long and gradual hollowing-out of the policy development capacity in departments. It is difficult to obtain good data to firmly establish the extent of this. However, most senior deputy ministers would confirm that it has been happening since the 1980s. It has occurred as part of the continuing pressure on the size of the public service, associated with attempts to reduce expenditures. Policy analysts and advisers have been extremely vulnerable as budgets have been trimmed. Only in the premiers' offices and the cabinet secretariats has there been a trend toward increases in the number of experts explicitly devoted to policy. In all provincial governments, there has been a significant increase in the numbers of central policy analysts since the beginning of the 1990s, which is coincidentally the period during which expenditure reductions have been the largest.

There has been little scholarly attention devoted to the centralization of policy deliberations in provincial governments (Bernier, Brownsey and Howlett 2005). It does raise important questions, some of which relate to the changing role of the premier, since in general the greater the centralization of the policy process, the greater the power of the premier to control the agenda. While conventional analyses emphasize this aspect of the trend, more important is the fact that it enhances the policy capacity of the governments involved. Analysis in support of policy formulation and decision making at the centre has had a positive affect on the deliberative capacity of governments. The very fact that priorities and planning committees are almost universally present in provincial governments is a good sign for deliberative practice. It suggests that there is a concern with review, analysis, and debate. Governments generally have difficulty devoting quality time to policy deliberations, as time is scarce and the number of policy issues is large.

An interesting question is whether the nature of processes for policy deliberation within provincial governments has any impact on the degree of policy innovation. A plausible theory is that smaller governments with highly centralized policy processes will be more innovative. The centralization of policy is most real and meaningful in the provinces, which also helps to explain rapid policy change and innovation at the provincial level.

A related question is whether the types of processes observed to be common in provincial governments contribute to a higher level of policy success. A plausible theory in this respect is that the more centralized the policy process, the more likely is it that due diligence will be performed with more success, information will be more complete, and checks and balances will be more effective. This is likely to be the case because more effective rules are likely to be in place requiring comprehensive analysis and meaningful deliberation. A plausible conclusion is that cabinet-based review and deliberation, supported by good analysis, is essential to policy success.

Analytical Technique and Public Policy Development within the Provincial Bureaucracy

For most of the third quarter of the twentieth century, a discussion of the policy process was treated as virtually synonymous with a discussion of policy analysis. The conviction that analysis would provide a solution to intractable policy problems gradually became an article of faith among scholars. Analysis promised to be a platform from which any number of issues could be addressed, including the irrationality of politics, the undue power of special interests, and knowledge and information gaps. The enthusiasm for analysis can be traced directly to the work of Lasswell and scholars who worked the same vein; they were impressed by the success of analysis in resolving complex policy challenges in large bureaucracies, particularly in the military and defence areas.

Two specific initiatives were of particular importance. One was Benefit Cost Analysis (B/C), and the other was Programming, Planning and Budgeting Systems (PPBS) (Boardman et al. 2001; Wildavsky 1969). The federal government formally adopted PPBS as an integral tool for policy development and expenditure planning in 1969. At about the same time, B/C was mandated as a procedure to be adopted by departments in planning major new initiatives. B/C was promoted as an essential ingredient in PPBS. A drawn-out and tortuous attempt to integrate sophisticated analysis into the policy process through this approach essentially ended in failure with the adoption of the Operational Performance Management System and Management by Objectives in 1974. This was followed by the Policy and Expenditure Management System (PEMS) in 1980, when expenditure envelopes were developed and cabinet committees reviewed and approved policy initiatives. Analysis still played a role, but in a much more generic way (Van Loon 1984; Borins 1983). Eventually, the emphasis shifted to judgment and deliberation by decision makers in a way that did not include the complex systems of PPBS and its derivatives.

The contrast with the provinces was marked. In general, the provinces never made the assumption that analysis, using the sophisticated techniques of PPBS and B/C, would provide a solution to the ever-increasing complexities of policy making. Some provinces were early enthusiasts for B/C analysis, but mostly for the purposes of evaluating major capital projects. In the early 1970s British Columbia published its own guide to cost benefit analysis. References to the use of cost benefit analysis for budgeting purposes can be found in the budget directives and guidelines of most provinces during the 1970s, but it was primarily at the federal level that cost benefit was emphasized. In general B/C analysis was treated by the provinces as an adjunct to the budgeting process, with the most common applications being to assist decision makers with water management and use projects. It was never treated as an integral part of policy making in any of the provinces. And when it was used, for example to assess irrigation, flood control, and drainage projects, results suggesting that projects were not economically sound were more often than not ignored (Gunton 2003).

Drivers of Provincial Policy Analytical Capacity: Budgetary Systems, Program Review, and New Public Management in the Provinces

Some of the trends prevalent in the federal system also found their way into provincial systems. However, differences were also clear. Professional economists and systems analysts never assumed the importance that they did in the federal system in designing procedures. Cabinet committees were relied upon to do the heavy lifting, with analysis taking the form of a support to inform the decisions. The main developments in the 1980s and early 1990s were in the area of budgeting. All provinces made attempts to reform the budgeting process so that the concentration was not solely on setting line-by-line expenditures. Various procedures were adopted to review budgets on a program basis, and to include information on what the programs achieved as well as what they cost (Maslove 1989).

No common system emerged, but there were marked similarities across the provinces. Treasury boards were the main vehicle for assessing and using the results of the analyses that were undertaken. One popular idea was zero-based budgeting, in which treasury boards evaluated all programs annually to find savings or potential program eliminations (Cutt and Ritter 1984). Budget analysts provided reports to treasury boards with recommendations for savings or cuts in programs, with mixed results. Over time, treasury boards and cabinets became familiar with the 'shopping lists' that appeared each year in the analysts' reports, and that were repeatedly partially or wholly rejected because of the expected political implications. But budgeting was becoming ever more rigorous as a result of the work of highly skilled analysts and conscientious treasury boards. Indeed, it was remarkable how knowledgeable and demanding cabinet members became in the performance of a difficult and thankless task.

The results were not necessarily obvious, as deficits grew at an alarming rate in the late 1980s and early 1990s. The finances of conservative, business-oriented governments, such as those in British Columbia, Saskatchewan, and Alberta, as well as the left-leaning governments in Ontario and Quebec, suggested that budgeting itself was becoming a lost art. Strong analytical support and dedicated treasury boards seemed to be making little difference; budget deficits were getting out of control (Savoie and Veilleux 1988).

The problem of course was that the existing systems and processes could not control the big budget drivers. Major political judgments were required and extremely difficult decisions needed to be made. However, during the 1980s, cabinets and ministers were reluctant to make the hard decisions. Indeed, the opposite too often happened, with politically driven expenditures and tax cuts adding immense additional budgetary burdens, as in the case of Saskatchewan, Alberta, and Ontario. Cuts in federal transfer payments and growing interest payments to service the accumulating debts simply made things worse (Ismael and Vaillancourt 1988).

By the mid-1990s, in response to increasingly severe budget crises (Saskatchewan came close to financial receivership) (Ip 1991), analysis had gained a new level of importance. The focus, however, was not on a particular technique as much as it was on a framework in which analysis was the essential ingredient, but within which any number of procedures and techniques could be applied. This approach became popularly known as 'program review.' The essential elements of the program reviews were:

- across-the-board cuts in the budgets of all departments and agencies, often in the range of 25 per cent;

- cuts of a similar magnitude in the size of the public service;
- the virtual elimination of intergovernmental transfers, which in the provinces' cases meant largely transfers to local governments (this became popularly known as 'downloading');
- the identification of programs that could become the responsibility of the benefiting citizens or businesses, and thus targets for elimination from the government budget;
- the identification of new or additional revenue sources, in which beneficiaries assumed a greater share of the costs of programs benefiting them;
- the shifting of capital expenditures to private-sector 'partners'; and
- the postponement of major infrastructure expenditures.

Obviously, in carrying through with these initiatives, very difficult and complex political decisions had to be made. But it was not easy to decide precisely what these should be. An often-overlooked aspect of these program reviews was that very few decisions were obvious without a lot of detailed analytical work. Policies, programs, and expenditures had to be scrutinized, evaluated, and reported upon in great detail (Kneebone and McKenzie 1999).

With the advent of the program reviews, analysis finally achieved respectability in the provinces. Until this time, as much as there were valiant attempts to secure a position for professional analysis in the policy development and budgeting processes of government, analysis did not enjoy the respect and commitment that had long been hoped for by its advocates in universities and central agencies. The arrival of the 'program reviews,' with the hard and detailed work needed to assess the feasibility and impacts of many of the cuts, finally placed analysis in a central position. It was embraced by politicians as useful and necessary, no longer seen simply as a way to justify spending and to thwart political wants. However, for a quarter of a century or more after the Second World War, the procedures did not conform to the technique-oriented approaches advocated by experts. None of the provinces, so far as one can tell from an admittedly incomplete record, adopted rigorous and complicated techniques that required specialized textbook knowledge (Kelly 2000). The emphasis was on good and effective oversight and review by responsible officials, elected and appointed. Most provinces developed approaches that were designed to accommodate the personalities, character, and culture unique to each of them.

The procedures did, however, all adopt a relative standard form of the policy analysis brief to frame the work that had to be done.

The status of the technically oriented professional economist declined considerably in the face of these new challenges, while those with training, ability, and experience in reasoning and critical thinking, regardless of discipline, saw their status increase considerably. A new path to recognition and success within governments opened, based on proven ability in the program review process. Many were managers long occupied with making programs work; others were analysts in central agencies and departments; and even others were people who had served in professional advisory roles such as law and finance (Good 2003).

The program reviews forced an integration of policy and budget analysis in a way that none of the previous technique-oriented initiatives were able to do. The professional skills that were sought were those related to rational models of analysis supporting effective deliberations by people searching for difficult answers to hard questions. The policy analyst as a generalist, task-oriented, flexible, and non-ideological, able to work in multi-disciplinary teams and to integrate qualitative and qualitative data, able to assess costs and implications relative to outcomes and impacts, and able to communicate clearly and effectively, became a valued human resource.

Efforts at program review overlapped considerably with other government reform initiatives, sometimes referred to collectively as 'New Public Management' (NPM). While program review promoted policy analysis, however, NPM pushed governments in the opposite direction (Aucoin 1995; Charih and Daniels 1997; Christensen and Laegreid 2001). NPM was, among other things, expected to transform the relationship between policy and the operations of government. Key ideas were:

- 'steering,' which meant that the central government established policy direction, leaving program management to arms-length agencies;
- institutional and process reform to reduce self-interested strategic behaviour of actors in policy making; and
- a transformation in the way choices were made, with a reduced reliance on government-driven choices, and more opportunities for citizens to make their own choices.

Ontario subscribed to NPM during the last half of the 1990s, when NPM was at its zenith as a new idea for redefining government (White and Cameron 2000). In a major publication in 1999, the government stated that the 'new' public management provided a rationale for its new approach to government. The document sets out what is involved in the 'transformation of government' resulting from the adoption of NPM, described as follows:

- planning the business of government by means of business plans that include performance measures;
- identifying the core and doing business differently;
- refining accountability in a new context, in which managing externally delivered services and performance expectations are addressed; and
- developing and disseminating a vision based on a smaller government focused on the core business, service quality, flexibility, cohesiveness and accountability (Ontario Cabinet Office 1999).

An interesting question is whether the Ontario model in fact involved a coherent formulation of NPM consistent with its standard formulation.[4] Notwithstanding this, however, an important point not often fully recognized by those examining NPM, but evident in the above, is that NPM reflected a deep discomfort with the 'age of analysis,' which roughly extended from the 1960s to the 1980s. During this period, as has been already stated, considerable emphasis was placed on better supporting decision systems within government through improved and more extensive analysis. NPM theorists had little faith in such systems, believing they were everywhere corrupted by particular interests and, for all practical purposes, tools supporting the growth of government. Thus, a need was seen for the policy process to be fundamentally altered, and not simply made 'bigger and better.' A bigger and better policy process was anathema to NPM theorists, although there was support for more diversity and competition.

There has been considerable debate in Canada about the role that NPM has played in policy outcomes. It is now generally accepted that NPM has had only limited influence within the federal government. A less settled question is that of the impact of NPM on provincial systems. Despite a great deal of rhetoric to the contrary, there is little evidence of a significant impact of NPM thinking in the provinces. Nevertheless, there are two developments common at the provincial level that have almost certainly been influenced by NPM ideas, whatever the formal ancestry.

The first of these relates to the famous distinction in the NPM literature between 'steering' and 'rowing.' Formal adherents to NPM advocated models for the public service in which departments responsible to ministers were transformed into policy agencies, and program delivery was devolved to corporate bodies operating on a contract basis, more or less independently of political direction. The last ten to fifteen years have seen the adoption of models at the provincial level that have many features in common with the NPM models. The delivery of health care, for instance, is now managed in all provinces by authorities with separate management boards, with health departments operating almost exclusively as policy agencies. Similar arrangements are also becoming more common in the delivery of child protection services, tourism services, and parks administration. When taken together with the longstanding approaches to schooling, universities, and colleges, it is now the case that over three-quarters of provincial services are delivered under arrangements that generally meet the criteria set out under the NPM in terms of the separation of 'steering' and 'rowing.' By way of contrast, the proportion of services provided by the federal government in a similar way is below 25 per cent.

One significant development in this regard has been the move toward alternative service delivery (ADS); another has to do with performance and accountability measurement. Both of these appeal to some of the underlying concepts and ideas of NPM, and are referenced in most NPM-based reforms. The majority of the provinces have issued guides and directives with respect to ADS. Privatization has been the most popular form of ADS, and is usually emphasized in provinces where conservative, business-friendly governments are in office. All provinces have paid lip service to so-called 'special operating agencies,' and most have developed guidelines and procedures for Public-Private Partnerships (PPPs or P3s). But the adoption of such measures turns out on closer examination to be justified in terms of the 'make or buy' principle (Ford and Zussman 1997; Kernaghan 2000).

Finally, NPM thinking has led to the creation and adoption of business plans. Interestingly enough, the focus in the development of these has actually been on planning and policy, including evaluation of policy. The majority of provincial governments now require departments, ministries, and agencies to prepare annual business plans. In some cases, as in Alberta and Ontario, the business plans are acknowledged as an outgrowth of NPM. In general, however, business plans are simply set as required products of the traditional planning cycle.

A representative case of what the new business planning and performance measurement involves can be seen by examining the case of Alberta. All departments and the government as a whole are required to produce annual business plans. The business plan is a document that records the results of a department's analysis and review of its undertakings and of strategic planning to set directions and priorities. Each department is also required to prepare an annual report on performance measures (Bruce, Kneebone, and McKenzie 1997).

The heady days when program reviews were at their zenith have passed, and NPM no longer has a significant impact on government actions. However, the legacy of the program reviews and business plans continues. The logic of policy analysis has become embedded in the decision-making process, to a much greater degree than was the case previously. The integration of policy and budget deliberations is now accepted as evident and practical. A new culture of analysis and deliberation has taken hold within provincial governments.

The permanency of this culture is by no means secure, however. Nothing permanent came even close to being achieved in previous attempts by experts to impose technical systems that would force decision making based on analysis. The values and practices that have developed from the program reviews may not be sustained if a professional attraction to abstract analysis and specialized expertise again produces analysis that is not relevant to the political executive.

Beyond Program Review and NPM: Policy Negotiations as Policy Analysis

Another area where the provinces have made a unique contribution to evolving practice in the policy development area is in the use of networked policy processes. Differentiating between consultation and network policy processes is somewhat challenging, since at a certain point they tend to blend into one another. However, the most important characteristic of networked processes is that of shared or collaborative decision making.

Virtually all policy decisions of any import are located at some point within a network. While most practitioners would say this is a matter of consultation, many critics of government say that these complex inter-actions in fact constitute transactions in which competing interests make their bargains. This is not the place to delve further into the theory and practice of networks (Klijn 1996; Klijn and Koppenjan 2000; Klijn, Koppenjan, and Termeeer 1995). However, innovation in the manage-ment of networks is of considerable relevance when examining policy organization and innovation at the provincial level. Whenever concerns and interests are diverse and diffuse and when conflicts are intense, existing analytical approaches have proven incapable of yielding rea-sonably acceptable policy outcomes, and governments have found it impossible to achieve stable policy in the absence of substantive en-gagement with key interests. In these situations, governments have turned to special processes to find a solution. Mandated negotiations, for example, have been used in order to achieve outcomes that are workable and lasting. These approaches challenge the now standard model, which involves deliberations supported by analysis undertaken by professionals.

The most prominent examples of this sort of conflict can be found regarding the use of public lands and environment and resources. Pro-vincial lands and resources are typically considered by numerous ac-tors to be commonly owned, and thus a balanced consideration of interests is difficult to achieve. The standard mechanisms for creating and distributing interests, based on professional analysis and executive deliberation, do not offer an acceptable solution. A number of provinces have experimented with unique models of joint stakeholder negotia-tions to try to arrive at a policy framework in these kinds of situations. In these cases, negotiations are not only explicitly recognized as a means of resolving the policy questions, but attempts are made to make them work more efficiently and effectively. The most prominent ex-amples of the use of such approaches have been in the foothills area of Alberta, the northern forests of Ontario, and the land and resources and environment planning processes in British Columbia (Wilson 1998; Stefanick and Wells 2000).

Some of the new and innovative aspects of these negotiated net-worked policy processes include:

1 The finding that an explicit commitment to negotiate policy out-

comes can be made to work, at least in specific circumstances in which stakeholders are well organized and knowledgeable.

This may seem obvious now, but it certainly was resisted prior to these new processes being adopted. There was intense opposition within the government departments that were most intimately involved.

2 Cabinets and political executives willing to relinquish a considerable amount of the policy discretion normally retained in the policy process.

3 Participants given the resources and opportunity to deliberate as part of the negotiations, and the use of analysis in the deliberations. Indeed, it is the acknowledgement of the importance of analysis-based deliberations that seems to make truly integrative negotiations work. Joint problem solving using analysis is the key to success.

4 Government provision of appropriate discipline and rules. Broad objectives, rules of participation, time frames, a process framework, resources, commitment, and the default option were all important to success.

Conclusion

As one traces developments at the provincial level, one finds that to some degree they track those at the federal level. However, they also differ in important ways. A common feature of attempts to improve the policy and planning processes of provincial governments has been a reliance on less formal techniques of analysis. Objective/instrumental techniques such as benefit cost analysis, cost effectiveness analysis, program-based budgeting, performance-based budgeting, and other technique-oriented approaches have displayed little staying power. Provincial governments have been reluctant to adopt these more highly technical approaches, favoured at different times in Ottawa and other large bureaucracies. But in more pragmatic and practical forms, policy analysis has endured at the provincial level.

The small size and ever-changing demands placed upon provincial governments, however, may serve as absolute limits to the kind of professional policy analysis practised in other jurisdictions (Radin 2000; Mayer, Bots, and van Daalen 2004).

In order to deal with these limits, provincial governments in recent years have experimented with a new focus on negotiation and deliberation. Regrettably, the state of theory with respect to each of these processes, as they apply to government policy making, is very underdeveloped (see, however, L. Salter's chapter in this volume).

NOTES

1 Few works exist which examine these differences. See Dunn 1996. This situation has not changed dramatically since the first major comparative works of the mid-1970s. See, for example, Bellamy, Pammett, and Rowat 1976.
2 See, for example, collections and studies like Gagnon and Montcalm 1990; MacDonald 1985; Thorburn 1961; Jamieson 1984; Smitheram, Milne, and Dasgupta 1982; Noel 1971; Silver and Hull 1990; Biggs and Stobbe 1991; Tupper 1992; Morley, Ruff, et al. 1983; Carty 1996.
3 It is of interest to note that it was not until 1968 that the federal government created a Planning and Priorities Committee, with similar system of bureaucratic support, to 'set broad priorities and directions and guide the work of the cabinet committees' (Carin and Good 2000).
4 As a description of NPM, the document is curious in regard to what is omitted or de-emphasized. Many of the main ideas of NPM are largely ignored after a strong start. Little attention is devoted to important ideas like policy competition, the separation of policy functions from delivery, strategic planning, breaking down public service monopolies, and the development of internal markets. The main focus is on vision, business planning, performance measurement and accountability, program review, and alternative service delivery, including privatization.

REFERENCES

Aucoin, Peter. 1995. *The New Public Management: Canada in Comparative Perspective*. Montreal: Institute for Research on Public Policy.

Balls, Herbert R. 1976. 'Decision-making: The Role of the Deputy Minister.' *Canadian Public Administration* 19(3), 417–31.

Bellamy, David J., Jon H. Pammett, and Donald C. Rowat, eds. 1976. *Provincial Political Systems: Comparative Essays*. Toronto: Methuen.

Bernier, Luc, Keith Brownsey, and Michael Howlett, eds. 2005. *Executive Styles*

in Canada: Cabinet Structures and Leadership Practices in Canadian Government.
Toronto: University of Toronto Press.

Biggs, Leslie, and Mark Stobbe, eds. 1991. *Devine Rule in Saskatchewan.* Saskatoon: Fifth House Publishers.

Boardman, Anthony E., et al., eds. 2001. *Cost-Benefit Analysis: Concepts and Practice.* Upper Saddle River, NJ: Prentice-Hall.

Borins, Sanford F. 1983. 'Ottawa's Expenditure "Envelopes": Workable Rationality at Last?' In G.B. Doern, ed., *How Ottawa Spends Your Tax Dollars 1982: National Policy and Economic Development,* 63–86. Toronto: Lorimer.

Bourgault, Jacques, Maurice Demers, and Cynthia Williams, eds. 1997. *Public Administration and Public Management: Experiences in Canada.* Quebec, QC: Les Publications du Quebec.

Bourgault, Jacques, and Stephane Dion. 1989. 'Governments Come and Go, But What of Senior Civil Servants? Canadian Deputy Ministers and Transitions in Power (1867–1987).' *Governance* 2(2), 124–51.

Boychuk, Gerard. 1998. *Patchworks of Purpose: The Development of Social Assistance Regimes in Canada.* Montreal and Kingston: McGill-Queen's University Press.

Brownsey, Keith, and Michael Howlett. 1992. 'Introduction: The Provincial State in Canada.' In K. Brownsey and M. Howlett, eds., *The Provincial State: Politics in Canada's Provinces and Territories,* 1–8. Toronto: Copp Clark Pitman.

Bruce, C.J., R.D. Kneebone, and K.J. McKenzie, eds. 1997. *A Government Reinvented: A Study of Alberta's Deficit Elimination Program.* Toronto: Oxford University Press.

Carin, Barry, and David Good. 2000. *An Abridged History of Major Expenditure Management Reforms in the Canadian Federal Government.* Ottawa. Consortium for Economic Policy Research Advice.

Carty, R.K., ed. 1996. *Politics, Policy and Government in British Columbia.* Vancouver: UBC Press.

Charih, Mohamed, and Arthur Daniels, eds. 1997. *New Public Management and Public Administration in Canada.* Toronto: IPAC.

Christensen, Tom, and Per Laegreid, eds. *New Public Management: The Transformation of Ideas and Practice.* Aldershot: Ashgate, 2001.

Cutt, James, and Richard Ritter. 1984. *Public Non-Profit Budgeting: The Evolution and Application of Zero-Base Budgeting.* Toronto: Institute of Public Administration of Canada.

Dunn, Christopher. 1995. *The Institutionalized Cabinet: Governing the Western Provinces.* Montreal and Kingston: McGill-Queen's University Press.

- 1996. 'Premiers and Cabinets.' In C. Dunn, ed., *Provinces: Canadian Provincial Politics*, 165–204. Peterborough, ON: Broadview.
- 2002. 'The Central Executive in Canadian Government: Searching for the Holy Grail.' In C. Dunn, ed., *The Handbook of Canadian Public Administration*, 305–40. Don Mills, ON: Oxford University Press.

Dyck, Perry Rand. 1992. *Provincial Politics in Canada.* Toronto: Prentice-Hall.

Ford, Robin, and David Zussman. 1997. *Alternative Service Delivery: Sharing Governance in Canada.* Toronto: IPAC.

Gagnon, A.G., and M. Montcalm. 1990. *Quebec: Beyond the Quiet Revolution.* Toronto: Nelson. .

Good, David. 2003. *The Politics of Public Management: The HRDC Audit of Grants and Contributions.* Toronto: University of Toronto Press.

Government of Alberta. 2004. *Strategic Business Plan.* Edmonton.

Gunton, Thomas. 2003. 'Megaprojects and Regional Development: Pathologies in Project Planning.' *Regional Studies* 37(5), 505–19.

Imbeau, Louis M., and Guy Lachapelle. 1996. 'Comparative Provincial Public Policy in Canada.' In C. Dunn, ed., *Provinces: Canadian Provincial Politics*, 401–422. Peterborough, ON: Broadview.

Imbeau, Louis M., et al. 2000. 'Comparative Provincial Policy Analysis: A research Agenda.' *Canadian Journal of Political Science* 23(4), 779–804.

Ip, Irene. 1991. 'An Overview of Provincial Government Finance.' In M. McMillan, ed., *Provincial Public Finances.* Toronto: Canadian Tax Foundations.

Ismael, Jacqueline S., and Yves Vaillancourt, eds. 1988. *Privatization and Provincial Social Services in Canada: Policy, Administration, and Service Delivery.* Edmonton, AB: University of Alberta Press.

Jamieson, Barbara, ed. 1984. *Governing Nova Scotia.* Halifax: Dalhousie University School of Public Administration.

Johnson, A.W. 2004. *Dream No Little Dreams: A Biography of the Douglas Government in Saskatchewan, 1944–61.* Toronto: University of Toronto Press.

Kelly, J. 2000. 'Budgeting and Program Review in Canada 1994–2000.' *Australian Journal of Public Administration* 59(3), 72–8.

Kernaghan, Kenneth, Brian Marson, and Sandford Borins. 2000. *The New Public Organization.* Toronto: Institute of Public Administration of Canada.

Klijn, Erik-Hans. 1996. 'Analyzing and Managing Policy Processes in Complex Networks: A Theoretical Examination of the Concept Policy Network and Its Problems.' *Administration and Society* 28(1), 90–119.

Klijn, Erik-Hans, and Joop F.M. Koppenjan. 2000. 'Public Management and

Policy Networks: Foundations of a Network Approach to Governance.' *Public Management* 2(2), 135–58.

Klijn, Erik-Hans, Joop Koppenjan, and Katrien Termeer. 1995. 'Managing Networks in the Public Sector: A Theoretical Study of Management Strategies in Policy Networks.' *Public Administration* 73, 437–54.

Kneebone, Ronald, and Kenneth McKenzie. 1999. *Past (In)Discretions: Canadian Federal and Provincial Fiscal Policy.* Toronto: University of Toronto Centre for Public Management.

Lerner, Daniel, and Harold D. Lasswell. 1951. *Policy Sciences: Recent Developments in Scope and Method.* Stanford, CA: Stanford University Press.

Lindquist, Evert, ed. 2000. *Government Restructuring and Career Public Services.* Toronto: Institute of Public Administration of Canada.

Lipset, S.M. 1959. *Agrarian Socialism: The Co-operative Commonwealth Federation in Saskatchewan – A Study in Political Sociology.* Berkeley, CA: University of California Press.

MacDonald, Donald C., ed. 1985. *Government and Politics of Ontario.* Toronto: Macmillan.

MacRae, Duncan, Jr, and James A. Wilde. 1985. *Policy Analysis for Public Decisions.* Lanham, MD: University Press of America.

Maslove, Allan M., ed. 1989. *Budgeting in the Provinces: Leadership and the Premiers.* Toronto: Institute of Public Administration of Canada.

Mayer, I., P. Bots, and E. van Daalen. 2004. 'Perspectives on Policy Analysis: A Framework for Understanding and Design.' *International Journal of Technology, Policy and Management* 4(1), 169–91.

Michelmann, Hans J., and Jeffrey S. Steeves. 1985. 'The 1982 Transition in Power in Saskatchewan: the Progressive Conservatives and the Public Service.' *Canadian Public Administration* 28(1), 1–23.

Molot, M.A. 1988. 'The Provinces and Privatization: Are the Provinces Really Getting Out of Business?' In A. Tupper and G.B. Doern, eds., *Privatization, Public Policy, and Crown Corporations*, 399–426. Montreal: Institute for Research on Public Policy.

Morley, J.T., N. Ruff, et al. 1983. *The Reins of Power.* Vancouver: Douglas and McIntyre.

Noel, S.J.R. 1971. *Politics in Newfoundland.* Toronto: University of Toronto Press.

Ontario Cabinet Office. 1999. *Transforming Public Service for the 21st Century: An Ontario Perspective.* Toronto: Government of Ontario.

Privy Council Office. 1998. *Reports on Provincial and Territorial Decision-Making Processes.* Ottawa: Government of Canada.

Radin, Beryl A. 2000. *Beyond Machiavelli: Policy Analysis Comes of Age*. Washington, DC: Georgetown University Press.

Richards, J., and L. Pratt. 1977. *Prairie Capitalism: Power and Influence in the New West*. Toronto: McClelland and Stewart.

Savoie, Donald J. 1990. *The Politics of Public Spending in Canada*. Toronto: University of Toronto Press.

– 1999a. 'The Rise of Court Government in Canada.' *Canadian Journal of Political Science* 32(4), 635–64.

– 1999b. *Governing from the Centre: The Concentration of Power in Canadian Politics*. Toronto: University of Toronto Press.

– 2003. *Breaking the Bargain: Public Servants, Ministers and Parliament*. Toronto: University of Toronto Press.

Savoie, Donald J., and Gerard Veilleux. 1988. 'Kafka's Castle: The Treasury Board of Canada Revisited.' *Canadian Public Administration* 31(4), 517–38.

Silver, James, and Jeremy Hull, eds. 1990. *The Political Economy of Manitoba*. Regina: Canadian Plains Research Centre.

Smitheram, V., D. Milne, and S. Dasgupta, eds. 1982. *The Garden Transformed: Prince Edward Island 1945–1980*. Charlottetown, PEI: Ragweed Press.

Stefanick, Lorna, and Kathleen Wells. 2000. 'Alberta's Special Places 2000: Conservation, Conflict, and the Castle-Crown Wilderness.' In S. Bocking, ed., *Biodiversity in Canada: Ecology, Ideas and Action*. Peterborough, ON: Broadview.

Thorburn, Hugh. 1961. *Politics in New Brunswick*. Toronto: University of Toronto Press.

Tribe, Laurence H. 1972. 'Policy Science: Analysis or Ideology?' *Philosophy and Public Affairs* 2(1), 66–110.

Tupper, Allan, and Roger Gibbins, eds. 1992. *Politics in Alberta*. Edmonton, AB: University of Alberta Press.

Van Loon, Richard. 1984. 'Ottawa's Expenditure Process: Four Systems in Search of Co-ordination.' In G.B. Doern, ed., *How Ottawa Spends 1983: The Liberals, The Opposition and Federal Priorities*, 93–120. Toronto: Lorimer.

Walkom, Thomas. 1994. *Rae Days: The Rise and Fall of the NDP*. Toronto: Key Porter.

White, Graham. 2001. 'Adapting the Westminster Model: Provincial and Territorial Cabinets in Canada.' *Public Money and Management* 21(2), 17–24.

– 2005. *Cabinets and First Ministers*. Vancouver: UBC Press.

White, Graham, and David R. Cameron. 2000. *Cycling into Saigon: The Conservative Transition in Ontario.* Vancouver: UBC Press.

Wildavsky, Aaron. 1969. 'Rescuing Policy Analysis From PPBS.' *Public Administration Review* (March-April), 189–202.

Wilson, Jeremy. 1998. *Talk and Log: Wilderness Politics in British Columbia.* Vancouver: UBC Press.

11 Immature Policy Analysis: Building Capacity in Eight Major Canadian Cities

KENNEDY STEWART AND PATRICK J. SMITH

Introduction[1]

Policy analysis in Canada's municipalities varies significantly from that undertaken at senior governmental levels, mainly because of the three communities of actors involved: *decision makers, knowledge generators,* and *knowledge brokers.* The first operates under a much more debilitating set of institutional arrangements while the other two are either less populated or, at worst, non-existent. As the bulk of this chapter explains, the capacity of local decision makers to direct, receive, and act upon sophisticated policy advice is severely hampered by an antiquated approach to local governing. When coupled with a paucity of knowledge-generating researchers and knowledge-brokering commissions, task forces or city-specific think tanks, the result is that un- or under-supervised civil servants drive and dominate the policy analysis process. While an engaged public service is not inherently problematic, at the senior levels of government this aspect of the policy analysis process is balanced by other institutional forms and broader policy communities than is the norm in Canada's cities.

By comparing electoral and legislative arrangements in eight of Canada's largest cities, this chapter also demonstrates that some metropolitan decision-making communities lag far behind others in terms of capacity. It also suggests that all require significant modernizing before they will be able to play the same role as their senior counterparts and even where the actor communities are adequately populated, local policy analysis is still liable to be truncated and unsophisticated.

Local Governmental Policy Analysis in Canada

This book seeks to explain how three sets, herein deemed 'communities,' of policy actors design, develop, implement and/or evaluate public policies at all levels of Canadian government. As described in the introduction, the book explores how 'decision makers,' 'knowledge generators' and 'knowledge brokers' interact to improve the rationality of the policy-making process by using increasingly sophisticated and integrated policy analysis techniques (Lindquist 1990). Chapters about senior governmental levels explain, for example, the inner workings of national knowledge brokers such as think tanks, or how all three communities interact to generate policy analysis in particular provinces.

Following these ideas, readers might expect a chapter on policy analysis at the local level to follow a similar path, with local mayors and councils seen as the decision makers, academics, and research institutes as knowledge generators, and local commissions, task forces, or organized interest groups as knowledge brokers. However, this analytical framework is mismatched with the local policy analysis process due to the underdeveloped nature, or even complete absence, of knowledge generators and knowledge brokers in most of the country's municipalities. Canada's handful of urban academics could not possibly act as knowledge generators for thousands of municipalities. As municipal commissions and task forces are extremely rare, very few local-specific knowledge brokers exist outside of omnipresent local boards of trade and service clubs. Where local interest groups are often powerful, they are seldom long-lived, well organized, or based on more than emotive responses to local policy problems.

Even in Canada's largest cities, knowledge brokers are far less plentiful than in provincial or national policy-making arenas, and where they do exist their focus is seldom concentrated on solving the problems of a single municipality. For example, Vancouver-based Better Environmentally Sound Transportation (BEST) often lobbies Vancouver City Council to promote 'sustainable transportation and land-use planning, and pedestrian, cycling and transit oriented neighbourhoods,' but as their efforts are aimed at all of Western Canada, what lobbying efforts they do manage are more wide than deep (BEST 2005). Knowledge generation about local problems is usually handled by local planning and policy staff; however, on rare occasions external agencies do generate reports that are adopted at a local level. For example, while the City of Vancouver's homelessness action plan was generated using data gathered by internal planning staff, the Greater Vancouver Regional District's homelessness plan is based on counts taken by consultants who were in turn commissioned by the non-profit Social Planning and Research Council of British Columbia (City of Vancouver 2005; Greater Vancouver Regional District 2003).

As the local governmental knowledge generation and brokerage communities are far smaller than those at senior governmental levels, we feel it might be more instructive to explore the state of decision-making communities in Canada's largest cities. While this may deviate from what has been written elsewhere in this book, capacity in this actor community cannot be taken for granted. For example, federal and provincial politicians set at least a portion of the governmental agenda and steer the work of generators and brokers by campaigning on platforms that they promise to implement if their party forms government. However, as local politics are often bereft of political parties, manifestos are virtually absent from local elections and policy is made on a more ad hoc basis. Or, more disturbingly, where parties do exist, their literature baldly states that elected party officials are not under any 'obligation to policies or platforms' (Non-Partisan Association 2005).

Lack of capacity in local decision-making actor communities may have been less of a problem during much of the twentieth century, when local governments often, and accurately, characterized themselves as administrative wings of senior governments (Federation of Canadian Municipalities 1976). But twenty-first-century municipal governments in Canada, especially those in our largest urban settings, have not only gained more responsibilities through offloading, but have also become increasingly financially independent of former provincial masters. For example, while the City of Vancouver's annual budget has risen to almost $1 billion, the provincial government contribution has dropped to a mere one per cent of total revenues (City of Vancouver 2003, 17). This decline in the provincial contribution to the local authority has left the City of Vancouver to fend for itself on the revenue side, which has happened at a time of more policy-making freedom (Smith and Stewart 2005).

While it would appear that investigating the capacity of Canadian local government decision-making communities is a necessary first step in understanding local policy analysis, this type of investigation is far from straightforward. There is the difficulty of determining what institutional arrangements might hinder or facilitate such capacity and the fact that examples from which to draw guidance for comparative studies of Canadian local government of any size are rare. Where little previous investigation has been undertaken, descriptive accounts of institutional behavioural features usually suffice. However, this chapter attempts to move beyond mere description by ranking Canadian cities according to the arrangements surrounding the capacity of their decision makers to effectively fulfill their role in the local policy analysis process. As explained in more detail in the next section, eight categories of data are generated for eight of the largest municipalities in Canada: Halifax, Montreal, Ottawa, Toronto, Winnipeg, Edmonton, Calgary, and Vancouver. After comparing these cities, the chapter concludes by offering suggestions for further research as to how to improve local governmental policy analysis. Although our ranking may not appeal to all readers, we hope that those who disagree can at least gain some benefit from the new descriptive data. As John Griffith cautions, anyone trying to compare local governing and policy making could find that 'every example can be shown in some way to be unrepresentative and ill-chosen. Any generalization evokes shouts of protest.' Griffith suggests the way out of this dilemma is to recognize that 'some aspects ... are more important and universal than others' (1966, 17). To us, capacity to properly direct and oversee local policy analysis is arguably 'more important,' and this forms the basis of our investigation.

Evaluating Local Governmental Decision Makers' Capacity

From our perspective, the job of decision makers during the process of policy analysis is to set the direction of research and supervise the development and implementation of appropriate policy options. There are two main stages in which to evaluate the capacity of local councils to effectively play their role. During the *electoral stage*, politicians generate a governmental policy agenda through the competitive struggle for votes. During the *legislative stage*, politicians further develop this agenda and oversee the work of civil servants. Although this heuristic description does not include interaction between these two stages, nor how governments respond to mid-term policy demands, the outline does provide broad clues as to where institutional deficiencies undermining capacity might be found.

Electoral Stage Capacity

The question of which type of electoral system *best* builds the capacity of decision makers to set agendas is a source of constant debate in

Canada and elsewhere. However, there has been much agreement about essential institutions and what types of rules and processes to *avoid*. As discussed and contextualized below, three minimum standards stand out in the electoral stage in most recognized democracies: competitive party systems; fair electoral formula; and limits to the amount that candidates can spend during elections.

It is almost impossible to imagine national and provincial elections without political parties. One might even agree with the statement by the (Lortie) Royal Commission on Electoral Reform and Party Financing, that 'without political parties there can't be true democracy' (1991, 207). Parties are primary political organizations that organize an often diverse array of views into more coherent policy packages, which citizens can vote for or against, and which eventually form the governmental agenda. However, in many Canadian cities there are often strong non-partisan traditions and overarching provincial legislation regulating local elections, which actively discourages party formation.

The Canadian tradition of non-partisan local elections is an offshoot of the late nineteenth- and early twentieth-century municipal reform movement in the United States that sought to separate 'politics,' and the perceived municipal corruption associated with it, from city government by removing local parties from the electoral process (see, for example, Riordan 1963). The American movement followed an even longer trend of divorcing administration from politics, at least traceable to Woodrow Wilson's seminal 1887 essay, *The Study of Administration*, in which he argued that 'the field of administration is a field of business. It is removed from the hurry and strife of politics ... Administrative questions are not political questions ... Policy does nothing without the aid of administration but administration is not therefore politics ... The province of administration ... lies outside the proper sphere of politics' (1887/1966, 2, 28–9).

The rationale of the reform movement was to free public administration from the corrupt practices of 'pal-tronage' by creating a politics/administration dichotomy. As Kernaghan and Siegel argue, 'Wilson's distinction between politics and administration was accepted and perpetuated' (1987, 269) to the point that 'the politics-administration dichotomy was assumed both as a self-evident truth and a desirable goal' (Sayre 1958, 103; for some of that 'perpetuation' see also Goodenow 1893, 1905, 1914; White 1926; Willoughby 1927). Kernaghan and Siegel also note: 'During the late 19th and early 20th centuries, administrative reform efforts in both the United States and Canada were devoted to eradicating patronage from the public service, with a view to promoting efficient administration ... In both the United States and Canada, the two elements of the reform movement – efficiency through the elimination of patronage and efficiency through (rational) scientific management – reinforced one another and became integral components of the merit system' (1991, 341).

In senior governmental terms, such reforms allowed party politics and administration to coexist, even as the dichotomy itself was challenged by the 1960s and early 1970s (see, for example, Gawthorp 1971; Dvorin and Simmons 1972). This was not so at the local governmental level, which has almost exclusively remained non-partisan. Donald Rowat (1975, 29–30) suggests that the reason for this senior/local governmental divergence is because 'Canadian cities have tended to copy forms of local government developed in the United States. They have been influenced far more than have the higher levels of government by American democratic experiments.' Rowat concludes that the longevity of the local government non-partisan tradition in Canada might be because it was 'imported near the end of the last century after the local non-partisan movement had become strong, but before the party battle was well established in English local politics.' Warren Magnusson (1983, 10) agrees, suggesting that this upper/lower-tier divergence is because local politicians themselves found this arrangement convenient, as it allowed them 'greater freedom of action' once in office. It also meant that property interests came to predominate. Whatever the reason for continuing the local non-partisan tradition, this type of arrangement is clearly out of step with what has come to be accepted as a common Canadian norm.

Non-partisan systems remove the commonly held view that electoral democracy – and democratic policy making – rests on a competitive party system. As noted by Lortie (Canada 1991), Banfield and Wilson (1985) and others, political parties and politics play the vital role of aggregating preferences into policy choice and providing labels that can be easily identified by voters.[2] Non-partisan elections are generally personality contests devoid of substantive policy discussion, as candidates do not fight under one common banner and have little capacity to develop policy platforms on which they collectively campaign or for which they can be held politically accountable. As such, once elected, candidates often have no common policy goals and are either free to forward their own private agendas, or, more commonly, to react to pressures from organized interests or civil servants. Simply stated, non-partisan politics in large cities undermine the capacity of decision makers to generate a public agenda for elected officials to transform into a governmental agenda.

In the same vein as non-partisanship runs a tendency to reject constituency-based, 'ward' systems for 'at-large' elections in which municipalities are treated as a single, all-encompassing multimember constituency. Again, borrowed from American municipalities, at-large electoral arrangements, particularly when coupled with a first-past-the-post system of vote counting, have had the effect of disenfranchising racial and ethnic minorities and lowering voter turnout. The end result is that the local governmental agenda often only includes the preferences of a small portion of residents within the municipality (Smith and Stewart 1998). According to Howard Scarrow, at-large elections 'cancel out the strength of geographically concentrated groups of voters (e.g. party groups, racial groups), and they make it difficult for a voter to vote for an individual candidate, rather than for one of the competing list of candidates' (1999, 557). Although at-large systems have been replaced by wards systems by court orders in a large number of U.S. municipalities, and have been all but eradicated in Canada, they still exist in some cities, such as Vancouver (for a detailed account of the U.S. experience see Grofman, Bernard, Davidson, et al. 1992).

As found at the national and provincial levels, unlimited election spending opens the door for wealthy groups and interests to have undue influence on setting the governmental agenda and often closes out those with fewer resources. Election spending limits have been common practice for decades in Canadian federal and provincial elections, yet spending in many local electoral contests in Canada remains uncapped and sometimes even unmonitored. This is problematic, given that although local elections are often perceived as inexpensive competitions between local candidates, the reality can be quite different. Elections in large Canadian cities can generate campaign spending in the millions. For example, the two major parties contesting the 2002 Vancouver civic elections spent almost $3 million on advertising and election-related spending (Bula 2004, B1). These high expenditures by local 'parties' all but eliminate independent candidates or less established parties and put enormous pressure on local politicians to raise funds, badly biasing the local electoral process (Smith and Stewart 1998; Stewart 2003). According to the 1991 Royal (Lortie) Commission on Electoral Reform and Party Financing, limiting election expenditure is essential to ensuring fairness during the electoral process:

Freedom of expression in the electoral process ... cannot be meaningfully achieved unless the laws that govern this process explicitly seek to promote fairness in the exercise of this freedom. In this critical respect, the electoral law should not presume that all participants will have equal resources to communicate with the electorate. To do so would be to ignore the fact that different participants draw upon different bases of political support to finance their campaigns. Nor should electoral law assume that inequalities among participants are irrelevant to the outcome of elections. To do so would be to ignore the known effects of political communication: the capacity to communicate often, to use different media and to develop messages with the assistance of marketing and advertising experts is a significant factor in the political persuasion of voters ... In these respects, the political process must not be equated with the economic marketplace. (Canada 1991; 324)

In sum, free, fair, and competitive elections generate mandates for governments that guide their actions while they hold office. Most readers will probably appreciate the chaos that would ensue if national or provincial elections were held without parties, under at-large systems with unlimited spending. Elected politicians would be directionless and held hostage to either the demands of a small constituency of voters on whom they rely for support or a small constituency of funders who provide them with the monies needed to win expensive election contests. At the very least, they would be less able to play an effective role in participating and leading the policy analysis process.

Legislative Stage

During the legislative stage, decision makers further refine and implement their agenda. It is also during this stage that they interact with existing knowledge generators and brokers and evaluate the value of their advice. As refining and implementing efforts are contingent on the resources decision makers have at their disposal, it is this factor on which we concentrate our efforts.

One way of ensuring that politicians have enough time for their consultative and supervisory roles is to offer adequate incentives or remuneration. It has been long established that an adequate wage and benefit package is essential to keep public servants committed to their jobs, with political officials being no exception (Girth and Mills 1963; Dowding 1995). However, the Canadian local government tradition has been to elect a small number of politicians to part-time positions. Canadian local council positions have traditionally been under-rewarded for the work involved, and they frequently supplement their income by working other jobs. As Crawford (1954, 101) notes, in the early 1950s the norm was clearly for part-time municipal politicians who were elsewhere in full-time occupations and who received little in the way of remuneration. In some provinces, payment to municipal councillors was actually prohibited.[3] Connected to above-noted notions of non-partisanship in local governing, the reason for part-time politicians was clear: 'It is claimed by the advocates of pay for councillors that it would make it possible for men to serve who could not otherwise afford to lose the required time from their work. One of the objections to such payments is that they may be an inducement to persons who have little to contribute but who are primarily interested in the extra income. The type of representative who is most needed is not likely to be influenced to seek office by the pay involved' (Crawford 1954, 104).

This view echoed a 1947 (Lindsay Committee) Report, *Expenses of Members of Local Authorities* (1947a), in England: 'The health of this democracy depends upon the fact that large numbers of men and women give their time and trouble to all sorts of voluntary work, and it is from such public-spirited people that the members of public authorities should be recruited. Such voluntary work must involve sacrifice, and indeed would lose its savour if it did not.'

And while Lindsay did recommend that 'local authorities should have power to pay actual fares reasonably incurred on public transport, reasonable mileage allowance ... and subsistence expenses ... allowances for loss of remunerative time should be at a maximum of one pound per day (with) details of the payments ... published in the minutes.' That same year, the Minority (Turton) Report for the Lindsay Committee (1947b) also argued 'that the voluntary character of local government work should be preserved.' This view of part-time politicians had begun to shift a little by the 1970s. Rowat has noted that this change began with local administration in Canada's cities:

Especially in cities, where the job of councillor should be full-time or nearly so, the salaries are far too low to match the responsibilities of the job. An undesirable result of regarding the job as part-time, with only part-time pay, is that salaried professionals and other employees don't run for office ... Hence, the candidates are mainly self-employed professionals or businessmen ... who are more likely to represent the interests of business and the developers than ... the whole community ... Councillor's pay must be high enough not only to attract the most capable people ... but also to help give the office the dignity and esteem that it deserves. (1975, 40)

A second potential problem is that even if financial compensation is adequate, municipal councillors may not see the value of making a long-term commitment to their positions. At federal and some provincial positions in Canada, for example, politicians are provided with additional benefits such as pensions after a number of years in service. As is the case with higher salaries, this additional remunerative component provides incentives to develop longer-term political careers and commit to developing and implementing policy platforms with sufficient public support to secure and maintain office. An inadequate salary and benefit package structure heightens the risk of politicians either looking elsewhere for reward, lessening the incentive to keep their word, or being less attentive to their public office duties. Here again, contemporary local governments in major Canadian cities vary significantly from the clear benchmarks established for provincial and federal governments.

Like their federal and provincial counterparts, once in government local politicians rely substantially on the civil service to implement their election promises and for detailed policy advice. At the local governmental level staff may be even more important due to the previously mentioned lack of external knowledge generators and brokers. One of the classic public administration problems is how political 'principals' can compel their bureaucratic 'agents' to implement a political agenda, especially in large polities. Much of the literature on political/bureaucratic relations focuses on the problems of civil servants hiding or controlling information in order to budget maximize or bureau shape (Niskanen 1973; Dunleavy 1991). As Max Weber (Gerth and Mills 1963, 233–4) summarizes, 'every bureaucracy seeks to increase the superiority of the professionally informed by keeping their knowledge and intentions secret.' This can become a feature *within* government itself, particularly between politicians and bureaucrats: '... the pure interest of the bureaucracy in power ... is efficacious far beyond those areas where purely functional interests make for secrecy ... In facing a parliament out of sheer power instinct, the bureaucracy fights every attempt of the parliament to gain knowledge by means of its own experts, or from interest groups. The so-called right of parliamentary investigation is one of the means by which parliament seeks such knowledge. Bureaucracy naturally welcomes a poorly informed and powerless parliament – at least insofar as ignorance somehow agrees with the bureaucracy's interests.'

At the extreme end, the capacity of bureaucratic actors to significantly influence policy outcomes has been called 'bureaucratic capture.' As Thomas Dye (2001, 140) has recently suggested: 'bureaucracies grow in size and gain in power with advances in technology, increases in information, and growth in the size and complexity of society ... The power of the bureaucracy is also enhanced when ... policymaking responsibility ... [is] deliberately shift[ed] ... to the bureaucrats [by politicians] ... The internal dynamics of bureaucratic governance also expands bureaucratic power. Bureaucracies regularly press for increases in their own size and budgets and for additions to their own regulatory authority ... Finally, bureaucratic expansionism is facilitated by the 'incremental' nature of most policymaking.'

Canadian political scientist Ted Hodgetts' idea that the bureaucracy accurately reflects and responds to societal pressure (1973, 344) suggests that Weber overstates the case, but Dye and others continue to note the potential of 'bureaucratic influence' and 'capture' (see, for example, Albrow 1970; Blau and Meyer 1971; Downs 1967). Guy Peters concludes that the truth probably lies 'somewhere in between':

> bureaucratic institutions ... do have some influence in the redistribution of powers away from elective institutions and in the direction of bureaucracy itself ... This capacity ... of the permanent staff ... essentially to determine the agenda of their political masters ... becomes especially important in the presence of an agency ideology concerning the proper goals for the agency to pursue and the proper means of attaining those goals. Through the ability to control information, proposals for policy, and the knowledge concerning feasibility, the bureaucracy is certainly capable of influencing agency policy, if not determining it. It requires an unusual politician to be able to overcome this type of control within an agency. (2001, 23–4)

Where federal and provincial politicians are provided with both the administrative and political staff necessary to aid their participation during the policy analysis process, this is often not the case in most local governments. In smaller towns and villages, part-time politicians often rely on the advice of a single city clerk and can perform many adminis-

Table 11.1 Eight Detrimental Electoral and Legislative Institutional Arrangements

A. Election Stage	B. Legislative Stage
A1. Non-partisan electoral systems	B1. Inadequate pay for councillors
A2. At-large elections	B2. Absence of council pension scheme
A3. Unlimited election spending	B3. High supervisory load
	B4. Inadequate support staff
	B5. Inadequate policy staff

trative duties themselves. This lack of staff not only forces elected officials to dedicate their time to more mundane issues, but does not allow them to garner advice from those concerned with their electoral mandate or re-election.

The Capacity of Local Decision Makers in Eight Major Canadian Cities

The last section described how local decision makers' efforts to effectively generate and implement governmental agendas might be undermined by inferior institutional arrangements and under-resourcing. Table 11.1 sets out the above-discussed details in order to investigate these problems in eight Canadian cities. It has been argued that non-partisan elections conducted under at-large arrangements with no election expense limits will greatly undermine the ability of local politicians to develop broad-based governmental agendas through which to direct later policy analysis. Likewise, under-compensated, understaffed politicians are less able to direct and supervise staff or interact with local knowledge generators or brokers.

Electoral Stage Institutions

The three core factors of any electoral process are the party system, vote-to-seat conversion method and resource regulation (i.e., election expenses). Of particular interest in this study are non-partisan systems, which here are defined as those contests which prohibit candidates from placing a party name, acronym or symbol beside their own name on the ballot.[4] While local political candidates often have other political alliances that might reveal their political leanings, the lack of a party identification on the ballot has been shown to stifle – if not completely

Table 11.2 Population, Council Structure, and Partisanship in Eight Canadian Cities

City	Population (2001)	Mayor	Councillors	Non-Partisan	At-Large	Unlimited Spending
Vancouver	568,442	Y	10	No	Yes	Yes
Montreal	1,812,723	Y	73	No	No	No
Calgary	878,866	Y	14	Yes	No	Yes
Toronto	2,481,494	Y	44	Yes	No	No
Edmonton	666,104	Y	13	Yes	No	Yes
Winnipeg	619,544	Y	15	Yes	No	No
Ottawa	774,072	Y	21	Yes	No	No
Halifax	359,111	Y	23	Yes	No	Yes

eliminate – parties from the local election process (Smith and Stewart 1998). The point here is not that candidates in non-partisan political systems do not have distinct political preferences or ideological leanings, but rather that the lack of organized – and electorally identifiable – parties remove the incentive for candidates to organize under identifiable party labels and, subsequently, present common policy proposals to the public during elections.

In addition to the population and council structure, table 11.2 identifies each study city as partisan or non-partisan, whether each system uses an at-large configuration and whether or not election spending is limited. As shown above, where all cities have a mayors and councillors, only Vancouver and Montreal have fully partisan systems. Where identifiable local parties may have existed for short periods in some cities, such as Winnipeg, the absence of party names on local ballots makes these affiliations difficult, if not impossible, to maintain, and are of little benefit to the local voter as the main source of information, because affiliation is absent from the ballot.

Table 11.2 also indicates that Vancouver is the only major Canadian city to have an at-large electoral system. The subject of much debate and local plebiscites, the at-large system has remained in place despite concerted council efforts to replace it with a ward system as allowed under the *Vancouver Charter* (British Columbia 2004a). On 16 October 2004, 22.6 per cent of registered voters rejected changing to a ward system by a margin of 46 per cent 'Yes' to 54 per cent 'No.' A local electoral commission struck to review the citizen participation in the local decision-making process decided to recommend a vote be held despite warnings that low turnout and skewed results would be the result of an off-election year vote (City of Vancouver 2004). These problems were further compounded by the lack of any 'electoral' spending limits. While other cities have used full at-large systems or multi-member wards in the past, all have abandoned what have been shown to be discriminatory systems in favour of wards. Although discussions of proportional representation have started at the national and provincial levels – such as British Columbia's Citizen Assembly proposals for STV electoral reform provincially (British Columbia 2004b) – they have yet to be undertaken with any seriousness in Canada's major cities.

Finally, table 11.2 also shows that many cities now employ spending limits during local elections. Where all eight cities now compel candidates to disclose donors, only Montreal, Toronto, Winnipeg, and Ottawa cap the amount of money candidates may spend in their struggle to gain office. Following the long-established lead of their federal and provincial counterparts, these four cities also partially reimburse candidates for election expenses. Out of all cities, only Montreal avoids the pitfalls of non-partisanship, at-large systems, and unlimited election spending and, from an electoral perspective at least, can be considered the study city most likely to play an effective role in the policy analysis process.

Legislative Stage Institutions

According to the previous sections, politicians need to be adequately resourced if they are going to be able to effectively develop policy, supervise staff and interact with knowledge generators and knowledge brokers. The tables and discussion below examine pay and staffing levels for local politicians in Canada's eight major cities. Salaries, pensions and administrative and political staffing levels all play an important role in determining the attentiveness of local decision makers. Table 11.3 shows mayoral salaries (in 2004 dollars) for the eight cities, in 1950, 1975, and 2004. These figures reveal some clear patterns. First, while salaries for mayors were low in many of Canada's larger cities in 1950, they had climbed considerably by 2004, averaging $116,000. Second, salary strongly correlates with the population. Mayors from larger Canadian cities are paid more than mayors of somewhat smaller cities. For the purposes of this chapter, it would appear that the financial incentives for remaining mayor are high in all study cities. At least in terms of pay, the incentive structure would seem to be conducive to hardworking, attentive, and full-time mayors. As demonstrated in table 11.4, councillors have less incentive than mayors to perform as full-time

Table 11.3 Mayoral Salaries 1950–2004 (2004 dollars)

City	2004	% Increase	1975	% Increase	1950
Toronto	$142,539	75%	$81,341	–27%	$111,822
Montreal	$130,000	74%	$74,781	0%	$74,548
Calgary	$122,658	56%	$78,717	76%	$44,729
Vancouver	$115,617	26%	$91,837	64%	$55,911
Edmonton	$111,803	42%	$78,717	n/a	n/a
Ottawa	$110,000	62%	$67,891	n/a	n/a
Winnipeg	$101,850	11%	$91,837	54%	$59,638
Halifax	$96,693	36%	$70,845	90%	$37,274
Avg.	$116,395	48%	$79,496	43%	$63,987

Table 11.4 Council Salaries 1950–2004 (2004 dollars)

City	2004	% Increase	1975	% Increase	1950
Toronto	$84,068	78%	$47,230	252%	$13,419
Montreal	$45,000	243%	$13,120	193%	$4,473
Calgary	$61,329	160%	$23,615	322%	$5,591
Vancouver	$50,932	62%	$31,487	135%	$13,419
Edmonton	$58,405	69%	$34,635	n/a	n/a
Ottawa	$56,000	106%	$27,220	n/a	n/a
Winnipeg	$54,325	216%	$17,200	28%	$13,419
Halifax	$39,089	49%	$26,239	487%	$4,473
Avg.	$56,144	103%	$27,593	202%	$9,132

politicians. Although salaries have dramatically increased in most cities since 1950, they are still much lower than mayoral salaries. For example, at just under $51,000, the salary for a Vancouver city councillor is just $5,000 higher than the salary of the average full-time worker in the city. Considering the stress and high profile of the job, this remuneration would not seem to be enough to keep politicians interested in sticking to their policy agendas or staying attentive to their jobs while in office. The $84,000 salary of a Toronto city councillor might be expected to provide more incentive to pursue the job in the long term and to be attentive to democratic aspects of the process of governing. As shown in table 11.5, only three cities do not offer pensions to local council members: Vancouver, Halifax, and Ottawa. The other cities offer a variety of schemes of variable benefit. Again, pension schemes would be expected to provide politicians some incentive to pursue their posts over the long term and make extra effort to implement election prom-

Table 11.5 Pension Benefits

City	Pension	Terms
Vancouver	N	
Halifax	N	
Ottawa	N	
Winnipeg	Y	1.5% of best years at age 55 after 30 years of service
Edmonton	Y	6%
Toronto	Y	Same as regular city employees
Calgary	Y	2% final term's average earnings after age 60
Montreal	Y	2% of annual gross salary for every year of service at age 60 and after 2 years of service

Table 11.6 Supervisory Capacity

City	Total city employees	Full-time councillors	Part-time councillors	Total councillors	Ratio
Halifax	3,700	0	24	12	308:1
Montreal	29,000	53	20	63	460:1
Ottawa	12,000	22	0	22	545:1
Winnipeg	8,300	15	0	15	663:1
Edmonton	9,785	13	0	13	753:1
Calgary	11,295	14	0	14	941:1
Toronto	46,000	44	0	44	1045:1
Vancouver	9,000	0	10	5	1800:1

ises while holding office. In terms of overall legislative stage arrangements, it would appear that Toronto, Edmonton, and Calgary are at least slightly ahead of other cities in this regard. Table 11.6 illustrates the supervisory capacity of councils in each of the eight study cities. Here the number of councillors is compared to the number of city employees. In building the ratio, part-time councillors are counted as half a full-time councillor. Thus a part-time councillor in Halifax is considered as available to do half the workload of a full-time councillor in Ottawa. In terms of ratios, then, Halifax's 24 part-time councillors equate to 12 full-time councillors and when dividing into the number of employees means that each full-time equivalent council position must oversee 308 staff members. Ottawa's 22 full-time councillors supervise 12,000 for a 545:1 ratio while Vancouver councillors face an 1800:1 ratio. In terms of policy analysis and planning capacity, the cities with the highest ratio appear to have a much heavier supervisory responsibility. Table 11.7 describes the number of support staff available to local coun-

Table 11.7 Political and Nonpolitical Council Support Staff (2004)

City	Total employees	Total council support staff	Political	Non-political	Employee/ support staff ratio	Employee/ political support staff ratio
Winnipeg	8,300	41	39	2	202:1	213:1
Toronto	46,000	153	106	47	301:1	434:1
Montreal	29,000	56	32	24	518:1	906:1
Calgary	11,295	16	9	7	706:1	1255:1
Ottawa	12,000	14	6	8	857:1	2000:1
Vancouver	9,000	12	3	9	750:1	3000:1
Edmonton	9,785	10	2	8	979:1	4893:1
Halifax	3,700	7	0	7	529:1	n/a

cils. Non-political support staff are regular city employees working in an administrative capacity for the mayor or council, including secretaries and receptionists. Political support staff are those appointed by mayors or councillors, such as political advisors or constituency office workers. A ratio has been devised for both categories by dividing the number of employees by both staff figures for each city. Here Winnipeg has the best support staff/employee ratio (202:1) where Edmonton's is worst (979:1), meaning that councillors in Edmonton will most likely have the most administrative/public correspondence tasks and the least 'political' support. The table also shows that with the exception of Halifax, all cities have some political staff to advise elected officials. In terms of the ability to provide a counter to the agendas of regular city staff, Winnipeg's institutional arrangements allow local decision makers to play a fuller role in the policy analysis process, while Edmonton offers the least opportunity in this regard.

Conclusion: Assessing Local Institutional Planning Incapacities

The purpose of this article was not only to take a first look at, but also to compare the capacity of local decision makers to be effective during the policy analysis process in eight major Canadian cities. The comparison in this section is only meant to identify whether cities are more or less likely to be so. While further exploration would be needed to test whether local politicians with perceived institutional weaknesses actually have less ability to participate fully, the work here suggests where such a study might start. Table 11.8 offers a ranking of each city based

Table 11.8 Policy-Analysis-Friendly City Rankings

City	Score	Non-partisan elections	At-large system	Unlimited election spending	Below salary median	No pension	Below supervisory capacity median	Below support staff median	Political support staff median
Montreal	1	0	0	0	1	0	0	0	0
Toronto	2	1	0	0	0	0	1	0	0
Winnipeg	2	1	0	0	1	0	0	0	0
Halifax	4	1	0	1	1	0	0	1	1
Ottawa	4	1	0	0	0	1	0	1	1
Calgary	4	1	0	1	0	0	1	1	0
Edmonton	5	1	0	1	0	0	1	1	1
Vancouver	7	0	1	1	1	1	1	1	1

on an indicator that combines scores from the previously explained eight factors. Where binary scores are entered '0/1,' other indicators have been reduced into 'above or below median' scores. Under this scheme, Montreal ranks most, and Vancouver least friendly in terms of how able decision makers are to meaningfully participate in policy analysis. Montreal would appear to have the set of institutions most conducive to elected politicians directing and supervising policy analysis in their city, with the only real problem being below median council salaries. With its at-large electoral system, unlimited election spending, low council salaries, no pensions, and low number of councillors and support staff, Vancouver City Council earns the least friendly ranking. Here local decision makers are not as likely to propose a government agenda, or supervise staff. Overall it would appear that some cities are clearly more favourably suited to policy analysis than others, but it is also evident that all need to examine the institutions that are supposed to enable local decision makers to effectively participate in the policy analysis process.

Taking this analysis further, the better prepared and resourced Montreal politicians are less likely to rely on city staff alone for direction and can challenge the policy advice of internal actors by taking advice from external knowledge generators and knowledge brokers. If these other policy community actors are scarce, Montreal city council could use local funds to help establish and enable these communities in order to facilitate better public policy analysis. It is arguable that the other cities are more, and some much more, reliant on internal staff for policy direction and generation. As stated earlier, not only might this lead to less fully developed policy analysis, but in the worst case it could mean that local politicians end up captured by their own civil servants. This lack of capacity to effectively participate and stimulate the local policy analysis process would appear to be problematic in an era when cities are gaining more powers and more independence from senior levels of government.

NOTES

This research was partly funded through the Social Sciences and Humanities Research Council MCRI grant on Multilevel Government and Public Policy in Municipalities project.

1 The authors presented an earlier version of this work, titled 'Unaided

Politicians in Unaided City Councils? Explaining Policy Advice In Canadian Cities,' at the British Columbia Political Studies Association, Richmond, BC, May, 2004 and are grateful for the comments of Don Alexander and Doug McArthur and the research assistance of Matthew Bourke of the SFU/MPP program.

2 In *City Politics*, Banfield and Wilson (1963, 20) argue that 'politics, like sex, cannot be abolished, no matter how much we deny it.'

3 Provinces prohibiting councillor payments were Nova Scotia and New Brunswick (for *town* councillors), Quebec (for *local* municipalities) and British Columbia (for *village* councillors).

4 Elections legislation regulating voting in Calgary, Edmonton, Ottawa, Toronto, and Winnipeg allow only the names of candidates to be printed on ballots (Local Authorities Election Act, R.S.A. 2000, c. L-21; Municipal Elections Act 1996; Manitoba The Local Authorities Election Act 2005) whereas section 77 of the *Vancouver Charter* allows the inclusion of 'the abbreviation or acronym of the endorsing elector organization for a candidate, as shown on the nomination documents for the candidate.'

REFERENCES

Alberta. 2004. *Local Authorities Election Act, R.S.A. 2000.* Edmonton: Queen's Printer.
Albrow, Martin. 1970. *Bureaucracy.* London: Macmillan.
Banfield, Edward, and James Q. Wilson. 1963. *City Politics.* New York: Random House.
Better Environmentally Sound Transportation. 2005. www.best.bc.ca.
Blau, Peter, and Marshall Meyer. 1971. *Bureaucracy in Modern Society.* New York: Random House.
British Columbia. 2004a. *Vancouver Charter.* Victoria: Queen's Printer.
British Columbia. 2004b. *Citizens' Assembly on Electoral Reform. Making Every Vote Count: The Case for Electoral Reform in British Columbia.* Victoria: Queen's Printer.
Bula, Frances. 2004. 'Don't Count Out COPE Yet, Analysts Say.' *The Vancouver Sun*, 19 October, B1.
Canada, Royal (Lambert) Commission on Financial Management and Accountability. 1979. *Report.* Ottawa: Minister of Supply and Services.
Canada, Royal (Lortie) Commission on Electoral Reform and Party Financing. 1991. *Reforming Electoral Democracy.* Volume 1. Ottawa: Minister of Supply and Services.

Canadian Federation of Mayors and Municipalities. 1976. *Puppets on A Shoe-string.* Ottawa: CFMM (April).

City of Vancouver. 2003. *Budget 2002.* Vancouver: City of Vancouver.

– 2004. *A City of Neighbourhoods: Report of the 2004 Vancouver Electoral Reform (Berger) Commission.* Vancouver: City of Vancouver.

– 2005. *Homeless Action Plan.* Vancouver: City of Vancouver.

Crawford, K. Grant. 1954. *Canadian Municipal Government.* Toronto: University of Toronto Press.

Dahl, Robert. 1991. *Democracy and Its Critics.* New Haven, CT: Yale University Press.

Dowding, Keith. 1995. *The Civil Service.* London: Routledge.

Downs, Anthony. 1967. *Inside Bureaucracy.* Boston: Little, Brown.

Dunleavy, Patrick. 1991. *Democracy, Bureaucracy and Public Choice: Economic Explanations in Political Science.* New York: Harvester Wheatsheaf.

Dvorin, Eugene, and Robert Simmons. 1972. *From Amoral to Humane Bureau-cracy.* San Francisco, CA: Canfield Press.

Dye, Thomas R. 2001. *Top Down Policymaking.* New York: Chatham House.

Easton, David. 1965. *A Systems Analysis of Political Life.* New York: Wiley.

Gawthorp, Louis. 1971. *Administrative Politics and Social Change.* New York: St Martin's.

Gerth, H.H., and C.W. Mills. 1963. *Max Weber: Essays in Sociology.* New York: Oxford University Press.

Goodenow, Frank. 1893. *Comparative Administrative Law.* New York: Putnam.

– 1905. *The Principles of Administrative Law in the United States.* New York: Putnam.

Greater Vancouver Regional District. 2003. *3 Ways to Home: Regional Homelessness Plan for Greater Vancouver.* Vancouver: Greater Vancouver Regional District.

Griffith, J.A.G. 1966. *Central Departments and Local Authorities.* London: Allen and Unwin.

Grofman, Bernard, and Chandler Davidson, eds. 1992. *Controversies in Minor-ity Voting: The Voting Rights Act in Perspective.* Washington, DC: The Brookings Institute.

Hodgetts, J.E. 1973. *The Canadian Public Service: A Physiology of Government.* Toronto: University of Toronto Press.

Howlett, Michael, and M. Ramesh. 2003. *Studying Public Policy: Policy Cycles and Policy Subsystems.* Toronto: Oxford University Press.

Kernaghan, Ken, and David Siegel. 1987. *Public Administration in Canada: A Text.* Toronto: Methuen.

– 1999. *Public Administration in Canada.* Toronto: ITP Nelson.

Lindquist, Evert. 1990. 'The Third Community, Policy Inquiry, and Social
   Scientists.' In Stephen Brooks and Alain-G. Gagnon, eds., *Social Scientists,
   Policy, and the State,* 21–51. New York: Praeger.
Magnusson, Warren. 1983. 'Introduction: The Development of Canadian
   Urban Government.' In Warren Magnusson and Andrew Sancton, eds., *City
   Politics in Canada.* Toronto: University of Toronto Press.
Manitoba. 2004. *Local Authorities Election Act.* Winnipeg: Queen's Printer.
Non-Partisan Association. 2005. www.npavancouver.ca.
Niskanen, William. 1973. *Bureaucracy: Servant or Master? Lessons from America*
   London: Institute of Economic Affairs.
Ontario. 2004. *Municipal Elections Act, 1996.* Toronto: Queen's Printer.
Pal, Leslie A. 1997. *Beyond Policy Analysis: Public Issue Management in Turbulent
   Times.* Toronto: ITP Nelson.
Peters, B. Guy. 2001. *The Politics of Bureaucracy.* New York: Routledge.
Riordan, William. 1963. *Plunkett of Tammany Hall.* New York: E.P. Dutton.
Rowat, Donald. 1975. *Your Local Government.* Toronto: Macmillan.
Sayre, Wallace S. 1958. 'Premises of Public Administration: Past and Emerg-
   ing.' *Public Administration Review* 18(1), 102–5.
Scarrow, Howard. 1999. 'The Impact of At-large Elections: Vote Dilution or
   Choice Dilution?' *Electoral Studies* 18, 557–67.
Schumpeter, Joseph. 1976. *Capitalism, Socialism, and Democracy.* 6th ed. Lon-
   don: Allen and Unwin.
Smith, Patrick J., and Kennedy Stewart. 1998. *Making Local Accountability Work
   in British Columbia.* Vancouver: Institute of Governance Studies, Simon
   Fraser University. Government-commissioned report for British Columbia
   Ministry of Municipal Affairs and Housing.
– 2004a. 'Unaided Politicians in Unaided City Councils? Explaining Policy
   Advice in Canadian Cities.' Paper for the British Columbia Political Studies
   Association, Richmond, BC, May.
– 2004b. 'Beavers and Cats Revisited: Has the Local-Intergovernmental Game
   Shifted to the Mushy Middle?' *Korean Local Government Review* 6, 123–56.
– 2005. 'Local Government Reform in British Columbia, 1991–2005: One Oar
   in the Water.' In J. Garcea and E. Lesage Jr., eds., *Municipal Reforms in
   Canada: Dimensions, Dynamics, Determinants.* Toronto: Oxford University
   Press.
Stewart, Kennedy. 2003. *Think Democracy.* Vancouver: Institute of Governance
   Studies.
Tindal, C. Richard, and Susan Nobes Tindal. 2004. *Local Government in Canada.*
   6th ed. Toronto: Nelson.

UK. 1947a. *(Lord Lindsay) Report of the Interdepartmental Committee on Expenses of Members of Local Authorities.* London: HMSO.
– 1947b. *Turton Minority Report for the Interdepartmental Committee on Expenses of Members of Local Authorities.* London: HMSO, April.
Weir, Stuart, and David Beetham. 1999. *Political Power and Democratic Control in Britain: The Democratic Audit of the United Kingdom.* London: Routledge.
White, Leonard D. 1926. *Introduction to the Study of Public Administration.* New York: Macmillan.
– 1955. *Introduction to the Study of Public Administration.* 4th ed. New York: Macmillan.
Willoughby, William F. 1927. *Principles of Public Administration.* Baltimore: Johns Hopkins Press.
Wilson, V. Seymour. 1981. *Canadian Public Policy and Administration.* Toronto: McGraw-Hill Ryerson.
Wilson, Woodrow. 1887. 'The Study of Administration.' *Political Science Quarterly,* 2. Reprinted in Peter Woll, ed. 1966. *Public Administration and Policy,* 15–41. New York: Harper and Row.

PART IV

Committees, Public Inquiries, Research Institutes, Consultants, and Public Opinion

Governments do not always get the information and analysis they need for planning ahead from their 'in-house' analysts. Commissions of inquiry, research councils, and parliamentary committees provide institutional settings for conducting policy research that is more or less independent from both governments and private interests and that can be made available to opposition parties, the media, and the public at large. More informal methods of probing public opinion, such as polls or the work done by consultants, also contribute to policy deliberations by generating ideas or ways of framing problems. But these sources are less transparent and, consequently, incite more criticism.

As Liora Salter shows, public inquiries can serve very different functions. Depending on the mandate of a public inquiry, and on how that mandate is interpreted by commissioners or the stakeholders, the 'public' in public inquiries can be constructed in ways that lead to quite distinct recommendations. Salter's typology in this regard opens interesting research perspectives. She identifies six possible types; here, mention can be made of two examples that illustrate the kind of contrasting uses to which inquiries can be put. If the 'public' is viewed as being composed of individuals and groups who know something that policy makers wish to learn about – the 'public' as experts, as can be the case when an inquiry is held about issues concerning Aboriginal people – the recommendations will be meant to translate the information gathered in ways that are relevant to policy makers and all Canadians. On the other hand, if the 'public' is viewed as the proverbial layperson, the inquiry will usually be designed to educate the public regarding issues about which they were poorly informed. The sort of analysis being conducted, and the political implications of inquiries' recommendations, will thus differ in significant but not always clearly acknowledged ways from one type to another.

Most federal or provincial research councils established in the postwar decades as permanent commissions of inquiry about important policy issues, such as the Economic Council of Canada or the Science Council of Canada, have been disbanded. Dobuzinskis considers whether there are grounds for re-establishing these councils, now that the budgetary constraints that largely account for this turn of events have eased. On the basis of the historical record and of a set of commonly used norms of moral and political discourse, the author concludes that there is indeed a case for re-establishing the Science Council, but not the Economic Council.

Committees of provincial legislatures operate in relative obscurity as compared to the institutions discussed by the two previous authors but, as Josie Schofield and Jonathan Fershau argue, there is much to be gained by paying more attention to the varied roles they play in the policy process.

Public opinion is often considered an important determinant of policy in liberal democracies, but as François Pétry shows, there are many distinctive ways for Canadian policy makers to assess credible expressions of public opinion on any issue. Although public opinion polls constitute an important tool in their kit, polls are far from being the only such tools.

Perhaps the most vexing question concerning the relevance and quality of the information at the disposal of policy makers has to do with the role played by consultants. Kimberley Speers examines the various issues raised by the increasing use of consultants, paying particular attention to the issue of accountability. She concludes that these issues need to be more thoroughly investigated and openly debated.

12 The Public of Public Inquiries

LIORA SALTER

Just when it looks like inquiries have fallen into disuse as tools of policy making, along come a slew of new ones. Then, when it looks as if inquiries have become a mainstay of policy making, the pundits suggest that inquiries have had their day, being too expensive and unpredictable for those who commission them. Meanwhile, many of the same issues – accountability, cost, the relationship of inquiries and the courts, etc. – continue to be raised regularly.[1]

But something new has happened. The literature on public policy has advanced considerably in the last decades, driven by new theory and by the need to respond to both globalization and the deregulatory state. This literature suggests new ways to look at public inquiries.

From time to time, law reformers have turned their attention to the untidy state of the law as far as inquiries are concerned. Their preoccupation seems mainly to be about the much-vaunted independence of inquiries versus their possible impact on the policy process. Both relate to the dual nature of inquiries, their insider-outsider status as instruments of policy making. It is worth recalling in this regard that Simmel (1971) argued that those who were simultaneously insiders and outsiders had enormous advantages when it came to the acuteness of their observations. Those who conduct inquiries are close enough in to see things that outsiders might never see, he might have said, but less thoroughly bound to the policy process.

Inquiries are, of course, commissioned by the state. They are designed to serve the purposes of the state by churning up recommendations for policy. At the same time, their primary characteristic (true across the board) is that inquiries are supposed to be free of state control. In other words, the strength of inquiries may come from what the law reformers have regarded as a problem.

I suspect that those of us in Canada who focus our attention on public inquiries agree with Simmel, even if we also recognize how often inquiries are used for the crassest political purposes and how often they seem to have minimal effect. We might answer, were we polled, that an inquiry commissioned for all the 'wrong reasons' often achieves something valuable (good research, for example), while inquiries with stellar mandates often run aground of politics. We might also say that one cannot judge an inquiry by the fate of its specific recommendations; however many are eventually adopted. Inquiries have an impact on both the climate of opinion and the conceptual frameworks that are used for policy analysis. Changes to policy, we would say, often come from new ways of speaking about policy issues, as much as they do from specific recommendations.

Above all, we might say, inquiries should be examined in light of what they, and they alone, add to the policy process. Inquiries often represent the only opportunity for well-structured, well-informed conversations about policy. They bring to the table members of the public who otherwise have no place or role in policy analysis. It is this last point, the public nature of inquiries, that offers me a new point of departure for a discussion of inquiries as instruments of policy analysis. The lens I want to use for this paper is deliberative democracy, which is all about the ways that members of the public become part of the policy process.

It must be stated at the onset that I am using the phrase deliberative democracy somewhat differently from many people writing in the literature, where deliberative democracy has a long and torturous history of theoretical entanglements and value-soaked controversies. In this literature, deliberative democracy and the public sphere are closely aligned with each other in various conceptual formulations, but the public sphere is treated as a single construct in its own right, standing for the various theorists' basic contentions about the nature of the democratic polity, state/non-state distinctions, the role of associations and civic society, and the nature of the judicial state. In virtually every example of authors writing on deliberative democracy, the tone is almost exclusively normative and prescriptive.

Almost none of this theoretical debate will show up in this article. Indeed, I propose to use the criteria for deliberative democracy laid out in this theoretical literature (about which most theorists agree) in an empirical context, something most of these theorists would be loathe to do. If I refer to the public sphere, for example, it is as the phrase might be used in everyday conversation. Public sphere refers to venues for public debate about important political issues. Ku's definition of public sphere (2000) serves the purpose of this paper if one needs a more theoretically grounded definition: she thinks of deliberative democracy as involving venues to receive and discuss issues, define them in light of collective experience, and finally to arrive at civil judgements with collective weight.

There is another issue to be laid aside before I can proceed. Some theories, Habermas's included, suggest that the public sphere develops in contradistinction to the state; it is about civil associations functioning on the private side of the public/private distinction. Other theorists argue that the public sphere is inherently connected to state actions. It is already obvious that I break ranks with those who regularly write about deliberative democracy, and the public sphere associated with it, as antithetical to state action. In speaking about inquiries, I have already mentioned the usefulness of Simmel's discussion of marginality in suggesting that inquiries are both inside and outside the state. In doing so, I am joining a small group of theorists who argue, as Agnes Ku does so cogently, that 'the modern notion of the public sphere should be tied to both state and civil society. Today state and civil society are so deeply intertwined with each other in shaping the political and moral boundary of public life (that) they are simultaneously subject to a common cultural field that constitutes and regulates public life' (2000, 221).

I cannot imagine what the grand theorists of deliberative democracy might make of inquiries, mainly because I cannot imagine them paying attention to inquiries in the first place. In my view their assessment is a mistake. I think a case can be made that inquiries are exemplars of deliberative democracy; they are the public sphere in action. Think about it. Their primary function is to get issues out into the open, to bring evidence to light in a very public domain. They encourage participation from a broadly interested public, stimulate free-flowing discussion among people whom they treat (at least in theory) as equals, and they provide informed recommendations to government. Seen in this light, inquiries lift the routine, and not so routine, business of government out of the closed world of government departments and their regular consultants, and transform this business into a matter for public debate.

However, inquiries are not yet on solid ground with respect to their contribution to deliberative democracy. The concepts of the public and the public sphere, always associated with deliberative democracy, are the source of trouble. Not knowing why the public is participating (but only that it *should* participate) or who indeed properly constitutes *the public,* inquiries undermine their own stated goals of being both public and democratically deliberative. Earnest though the intentions of their commissioners and staff may be, inquiries easily diminish what they should be enhancing.

I begin with the notion of the public, which is central to every discussion of deliberative democracy. It cries out for examination, and always has. The literature is vast, but this fact need not be a deterrent. My discussion is not meant as a contribution to theory or political philosophy, but instead aims to lay the foundation for a very practical discussion of inquiries. I want to consider how various conceptions of the public affect what inquiries do and say. I will refer to a number of inquiries, but will not provide a detailed description or analysis of any one of them. I am counting on readers to know a little about these inquiries through their own newspaper reading, and have provided a list of final reports in the reference section. I am using this overview and comparison of inquiries for the simplest of illustration purposes only: only to remind these newspaper readers how inquiries are differently oriented with respect to how they operate. Towards the end of this paper, I will come back to my central contention: that inquiries are, or could be, exemplars of deliberative democracy, but often are not. And I will test this proposition against the arguments I have made. In doing so, I will compare inquiries with other instruments of policy analysis in order to highlight their strengths and weaknesses as instruments of *public* policy.

Dealing With the Terminology

Connolly (1993) lays out the first problem to be dealt with when he lists 'public' among the essentially contested concepts that confound political discourse. His point is as follows: some words, such as *public,* can no longer serve as ordinary words, closely tied to their dictionary definitions with widely shared understandings of their meaning. These words are instead elevated to a different plane of language, where they serve as proxies for the political philosophies that underlie political discourse. This would not be a problem but for the fact that the same words are used by groups with diametrically different political philosophies. Such words become emblematic of their very different theoretical assumptions, radical agendas and practical advice. The example that springs to mind is *democracy*. Recall that East Germany was once called the German *Democratic* Republic, even as the Cold War was being waged by the West under the banner of *democracy*. Democracy is undoubtedly an essentially contested concept.

Connolly argues that essentially contested concepts are fundamentally open-ended with respect to the characteristics that can be added and subtracted from their definitions. For example, virtually anything can be said to be *the* defining characteristic of *democracy*. Recall C.B. Macpherson's now classic study of *The Real World of Democracy* (1966), in which he attempts to argue (successfully for its time) that the emerging one-party states of post-colonial Africa had as much claim to being democratic as the multi-party states of the Western industrialized countries. Macpherson also claims that the countries of the then Soviet bloc are democratic, albeit using a different conception of democracy. Each political system, Macpherson suggests, grounds its conception of democracy in its own political philosophy, and thus uses the term not capriciously or merely rhetorically but as an integral part of a coherent conceptual framework. For Macpherson, words like *democracy* play a pivotal role in politics, and cannot not be disconnected from the philosophies or conceptual frameworks that give them meaning. There is no solid ground to be found for any common definition of democracy, or indeed for any other essentially contested concept.

That said, those who use essentially contested concepts like democracy are so deeply attached to their own conceptions that these words cannot simply be discarded. This is Connolly's point as well. These words are somewhat like a flag or logo. They stand for and act as a symbol of the whole. The German Democratic Republic distinguished itself precisely because it was *democratic* in a way that Western market democracies could never be. The one-party states were *democratic* in a way that captured, for their leaders of the time, what it meant to break away from colonialism. They would say: democracy is worth nothing if it is not indigenous to, and shaped by, the communities in which it takes root. What is really at stake, for Macpherson and Connolly alike, are conflicting definitions of democracy. The terminology masks a struggle over philosophy, but it plays out as a conflict over words or, more specifically, over the right to control the definition of emblematic words. The political philosophies that churned up the label *democratic* would have been lost without their *democratic* moniker.

Connolly argues that essentially contested concepts are not just essential and contested, in the sense I have just described, but also serve another function. They lay the foundation for moral judgements, even about seemingly unrelated matters. As such, they are the lynchpins of the value debates that permeate all political discourse, the bearers of moral judgements about all kinds of things, in all kinds of circumstances. These terms set standards against which all behaviour (state behaviour, company behaviour, and even individual behaviour) can be judged. To be *democratic* is good, regardless of what democracy means in practice. To be successful in attaching the label *democracy* to one's actions or beliefs is to bless all one's beliefs, regardless of any connection they may have to democracy, however it might be defined.

It must be emphasized that neither Connolly nor Macpherson disparage the use of the essentially contested concepts in political discourse, and neither do I. They do not argue that essentially contested concepts render politics meaningless, nor does either writer rail against the drift of modern media-soaked politics. According to the two authors, essentially contested concepts are the way that differences in values and philosophies are factored into political discourse, and philosophical differences are telegraphed from one group to another. These shortcut words are necessary for making sense of political debate, abbreviations for the deep-seated issues and values that divide countries, blocs, and political opponents. Political struggles about the proper definition of words like *democracy* are never really about the word or its definition. That said, words are a useful proxy for conflict, given that the alternative is often war.

As noted, Connolly lists *public* as an essentially contested concept. By *public* he mean all of the following: the *public interest, the public sphere,* and *public participation.* All these terms are emblematic of what Dewey (1954) once referred to as searching for public policies that reflect 'the good of all.' However, something about *public* makes it a special case, unlike *democracy.*

Here Raymond Williams (1983) provides some guidance. *Public* is, as Williams would say, also a key word. That is, it is a word whose presence (as opposed to definition) symbolizes what political systems stand for at any moment in history. These monikers describe the political system as a whole, but only temporarily. They orient political discourse at one time, but not at others. Particular key words ebb and flow in political discourse. Their salience changes over time in ways that signify the preoccupations and ethos of the era in which they are used. Let me play this out, using the term *public.* At one moment in time, *public* was attached to almost every government action (public interest), every organization with altruistic motives (public groups), and indeed every government policy (public policies). Then, seemingly without warning, *public* all but disappeared from political discourse. References to *the public interest* were dropped, public groups became NGOs or 'special interests,' *the public* became citizens, voters, or consumers, and policy replaced *public policy*.

This all-too-brief discussion of key words and essentially contested concepts serves a specific purpose for this paper. I think that the ebb and flow of keywords, and also the clash reflected in essentially contested concepts, can be used to identify the ideas, values, and philosophies that underpin political discourse at any moment in time The fact that the same word is used to mean radically different things, and that this word is emblematic of whole political philosophies and values, makes it a window onto differences that are normally hidden from view. If a word resonates politically at one moment in time, and later becomes the centrepiece of political controversy at another, obviously something important is happening to cause the change. Alerted to the fact that there is change, I can search for the reasons why it is happening.

In other words, if I can locate the unspoken ideas and assumptions that are being called into play each time *public* is invoked, and if I can line up these many ideas and assumptions alongside each other, I can see where *public* inquiries might differ quite radically from each other, despite their common allegiance to being public. I might make sense of their quite different approaches to encouraging public participation. If I then can trace, even in an impressionistic way, the changing conceptions of public that are used by inquiries, and note when the public aspect of inquiries is not being discussed, I have another avenue of approach. I can usefully comment on the implications of adopting one conception of the public over others. My goal becomes to lay bare some of the assumptions that drive individual inquiries, assumptions otherwise hidden by their common description as *public* inquiries.

Remember, almost all inquiries today claim to being public and to making contributions to public policy. Not all inquiries do the same things, the same ways, or even have the same kinds of goals, as far as including the public is concerned. They do not reach similar conclusions, or reflect the same politics, values, or philosophy. Public means something different in every case. The job here is to tease out just what this difference might be.

It is time to hold inquiries up to scrutiny in light of their claim to be public and to include members of the public. This claim is, I have suggested, key to understanding inquiries as the essence of deliberative democracy in action. I have also said that there is, and can be, no commonly accepted definition of *the public,* because *public* is both a key word (thus emblematic for the whole of society and changing in its salience) and an essentially contested concept (thus the centrepiece of debates about philosophy and values). I have then suggested that *public* can be used as an indicator of the underlying politics, values and philosophies that guide each inquiry, shaping its procedures, reflecting its preoccupations and influencing its recommendations. My analytical strategy will be to create a rough typology of possible conceptions of *the public.* I will ask: Which of these conceptions animates particular inquiries? I will look at the implications of choosing one conception of the public over others. Finally, I will comment on what each conception does to the broader assessment of inquiries as the essence of deliberative democracy.

Conceptions of the Public That Animate Inquiries

Six quite different conceptions of *the public* can be identified from the practice of inquiries.

Public as interest groups. By far the most commonplace notion of *the public* today is one that associates the public with interest groups, and public participation (or consultation as it is more routinely called) with interest groups. That some of these so-called interest groups are less likely to have personal, legal, or economic interests than others is not important. Obviously, the Canadian Manufacturers Association and the National Council on Business Issues have different interests than Pollution Probe. Followers of this notion of *the public* think both kinds of groups do have interests. Either the members of advocate groups do have personal (power and influence) interests at stake, regardless of their stated altruistic motives, or it is suggested that by elevating groups such as Pollution Probe to the status of stakeholder, the goals of environmentalism are best served. By including spokespeople from Pollution Probe in stakeholder consultations, by seating them at the table, so to speak, it is argued that these groups have more influence on policy than they would otherwise. However, it should also be noted that stakeholder consultations/negotiations are seldom open to public view. This fact seems not to matter much in this conception of *the public. The public interest* is seen as being properly represented because of the presence of all the possible stakeholder groups at the table. Pollution Probe is a proxy for the *environmental public*, just as the officials from Alcan serve as proxies for *the industry interest*. Underlying this conception of the public is a notion that politics is the negotiated compromise of interests.

Public as the disaffected. The most compelling alternative to the stakeholder version of *the public* is one that places emphasis on those who have been dislocated, harmed or disaffected by the policies of government, and perhaps also the actions of private parties. Think of the abused children of Cashel (see the report of the Royal Commission of Inquiry into the Response of the Newfoundland Criminal Justice System to Complaints), the parents of the dead babies whose views were reflected in the Grange Inquiry (see the report of the Royal Commission of Inquiry into Certain Deaths at the Hospital for Sick Children and Related Matters), or the people who received contaminated blood who spoke to the Krever Inquiry (see the report of the Commission of Inquiry into the Blood System of Canada). These are the disaffected; they best reflect *the public* in the case of these specific inquiries. Virtually every inquiry today makes provision for these disaffected groups or individuals to testify, to tell their stories to a sympathetic audience. The *public* function of the inquiry lies in providing an opportunity for those who have been harmed to speak out about their harm. Public participation is often compared to healing or therapy, even while it may also serve as a platform for a radical critique (Salter 1990).

Public as about discourse. This notion of *the public* is most closely associated with Habermas and other theorists of democracy who speak about *the public sphere.* Seen from this perspective, democracies become legitimate only to the extent that they facilitate an unfettered communication about the ideas and values that permeate public policies. In this case, *public* equates with dialogue, dialogue amongst informed citizens about the issues they deem important. The ideas brought forward by *the public* stand or fall on their merit, judged in the by-play of debate. Those who advance them are not necessarily interested parties, nor are they always representatives of formal groups. They are not necessarily disaffected, except inasmuch as everyone might be seen as disaffected or, as it is more commonly stated, 'alienated.' At the same time, dialogue amongst informed citizens (*the public sphere*) counts for little if some people and some groups are excluded from participating by virtue of their race, class, social circumstances, or gender. Discourse (the way that issues are spoken about) is the most common way that such groups are excluded, at least in Western industrial democracies. To be *public*, both discourse and *the public sphere* must be challenged to become more inclusive, even though the dialogue is about ideas, and even though the representation of groups (group interests) does not matter much in this conception of *the public*.

Public as expert. Canada's most famous inquiry is the Berger inquiry (see the report of the Mackenzie Valley Pipeline Inquiry), and its commissioner, Thomas Berger, had a different conception of *the public*. Berger was convinced that the people in the communities of the Mackenzie Valley had something both specific and useful to offer his inquiry in terms of actual information about wildlife and habitat, land use and occupancy, the nature of their communities and the role of the landscape in their culture. This specific information was crucial if he was to evaluate the desirability of proposals for a gas pipeline to be built through this northern territory of Canada. It was expertise, no less than the submissions of the scientists were expertise. However, Berger believed that this expertise had never been properly marshalled and analysed, despite some exceptional social science research. Collecting it was the job of the inquiry, Berger said. Doing so meant talking to people individually about the things that they had seen, experienced or about what mattered most to them. Gaining *public* expertise meant the Berger inquiry needed to go into each community, hold evening sessions, and welcome everyone to speak in the language of his or her choice. The Berger inquiry dealt with the special circumstances of the Mackenzie Valley only, but the contention that members of the public are a repository of specific expertise, expertise otherwise not available, has wider applicability. Needless to say, it takes a special kind of inquiry to seek public expertise of the kind referred to here. This type of inquiry needs to be able (in addition to collecting information) to translate public expertise into something useable for a public policy and to guard against the power of anecdote.

Public as the non-expert, layperson. It is not unusual for *public participation* to be translated into a call for the dissemination of information to the public, by politicians or anyone else – that is, providing some form of adult education. There is now also a considerable literature on, for example, communicating science to the public. Here the emphasis is on creating the conditions for informed political decision making. Scientists and interested parties (such as industry) are already informed. They can be distinguished because of what they know. By contrast, *the public* lacks familiarity and/or even the capacity to handle disciplinary knowledge properly, and to appreciate the true circumstances of industry. Note that this notion of *the public*, as needing and awaiting information and education, is the opposite of *the public as expert*. In the conception of public as layperson, expertise is seen to reside with scientists and policy makers exclusively. The presumption is not that these 'more expert' views must prevail so much as it is that the public must be educated about what scientists, governments, industry and 'producers and major users' have learned, especially about what is at stake in policy decisions. Armed with this knowledge, a newly educated public will then be in a better position to vote, join pressure groups, and otherwise participate in politics.

Public as in public opinion. Along with the conception of *the public as interest groups*, the equation of *the public* with public opinion makes intuitive sense and, as a result, this conception of the public is very popular. To the extent that an inquiry can gauge public opinion, public opinion can be reflected in its recommendations. However, inquiries do not typically conduct public opinion polling (Hauser 1998). Inquiries' assessment of public opinion are usually based on their public hearings, on the testimony of groups purporting to represent *the public* in some way, and on the inquiries' own reading of the situation. Not having themselves been elected, but being challenged with the task of finding politically acceptable solutions to tricky and complex political problems, the inquiries' commissioners and staff see the inquiry as being a forum for public opinion to express itself, albeit in non-scientific ways. Some commissioners and staff might go so far as to argue that inquiries are a better choice than public opinion polls in gauging public opinion. They would claim that only through forums where people can speak in their own vernacular 'can the complex process whereby a public opinion is formed and communicated be appreciated' (Hauser 1998). Hauser believes that one must account for the dialogic engagements by which an active populace participates in issue development, the contours of the public sphere that colour their levels of awareness, perception, and participation, the influence of opinion formation of sharing views with one another, and the terms of expression warranting the inference that a public has formed and has a dominant opinion. Seen in this light, public opinion is far better captured through an inquiry than a scientific public opinion poll.

How Do Inquiries Conceive of the Public?

It is easy to see how adopting any of these notions of *the public* might shape what inquiries do, even in a most practical sense. Procedures designed to attract members of the 'public as experts' will be different from those that bring stakeholder representatives to the table. An inquiry that sees itself as a reasonable facsimile of a public opinion poll will organize itself to capture public opinion, not as a dialogue of ideas.

Following this logic, one would expect the Berger inquiry to look nothing like the MacDonald inquiry (Royal Commission on the Economic Union and Development Prospects for Canada), even though both held hearings, nothing like the Walkerton inquiry or the Krever inquiry. Each of these inquiries had a different conception of *the public* and of the kinds of roles that citizens might play in determining its recommendations.

The difference could not be clearer than in the contrast between Berger and Bayda inquiries (see the report of the Cluff Lake Board of Inquiry). Justice Bayda was charged with deciding the fate of uranium mining in Saskatchewan, and he told me that he intended to follow in Berger's footsteps. Like Berger, he took his inquiry into indigenous communities in the north, and he opened the microphones to all comers. In my assessment at the time, his mindset was fundamentally different from Berger's. Justice Bayda equated the public with the representatives of the groups who appeared before his inquiry. In my estimation, his conclusions are more reflective *of the public as public opinion* than *the public as expert*. Saying this is not to fault the Bayda inquiry, but only to point out that, in my opinion, Justice Bayda never really came to terms with the expertise that the public was supposed to contribute. He confused public expertise with public opinion, as many are wont to do. Moreover, he was not entirely in control of the situation, because the long-established advocate groups had learned their lesson from the Berger inquiry, and they participated strongly to influence Justice Bayda's recommendations. Bayda saw mainly only the advocate groups, and he had, despite his best intentions, precious little opportunity to speak to anyone else.

The commissioner and staff of the Krever inquiry (which explored the roots of the tainted blood tragedy in Canada) were openly committed to using their inquiry as a safe haven, a place where those who had been harmed could speak out. The disaffected were welcomed in community hearings, which were explicitly designed to elicit their personal testimony. However, the community hearings were only one element of this inquiry (as indeed was also the case in the Berger and Bayda inquiries). The focus in the Krever inquiry was on its lengthy formal hearings, which were decidedly of a different kind. Here the inquiry adopted an approach that brought it close to being a criminal trial, in my view. This inquiry depended upon testimony from organized groups, and they all used legal counsel as much to protect as to represent their interests. But ask any staff member from the Krever inquiry, as I have done, where the public interest lay in relation to this inquiry. The task for the inquiry in its formal hearings was determined by the questions raised in the personal testimonies, they said. The inquiry's real job was, they believed, to issue the report that the people who had been harmed might have issued, had they been in a position to write it. If that meant conducting the formal hearings in a court-like manner and 'going after those responsible,' it was a strategy dictated by the disaffected themselves, who wanted to see their concerns addressed in a vigorous manner and concrete results emerging, including punishing those who had, in their view, caused their suffering.

The Walkerton inquiry held public hearings, but its orientation was different yet again. As I understand it, it saw its mandate as fundamentally investigatory. It viewed members of the public as being in a position to provide some of the evidence it needed about changing farming practices and the political economy of industrial farming. Individuals could speak about what they had seen in the way of inspections, or the illnesses they had suffered. Individuals were, in other words, potentially experts in their own right. Contrast the Walkerton inquiry to a typical environmental assessment hearing, in which it is the job of the inquiry (environmental assessment hearings are inquiries) to arrive at an accommodation of interests, if at all possible, so that the necessary approvals and permits can be granted. Whether individual members of the public have any role to play in an environmental assessment hearing is open to question, because everyone is treated as a stakeholder, and interest group, best represented by properly resourced stakeholder groups.

Now think back to the Aird Commission, an inquiry that set the terms of reference for broadcasting in Canada for many years, or consider the inquiry (not a formal Royal Commission) that produced the

Caplan-Sauvageau report. Neither was a stakeholders' negotiation, despite the fact that industry lobby groups participated in full force in both. The ideas that found their way into these final reports did not necessarily come from the interested groups, in my opinion. They emerged instead from a dialogue, conducted inside and outside of public meetings. The whole inquiry was attuned to producing dialogue and drawing ideas from it. This dialogue necessarily involved individuals who were representative of no one other than themselves.

What was the MacDonald inquiry? A dialogue of ideas to be sure, but mainly among the experts. A stakeholders' negotiation? To some extent. Certainly the MacDonald inquiry did not see individual members of the public as having any particular expertise to contribute. Rather it sought to disseminate information and to educate the public.

I could go on making quick observations on inquiry after inquiry, but this is not the proper place to do so, nor to back up my observations with the data that supports them. The point to be made here is a different one. Inquiries orient themselves around their own particular conceptions of *the public*. They encourage the kind of participation that matches their conception of *the public's* role. They seek out some kinds of public input, while barely acknowledging others. They think of themselves as acting *in the public interest* without specifying what this interest might be, other than what is in evidence in their mandates and recommendations. They do all this in the name of *the public*, which (generally speaking) they see as a phenomenon requiring little further thought. They fully accept and endorse the public dimension of their own work, regarding the design of their procedures, deliberations and recommendations as solutions to essentially pragmatic problems, such as how to control the length of the hearings while still hearing from everyone. They act as if the meanings of *the public* and public participation were self-evident.

What Are the Trade-Offs?

It is hardly surprising that different inquiries hold differing conceptions of *the public* and constitute themselves and their recommendations differently as a result. What is less obvious is the price to be paid for following one route, emphasizing one conception of *the public*, as opposed to another. Let me work through each conception of *the public* again, showing what is *not* likely to be encouraged as a result of adopting it.

Public as interest groups. An inquiry that mainly treats *the public* as interested parties and that treats its deliberations as a means of arriving at a compromise of interests is unlikely to foster much dialogue. Indeed, many of its most important deliberations will not be held in an open forum (any more than labour negotiations are conducted in an open forum), because that is not where true compromises get hammered out. Nor, interestingly enough, are such inquiries likely to offer up more than predictable opinions from the groups that can be counted on to show up everywhere policy recommendations are being determined. These groups show up (resources permitting) regardless of whether they have very specific interests at stake. From the inquiry's own point of view, there would be no particular value in encouraging broad-ranging dialogue, and this type of inquiry would also have little reason to identify the particular sorts of expertise that individuals might offer. Weighed against these limitations, the advantage for an inquiry of seeing *the public* mainly as a collection of interest groups is that its recommendations, if well crafted, have something very important to offer government, that is, a set of conclusions that all interest groups can agree to. This kind of inquiry is perhaps the most well suited to the needs of policy analysis. It adds something important – the fashioning of compromise – to what policy analysts would otherwise bring to the table.

Public as the disaffected. The inquiry that courts the participation of the disaffected and offers itself up as a place where stories can be told is not any more likely to foster dialogue, because it does not really address the situation of those not harmed. Valuable as these disaffected people certainly are, they are also not likely to be representative of interested groups, so a compromise of interests is unlikely. Indeed, such inquiries tend to focus instead on proposals for redress, not policy making in general. The specific expertise of members of the public is indeed being actively sought, but only one kind of public expertise, that which emerges from the experience of being harmed. Other kinds of expertise seem out of place. The Grange inquiry is a good example of what I mean. There is no doubt that those who lost their babies at the Sick Children's Hospital found the Grange inquiry to be a welcoming place. However, what is striking about this inquiry, to us inquiry watchers, is how little empha-sis was given to the working conditions in the hospital and the relation-ships between its many health practitioners, about which nurses, nurse practitioners, doctors, and hospital cleaners alike might have had important things to say. The distraught parents were 'experts,' unlike those actually working at the hospital. Weighed against these disadvantages, an inquiry that emphasizes the role of the public as disaffected is seen to be a just inquiry, itself a kind of redress for those who have been harmed.

Public as about discourse. An inquiry that sees itself primarily as a forum for discourse is not very likely to reach an accommodation of interests for the simple reason that its recommendations may veer in an entirely different direction than its interest group participants have in mind. Who, among the major industry groups, cheered the release of the Caplan-Savigeau Report? Some, to be sure, but not everyone. It was not a consensus document, nor was it intended to be. Needless to say, an inquiry that positions itself as a catalyst for dialogue is also on less firm ground as far as acceptance of its recommendations is concerned. An inquiry with a conception of *the public* that emphasizes dialogue of ideas has a difficult time staying on course. Even its own commissioners can easily fail to distinguish between new ideas versus long-established beliefs and opinions. I have observed that they routinely ask who is being represented, as if the value of an idea lay only in the number of people who held it, and as if their mission was to conduct a public opinion poll. Weighed against these limitations, the advantage for an inquiry of seeing itself as the sponsor of dialogue is that this kind of inquiry allows truly new ideas to emerge. It offers the possibility of new ways of approaching problems. It brings to light new dimensions of issues. This type of inquiry, being focused on public dialogue, contributes a kind of policy analysis that is, sadly to say in my view, often not in evidence in the policy process, nor even welcomed by government officials charged with making policy. It may be what they need, but it is seldom what they want.

The public as expert. The inquiry that treats *the public* as expert has possibly the most difficult task of all, and it would not be surprising if these kinds of inquiries sometimes failed, or turned away from the task they set themselves, as was the case with Justice Bayda's inquiry, in my view. Seeing the public as an expert in its own right means convincing people that what they know, as a matter of routine, is important. It means encouraging people to participate in a public process when they are unaccustomed to doing so. It means holding the advocate groups at bay, not because they are unimportant, but because their well-packaged expression of ideas is likely to overshadow the much more tentative description of what actually happened on the ground. An inquiry that sees the public as expert must also conceive of itself as doing social science. Experiential information must not only be collected, it must be weighed for its value and veracity. The differences between this kind of inquiry and the others could not be more striking. The individual who is expert on his or her own working conditions or hunting and trapping routes is not necessarily representative of anyone else; he or she is not really an interested party. He or she is not reflective of public opinion. He or she is not interested in a dialogue of ideas. Weighed against these limitations, the inquiry that puts emphasis on the expertise of individuals has access to a wealth of information seldom matched in the political process. It can produce a genuinely new contribution to policy analysis.

The public as non-expert, in need of information and education. An inquiry that takes as its mission to educate *the public* is bound to meet resistance in an age where the expertise of scientists, lawyers and policy makers is often suspect. Truth be told, most people are not lining up for the kind of adult education that an inquiry can offer. Their strongly held views are more likely to be buttressed by their existing own good reasons. Their views are unlikely to be changed by virtue of the information presented to them by the experts. Of course it is true that informed debate is better than uninformed. Also, some inquiries do have an admirable record of putting new, and often quite sound information, into circulation. That said, to the extent that inquiries present themselves as a kind of mobile classroom, providing education about matters that are inherently controversial, they are likely to be ignored. Setting out to be educative in nature, such inquiries easily turn into interest group negotiations or public opinion polls in disguise. Weighed against these limitations, it is worth emphasizing that inquiries do educate; this is one of their more important functions.

The public as public opinion. An inquiry that sees its recommendations as a measure of public opinion easily falls into the trap of seeing the people who choose to appear in its public hearings as being representative of everyone else. Once the fallacy of 'those who show up are representative' is exposed, cynicism sets in. Everyone who does show up becomes 'a special interest.' An inquiry that sees itself as akin to a public opinion poll is also unlikely to foster a dialogue. Weighed against these limitations, an inquiry that sees itself as gauging public opinion can do a reasonable job because, unlike public opinion polling, an inquiry can ask follow-up questions and observe changes in opinion over time. It can listen long enough to hear what people truly think.

Before moving on to the conclusion of this article, it must be emphasized that the exercise of identifying the various conceptions of *the public* used by inquiries, and of listing some of the weaknesses of each, is not to suggest that there is one right way for inquiries to proceed. In fact, inquiries follow more than one approach, using their different kinds of hearings and their own research to do so. (It is hard to imagine an inquiry that follows all of them, however.) I have chosen to focus on the 'weaknesses and strengths' of each approach to illustrate the trade-offs that invariably face each inquiry as it goes about determining its conception of *the public*.

Inquiries as Exemplars of Deliberative Democracy?

There remains one important task for this paper, as suggested in the introduction. This is to examine whether, and if so how and under what conditions, might inquiries be exemplars of deliberative democracy. Is this their most important contribution to policy analysis, and if so, are they very successful in making it? Recall that I have put aside the weighty questions raised by the theorists of deliberative democracy and its companion concept, *the public sphere*, using an approach that probably none of them would endorse. I want to treat their contentions about the essential criteria of deliberative democracy as propositions to be tested in a real world context, one involving a state-related but somewhat independent institution.

However, even if I put aside the theoretical debates, in dealing with deliberative democracy, I am immediately cast back into the quagmire of essentially contested concepts that I described at the beginning of this paper. I have already said that *democracy*, deliberative or otherwise, is an essentially contested concept, and so too is *the public*. At first, it seems like the problem I have set myself offers ample opportunity for political and language philosophers (which I am not) but not much else. I do think that it is possible to step outside the fray, as long as no one thinks that the deeper philosophical issues are being addressed or resolved. Remember, this paper is not about deliberative democracy, but about inquiries and policy analysis. I am interested in deliberative democracy only for the types of questions it raises about the shape and the contribution of inquiries to policy analysis.

So what would be the elements of deliberative democracy that are of special relevance to inquiries and policy analysis? Here is what one commentator listed as the criteria that should be attended to: 'Deliberative democrats and discourse theorists emphasize, in the Arendtian tradition, the importance of a free public sphere, separate from the apparatus of the state and economy, where citizens can freely debate, deliberate, and engage in collective will formation' (Charney 1998, 97).

Following this logic, one criterion for deliberative democracy is openness, the capacity of the inquiry commissioners and staff to keep an open mind, to be reflective, to be accessible and to permit the reciprocal exchange of views among people (and groups) treated as equals. Openness would certainly mean the inclusion of people without imposing the usual barriers of race, class, gender, or circumstances. Ethical issues could not be set aside in favour of information or negotiating a compromise of interests (Seyla 1996). The public dialogue being fostered would also need to be 'unfettered.' No one should be precluded from dealing with any issue or argument, or from addressing these issue in new or unusual ways. The state would have to hold back from influencing the outcome, treating the inquiry as an outsider, not insider to policy analysis. The goal would be to arrive at a common understanding that could serve later as the basis for public policy. As well, participants would need to cast their own good reasons in terms that were intelligible to other participants who did not share them. The expertise of people other than scientists, lawyers, and government officials would have to be recognized as legitimate and authoritative. All the unfettered dialogue would have to have some impact, or at least the potential of making an impact. Unfettered dialogue must not be rhetoric for rhetoric's sake, relegated to window dressing for decision making.

In a general sense, these criteria are precisely what *public* inquiries are all about. But the question about whether inquiries meet these tests of being *public,* and thus deliberatively democratic, is not so simply answered. These criteria of deliberative democracy have to be applied, one by one, as measures against which the contributions of specific inquiries can be assessed.

On closer examination, not all inquiries make a contribution to deliberative democracy. For example, some inquiries mainly generate a considerable body of high quality research. Doing so is undoubtedly valuable, but it has nothing to do with deliberative democracy per se, that is, unless this research is fed back into dialogue directly. Other inquiries are quite adept at influencing policy makers through the back channels, but they are hardly examples of deliberative democracy, although they might be very useful for policy analysis purposes. Yet other inquiries so limit access to their stakeholders' negotiations that nothing emerges from behind the closed-door sessions into an open forum for deliberation. Are such inquiries useful for policy analysis purposes? Perhaps. Are they examples of deliberative democracy? No.

Let me continue with this thought: some inquiries are so intent on capturing public opinion that they fail to listen when individuals present entirely new ways of conceiving of issues or when individuals (representing no one but themselves) raise concerns that have yet to register significantly among the broader public. One can also imagine an inquiry that so modelled itself after the Berger inquiry in terms of treating its participants as experts that it failed to engender much of a dialogue about anything else. Or an inquiry that was so caught up in being a safe haven for people who had been harmed that it lost sight of its mandate to deal with any policy issues other than redress. One can easily imagine an inquiry that was all dialogue and no effect. An inquiry that views itself as a classroom for an ill-informed public hardly meets the standard of deliberative democracy. Clearly, the link between inquiries and deliberative democracy is not so tight after all.

What Are the Options?

It cannot be emphasized too strongly that inquiries make all kinds of contributions to policy analysis, some connected to their role in resolving controversies, some to their research, and some connected to policy recommendations that eventually get implemented. What is at issue in this paper pertains directly to the *public* dimension of inquiries only, that is, to how inquiries chose to understand and include *the public* in their sense of themselves and in their actual deliberations. My question has been whether public inquiries are examplars of deliberative democracy: whether their unique 'insider/outsider' status and preoccupation with all things public makes them so.

The usefulness of any instrument for policy analysis can only be gauged in relation to the options available. What are the alternatives to an inquiry? Parliamentary committees, consultant reports, expert committees, and government-sponsored policy institutes all come to mind. But who could argue that a parliamentary committee was a better exemplar of deliberative democracy than an inquiry, according to the criteria I have laid out here? Is any consultant a contributor to deliberative democracy? Of course not. If we were to bring back the science and economic councils, would this enhance deliberative democracy? Not likely. If we were to designate the Royal Society as a national science body, would this contribute to deliberative democracy? Not likely, again. What about the now ubiquitous consultations, or advisory councils? Surely they too would fail the deliberative democracy test, at least some of the time.

The bottom line is this: inquiries are not always as unabashedly public as their commissioners and staff would like to believe. Despite the intensive thought given to the public by virtually everyone who comes into contact with inquiries, the *public* role of inquiries cannot be taken for granted. Inquiries are not always open; they do not always foster unfettered dialogue or the free play of debate about social values. Inquiries often fail to acknowledge the expertise and authority that lies with their non-scientist, non-lawyer, or government participants. They do not always deliver an invigorated and refashioned discourse about important issues. They do not always have good links to the electoral process or the rule of law, and occasionally they can be truly irrelevant to governing.

What makes inquiries unique is that they want to be *public;* they want to be exemplars of deliberative democracy in practice. This is what distinguishes them from other bodies that also make recommendations for policy analysis. I have argued here that inquiries also make decisions that move them closer or further from the deliberative democratic ideal. Overall, inquiries are less deliberatively democratic than their idealistic proponents would like to believe. Moreover, some inquiries are much more clearly exemplars of deliberative democracy than others, even when all espouse the intention to be so. Those who design and carry out inquiries take steps to move their particular inquiry closer to or farther away from the deliberatively democratic ideal that they have espoused in choosing inquiries as a mode of policy analysis in the first place.

I do not believe that these choices are made explicitly. No one sits down and says to herself: 'Well, here is an opportunity for deliberative democracy, but lets put deliberative democracy aside this time around, and concentrate instead on all the other contributions that this inquiry might make to policy analysis.'

In fact, it would be better to do just that. It would better that those who commission and run inquiries abandon the rhetoric of inquiries as being 'public inquiries' until they have answered, for themselves and others, why their inquiries deserve to be called *public* inquiries. It would better that they put more thought into the actual conception of the public that underwrites their inquiries, and to the trade-offs they make in choosing one conception of the public over another.

Deliberative democracy demands that we be deliberative about the democratic potential of policy analysis. This demand extends to the scrutiny of inquiries.

NOTES

1 For some writing on inquiries see Hickman 2004, 183; Manson and Mullan 2003; Van Harten 2003, 242; Aucoin and Goodyear-Grant 2002, 301; Bradford 2000, 136; Desbarats 1999, 106; Schwartz 1997, 72; d'Ombrain 1997, 86; Desbarats 1997, 252; Roach 1995, 268; Jenson 1994, 39; Ontario Law Reform Commission 1992.

REFERENCES

Aucoin, P., and E. Goodyear-Grant. 2002. 'Designing a Merit-Based Process for Appointing Boards of ABCs [agencies, boards, and commissions]: Lessons from the Nova Scotia Reform Experience.' *Canadian Public Administration* 45, 301.

Berger, Justice Thomas R. 1978. *Commission of Inquiry and Public Policy.* Speech delivered at the 1977–78 Public Administration Lecture Series at the School of Public Administration, Carleton University. Ottawa: 1977–78 Lecture Series.

Bradford, Neil. 2000. 'Writing Public Philosophy: Canada's Royal Commissions on Everything.' *Journal of Canadian Studies* 34, 136.

Calhoun, Craig. 1992. *Habermas and the Public Sphere.* Cambridge, MA: MIT Press.

Charney, Evan. 1998. 'Political Liberalism, Deliberative Democracy and the Public Sphere.' *American Political Science Review* 92(7), 97–110.

Connolly, William E. 1993. *The Terms of Political Discourse.* 3rd ed. Princeton, NJ: Princeton University Press.

Desbarats, Peter. 1996. 'Public Inquiries: A Case Study.' In Martin W. Westmacott and Hugh P. Mellon, eds., *Public Administration and Policy.* Scarborough, ON: Prentice-Hall Allyn and Bacon Canada.

– 1997. 'The Independence of Public Inquiries.' *Alberta Law Review* 36, 252.

d'Ombrain Nicholas. 1997. 'Public Inquiries in Canada.' *Canadian Public Administration* 40, 86.

Hickman, T. Alexander. 2004. 'Wrongful Convictions and Commissions of Inquiry: A Commentary.' *Canadian Journal of Criminology & Criminal Justice* 46, 183.

Jenson, Jane. 'Commissioning Ideas: Representation and Royal Commissions.' In Susan D. Phillips, ed., *How Ottawa Spends 1994–95: Making Change,* 39. Ottawa: Carleton University Press.

Ku, Agnes S. 2000. 'Revisiting the Notion of "Public" in Habermas' Theory – Toward a Theory of Politics of Public Credibility.' *Sociological Theory* 18(2), 216–40.

MacPherson, C.B. 1966. *The Real World of Democracy.* Oxford: Clarendon Press.

Manson, Allan and David Mullan. 2003. *Commissions of Inquiry: Praise or Reappraise?* Toronto: Irwin Law.

Ontario. Ontario Law Reform Commission. 1992. *Report on Public Inquiries.* Toronto: Ministry of the Attorney General.

Roach, Kent. 1995. 'Canadian Public Inquiries and Accountability.' In Philip C. Stenning, ed., *Accountability for Criminal Justice.* Toronto: University of Toronto Press.

Salter, Liora. 1990. 'The Two Contradictions in Public Inquiries.' In *Commissions of Inquiry.* Toronto: Carswell.

Schwartz, Bryan. 1997. 'Public Inquiries.' *Canadian Public Administration* 40, 72.

Seyla, Benhabib. 1996. 'Towards a Deliberative Model of Democratic Legitimacy.' In Benhabib Seyla, ed., *Democracy and Difference: Contesting Boundaries of the Political.* Princeton, NJ: Princeton University Press.

Simmel, Georg. 1971. *On Individuality and Social Forms.* Chicago: The University of Chicago Press.

Van Harten, Gus. 2003. 'Truth before Punishment: A Defence of Public Inquiries.' *Queen's Law Journal* 29, 242.

Williams, Raymond. 1983. *Keywords: a Vocabulary of Culture and Society.* London: Fontana Paperbacks.

INQUIRIES CITED

Aird, John. Royal Commission on Radio Broadcasting. Canada. 1929. *Report of the Royal Commission on Radio Broadcasting.* Ottawa: F.A. Acland, Printer to the King.

Bayda, E.D. Cluff Lake Board of Inquiry. Saskatchewan. 1978. *The Cluff Lake Board of Inquiry Final Report.* Regina: Cluff Lake Board of Inquiry.

Berger, Thomas R. Mackenzie Valley Pipeline Inquiry. Canada. 1977. *Northern*

Frontier, Northern Homeland: The Report of the Mackenzie Valley Pipeline Inquiry. Ottawa: Minister of Supply and Services Canada.

Caplan, Gerald L., and Florian Sauvageau. Task Force on Broadcasting Policy. Canada. 1986. *Report of the Task Force on Broadcasting Policy.* Ottawa: Minister of Supply and Services Canada.

Grange, Samuel G.M. Royal Commission of Inquiry into Certain Deaths at the Hospital for Sick Children and Related Matters. Ontario. 1984. *Report of the Royal Commission of Inquiry into Certain Deaths at the Hospital for Sick Children and Related Matters.* Toronto: Ontario Ministry of the Attorney General.

Hughes, Samuel H.S. The Royal Commission of Inquiry into the Response of the Newfoundland Criminal Justice System to Complaints. Newfoundland. 1992. *Royal Commission of Inquiry into the Response of the Newfoundland Criminal Justice System to Complaints* (report). St John's: The Commission.

Krever, Horace. Commission of Inquiry on the Blood System in Canada. Canada. 1997. *Commission of Inquiry on the Blood System in Canada: Final Report.* Ottawa: The Commission.

MacDonald, Donald S. Royal Commission on the Economic Union and Development Prospects for Canada. Canada. 1984. *Challenges and Choices: Report of the Royal Commission on the Economic Union and Development Prospects for Canada.* Ottawa: The Commission.

O'Connor, Dennis R. Walkerton Inquiry. Ontario. 2002. *Report of the Walkerton Inquiry: A Strategy for Safe Drinking Water.* Toronto: Ontario Ministry of the Attorney General.

13 Back to the Future? Is There a Case for Re-establishing the Economic Council and/or the Science Council?

LAURENT DOBUZINSKIS

In 1992, the Economic Council of Canada (ECC), the Science Council of Canada (SCC) and the Law Reform Commission fell victim to the budget cutters' axe.[1] Although at the time many observers felt that this was a regrettable decision, especially in the case of the ECC, the issue of whether there is still a need for institutions such as these has quietly disappeared from the policy agenda. This would seem to suggest that the decision to abolish them was not, after all, without grounds. Since then the Law Commission of Canada, which looked rather similar to the Law Reform Commission of old, was re-established in 1997 (only to be abolished itself in 2006). The purpose of this paper is to examine the case, if any, for recreating either the ECC or the SCC, or both.

The question of whether something equivalent to the ECC or the SCC is needed today depends obviously on a judgment concerning not only the value of that legacy but also the present circumstances, the extent to which they are significantly different from the situation that prevailed about 12 years ago, and on whether or not existing institutions fill the gap left vacant by their demise. The term 'judgment' clearly implies that it is not a strictly factual question. Policy problems always involve value choices because policy making aims at the achievement of some more desirable goals among the myriad of possible ones, and further down the choice of better means of achieving these goals in some sort of recursive loop endlessly relinking ends and means. Indeed, contemporary policy studies literature is replete with works that undermine the positivist faith in the possibility of solving policy problems in a techno-cratic manner and stress the interplay of empirical and normative con-siderations (Fisher 1980; Goodin 1982; Amy 1984; Bobrow and Dryzek 1987; Gilroy 1993; Pal 2001; Imbroscio 2004). Section 3 offers an analysis of what is minimally needed in formulating a policy recommendation, such as deciding whether to recreate either one or both of these councils. My contention is that it is not enough to pay lip service to the importance of norms and values; one has to carefully articulate the relevant values and examine their (often contradictory) implications. But if policy problems inevitably raise difficult normative questions, it does not mean that one can dispense with an analysis of the relevant facts. Thus what follows in the next two sections is an examination of the historical record, which prepares the ground for a reflection on the desirability of re-establishing these agencies in the final section.

Historical Background

For more than a century, governments in Canada have used commissions of inquiry to investigate a wide range of problems. As the administrative state developed in the postwar decades, however, the need for more permanent institutions became more obvious. Many arms-length advisory councils were established at both the federal and provincial levels in the 1960s and 1970s. Their members could only be dismissed for 'just cause' and they had control over their research agenda, research publication and hiring practices (Pal 1986, 78–9). Most of them have since then been abolished, as the determination of all levels of government to reduce or eliminate their budgetary deficits became firmer in the 1990s. Other, more political, factors also played a role: bearers of bad news are rarely welcome at the prince's court, and in the 1980s and 1990s criticisms expressed by advisory councils became more pointed, even if they often diverged significantly.

The Economic Council

The Economic Council of Canada was established in 1963, after the return to power of the Liberals. Arthur J. Smith, who became one of the council's first two directors, recalls that 'Parliament moved relatively quickly to pass the *Economic Council Act*. Indeed, the act was unanimously endorsed and approved by all parties represented in Parliament. It also received widespread public support and acclaim' (1981, 76). However, unanimity was achieved at the cost of considerable vagueness in the wording of the council's objectives.

Long-term planning was a popular concept then. Thus, one of the objectives of the newly formed council was to serve as a means of building a consensus on social and economic goals. More than a decade of sustained economic growth and high levels of employment had created new expectations and a belief that long-term planning was required to sustain such favourable economic conditions. Foreign examples seemed to point in this direction (e.g., the French General Planning Commissariat and the then recently established British National Economic Development Council, which was composed of representatives from government, unions, and employers. (For an analysis of these planning systems, see Thorburn 1984, chapter 4.) In Canada, the Diefenbaker government had created the National Productivity Council to improve labour-management relations and to facilitate economic growth.

Medium- to long-term planning, at least in an advisory capacity, and consensus building figured prominently among the statutory responsibilities of the Economic Council.[2] Each *Annual Review* outlined the economic trends supposed to prevail over the next five to ten years. At the time when the ECC was set up, it was envisioned that the Department of Finance would play a complementary role: the council would be in charge of long-term projections while Finance would focus on short-term issues. However, it was not long before Finance began to work on the preparation of multi-year economic projections of its own.

The council was composed of three full-time members (a chairman and two directors) and not more than 25 part-time members. They were appointed by the governor-in-council. Partisan considerations played a part in the selection process; nevertheless, the council's members represented a variety of social, professional, and regional interests. Labour union officials sat on the council until the implementation of the anti-inflation program of 1975. They never returned officially but labour's point of view was not ignored during all these years, as retired labour leaders were appointed to the council from time to time (e.g., Paul-Emilien Dalpé); closer working relations between the Economic Council and the labour movement developed in the last few years of its existence.

The Economic Council was a Crown corporation that reported to Parliament through the prime minister. This status provided the council with a fair degree of autonomy in its internal affairs, especially as far as its research program and policy recommendations were concerned. Throughout its existence the council received rather substantial funding; in 1991 its operating budget amounted to approximately $11.2 million, which was considerably larger than the budget of any other policy research organization in Canada at that time, and would still be large by today's standards.

The chair – always a professional economist – was appointed for seven years. He or she – two women held this position: Dr Sylvia Ostry and the last incumbent, Judith Maxwell – '[was] the Chief Executive Officer ... and has supervision over and direction of the work and staff of the Council.'[3] (The size of the staff varied over the years; it was above 130 in the early 1980s, but it fell below that mark in the late 1980s.) The chair was most directly involved in the preparation of the *Annual Review*, and in the screening of research topics.[4] He or she also played a 'managerial role ... by mediating between the technical and the representative elements on the Council' (Phidd 1975, 430).

Dr John J. Deutsch, who chaired the council from 1963 to 1967, is widely credited for having successfully launched the council and for steering it away from political and bureaucratic sandbars. He had the advantage of considerable experience with bureaucratic politics, and he believed in consultative planning. He was convinced that one of the most important roles of the council was 'to improve public understanding of basic economic policy' (quoting Dr Sylvia Ostry's recollection of John Deutsch's term at the helm of the council; see Economic Council of Canada 1992, 10). Dr Arthur J.R. Smith (1967–71) found it more difficult to gain influence with the policy makers, largely because 'he had never been involved with the Canadian governmental bureaucracy or research commissions to the degree that his predecessor was' (Phidd 1975, 445). In fact, conflicting relations between the Economic Council and the Department of Finance developed during his tenure. On a more positive note, CANDIDE, an econometric model of the Canadian economy that was used in the preparation of the *Annual Reviews*, was developed under Dr Smith's leadership (after 1986, however, the council contracted out econometric forecasts to the Conference Board). Under the next four chairs – André Raynauld (1971–76), George Post (1976–77), Sylvia Ostry (1977–79) and Dr David W. Slater (1980–85) – the council was slowly transformed into a policy research institute staffed by economists and producing research relevant mostly to other economists.

Judith Maxwell's appointment as chair of the council in 1985 marked the beginning of a period of renewal. Indeed, government officials had indicated to her at the time of her appointment that they felt the council did not have as much impact on the policy debates of the day as they wished; her mission was to enhance its profile (interview,

21 March 1994). Earlier in her career, she had held a senior research position at the C.D. Howe Institute, but she had left the institute in the early 1980s, before it took a turn toward a resolutely more market-oriented approach. Her priorities differed in subtle ways from those of her immediate predecessors or of private-sector think tanks in the late 1980s. The subtlety of these differences stems from the rather muted but apparent contrast between the council's economic policy goals that continued to be entirely consistent with mainstream economics, on the one hand, and a distinctive concern with the social policy implications of this orientation. Under Judith Maxwell's leadership, 'the Council ... diversified its research agenda in order to address simultaneously a range of topics of interest to Canadians and to take advantage of the insights of other disciplines such as sociology and political science' (Economic Council of Canada 1991a, 8).[5] Maxwell was also committed to making council's reports more readable and more topical.[6]

The news of the council's termination came as a total surprise to its members when the budget was presented to the House of Commons on February 25, 1992. Apart from the general argument about deficit reduction – an argument that, ironically, the council itself had made repeatedly – the specific justification given by the minister of finance, Don Mazankowski, was that advice on economic policy matters was available from universities and private-sector think tanks. He mentioned in particular the C.D. Howe Institute and the Conference Board of Canada (Dowling 1992). Many commentators suggested that other motives lay behind the decision. It was known that the council had few friends in the Department of Finance or the Bank of Canada, i.e., the two other sources of economic advice to the government. And most observers of the Ottawa scene agree that since the mid-1980s the Department of Finance has regained most of the influence and power it had lost in the previous decade and a half or so. Several Conservative backbenchers also had voiced criticisms of the council for years. The most often heard explanation in terms of retribution, however, was that the council had miscalculated badly when it issued its 1991 report on *The Economics of Constitutional Options.* According to that report, the economic cost of Quebec's separation would not have been very severe. Rumour had it that this analysis had infuriated Prime Minister Mulroney but, as could be expected, he denied it. Responding to critics who implied that the government was trying to silence critics, the prime minister argued that, in fact, the council had supported the government's economic priorities (Howard 1992, A2).

Reactions to the announcement of the elimination of the Economic Council were generally negative, even from the business community, which is usually supportive of cost-cutting measures.[7] Most commentators[8] pointed out that the ECC had acquired a good reputation for producing timely and rigorous studies. Many also noted that its budget, although large by comparison with other research institutes, was merely a drop in the bucket of the federal deficit. A few critics, however, suggested that the council had been severely handicapped by its attempt at finding a middle road between the divergent positions of its members, and thus had not been able to speak with a strong voice on crucial issues (Dowling 1992, B2). Michael Walker of the Fraser Institute portrayed the Economic Council as a bureaucratic agency that was 'largely reflective of a public sector viewpoint'[9] and suggested that it was too expensive for what it was worth.

The Science Council

The Science Council was created three years after the Economic Council in 1966, at a time when rational policy analysis was an idea whose time had come. Until the end, the Science Council demonstrated a commitment to rational planning and certain scepticism with respect to the capacity of market mechanisms to produce spontaneously the desired response to changing circumstances. We live in a scientific and technological age and, therefore, science policy touches upon a wide range of issues. The broad mandate of the Science Council reflected this reality. It was expected to make recommendations concerning:

1 the adequacy of the scientific and technological research and development being carried out in Canada;
2 the priorities that should be assigned in Canada to specific areas of scientific and technological research;
3 the effective development and utilization of scientific and technological manpower in Canada;
4 long-term planning for scientific and technological research and development in Canada;
5 the factors involved in Canada's participation in international scientific or technological affairs;
6 the responsibilities of departments and agencies of the government of Canada, in relation to those of universities, private companies, and other organizations, in furthering science and technology in Canada;

7 information on scientific and technological research and development that should be obtained in order to provide a proper basis for
the formulation of government policy in relation to science and
technology in Canada; and
8 the best means of developing and maintaining cooperation and the
exchange of information between the council and other public or
private organizations concerned with the scientific, technological,
economic, or social aspects of life in Canada.

The *Science Council of Canada Act* was amended in 1978 to add a further
responsibility with respect to public awareness of science and technology, and of the interdependence of the public, governments, industries,
and universities in the development and use of science and technology
(Doern 1971, 247; and Science Council 1982, 17).

Research in any established scientific discipline was never an objective of the Science Council. The function of the Science Council consisted in doing science *policy* research, i.e., research intended to explore
policy options concerning the development and utilization of science
and technology in Canada. For example, the council's study on genetic
predispositions to disease did not contribute new knowledge about
genetics nor did it help in developing new medical technologies; rather,
it was concerned with the importance given to these questions in the
curriculum of medical schools, the economic impact of further investment in this area, the ethical and legal aspects, etc (see Science Council
of Canada 1991). The difference between these two activities is perfectly
rational. However, it proved to be a source of ambiguity that made it
harder for the Science Council to gain acceptance in the bureaucratic
environment or to build a constituency outside of it. Even the members
of the council – who, for the most part, were practicing scientists or
engineers rather than policy analysts – felt unsure about its mandate.
This situation was not helped by the fact that science policy is a more
unfamiliar concept than, say, economic policy, and is not a matter of
urgent concern to most Canadians.

When it was first established, the Science Council reported to the
prime minister via the Science Secretariat, which was located within the
Privy Council Office (PCO). Thus, the relatively marginal nature of the
Science Council's activities was balanced by its strategic place in the
policy-making system. However, as G.B. Doern explains, 'This relationship created many difficulties, not the least of which was the strain and
ambivalence which the confidential and secretive PCO environment
placed on a supposedly open and public body such as the Science

Council was intended to be. The relationship also often meant that the Science Secretariat would be called upon to evaluate Science Council recommendations, recommendations which Science Secretariat personnel had already helped to formulate' (1982, 248).

The council acquired more independence in 1968, when it was made an autonomous body. It was established as a departmental corporation. After the creation of the Ministry of State for Science and Technology (MOSST) in 1971, a measure that the council itself had recommended, it reported to Parliament through the minister in charge of MOSST.[10] (After that ministry had been eliminated, the Science Council reported through the Minister for Science.) However, according to Ray W. Jackson, 'A difficult choice presented itself. The Council could remain internally oriented, and quite possibly be ignored, or it could do its studies and reach its conclusions in public, so that it could be seen to be advising and its ideas could be publicly seen to have merit ... The public mode was the one chosen by its first chairman, Omond Solandt' (1985, 33).

The Science Council was not well prepared to take advantage of this strategy. Commenting on these early years, G.B. Doern noted that it was 'operating in an intensely political environment but its own political skills and strategies regarding [the question of how to function as a public forum] seem[ed] to be undeveloped' (1971, 264). It failed to realize early enough the difference between authoritative advice given in confidence and recommendations expressed publicly. Since most of these recommendations involve some degree of criticism of government policies, 'it is hardly surprising that the reactions of the bureaucrats and politicians ranged from annoyance, to ignoring or belittling the work of the Council, to outright animosity' (Jackson 1985, 33). Over the years the council learned to play the political game but it seems to have been a case of 'too little too late.'

The council was composed of 28 (originally 23) part-time members, appointed by the governor-in-council for a three-year term, as well as a vice-chairman and a chairman, who served for five years. The membership varied somewhat over the years but it included academics, individuals who came from the private sector, and a few public servants. The first four chairmen – Dr O.M. Solandt (1966–71), Dr Roger Gaudry (1971–75), Dr Josef Kates (1975–78), and Dr Claude Fortier (1978–81) – were only part-time officers. This placed the council in a position of relative weakness in the bureaucratic system. Dr Stuart Smith, a psychiatrist and former leader of the provincial Liberal Party in Ontario, became the first full-time chairman in December 1981. Dr Geraldine A.

Kenney-Wallace, a physicist, succeeded him in October 1987, but she did not complete her mandate.[11] Janet E. Halliwell was appointed in 1990 to replace her.

The staff, numbering 29 in 1990–91 and including less than a dozen policy analysts, was headed by two directors (one for policy analysis, and one for programs). The number of person-years in 1985–86 had stood at 67, but 'severe and unjustified' budget cuts were forced upon the Science Council in the fiscal year 1986–87, when its budget was cut almost in half, from $4.7 million to just under $2.6 million (Science Council of Canada 1986, 3; see also *Vancouver Sun* 1985, A11; and Immen 1985, A1). The budgetary situation of the council improved modestly in the late 1980s but never returned to the pre-1987 level.

An attractive feature of the Science Council was the multidisciplinary nature of its research personnel. Practically all the disciplines that are relevant to policy research were represented, at one time or another. Some researchers with a background in the natural sciences were included but social scientists formed a clear majority. This created occasional tensions between the council and its staff, since they shared neither the same vocabulary nor the same outlook on science and technology. The difference between the Science Council and the Economic Council in this respect was evident. While economists and business people cannot be expected to agree on everything, they share many assumptions and concepts. Engineers and scientists have far less in common with social scientists trained in the policy sciences. It was the chairman's role and that of the council's senior executives to act as bridges between these two camps.

The Science Council covered a wide range of topics (see next section). Too many, in fact: the council failed to position itself among the various policy communities that were its potential audience. The constituencies that had been the objects of its attention at one point in time, and with which it could have established lasting contacts, lost interest in the council as it kept on moving in different directions. The council's fuzzy identity was one of the factors explaining the relative indifference that greeted the announcement of its closure. This is not to say that no one objected to it[12] but typically the press devoted far more attention to the disappearance of the Economic Council than to that of the Science Council. As for the scientific community, it was more directly concerned with the fate and the budgetary allocations of the granting councils than with the Science Council. Even Dr Solandt, the council's first chairman, was reported as saying that over the years it had become 'just another think tank,' adding that 'we lost the rudder, that's true, but maybe it wasn't a very good rudder anymore' (cited in Egan 1992). With friends like these, who needs enemies?

It was stated at that time that the council's advisory function would continue to be performed by the National Advisory Board on Science and Technology (NABST). These two organizations, at first sight, appeared to have overlapping mandates. The members of the NABST, and of its successor, the Advisory Council on Science and Technology (ACST), however, enjoy less independence than did the members of the SCC and lack the support of a comparable research staff.

The Evolution of Policy: The Councils' Research Agendas

The research produced by the Economic Council offers an interesting window on the evolution of economic policy analysis in Canada. The council gradually moved from a lukewarm but undeniable commitment to long-term economic planning in the 1960s and early 1970s to a more resolute advocacy of market-oriented approaches in later years. The Science Council, by contrast, was always more interventionist – indeed its mandate presupposed the validity of the market failure paradigm. Its demise at the hands of a government that had turned away from the market failure model was not very surprising.

The Economic Council's Contribution to Policy Research: An Overview

The publications of the Economic Council fell under five categories. First, one of its statutory obligations was to produce an annual review. It used to be released in September, that is, before the traditional date of the Budget Speech, in order to give government a chance to consider the council's policy recommendations, and to provide the attentive public with the information needed to evaluate the government's stated economic objectives. Although the council's mandate was to analyse the medium- and long-term prospects of the economy, its annual reviews often dealt with more immediate concerns.

Council reports on specific topics were also issued frequently. The council assumed responsibility for both the annual reviews and the council reports (after 1978 dissenting comments were added when necessary). Research studies, discussion papers, and conference proceedings were documents attributed to individual authors and did not engage the responsibility of the council. With the exception of authored discussion papers that were available only in the language of preparation, all Economic Council publications were printed in both official languages. This enhanced the visibility of the council in Quebec, where it was probably the best-known Canadian policy research organization.

The scope of the Economic Council's interests and concerns was impressive. An analysis of its output supports the impression held by a majority of academic policy researchers in the 1980s that no competing policy research organization had a broader research program.[13] The breakdown of the council's publication list in table 13.1 shows that it had either initiated or sponsored studies ranging from highly theoretical problems to quite specific policy issues, e.g., mortgage finance. Also, the research effort was well balanced: no category accounts for more than 12 per cent of the total number of citations. (Of course, this is due in part to my somewhat arbitrary choice of categories; nevertheless, it should be obvious that the Economic Council avoided putting all its eggs in the same basket.)

That many publications dealt with the medium- or long-term economic horizon is not surprising. This was consistent with the council's mandate. But more immediately pressing issues were addressed from time to time, such as the extent to which the government should attempt to control or reduce its budgetary deficit.

It is difficult to fault the council for obvious or systematic bias. Examples of apparent bias are rather counter-intuitive. For instance, the council produced more studies of the Newfoundland economy than of the Ontario economy. (Admittedly, many studies not explicitly concerned with Ontario deal at length with economic sectors that are essential to the economic well being of that province.) Similarly, the Western provinces were the subject of a fair number of studies and reports. Or, to choose another sensitive topic, the place of women in the Canadian economy received significant attention (for example, Boothy 1986; Boulet and Lavallée 1981; 1984; Breton 1984, 1985; Economic Council 1985; Cloutier 1986; Alexander 1984; Boyd and Humphreys 1979). Only about one per cent of the titles could be regarded as being primarily concerned with ecological issues; however, in absolute terms, the Economic Council's output on environment-related topics was far from negligible.

Nevertheless, there were some noticeable gaps in the research output of the council. The attention granted to savings and investment outweighed the resources devoted to the study of poverty. The small number of studies dealing exclusively with the latter did not even

Table 13.1 Classification by Subject of the Publications (1964–92) of the Economic Council of Canada,[a] N (%)

Economic Theory/ Methodology	Canadian Economy	Regional and Provincial Economies	International Trade Global Issues	Miscellaneous
55 (6.78)	Planning and economic management techniques[b]: 10 (1.23)	Federal-provincial relations; regional disparities: 30 (3.7)	Global issues; comparative studies: 15 (1.85)	41 (5.06)
	Governing instruments, other than regulation[c]: 23 (2.84)	Atlantic region, or Maritimes (as a whole): 3 (0.37)	Canada and world markets: 12 (1.48)	
	Government regulation; competition policy: 71 (8.75)	Newfoundland: 20 (2.47)	Canada and the US market: 9 (1.11)	
	Public finance: 1) fiscal policy; monetary policy; public debt: 35 (4.32); 2) budgetary process and government expenditures: 9 (1.11)	Quebec: 5 (0.61)	Canada and the developing world: 11 (1.36)	
	Macroeconomic trends; economic growth; medium- and long-term strategies[d]: 50 (6.16)	Ontario: 3 (0.37)	International monetary system; balance of payments: 2 (0.25)	
	Short-term (stabilization) strategies: 10 (1.23)	Western region (as a whole): 18 (2.22)		
	Technological change; productivity: 41 (5.06)	British Columbia: 2 (0.25)		
	Employment; industrial relations[e]: 90 (11.1)	Alberta: 10 (1.23)		
	Incomes (real wages, etc.): 40 (4.93)	Saskatchewan: 4 (0.49)		
	Pricing and inflation: 25 (3.08)	Manitoba: 3 (0.37)		

Table 13.1 (*concluded*)

Economic Theory/ Methodology	Canadian Economy	Regional and Provincial Economies	International Trade Global Issues	Miscellaneous
	Savings, investment; banking; mortgage financing: 29 (3.58)	Urban economics: 17 (2.1)		
	Environmental issues: 9 (1.11)	The North: 4 (0.49)		
	Social programs: education: 19 (2.34); health care: 6 (0.74); income support programs and pensions: 15 (1.85) Sectoral policies: natural resources, energy: 19 (2.34); agriculture: 10 (1.23); fisheries: 3 (0.37); construction, housing: 11 (1.36); manufacturing: 17 (2.1); services (including transportation): 8 (0.99)			

a) All publications categories are included here: annual reviews, council reports, conference papers and reports, candid project reports, staff studies, research studies, and discussion papers. As some of the documents overlap several categories, the total number of citations (811) is greater than the total numbers of titles. Percentages do not add up to 100 per cent because of rounding error.
b) For example, social indicators.
c) For example, Crown corporations.
d) Includes all 28 annual reviews.
e) Including annual reviews dealing very explicitly with this subject, even though all deal with it to some extent.

warrant the definition of a separate category; they are subsumed under the rubrics 'incomes' and 'income support programs,' accounting respectively for 4.93 and 1.85 per cent of all titles. Poverty in Canada was identified as a serious problem in three consecutive annual reviews, in 1968, 1969, and 1970, all of which were prepared when Dr Smith was chairman. 'As a result of the Council's studies in the poverty area,' noted R.W. Phidd, 'the Senate established a committee which published a report entitled *Poverty in Canada*' (1975, 465). But, after having initiated the debate, the council did not return to it until the very final year of its existence, when it revisited the issue *in extremis,* as it were. The unpublished 1992 *Annual Review* would have dealt with this issue, as I indicated already.[14]

It could be retorted that poverty is not so much an economic problem as it is a social and moral issue. What economists can do about it is to suggest ways of accelerating economic growth, and of achieving full, or near-full employment; there is no doubt that these matters are addressed and dealt with at great length by the council (see table 1). The social aspects of poverty are more adequately being studied by other bodies, such as the National Council of Welfare. As for environmental issues, they only become an economic problem when they have a noticeable impact on the price structure. Yet, if policy issues form a seamless web, the Economic Council's rather literal reading of its mandate prevented it from fulfilling its mission as a *public* institution. The last chair tried to overcome the constraints inherent in the economists' worldview. However, the change of direction for which she was responsible possibly came too late or was too modest to generate the kind of political support the council would have needed.

Contrary to the Science Council, the Economic Council argued on many occasions *against* an interventionist industrial policy. It consistently supported trade liberalization, if possible on a worldwide basis but, as a matter of priority, with the United States. With the publication of *Looking Forward* (1975) by the Economic Council and *The Weakest Link* (1978) by the Science Council, the lines between the proponents and opponents of free trade were drawn. From then on, the two councils never moved very far from their respective positions.

So far, the emphasis has been placed on some of the most obvious gaps in what was an otherwise comprehensive and rather well-balanced research and publication program. What follows is more concerned with the content of that program.

The Economic Council Outlook: From Long-Term Planning to (Almost) Laissez Faire

The themes raised in the annual reviews have changed as a result of a variety of factors, including the preferences of the Economic Council's chairmen, the domestic economy, and international influences. One can also discern interesting shifts in the theoretical and practical concerns of professional economists.

Employment and human resources were always significant preoccupations of the council. The first two reviews paid considerable attention to full employment and to the means of achieving it (e.g., education); the eighth review dealt with the structure of the job market and manpower training (to use the vocabulary of the times). Paradoxically, however, this theme became less central in the 1980s, when unemployment worsened. Employment continued to be an important theme, but it was more typically discussed in relation to other dimensions of economic policy, namely, free trade, the budgetary deficit, investment, productivity, inflation, and so on. Thus, the nineteenth annual review, *Lean Times – Policies and Constraints* (1982), gives the impression that the council was rather more preoccupied with inflation than with unemployment. The twenty-fourth annual review, *Reaching Outwards* (1987), strongly endorses the idea of 'reaching out to new markets' by entering into a comprehensive free trade agreement with the United States. The rationale offered is that the single-minded pursuit of an objective (e.g., full employment) without regard for the new global environment risks bringing about unexpected, and potentially damaging, consequences. This argument was bitterly criticized by several dissenting council members, in whose opinion free trade could not improve Canada's unemployment situation.

This shift reflected a change in the value system of the present generation of economists who, contrary to those of John Deutsch's generation, have not experienced the Great Depression and are perhaps more condescending toward unemployed people. In its fifteenth annual review, *A Time for Reason* (1978), the council stated that the unemployment rate at the time did not 'portray the same economically, socially, or politically trying conditions that prevailed when a family's sole income earner was out of work in the 1930s' (83). This is true to an extent, of course, but it is also a way of ignoring the real social and political problems linked to it. Beginning with the twenty-seventh annual review, *Transitions for the 90s* (1990), the seriousness of the problems posed at that time by the persistence of unemployment was acknowledged. But this did not exactly mean that full employment was put back on the agenda.

Not surprisingly, inflation and energy are two themes that reoccur often in the reviews issued in the late 1970s and early 1980s. The council made a rather positive assessment of the anti-inflation program of 1975 (1978, 19). In the early 1980s, the council recommended a policy of expenditure restraint. It also supported the federal government's policy objective of maintaining the domestic price of oil below the international level, although it did not always approve of the chosen margin of difference.[15] While the nineteenth annual review (1982) did not contain any ringing condemnation of the Liberal government's National Energy Program, it affirmed the principle that government interference with the rules of the market has destabilizing effects.

On the subject of the budgetary deficit, the Economic Council was careful in the early 1980s not to insist on immediate corrective measures when even more severe problems needed to be tackled. But as of the late 1980s, the council became more insistent about the need to put Canada's public finances in order. It recommended spending cuts or, at a minimum, firmness in resisting pressures to increase spending.[16]

Competitiveness and trade were the dominant themes of the twenty-second (1985) and twenty-third (1986) reviews. Like almost everyone else, the Economic Council stressed the need to adjust to a changing technological and international environment. In that new environment, government was supposed to play a less active role, concentrating on ways of creating a more favourable climate for free enterprise. The council had previously addressed the attendant problems caused by costly social programs. For example, it had suggested a tightening of unemployment insurance. That program was criticized for not being more closely connected to job training and labour reallocation programs (see the twentieth annual review). Competitiveness also requires a stronger economic union, a theme that the council picked up in its twenty-eighth annual review, titled *A Joint Venture – The Economics of Constitutional Options* (1991b). The council tried to avoid taking sides in the constitutional debate: it took the view that a strong economic union can be achieved, at least in principle, either through centralized or decentralized mechanisms for delivering social programs, but it acknowledged that the Atlantic provinces have much to lose from a shift toward a more decentralized regime.

This last annual review exemplified Maxwell's willingness to tackle relevant issues. Unfortunately, the effort also revealed the ECC's lack of political savvy. By stating that sovereignty-association was one of several options, and by further asserting that such an option might prove beneficial to Canada and not exaggeratedly costly for Quebec, the council appeared to contradict the long-standing position of the federal government (Economic Council of Canada 1991, 22). Even if it might have been a well-reasoned and objective statement, coming from a federal agency, it could be interpreted as legitimizing the position of the sovereignists.

Space constraints allow me to provide only a brief discussion of the most salient points in a selection of council reports from the 1980s and early 1990s (Economic Council of Canada 1981; 1982a; 1986a; 1986b; 1990; 1992). What is striking is the extent to which the ideas scattered through these reports continue to be relevant to today's policy problems. The ECC can in hindsight be looked at as a microcosm of the policy-making system. An institution that was founded on interventionist, Keynesian, and quasi-corporatist premises ended up advocating something that it has become conventional to call the 'neo-liberal paradigm.' By that I mean a preference for non-interventionist market-oriented solutions like deregulation and free trade and a more pronounced concern with inflation than with full employment. (I must add, though, that the council's recommendations were generally expressed in a carefully measured tone.)[17] Reports exemplifying that shift include *Reforming Regulation* (1981), in which the council declared that 'our approach is to favour individual choice and non-coercive exchanges that are a part of the market process' (10); *Financing Confederation* (1982), in which the council expressed criticism of provincial practices, such as preferential tax treatment for the purpose of attracting investment; *Minding the Public's Business* (1986), which is arguably the council's most direct attack on the merits of government intervention in the management of the economy;[18] and *Road Map for Tax Reform* (1986), which favoured replacing the then current manufacturers' sales tax by a value-added tax.

Under the leadership of Maxwell, the council seemed to be ever so slightly veering in a different direction, one that evokes the 'Third Way' advocated by Anthony Giddens (1999). However, that parallel remains tentative and it certainly was never explicitly articulated by the council itself. Reports that support this point include *From the Bottom Up: The Community Economic-Development Approach* (1990), which advocated government support for community development projects while stressing the need to preserve community leadership and flexibility; and *The New Face of Poverty* (1992), which, although it implied that it was not the time for a major effort toward reducing poverty in Canada, in light of the growing fiscal stress (11), nevertheless is noteworthy because it was a report on *poverty* as such, and not on the inefficiency of social programs.

When the winding down of the council was announced, many commentators expressed dismay and some ventured that it would be reinvented sooner or later. The void left by the council is indeed noticeable, but it is not as large as one would have thought. A useful coordinating mechanism has been lost, and an important source of funding for independent scholarly research on comprehensively defined problems (e.g., education or health) is now gone. However, the view of the policy world shared by most economists has become so influential and so pervasive nowadays that the loss of the Economic Council makes relatively little difference in the end.

As Michel Foucault argued, the term 'discipline' conveys a double meaning: it refers to a branch of knowledge and to the harsh treatment reserved for those who transgress the rules, i.e., the standards set by exemplary scholars and enforced through the peer review process.[19] Economists' worldviews shifted in the direction of a more determined emphasis on market solutions during the 1980s, and so did the Economic Council's philosophy. Evidence of this shift is evident in the twenty-third annual review, *Changing Times* (1986), which provided a report on the taxation of savings and investments, as well as in a research project on 'adjustment and adaptation,' which was predicated on the assumption that Canada has no choice but to adapt to external pressures by relaxing the controls and social commitments inherent in the concept of the 'welfare state.' In the early 1990s, discussions of the desirability and feasibility of full employment, and the interest in community-based economic development signalled a realignment of sorts, albeit not a radical one. Judith Maxwell tended to think that instead of an 'either-or' choice between economic orthodoxy and political sensitivity, the council had to embark on a more creative course, taking different dimensions of analysis into account without seeking to force them into a Procrustean bed. More non-economists began to receive research contracts under Maxwell's term in office.[20] However, more time would have been required to allow these changes to leave their mark on the identity of the council. The council had evolved in a rather incremental way and without seeking to attract much attention beyond its usual public in the academic community. Therefore, it did not succeed in convincing government or the public at large that it had embarked on a new course. In any event, the Mulroney government had other priorities and was not ideologically disposed to look for a third way between *dirigisme* and laissez faire.

The ECC, of course, leaves an important legacy of high-quality research. It remains a sort of icon, defining an era of forward-looking economic and social planning in a context of sustained economic growth. As I have suggested, however, it failed to position itself in the new pluralistic, postmodern and more international environment in which we now find ourselves. Judith Maxwell was well aware of the challenge (see, for example, Economic Council of Canada 1992, 16–18); however, in order to have achieved a successful transition, the council would have needed stronger direction and support from senior bureaucrats in the central agencies and from the cabinet.

Canadian Policy Research Networks: The Economic Council Redux?

The talents that revitalized the Economic Council during its final years were dispersed after the council was wound down. Judith Maxwell, however, has been instrumental in regrouping some of them around the Canadian Policy Research Networks (CPRN), an organization she founded in December 1994. As its name suggests, the CPRN is not a think tank conducting all its research by its own means, but rather a co-ordinating mechanism linking researchers and policy makers in universities, other think tanks, and government departments across the country.

The search for a new equilibrium between the more individualistic culture that now prevails in the new global economy, and the need for some form of social cohesion, defines the CPRN philosophy. It is exemplified in reports like Betcherman and Lowe (1997), Jenson (1998), and Beauvais and Jenson (2002). What such efforts seem to aim for is an alternative to privatization as a solution to the problem of government failure by, in particular, stressing the new role that the voluntary sector and community-based initiatives could play in the new economy. At the same time, the CPRN wishes to encourage a more active role on the part of the public sector, not necessarily as a doer, but as a facilitator and catalyst. The CPRN has also taken the lead in promoting citizens' engagement and dialogue (e.g., *Citizens Willing to Work with Queen's Park to Meet Budget Challenge* [27 April 2004], described as an 'unprecedented pre-budget consultative dialogue').

Table 13.2 Classification by Subject of the Publications (1966–92) of the Science
Council of Canada, N (%)

	N	%
Agriculture	5	2.2
Aquaculture, fisheries and oceanography	9	3.9
Biotechnology and the life sciences	7	3.0
Computers, communications and the information society	10	4.3
Education and university research		16.1
Energy	10	4.3
Environment	16	6.9
Health care and occupational safety	14	6.1
International issues	9	3.9
Natural resources	20	8.7
Northern issues	8	3.5
Physical sciences	8	3.5
Science (generalities) and science policy (including support for basic research)	21	9.1
Technological innovation, R&D and industrial development strategies	39	16.9
Transportation	7	3.0
Unclassified	10	4.3

The Science Council's Crusade for an Industrial Policy

As with the Economic Council, the publications of the Science Council
fell under two categories: those which directly involved the responsibility of the council, and those which did not, namely, background studies
and other discussion papers signed by individual authors. The Science
Council did not publish as many of these authored papers as the Economic Council, and the range of opinions expressed in them was somewhat less wide.

The eclectic nature of the Science Council's research program is well
illustrated in table 13.2. From the mid-1980s until the early 1990s, the
council's research program targeted the following themes:

- an assessment of Canada's progress in developing and applying
  technology, and of Canada's future needs and requirements;
- water policy;
- cooperation between Canada and Japan in R&D;
- university/industry interaction in Canada;
- the policy implication of food irradiation technology;

- genetics in health care and use of medication in Canada;
- 'sustainable agriculture';
- cold climate technologies, and the importance of science and technology for the social and economic development of northern communities; and
- 'The Technology Engine in Community Economic Development' (a series of workshops were held across Canada on that theme).

This overview gives an idea of the breadth of the council's research interests. It also confirms the criticisms that the council tackled too many disparate subjects. In its final years, it focused a little more clearly on the relationship between technology and competitiveness, as a result of having adopted in 1988 two unifying themes for its research agenda: 'competitiveness and caring.' The second element of this diptych, however, was vague enough to embrace almost anything!

The Science Council made a valuable contribution to socio-economic policy analysis in that it explored certain issues that had been ignored or downplayed by other think tanks. For example, the council (1988b, 1991) undertook a project on the use and conservation of land and water resources, and it sided with the Brundtland Commission in calling for 'a sustainable economy.'

Perhaps because the kind of problems inherent in science policy require some degree of planning and guidance by the public sector, the Science Council developed a favourable approach to government intervention in more traditional policy fields as well. In the late 1970s, a report entitled *Forging the Links: A Technological Policy for Canada*, together with an accompanying background paper by J.N.H. Britton and J.M. Gilmour (1978), generated a controversy that was fuelled by critical reviews appearing in publications from other think tanks. The council showed great concern for what it refers to as Canada's 'technological sovereignty.' Instead of depending on the research and development carried out in other countries, it urged that government policies should encourage innovation in domestic firms. To that end, government, business, and labour were advised to agree on means to 1) increase the demand for indigenous Canadian technology; 2) expand the country's potential to produce technology; 3) strengthen the capacity of Canadian firms to absorb technology; and 4) increase the ability of Canadian firms to import technology under conditions favourable to Canadian industrial development (Science Council of Canada 1979).

In *Hard Times, Hard Choices* (1981), the council singled out Canada's poor performance in exporting manufactured goods and our dependence on imported technologies. In *Canadian Industrial Development* (1984), it recommended that the federal government find ways of inciting multi-national corporations to do more research in Canada, and to encourage Canadian entrepreneurs to 'look forward,' for example, by sharing some of the risks with them. The (then) vice-chairman of the council, J.J. Shepherd, also called for a 'total product mandate' (1978, 4) for Canadian subsidiaries of foreign multinationals. This statement did not necessarily reflect the views of the council, but it was revealing of the protectionist orientation of one of its most influential members at that time. (The fact, incidentally, that Magna International has become a giant in the parts industry shows that protectionist sentiments of that sort are often illfounded.) In a 1986 statement on the bilateral trade negotiations, the council declared that a free trade agreement ought not to preclude the possibility of protecting 'infant industries,' and reminded the Canadian negotiators of the considerable extent to which the US government indirectly subsidizes research and development through defence contracts and special tax provisions (Science Council of Canada 1986). Similarly, Michael Jenkins (1983) strongly recommended that the federal government play a 'catalytic' role in the development of an industrial policy that would respect Canada's regional diversity.

The council never gave up its commitment to technological sovereignty. However, beginning in the late 1980s, it showed less willingness to promote an interventionist industrial policy. This was partly due to the budget cuts imposed on it in 1986. It was obliged to use its diminished resources more sparingly, and it had to play its cards more prudently. By that I do not mean that the council lost its independence and simply adopted the priorities and viewpoints of the Mulroney government, but it did move slightly closer to the Economic Council's position. In its final years, the Science Council emphatically stressed the importance of technological innovation for international competitiveness – a criterion for evaluating science and technology that it did not weigh as heavily in earlier years. It also alluded more frequently to industry self-help strategies, perhaps acknowledging in this indirect way that government is not necessarily the prime agent of change (see, for example, Science Council of Canada 1989, 12). Concepts like 'partnership' or 'cooperation' became buzzwords in its publications. According to the council (1988), in the last decade of the twentieth century, one of the prime innovations for change would be the 'new university,' i.e., an institution which is engaged in research that is relevant to the needs and expectations of industry, which is open to the local community and attracts students from a variety of backgrounds, and whose professors are actively engaged in consulting activities. The villain that the Science Council could not resist condemning time and time again was the proverbial academic 'ivory tower.' This message was somewhat prophetic in view of the current (and questionable) trend toward applied research in the allocation of research grants, not only in the natural sciences but increasingly in the social sciences as well.

One of the most valuable initiatives that the council undertook under the guidance of Janet Halliwell began just one year before it was closed. In 1990, the SCC announced its commitment to the publication of an annual series, *Science and Technology Policy in Canada*, which was intended to offer an overview of 'the integration of science and technology into the fabric of our society and economy.' The first and last of these reviews, *Reaching for Tomorrow*, appeared in 1991. This report surveyed trends and events in education and training, industrial innovation, the infrastructures for science and technology, the environment, and 'new frontiers.' Although a step in the right direction, this was probably another case of 'too little, too late.'

The Legacy of the Science Council

In the late 1960s, the Science Council advocated a rational planning style that required the precise identification of policy goals – a task that has been shown to be 'easier said than done.' (Its attempt, in its fourth report, to spell out *the* national goals stood as an example of political naivety and irrational rationalism.) The irony is, however, that it did not apply this recommendation to itself. For a while, it even appeared as if the council had lapsed into a scatter-gun approach to many interesting but loosely connected problems.

Fiscal restraint compelled the council to concentrate its efforts on a narrower range of priorities. Canada's international competitiveness became its first priority. Indeed, with its futuristic outlook, the council took on the role of prophet of the coming of the global information-based economy. This messianic tone was softened by the expressions of concern for the environment and health care. This was an appealing, albeit not particularly original, discourse. On the whole, however, the record of the Science Council, both in terms of the research it carried out and of the influence it had on the policy-making process, is not very impressive.

A distinctive and original commitment to 'technological sovereignty' and a willingness to foster the full development of the incompletely realized potential of Canadian science and technology are the traits for which the Science Council will be remembered. But if that message was not as well received as the council would have hoped, and if many of its policy recommendations were never acted upon, this was in part the council's own fault. The message lacked clarity of purpose and, occasionally, sounded rather hollow. For example, *Water 2020: Sustainable Use of Water in the 21st Century*, in spite of its rather grandiloquent title, is a disappointingly thin text, replete with platitudes. (But it was nicely illustrated!)

The Case for Re-establishing the Science Council

Just as the fact that moral judgments are irremediably subjective does not mean that all such judgments are equally valid or convincing, judgments concerning the merits of a policy must be justifiable. I suggest that they must be assessed on at least two grounds: the logical rigour of the arguments and the reasonableness of the criteria used to support a recommended option. Matters of logic and method are important and sometimes raise interesting epistemological questions about which specialists can disagree. But since my topic does not raise any such question, the only angle from which my conclusion could be challenged is the criteria I intend to apply. Therefore, it is incumbent on me to briefly spell these out. Indeed, a secondary objective of this paper is to underline the need to pay careful attention to the empirical and normative threads that necessarily run through policy analysis. While this observation is rather trite, I hope to show by treating what is apparently a straightforward and not very pressing issue that the normative side of the exercise is never simple. There is no easy way to lighten what Rawls calls 'the burden of judgment.'

The standpoint from which I work is that there is no Manichean division between the public and the private sectors (the latter should itself be divided into a commercial sector and a 'not-for-profit' sector). Thus, in the case at hand, there is no obvious reason to conclude that research on economic policy or science policy is necessarily always better carried out from within government, except perhaps that one ought not to burden the state with more responsibilities than it can perform. But if pragmatism must prevail, it needs to be defended. It can lead to relativism: if the only criterion is 'whatever works' for me or for the group I belong to, then pragmatism may fail to provide sufficient protection against arbitrariness or prejudice.[21] On the positive side, pragmatism encourages the use of democratic, consultative, and pluralistic means to solve moral dilemmas and policy problems. Since the truth is not given a priori, it must be worked out through critical engagement with the claims made by all those who have an interest in seeking a solution. John Dewey (1927) was very concerned about the quality of public debates and the obstacles that citizens face in trying to fulfill their roles. So the good can be defined as what works for the public interest. Whether something 'works' or not, and in particular, whether it contributes to the public interest, is not an easy question. Obviously, in a liberal democracy, a policy recommendation must not offend democratic values. But that is still not saying much. It is often quite difficult to assess with any degree of certainty where the Canadian public stands on a whole range of issues.[22] With some safeguards, very technical issues about which the public knows little can be delegated to experts. Few issues, however, fall entirely within the narrow limits of expert knowledge, and only the most salient ones can realistically be the object of extensive public consultations or parliamentary debates. The rather unimportant, albeit not trivial problem of whether it would make sense to re-establish one or both of the research councils mentioned above is worth exploring precisely because it serves to illustrate the difficult challenges that policy analysts (and all social scientists) confront in trying to provide judicious advice to policy makers or in bringing an issue to the attention of the academic community.

A careful reflection on the criteria that should be applied to such cases is imperative. In my case, I propose three norms: a) a modified Rawlsian framework, according to which public policy must attempt to achieve a greater degree of fairness in social arrangements aimed at improving the conditions of the most disadvantaged citizens (Rawls 1971) when it is both feasible and appropriate (the meaning of these two terms is given below) to do so, and provided that doing so does not violate the fundamental rights of others; b) opportunity costs must always be applied to comparisons between alternatives, which is to say that if reaching a trivially fairer situation would divert resources that would be better used to achieve a different goal, then that goal is not feasible;[23] and c) since any attempt at constructing a fairer society is likely to involve not only complicated but truly complex issues – i.e., problems that are characterized by uncertainty and indeterminacy – Popper's 'piecemeal engineering' is more appropriate than comprehensive planning. These three points are in tension:[24] one might be inclined to think that a reborn ECC would defend the interests of disadvantaged Canadians marginally better than, say, the Fraser Institute or the C.D. Howe Institute, but the opportunity cost of investing several millions of dollars annually in the new agency might not be justifiable and since the federal government's economic management ambitions are more modest than they were 30 years ago, there may not be a need for a planning instrument like the ECC. But most policy problems give rise to even more challenging dilemmas.

As I explained above, by the time the ECC was abolished, the research it produced was not markedly different from what other think tanks were offering, and the consensus building goals of its original mandate had ceased to be its defining characteristics. This is not to say that the policy research community was unaffected by its disappearance, nor that no benefit would flow from the re-establishment of a similar institution. A well-funded council would be able to attract well-trained economists and, as in the past, it could also be counted on to produce somewhat more balanced or seemingly less ideologically charged reports than, say, the Fraser Institute or the Canadian Centre for Policy Alternatives. However, the case for recreating the ECC is weak.

The creation of a Law Commission shows that when there is a demonstrable case for reverting to the decisions made in 1992, the federal government and, more specifically, a Liberal government sitting on a budget surplus is prepared to do just that. But even if there are no obvious constraints preventing it, the probability that any government will be inclined to re-establish an institution that has not been very much missed for more than ten years is virtually nil. And even if serious consideration were given to an initiative of this sort, it would not be advisable to go ahead with it. To elaborate on this point, I must present an analysis of the facts of the case as well as a discussion of its normative aspects.

The policy research environment is very different today from what it was some thirty years ago. Research intended to lead to the articulation of a broad-based, quasi-corporatist consensus is no longer considered to be relevant to the present circumstances. In a globalized world, this sort of consensus-building exercise would be rather futile, and comprehensive macroeconomic planning sounds like an obsolete idea. Of course, the mandate of a re-created ECC could be written in a way that would reflect this new reality. As I explained, even the old ECC had in its last decade abandoned the vision that had inspired its designers. But then there is no need for another policy research institute specializing in economic policy. The field is already rather crowded, with more than half a dozen think tanks commenting on more or less the same issues (e.g., the C.D. Howe Institute, the Fraser Institute, the Atlantic Institute for Market Studies, the Institute for Research on Public Policy, the Montreal Economic Institute, the Canadian Centre for Policy Alternatives, the Parkland Institute). It could be argued that a larger institution could play a useful co-ordinating function, as the old ECC did to some extent, but, then again, the already mentioned CPRN offers policy analysts some means of 'networking.'

From a normative standpoint, the case for recreating the ECC does not appear to be very convincing either. Would it bring to economic policy research a greater emphasis on fairness? This is very doubtful. The role played by the ECC in its early years, i.e., the search for a consensus that could guide the management of the national economy, contributed to the achievement of a greater degree of fairness by highlighting the problems emerging at the interface of economic policy and social policy. But, as I have shown above, the council moved away from that goal when the circumstances changed. It is more than likely that the voice of a recreated ECC would be the voice of mainstream economists; it would not contribute anything really new to ongoing debates. I am not trying to imply that mainstream economics is antithetical to fairness – indeed, economic growth, even unequally distributed, works more to the advantage of the least advantaged than economically unsound redistributive schemes, and contemporary economists, in any event, have developed a new interest in issues like social cohesion, altruism, the voluntary sector and other related issues that touch more or less directly on fairness (see, for example, Gérard-Varet et al. 2000; and Dobuzinskis 2003). My point is that these issues have become so complex that the standpoint of fairness can only be moved forward by inventing new forms of interdisciplinary dialogue. The economists' voices are already quite well heard; what is missing is a theoretical approach for articulating a far broader dialogue, as well as an institutional framework for achieving it. A reborn ECC would not fit the bill even if, as I have underlined above, under Judith Maxwell's leadership, it began to pay more attention to redistribution. Her vision, in any event, has now become well entrenched in the CPRN.

Therefore, the opportunity costs of re-establishing the ECC would be rather high, since there are obviously more efficient ways of promoting fair societal ends (e.g., more investment in students' access to higher education). Moreover, it would seem that the Hayekian lesson that comprehensive planning is futile has been well learned; in other words, there is simply no need for a version of a super-think tank at the top. However, a more in-depth investigation of this question, using questionnaires to determine where the policy research community stands in relation to it, might reveal another picture.

The case for recreating the Science Council looks stronger, though this does not make the probability any higher that a given government will act in that direction. It is, however, worth articulating an argument for reversing this inertia. I do not mean to say that what we need today is an advocate for the outdated idea of an interventionist industrial policy or another cheerleader for applied research, as the SCC was for many years. Rather I want to suggest that an institution with a mandate comparable to that of the defunct SCC would be able to bring into view a whole range of new issues that have not received the attention they deserve. The fact that the SCC has not performed that role, as I showed, does however imply that a recreated council should be given a new mandate, one more specifically oriented toward engagement with the public and democratic deliberation.

The budget surplus opens up some opportunities for policy innovation. The original mandate of the old SCC has never really become obsolete; even if the era of comprehensive macroeconomic planning has passed, there is still room for well-targeted interventions, especially with respect to science and technology. (More often than not, private-sector firms tend to 'free ride' on the research carried out by publicly funded institutions.) Indeed, G.B. Doern and T. Reed (2000, 6) have suggested that Canada is experiencing a 'science deficit' that needs to receive as much attention as the fiscal deficit of the last decade. Even if recent pronouncements by both the Martin and Harper governments are encouraging as far as funding for research and development is concerned, there are reasons to think that the more fundamental problem identified by William Leiss remains, namely, that 'recent experience indicates that there is some serious misalignment between science and public policy' (2000, 49). A correction would require, according to Leiss, something like a paradigmatic shift, whereby government's role would be limited to the management of health and environmental risks, leaving the responsibility for actual scientific research to other institutions, since scientists need autonomy to do their work. Critics (Leiss 2004; Nikiforuk 2005) have charged, for example, that the Canadian Food Inspection Agency mishandled the Bovine Spongiform Encephalopathy (BSE) crisis because its overlapping mandates prevented it from clearly distinguishing risk prevention from trade-related issues. I agree entirely with Leiss's diagnosis but since a reborn SCC would only be involved in policy research, it would fit very well within this new structure by playing a much-needed advisory role informed by democratic inputs. In sum, there seems to be good factual reasons for bringing back some modified version of the original SCC.

Can this wish be justified in a coherent manner? I want to suggest that it can. As far as the goal of fairness is concerned, the status quo could most certainly be improved upon. In spite of the fact that all Canadians are potentially at risk from a variety of sources – and threats to public health seem to be becoming more prevalent, as the examples of SARS, BSE, the spread of the West Nile Virus, the contamination of drinking water, and so forth, suggest – children, the elderly, and the poor are often more at risk. Their immune systems are less capable of coping with viral, bacterial, or chemical threats.[25] Besides, there are other aspects of the science/policy interface that raise issues of fairness; women's access to education and professional opportunities in engineering comes to mind. One would hope that government agencies responsible to Parliament (e.g., Health Canada) would feel compelled to take these dimensions into account. But they are also subject to a whole range of short-term pressures and all sorts of political and economic incentives prevent them from focusing on fairness in a sustained manner. Of course, there is no guarantee that a newly re-established Science Council would be much more concerned with fairness – the old SCC's record in that respect is not very impressive – but its arms-length status would give it an advantage.

Another aspect of fairness concerns the imbalance between basic research, for which there are too few advocates today, and applied research. A new agency might be able to do something about this imbalance even if, admittedly, the record of the SCC in that respect was not impressive. Most importantly, fairness and 'publicness' are related. By publicness, I mean the extent to which public affairs are conducted in public and the extent to which citizens are able to hold public officials accountable for their decisions. Science and technology are areas characterized at the moment by a lack of publicness in that sense; the ACST, for example, reports to the prime minister and is only incidentally involved in public debates. One would hope that recreating the SCC could help to turn things around in that respect. After all, the difficulty here is political indifference rather than a lack of theoretical reflections on the subject, since one could almost say that from Dewey to Jürgen Habermas (1996,

1998), the subject of how to improve deliberative democracy has been exhausted (on the subject of deliberative democracy in relation to policy analysis, see Liora Salter's chapter in this volume).

This project would be feasible because the opportunity costs are low. The budget of the SCC was never very big and since there is no competing institution at the moment, the creation of a new SCC would probably be a Pareto efficient measure. The only serious objection I can see to an initiative of this sort would be that it perhaps puts too much faith in our capacity to approach risk management and science policy in general in a dispassionate manner. Given the degree of uncertainty that characterizes the issues at stake, and given the propensity of many pressure groups to press their often questionable claims (e.g., the campaign against vaccination based on the now disproved assumption that vaccination is linked to autism; on this subject, see Wildavsky 1995), this concern must be weighed against the advantages mentioned above. There would be little to gain from the establishment of a policy research and consultation mechanism that would legitimize what some critics of fashionable causes call 'junk science.' The solution to this problem might require a more balanced mix of policy researchers and natural scientists on the staff of the new agency than was the case in the old SCC.

To conclude, the two councils have left a valuable legacy that vividly illustrates changing trends and recurrent themes in policy research. In particular, they bear witness to the demise of the postwar planning approach. I have argued that the case for recreating the SCC with a more focused mandate would be a defensible idea. I hope I have also shown that making even such a narrowly circumscribed recommendation requires the careful consideration of a broad range of factual and normative considerations. When the complexity of the problems under review reaches another order of magnitude, policy analysis becomes an immensely challenging exercise that should at some point be merged with deliberative processes involving as many participants as possible. In the case of risk management, for example, I have argued that this is precisely why we need a redesigned SCC.

NOTES

1 In his 25 February 1992 budget speech, Finance Minister Don Mazankowski announced that 21 public bodies were to be closed down; among these, the following advisory councils were included: the Canadian Institute for

International Peace and Security, the Canadian Environmental Advisory Council, the Economic Council of Canada, the Law Reform Commission and the Science Council of Canada. Since then other advisory agencies, notably the Advisory Council on the Status of Women, have been abolished by the Chrétien government.

2 The *Economic Council Act* stated that, among other functions, the mandate of the Council was 'regularly to assess ... the medium-term and long-term prospects of the economy, and to compare such prospects with the potentialities for growth of the economy'; and 'to encourage maximum consultation and co-operation between labour and management.'

3 This is an excerpt from a notice that can be found in many of the council's publications.

4 The chair could devote his or her attention only to a few priority items. Much of the research was carried out by the staff under the two directors' supervision. The appointment in 1986 of a corporate secretary responsible for all support services freed the two directors of practically all administrative duties.

5 In an interview, Janet Maxwell also indicated that in her view the council should have been named the 'Social and Economic Council' (March 21, 1994).

6 Maxwell puts her appointment down to her communication skills, which she demonstrated during her years on the staff of the C.D. Howe Institute and later as an economic consultant. She has put in place 18-month deadlines for all research projects, requested that researchers turn over their manuscripts to professional writers who can 'translate' them into plain English (or French), and suggested that interim reports be issued more frequently to keep the public better informed of on-going projects.

7 For example, both Tom d'Aquino, of the Business Council on National Issues, and Tim Reid, president of the Canadian Chamber of Commerce, said that agencies like the ECC were serving a useful purpose. See Allan Thompson, 'Business Reaction Mixed, Some Fear "Wrong Message,"' *Toronto Star* 26 February 1992, B2, and David Pugliese, 'Government Plans Further Cuts and Mergers,' *Ottawa Citizen*, 27 February 1992.

8 With only a few exceptions (e.g., Terence Corcoran of the *Globe and Mail*), most editorialists (including Jeffrey Simpson in the *Globe and Mail*) penned articles deploring the death of the council.

9 Quoted by John Geddes, 'Axed Economic Council Will Leave "Terrible Gap,"' *Financial Post*, 27 February 1992.

10 Considering the nature of their respective mandates, these two organiza-

tions were bound to be rivals, and indeed relationships between the council and MOSST were often conflictive (interview with Dr Stuart Smith, April 1986).

11 Dr Kenney-Wallace left the SCC to become president of McMaster University.

12 Nobel laureate John Polanyi expressed strong criticisms of the government's action. And Howard Tennant, then president of the University of Lethbridge, requested a meeting with Mr Mazankowski to urge him to reconsider his decision to close the SCC (*Lethbridge Herald*, 28 February 1992, A1).

13 This assertion is based on the results of a survey conducted in the spring of 1985. Five hundred questionnaires were mailed to named individuals and/or to the chairmen of Political Science, Economics and Public Administration departments/schools, with a request that these be communicated to those involved in policy research. One hundred and five answers were received.

14 In addition to this unpublished review, the council managed to publish *The New Face of Poverty* (1992), which received substantial press coverage when it was released.

15 See the sixteenth annual review (1979) and the seventeenth annual review (1980).

16 In the twenty-sixth annual review, Diane Bellemare and Marcel Pepin registered their dissent concerning the suggested attack on the deficit, arguing instead that a radical change in the direction of Canada's monetary policy was needed.

17 The council entered the 1980s with a report (1982b) that still attested to the persistence of an interventionist streak in its thinking: it suggested that the federal government should offer direct cash wage subsidies to private employers for the purpose of job creation.

18 In this report, the council advocated ending government monopolies in telephone services. It also recommended that urban transit systems be contracted out to private firms and that railways, airline companies, and Petro Canada should be privatized.

19 On the relevance of Foucault's work to policy analysis, see Pal (1990).

20 Two political scientists, for example, contributed studies to the Government and Competitiveness project: G.B. Doern and R.W. Phidd.

21 There is no space here to launch a critique of Richard Rorty's efforts to revive pragmatism from a relativist standpoint, but suffice to say that I do not intend to follow him down that path.

22 Dewey (1927) dealt at length with the problem of determining the public

interest in situations where the public itself knows little about issues that concern it.

23 For a critique of Rawls's maximally prudent approach to the defence of the interests of the least disadvantaged, see Harsanyi (1975).
24 A tension that reflects, more generally, the opposition between a deonto-logical and a utilitarian approach; my preference for pragmatism owes much to the fact that I see no reason to consistently side with either one of these two dogmatic positions.
25 This would not be the case with BST, admittedly.

REFERENCES

Alexander, J.A. 1984. *Equal-Pay-for-Equal-Work Legislation in Canada*. Ottawa: Economic Council of Canada (Discussion Paper no. 252).
Amy, Douglas J. 1984. 'Why Policy Analysis and Ethics are Incompatible.' *Journal of Policy Analysis and Management* 4, 573–91.
Betcherman, Gordon, and Graham Lowe. 1997. *The Future of Work in Canada*. Canadian Policy Research Network.
Blais, André. 1986. 'The Debate on Canadian Industrial Policy.' In A. Blais, ed., *Canadian Industrial Policy*. Toronto: University of Toronto Press.
Bobrow, David B., and John S. Dryzek. 1987. *Policy Analysis by Design*. Pittsburgh: University of Pennsylvania Press.
Boothy, Daniel. 1986. *Women Re-entering the Labour Force and Training Programs: Evidence from Canada*. Ottawa: Economic Council (EC22–129/1986E9).
Boulet, Jac-André, and L. Lavallée. 1981. *Women and the Labour Market: An Analytical Framework*. Ottawa: Economic Council of Canada (Discussion Paper no. 207).
– 1984. *The Changing Economic Status of Women*. Ottawa: Economic Council of Canada (EC22–122/1984E).
Boyd, M., and E. Humphreys. 1979. *Labour Markets and Sex Differences in Canadian Incomes*. Ottawa: Economic Council of Canada (Discussion Paper no. 143).
Breton, A. 1984. *Population, and the Labour Force Participation of Women*. Ottawa: Economic Council of Canada (EC22–117/1984E).
– 1985. *Toward Equity – Proceedings of a Colloquium on the Economic Status of Women in the Labour Market*. Ottawa: Economic Council of Canada (EC22–26/1985E).
Britton, John N., and James M. Gilmour. 1978. *The Weakest Link: A Technological Perspective on Canadian Industrial Underdevelopment*. Background Study 43. Ottawa: Supply and Services.

Cloutier, Eden. 1986. *Taxes and the Labour Supply of Married Women in Canada*. Ottawa: Economic Council of Canada (Discussion Paper no. 305).

Dewey, John. 1927. *The Public and Its Problems*. Denver, CO: Allan Swallow.

Dobuzinskis, Laurent. 2003. 'Social Norms in Transition: Gift-Giving and Reciprocity in the Global Era.' In L. Dobuzinskis and J. Busumtwi-Sam, eds., *Turbulence and New Directions in Global Political Economy*. London: Palgrave.

Doern, G.B. 1971. 'The Role of Central Advisory Councils: The Science Council of Canada.' In G.B. Doern and P. Aucoin, eds., *The Structures of Policy-Making in Canada*. Toronto: Macmillan.

Doern, G.B., and T. Reed. 2000. 'Canada's Changing Science-Based Policy and Regulatory Regime: Issues and Framework.' In G.B. Doern and T.Reed, eds., *Risky Business: Canada's Changing Science-Based Policy and Regulatory Regime*. Toronto: University of Toronto Press.

Dowling, Deborah. 1992. 'Closing Down the Economic Council,' *Ottawa Citizen*, 9 March 1992, B1–2.

Economic Council of Canada. 1983. *The Bottom Line: Technology, Trade and Income Growth*. Ottawa: Canadian Government Publishing Centre.

– 1991a. 'The Role of the Economic Council of Canada.' In *Annual Report 1990–91*. Ottawa: Supply and Services.

– 1991b. *A Joint Venture: The Economics of Constitutional Options-SUMMARY*. Ottawa: Supply and Services.

– 1992a. *The New Face of Poverty: Income Security Needs of Canadian Families*. Ottawa: Supply and Services.

– 1992b. *Annual Report, 1991–92*. Ottawa: Supply and Services.

Egan, Kelly. 1992. 'Science Council Was Far Ahead of its Time.' *The Ottawa Citizen*, 8 March.

Fisher, Frank. 1980. *Politics, Values, and Public Policy*. Boulder, CO: Westview.

Gérard-Varet, L.-A. et al., eds. 2000. *The Economics of Reciprocity, Giving and Altruism*. London: Macmillan.

Giddens, Anthony. 1999. *The Third Way: The Renewal of Social Democracy*. Malden, MA: Polity.

Gilroy, John Martin, ed. 1993. *Environmental Risk, Environmental Values, and Political Choices: Beyond Efficiency Tradeoffs in Public Policy Analysis*. Boulder, CO: Westview.

Goodin, R. 1982. *Political Theory and Public Policy*. Chicago: University of Chicago Press.

Habermas, Jürgen. 1996. *Between Facts and Norms: Contributions to a Discourse Theory of Law and Democracy*. Cambridge, MA: MIT Press.

– 1998. *The Inclusion of the Other: Studies in Political Theory.* Cambridge, MA: MIT Press.

Harsanyi, J.C. 1975. 'Can the Maximin Principle Serve as a Basis for Morality? A Critique of John Rawls' Theory.' *American Political Science Review* 69, 594–606.

Howard, Ross. 1992. 'PM Denies Critics Targets of Council Cuts.' *Globe and Mail*, 27 February, A2.

Imbroscio, David L. 2004. 'Fighting Poverty with Mobility: A Normative Policy Analysis.' *Review of Policy Research* 21(3), 447–61.

Immen, Wallace. 1985. 'Science Council Slashed.' *Globe and Mail*, 9 August, A1.

Jackson, Ray W. 1985. 'The Lure of Power.' *Policy Options* 6(9), 32–35.

Jenkins, Michael. 1983. *The Challenge of Diversity: Industrial Policy in the Canadian Federation.* Background Study no. 50. Ottawa: Supply and Services.

Jenson, Jane. 1998. *Mapping Social Cohesion.* Ottawa: Canadian Policy Research Network.

Jenson, Jane, and Caroline Beauvais. 2002. *Social Cohesion: Updating the State of Canadian Research.* Ottawa: Canadian Policy Research Network.

Leiss, William. 2000. 'Between Expertise and Bureaucracy: Risk Management Trapped at the Science-Policy Interface.' In G.B. Doern and T. Reed, eds., *Risky Business: Canada's Changing Science-Based Policy and Regulatory Regime.* Toronto: University of Toronto Press.

– 2004. 'BSE Risk in Canada, Part 4: A Closer Look at CFIA's Risk Estimation.' http: www/leiss.ca/bse/155.

Matthews, R.A. 1985. *Structural Change and Industrial Policy.* Ottawa: Canadian Government Publishing Centre.

Nikiforuk, Andrew. 2005. 'Beef Up the Science.' *Globe & Mail*, 26 January, A17.

Pal, Leslie. 1986. *Public Policy Analysis: An Introduction.* Toronto: Methuen.

– 1990. 'Knowledge, Power and Policy: Reflections on Foucault.' In Stephen Brooks and Alain-G. Gagnon, eds., *Social Scientists, Policy and the State.* New York: Praeger.

– 2001. *Beyond Policy Analysis: Public Issue Management in Turbulent Times.* Scarborough, ON: Nelson Thompson.

Phidd, R.W. 1975. 'The Economic Council of Canada: Its Establishment, Structure, and Role in the Canadian Policy System, 1963–74.' *Canadian Public Administration* 18(3), 428–73.

Rawls, John. 1971. *A Theory of Justice.* Cambridge, MA: Harvard University Press.

Science Council of Canada. 1976. *Canada as a Conserver Society: An Agenda for Action.* Ottawa: Information Canada.
– 1979. *Forging the Links: A Technology Policy for Canada.* Ottawa: Supply and Services.
– 1981. *Biotechnology in Canada Promises and Concerns.* Ottawa: Supply and Services.
– 1982. *Annual Review, 1982.* Ottawa: Supply and Services.
– 1985. *Seeds of Renewal: Biotechnology and Canada's Resource Industries,* Report 38. Ottawa: Supply and Services.
– 1986a. *Annual Report, 1985–86.* Ottawa: Supply and Services.
– 1986b. *Placing Technology Up Front: Advising the Bilateral Trade.* Council Statement. Ottawa: Supply and Services.
– 1987. *Food Irradiation: Prospects for Canadian Technology Development.* Ottawa: Supply and Services.
– 1988a. *Winning in a World Economy: University-Industry Renewal in Canada.* Report no. 39. Ottawa: Supply and Services.
– 1988b. *Water 2020: Sustainable Use of Water in the 21st Century.* Report no. 40. Ottawa: Supply and Services.
– 1989a. *Annual Report, 1988–89.* Ottawa: Supply and Services.
– 1989b. *Enabling Technologies: Springboard for a Competitive Future* A Statement by the Science Council of Canada. Ottawa: Supply and Services.
– 1991a. *Genetics in Canadian Health Care.* Report no. 42. Ottawa: Supply and Services.
– 1991b. *Sustainable Farming: Possibilities 1990–2020.* Ottawa: Supply and Services.
Shepherd, J.J. 1979. *The Canada-U.S. Auto Pact: A Technological Perspective.* Ottawa: Supply and Services.
Smith, Arthur J. 1981. 'The Economic Council of Canada.' In David C. Smith, ed., *Economic Policy Advising in Canada.* Montreal: C.D. Howe Institute.
Thorburn, H.G. 1984. *Planning and the* Economy: *Building Federal-Provincial Consensus.* Toronto: Lorimer.
Vancouver Sun. 1985. 'Layoffs, Projects Cuts Rile Head of Science Council.' 8 August, A11.
Wildavsky, Aaron. 1995. *But Is it True? A Citizen's Guide to Environmental Health and Safety Issues.* Cambridge, MA: Harvard University Press.

14 Committees inside Canadian Legislatures

JOSIE SCHOFIELD AND JONATHAN FERSHAU

Introduction

Committees operating inside Canadian legislatures can and do shape public policy, yet their contribution is often downplayed in policy studies and by the news media. This chapter seeks to rectify this situation by demonstrating that parliamentary committees can play an important role in the policy process. Another aim is to identify some of the criteria that need to be taken into account when assessing their policy-making capacity.

At the outset, we think it is important to explain why we qualify as policy analysis 'insiders.' We are both political scientists, who specialized in public policy analysis in our graduate work and who now work in the committee secretariat of the Legislative Assembly of British Columbia. Our co-workers and research staff in other legislatures have diverse backgrounds and qualifications ranging from social scientists to lawyers and planners.

The primary role of legislative research staff is to provide analysis and research services for private members (backbenchers) who serve on committees appointed by the House to conduct an inquiry of some kind. Committee work involves performing a variety of tasks, such as preparing briefing notes and highlighting issues, suggesting expert witnesses to be called, summarizing testimony, providing legal and issue analysis, monitoring progress on the issues under consideration by the committee, and drafting reports under the direction of the committee members.[1]

As contributors to this book, we have also become aware that the job description of legislative research staff is similar in some respects to the 'policy fire-fighting work' and 'executive assistant support' provided in the public service, which Michael Prince describes in chapter 7. For example, committee work can involve doing rush assignments, working under tight deadlines, doing research and analysis of 'hot topical issues,' preparing articles and speeches, drafting correspondence, and helping to organize interparliamentary visits. All these tasks are performed in a working environment of ambiguous goals, resource constraints and competing interests, ideas and policy agendas, which is similar to a public service setting.

We are also struck by the tendency in policy analysis to downplay the role of parliamentary committees, which are the main focus of this chapter. For example, in the course of preparing this chapter, we have encountered questions about their effectiveness – in particular, concerns about their use as partisan tools to defuse controversial issues.

In chapter 12, Liora Salter also casts doubt on the validity of committee consultations, by claiming that public inquiries are the only mechanisms capable of fostering citizen participation. To counter this claim, we would point out that policy-oriented parliamentary committees have similar capacities to reach the 'disaffected' public, via traditional consultation methods (public hearings, call for written submissions) and the increasing use of e-consultation. Furthermore, committees inside legislatures consist of elected representatives, not appointed officials. This democratic quality of their membership not only enhances their legitimacy but also distinguishes them from public inquiries and the other quasi-independent institutions discussed in part 4.

Based on our own work experience, we would argue that the committee system is an important, if submerged, feature of parliamentary life and needs to be recognized as part of the institutional context of policy making. Having the opportunity to work as committee researchers in a parliamentary setting has also made us more conscious of the gap between the theory and practice of policy analysis. However, while parliamentary committees are under-appreciated in policy studies, we do not go so far as to claim that a committee system is 'the engine room which powers Parliament' (Reid 2001–2, 1). On the other hand, we also reject the cynical depiction of parliamentary committees as merely 'a collection of the unfit appointed by the unwilling to perform the unnecessary' (A.M. Young, cited by Dignam 2003, 55).

Instead, our position is that committees inside Canadian legislatures can inform democratic debates about policy choices. The two key questions we seek to answer in this chapter are: What are parliamentary and caucus committees capable of doing in the policy cycle? What are the key institutional constraints and political factors that influence their effectiveness as agents of public policy?

Our analysis, however, is not intended to be either definitive or exhaustive. It is difficult to generalize about the policy-making influence of parliamentary committees, because it differs markedly depending on the type of committee, the nature of the inquiry being undertaken, and the parliamentary environment – i.e., the formal rules, the traditions, the internal culture, and the day-to-day practices of a particular legislature. Also, as John Uhr, an Australian academic, points out, the 'fascinating variety' of parliamentary committees poses a significant challenge in evaluating their performance: 'Committees are confusing: there are many types, each with many potential forms of operation and impact ... committee systems vary, even if only in subtle ways, across ... elected assemblies. There is no one prevailing model' (J. Uhr cited in Duffy and Thompson 2003, 5.5).

Another challenge is the paucity of policy studies on why committees exist, what roles they play in the parliamentary and wider policy process and on how well they do their work. One reason why these questions are neglected is because most legislative studies in Canada concentrate on House-related activities, which are more visible than committee work. In addition, the relatively few secondary sources on committee systems focus almost exclusively on the Parliament of Canada, whether they are included in cross-national studies (Rush 1979; Shaw 1979; Franks 1997; Milliken 1999; Smith 2003) or their primary focus is the bicameral Canadian Parliament (Lee 1999; Robertson 1999; McInnes 1999; Milliken 1999).

Nonetheless, there is some descriptive information available on how parliamentary committees inside Canadian legislatures conduct their work. As well, there is a democratic audit of Canadian legislatures (Docherty 2005), plus comparative studies of provincial and territorial assemblies (White and Levy 1989; White 1996) and of the administrative structures of all Canadian legislatures (Fleming 1992). Also available are comparative analyses of Canadian public accounts committees (McInnes 1977; Malloy 2004) and committee systems in Ontario and Québec (Pelletier et al. 1996).

An additional resource is procedural research, a body of knowledge prepared by and for table officers serving in Commonwealth parliaments.[2] Relevant examples of published works in this area are a comparative report on parliamentary committees (Barnhart 1999) and two international studies of audit committees (McGee 2002; Gay and Wintrobe 2003). Useful primary source materials include the reports on the proceedings of the 1999 and 2003 conferences on Canadian parliamentary committees, the first ones to be devoted to this topic.[3]

In contrast to most legislative studies, the scope of our inquiry extends to caucus committees created by intraparliamentary parties. They are included in our analysis because caucus committees perform policy-making functions similar to those undertaken by conventional parliamentary committees inside Canadian legislatures. As Thomas (1998) points out, though, both the variation in caucus structures and the secrecy surrounding their meetings make it difficult to generalize about their influence.

In the first part of this chapter, we define the common and distinctive features of parliamentary and caucus committees. We then turn our attention to developing a typology for classifying these committees, based on their role within the policy cycle.

The second part identifies the institutional constraints and political factors that influence the policy-making capacity of committees. Our analysis involves refining the criteria developed by Graham White, a former committee clerk in the Ontario legislature, to explain variations among Canadian assemblies.

Defining Committees

As stated in the introduction, we believe that the lack of scholarly attention paid to committees inside Canadian legislatures has resulted in the neglect of an important set of institutional actors in the policy process. Our first task therefore is to demonstrate that committees operating in Westminster-style parliaments are amenable subjects for comparison. We will show that they share a common purpose and generic functions, even though their powers, operating procedures and practices may vary significantly within, as well as across, Canada's 14 elected assemblies.

For the purpose of our analysis, the range of committees active within assemblies covers both parliamentary and caucus structures. The key difference between the two types is that a parliamentary committee represents the members of all officially recognized parties (and independents), while the members of a caucus committee are drawn exclusively from the ranks of a single parliamentary party. The nature of their proceedings and deliberations also differ in that meetings of parliamentary committees are often open to the public, whereas caucus committees usually meet in secret – unless they are caucus task forces seeking public input on a topical policy issue.

There are different types of parliamentary committees. The traditional form is the committee of the whole House, which consists of all elected members of an assembly. Its primary functions are to review draft legislation and spending estimates. A chairperson, not the speaker, presides over its proceedings, which are more informal than House debates.

By contrast, parliamentary committees that meet outside the chamber consist of a small group of private members (backbenchers) representing all officially recognized parties in proportion to their respective seat totals. They share a common purpose: namely, to investigate a matter referred for inquiry by the House. The traditional inquiry process can include hearing witnesses, receiving submissions, sifting and weighing evidence, discussing matters in detail, and formulating conclusions and recommendations. According to Duffy and Thompson, how a parliamentary committee interprets its mandate 'may be influenced by members' sense of the broader role of committees in parliamentary democracy, for example in relation to ensuring accountability or strategically influencing policy' (2003, 45).

There are two types of parliamentary committees that conduct their activities outside the House: standing and special. Standing committees are relatively permanent structures in the sense that they are reappointed in each parliament. They are authorized by the standing orders of a chamber, or via a sessional motion, to conduct an inquiry – whether it is to review draft legislation or estimates, to investigate and report on a particular area of public policy, or to scrutinize certain government operations.

Special (select) committees, on the other hand, are temporary structures that are established for a specific purpose, and they cease to exist once they have reported back to the House. Special committees may be struck to fill a vacancy for an independent officer of parliament; to review existing legislation; or to investigate a particularly controversial or complex issue.

Turning now to caucus committees, it is important to highlight again the difficulty that researchers face investigating any activities of a caucus, which is essentially a private meeting of all the elected members from a single political party. First, parliamentary party caucuses, particularly large ones, have any number of ways of dividing into smaller subsets such as regional caucuses and, more importantly for our purposes, caucus committees that review topical policy issues, as well as proposed laws and draft regulations in advance of their introduction in the House. Members of a governing or opposition party caucus may also be involved in other informal caucus structures, such as a women's caucus, or an election planning committee.

However, due to the secrecy surrounding party caucus activities, little is known about how these informal structures operate. Furthermore, as Thomas (1998, 3) points out, the role of a party caucus in the parliamentary process varies from legislature to legislature and the extent of its influence depends upon a number of factors, including the status of the party, the size of the caucus and its regional representation, the traditions and internal political culture of the caucus, and the 'wild card' of the mix of personalities.

Classifying Committees

From our perspective as policy analysis 'insiders,' the purpose of classification is essentially to make sense of the array of committee types within and across Canadian legislatures. There are several ways of classifying parliamentary committees. In our own professional work, for example, we use a simple scheme that categorizes parliamentary committees according to their function – whether it is appointment of an officer of parliament, scrutiny of government activity, public consultation on a policy matter, or review of an existing statute. While this method of classification focuses on generic functions rather than the goals of a particular inquiry, it does not link committee activities to the wider policy process.

Policy Cycle Model

A more useful way of classifying committee activities is by outlining their role in the policy cycle, using the model developed by Howlett and Ramesh (2003). Their five-stage model demonstrates how an issue moves from the idea stage to implementation as policy or law by institutional actors. The five stages of the policy cycle are agenda setting, policy formulation, decision making, policy implementation, and policy evaluation.

By their very nature, committees, with their limited terms of reference and short tenure, generally have the resource capacity to participate in only one stage of the policy cycle during the life of a parliament. Yet the model is flexible enough to accommodate their activities because each stage (or substage) 'can be investigated alone or in terms of its relationship to any or all [of] the other stages of the cycle' (Howlett and Ramesh 2003, 14).

The model also recognizes that a committee report – the output of an inquiry – can have an impact elsewhere in the policy cycle. Rather than just an end product, a report can be seen as the penultimate output of an active parliamentary or caucus committee. The recommended course of action (set an agenda for political activity, define a problem, make changes to a draft bill or an existing law, implement a policy or a hiring decision, or conduct a follow-up review) can be more important at the end of the day than the various inputs used during a committee's deliberations (financial resources, number of witnesses heard from, reports commissioned, or extent of media coverage). From this perspective, the key adjudication criterion will be whether, say, an investigative committee is successful in advancing its recommended course of action to the next stage of the policy cycle. The policy cycle model is also a potentially useful guide for decision makers, providing them with the means to assess whether a parliamentary committee or a caucus structure is an appropriate mechanism for achieving specific objectives.

Agenda setting is the first stage of the policy cycle and is defined by Howlett and Ramesh as 'the process by which problems come to the attention of governments' (2003, 13). This definition effectively excludes parliamentary committees, since agenda setting is the domain of the governing party in a Westminster-style parliamentary democracy. Instead, the inquiry of a parliamentary committee usually focuses on a topic that has already received some attention from government, and its work will often be based on the need for an expected outcome, whether it is to study an issue in more detail, to evaluate proposed legislation, or to scrutinize government activity.

On the other hand, caucus committees, particularly those established by the governing party, can play a more important role in the agenda-setting stage. As Paul Thomas points out, 'the influence opportunities' for party caucuses are different in government than in opposition. He also concludes that while the governing caucus seldom initiates policy, 'it does contribute to setting the agenda of government and to the parameters of policy choice' (1998, 3). In the case of one-party dominant legislatures, which are quite common at the provincial level, the opportunities for government caucus committees to influence the cabinet's policy agenda are quite considerable, as we show in the next section.

The formulation of policy options by government is the second stage of the policy cycle, as defined by Howlett and Ramesh (2003, 13). Committees that conduct inquiries into matters of public policy are active in this stage of the cycle, either as caucus committees helping the government establish priorities on issues for which no policy has been formulated, or as parliamentary committees helping gauge reactions to a particular set of policy proposals.

As well as assisting in setting the government agenda, caucus committees also play a role in the development of public policy. Based on a survey of five provincial caucuses, Ray White found that government party caucuses in Alberta, Nova Scotia, Ontario, and Saskatchewan (but not PEI) utilized the committee structure to increase members' input in developing policies and legislation. In his opinion, a caucus that allows its members meaningful input by incorporating committee reports fosters effective communication, 'an invaluable tool in securing support for government and opposition agendas' (White 1997, 311).

Multi-party parliamentary committees are also active in the policy formulation stage. Since their mandate generally allows for wide-ranging public consultation on a topical policy matter, they tend to exert considerable influence. Indeed, some legislative researchers claim that public participation 'means that an inquiry is likely to be more grounded in reality, to have more legitimacy with government, and to have a greater impact on policy' (Duffy and Thompson 2003, 6).

The policy development function of parliamentary committees is also becoming an important and increasingly popular one among elected officials in Canadian legislatures. Robertson (1999), for example, points out that by undertaking special studies and investigations, committee members in both chambers of the Parliament of Canada feel that they are helping to develop policy and participating in the governing of the country, rather than merely reacting or responding to government initiatives. He also agrees with O'Keeffe (1992) that the forte of legislators serving on parliamentary committees is in the cross-matching of opinions and information for political implications and significance: 'Committee members are uniquely equipped to bring a political perspective to their assessment of an issue; far more than public servants – or even cabinet ministers – they can see the political implications of a proposal' (Robertson 1999, 6–7).

Decision making is the third stage of the policy cycle and is defined by Howlett and Ramesh as 'the process by which governments adopt a particular course of action or non-action' (2003, 13). Parliamentary committees charged with the task of reviewing legislation are active in the decision-making stage. In several Canadian jurisdictions, government bills are referred to standing committees, after second or first reading, rather than being debated in committees of the whole House. These standing committees may call witnesses, conduct public hearings, or choose to question a minister on the content of proposed legislation, before conducting a clause-by-clause analysis of a draft bill. Like committees of the whole, they make the following types of decisions as to future action or non-action: to move the government bill forward to second or third reading without amendments, to recommend amendments to the bill, or even to reject the bill outright.

Special committees may also be delegated the task of making the key decisions to appoint officers of parliament, such as an auditor-general, a chief electoral officer or an ombudsman. While appointment committees are not directly involved in setting government policy, the 'public watchdogs' they select can have a significant impact when scrutinizing the operations of government. These multi-party committees must unanimously recommend the appointment of a qualified candidate to the House. Due to concerns about preserving the confidentiality of prospective applicants, most of their proceedings take place in camera.

Policy implementation is the fourth stage of the policy cycle and 'relates to how governments put policies into effect' (Howlett and Ramesh 2003, 13). It does not involve either parliamentary committees or caucus committees. Instead, implementation is largely the preserve of the public service, which has the resources to effectively carry out policy decisions and deliver programs and services for those affected by them.

Policy evaluation is the final stage of the policy cycle and refers to 'the processes by which the results of policies are monitored by both state and societal actors, the outcome of which may be reconceptualization of policy problems and solutions' (Howlett and Ramesh 2003, 13). Standing committees that perform the scrutiny function or review existing statutes are engaged in different forms of policy evaluation.

Scrutiny of government activity is a traditional function of parliamentary committees and, as Stilborn (2002) points out, the trend towards increased scrutiny is grounded on parliament's 'power of the purse.' Audit or public accounts committees are the best-known examples of scrutiny committees. They are charged with reviewing the reports of the legislative auditor and usually hear from witnesses representing the independent audit office and government organizations. Similarly, standing committees struck to review the activities of Crown corporations will hear from senior management, question witnesses and then issue a report to the House, often containing recommendations on how to improve the agencies' operations.

Statutory review committees are also involved in the policy evaluation stage. They are special committees struck by the House to conduct a comprehensive review of the legislation governing the activities of some independent officers of parliament (e.g., information and privacy commissioner, police complaint commissioner). Usually, they will receive submissions from interested parties on whether the existing legislation needs to be amended. The committee will then deliberate on what they have heard and issue a final report to the House.

As with many other committee reports, it is usually left up to government to decide whether the recommendations are implemented or ignored. A survey conducted by Docherty (2005) found that six jurisdictions – the Parliament of Canada, Prince Edward Island, Ontario, Saskatchewan, the Northwest Territories, and Nunavut – have adopted procedures that require a government to respond to parliamentary committee reports within a specified time limit. However, 'there is no requirement that the recommendations of the committee actually be implemented, even if the committee report represents an all-party consensus' (Docherty 2005, 170).

Our analysis has shown that caucus committees play a role in agenda setting and the formulation of policy, and that parliamentary committees are active in three stages of the policy cycle: policy formulation, decision making, and policy evaluation. It has also confirmed that committees operating inside legislatures are not active at all in the policy implementation stage. In figure 14.1, we provide a summary of caucus and parliamentary committee activities in relation to their position in the policy cycle.

Assessing the Effectiveness of Committees

Having shown that committees inside Canadian legislatures are active in four stages of the policy cycle, we now turn our attention to examining the key institutional constraints and political factors that influence their effectiveness as active participants in the policy-making process.

Figure 14.1 Role of Committees in the Policy Cycle

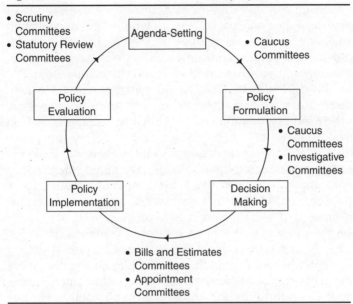

- Scrutiny
  Committees
- Statutory Review
  Committees

Agenda-Setting

- Caucus
  Committees

Policy
Evaluation

Policy
Formulation

- Caucus
  Committees
- Investigative
  Committees

Policy
Implementation

Decision
Making

- Bills and Estimates
  Committees
- Appointment
  Committees

Policy cycle model adapted from Howlett and Ramesh (2003)

Institutional Constraints

There are two factors related to the system of governance we share in Canada that constrain committee activity in all 14 jurisdictions that make up the federation. The first institutional constraint is federalism itself. Under the constitutional division of powers, a parliament – and, by extension, its committees – cannot inquire into a matter that is outside its jurisdiction (Lee 1999). While the lines between federal and provincial responsibilities have become blurred over the years, matters of foreign policy and international trade, for example, still remain largely off limits for committees in subnational parliaments. One notable exception was the BC Legislative Assembly's Special Committee on the Multilateral Agreement on Investment (see Smallwood 1998).

The other major institutional constraint is the Westminster style of parliamentary government inherited from the United Kingdom. Under the Westminster model, the cabinet controls the legislative agenda and the House determines the composition and mandate of each parliamentary committee, on the advice of a government-dominated selection committee. In a similar fashion, it is the parliamentary House leaders of the governing or opposition parties that determine the membership and terms of reference of caucus committees. Therefore, like their counterparts elsewhere, committees inside Canadian legislatures are certainly not autonomous structures. Instead, they are essentially subordinate advisory bodies that may consider matters referred to them either by the House or the parliamentary party caucus. Once they have completed their inquiry, committees are obligated to report back on their findings.

As a result, some Canadian academics are quite pessimistic about the ability of parliamentary committees to undertake independent policy making. For example, Graham White, in his comparative study of provincial legislatures, concluded that the overall pattern of executive dominance imposed 'debilitating restrictions on the powers of committees to determine public policy or to control government activities' (1996, 206). He also noted that cabinet domination of the policy-making process is particularly prevalent in the federal House, which has more elaborate and better-resourced committees with procedural mechanisms that offer greater opportunity for influencing public policy, such as open committee mandates.

Political Factors

Besides the institutional constraints, there are other factors that affect the policy-making capacity of committees operating inside Canadian legislatures. The two earlier studies of provincial and territorial assemblies (White and Levy 1989; White 1996) identified four political factors that affect parliamentary committee systems: the size of a legislature, the number of parties, the degree of legislative independence from government, and the level of resources and services available for legislators.

We think this list is a useful starting point for our study, but it is by no means exhaustive. Based on our experience as policy analysis 'insiders,' we would suggest that other factors also help to explain the effectiveness of committees: namely, the personality traits and talents of individual committee members, the role of government caucus committees in one-party dominant legislatures, and the procedures of parliamentary committees.

Table 14.1 Composition of Canadian Legislatures, August 2005

Distribution of Members

	Total	Govt.	Oppos.	Third party	Other	Vacant
H of C	308	133	98	54	22	1
BC	79	46	33	0	0	0
Alta.	83	62	16	4	1	0
Sask.	58	30	28	0	0	0
Man.	57	35	20	2	0	0
Ont.	103	70	24	8	0	1
Que.	125	72	45	5	1	2
NL	48	33	12	2	1	0
NB	55	28	26	1	0	0
NS	52	25	15	11	1	0
PEI	27	23	4	0	0	0
Yukon	18	11	5	1	1	0
NWT*	19	19	0	0	0	0
Nunavut*	19	19	0	0	0	0

* Consensus government

SIZE OF A LEGISLATURE

One of the findings of the two earlier studies is that the size of a legislature appears to have greater influence on its operation and performance than any other structural or organizational variable. In this respect, Canada qualifies as 'a veritable laboratory of parliamentary government' (White and Levy 1989, 1). Canadian legislatures cover a wide spectrum, ranging from small assemblies in the three territories and Prince Edward Island, through to relatively large houses in Ontario and Québec, which are less than half the size of the federal House of Commons, as table 14.1 shows. According to White (1996), there are several consequences for a committee system that flow from this variation in size. First of all, the size of a legislature greatly affects the scope and effectiveness of committee systems. White concludes that in small provincial legislatures, there are simply too few private members available for committee work and so 'an extensive committee system is simply not possible ... Moreover, governments in the smaller assemblies will be disinclined to sanction extensive committee activity because most of the talent in caucus will be in cabinet, so that few able backbenchers are left to protect government interests in committee' (White 1996, 212).

Obviously, the impact of size is even more pronounced in the three territorial assemblies, which have a smaller membership than all provincial legislatures. For example, in the Yukon – the only one of the three territories with a party-based legislature – there were only 12 private members available to serve on the five standing committees during the 31st Parliament. In the recent past, having so few private members has meant that standing committees met infrequently, if at all, due to the conflicting pressures of parliamentary and constituency work.

However, while the small size-limited scope linkage is obviously a strong one, it does not automatically preclude smaller houses from having effective parliamentary committees. The speaker of the non-partisan Legislative Assembly of Nunavut, for example, claims that the capacity of its four standing committees to influence government decisions is greater than in other Westminster parliaments for the following reason: they are routinely provided by cabinet with confidential information 'that committees in Ottawa and the provincial capitals could only dream of receiving,' and this practice 'gives MLAs genuine influence – though by no means the final say – in important government decisions' (O'Brien 2003–04, 8).

Besides scope, the size of a legislature also affects procedure. White (1996) points out that generally speaking, larger provincial houses require more complex rules and procedures and can support active committee systems, which means that legislation and spending estimates will be handled differently than in small houses. They are more likely to refer legislation or estimates to standing committees, which are less partisan than committees of the whole and permit citizen participation. However, a recent survey reveals that only five provinces – Nova Scotia, Québec, Ontario, Manitoba, and Saskatchewan – routinely send public bills to standing committees after second reading (Docherty 2005, 149).

At the federal level, most bills and all spending estimates have been referred to standing committees since the reform of the committee system in 1968. According to a former clerk of the House of Commons, the period from 1968 through to 1979 was a major watershed: 'When you compare what committees did in those days with the years prior to 1968 it was a revolution. Committees were smaller and they got into amending legislation. They built up a head of steam to have more and more autonomy in the studies and inquiries. They used the supply process as an excuse to get at issues in a timely fashion without an order of reference from the House' (Marleau 1999, 5).

Finally, the size of a legislature can have an impact on the interpersonal dynamics among members. White (1996) suggests that cross-party relationships among members can be less hostile and antagonistic in larger legislatures, where there is more opportunity for members to get to know one another through committee work. Others, though, are skeptical of this type of claim. Robert and Doreen Jackson (1990), for example, point out that it is part of the conventional wisdom that the less formal environment of committee work, and the relative absence of publicity surrounding committee deliberations, can permit the development of a less partisan atmosphere and enhance corporate identity. However, they suggest that collegiality varies according to function, rather than size per se: 'It is in the performance of ... the investigative function that Canadian parliamentary committees most often live up to the conventional wisdom by displaying non-partisanship, group cohesion and autonomy from party and government control' (Jackson and Jackson 1990, 350–51).

PERSONALITY TRAITS
We would argue that the personality traits and talents of individual members also affect the cross-party relations within parliamentary committees. The skills and temperament of a committee chair, for example, can make an important difference (see O'Keeffe 1992). Don Blenkarn, MP (1979–93), is widely recognized as having been a powerful chair of the House of Commons finance committee during two parliaments (see Marleau 1999; McInnes 1999). In British Columbia, Fred Gingell, MLA (1991–99) was well respected as an effective chair of the public accounts committee at the time of a polarized house. Based on our own work experience, we would add that the forceful personality of an individual member can also influence the outcome of a particular committee inquiry.

NUMBER OF PARTIES
The number of parties is another political factor that can critically affect the effectiveness of committees inside Canadian legislatures. In their pioneering study of provincial and territorial assemblies, White and Levy (1989) point out that any generalizations about the impact of party composition apply to only the Yukon territorial assembly and the provincial and federal houses in Canada, legislatures where members are first and foremost party representatives. In the other territories – NWT

and Nunavut – there are no parliamentary political parties in their consensus-based assemblies.

Within the partisan legislatures, White and Levy (1989) claim that the effectiveness of a parliamentary committee system is limited when, as often happens, the private members on one side substantially outnumber those on the other side. In such a situation, the opportunities available to opposition members to contribute to the policy process are obviously restricted. While their claim is valid, we think there is still an opportunity for a tiny opposition to exert a modicum of influence in one-party dominant legislatures. In British Columbia, for example, the committee system in the 37th Parliament (2001–05) provided the two opposition members with an alternative forum to continue House debate and to perform the scrutiny function.

ONE-PARTY DOMINANT LEGISLATURES

Furthermore, what the two earlier studies of Canadian legislatures overlook is the fact that in one-party dominant legislatures, the opportunities for government caucus committees to influence agenda setting and policy formulation increase considerably. In the case of the Alberta legislature, where one-party dominance is firmly established, the pattern has been to have powerful government caucus committees and relatively weak parliamentary committees (see Engelmann 1992; Speaker 1998; Cooper and Kanji 2000).

In Alberta, the six standing policy committees (SPCs) are chaired by a private government member, with appropriate ministers acting as co-chairs. The consensus seems to be that these committees are essentially where the policy-making action occurs. For example, all the Alberta ministers and MLAs interviewed in the spring of 1995 'agreed that the power of SPCs lies not only in the vetting of ideas coming from the ministries, but also in their ability to introduce new ideas into the policy process' (Kneebone and McKenzie 1997, 186).

Following the 2001 provincial election, when the BC Liberal Party won 77 of the 79 seats, the governing party in British Columbia established quite an elaborate caucus committee system, based on the Alberta model. During its first term of office, there were five government caucus committees organized on a sectoral basis (economy and government operations, education, health, cross-government initiatives, communities, and safety), as well as task forces on topics as diverse as land use planning, Asian economic development, multiculturalism, and seniors' issues. According to media reports, private members had considerable influence in developing legislation and policies that helped their communities (see Willcocks 2005).

COMMITTEE PROCEDURES

In addition to the number of parties, the procedures governing committee activity in a particular jurisdiction can also affect the capacity of parliamentary committees to influence public policy. For example, a formal rule banning minority reports may be more significant than the party composition of a legislature in building cross-party consensus, which enhances the impact of a committee report in the eyes of government and the public (see Quigley 2000).

In Canada, only the Legislative Assembly of Ontario and the House of Commons routinely permit dissenting opinions or minority reports, which can make it more difficult to achieve consensus in those jurisdictions. For example, the 2002 report on the pre-budget consultation process by the Ontario Standing Committee on Finance and Economic Affairs did not contain any joint recommendations. Instead, it simply included three separate opinions of the Progressive Conservative, Liberal, and New Democratic members.

At the federal level, the introduction of minority reports into the House of Commons committee system was recommended by the McGrath committee in 1985 and introduced in the 34th Parliament (1988–93), when the official opposition offered a clear alternative and represented a government-in-waiting. In the next two parliaments, the main opposition parties were the Bloc Québécois and the Reform Party, so the political dynamics were different. In the 35th Parliament (1993–97), the widely diverging views of the two opposition parties resulted in minority reports being the more common practice than unanimous ones (Finsten 1996, 18). Likewise, a striking feature of the 36th Parliament (1997–2000) was the proliferation of minority reports or dissenting opinions, which resembled pre-election platforms.

LEGISLATIVE INDEPENDENCE

Another political factor that needs to be taken into account in assessing the effectiveness of parliamentary committees is the degree of legislative independence from the government. Obviously one important measure of this is whether ministers serve on parliamentary committees, as opposed to taking part in committee proceedings as witnesses. Nowadays in Canadian legislatures, the convention is that ministers are not considered eligible for standing or special committee membership.

For White and Levy (1989), another important aspect of legislative independence is the ability of parliamentary committees to determine their own agendas. They claim that private members can more readily influence public policy and enhance government accountability if parliamentary committees do not need authorization from government to embark on policy studies or to hold investigations. The majority of provincial and territorial houses grant committees the power to inquire into any matter within their mandate, except for Alberta, Saskatchewan and New Brunswick. At the federal level, House of Commons committees were given the power to initiate their own inquiries as a result of the amendments made to the standing orders to incorporate the 1985 McGrath proposals (see Marleau 1999).

However, in the case of those jurisdictions where committees have been delegated considerable independence, it is not always clear how much of a difference the new autonomy has made. For example, a 1993–94 study of committee systems in Québec and Ontario indicates that 'while the degree of initiative and autonomy exhibited by Ontario committees was higher than in Québec, it still represented only a tiny fraction of committee business as a whole' (Pelletier et al. 1996, 26). Furthermore, it would be wrong to conclude that the ability to initiate an inquiry is a prerequisite for committee effectiveness. As Robertson points out, jurisdictions like the Canadian Senate that require an order of reference from the chamber can also produce 'meaningful and productive committee studies' (1999, 42).

Another indicator of legislative independence, discussed by White (1996), is the increasing use of committees to appoint independent officers of parliament, including ethics commissioners. In many Canadian legislatures, special committees now make the effective decisions on such key appointments, whereas previously cabinet alone decided on these important staffing matters.

In fact, the extent of legislative control vis-à-vis independent officers of parliament extends beyond the selection process. The federal House and several provincial and territorial assemblies – Alberta, BC, Manitoba, and Nunavut, to name a few – also review the estimates, service plans, and performance reports of independent offices. As well, the legislation that governs the officers' activities is also subject to periodic statutory review by multiparty parliamentary committees, as we discussed earlier.

Finally, we would propose that legislative autonomy is also enhanced in a minority-government situation, such as the ones prevailing in the

House of Commons since the 2004 federal election. One consequence of having such a balanced House is that opposition parties can have a majority of members on standing committees and the ability to work together to control a committee's timetable, call witnesses, and make amendments to key pieces of government legislation (Strahl 2004, 8).

LEGISLATIVE RESOURCES AND SERVICES

Another point of comparison between Canadian legislatures is the level of resources and services available for members. White calls this factor 'legislative professionalization' and defines it as 'a set of attitudes and procedural/administrative arrangements supporting elected members' capacity to carry out their duties' (1996, 217). Indicators of a professional legislature include adequate levels of pay, legislative sessions of reasonable duration, sufficient professional staff support, caucus research facilities, and professional non-partisan committee support.

Generally speaking, Canadian legislatures attained an adequate level of resources and services for members during the 1979 to 1992 period. According to a former administrator of the Ontario Assembly, they grew 'like topsy' in those 15 years in terms of members, staff, budgets, and services (Fleming 1992, 77). However, there were exceptions to this general trend. For example, in 1989, White and Levy concluded that smaller houses in the Maritimes had yet to attain the minimum level of resources and services to enable members to perform their duties effectively. More recently, an unpublished survey of audit committees across Canada, conducted in July 2004, reveals that seven of the 14 jurisdictions still do not have in-house research support.

While admitting our own bias here, we would propose that the relative lack of professional and non-partisan research services for parliamentary committees qualifies as perhaps the last obstacle to becoming a 'professionalized' legislature. Our claim is supported by a number of legislators in the Québec National Assembly, who concluded that the lack of sufficient staff prevents parliamentary committees from fulfilling their existing functions adequately and from taking on new tasks related to parliamentary reform and surveillance work (see Pinard et al. 2000–1).

Conclusion

At the outset of this paper, we posed two questions concerning the potential and actual capacity of committees to influence the policy process. The first section demonstrated that caucus and parliamentary committees inside Canadian legislatures do play a role in four of the five stages of the policy cycle: agenda setting, policy formulation, decision making, and policy evaluation. Policy implementation is the only stage that is off limits to committees.

Our analysis has also shown that the policy-making capacity of committees is constrained by the federal system of parliamentary government. It has confirmed that the size of a partisan legislature influences the scope, procedures and interpersonal dynamics of standing and special committees, that the number of parties can affect the relative influence of parliamentary and caucus committees, that a degree of legislative independence is necessary for a parliamentary committee system, and that parliamentary committees require research services to perform their investigative and scrutiny functions.

These constraints and political factors need to be taken into account when assessing the contribution committees can make towards the democratic renewal of parliamentary institutions. Nonetheless, we believe that policy formulation committees, in particular, are important mechanisms for engaging citizens in the routine work of Canadian legislatures. They provide a unique venue for organized groups and the 'disaffected' public to voice their views directly to elected officials, with their input influencing policy choices. Indeed, like public inquiries, such committees are open, encourage public and group participation, and provide informed recommendations to government.

However, as researchers working in a parliamentary setting, we are also conscious of the fact that legislators tend not to engage in self-evaluation. Pending the development of useful indicators to measure the outcomes of their committee work, our study remains incomplete. Nonetheless, we will judge our approach to be a success if we have managed to stimulate the interest of policy analysts – whether they are academics, 'insiders' or 'outsiders' – in the 'fascinating variety' of committees operating inside Canadian legislatures and other Westminster-style parliaments.

NOTES

We would like to acknowledge the helpful feedback and support we have received for this research project from the legislative clerks E. George MacMinn, Craig James, and Kate Ryan-Lloyd; our co-workers, Wynne

MacAlpine and Brant Felker; and from our partners, John Schofield and Terri Evans.

1 See Canadian Study of Parliament Group and the Association of Parliamentary Librarians in Canada, 'Research and Information for Parliamentarians,' Ottawa, October 24–25, 1988, Panel VI: Serving Committees, 13–15.
2 'Table officers' are the legislative clerks who sit at the table directly in front of the speaker's (or le président's) chair. Apart from their substantial administrative duties, they provide procedural advice during sittings of the House, keep the minutes of the proceedings, and record the votes. They include the clerk of the House, clerk assistants, law clerks, procedural clerks, and committee clerks.
3 Special Conference on Parliamentary Committees, 'The State of Parliamentary Committees at the End of the 20th Century,' Parliament Buildings, Ottawa, 13–14 September 1999; and 2003 Conference on Parliamentary Committees, Legislative Assembly of Ontario, Toronto, 11–14 November 2003.

REFERENCES

Barnhart, Gordon. 1999. *Parliamentary Committees: Enhancing Democratic Governance.* Report of a Commonwealth Parliamentary Association Study Group. London: Cavendish Publishing Ltd.
Cooper, Barry, and Mebs Kanji. 2000. *Governing in Post-Deficit Times: Alberta in the Klein Years.* Toronto: University of Toronto Press.
Dignam, Anthony. 2003. The Oireachtas Committee System: A Framework for Evaluation. MSc thesis in Economic Policy Studies, Trinity College, Dublin.
Docherty, David C. 2005. *Legislatures.* Vancouver: UBC Press.
Duffy, Beverly, and Merrin Thompson. July 2003. *Innovative Committee Methods: Case Studies from Two Parliaments.* A report prepared for the Conference on Parliamentary Committees, Legislative Assembly of Ontario, Toronto, 11–14 November 2003.
Engelmann, Frederick C. 1992. 'The Legislature.' In Allan Tupper and Roger Gibbins, eds., *Government and Politics in Alberta,* 137–65. Edmonton: University of Alberta Press.
Finsten, Hugh. 1996. 'Research Services for Parliamentary Committees.' *Canadian Parliamentary Review* 19(2), 15–19.
Fleming, Robert J. 1992. *Canadian Legislatures 1992: Issues, Structures and Costs.* Agincourt, ON: Global Press.

Franks, C.E.S. June 1997. 'Constraints on the Operations and Reform of Parliamentary Committees in Canada.' In Lawrence D. Longley and Attila Ágh, eds., *The Changing Roles of Parliamentary Committees*, 199–207. Working Papers on Comparative Legislative Studies II. Appleton, WI: Lawrence University.

Gay, Oonagh, and Barry Winetrobe. 2003. *Parliamentary Audit: The Audit Committee in Comparative Context*. A report to the Audit Committee of the Scottish Parliament. SP Paper 839, session 1.

Howlett, M., and M. Ramesh. 2003. *Studying Public Policy: Policy Cycles and Policy Subsystems*. 2nd ed. Oxford: Oxford University Press.

Jackson, Robert J., and Doreen Jackson. 1990. *Politics in Canada: Culture, Institutions, Behaviour and Public Policy*. 2nd ed. Scarborough, ON: Prentice-Hall Canada.

Kneebone, Ronald D., and Kenneth J. McKenzie. 1997. 'The Process Behind Institutional Reform in Alberta.' In Christopher J. Bruce, Ronald D. Kneebone, and Kenneth J. McKenzie, eds., *A Government Reinvented: A Study of Alberta's Deficit Elimination Program*, 176–210. Toronto: Oxford University Press.

Lee, Derek. 1999. *The Power of Parliamentary Houses to Send for Papers, Persons and Records: A Sourcebook on the Law and Precedent of Parliamentary Subpoena Powers for Canadian and Other Houses*. Toronto: University of Toronto Press.

Malloy, Jonathan. 2004. 'An Auditor's Best Friend? Standing Committees on Public Accounts.' *Canadian Public Administration* 47(2), 165–183.

Marleau, Robert. 1999. 'Keynote Address,' Special Conference on Parliamentary Committees, 13–14 September, Parliament Buildings, Ottawa.

McGee, David G. 2002. *The Overseers: Public Accounts Committees and Public Spending*. Report of a Commonwealth Parliamentary Association Study Group. London: Pluto Press.

McInnes, David. 1999. *Taking It to the Hill: The Complete Guide to Appearing before (and Surviving) Parliamentary Committees*. Ottawa: University of Ottawa Press.

McInnes, Simon. 1977. 'Improving Legislative Surveillance of Provincial Public Expenditures: The Performance of the Public Accounts Committees and Auditors General.' *Canadian Public Administration* 20(1), 36–86.

Milliken, Peter. 1999. 'The Future of the Committee System.' In Gordon Barnhart, *Parliamentary Committees: Enhancing Democratic Governance*, 135–59. Report of a Commonwealth Parliamentary Association Study Group. London: Cavendish Publishing Ltd.

O'Brien, Kevin. 2003–04. 'Some Thoughts on Consensus Government in Nunavut.' *Canadian Parliamentary Review* 26(4), 6–10.

O'Keeffe, Peter. 1992. 'The Scope and Function of Parliamentary Committees.' *The Parliamentarian* 73(4) (October), 270–5.

O'Neal, Brian. 1994. *Senate Committees: Role and Effectiveness*. Paper prepared for Parliamentary Research Branch, Library of Parliament of Canada, June.

Pelletier, Réjean, et al. 1996. 'Committee Systems in Quebec and Ontario: Part 1: Structure and Organization.' *Canadian Parliamentary Review* 19(1) (spring), 25–30.

Pinard, Claude, et al. 2000–01. 'Proposals to Revitalize Committee Proceedings of the Quebec National Assembly.' *Canadian Parliamentary Review* 23(4) (winter), 2–10.

Quigley, Derek. 2000. 'Seeking Consensus: Select Committees and Multiparty Policy-Making.' *The Parliamentarian* 81(2) (April), 132–4.

Reid, George. 2001–2. Foreword, The Scottish Parliament Annual Report.

Robertson, James R. 1999. *Functions of Committees: Special Studies and Legislation*. Paper prepared for Parliamentary Research Branch, Library of Parliament of Canada, 26 August.

Rush, Michael. 1979. 'Committees in the Canadian House of Commons.' In John D. Lees and Malcolm Shaw, eds., *Committees in Legislatures: A Comparative Analysis*, 191–241. Durham, NC: Duke University Press.

Shaw, Malcolm. 1979. 'Committees in Legislatures.' In Philip Norton, ed., *Legislatures*, 237–267. Oxford: Oxford University Press.

Smallwood, Joan. 1998. 'Trade Liberalization Marches On: Public Interest May Be Threatened by Global Investors.' *The Parliamentarian* 79(4) (October), 350–55.

Smith, Jennifer. 2003. 'Debating the Reform of Canada's Parliament.' In F. Leslie Seidle and David C. Docherty, eds., *Reforming Parliamentary Democracy*, 150–67. Montreal and Kingston: McGill-Queen's University Press.

Speaker, Ray. 1998. 'Party Caucuses behind Closed Doors.' *Canadian Parliamentary Review* 21(1) (spring), 4–6.

Stilborn, Jack. 2002. *The Roles of the Member of Parliament in Canada: Are They Changing?* Paper prepared for Parliamentary Research Branch, Library of Parliament of Canada, 31 May.

Strahl, Chuck. 2004–2005. 'Politics and Procedure in a Minority Parliament.' *Canadian Parliamentary Review* 27(4) (winter), 7–9.

Thomas, Paul G. 1998. 'Caucus and Representation in Canada.' Keynote Address to the Canadian Study of Parliament Group Fall Conference on Party Caucuses: Behind Closed Doors. Ottawa, 21 November 1997. *Parliamentary Perspectives* 1.

White, Graham. 1996. 'Comparing Provincial Legislatures.' In Christopher

Dunn, ed., *Provinces: Canadian Provincial Politics*, 205–27. Peterborough, ON: Broadview Press.

White, Graham, and Gary Levy. 1989. 'Introduction: The Comparative Analysis of Canadian Provincial and Territorial Legislative Assemblies.' In Gary Levy and Graham White, eds., *Provincial and Territorial Legislatures in Canada*, 1–12. Toronto: University of Toronto Press.

White, Ray. October 1997. 'The Role of Caucus: Comparing Canadian Practice.' *The Parliamentarian* 78(4), 311–13.

Willcocks, Paul. 2005. 'Campbell Kills His Brave Plan to Give Power to Backbenchers.' *Vancouver Sun*, 2 July, C7.

15 How Policy Makers View Public Opinion

FRANÇOIS PETRY

Introduction

Public opinion research and polling are not only indispensable features of election campaigning, they have also become an essential form of communication between government decision makers and their environment.[1] Politicians presumably take the pulse of public opinion in order to achieve some degree of harmony between government policy and the preferences of the public. This, however, begs the question of what exactly politicians take the pulse of.

Some readers might dismiss my question as irrelevant on the apparently reasonable grounds that public opinion has no visible effect on public policy, at least in Canada (Howlett and Ramesh 2003, 75–7). Unlike the United States, where politicians appear responsive to the preferences of their constituents, Canada operates under a Westminster system that was in part designed to insulate politicians from public opinion. The dismissive attitude is also supported empirically by recently uncovered evidence that politicians in Ottawa ignore the opinions of Canadians significantly more often than their U.S. counterparts (Pétry and Mendelsohn 2004).

However, the presumption that public opinion has no effect on policy is reasonable only in appearance, for two reasons. First, because it narrowly assumes that there must be a causal effect between public opinion (seen as the independent variable) and policy (viewed as the dependent variable). And second, because it narrowly equates public opinion with polling. Neither assumption is entirely correct. Constructivist scholars of public opinion and political communication (Herbst 1998; Glasser and Salmon 1995) have emphasized that the 'dependent vs. independent variable' metaphor is often a caricature that does not give a correct account of the complexities involved in the opinion/policy relationship. They argue that the relationship is better understood as a social construction, a conversation between the public, the media, and policy makers about the meaning of government actions. Constructivist scholars also view public opinion as larger than polling alone. A government's mandate to implement a policy agenda does not come only from actual – or simulated – support as measured by polls, but also from a societal understanding of whether public support exists, which is constructed from many elements other than polling, such as media reports and demands from interest groups. Thus, the question of how policy makers view public opinion is relevant if one adopts a constructivist framework, which I do, at least in part, in this chapter.

How do Canadian officials view public opinion? Do they define it primarily in terms of mass surveys? What alternative indicators do they use to operationalize public opinion? There is a growing body of research in the United States (Herbst 1998; Kohut 1998; Powlick 1995; see also Fuchs and Pfletsch 1996 for German evidence) but so far the published Canadian evidence on this question is nonexistent. As a move toward advancing our knowledge, this chapter uses the data from a questionnaire and from interviews with federal officials to find out what indicators Canadian policy makers use to know more about the state of public opinion, and what implications follow for policy analysis.

Methods

This research starts with the premise that public opinion is at least in part a social construction whose meaning is shaped by a variety of forces, including the methodology used to assess public opinion, the occupations of respondents, their shared notion of democracy, as well as the institutional set-up within which they operate. To find out how these variables shape decision makers' attitudes toward public opinion, a close-ended mail questionnaire was sent out in early 2003 to 522 federal officials in Ottawa.[2] English and French versions of the questionnaire were sent out to elected members of Parliament (senators were not included in the study), to deputy and assistant deputy ministers and general directors, communications officers in central agencies (PMO, PCO) and several line departments, and executive assistants in the same departments.[3] There were 105 usable responses (the response rate is therefore 20 per cent) from 35 Liberal MPs (including two cabinet ministers), 28 MPs from the opposition, 12 senior officials at the rank of assistant deputy minister or general director, and 7 communications experts. Twenty executive assistants and party activists also returned the questionnaire. There are three times as many male as female respondents and there are also three times as many anglophones as there are francophones. These numbers roughly coincide with the observed gender and language distributions in the population that was targeted in this study. The age distribution in the sample is also fairly representative of what is observed in the higher echelons of the federal civil service. The modal age category in the sample is between 50 and 59.

Twenty-eight informants were subsequently interviewed in 2003 and 2004. Unlike the close-ended questionnaire, which gave relatively little choice to the respondents, the interviews allowed subjects to provide spontaneous ideas and to give a more detailed and personal account of their attitude toward public opinion. The interviews were also used to validate the results of the questionnaire. Well-prepared open-ended interviews are much better than close-ended questionnaires at eliciting self-conscious responses from officials, thereby allowing for more nuanced and valid conclusions. The occupations of the interview informants are: six executive assistants, five communications experts, four pollsters, two journalists, two elected representatives, one legislative clerk, and eight high-ranking bureaucrats.[4]

Included in the questionnaire is a prompt designed to measure how federal officials define public opinion. Survey respondents were not asked to provide their own abstract definition of public opinion. In view of the highly contested nature of the concept,[5] such an exercise would prove futile in all likelihood. Instead, the prompt presents the respondents with a 'list of items [they] might use to understand what the public thinks,' and asks them to 'indicate the importance they give to each item when it comes to knowing what the public thinks.' The items in the list include several indicators of public opinion that have appeared in previous studies of how American policy actors view public opinion: elected officials, newspaper articles, survey results, people you know, lobbyists. The list also features specific groups of self-selected outspoken citizens – protesters, for example, or this could also be said of radio talk shows – that are intended to reflect the opinions of the vocal public. Respondents were also asked to evaluate the importance of focus groups, election results, and public consultations. When asked how they understood public consultations, several interviewees made

Table 15.1 Sample Distribution

	N	%
Occupation		
Majority MP	35	33.3
Opposition MP	28	26.7
Assistant deputy minister	12	11.4
Executive assistant	20	19.0
Communications officer	10	9.5
Gender		
Female	26	24.8
Male	79	75.2
Language		
Anglophone	79	75.2
Francophone	26	24.8
Age		
29 or less	4	3.8
Between 30 and 39	11	10.5
Between 40 and 49	35	33.3
Between 50 and 59	53	50.5
60 and above	12	11.4
Consult public opinion		
Always/almost always	7	6.6
Often/regularly	39	37.1
Sometimes/occasionally	50	47.6
Never/almost never	9	8.6
Governments make policy in order to respond to public demands		
Strongly agree	6	5.7
Agree	37	35.2
Unsure	14	13.3
Disagree	38	36.2
Strongly disagree	10	9.5
Total	105	100.0

specific mention of the roundtable discussions in the preparation phase of Paul Martin's budget, the strategic defence forum meetings, and public consultations on youth justice. Other informants understood 'public consultation' to mean 'referendum.' Only one spontaneously proposed public inquiries as a definition of public consultation. Although the notion of public inquiries as forums for voicing public opinion has intuitive appeal (see the chapter by Liora Salter in this volume), it does not appear that our informants think of public inquiries as indicators of public opinion unless prompted to do so.

The Sources of Public Opinion

Figure 15.1 displays questionnaire respondents' ordering of indicators of public opinion based on the number of officials who declare that the indicators are 'very important' and 'important.' Looking at the bar graphs, we see very large numbers of officials in this study expressing operationalizations of public opinion that include elected officials, public consultations, election results and the news media.

The most recognized indicator of public opinion is elected officials (93 per cent). This is hardly surprising. Elected representatives are a readily available source of well-informed opinions, at least compared with the uninformed opinions of the masses. Unlike the public that elected them, they can be contacted easily by officials who want to solicit their views on policy issues. Elected officials are also important in their role as representatives of the opinions of their constituents. The following quote by the executive assistant of a senior member of the Chrétien cabinet is a good example of public opinion operationalization in terms of elected officials: 'The best barometer, in my view, of public opinion are members of the legislature and cabinet ministers. They were the ones that had the best feelings in so far as opinions there in the ridings – just as a means of measuring the impact upon particular policies that the government was launching, as it might affect us politically.'

An assistant deputy minister sees elected officials as a crucial channel of communication between government and society: 'Elected officials tend to know what people are thinking. I mean that is their business. I think every decision that a minister takes, he looks at it (*public opinion*). These are people that read the newspaper everyday. They live, they eat, they breathe the radio, the TV, you know. They get their morning clippings. That is what they want to know right away. What is the public out there saying? What are the journalists out there saying? And what are the polls saying?' The above quotes are illustrations of a conception of elected representatives as 'barometers' or 'surrogates' of public opinion. But this cannot be the whole story, because other political actors aside from elected representatives, such as the media and organized groups, can also play the role of barometers of public opinion. However, what makes representatives better surrogates than these

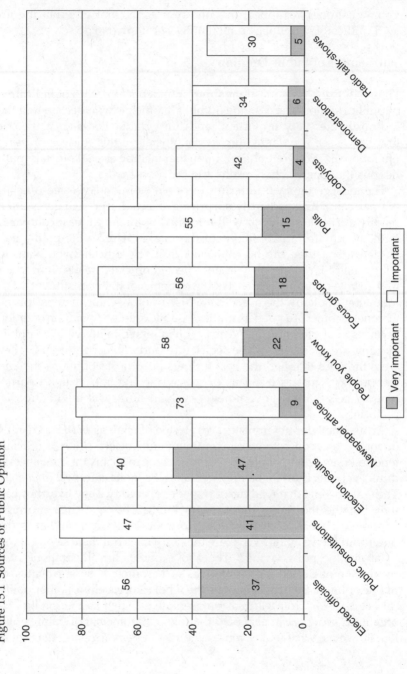

Figure 15.1 Sources of Public Opinion

other actors, several informants pointed out, is that they are elected. Being nominated as a candidate by the party and then getting elected means that you and your party are better than the competition at sensing the public mood, or, as one pollster we interviewed put it, 'to be elected you have to know where public opinion will be at election time.' The important role that elections play in Canadian officials' definitions of public opinion is confirmed by the high number of questionnaire respondents (87 per cent) who think that election results are an important or very important indicator of what the public thinks (see figure 15.1).

Eighty-two per cent of respondents in the study thought that newspaper articles were an 'important' or a 'very important' indicator of public opinion. The news media are, by definition, transmitters of information, but they are also an important indicator of public opinion. This is obviously true in the sense that the news media are the primary source of information on which citizens form their opinions (Zaller 1992). But the news media are also an important source of public opinion in the sense that the stories that are reported by journalists are themselves interpreted by officials as an indicator of where the public stands on issues (Iyengar and Kinder 1987; see also the chapter by Catherine Murray in this volume). The following quote from an assistant deputy minister summarizes well the role of the media as a source of public opinion: 'The media analysis and the clipping service is always important in government. Every day, any bureaucrat of any stature basically has the clippings in front of him, and that is the print and the electronic media for the day. If you are a senior decision maker in any department you look at these things every day to see what is in them and you keep an eye on them. And that gives you, I think, a good sense of what the public attitude and views are in general. Not just public opinion but also how public opinion is being viewed by the media.'

Public opinion scholars have often pointed out the importance of elites as sources of public opinion on which decision makers can rely. Elite opinion is generally seen as more knowledgeable and articulate than mass sentiment. The organized elites also have more influence on policy decisions than the unorganized masses (Olson 1965). Elite influence on policy is seen in a favourable light by some precisely because elite opinion is perceived as being better informed and more articulate (Lippman 1925). This study operationalizes elite opinion by asking respondents whether they consider people they know (friends and colleagues) as an important indicator when it comes to knowing what the public thinks. Eighty per cent of officials in the study cited people they know as 'important' or 'very important.'

Only seventy per cent of questionnaire respondents declare polls to be a 'very important' or 'important' source of public opinion. That is a considerably lower number than the percentages for 'elected officials' (93 per cent) and 'public consultations' (88 per cent) and still below 'people you know' (80 per cent) and 'focus groups' (74 per cent). Furthermore, the interviews reveal that officials who think that mass surveys are an important indicator of public opinion simultaneously express misgivings about them. This is what an executive assistant has to say about the use and limits of mass opinion surveys: 'Obviously polls are important to reflect the mood of Canadians. But I think you can't just rely on polls – I mean quantitative survey research – and figure that you know what the Canadian public thinks; what policies Canadians prefer. I think you have to use a variety of methods: media analysis, roundtables, academic reports.'

The relatively low priority that Canadian officials assign to public opinion polls may come as a surprise in view of the central role they occupy in the academic literature. The vast majority of academic studies of the relationship between public policy and public opinion rely exclusively on poll results as an indicator of public opinion, as if they were the only relevant measure of people's attitudes toward policy issues (for Canada, see Pétry 1999; Pétry and Mendelsohn 2004). The questionnaire data clearly indicate that this is not the case. And many of our informants agree that polls are not very useful or important to them, mainly because they consider polling as a science, whereas governing is an art. Other familiar reasons that were offered for not considering polls as important indicators of public opinion included the unsophisticated nature of mass opinion, and the suspicion that polls do not always represent what the people truly believe (these will be discussed in a later part of the chapter). Another, less familiar, reason that emerged from our conversations with pollsters and journalists (who are more openly critical than government officials) has to do with the way polls are used by decision makers in Ottawa. Commenting on the difference between his public and private sector clients, one pollster observed that: 'Politicians only want to hear good news because they have political agendas; managers of private corporations don't. The basic problem is that communication with business is more honest than [with] the public sector ... Pollsters who find themselves dependent on

the government for their livelihood have an incentive to only emphasize poll results that put their government client in a favourable light.'

The Access to Information Law and the recently enacted communication policy of the federal government have helped exacerbate the problem. Access to information requests (ATIR) now envelope almost all
polling activity (see note 2) and have contributed to a climate in which
government officials only commission polls whose results they know
they can construct in favourable ways. Because those drafting the poll
questions are aware that the results will become public, they are highly
resistant to asking certain kinds of questions that may subsequently
embarrass the government. One of our informants (a journalist), who
jokingly referred to polls that fall under ATIR as 'weapons of mass
distraction,' had this to say: 'The general rule is that the polls that fall
under Access to Information have become basically polls on issues we
all know the answers to and therefore they are only for one purpose,
and that is to make the government look better in its communication.'

So far the data from the questionnaire indicate that large proportions
of officials in Ottawa (74 per cent or more) agree to define public
opinion in terms of a series of indicators that include election results
and elected representatives, survey results and focus groups, news
media, and people they know (elites). Canadian officials also agree
about what public opinion is not. As figure 15.1 shows, only 40 per cent
of respondents think that public protests and demonstrations are 'important' or 'very important' indicators of public opinion, and the numbers are even lower for radio talk shows (35 per cent). One reason why
our informants do not consider these items as important indicators of
public opinion is that they represent the opinion of vocal minorities, not
the will of the majority. As one communications officer puts it, 'public
protests and demonstrations cannot qualify as a reflection of the public
will.' One national defence official adopts the typical attitude toward
radio talk shows when he dismisses them as 'the uninformed talking to
the ignorant.' As another high-ranking official in Ottawa explains, 'no
one really listen[s] to those here in Ottawa. In the West perhaps but back
in Ottawa, you don't really pay much attention to that.'

Another item that receives little recognition from officials as an indicator of public opinion is interest groups. Forty-two respondents consider lobbyists an 'important' source of public opinion and only four
view them as 'very important.' That is the lowest proportion of 'very
important' responses in any of the ten sources of public opinion in
figure 15.1. These low numbers are in stark contrast with the high

percentages of U.S. officials who believe that interest groups are an important indicator of public opinion. In his study of how U.S. foreign policy officials conceptualize public opinion, Powlick (1995) reports that a large proportion of respondents find interest group opinion to be the most reliable indicator of popular sentiment. He attributes this in part to the unavailability of survey results on many foreign policy issues, interest groups therefore becoming the only 'public' upon which a foreign policy official can rely. However valid this interpretation, it cannot represent the whole picture. In her study of how state decision makers conceptualize public opinion in America, Herbst (1998) finds that a majority of legislative staffers equate interest groups with public opinion. These staffers are concerned exclusively with domestic decisions, so Powlick's argument does not seem to apply.

The reason why so few Canadian officials consider lobbyists as important indicators of public opinion is twofold. First, Canadians in general have a somewhat negative attitude toward lobbyists, which explains their reluctance to recognize the representative role of interest groups. Unlike their American counterparts, Canadian officials tend to view lobbying by interest groups as influence peddling by the organized rich, often at odds with public sentiment. This attitude is reflected in the following quote from the executive assistant of a senior member of the Chrétien cabinet: 'Lobbyists play a role but I cannot say they are very influential, for me anyway. They come in here all the time but they have a set of goals that they want and they have only one point of view that is very predictable. And what they want is it the public interest? It is usually somebody's interest, and a very narrow interest, that they want.'

The second reason why Canadian officials do not consider interest groups as useful indicators of public opinion is institutional. Unlike the U.S. system of separation of power, where elected officials at the federal and state levels have constant and intense interactions with lobbyists, the Canadian parliamentary system is not conducive to intense interaction between elected officials and lobbyists (see also Andrew Stritch's chapter in this volume for evidence that Canadian business associations do little policy analysis). A high-ranking official puts it as follows: 'Lobbyists rarely consult with me and my department here in Ottawa. Things are different in Washington.'

Given the relatively low intensity of contacts between lobbyists and officials in Canada, it is no coincidence that, whereas U.S. officials often name interest groups and lobbyists as the most useful indicator of public opinion, a majority of Canadian officials do not even consider lobbyists as an important part of the definition of public opinion.

Three Conceptions of Public Opinion

So far we have only looked at the relative frequency of responses to questionnaire items. This allows us to tell salient indicators of public opinion from less salient ones. Now we want to see which indicators measure fundamentally similar, and which separate, conceptions of public opinion. For example, many respondents operationalize public opinion in terms of the news media, and many in terms of polls. But that does not mean that the two indicators are components of a similar underlying attitude toward what best defines public opinion. We cannot be sure whether these two items measure separate or similar attitudes until we perform some kind of data reduction analysis that will reveal underlying regularities across individual indicators of public opinion.

Factor analyzing the ten indicators of public opinion allows us to reduce the complexity of the data and to use a smaller set of dimensions to make comparisons with previous classifications of measures of public opinion found in the academic literature. One well-known typology contrasts definitions of public opinion as elite opininion emanating from organized groups (Blumer 1948), on the one hand, and mass opinion from polling (Converse 1986), on the other hand. Unlike Converse, who thinks that, whether we like it or not, polls are and should be the dominant channel of transmission of public opinion, Blumer argues that public opinion deserves to be counted as such only if it is 'socially embedded' and if it can be demonstrated that it affects policy decisions. According to Blumer, mass polling, the aggregation of the opinions of unconnected and uninformed individuals, does not 'fit the bill'; he only considers organized elite opinion as a valid source of public opinion. Other scholars have also argued that mass opinion as reflected by polling is a 'phantom' (Lippman 1925) or an artificial construct that has no independent existence (Bourdieu 1979) and that it would therefore be a mistake to reify mass opinion and rely on it to guide policy decisions.

Do Canadian officials' underlying attitudes toward public opinion reflect the Blumer vs Converse controversy? Table 15.2 displays the results. The ten indicators generate three factors that together explain 54.5 per cent of the total variance. The first factor (21.1 per cent of the total variance explained) picks up the indicators of public opinion that appear least salient in figure 15.1: lobbyists, protests and demonstrations, and radio talk shows. These items appear strongly correlated, in part by virtue of their low salience as opposed to the other highly salient items. Their intercorrelation is therefore somewhat coincidental. More theoretically significant are the positive loadings of 'people you know' and 'the news media' in the first factor. What this all suggests is a Blumer-like conception that originates in the informed discourse of organized elites transmitted through the news media. The conception also resembles closely Entman and Herbst's (2001) notion of 'articulated opinion' defined as 'the opinions of engaged, informed, and organized citizens – those who are mobilizable during campaign periods and between elections as well.' The first factor is labelled accordingly. The highly positive loading of polls (and the highly negative loading of public consultations) along the third factor (15.0 per cent of variance explained) is self-explanatory. The dimension refers unambiguously to Converse's conception of public opinion measured by random polling of the citizenry. This also closely coincides with what Entman and Herbst call 'mass opinion.' The factor is labelled accordingly. Two items are highly loaded along the second factor (18.4 per cent of variance explained): elected officials and election results. The conceptualization emerging from this factor appears predicated on the notion that public opinion materializes itself through the election of representatives in a parliamentary system. The second factor is therefore labelled 'ballot opinion.' Crucially, this conceptualization of public opinion in terms of casting a ballot in order to elect a majority government is not anticipated in the Blumer vs Converse controversy and neither is it part of the Entman and Herbst typology.[6] Perhaps this oversight can be explained by the fact that these are American authors, who are more familiar with the U.S. presidential system of separation of powers than with parliamentary systems like ours.

As pointed out earlier, polling has come to dominate popular discourse, and is now synonymous with public opinion, as other sources of public opinion have been displaced by the sample survey (Converse 1986; Ginsberg 1986). If it is true that 'articulated opinion' and 'majority ballot opinion' have been displaced by 'mass opinion' through polling in the popular mythology, then why have the older conceptions survived in the minds of Canadian policy makers? The presumption is that articulated opinion and ballot opinion continue to be useful channels of communication between policy makers and the public because they

Table 15.2 Factor Scores from Components of Sources of Public Opinion (Varimax Rotation)

	Factor 1 'Articulated opinion'	Factor 2 'Ballot opinion'	Factor 3 'Mass opinion'
Elected officials	.052	.796	.044
Public consultations	−.065	.406	−.619
Public opinion polls	−.109	.240	.746
Election results	−.012	.791	−.010
Focus groups	−.033	.147	.255
People you know	.727	−.099	−.177
Newspaper articles	.598	.246	.317
Lobbyists	.599	−.045	.323
Protests and demonstrations	.230	−.060	−.123
Radio talk shows	.768	−.008	−.043
Explained variance before rotation	21.05	18.41	15.01

Total variance explained = 54.47

fulfill some needs that mass opinion fails to answer. In the rest of this section, I propose several hypotheses to explain why some policy makers find mass opinion less important and useful than articulated opinion or majority ballot opinion. These hypotheses will be tested in the next section.

Federal officials may find articulated opinion more important and useful than mass opinion by polling because they believe the mass public is not sufficiently informed and sophisticated about policy issues. There is ample scholarly evidence to show that mass opinion is not informed, deliberative, or reliable opinion (Delli Carpini and Keeter 1996; Althaus 2003). Policy makers may find informed and deliberative sources particularly useful because they need to know when public opinion is consciously constructed through active cognition and discussion and when it is not. Mass surveys do not fulfill this need. Therefore, with polls alone, policy makers may find it difficult to know whether they get the 'real' picture or simply the unconscious reactions to symbols and manipulation. One way to avoid this problem is to rely on the articulated opinions of organized groups, journalists, and elected officials, because they are typically informed about the issues for which they speak and aware of the needs of policy makers and the sort of constituencies they must be accountable to. In addition, and unlike mass opinion measured by polls, elite groups, elected representatives, and the journalists that transmit their messages are clearly identifiable by decision makers, and this is a powerful incentive for them to provide accurate, reliable, and verifiable information to politicians. A look at federal officials' attitudes toward the public's sophistication helps put things in perspective. Included in the questionnaire is a prompt designed to assess how much policy knowledge federal officials grant the Canadian public. It turns out that 26 per cent of the officials in the sample agree or strongly agree with the statement that 'policy issues are simply too far removed from the everyday experience of Canadians for them to understand' (69 per cent disagree or strongly disagree with the statement while the remaining 5 per cent are unsure).

It is hypothesized that officials who think that the mass public does not understand policy issues (i.e., officials who agree or strongly agree with the statement) will have a tendency to disregard mass opinion as measured by polls for fear that poll results will only give them the random reflection of citizens' nonattitudes. On the other hand, officials who think that the mass public understands policy issues (and therefore disagree with the statement) will tend to be more attentive to mass opinion as measured by polls because they believe that survey responses represent informed public opinion.

Another reason why policy makers may ignore or minimize the importance of polling and rely instead on other indicators of public opinion is that they think that mass polling does not reflect what 'true' public opinion is as well as these other indicators. As a matter of fact, 22 per cent of the officials in the sample agree or strongly agree with the statement that 'poll results do not really represent what the public truly believes' (66 per cent disagree or strongly disagree with the statement while the remaining 12 per cent are unsure). It is hypothesized that officials who think that poll results do not report what the public truly believes (and therefore agree with the statement) will tend to disregard mass opinion polls for fear that poll results misrepresent true public opinion. On the other hand, officials who believe that poll results report what the public truly believes (and therefore disagree with the statement) will be more attentive to mass opinion as measured by polls.

Do elected officials differ from nonelected officials in their definitions of public opinion? Herbst (1993, 120) argues that the American national parties, and the candidates they support, find surveys about public attitudes on issues to be of great instrumental value not only at election time but also between elections. It is therefore to be expected that polling – especially polls conducted by party organizations – will be more critically important to elected officials than to nonelected officials working for the civil service, the latter relying more on other sources of information about the state of public opinion. However, Herbst theorizes in an American context where Congress members are reelected on their own merits and are therefore quite sensitive to constituency opinion. By contrast, MPs in Ottawa operate in a parliamentary setting of strong party discipline. They have little individual control over their electoral fate, which coincides with the ups and downs of their party, so they are probably less sensitive to mass polling. Perhaps the dividing line is not between elected and nonelected officials but rather between majority and opposition MPs. It is therefore hypothesized that majority MPs are significantly more likely than opposition MPs to identify with a view of public opinion in terms of election results that put them and their party in power.

Explaining Variation in Conceptions of Public Opinion

The rest of the chapter quantitatively explores several variables that may explain differences in the way officials define public opinion. As a first step, table 3 cross-tabulates the ten indicators of public opinion with individual respondents' occupations. The entries in the table report the percentage of respondents within each occupation category who declare that a particular item is 'important' or 'very important.' From the table we see that the different occupations of respondents generate only a moderate variation in their responses. Some values stand as outliers, however, and deserve notice. Taking the values in the column for assistant deputy ministers as a reference, we see that opposition MPs are more likely than deputy ministers to consider radio talk shows as important sources of public opinion. Opposition MPs are less inclined to believe polls are important tools for their definition of public opinion. Majority MPs associate public opinion more often with people they know and less often with public consultations than assistant deputy ministers. Finally, executive assistants are more likely to consider polls and lobbyists as important sources of public opinion. Note that assistant deputy ministers are unusually restrained in their responses. They are typically more reluctant than other respondents to consider a particular indicator as very important.

The data of table 15.3 can only suggest associations between officials' occupations and their definitions of public opinion. Can their occupations also explain in a causal fashion how officials conceptualize public

Table 15.3 Sources of Public Opinion Cross-Tabulated With Respondent Occupation

	Majority MPs	Opposition MPs	Assist. deputy minister	Executive assistant	Communi-cations officer
Elected officials	91	86	100	92	86
Public consultations	60	86	100	84	86
Election results	89	80	75	88	86
Polls	80	36	92	84	86
Focus groups	74	64	92	88	86
People you know	100	89	50	64	57
Newspaper articles	74	82	67	76	86
Lobbyists	57	57	8	84	57
Demonstrations	34	43	42	28	57
Radio talk shows	31	64	8	32	29

Note: Entries are the number of 'important' and 'very important' responses as a percentage of the total.

opinion? Multiple regression is used to examine this question. Three OLS regression models are run in which the dependent variables are indices constructed on the basis of the positive loadings in the three factors identified above. Each index is constructed by giving scores of 4 for 'very important' responses, 3 for 'important,' 2 for 'not very important,' and 1 for 'not important at all.' Because the number of items varies between indices, the scores for each item are averaged to produce final scores ranging from 1 (lowest possible rating) to 4 (highest possible rating) in each index.[7] It is hypothesized that ballot opinion correlates positively with majority MPs and negatively with opposition MPs. Aside from the variables for occupations, there are two additional explanatory variables in the models, one measuring whether decision makers believe that polls represent the true opinions of Canadians, and one measuring how sophisticated they believe the mass public to be.[8] It is hypothesized that the two variables correlate positively with 'mass opinion' and negatively with 'ballot opinion' and 'articulated opinion.'

There are four control variables in the models: one for age, one for language, one measuring officials' attitudes toward government responsiveness,[9] and one measuring how often they consult public opinion on issues related to their work.[10] Exploratory bivariate analyses suggest that older francophone officials who consult public opinion often and who believe government should be responsive to public demands give significantly more 'very important' and 'important' rat-

Table 15.4 Determinants of Variation in How Policy Makers View Public Opinion

Dependent variables	Articulated opinion (1)	Ballot opinion (2)	Mass opinion (3)
Explanatory variables:			
Francophone	.276 (2.59)[a]	−.002 (.61)	.477 (2.87)[a]
Consult opinion more	.102 (2.33)[a]	.090 (1.53)[c]	−.014 (−.10)
Responsive government	.130 (1.10)	.110 (1.22)	.145(1.33)
Older	.032 (1.59)[c]	.075 (1.56)[c]	.050 (1.10)
Majority MP	.076 (.49)	−.077 (−.49)	.078 (.37)
Opposition MP	.420 (2.98)[a]	−.275 (−1.76)[b]	−.309 (−1.50)[c]
Executive assistant	.368 (1.79)[b]	.090 (.33)	.280 (1.00)
Communications officer	.421 (2.20)[b]	.010 (.50)	.310 (1.40)[c]
Representative polls	−.025 (−.41)	−.167 (−1.52)[c]	.209 (1.47)[c]
Sophisticated public	−.225 (−1.50)[c]	−.346 (−1.77)[b]	.080 (.96)
Constant	1.976 (3.36)[a]	3.354 (5.65)[a]	3.245 (4.98)[a]
Adjusted r-square	.31	.04	.22
F-ratio	3.60[a]	1.35 [c]	2.57[a]

Note: Cells are the OLS coefficients and (corresponding *t* ratios). N = 105. The reference occupation category is assistant deputy minister.
[a] Significant at the 1% level (one-tailed t test).
[b] Significant at the 5% level.
[c] Significant at the 10% level.

ings in their evaluations of indicators of public opinion than other officials. These variables may introduce biases in the data and these biases may have an impact on the regression estimates. It is therefore necessary to add them in the regression equations as controls. Bivariate tests show that ideology and gender have no statistical impact on how officials define public opinion. These variables are therefore left out of the analyses.

Table 15.4 presents the results. Looking first at the control variables, we see that, with a few exceptions, age, language, support of government responsiveness, and frequent opinion consultation tend to correlate positively with the dependent variables as hypothesized. From model 1 (articulated opinion) we see that the dependent variable correlates negatively with public opinion sophistication as hypothesized. We also see that opposition MPs, executive assistants, and communications officers are more likely to define public opinion in terms of articulated opinion than assistant deputy ministers (the reference group). From model 2 we see that officials' rating of ballot opinion as a channel of transmission of public opinion is negatively affected by their belief that the public is sophisticated and by the feeling that polls are representative of true public opinion, as hypothesized. Model 2 also indicates that opposition MPs conceptualize public opinion as ballot opinion significantly less often than assistant deputy ministers (the reference category). The other coefficients for respondents' occupations all fail the conventional test of statistical significance. This suggests that all occupations that were included in the survey, except opposition MPs, tend to view public opinion in terms of ballot opinion. From model 3 we see that, contrary to the previous model, officials' conceptualization of public opinion in terms of mass surveys is positively influenced by their belief that polls represent what the public truly believes, but it remains unaffected by their attitude toward public opinion sophistication. Like model 2, however, the data show that opposition MPs are significantly less likely than assistant deputy ministers to conceptualize public opinion in terms of mass opinion.

Several results stand out. First, we know that Canadian officials view elections as one of the most important channels through which they get their information about, and construct their image of, the state of public opinion. Tables 15.3 and 15.4 confirm that this is true of all occupations except opposition MPs. The wide consensus about the importance of elections as sources of public opinion is reflected by the absence of explained variance in the equation of model 2 (ballot opinion). There is considerably more explained variation in the two other models. Articulated opinion is less important in the eyes of majority MPs and assistant deputy ministers than it is with other officials, especially opposition MPs. On the other hand, assistant deputy ministers agree that mass opinion is important more often than opposition MPs but less often than communications officers.

Second, opposition MPs appear to differ most from other officials in their definition of public opinion. They are more likely to view public opinion as articulated opinion than any other occupation category. They are also less inclined to define public opinion in terms of majority ballot opinion and mass opinion than other occupations, including majority MPs. Having lost the 1993, 1997, and 2000 federal elections by a larger parliamentary seat margin than the popular vote margin, one can speculate that MPs from opposition parties were holding a grudge against the Liberal majority and less willing than majority MPs to consider the verdict of recent electoral consultations as synonymous with pubic opinion. A related explanation is that opposition MPs, who represent primarily regional interests (Quebec and Western provinces), are more likely than majority MPs to conceptualize public opinion in terms of regionally articulated elite opinions than in terms of national election results or mass surveys. Whatever the case may be, further statistical tests show that the ten *Bloquistes* in the sample are not significantly different from the other opposition MPs in their definition of public opinion.

Third, the negative coefficients for the variable for sophisticated public indicate that officials who believe that the public is informed and sophisticated are significantly less likely to view public opinion in terms of articulated opinion and majority opinion than officials who believe the public is unsophisticated. This makes sense. Officials who believe that the mass public is sophisticated are probably satisfied that mass surveys give them sufficiently accurate and reliable information about the state of public opinion. They do not need to rely on elite opinion or election results as often as those officials who believe that the public is unsophisticated. By contrast, officials who believe that the mass public is uninformed and unsophisticated do not find polls to be a reliable or valid source of public opinion. They prefer to rely on the opinion articulated by the elite and the news media and on election results, because these measures do not require a belief that the masses are informed and sophisticated.

Conclusion

When it comes to knowing what the public thinks, officials in Ottawa use a variety of sources that can be summarized in terms of three easily recognizable dimensions of public opinion. The most salient dimension, labelled 'ballot opinion,' associates public opinion with elections. This is an important point of divergence between Canada and the United States. There is no published evidence that American policy makers conceptualize public opinion in terms of election results. The second most salient dimension correlates positively with polls and is therefore labelled 'mass opinion.' The relatively low saliency of this dimension is consistent with the finding from figure 15.1 that Canadian government officials do not rely primarily on mass polling as a source of information on public opinion. The third dimension is comprised of disaggregated forms of 'articulated opinion' that are not always salient among our informants. Canadian officials do not consider interest groups as a major source of public opinion, and this is another point of divergence with the United States.

The evidence that was presented in this chapter supports a scenario whereby Canadian government officials recognize the problems associated with the low information level among the mass public[11] and are therefore reluctant to rely too much on mass surveys as a source of information about public opinion. However, this reluctance on the part of Canadian officials to use mass opinion surveys as a source of public opinion does not translate into more reliance on articulated opinion as is the case in the United States. Instead, Canadian government officials use election results to shape their perception of where majority opinion stands on issues and to persuade others and themselves that the public is onside. If correct, the scenario has obvious implications for democratic representation and governance in Canada. The absence of checks and balances and the strong party discipline in the Canadian system, compounded by an ineffective parliamentary opposition (at least until 2004), have contributed to a concentration of powers to an extraordinary degree in the hands of the prime minister. The Canadian government is sheltered from public opinion and this permits its officials to downplay mass opinion and the preferences of organized groups and to look instead to their belief in an electoral mandate to govern as guidance on policy direction. Whether the same pattern will persist under minority governments is still unclear.

Based on evidence from the United States (Powlick 1995; Herbst 1998), it was assumed at the start of the study that their occupations have a major influence on how officials view public opinion. In reality, however, with the exception of opposition MPs and pollsters, our informants do not differ much in their definition of public opinion (at least not as much as expected based on comparable U.S. studies). In fact, they appear remarkably like-minded in this regard. The relative similarity of views about public opinion may be a reflection of the relative similarity of occupations in the sample of respondents. Respondents in the study work, for the most part, in the same environment and share the same institutional culture. It would be interesting to investigate further how the views of journalists, opposition party activists, and pollsters differ from those of government officials.

There is a firmly anchored belief in the popular folklore of politics that decision makers are highly attentive to public opinion. This is apparently confirmed by the data in our survey. Forty-four per cent of officials declare that they consult public opinion regularly and 93 per cent at least occasionally (see table 15.1). However, the presumption of attentiveness stands in stark contrast with recent evidence that politicians in Ottawa have largely ignored the preferences of the Canadian public measured by mass surveys (Mendelsohn 2003; Pétry and Mendelsohn 2004). Have Canadian politicians truly become unresponsive to public opinion? Or is the observed lack of responsiveness to public opinion simply a methodological artifact of the use of mass surveys as a measure of public opinion? Policy might appear to be more in harmony with public opinion measured by other means. What this research suggests is that this appearance-of-harmony effect is probably at work among government officials in Ottawa. A definition of public opinion that gives centre stage to election results allows government decision makers to feel as if they are more attentive to public opinion than they would otherwise appear to be, if using a narrow definition of public opinion in terms of mass polling.

NOTES

I wish to thank Evert Lindquist, Doug McArthur, Matthew Mendelsohn, and the editors of this volume for their stimulating insights. I would also like to thank Derry O'Connor for his able research assistance. Needless to say, any errors remain my own.

1 According to the auditor general of Canada, Communication Canada co-ordinated 576 public opinion research projects in 2002–03, at a cost of $23.7 million. The departments that spent the most were Health Canada, Human Resources and Development, Natural Resources Canada, and Industry Canada. More than 80 per cent of this amount was spent on custom public opinion research commissioned from polling firms to fit the research needs of government departments and agencies. The rest was spent on so-called syndicated polls that, unlike custom polls, are not available to the public.

2 The number of questionnaires actually returned was 125, but 20 were rejected because they were not complete (in most cases the respondent failed to identify an occupation).

3 The departments are Human Resources and Development Canada, Department of Foreign Affairs and International Trade, Department of National Defence, Department of Justice, Department of Finance, Intergovernmental Affairs, and the Privy Council Office.

4 Not all the people targeted for an interview were willing to answer our questions. Informants who were willing to be interviewed were most

generous with their time and many went to great length to accommodate our questions.

5 Childs (1965) compiled over 50 definitions of public opinion. Forty years later, the conceptual landscape has become even more confusing. The academic literature on the nature of public opinion – indeed its very existence – and its relation to voting and public policy is divided by several apparently irreconcilable theoretical and methodological fault lines and wrought with a myriad of unanswered questions.

6 Entman and Herbst (2001, 208–9)'s classification includes two additional referents. They define perceived majorities as the perceptions of political actors of where majority opinion stands on issues. The other referent is latent opinion, which is shaped by the underlying beliefs behind opinions and is where the collective stance ends up after debate. Without denying their importance in a post-positivist framework, these definitions are of little help because, unlike mass opinion and articulated opinion, they cannot be operationalized with the method used in this chapter.

7 Factor scores of individual respondents were used instead of indices in an exploratory analysis. The use of indices produces slightly better results but the basic findings are similar in both analyses.

8 Respondents' belief in the representative nature of polls was measured by the following prompt: 'Please indicate whether you Strongly Agree, Agree, Disagree, Strongly Disagree or are Unsure with the statement: "Most poll results do not really represent what the public truly believes."' The prompt about public opinion sophistication reads as follows: 'Please indicate whether you Strongly Agree, Agree, Disagree, Strongly Disagree or are Unsure with the statement: "The public simply does not have the sophistication necessary to make reasonable decision on most policy issues."' The variables are constructed by giving scores of 1 for 'strongly agree' responses, 2 for 'agree,' 3 for 'disagree,' and 4 for 'strongly disagree.' 'Unsure' responses are reported as missing values.

9 The corresponding prompt reads as follows: 'Please indicate whether you Strongly Agree, Agree, Disagree, Strongly Disagree, or are Unsure with the statement: "We make policy in order to respond to public demand."' The variable is constructed by giving scores of 4 for 'strongly agree' responses, 3 for 'agree' 2 for 'disagree' and 1 for 'strongly disagree.' 'Unsure' responses are reported as missing values. See table 1 for the distribution of responses on this item.

10 The corresponding prompt reads as follows: 'When thinking of issues related to your work, how often do you consult public opinion before making a decision or a recommendation on those issues? Please check one

answer: Always/almost always; Often/regularly; Sometimes/occasionally; Never/almost never; Unsure.' The variable is constructed by giving scores of 4 for 'always/almost always' responses, 3 for 'often/regularly,' 2 for 'sometimes/occasionally,' and 1 for 'never/almost never.' 'Unsure' responses are reported as missing values. See table 15.1 for the distribution of responses on this item.

11 For evidence that the Canadian public remains as uninformed as the U.S. public, see Fournier 2002 and Johnston et al. 1996.

REFERENCES

Althaus, Scott. 2003. *Collective Preferences in Democratic Politics: Opinion Surveys and the Will of the People.* Cambridge: Cambridge University Press.

Blumer, Herbert. 1948. 'Public Opinion and Public Opinion Polling.' *American Sociological Review* 13, 542–554.

Bourdieu, Pierre. 1979. 'Public Opinion Does Not Exist.' In Armand Mattelart and Seth Siegelbaum, eds., *Communication and Class Struggle*, Vol. 1, *Capitalism, Imperialism*, 124–30. New York: International General.

Converse, Philip E. 1964. 'The Nature of Belief Systems Among Mass Publics.' In David Apter, ed., *Ideology and Discontent*, 206–21. New York: Free Press.

– 1987. 'Changing Conceptions of Public Opinion in the Political Process.' *Public Opinion Quarterly* 51, S12–S24.

Childs, Harwood, L. 1965. *Public Opinion. Nature, Formation, and Role.* Princeton, NJ: Van Nostrand.

Delli Carpini, Michael X., and Scott Keeter. 1996. *What Americans Know About Politics and Why it Matters.* New Haven, CT: Yale University Press.

Entman, Robert M., and Susan Herbst. 2001. 'Reframing Public Opinion As We Have Known It.' In Lance Bennett and Robert M. Entman, eds., *Mediated Politics: Communication and the Future of Democracy*, 203–25. New York: Cambridge University Press.

Fournier, Patrick. 2002. 'The Uninformed Canadian Voter.' In Joanna Everitt and Brenda O'Neill, eds., *Citizen Politics: Research and Theory in Canadian Political Behaviour*, 92–109. Don Mills, ON: Oxford University Press.

Fuchs, Dieter, and Barbara Pfetsch. 1996. *The Observation of Public Opinion by the Governmental System.* Science Center Berlin. http://skylla.wz-berlin.de/pdf/1996/iii96–105.pdf.

Ginsberg, Benjamin. 1986. *The Captive Public: How Mass Opinion Promotes State Power.* New York: Basic Books.

Glasser, Theodore, and Charles Salmon, eds. 1995. *Public Opinion and the Communication of Consent*. New York: Guilford.

Herbst, Susan. 1993. *Numbered Voices: How Opinion Polling has Shaped American Politics*. Chicago: University of Chicago Press.

– 1998. *Reading Public Opinion: How Political Actors View the Democratic Process*. Chicago: University of Chicago Press.

Howlett, Michael, and M. Ramesh. 2003. *Studying Public Policy. Policy Cycles and Policy Subsystems*. 2nd ed. Toronto: Oxford University Press.

Iyengar, Shanto, and Donald Kinder. 1987. *News That Matters*. Chicago: University of Chicago Press.

Johnston, Richard, André Blais, Elisabeth Gidengil, and Neil Nevitte. 1996. *The Challenge of Direct Democracy. The 1992 Canadian Referendum*. Montreal and Kingston: McGill-Queen's Unversity Press.

Kohut, Andrew. 1998. *Washington Leaders Wary of Public Opinion*. Washington, DC: Pew Research Center for People and the Press.

Lippman, Walter. 1925. *The Phantom Public*. New York: Harcourt Brace.

Mendelsohn, Matthew. 2003. *Listen Up Canada*. Toronto: Friends of Canadian Broadcasting. www.friends.ca/news/articles 07020306.

Olson, Mancur. 1965 [1971]. *The Logic of Collective Action. Public Goods and the Theory of Groups*. New York: Schocken Books.

Pétry, François. 1999. 'The Opinion-Policy Relationship in Canada.' *The Journal of Politics* 61, 540–50.

Pétry, François, and Matthew Mendelsohn. 2004. 'Public Opinion and Policy-making in Canada 1994–2001.' *Canadian Journal of Political Science* 37, 1–25.

Powlick, Philip J. 1995. 'The Sources of Public Opinion for American Foreign Policy Officials.' *International Studies Quarterly* 39, 427–51.

Zaller, John R. 1992. *The Nature and Origins of Mass Opinion*. Cambridge: Cambridge University Press.

16 The Invisible Private Service: Consultants and Public Policy in Canada

KIMBERLY SPEERS

Introduction

In 1967, John Deutsch contended that civil servants would have a reduced role in the development of new policies because of the 'increasing use of private consulting firms, research institutes and the latest phenomenon, the so-called think tank' (Meredith and Jones 1970, 383). Almost forty years later, the rise of the consultant has been one of the most significant changes in Canadian public policy analysis, evaluation, development and implementation. The latest figures available state that as of 1998, 70 per cent of all business and government organizations in Canada have used the services of a management consultant at least once in the period 1993–98. Especially in North America and Britain, the management consulting industry has experienced tremendous growth in both the size and services offered (Buono 2001) over the past two decades. Numerous reasons have been given for the increased use of consultants, including the increased deregulation and outsourcing of services, the impact of globalization, the increased use of information technology to manage and operate services, and the international management trends emphasizing competition, re-engineering, downsizing, performance measurement, and information management (Wooldridge 1997). Specific to the public sector, these factors, to varying degrees, have all had an impact on how governments manage personnel, deliver services and develop policy. Furthermore, all levels of government have purchased management consultant services, ranging from the delivery and analysis of policy advice to the implementation and evaluation of policy directives, services and programs.

This chapter introduces the reader to the increasing participation of the consulting industry in Canadian policy development and analysis, a field of study that is neither well understood nor well defined (Buono 2001), especially from a Canadian perspective (Saint-Martin 2000; Bakvis 1997). In one of the few pieces on the impact of consultants on public policy, Herman Bakvis argues the federal government executive is increasingly demanding more political and less formal advice from a variety of external advisors instead of the traditional means of relying on one trusted advisor for policy advice (1997, 84–85). He questions whether the rise in the prominence and importance of external policy agents (think tanks, polling firms, and management consulting organizations) have 'helped to strengthen the capacity of the core political executive to direct the affairs of state or whether it undermines the capacity of the executive to do so, that is contributing to the hollowing out of the centre of government' (85). Management consulting firms have carved a niche in government where they are not, according to Bakvis, seen as challenging the power within the core of government; instead, consultants are viewed as 'instruments that executives can use to help implement their agendas' (112).

The primary reason for the dearth of research on the role of consultants in public policy is the difficulty of garnering hard data. Neither the federal or provincial levels of government are currently able to estimate annual expenditures on management consultants. Although some governments listed such firms and related contract values in their public accounts, information regarding the nature of the services provided was starkly absent. Sometimes, as in Manitoba, information on total spending on external consultants was not available at all. In most other cases, Canadian governments will only provide information on contracts above $10,000.

Another related challenge for researchers is that even when monetary figures are available, it is impossible to determine how much money is spent specifically on policy-related contracts. Further, even contracts not categorized as 'policy oriented' may nonetheless require a certain amount of policy analysis. And depending on how contracted service work unfolds, policy analysis may be warranted – and undertaken – even though it was not requested in the government proposal. It should also be noted that those attempting to assess how much policy analysis is undertaken by consultants for governments may be misled by government officials' over-classification of some areas of government work as 'internal administrative policy,' when it is clear that consultants hired to develop and assess such policy could also have an impact on the public in some manner.

Research on this topic is further challenged by the lack of results-based analysis. As noted, information on government spending on consultants varies across jurisdictions and, when available, this information only tells the researcher about the inputs (i.e., money spent on consulting) and nothing about the processes or results of the consulting contract. Consequently, questions about consultants' involvement in policy analysis, as compared to their work in more management-related processes, have yet to be answered. Also lacking is information about specific research methodologies employed by consulting firms, while the extent to which consultants make palpable recommendations and propose substantive policy options remains equally unknown. Finally, the dynamic and multifaceted relationship between consultants and government clients often transcends their purely legal, contractual relationship. As a result, the amount of client/government control over the research process and the ability of consultants to influence policy through analysis remains unknown outside of these legal relationships, at least until further research can be done on this topic. Lindquist comments on the need for research to examine the spending patterns of policy units during the last decade, including envelopes for contracts issued to external free agents for policy analysis (forthcoming).

To develop a better understanding of the consulting industry's role in policy analysis and development, the first part of this chapter will describe different types of consulting work conducted for government clients. Following this, the question of why governments hire consultants will be considered. In closing, a brief analysis of the impact of such consultants' contributions to government policy analysis will be offered. It will be argued that governments at all levels should track spending on consultants, and that further research and discussion needs to take place to determine the appropriate level of input and influence the private sector consultant has on policy analysis in Canada. If politicians and citizens alike are lamenting a democratic deficit in Canadian politics, one way of addressing it is to ensure that the politicians and civil servants still control and have primary influence over the public policy agenda and process.

Defining Consultants

A consultant is an individual, partnership, or corporation engaged to give professional advice or services for a fee or, in the case of an internal consultant, give advice in return for a career. The services of a consultant may include sharing knowledge, experiences, processes, models, behaviours, technology, or other assets (Weiss 2003). Defined this broadly, consultants are engineers, lawyers, accountants, and professionals in the areas of information technology, government relations, and public relations. This chapter will focus on management consultants, with some attention to the increased blurring of services offered by some of the government relations firms in Canada.

The Institute of Management Consultancy (IMC) in Britain defines management consultants as 'those organisations and/or individuals that participate in the process of management consultancy within a framework of appropriate and relevant professional disciplines and ethics designed for the activity of management consultancy' (2004). The IMC further explains that management consultancy is 'the provision to management of objective advice and assistance relating to the strategy, structure, management and operations of an organisation in pursuit of its long-term purposes and objectives.'

Typically, management consultants identify who they are to clients by describing what level or type of services they offer. Some consultants identify themselves as generalists whereas others self-identify as specialists. This former type of consultancy offers a broad range of services to clients that may include organization management, policy analysis, leadership development, change management, information management and systems, evaluation, risk management, and human resources training. While a firm or individual may offer these general services, other firms and individuals specialize in one or more of these fields. In a large consulting practice, individual consultants may focus on a geographic region, a policy issue (e.g., health, immigration, policing, education), or a process such as hospital restructuring, the implementation of smart cards, and performance measurement in local governments. Some consulting firms deliver a wide array of services at the national and international levels, whereas other firms or individuals offer specialized 'boutique' services and perhaps only consult within a province or regional area. Finally, some management consultants and firms tend to deal with either the private or public sector, while others consult in both sectors. More attention is being paid by management consultants to the third sector as potential markets, but many management consultants are also aware that this sector has limited funding and hence, some consult on a voluntary basis or do not target this market at all.

It is also important to distinguish between management consultants and government relations consultants or 'lobbyists.' According to the Government Relations Institute of Canada (GRIC), government relations professionals 'facilitate the exchange of information, experience and ideas between decision makers and those affected by the decisions contributing to the development of public policy' (GRIC Web site). Government relations consultants are hired by private sector or not-for-profit organizations and assist their clients in navigating the political system for a specific reason. Reasons for hiring a government relations consultant may include a client's desire to influence a piece of legislation, regulation, policy or some other type of government decision. As noted by the GRIC, lobbyists represent their clients' views and assist them by educating them about the political and decision-making processes of government, conducting research, proposing policies for clients to consider, and, when appropriate and relevant, introducing their clients to decision makers within government.

A government relations consultant can either work for a firm that is in the primary business of lobbying or for a firm or not-for-profit organization as a full- or part-time government relations consultant. For example, many of the global pharmaceutical companies have at least one person who deals with government relations in some capacity. While the government relations consultant tends to concentrate on providing advocacy services on behalf of their clients, management consultant services are geared toward solving management and organizational issues. Depending on the project, however, these separate lines of business can become blurred. A management consulting firm may also provide strategic advice on how a client should interact with the government or how it needs to develop stronger relationships within a policy community to achieve its goals. Likewise, a government relations consultant can also provide advice and direction to a client on policy or organizational issues. Nonetheless, the differences between an advocacy firm and a management consulting firm are fairly well known to clients, who choose among specialized firms accordingly. Importantly, though, both the management and government relations consultant can have a significant impact on public policy.

Another relevant difference in this field is between external and internal consultants. Evert Lindquist describes external free agents as consisting of 'policy experts from consulting firms, think tanks, other governments, or universities from outside the public service ... whereas internal free agents are experts from elsewhere in the public service' (forthcoming). Meredith and Jones argue that even in the late 1960s, both the federal and provincial levels of government were classifying some of their positions as management consultants because they recognized the need to build in-house capacity to promote cost-effectiveness and to support staff training and learning. Furthermore, some government employees believe that they are the only people intimately familiar with their organizations, and that only they can fully understand the organization's needs and make pertinent recommendations. In this case, the government client would prefer to hire an internal consultant over an external consultant since it takes time and money to educate an external consultant about the current state within a government department.

This practice of classifying certain positions within the public service continues as governments recognize the value of their own employees' expertise and experience. For example, the government of Canada has established its own consulting agency, Consulting and Audit Canada. This agency has approximately one hundred professional consultants who offer the following services to the rest of government: advice, research, consultation, analysis, surveys, facilitation, evaluation, review, problem diagnosis, business case development, training, benchmarking, environmental scanning, preparation of government documents and discussion papers, and direct participation in public-service management tasks (Consulting and Audit Canada 2002). Although not designed to compete with the private sector, this new agency is able to market itself as a body that has the experience and expertise with Canadian federal government issues. The agency also provides consulting services to other governments and, according to Consulting and Audit Canada (2002), they have had client engagements with over forty countries and international organizations. No provincial government has established an equivalent to Consulting and Audit Canada, but they do have departments in which positions are classified as consultants.

Finally, it is important to distinguish the firm consultant from the individual consultant. Consultants in a firm offering consulting services have a wide range of services and knowledge available to them. Depending on the size of the firm, international knowledge management databases may be available and consultants may be assigned to projects anywhere in the world. In contrast, individual consultants do not have access to a shared knowledge management database and rely on their own expertise and experience to sell consulting services. Individual management consultants must be able to market their skills and knowledge to clients. Hence, individual consultants tend to be well-connected retired public servants and politicians, former management consultants from the larger firms, and senior-level management from quasi-government agencies and the private sector in general. In some cases, an individual consultant may also contract his or her services to a firm if the firm does not have the individual's expertise.

History of Consulting in Canada

The consulting business has existed in Canada for almost a century. Despite more awareness about the complexities of governing and the elaboration of consulting services offered to clients, the negative perception of the consultant developed in the pre-WWII period was further exacerbated in the 1940s and 1950s by a business that was 'attractive to charlatans and quacks who preyed upon the gullible' (Mellett 1988, 5).

This negative image has not been entirely shed but was somewhat alleviated in the 1960s when reputable accounting firms began to offer management and information control consulting services. At the same time, the Royal Commission on Government Organization (often called the Glassco Commission) in 1960 was an important catalyst for the growth and acceptance of management consultants in government (Mellett 1988; Tunnoch 1964; Saint Martin 1998). The Glassco Commission was established to 'inquire into and report upon the organization and methods of operation of the departments and agencies of the Government of Canada and to recommend the changes therein which they consider would best promote efficiency, economy, and improved service in the dispatch of public business' (Government of Canada 1963, vol. 5). The commission made many recommendations to improve the economy of the public sector and to shape the overall climate of governing. One of the most controversial themes in the final report was its support for the application of business principles and practices to certain government operations. With these recommendations came the need to learn more about how business operations and principles could be applied to government. Management consultants were then hired to work with and in numerous government departments.

Denis Saint-Martin (2000) notes that many of the management consultants hired to work on the commission ended up working in senior management positions in the Civil Service Commission and in the newly created central agency, the Treasury Board Secretariat. A.W. Johnson, the deputy provincial treasurer with the province of Saskatchewan at the time of the Glassco Commission, recognized the impact the commission had on the growth of consulting and wryly commented that, 'For a few – the management consultants – the reports and the public interest which they have aroused create a happy hunting ground where new commissions and new studies can be proposed with confidence – all of them requiring the specialized skills of management consultants' (Tunnoch 1964, 393).

As business principles became more accepted in government, the 1960s saw management consultants become more institutionalized in the processes of government. Major changes to information technology (IT) did not really significantly influence the public sector until the 1990s, when the Internet became publicly available and system-wide technologies were available for organizations to implement. Consulting firms employed thousands of people with a computer background and while the technology 'boom' ended in 2000, many consulting firms are still making healthy profits offering this type of consulting. Over the past decade, consulting firms have further diversified their service offerings to include services such as polling and branding to their public-sector clients (see Petry's chapter in this volume). Along with offering consulting services on information technology, management consultants also offered side services such as strategic advice, change management and business process reviews to complement the IT-related contracts.

While IT-related projects were important to the growth of the management consulting industry, the most significant factor influencing the industry's growth in government in the past two decades has been the acceptance that private-sector principles and practices – those embedded in 'new public management' – trump those of government (Hood 1995). New public management (NPM) reforms have, in one sense, forced governments to look to consultants for assistance in a multitude of activities. In the 1980s and 1990s, most Canadian governments experienced massive cutbacks in financial resources, services offered, and in the number of civil servants delivering programs and services. Increasingly, governments became focused on showing the public how accountable and successful they were through the results they achieved. Planning, policy and research branches seemed to be particularly under attack because it was difficult for politicians to always determine the immediate outcomes or results from these areas, because of heightened 'public servant' bashing in the 1980s and early 1990s, and because of the broadening perception that civil servants had hijacked the policy agenda. Some politicians may have intentionally cut the policy capacity of the civil service to create the impression that they were taking back control of the political agenda (Speers forthcoming). Yet because the tasks of policy analysis, development and implementation still remained necessary, cutbacks made to most of the civil services across Canada gave management consultants an opportunity to fill those policy, planning and research gaps.

Another area targeted for change was the government's direct delivery of services to the public and, in some cases, the internal services within government itself. Even though citizens wanted a more streamlined and efficient government, for the most part citizens still expected governments to maintain most services and programs. Recognizing the political ramifications of simply stopping certain government programs and services, and advocating the 'steering not rowing' philosophy of new public management, many governments looked for ways to deliver services in a more cost-efficient and customer-oriented manner (Gaebler and Osborne 1992). Indeed, part of the mantra of new public management has been for the public sector to 'get out of the business' of delivering services if some other entity can deliver them. Services traditionally delivered by government, such as the sale of liquor, tire recycling, and road repair, were often privatized or some other partnership arrangement between business and government was developed to deliver the rejected services.

Consultants were an integral part of this process, involved either in managing the transition between the old and new ways of delivering services, or as direct participants in new service delivery arrangements. Indeed, consultants have played an important role in packaging, selling and implementing NPM techniques. Governments contemplating institutional change often enlisted the services of consultants to clarify available options and recommend courses of action (Greer 1994). In summary, management consultants have gone from having a limited role in offering services to a government to having a somewhat stable, ubiquitous role in government, while at the same time remaining somewhat invisible to the public eye.

Why Governments Hire Management Consultants

The actual reasons why clients hire consultants are varied and can change throughout the course of a consulting project (Lindquist 2007). While the particulars of a project depend on the client's needs and goals, there are some common reasons for engaging a consultant. One is that the public sector does not have the particular skills or expertise needed to undertake a task. For example, as governments have taken advantage of information technology systems since the early 1990s, they have often not understood what systems were needed, what might be done with them, or how to make those changes. Both technology and management consultants, often from international firms, were then engaged by governments to develop information management systems, e-government frameworks and related policies, despite the dearth of experience in these areas among private-sector consultants. There was hesitancy to create new positions in the civil service for IT-related positions because it was an era when it was politically responsible to be seen reducing, not expanding, the size of government. Furthermore, the IT-related work was seen to be, for the most part, temporary.

Significant internal government cuts and streamlining have considerably reduced the pool of people available to do the work required by legislation or expected by politicians and citizens, thereby also fuelling government demand for management consultants. Hence, consultants may be hired to carry out research projects; to develop, administer, and assess client satisfaction surveys; to develop best practices and benchmarking databases; and to conduct feasibility and risk assessment studies or change management projects. Another impact of downsizing the civil service is that undertaking projects of short duration may be more cost-efficient, resulting in the hiring of more external consultants for the length of these projects. To increase the internal capacity of remaining career civil servants, a consultant may also be engaged to train civil servants to do the jobs themselves. Knowledge transfer is increasingly becoming important to government clients purchasing consulting services, in areas such as computer training, information management, board governance, evidence-based decision making, and protection of privacy.

Governments may also hire consultants when they need independent opinions. New Public Management was characterized by a view that politicians are right to distrust civil servants. In hiring management consultants, politicians can use their perspective as a 'check' on the civil service; likewise, if the civil service hires a management consultant, doing so helps to legitimate its work. For example, a government department may seek the services of a larger, well-known consulting firm because the 'higher-ups' the department reports to want a 'big name' firm to conduct research and provide recommendations. Alternatively, individual management consultants with smaller practices may be sought out for their reputations and expertise. This can be a rather frustrating situation for civil servants if retired or laid-off public servants have been hired on as management consultants and then return to offer an independent opinion. Civil servants also cringe when they are required to inform consultants of the relevant situation, only to see their own informal suggestions echoed in that consultant's formal recommendations.

Government departments also occasionally hire a management consultant to facilitate a strategic, business or operational planning exercise. It is generally easier for a person external to the organization to assist the group in finding solutions and to deal with difficult situations or personalities. Using a consultant also helps to ensure that everyone participates, that the issue at hand is being addressed, that consensus is reached among the different positions, and that hidden agendas do not dominate the process and outcomes. The consultant's experience in working with other groups in similar exercises can prove to be decisive in such sensitive situations. Nonetheless, it is important to appreciate that unanticipated consequences for internal policy analysis may flow from this management consultant facilitation; a consultant can influence how policy analysis is perceived and prioritized depending on his or her personal biases and style of facilitation.

An example of a management consulting firm conducting a review for the federal government illustrates their potential impact. KPMG recently conducted a review of Aboriginal Tourism Team Canada (ATTC), on behalf of Aboriginal Business Canada (a branch of Industry Canada). As noted in their report, a review of the ATTC was undertaken 'to determine to what extent ATTC has been successful in influencing and developing tourism policy and programs for the benefit of Aboriginal people' (Rostum 2002). In preparation for the final report on ATTC, KPMG conducted a review of relevant documents and databases, did a survey of Aboriginal tourism sector organizations, developed a literature review, and conducted interviews with ATTC Board members, regional Aboriginal tourism associations, and government partners. Upon completion of the research, KPMG made several recommendations to further enhance Aboriginal tourism in Canada. This experience suggests how a management consulting firm has numerous opportunities to conduct influential policy analysis and thus shape government policy directions.

Finally, in the past decade, consultants have been increasingly asked by the public sector to facilitate and manage public consultations, which involve communicating with the public and conducting focus groups, workshops, townhall meetings, interviews, and surveys. While a government may engage management consultants in a public consultation to reduce any biases, they may also be involved so that the government can distance itself from any controversial issues that require public consultation. Once the final recommendations or decisions are made, there will likely be some individuals or groups disappointed with the results. A government can then state that a private-sector firm developed the survey instrument, administered the survey, and developed the final report outlining the major policy issues at stake, the available policy options, and a list of recommendations. The hope often seems to be that making a policy decision can become less politicized as management consultants become more involved in the policy process.

Impact of Consultants on the Policy Process and Policy Analysis

The relationship between management consultants and the public sector is characterized by both tension and opportunity. On the one hand, the increase of management consultants working with civil servants has given the latter an opportunity to gain external knowledge to improve their processes, programs, services, and policies. It is also an opportunity for management consultants to hone their skills and expand their practice and service offerings. There is also the opportunity for programs, services, processes, and policy to improve and to better reflect the goals of the politicians and citizens. On the other hand, there is also tension and concern about the impact of management consultants on policy issues, processes and structures in Canada.

As noted at the outset of this chapter, the numerous reforms to the Canadian federal public service since the 1980s have made management consultants an integral part of how the civil service develops, implements, analyses, and evaluates policy, and how it operates and delivers services. The biggest concern about this development reflects the different goals of the private and public sectors. Recognizing that profit is the primary motive for a private-sector company, there is a concern about how this profit focus conflicts with government's wider goals. Remembering that a private-sector consultant's goal is to sell services and make a profit, we must acknowledge that in their quest to develop business, management consultants also create management trends or problems to fix. There is thus a tension between creating problems and selling solutions. It then becomes part of the management consultant's job to tell organizations, including government, that there are better ways of strategizing, developing policy and plans, running services, and delivering programs – and that management consultants are best positioned to provide such solutions.

Abrahmson (1991) comments that management consultants are partially responsible for setting many managerial and operational trends in the economy. Bertrand Venard further argues that while the establishment of such trends often improves management thought, 'the underlying danger is when these concepts are simplified and utilized without full and proper diagnosis, as they are typically offered to enterprises [or governments] as universal, scientific, and efficient means of improving organizational performance' (2001, 171–172). Especially within the larger consulting firms, templates of consulting processes and solutions are often shared among consultants to market to their current and potential clients. These 'one-size-fits-all' approaches to consulting are often developed with the private sector in mind, so when marketed to the public sector, few, if any, changes are made to reflect the differences between the two sectors. This should be a cause for concern if the focus of the service being delivered to government is customers and not citizens, with rights and obligations different from those of customers.

Another related area of concern is the background of those consulting for government. While the private and public sectors overlap somewhat in terms of processes and systems, consulting for the two sectors also entails some significant differences. Consultants trained in business, or with engineering and computer degrees, typically have little training in how a government works. Such consultants thus find it difficult to identify the fundamental differences involved in working in private- and public-sector environments. Hence, public-sector reporting mechanisms may seem to be 'burdensome' and full of 'red tape,' but to those more familiar with the decision making and reporting processes within government, they are deemed to be essential in fulfilling the requirements of accountability and ministerial responsibility and meeting requirements mandated by legislation and regulations. Further, legislation, regulations or political or cultural conventions often shape the projects consultants take on. External consultants hired to assess a policy with an eye to developing policy options for a government department thus need to be aware not only of the substance of the policy, but also of government culture, legislation and regulations, and conventions. Training in political science, public policy, or public administration may thus be necessary for those who consult with government and lack experience working with government in some other capacity.

The ultimate goal in business is to make a profit, whereas in government, the goals of a policy or decision are usually a great deal more complex, involving multiple stakeholders with different goals and interests. Consequently, highly regarded qualities in the private sector, such as efficiency and speediness, have to be balanced with equity and effectiveness in the public sector.

Engaging management consultants in government unavoidably undermines institutional memory and policy capacity. For example, management consultants often conduct an environmental scan and write a report recommending new benchmarks and performance measures for a policy sector. In the course of conducting the research, the management consultant often takes away the contacts made during the research. Unless these contacts are carefully documented, the government department or agency may be left without clear reasons as to why some information was not included, and whether and why the performance measurement benchmarks might evolve. Thus, many nuances may be lost that might benefit the project in either the short or long term. Moreover, when management consultants complete a project, they take away part of the institutional capacity for the organization to conduct the work in the future or for the organization to benefit from learning about a specific issue. Finally, department evaluations suffer when, as is typically the case, information or materials are incompletely passed from the management consultant to the client at the end of the project.

Ethical behaviour in the workplace has become increasingly important in recent years. Given that management consultants are not part of the public service, it is important to identify their own codes of conduct and to determine if management consultants are bound by the ethical codes of a department or government when hired. Some management firms adhere to a code of ethics, and management consultants who belong to the Canadian Association of Management Consultants are committed to a common code, but many management consultants are not bound by any professional code of ethics. The issue of ethics can arise in a consulting engagement in many ways. For example, some may argue that underbidding a project may not be ethical (Pfeiffer and Jones 1985). Having inexperienced consultants do the majority of work where the proposal stated the expertise utilized would be from the senior management consultants is also unethical (Robinson and Zody

1988/89). Even if the senior consultant provides quality control in supervising any documents released to the client, it is ethically important for consultants to be explicit about the experience of those consultants who will actually be doing the work.

Revelations in the Gomery Commission hearings in the spring of 2005 raised high-profile ethical issues concerning government contracts with consultants (of all kinds), the level of political involvement in the awarding of contracts to external consultants, and access to information about contracts between government and an external consultant. Whereas before consultants were somewhat invisible to the average citizen, the commission hearings made citizens aware of the extent to which consultants are involved in developing, marketing and delivering services on behalf of government. The government has been criticized for its lack of ethics, accountability, and access to information regarding this case. The Gomery Commission has also tarnished the image of consultants in the sense that it highlighted kickbacks, consultants not performing the work required in a contract, and people being hired because of their familial or political relations. Perhaps most importantly, the federal Liberal sponsorship scandal emphasized the accountability gaps between government and consultants and between politicians and civil servants. The full impact of the Gomery Commission has yet to be determined, but it is clear that the federal government's procurement processes have become more formalized and stringent, and accountability procedures and guarantees strengthened. We thus have good reasons to expect that such changes will significantly constrain the activities of management consultants in federal departments.

Management consultants' involvement in policy and decision making also has an impact on accountability. Donald Savoie argues that 'policy issues no longer respect organizational boundaries and, as a result, policy-making has now become horizontal, consultative and porous' (2004, 7), with management consultants being an important part of this change. Although Savoie focuses more on implications for civil servants' accountability to their ministers, he makes a strong case for developing new ways to understand accountability that take into account the roles played by various policy process actors. The challenge of holding consultants accountable is that 'consultants do not have a minister, they have clients; however, career officials not only have ministers, they must also live with the consequences of their policy advice'

(2004, 11). Usually the only consequence of a poorly managed consultant engagement is that the reputation of the consultant is tarnished,
thus diminishing work opportunities with the affected department or
government.

What of management consultants' accountability to citizens? Given
that management consultants are involved in every stage of the policy
process (policy agenda setting, development, implementation, analysis,
evaluation and communication) and have consulted for all levels of
government, citizens who want to get involved in the decision-making
process or want to learn more about why decisions were made (e.g.,
through an access to information request) may be at the mercy of the
private sector. The public still has access to records concerning specific
policy decisions; however, the files may not contain all of the information pertinent to the decision, as some is 'privatized' within the consulting firms. The federal Privacy Act provides citizens with the right to
access personal information held by the government and to protection
of that information against unauthorized use and disclosure. But there
are still loopholes. As noted in the 2003 Auditor General's Report, the
office did not audit the records of the private-sector contractors in the
well-known sponsorship scandal.

One of the most challenging aspects of management consultants'
accountability to government is the private/public partnership. Research in the evaluation of these relatively novel partnerships is still
rare. In one of the few studies of a partnership between a government
department and a management consulting firm, David Whorley (2001)
explores the partnership between Ontario's Ministry of Community
and Social Services (COMSOC) and Andersen Consulting, with particular attention to accountability issues. He finds that collaborative
partnerships and democratic accountability are in tension and that the
'Andersen-Comsoc affair suggests an important power imbalance between the partners and the associated displacement of public concerns
for private ones' (328). Whorley notes that the goals of each party
collided in that COMSCO was trying to support the agenda of the
Conservative government of reducing overall costs whereas Andersen's
interest was profit. He observes that other studies conducted on pri-
vate-public partnerships reveal that accountability is often an issue
between both sectors.

In a recent scandal concerning Hydro One in Ontario, former Progressive Conservative minister Frank Klees argued that the awarding of over
$6 million worth of untendered contracts for consulting contributed to

the Conservative Party's defeat in the last Ontario election. 'Who is accountable to the public? It's always going to be the person who has their name on the ballot. It's never going to be 'Mr. Consultant.' They wander off in to the sunshine, and they'll be drinking their tequilas on the beach while we answer to the people who elected us' (Hiscox 2004). Klees's comments underscore the sense in which policy oversight and accountability issues must be taken seriously in all consultant/government relationships, by both political parties and the general public.

Consultants and Public Policy

Others in this book raise the question of who should play which roles in the development of public policy. This question is extremely important in assessing the relationship between management consultants and government. Remembering that the ultimate goal for the private sector is increasing profit margins, and that the vast majority of management consultants come from a business and accounting background, we should not be surprised that consultants may not be familiar with the democratic principles of equity, equality, fairness and justice that are central to government operations in Canada. Yet if consultants simply implemented what governments desired, the issue of policy orientation or one's background would not be of concern.

Anthony Buono takes a different perspective, arguing that for management consultants, 'the boundary between dispensing advice and managing systems is becoming increasingly blurred' (2001, viii). Numerous consulting firms now advertise an ability to give policy advice to governments as a key part of their service offerings. For example, on their Web site, XIST lists numerous services, including: 'information policy and legislative compliance auditing, preparation of Treasury Board funding submissions, and writing ministerial briefing notes and reports for senior management' (XIST, http://www.xist.com/01/services.php). Another consulting firm, Kaufman, Thomas + Associates (KTA) established the Centre for Collaborative Government within their firm, with the intention of making the centre 'a vehicle for a more independent approach to public policy research, dialogue and development' (KTA, http://kta.on.ca/ktacenter.html). According to their Web site, the KTA Centre 'has achieved a national reputation for generating important new perspectives and policy directions in areas of accountability, government transformation, Aboriginal capacity building, and democratic renewal' (KTA, http://kta.on.ca/ktacenter.html). And the

Stratos consulting firm states: 'We provide a diverse set of consulting skills and services to support the full spectrum of public policy, from strategic advice and the development of new policies, to program implementation and instrument design through to program evaluation and institutional reviews' (Stratos, http://www.stratos-sts.com/pages/services_003.htm). Indeed, the federal government has become porous as management consultants are infiltrating every policy area of government.

Some policy areas are more porous than others, largely because some government departments have more funds to spend on consultants. For example, provincial health and education departments usually obtain the most funding and also tend to hire the most consultants. Other departments that hire management consultants on a regular basis tend to be those dealing with justice, economic development, infrastructure, Aboriginal affairs, and municipal or intergovernmental affairs. Increasingly, consulting projects have dealt with cross-government policy issues such as children's welfare, Aboriginals, information management, communication, and management issues in general. Within the consult ing world, the larger firms tend to focus their energy on building relations with government departments that have the largest consulting budgets and compete on projects that are $60,000. Smaller firms or individual management consultants tend to compete with one another on projects under $60,000.

Larger consulting firms develop relationships with federal and provincial government departments in the hope of developing a long-term working relationship. Federal and provincial methods of tracking and reporting on external contracts do not allow us to determine the exact amount of money spent on external consulting contracts annually by each government. Unsurprisingly, however, we can say that the federal government and the provincial governments of Alberta, British Columbia, Quebec, and Ontario are the biggest purchasers of external consultants in Canada. In some jurisdictions, particularly in Ontario and at the federal level, the cost of consulting services has become a concern for the auditor general, the media, and the public. For example, an article that appeared in the *Ottawa Citizen* notes that, 'the [federal] government spends nearly $7 billion a year on professional services, the army of for-hire consultants dubbed the shadow public service' (May 2004). Furthermore, the Office of the Auditor General's (OAG) reports in the past several years are filled with references to overspending on consultants and project overruns. In its 1996 report, the OAG commented that for one project, the consulting costs doubled, from a projected $8.75 million to a final tally of $15.4 million (Auditor General of Canada 1996, sec. 8:49). The 2003 OAG report offered extensive observations on questionable management and reporting standards, and drew attention to the lack of standards, ethics, and accountability in several government programs and offices.

In response to the negative publicity surrounding the federal Liberal sponsorship scandal and the overall desire to improve transparency and accountability of the government-consulting relationship, the federal government's 2004 budget announced a new policy on the mandatory publication of contracts over $10,000 for each government department (Treasury Board Secretariat 2004). The contract information to be reported by each department includes: vendor name, number used in the financial system, contract date, description of work, contract period for services, delivery date of goods, and contract value. This information is still too vague to offer precise and comprehensive information regarding the types of consulting being undertaken. For example, on Environment Canada's website, numerous contracts were described as 'other professional services – management consulting – OGD or programs.' This generic description is designed to represent all services purchased by any government department categorized as: 'consulting services for financial management, transportation, economic development, environmental planning, public consultation and other consulting services not specifically mentioned in other objects' (Public Works and Government Services Canada 2003). Other vague categories make it problematic to determine how much money is spent on policy analysis and what types of projects governments contract out.

Finally, it is also important to note that management consultants are not only hired by governments to work in specific policy areas; they are also employed by actors wishing to influence public policy. For example, as noted by Stritch, business associations employ management consultants to conduct policy analysis in ways that ultimately affect government operations. Interest groups, polling firms, and think tanks have also employed management consultants. Adding to the complexity of influence, at times these external policy agents may be in competition with each other for the government's attention, but at other times, they may act in complementary ways. This policy actor matrix, where external consultants work for government, quasi-government agencies, think-tanks, policy institutes, business associations, nonprofit organizations, and the private sector, can give external management consultants a great deal of influence over policy analysis. So depending on what type of policy one is investigating, it can be important to consider the role and impact of other external policy agents and their relationship to external consultants.

Closing Thoughts

In the past several decades, management consultants have become involved in every stage of the Canadian policy process; in some government departments, they have been involved in the analysis of policy. In one sense, management consultants have become the private service to the public service. The impact of this public/private relationship needs to be further explored to determine the repercussions of contracting out policy services to external consultants on government performance, policy development, program delivery, and government accountability to citizens. As Andrew Stritch eloquently notes in this book, a larger question looms over the business/government relationship, namely, the uneasy marriage of competing distributive mechanisms. This observation underscores a key theme of this chapter: instead of characterizing external consultants as rational and apolitical, perhaps more attention should be paid to the personal interests and biases they bring to government when making recommendations on policy. Bakvis comments that 'it is extremely rare ... to find among current management consultants recommendations that run counter to market-driven, client-centred solutions' (1997, 111). The bottom line for management consultants is profit – not accountability, not getting elected, and not ensuring services to citizens are equitable and fair. Instead, the good consultant is always thinking of a future opportunity to work with a client again, and making other governmental contacts during the course of a project to broaden his or her money-making network.

Management consultants have become important policy actors in all levels of government, and have worked for external policy actors such as interest groups, think tanks, research institutes, and professional associations in their attempts to influence public policy. As additional research into this increasingly influential aspect of Canadian policy analysis and development is conducted, the real value of management consultancy in these areas must be openly debated. Particular attention should be addressed to questions of accountability and the problematic fit between private- and public-sector culture and objectives.

REFERENCES

Abrahamson, E. 1991. 'Managerial Fads and Fashion: The Diffusion and Rejection of Innovations.' *Academy of Management Review* 16(3), 586–612.

Bakvis, Herman. 1997. 'Advising the Executive: Think Tanks, Consultants, Political staff and Kitchen Cabinets.' In Patrick Weller, Herman Bakvis, and R.A.W. Rhodes, eds., *The Hollow Crown*. London: Macmillan.

Buono, Anthony. 2001. 'Introduction.' In Anthony Buono, ed., *Current Trends in Management Consulting*. Greenwich, CT: Information Age Publishing.

Canada. 1962. The Royal Commission on Government Organization. *The Organization of the Government of Canada*. Volume 5. Ottawa: Queen's Printer.

Canada. Consulting and Audit Canada. 2004. 'Our Organization' and 'Our Services.' http://www.cac.gc.ca/corp/internet/cacinternet.nsf/vmain/pifler704?OpenDocument.

Canada. Public Works and Government Services. 2004. 'Master List of Objects for Fiscal Year 2003–2004.' http://www.pwgsc.gc.ca/recgen/gw-coa/0304/objtoc-e.html.

Canada. Treasury Board Secretariat. 2004. 'Proactive Disclosure.' http://www.tbs-sct.gc.ca/pd-dp/index_e.asp.

Canadian Association of Management Consultants. 2004. 'Code of Conduct.' http://www.camc.com/.

Gaebler, Ted, and David Osborne. 1992. *Reinventing Government: How the Entrepreneurial Spirit is Transforming the Public Sector Review*. Reading, MA: Addison-Wesley.

Goodsell, Charles. 1994. *The Case for Bureaucracy: A Public Administration Polemic*. 3rd ed. Chatham, NJ: Chatham House.

Government Relations Institute of Canada. 2004. 'About GRIC: What is Government Relations?' http://www.gric-irgc.ca/english/index.html.

Greer, P. 1994. *Transforming Central Government: The Next Steps Initiative*. Buckingham, UK: Open University Press.

Hiscox, Heather. 2004. 'Handling Scandal: The Other Scandals.' CBC news online. 5 April. http://www.cbc.ca/news/background/groupaction/handlingscanda11.html.

Hood, Christopher. 1995. 'Contemporary Public Management: A New Global Paradigm?' *Public Policy and Administration* 10(2), 104–17.

Institute of Management Consultancy. 2004. 'Introducing the New Management Consultancy Competency Framework.' http://www.imc.co.uk/our_standards/competence_framework.php.

Kaufman, Thomas, and Associates. Centre for Collaborative Government.

2004. 'KTA Centre for Collaborative Centre.' http://www.kta.on.ca/ktacenter.html.

Lindquist, Evert. (forthcoming).

Manheim, Jarol, Richard Rich, and Lars Willnat. 2002. *Empirical Political Analysis: Research Methods in Political Science*. 5th ed. New York: Addison Wesley Longman.

May, Kathryn. 2004. 'Ottawa Bears Brunt of Cuts.' *Ottawa Citizen*, 24 March. http://www.canada.com/national/features/budget_2004/story.html?id=8fb72cf9-ef78-4f2e-905f-09f90909565e.

McKinsey & Company. 2004. 'Consulting Roles.' http://www.mckinsey.com/aboutus/careers/applyingtomckinsey/consultingroles/index.asp.

Mellett, E.B. 1988. *From Stopwatch to Strategy: A History of the First Twenty-Five Years of the Canadian Association of Management Consultants*. Toronto: Canadian Association of Management Consultants.

Meredith, H., and J. Martin. 1970. 'Management Consultants in the Public Sector.' *Canadian Public Administration* 13(4), 383–95.

Office of the Auditor General of Canada. 2003. 'Matters of Special Importance.' Report of the Auditor General of Canada. http://www.oag bvg.gc.ca/domino/reports.nsf/html/03menu_e.html.

– 1996. *Report of the Auditor General of Canada*. http://www.oag-bvg.gc.ca/domino/reports.nsf/html/96menu_e.html.

onrec.com. 2003. 'Skills Shortage Could Threaten Modernisation of Public Services.' 12 March. http://www.onrec.com/content2/news.asp?ID=2170.

Pfeiffer, J. William, and John Jones. 1985. 'Ethical Considerations in Consulting.' In Chip Bell and Leonard Nadler, eds., *Clients and Consultants: Meeting and Exceeding Expectations*, 314–22. Houston: Gulf Publishing Company.

Praxis. 2004. 'Special Research Methodologies: Kananaskis Country Recreation Development Policy Review.' http://www.praxis.ca/praxis/Methods/methods.htm.

Robinson, Jerald, and Richard Zody. Fall 1988/Winter 1989. 'Consulting for the Public Sector.' *Business Forum* 14(1), 54–6.

Rostum, Hussein. 2002. 'Review of Aboriginal Tourism Team Canada.' Prepared for Aboriginal Business Canada, Industry Canada. http://www.ic.gc.ca/cmb/welcomeic.nsf/04f61971a986e735985256e13004fc951?OpenDocument.

Saint-Martin, Denis. 1998. 'The New Managerialism and the Policy Influence of Consultants in Government: An Historical-Institutional Analysis of Britain, Canada, and France.' *Governance* 11(3), 319–56.

– 2000. *Building the New Managerialist State: Consultants and the Politics of Public Sector Reform in Comparative Perspective*. New York: Oxford University Press.

Savoie, Donald. 2004. 'Searching for Accountability in a Government without Boundaries.' *Canadian Public Administration* 47(1), 1–26.

Speers, Kimberly. Forthcoming. 'Corporate Government: Accountability, Business Planning, and Performance Measurement in the Government of Alberta.' Dissertation (in progress), University of Alberta.

Stratos. 2003. 'Our Approach.' http://www.stratos-sts.com/pages/services_003.htm.

Tunnoch, G.V. 1964. 'The Glassco Commission: Did it Cost More Than it Was Worth?' *Canadian Public Administration* 7(3), 389–97.

United States. Department of Commerce. 1998. 'Industry Sector Analysis: Canada, Management Consulting Services.' June.

Venard, Bertrand. 2001. 'Transforming Consulting Knowledge into Business Fads.' In Anthony Buono, ed., *Current Trends in Management Consulting*, 171–88. Greenwich, CT: Information Age Publishing.

Weiss, Alan. 2003. *Great Consulting Challenges and How To Surmount Them*. San Francisco, CA: Jossey-Bass/Pfeiffer.

Whorley, David. 2001. 'The Andersen-Comsoc Affair: Partnerships and the Public Interest.' *Canadian Public Administration* 44(3), 320–45.

Wooldridge, A. 1997. 'Management Consultancy: The Advice Business.' *The Economist*, 22 March supplement, 1–22.

XIST inc. 2003. 'Government Online Info: Services for the Government of Canada.' 21 October. http://www.xist.com/01/newsItem.php?id=52.

Zussman, David. 1999. 'The Role of Management Consultants to the Federal Government.' Notes for an address at the Annual General Meeting of the Eastern Ontario Chapter of the Canadian Association of Management Consultants, Ottawa, 23 September 1999.

PART V

Parties and Interest Group-Based Policy Analysis

This section explores whether what appear to be influential policy contributions by political parties and organized economic and social group actors are backed by focused or systematic policy analytical work. Four authors inquire into the quantity, character, and impact of policy analysis in Canadian political parties, business associations, trade unions, and voluntary sector organizations.

William Cross shows that Canadian parties are generally uninterested in the kind of policy analysis that one sees conducted by many European parties. In chapter 17, he contends that neither internal party officials' time and resources, nor party members' potential to engage in serious consideration of policy alternatives, have been tapped. As a result, extra-parliamentary parties have developed low levels of policy analytical capacity, even in the Liberal 'government party.' Competitive party system dynamics, combined with extra-parliamentary parties' self-reinforcing perceptions as merely 'electoral machines,' will probably ensure that those interested in extra-governmental policy questions and analysis will gravitate to organized interests rather than parties.

In chapter 18, Andrew Stritch anchors an account of the policy analytic capacities of Canadian business associations in a discussion of a survey of several such associations. His review of 'the extent, means, focus, and dissemination of policy analysis by Canadian national business associations' shows that these associations seldom devote substantial resources to such tasks, except at the 'elite' level of major associations focusing on shared sectoral concerns. He finds that when such associations do conduct policy analysis, the work addresses matters of provincial, national and international jurisdiction and scope. But as much of this work is contracted out to consultants, it is extremely difficult to get a clear sense of the range and precise types of impact of policy analysis conducted for business associations on public policy.

Andrew Jackson and Robert Baldwin offer Canada's first clear survey of labour movement efforts at policy analysis in chapter 19, setting their portrait against the backdrop of a labour movement operating in a hostile environment. The authors show that trade union contributions to major policy discussions, reviews, and organized commissions of enquiry are often supported by policy analysis by affiliate union and Canadian Labour Congress (CLC) staff research. Their account of Canadian unions' refocused policy goals and partisan (NDP) support efforts offers a clear sense of the strategic environment within which Canadian unions undertake policy analysis.

Finally, in chapter 20, Susan Phillips uses a systematic overview of policy analytical work within the voluntary sector to ask whether policy processes in Canada are as open as widely promoted new models of participatory governance suggest. She argues that voluntary sector organizations' difficulties mobilizing resources for policy analysis, let alone effective advocacy, are a symptom of a structural bias against voluntary sector organizations within the expanding networks of collaborative governance. Endemic financial instability in voluntary sector organizations ensures that their participation in policy development is typically more weakly supported by sufficient policy capacity than is true in either the business community or in organized labour. Phillips urges readers to take seriously education regarding the potential role of voluntary sector organizations in policy development as part of an overhaul of public administration training.

17 Policy Study and Development in Canada's Political Parties

WILLIAM CROSS

Introduction

Given the primary place of political parties in modern democracies, it seems logical that a book about policy analysis should include a chapter about parties. Canadian political parties play a crucial gate-keeping role in the selection of elected officials, they dominate our election campaigns and our legislatures are structured along party lines. Many Canadians experience politics only through political parties: they vote for candidates chosen by the parties, volunteer to assist a party in its election campaigns, and, perhaps, petition an elected party member with a policy-related grievance.

Nonetheless, this chapter argues that Canada's political parties are not effective vehicles for policy study and development. They neither offer voters meaningful opportunity for involvement in the policy-making process nor do they regularly generate policy alternatives for consideration and examination by those in elected office or in the senior bureaucracy.

It is fair to say that Canadian parties have long seen their primary role as being that of electoral machines. The extra-parliamentary parties exist to choose candidates and leaders and to help them get elected to the provincial and federal legislatures. In between elections, these party organizations have never been particularly active in developing policy options. The lack of a significant role for party members in policy development may help to explain the sharp decline in party membership routinely experienced between elections, the increased attractiveness of interest groups to those Canadians interested in influencing public policy, and the general dissatisfaction of many partisans with the operations of their own party.[1] Though this disenchantment was particularly strong in the final years of the twentieth century, it is not a new phenomenon in Canadian politics. There have been repeated efforts by party activists to win a more influential role in policy making, dating back almost one hundred years. These demands will continue to fester and occasionally reach a boiling point, and they will continue to be frustrated, so long as the political parties have minimal interest in, and capacity for, inter-election policy development.[2]

Members and Party Policy Development

Canadian parties have traditionally taken the approach that policy making is a function of the parliamentary party, with only a weak advisory role assigned to the extra-parliamentary membership. The tensions between the membership party and the parliamentary group over policy making have usually been sharpest when a party is in government. Setting party policy during these periods is more meaningful because the party has the levers of the state at its disposal. And governing parties, cognizant of the disparate political interests that need to be accommodated, have argued that responsibility for the setting of public policy must lie with the Cabinet and parliamentary caucus, as they are the only bodies capable of brokering all of the varied interests into a coherent public policy. Opposition parties are freer to advocate the more narrow interests of their activist membership base as they are not charged with governing. The result has been that opposition parties are often responsive to the policy views of their members only to become substantially less so upon assuming the reins of government. Understandably, this often results in a frustrated and dispirited party membership.

This cycle has a long history in Canadian politics. The federal Liberal Party in the first half of the last century provides a good example. Finding itself in opposition, the party held a national convention in 1919 to engage its activists in policy discussion and to select a successor to Laurier as party leader (the convention was initially called for purposes other than leadership selection). The party subsequently won the general election of 1921 and spent most of the next 27 years in government under the leadership of Prime Minister Mackenzie King. During this period, the government ignored many of the policies adopted by the 1919 convention, and Mackenzie King never once called the party together in convention (see Whitaker 1977). During this long period of

Liberal Party rule, there was virtually no opportunity for the party's grassroots supporters to exert themselves in the policy field. Mackenzie King believed that the realm of policy making was solely within the purview of the parliamentary party. The strength of his conviction is apparent in the following passage from a speech he made in 1948: 'The substitution, by force or otherwise, of the dictates of a single political party for the authority of a freely elected Parliament is something which, in far too many countries has already taken place. It is along that path that many nations have lost their freedom. That is what happened in Fascist countries. A single party dictatorship is, likewise, the very essence of Communist strategy' (as quoted in Wearing 1981, 74–5).

The contemporary Liberal and Conservative Parties, the only parties to have governed federally, occasionally hold policy conventions at which their members debate and adopt policy positions, but these are in no way binding upon their parliamentary parties. Typically, these processes are ad hoc and not part of an ongoing policy development structure. The result is that their impact is often short-lived and negligible.

A relatively recent example of the typical process engaged in by these parties is instructive. In the early 1990s, the Conservative government of the day, in the follow-up to its second straight majority victory in 1988, decided to engage its membership in a policy-making process to produce ideas for what it hoped would be a continuing run in government. A rather elaborate process was put into place with policy resolutions working their way up through riding level, regional, and provincial party meetings before appearing on the agenda at a 1991 national policy conference. In total, 320 resolutions reached the national meeting out of more than 800 initially submitted by riding associations. While party members may have thought they were setting the future direction for the government, this was clearly not the case.

For example, in the immediate aftermath of the convention delegates voting in favour of privatization of the CBC, Communications Minister Perrin Beatty told the press that he opposed the resolution and that the government had no plans to follow the membership's directive. More importantly, there was no follow-up to the policy process. Typical of the Canadian practice, there was no permanent party body in place charged with policy study. The result was that the work of the party members in debating and adopting these policy resolutions was forgotten almost as soon as the convention adjourned. Within short order, Prime Minister Mulroney resigned the party's leadership and the new leader, Kim Campbell, appeared to give no particular regard to the recent policy process in setting out her platform for the subsequent general election. Instead it was a platform largely devoid of specific policy planks and written by a few senior aides working for the leader. This scenario is typical of governing parties.

This is not to suggest that governing parties have never tried to provide a significant role in policy making for their grassroots activists. The best example of such an effort at the federal level occurred in the first Trudeau government from 1968 to 1972. Upon coming to office the Trudeau Liberals set out several reforms aimed at providing an important role for their local partisans. These included a year-long constituency-level discussion of policy papers, a 1970 policy convention at which party members were to adopt policy resolutions uncontrolled by caucus or cabinet, regular reporting by cabinet ministers on the policies adopted by their ministries subject to a vote of approval by the membership in convention, and a promise that resolutions passed in convention would be included in the next election platform (this process is well described in Clarkson 1979). The participatory enthusiasm of the late 1960s that encouraged these reforms quickly turned into the reality of governing and ultimately the reforms had little impact. For example, instead of having individual ministers report on behalf of their departments and allowing for debate on each report, Trudeau quickly adopted the practice of presenting one report himself on behalf of the government. The result was that any criticism would be interpreted as a direct assault on the party leader. Similarly, the government rejected many of the key policy positions adopted at the 1970 convention. Stephen Clarkson sums up the subsequent disenchantment of party members when he writes: 'When it became clear that none of their policy positions would be adopted for the 1972 election campaign platform the morale of the party core fell noticeably. A survey of the most active Liberals in Ontario showed that it had been far harder to recruit volunteers in the 1972 election than it had been in 1968 and that campaign workers' morale had been far worse even in constituencies that successfully returned a Liberal member of parliament' (1979, 159).

While governing parties have long struggled with finding an influential role for their members, opposition parties have occasionally had more success. The federal Liberal Party under the leadership of Lester Pearson in the early 1960s and the Ontario Conservative Party under the leadership of Mike Harris in the 1990s provide two examples of parties using periods in opposition to consult widely on policy consideration, to engage both their membership and outside experts in the process, and to use the process to define a set of policy options for their subsequent years in government. Both were former long-term governing parties that looked forward to returning to government and used their time in opposition to prepare for that eventuality.

The case of the Liberals in the 1960s is well known. Finding themselves in opposition after nearly four decades in government, the party used the period between the 1958 and 1962 elections to develop a policy platform for its return to government. The highlight of this period was the party's 1960 Kingston conference, attended by 200 or so academics, party officials and others with an interest in social, economic and foreign policy. The conference sparked much policy discussion within the party, particularly around Tom Kent's call for a much-strengthened social welfare package. The following year the party held a much larger rally that was attended by close to 2000 party activists, at which these and other policy ideas were debated and adopted in preparation for the 1962 election. Some key members of the future Liberal government, such as Walter Gordon, were brought into the party during this policy development period and much of the policy agenda pursued in the first years of the Pearson government can be traced back to this period in opposition. However, once well established in government, the party reverted to form. Within days of a 1966 national convention, Pearson repudiated several of the policies adopted and 'in spite of what the party's constitution now said he declared that the convention's resolutions did not establish party policy' (Wearing 1981, 75).

The Ontario Conservative case in the 1990s is similar. After becoming leader of a then third-place party, Mike Harris authorized a party commission to travel the province, speaking to both party activists and policy experts, and to begin developing the foundation of a policy platform for a new Conservative government. The party later held a convention at which it reviewed the results of this consultation and adopted them as party policy (for more on this, see Cameron and White 2000). The resulting *Common Sense Revolution* platform that the party successfully promoted in the 1995 election, and subsequently implemented during its first term in government, was the product of this policy development exercise.

The Bloc Québécois and New Democratic Parties have argued for a more consistently influential role for their membership in policy development. In both parties, official policy positions are determined by the membership at regular policy conventions and not by the parliamentary caucus. For the most part, the parliamentary party is meant to follow the policy direction established by the membership party. For example, the federal New Democrats' constitution includes the following provision: 'The convention shall be the supreme governing body of the Party and shall have final authority in all matters of federal policy, program and constitution.'

This reflects the populist traditions of these parties and the fact that they are less interested in the practice of brokerage politics than are the Liberals and Progressive Conservatives. Of course neither of these parties has come close to forming a government at the federal level. Since they both represent rather narrow ideological (and regional) spectrums and have shown little real interest in expanding their ideological base, it is easier for them to cater to the views of their activists than it is for brokerage parties seeking to govern and maintain large, diverse coalitions.

However, even these newer parties, when forming governments at the provincial level, have struggled with providing a meaningful policy role for their members. The New Democrats experienced this difficulty in Ontario in 1990. Not expecting to win the upcoming election, the party entered the campaign with a policy platform reflecting the positions taken by its membership in convention. Having never before governed, the party had long argued it was more 'democratic' than its Liberal and Conservative opponents by virtue of taking its policy directions from its grassroots supporters. Once elected, the party quickly realized that it was now charged with representing the whole province and not simply the views of its partisan base of social activists and trade union members. As the party moved further away from the policy preferences of its members on issues such as a provincially run automobile insurance scheme, and implemented its social contract provisions that were wildly unpopular with organized labour, it struggled grandly and was widely criticized by its members for breaking with the party tradition of having the legislative caucus follow the policy views of the members. That was relatively easy to do in opposition but very difficult in government. The Parti Québécois has experienced similar tensions during its recent terms in power. The party's activist corps is more committed to the sovereignty cause than is the population at large. PQ governments, representing the entire electorate, are forced into a very delicate dance of keeping their committed activists satisfied while reflecting the views of the general populace.

The case of the new Conservative Party illustrates the different approaches to policy making taken by opposition parties and those positioning themselves as a potential governing party. The new Conservative Party is a direct descendant of the old Reform and Canadian Alliance Parties. The traditions of this political movement are deeply rooted in participatory, grassroots populism. Both of these earlier parties were firmly entrenched on the opposition benches and had elaborate processes in place to facilitate the participation of their grassroots supporters in party policy making (for a full discussion of Reform, see Laycock 2002). Nonetheless, when the new party was formed with the explicit purpose of expanding their voter base and challenging the Liberals for government, it completely ignored these principles.

The new party was formed without any meaningful policy discussion. Notwithstanding the fact that there were serious policy differences between the two merging parties (see Cross and Young 2003), their members were asked to endorse the creation of the new party before any policy positions, beyond a generic list of 'founding principles,' were enunciated. The new party then chose a leader, nominated candidates, waged an election campaign and served as the official opposition, all without holding a single policy convention, something that would have been inconceivable in the old Reform Party. The Conservative Party held its first policy convention in March 2005, more than a year after being formed.

There is also a structural barrier to Canadian parties being attractive institutions for voters interested in policy development, that is, the federal nature of Canadian politics. The party system reflects the highly decentralized nature of the Canadian federation. There are, essentially, different parties and party systems at the federal level and in each of the provinces. Two of the four major federal parties exist only at this level (the Bloc Québécois and Conservatives), while some important provincial parties exist only at that level (the Saskatchewan Party and the Parti Québécois). Even when the same party exists in name in different jurisdictions, policy positions are taken separately in each instance and there is often little coherence between them.

For example, the governing Liberal Parties in British Columbia and Quebec compete as right-of-centre alternatives in those provinces, while the national party typically places itself slightly left-of-centre in policy terms, as do many of the other provincial parties. Similarly, the Progressive Conservative Parties in provinces such as Alberta and Ontario (and the Conservative Party nationally) are often far to the right of their namesakes in the four provinces in Atlantic Canada. And there is no Conservative or Progressive Conservative Party at the provincial level in two of the three largest provinces – Quebec and British Columbia. Similarly, provincial Liberal governments feel absolutely no compulsion to adopt policy positions consistent with those taken at the national level. Indeed, they often see themselves as competitors of a federal party of the same name and seek electoral fortune by highlighting their policy differences.

Even in the NDP, which has considerably greater coherence between the federal and provincial levels, policy is made separately at each level, with the result that important differences can exist between different jurisdictions. This is particularly true in cases where the party is competitive at the provincial level and thus faces the policy restraints of governing – a phenomenon unknown to the party at the federal level and in many provinces.

The result of this is that party brand names do not represent distinct, consistent policy positions across the country. Even within a province, the voter interested in policy will find that parties of the same name at the federal and provincial level will often have very different policy positions. Coupled with the flexible policy positions that traditionally characterize Canada's brokerage parties, this does not make political parties particularly attractive vehicles for policy participation by voters who are motivated by policy concerns. One of the results is that those citizens wanting to influence public policy prefer to participate in interest groups rather than parties. Howe and Northrup found that by a three-to-one margin, Canadians think joining an interest group is a more effective way of working for political change than joining a party (Howe and Northrup 2000).

Policy Study within Parties: The Need for Policy Foundations

Not surprisingly, it is far more difficult for parties without an ongoing capacity for policy development to engage their members in policy-related activities. And, at least insofar as it relates to taking policy direction from their activist members, from a democratic perspective this may be a good thing. Governments are charged with being responsive to all of the citizens. And surely, there is merit to the accommodative approach that Canadian governments at the federal level have always attempted to take. The views of party activists are often more extreme (on both the left and the right) than are each parties' voters, and certainly more so than the electorate at large (see Cross and Young 2002). Governing parties have used this rationale to deny their membership significant influence in policy setting.

The cost of this behaviour, however, is the growing antipathy found among members towards a policy development process that they view as elite dominated and nonresponsive. Members of every federal party believe they have less influence in party decision making than they should (see Young and Cross 2002). A survey of party constituency associations following the 1993 election found that in half of local Conservative and one-third of Liberal constituency associations, members were offered no opportunity in the prior year for policy discussion. Not surprisingly, more than 80 percent of local associations were dissatisfied with the opportunities provided them in this regard (Cross 1998). Similarly, a 2000 party member survey found that three-quarters of members believe that they should play a greater role in developing their party's policy positions (Cross and Young 2002).

The challenge is to find a meaningful role for party members while preserving the parliamentary parties' responsibility for determining the ultimate policy positions. Turning responsibility for policy making over to a party's members will not result in an inclusive and responsive politics for the citizenry at large. Instead, a better approach is for the parties to invest in policy study and development on an ongoing basis, to include a wide array of views in these processes, and over time to build an ideological foundation for their party on which subsequent, shorter-term policies can be based.

The Royal Commission on Electoral Reform and Party Financing captured the status of policy development in Canada's parties when it concluded that: 'The dilemma is that the core of the party organization is concerned primarily with elections; it is much less interested in discussing and analysing political issues that are not connected directly to winning the next election, or in attempting to articulate the broader values of the party' (Royal Commission 1991, 292). In fact, most Canadian parties essentially have no capacity for ongoing policy study. Parties routinely lay off most of their staff immediately after each election and engage in little other than fundraising and housekeeping activities until the time arrives to begin preparation for the next election. This is not reflective of the preferences of party members. As described earlier, those members who remain in the parties between elections, regardless of party affiliation, overwhelmingly say that they would like more party-sponsored opportunity for policy study and discussion.

Unlike parties in some Western democracies, Canadian parties do not have policy institutes. Many European parties have either formal party institutes devoted to long-term policy study or have close ties with quasi-independent institutes committed to policy development. These organizations allow parties to engage their supporters in the policy process, to establish networks of policy experts, and to develop policy frameworks consistent with each party's overarching ideology. Of course, the operation of party policy institutes is costly. Many Canadian parties, particularly those in opposition, survive on shoestring budgets between elections. It is routine for parties to emerge from a general election campaign with a sizeable debt and to spend the following years raising funds to pay it off before the next election brings another spending binge. Dollars are scarce during these periods and, even if they wanted to (which has not often been the case), parties simply have not had the funds necessary to engage in serious policy study work.

Other Western democracies have shown their commitment to party policy development by providing annual public funding to parties between elections. This is the case in many European countries, including Austria, France, Germany, Italy, the Netherlands, and Sweden. A few provinces (including Quebec, New Brunswick, and Prince Edward Island) do provide modest annual funding to their parties, but these are the exception in the Canadian case. All Canadian jurisdictions allocate annual funding to party caucuses represented in the respective legislatures. These funds, however, are restricted to the parliamentary party and encourage both an elite-driven and short-term-focused policy development process. Party caucuses are understandably concerned with the cut and thrust of daily parliamentary debate and are not regularly engaged in longer-term policy study. The 2003 campaign finance legislation (Bill C-24) changes this situation by providing the federal parties with significant annual allowances of public money. What remains unclear is whether any of the parties will use this new funding to enhance their policy capacity.

The 1991 Royal Commission on Electoral Reform and Party Financing recommended that federal parties establish policy institutes but this has never been followed up on. In their post-1993 restructuring efforts, a Progressive Conservative Party task force proposed creation of a permanent policy foundation to act as 'a mechanism for Party member and riding level involvement in, and input to, the policy process' (Progressive Conservative Party 1994, 3). The party approved this proposal and committed itself in its new constitution to development of 'a continuous policy process and a permanent policy resource which respects and encourages the participation of members.' The party never acted on this commitment.

The 2004 New Brunswick Commission on Legislative Democracy made a similar proposal, recommending that the province provide both start-up and ongoing public funding to the parties for the purpose of supporting these activities. Their view is that this will both invigorate parties as preferred organizations for voters wanting to influence policy and will better serve elected members, as their parties will be better able to offer them policy support and alternatives (Commission on Legislative Democracy 2005, 81).

While Canadian parties typically do not have their own policy institutes, there are independent groups devoted to the study of public policy. These include groups such as the C.D. Howe Institute and the Fraser Institute on the right, the Canadian Centre for Policy Alternatives and the Caledon Institute on the left, and the Institute for Research on Public Policy in the centre. These groups, however, are fully independent of the political parties. The traditional governing parties, the Liberals and Progressive Conservatives, have no history of formal or even quasi-formal ties with any of these groups. This differs from countries such as the United States. While the American parties themselves have limited policy-making capacity, both the Democrats and Republicans have forged close ties with groups of policy think tanks on the left and right that fill this void (Thunert 2003).

By essentially ignoring political parties, other contributions to this volume, considering the roles of interest groups, think tanks, and industry associations in policy making, all buttress the argument that parties are marginal players in the policy-making process (Jackson and Baldwin 2007; Phillips 2007; Stritch 2007). The old Reform/Alliance Parties had established close ties with groups on the right-of-centre, including the National Citizens Coalition (NCC), the National Taxpayers Foundation (NTF), and the Fraser Institute. The party's last leader (and the Conservative Party's founding leader), Stephen Harper, is a former president of the NCC and veteran caucus members such as Jason Kenney, formerly with the NTF, have close ties with these groups. It is unclear whether the new Conservative Party will maintain these ties.

The New Democrats are the one federal party to have created a formal connection with a policy foundation, the Douglas-Coldwell Foundation. While the foundation is formally independent of the political party, the connections are apparent in the make-up of its board of directors, which has included former NDP premiers Alan Blakeney and Howard Pawley, as well as high-profile MP Bill Blaikie, and former NDP federal secretaries Jill Marzetti and David Woodbury. The founda-

tion played an important role in the policy renewal conferences the
party held following its electoral devastation in 1993. The NDP also has
long ties with the labour movement and has at times collaborated with
organized labour in developing policy (see Jackson and Baldwin 2007
for more on this).

The establishment of party policy institutes, or the development of
strong ties with quasi-independent groups, would allow a vehicle for
serious, ongoing policy study and development. This activity provides
many benefits to parties and to democracy generally. Five of the principal advantages they would provide are as follows:

1 Policy institutes allow parties to engage their members in the
   policy development process. The data recounted above are un-
   equivocal in showing party members' dissatisfaction with the role
   currently afforded them in the policy-making process within their
   parties.
2 Policy institutes generate policy alternatives for parliamentary
   parties to consider. Policy debate currently is dominated by the
   parliamentary parties but they have little capacity to develop new,
   detailed policy positions.
3 Policy institutes can assist a party in making the transition from
   opposition to government. Virtually overnight the task of the parliamentary leadership changes from one of primarily criticizing the
   government to identifying and implementing a policy plan. A party
   institute can help prepare for transitions to government by preparing detailed policy alternatives for the new government's consideration.
4 An institute can serve as a vehicle for reexamination of a party's
   policy positions and consideration of alternatives without drawing
   the same intensity of media attention and public scrutiny that inevitably results when such ruminations come from a parliamentary
   party. Parliamentary parties are loath to engage in reconsideration
   of their positions for fear of a public perception of them backtrack-
   ing on their promises or acknowledging that they were misguided
   in the first place. Policy institutes can provide the space for such
   deliberation, some distance removed from a party's immediate
   political imperatives.
5 In addition to providing a vehicle for policy participation for their
   ordinary members, institutes can serve to develop a network of

policy experts engaged in advising the party on long-term policy direction. This is somewhat less of a partisan activity than advising a parliamentary party on the immediate issues of the day and can result in the involvement of more academics and other serious students of public policy. Parties can also use this process to reach out to areas, regional and otherwise, where they have limited electoral support.

A party foundation also addresses one of the common arguments made against effective grassroots participation in party policy making in the Canadian context. The argument, as made by Prime Minister MacKenzie King, is that political parties need to be responsive to all voters, and not solely to their activist base. The result being that they cannot take their policy direction solely from the views of their own supporters. This argument is most often made by the traditional brokerage parties, with both the Progressive Conservatives and Liberals regularly arguing that they have to broker the wide array of interests found in Canada, accommodate the disparate views, and try to find common ground. A party-run policy foundation can be useful to a brokerage party by focusing party members' participation into the foundation and thereby providing otherwise frustrated members with an opportunity to participate in policy study and development. Channelling the participation into a policy foundation provides some necessary distance between the policy demands of the party's activist corps and its parliamentary party. The parliamentary party benefits from the policy work of the foundation but is ultimately free to set its own course. A well-run foundation also ensures that voices beyond the party's own members are considered in framing policy objectives. This may be particularly valuable in the Canadian case, where all of the federal parties have large areas of regional electoral weakness and thus gaping holes in regional representativeness in their parliamentary caucuses (and often in their grassroots membership).

Ironically, given the brokerage parties' reluctance to establish policy foundations, an argument can be made that parties are disadvantaged in fulfilling the brokerage function because of a lack of capacity for policy innovation. Groups that are not represented in the parliamentary party (or in the PMO) find it difficult to have their interests heard in the closed world of party caucuses and cabinet meetings. When party policies (and government policy) are made largely in a vacuum by a small group of party elites, interests not represented in that group may be shut out (Brodie and Jenson 1991). For example, Western Canadian interests argued that there was no place for their policy preferences to be considered in the later Trudeau governments that included almost no MPs from Western Canada. When outside interests are heard, they often come in the form of representations from single interest groups not concerned with compromise and accommodation. Policy foundations could ensure that voices are heard from all regions and segments of society and at their best generate alternative policy proposals for consideration by the party's parliamentary leadership.

One of the results of a lack of policy development capacity in the political parties is that governments rarely look to their own party for policy prescriptions and directions. A prime example of this was the federal Liberal Party's establishing of the Romanow Commission to provide a blueprint for reform of Canada's health care policies. The Chrétien government held no important party discussions on the issue; rather, an independent commission, led by a former NDP premier of Saskatchewan, was established to consider the issue and provide a policy prescription. This is typical. Governments almost never turn to their party when seeking serious policy advice; instead, they appoint independent or royal commissions. Policy foundations could make parties a more attractive alternative for the development of policy alternatives and in doing so provide a mechanism for ordinary voters to participate in policy development.

Policy foundations also serve, in the long term, to give parties a clearer ideological imprint and to bring some continuity to a party's long-term policy direction. Canada's parties are dominated by the personalities of their leaders. The leaders typically exercise substantial control over candidate selection, election campaigning, and policy adoption. Election campaigns largely revolve around the leader and are orchestrated by a small team of his or her close personal advisers. It is often difficult to ascribe characteristics to a party independent of those of its current leader, as the policy direction a party takes is largely determined by his or her preferences. And, too often, leaders and their operatives, in search of electoral success, avoid staking out specific policy positions for fear of alienating groups of voters. This results in voters having no clear idea of what a party stands for and parties therefore winning little mandate for tackling difficult policy issues (for more on this, see Clarke et al. 1996).

Conclusion

In arguing for a stronger policy development capacity for parties, Robert Young has written: 'In a self-reinforcing cycle, people with genuine policy concerns seek out interest groups to advance their causes, and the parties degenerate further into domination by leaders and their personal entourages, who play the politics of image and strategic vagueness, who take office with little sense of direction, and who end up as brokers among interest groups' (1991, 77). In this scenario, parties end up responding to special and single interest groups, as they often have greater capacity for policy development than do the parties themselves. All parties and governments eventually need to take policy positions and if they do not have the capacity to engage both experts and .the general citizenry in the policy development process, then they are reduced to responding to proposals made by organized interests.

This is particularly unsatisfactory in a country with a long tradition of brokerage politics. Parliamentary parties in both government and opposition would benefit from serious policy study undertaken by their extraparliamentary parties towards the purpose of providing policy alternatives and guidance to the parliamentary parties. Such activity would serve to encourage those Canadians interested in policy to participate in party activity rather than looking to interest groups as a way to influence public policy. A beneficial side effect may also be a weakening of the growing concentration of government party decision making within the PMO.

Recent months have seen considerable attention paid, both at the national and provincial levels, to a perceived 'democratic deficit.' The focus of this attention in the provinces has been on the electoral system and at the federal level on the role of MPs in the House of Commons. Five provinces – British Columbia, Ontario, Quebec, New Brunswick, and Prince Edward Island – have all recently undertaken comprehensive examinations of their electoral systems, suggesting that voter disgruntlement with the current state of democracy might be alleviated under an electoral system other than the single-member plurality one (Cross, 2005). With the exception of the New Brunswick case discussed above, none of these provincial projects have focused on the primary role of parties in Canadian democracy. At the same time, former prime minister Martin suggested that the democratic deficit might be reduced by weakening party discipline in the House of Commons, thus providing members with more opportunity to vote independently of their party. Both of these projects, weakening party discipline and electoral reform, have the potential of further diminishing the place of parties in policy study and development.

An increase in the number of free votes in Parliament would diminish the role of the party in policy making, as representatives would be increasingly free to ignore whatever positions their parties adopt (assuming they continue to take a position at all on these issues). Voters and groups interested in influencing policy outcomes would increasingly turn their attention away from parties and their leaders, and towards individual legislators. This is the case in the United States, where party discipline in Congress is significantly weaker and parties have long been criticized for failing to take consistent and coherent policy positions.

Depending on the details of any new system adopted, electoral reform might have the same effect. For example, the experience in Ireland with the 'single transferable vote,' the system recently endorsed by British Columbia voters, suggests that its adoption would have the effect of weakening the larger parties to the benefit of independent candidates and smaller parties. All of the varying proportional representation systems under consideration are likely to have the effect of significantly increasing the occurrence of minority and coalition governments. Prior experience in Canada, and the experiences of other jurisdictions around the world, suggests that such parliaments, often with multi-party government, require substantial negotiating among party leaders in the legislature. The result is that parties are not able to commit to a particular platform of policy positions and then stick to them in the subsequent parliament. One result may be an increase in voter cynicism towards participation in parties as an effective way of influencing public policy.

There is no quick fix to the dilemma facing our parties. Encouraging them to develop long-term policy-making capacity that is grassroots driven and arms-length from the elected caucus may provide them with the best opportunity of engaging voters in their policy study activities and better serving the policy needs of their elected representatives.

NOTES

This chapter is adapted from chapter 3 of William Cross, *Political Parties* (Vancouver: UBC Press, 2004). I thank UBC Press for their permission to reprint much of this material.

1 For data relating to political parties, see Cross 2004. For data relating more generally to voters' attitudes towards democratic institutions, see Howe and Northrup 2000.
2 For an overview of the historical efforts at increasing party members' role in policy making, see Carty, Cross, and Young 2000, chapter 6.

REFERENCES

Abelson, Don. 2007. 'Any Ideas? Think Tanks and Policy Analysis in Canada.' This volume.

Baier, Gerald, and Herman Bakvis. 2001. 'Think Tanks and Political Parties: Competitors or Collaborators?' *Isuma: Canadian Journal of Policy Research* 2(1), 107–13.

Brodie, Janine, and Jane Jenson. 1991. 'Piercing the Smokescreen: Brokerage Parties and Class Politics.' In Alain Gagnon and A. Brian Tanguay, eds., *Canadian Parties in Transition*, 52–72. Scarborough, ON: Nelson.

Cameron, David, and Graham White. 2001. *Cycling into Saigon: the Conservative Transition in Ontario.* Vancouver: UBC Press.

Carty, R. Kenneth, William Cross, and Lisa Young. 2000. *Rebuilding Canadian Party Politics.* Vancouver: UBC Press.

Clarke, Harold, Jane Jenson, Lawrence LeDuc, and Jon H. Pammett. 1996. *Absent Mandate: Canadian Electoral Politics in an Era of Restructuring.* 3rd ed. Toronto: Gage Publishing.

Clarkson, Stephen. 1979. 'Democracy in the Liberal Party: The Experiment with Citizen Participation under Pierre Trudeau.' In Hugh G. Thorburn, ed., *Party Politics in Canada.* 4th ed. Scarborough, ON: Prentice-Hall.

Cross, William. 1998. 'The Conflict Between Participatory and Accommodative Politics: the Case for Stronger Parties.' *International Journal of Canadian Studies* 17 (spring), 37–55.

– 2004. *Political Parties.* Vancouver: UBC Press.

– 2005. 'The Rush to Electoral Reform in the Canadian Provinces: Why Now? *Representation* 41(2), 75–84.

Cross, William, and Lisa Young. 2002. 'Policy Attitudes of Party Members in Canada: Evidence of Ideological Politics.' *Canadian Journal of Political Science* 35(4), 859–80.

– 2003. 'Party Membership on the Canadian Political Right: The Canadian Alliance and Progressive Conservative Parties.' In Rainer-Olaf Schultze, Roland Sturm, and Dagmar Eberle, eds., *Conservative Parties and Right-Wing Politics in North America: Reaping the Benefits of an Ideological Victory?*, 191–206. Opladen, Germany: Leske & Budrich.

Howe, Paul, and David Northrup. 2000. *Strengthening Canadian Democracy:*

The Views of Canadians. Policy Matters series vol. 1, no. 5. Ottawa: Institute for Research on Public Policy.

Jackson, Andrew, and Bob Baldwin. 2007. 'Policy Analysis by the Labour Movement in a Hostile Environment.' This volume.

Laycock, David. 2001. *The New Right and Democracy in Canada: Understanding Reform and the Canadian Alliance.* Toronto: Oxford University Press.

New Brunswick Commission on Legislative Democracy. 2005. *Final Report and Recommendations.* Fredericton, NB.

Phillips, Susan. 2007. 'Beyond Public Interest Groups: Rethinking Concepts and Assessing Capacities in Policy Participation.' This volume.

Report of the Royal Commission on Electoral Reform and Party Financing. 1991. Ottawa: Ministry of Supply and Services Canada, vol. 1.

Progressive Conservative Party of Canada. 1994. 'Background Paper on Restructuring.' Policy document, Ottawa.

Stritch, Andrew. 2007. 'Business Associations and Policy Analysis in Canada.' This volume.

Thunert, Martin. 2003. 'Conservative Think Tanks in the United States and Canada,' In Rainer-Olaf Schultze, Roland Sturm, and Dagmar Eberle, eds., *Conservative Parties and Right-Wing Politics in North America: Reaping the Benefits of an Ideological Victory?*, 191–206. Opladen, Germany: Leske & Budrich.

Wearing, Joseph. 1981. *The L-Shaped Party: the Liberal Party of Canada 1958–1980.* Toronto: McGraw-Hill Ryerson.

Whitaker, Reginald. 1977. *The Government Party: Organizing and Financing the Liberal Party of Canada, 1930–1958.* Toronto: University of Toronto Press.

Young, Lisa, and William Cross. 2002. 'The Rise of Plebiscitary Democracy in Canadian Political Parties.' *Party Politics* 8(6), 673–99.

Young, Robert. 1991. 'Effecting Change: Do We Have the Political System To Get Us Where we Want To Go?' In G. Bruce Doern and B. Bryne, eds., *Canada at Risk? Canadian Public Policy in the 1990s*, 59–80. Toronto: C.D. Howe Institute.

18 Business Associations and Policy Analysis in Canada

ANDREW STRITCH

One of the outstanding features of political economy in Western indus-trial societies is the uneasy coexistence of capitalist economies and democratic governments. The rocky marriage of competing distributive mechanisms – one based on the formal equality of political representa-tion, the other based on the right to unequal ownership of property – is a central problematic of capitalist democracies. The idea of popular control over 'who gets what' grates against massive disparities in wealth and income, and any theory of pluralism has to contend with the reality of pervasive corporate power.

Analysis of corporate power can be conducted on a number of differ-ent levels. In Canada, a significant amount of academic literature has focused on the structure of class/state relations and on the linkages between corporate and political elites (see, for example, Panitch 1977; Carroll 1986, 2004; Brym 1985; McBride and Shields 1997; Mahon 1984; Clement 1975; Veltmeyer 1987; Brownlee 2005). At a less macro level, relatively little attention has been directed towards the lobbying power of business interests or the role of business associations in policy mak-ing (Coleman 1988; Jacek 1986; Atkinson and Coleman 1989; Brownlee 2005, 72ff; Brooks and Stritch 1991, 208ff; Stanbury 1986, 244ff; Langille 1987; Clancy 2004).

At this latter level, the most detailed and useful study is William Coleman's (1988) *Business and Politics: A Study of Collective Action*, which focuses specifically on Canadian trade associations, and was itself part of a wider cross-national project. Coleman provides a picture of Cana-dian business associations that is highly fragmented in comparison with most other industrialized nations, with only the United States being similarly disaggregated (1988, 6). Representation was divided amongst a variety of general business associations covering broad sections of the economy, such as the Business Council on National Issues (now the Canadian Council of Chief Executives) representing large corporations; the Canadian Federation of Independent Business representing small business; the Canadian Chamber of Commerce representing a wide range of businesses organized into local chambers; and in the manufacturing sector, the Canadian Manufacturers' Association (now merged into Canadian Manufacturers and Exporters). At a less general level, a multitude of trade associations represent other industrial sectors, individual industries, and industry subsegments. There is much overlap here, making it difficult to determine exactly which organizations are responsible for what, and the extensive fragmentation is also an obstacle for Canadian governments in trying to devise a coherent industrial strategy in consultation with business interests. This structural policy problem is further exacerbated by the fragmentation of the Canadian state itself (Coleman 1988, 6–8).

Coleman allows for the possibility that this formal, structural fragmentation may be mitigated by elite linkages amongst an 'inner circle' of business leaders, as suggested by Michael Useem (1984) for the United States and Britain, or Wallace Clement (1975) and William Carroll (1986) in Canada, but he argues that there is still a need to demonstrate 'how and where such an elite participates in the policy process' (1988, 11). However, Coleman's focus on the overt structure of business associations may overstate their degree of fragmentation by overlooking informal and other ties that can help to bond the mosaic together. Using a typology devised by Philippe Schmitter and Wolfgang Streeck (1981, 195–9), Henry Jacek has pointed to various ad hoc and other more structured alliances between Canadian business associations (1986, 425–6). He found that ad hoc alliances involving irregular linkages were common amongst business associations in Canada and, beyond that, 46 per cent of them entered into more permanent forms of integration (1986, 425). These linkages can act as integrative mechanisms within a formally pluralist constellation of business groups. Another such linkage, revealed in the current study, is the extensive co-operation between business groups in the conduct of policy analysis, as will be seen later.

Furthermore, the very institution of a business association is an integrative mechanism for enterprises that would otherwise be even more fragmented. Such organizations play important collective roles for business in both economic and political realms. Trade associations perform vital economic functions for their members by providing a variety of information on new products, processes, and technologies, in addition to management and financial information and statistics gathering. They also engage in marketing and trade promotion activities, and are useful in planning and strategic development by identifying problems and trends, as well as economic forecasting. Such information is communicated to members through various mechanisms such as newsletters, magazines, websites, conferences, and personal contacts. Many of these services are selective benefits only available to group members, and they provide an incentive to join business associations beyond the collective benefits for the industry as a whole that might arise from political action.

On the political side, trade associations perform five main functions in regard to policy making: (1) monitoring political developments relevant to the association's members, including policy proposals, regulations, legislation, appointments, and the emergence of new issues; (2) direct lobbying of proximate policy makers, involving personal contacts and representations before various government agencies at home and abroad; (3) indirect lobbying – affecting policy indirectly by attempting to shape public opinion through media relations, advocacy advertising, public relations activities, etc.; (4) building alliances with other groups to broaden the base of influence; and (5) research and policy analysis to provide a solid basis for advocacy (Brooks and Stritch 1991, 221–2). In addition, trade associations can also play an important role in policy implementation, such as administering product standards and labelling regulations (Coleman and Jacek 1983, 268–71). In some respects, these political functions are easier to perform when an association's membership is relatively homogenous and is drawn from a single industry or business segment. Here, members' interests are more coherent and united, and advocacy can take a clear and forceful direction. Broader-based groups have to make policy compromises to accommodate a more diverse membership, and their voices can be more attenuated. However, broad-based groups have an advantage in representing a wider sector of the economy, and their input is harder for policy makers to ignore.

The issue of business unity or fragmentation is important because it is normally seen as influencing the level of business power in society (Vogel 1989, 12; Useem 1984, 6; Mizruchi 1992, 250; Brownlee 2005, 14).[1] However, even when fragmented, particular business associations can still have extensive influence over policy outcomes if they are able to achieve a privileged position of incorporation into policy subsystems with government agencies relevant to their interests. At one time, the idea of cozy, exclusive, clientele relationships between privileged groups and subsections of government enjoyed a considerable popularity in policy studies, particularly in the United States (see for example McConnell 1966; Greenwald 1977; Dodd and Schott 1979; Ripley and Franklin 1984; La Palombara 1964; Richardson and Jordan 1985; Schultz 1980; Bucovetsky 1975; Abonyi and Atkinson 1983). However, these closed, symbiotic relationships described some policy areas better than others and had a hard time surviving the explosion of consumer groups, environmental groups, and other 'public interest' groups in the 1970s, which had the effect of opening up the policy process to a variety of new participants. The idea of clientelism was challenged and generally superceded (or augmented) by concepts such as 'issue networks' or 'policy communities' which described wider, more nebulous, more fluid and less harmonious groupings of policy actors in different policy areas (see, for example, Heclo 1978; Coleman and Skogstad 1990; Atkinson and Coleman 1996).

In this more complex and competitive political environment, business has become less complacent in its relations with government and has had to engage more systematically in a battle of ideas with other groups and interests. The mobilization of knowledge gives well-resourced and well-organized groups an important potential for agenda setting and advocacy. The provision of reliable information from the private sector, particularly on specialized or technical issues, is useful for policy makers and is one of the key resources facilitating inclusion and influence of groups in the policy process. In addition, the cognitive dependency of government officials on private interests is likely to have increased over the last decade as federal and provincial budget cuts have eroded the state's own capacity for independent policy analysis. For business associations there are now greater opportunities for shaping official thinking, but there are also greater challenges in responding to the competing inputs of other groups. In both respects, there is an increased premium on research and policy analysis.

Yet despite its potential significance, very little is known about the scope and character of policy analysis by business groups. How much policy analysis is being done, and by what sorts of associations in which economic sectors? How has the extent of this activity changed? To what areas and levels of government do business groups direct most attention? What sorts of issues are important? And what use is made of the results? In an attempt to answer these questions a survey was carried

Figure 18.1 Frequency of Policy Analysis

How often does your association analyze public policies?

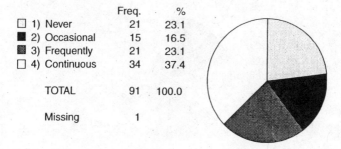

	Freq.	%
☐ 1) Never	21	23.1
■ 2) Occasional	15	16.5
▨ 3) Frequently	21	23.1
☐ 4) Continuous	34	37.4
TOTAL	91	100.0
Missing	1	

out of the policy analysis functions of Canadian national business associations, and this paper reports and discusses the results of that survey.[2]

The Extent of Policy Analysis

In an attempt to assess the extent of policy analysis, national business associations were asked both about the frequency of their analytical activities and about the number of full-time personnel employed in policy analysis functions. On both measures there was a considerable disparity within the business association universe, with some groups being heavily committed while others engaged in little or no analytical activity. From figure 18.1 it can be seen that for over 37 per cent of associations, policy analysis is something that is conducted on a continuous basis, while at the other end of the spectrum, 23 per cent never do any sort of policy analysis. If anything, this latter figure probably underestimates the case, as the response rate for groups with little interest in studying government policies is likely to be lower than for those for whom it is a major commitment.

Although trade associations commonly have functions in addition to their political and policy roles, the ability to represent an industry or sector to government, or to articulate industry views to a wider public, is an important part of the raison d'être for such groups. A capacity for analyzing policies, evaluating alternatives, and providing new information is something that would undoubtedly enhance the association's advocacy and representative roles, and it is thus somewhat surprising that nearly one-quarter of Canadian business associations eschew this

Figure 18.2 Number of Analysts (Groups Doing Analysis)

If analysis is done in-house, how many full-time analysts do you have?

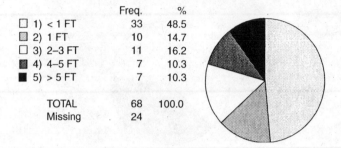

	Freq.	%
☐ 1) < 1 FT	33	48.5
▨ 2) 1 FT	10	14.7
☐ 3) 2–3 FT	11	16.2
▩ 4) 4–5 FT	7	10.3
■ 5) > 5 FT	7	10.3
TOTAL	68	100.0
Missing	24	

function even in a qualitative or unsystematic fashion. However, this significant minority should not obscure the fact that over 60 per cent of associations conduct policy analysis either frequently or continuously.

When we look at the number of personnel that each group allocates to policy analysis, a disparate pattern also emerges. As figure 18.2 illustrates, almost half of the organizations that do some in-house analysis have less than one full-time employee engaged in this function. This could be quite a senior person but someone who also has other responsibilities within the association. If we combine the first two categories, 63 per cent have the equivalent of one full-time person or less, and when we include the non-analytical groups (table 18.1), we are faced with the conclusion that for 72 per cent of Canadian national business associations, policy analysis is a one-person effort at best. This is perhaps not too surprising given William Coleman's earlier finding that the majority of Canadian business associations have fairly modest resources and employ only two or three non-clerical people in total, who are typically 'jacks of all trades' (1988, 45). Yet, despite this general pattern, there is also a small elite group of business associations that have more considerable analytical resources, and that employ four or more full-time analysts. This distribution suggests a hierarchy amongst Canadian business associations with regard to policy analysis, and if we combine the two intercorrelated variables (frequency and number of analysts) into a single measure, we can achieve a composite indicator of analytical intensity, as shown in table 18.2.[3] On this measure, the high-end group of 'super-analysts' constituting just under 16 per cent of the total is juxtaposed with the 64 per cent of groups that had a low or nonexistent level of policy analysis.

Table 18.1 Number of Analysts (All Groups)

	Freq.	%
0) None	21	23.6
1) 1 PT	33	37.1
2) 1 FT	10	11.2
3) 2–3 FT	11	12.4
4) 4+ FT	14	15.7
TOTAL	89	100.0
Missing	3	

Table 18.2 Analytical Intensity

	Freq.	%
0) None	21	23.6
1) Low	36	40.4
2) Moderate	18	20.2
3) High	14	15.7
TOTAL	89	100.0
Missing	3	

One factor that could possibly reduce the disparity in this associational class structure is the fact that many business associations use external bodies, such as consultancy or law firms, to carry out policy analysis in addition to their own internal resources. Groups that do little in-house analysis might compensate by relying more on external agencies. However, this plausible hypothesis is not supported by the data. There was only one instance of a group exclusively relying on external bodies for policy analysis, and for the rest, the propensity to use external resources was greater amongst the higher intensity associations than lower ones. For the top group of super-analysts, 85 per cent also went outside the organization, as opposed to 64 per cent in the low intensity category. Thus, those groups with fewer analytical resources were more likely to rely just on in-house analysis.

To further investigate these disparities, the level of analytical intensity was examined across different economic sectors and for different sizes of enterprise.[4] Although the numbers of groups in any particular sector were fairly small, the general pattern was that most sectors contained groups with different intensity levels. To the extent that there were sectoral divisions, a somewhat lower level of policy analysis took place in the sectors for agriculture and food, wood and paper, chemicals and textiles, and construction. At the high intensity levels, there was also a fairly widespread distribution across sectors, with a greater prominence of such groups in the two sectors of accommodation/recreation and health. However, the broad picture here is that high and low intensity associations were found in almost all sectors, and that sectoral variations had little impact in accounting for differences in the extent of policy analysis amongst business groups.

A different pattern emerged when the effect of size on analytic intensity was examined. Again, the numbers in any particular size category were limited, especially after eliminating those associations that represented businesses of all sizes. However, by dichotomizing both variables (small/large size; low/high intensity) significance problems were overcome and a strong positive relationship was revealed. Those associations whose members were larger companies were much more likely to do a lot of regular policy analysis than those groups whose members were predominantly smaller businesses (tau-b = 0.519; P < 0.000). This is fairly predictable given the more extensive resources of large corporations, although it could be argued that such enterprises have less need for trade associations to do policy research precisely because of their own individual capabilities. Such a hypothesis is not supported by the data here, and while large corporations may do more individual policy analysis than small companies, the associations where they dominate are also more active.

In order to provide a less static picture, associations were also asked to evaluate how the extent of policy analysis had changed over the last five years. As shown in figure 18.3, the results are heavily skewed. Of those groups that do some policy analysis, nearly 70 per cent reported that this function had become more extensive, while only 4 per cent reported a drop. This was true across all intensity levels, but was particularly pronounced amongst the super-analysts, where 92 per cent reported an increase. Clearly, policy analysis is an expanding area for Canadian business associations, and one factor that may help to account for this development is budgetary restraint in the public sector. As governments at all levels have cut back over the last ten years or so, resources for policy analysis have been affected, along with everything else. When business groups feel that government has lost the capacity to provide full and accurate analysis on important issues, then there is an incentive to redress the deficiency. In so doing, business associations achieve greater control over the research agenda, the nature of the analysis and the results, and ultimately greater influence over the direction of public policy. Government may achieve short-term savings but

Figure 18.3 Change in Extent of Analysis (Last Five Years)

Over the last five years, has your policy analysis function become more extensive, less
extensive, or stayed the same?

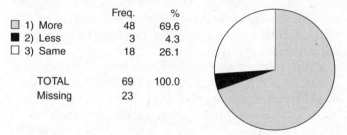

	Freq.	%
☐ 1) More	48	69.6
■ 2) Less	3	4.3
☐ 3) Same	18	26.1
TOTAL	69	100.0
Missing	23	

at the cost of an increasing dependency on business for information and
a decline in disinterested policy research.

Evert Lindquist has suggested that governments started to rely more
on external analysts in the 1980s, partly because new political leaders
did not completely trust their public servants but also because of 'significant expenditure restraint and delayering of senior management in
the public service' (1996, 222). Senior policy makers also became more
comfortable using outside policy advice as private sector analysts were
increasingly drawn from the ranks of former public officials (1996, 222–
3). Michael Prince similarly points to a decline in government in-house
research activities in the 1980s and 1990s as a result of downsizing, and
argues that the policy advice role of departmental officials is now
shared with a variety of actors inside and outside of government (2007,
9). Other contributors to this volume, such as Donald Abelson and
Kimberley Speers, also note the impact of budgetary cuts on government think tanks and policy research capabilities in this period. The
expansion of policy analysis by business associations over the last five
years suggests that the balance between private and public analysis
continues to shift, and if this is the case, then we are witnessing a
trend towards a growing privatization of policy analysis and a greater
empowerment of private-sector organizations in the policy-making
process.

Means and Mechanisms of Policy Analysis

Besides the extent of analytical activity by business associations, very
little is known about the techniques of analysis that these groups conduct when they address problems using their own resources. Nor is

there much information about the sorts of outside agencies used by business groups when policy analysis is conducted externally. This section briefly examines both of these issues, looking firstly at the use of formal analytical techniques such as cost-benefit analysis, and secondly at the importance of linkages between business associations and universities, research councils, consultancy firms, pollsters, law firms, and other business associations.

Cost-benefit analysis and other quantitative techniques are aimed at providing a systematic means of evaluating and comparing alternative policy options. While offering the promise of objective and scientific conclusions, they also have a number of shortcomings that serve to limit the utility of such methods. First, it is not always possible to identify all the consequences of different policy options, let alone translate them into monetary values. Second, rational analysis is circumscribed by the normative values of policy participants and the conflicts these engender. Third, rational economic analysis can easily be drowned out by the exigencies of the political process. And finally, where government is structurally divided, as in federal systems or where there is a separation of powers, rational planning can be difficult to implement (Heineman et al. 2002, 49–55, 105; Irwin 2003, 62).

Despite these shortcomings, it is still useful for business or other groups to claim that their policy demands are backed by empirical research based on rational analytical techniques. In the United States, cost-benefit analysis is widely used by practising policy analysts and has been touted as the 'single most important problem-solving tool in policy work' (Munger 2000, 134). Figure 18.4 shows that 42 per cent of the Canadian business associations that do some policy analysis claim to have used such techniques in the last two to three years. Given that the explicitness and comprehensiveness of cost-benefit analysis makes it expensive to use (Vining and Boardman 2007), we might expect these formal quantitative techniques to be more prevalent amongst groups with greater resources and a more intense commitment to policy analysis. This seems to be corroborated by the survey data, where 69 per cent of the high intensity groups used cost-benefit analysis or other formal quantitative techniques, as opposed to 37 per cent of the low intensity analysts. Of the groups representing mostly larger corporations, 62 per cent used these techniques, while this figure was only 14 per cent for associations whose members were mostly smaller businesses. Data on quantitative techniques were from business associations that do at least some of their policy analysis in-house, and there were very few analyti-

Figure 18.4 Cost-Benefit Analysis

For in-house policy analysis over the last two to three years, have you used formal
techniques such as cost-benefit quantitative analysis?

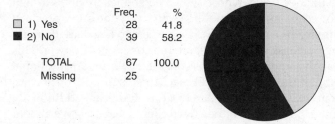

	Freq.	%
☐ 1) Yes	28	41.8
■ 2) No	39	58.2
TOTAL	67	100.0
Missing	25	

cally active associations that did not have some in-house capability.
However, the largest category contained groups that conducted analysis both internally and through external resources. This category comprised 68 per cent of active groups. All groups that also use external
bodies for policy analysis were asked to assess the importance of various institutions on a five-point scale from 1) not very important to 5)
very important. Table 18.3 reports the combined percentage of groups
answering in the top two categories (4 and 5), along with the mean
importance score for each institution.

Table 18.3 Importance of External Agencies for Policy Analysis

	% Important/ V. Important	Mean Importance (5-point scale)
Consultancy firms	63.8	3.6
Polling firms	19.6	2.4
Law firms	41.3	3.0
Other bus. associations	40.4	3.2
Research councils	43.5	3.0
Universities	25.5	2.4

Most notably, this table reveals the high degree of importance attached to consultancy firms as mechanisms for policy analysis. These
firms offer several advantages for trade associations and other business
clients who employ them on a continuing or ad hoc basis. Not only are
they sources of specialized expertise in various areas of public policy –
sometimes with a specific sectoral focus – they are also specialists in the
practice of government relations, normally with established networks

of personal contacts in politics and the bureaucracy. For business associations, policy analysis is not an academic exercise; it is a pragmatic, results-oriented endeavour aimed at shaping the course of public policy. The use of consultancy firms, whose senior personnel are often drawn from the higher echelons of the public sector, facilitates the practical application of policy research by providing access to key decision makers and helping business groups navigate the corridors of power. This dovetailing of analysis and access gives consultancy firms an additional utility over some of the other external mechanisms of policy analysis, such as university-based policy research. Consultants are additionally useful for business groups when they have clients that are government departments or agencies. In this role they work both sides of the street simultaneously – advising business clients about influencing government policy at the same time as they advise government policy makers about what to do. As noted by Kimberley Speers (2007), the federal government has become quite porous to this sort of infiltration by management consultants.

The larger consultancy firms can also deliver two other sets of benefits for business groups. First, these firms sometimes provide a variety of different consultancy functions under one roof, such as polling, public relations and market research in addition to policy analysis and government relations. Business clients can thus benefit from the synergies of 'one-stop shopping' for many of their public policy needs. Second, some consultancy firms are international consortia with operations in many different countries, and this allows them to offer services for Canadian business associations whose policy interests transcend national borders. The globalization of business operations puts a premium on policy analysis that is similarly international in scope.

Research councils and institutes also feature prominently as useful resources for business associations that use external agencies. More than 43 per cent of these business groups reported that such organizations were important or very important. As Donald Abelson (2007) reports, the perceived independence of these 'think tanks' enhances their credibility while at the same time many have become more extensively oriented towards policy advocacy. This combination of attributes makes them attractive vehicles for business associations in the conduct of policy analysis.

Another noteworthy finding in table 18.3 is that 40 per cent of the groups using external agencies considered other business associations to be important or very important in conducting policy analysis. This is

Table 18.4 Importance of Levels of Government for Policy Analysis

	% Important/ V. Important	Mean Importance (5-point scale)
Federal government	92.8	4.7
Provincial governments	71.0	4.0
Municipal governments	10.6	2.1
Foreign governments	25.4	2.6
International organizations	29.4	2.6

significant because it suggests a substantial level of co-operation amongst Canadian business groups in analytical activity, despite the fact that the business community is structurally fragmented, particularly in comparison with European countries (Coleman 1988, 219–23). Although Canadian business associations are institutionally disaggregated, informal mechanisms of co-operation may result in a higher level of integration than is otherwise supposed.

Analytical Focus

The focus of policy analysis by business groups can be divided into two sections. The first looks at where groups direct their attention in terms of federal, provincial and local governments, as well as foreign governments and international organizations. The second examines the sorts of issues that business associations address based on a series of open-ended questions.

Level of Government

Looking first at the governmental focus, associations were asked to rate the importance of different levels of government for policy analysis on the same five-point scale used for table 18.3. The percentage reporting in the two highest categories of importance and the mean score are shown in table 18.4. These data provide few surprises about the focus of attention for national business groups, with federal government policy handily dominating the list. However, 71 per cent of the national associations that are engaged in policy analysis put provincial government policy in the highest categories of importance. As Doug McArthur (2007) points out, more than half of all government activity in Canada takes place at the provincial level, yet there is a relative neglect of provincial policy making in the scholarly literature. While this may be a deficiency of academic policy analysis, it does not seem to be repeated by Canada's business associations, where the provincial level of government is given considerable attention. The importance of both levels of government reflects the reality of constitutional policy divisions in Canada as well as the *de facto* sharing of powers that characterizes most areas of Canadian public policy. It is also necessary to recognize the importance that provincial governments can have in shaping the national political agenda and pressuring Ottawa, even in areas of formal federal jurisdiction. Consequently, it is difficult for national business associations to ignore provincial policy.

Municipal governments, not surprisingly, get relatively little attention from national associations, although policy at this level does have important implications for some groups – for example, in home building or urban transit. Provincial trade associations may have more activity at this level, but the resources available for any sort of policy analysis are likely to be more restricted amongst subnational groups.

At the other end of the local-to-global spectrum, one interesting finding from table 18.4 is that over one-quarter of the active associations rated foreign governments and international organizations as important or very important. Policy analysis by these groups extends beyond the confines of domestic Canadian politics and has a strong outward-looking, international component. The increasing globalization of economic activity and the closer integration of the North American economy have given international organizations and foreign governments a greater impact on domestic policy outputs, and consequently it is more important for business associations to analyse policy at this level. To a significant extent, policy analysis has become extraterritorial and is likely to become more so.

Yet this endeavour poses problems for business groups. To engage in policy analysis at an additional, international level creates an extra layer of complexity and expense that places new burdens on the association's personnel. It is not just a matter of examining the policies of other governments and institutions themselves, but also involves analysis of how these policies interact with Canadian and provincial policy making, either as constraints or opportunities. With foreign governments, Canadian trade associations are venturing as outsiders onto less familiar territory, with shortcomings for both analysis and advocacy. Moreover, in both bilateral and multilateral forums, where government-to-government negotiations are the norm, private groups are one step further removed in the process. Their policy analyses may have some impact on positions taken by Canadian delegations, but these positions do not necessarily carry much weight at the bargaining table and may become subject to various compromises. Rational economic analysis can easily be lost in the give-and-take of international negotiation.

Issues

To get a sense of the substantive focus of policy analysis, Canadian business associations were asked to list the three most important issues on which they had conducted analysis over the last three years. As expected, this yielded a diverse array of topics reflecting the diversity of groups and economic sectors across Canada, but which still permitted some aggregate generalizations.

One set of questions concerns the specificity or generality of business group analysis. Are groups focused on narrow, sector-specific or industry-specific issues, or do they analyse broader policies that transcend particular industries and that affect business collectively? In this regard it is useful to consider Mancur Olson's distinction between collective or public goods and selective benefits. The former are benefits of group action from which no one is excluded regardless of group membership, while the latter accrue only to those who are members of a particular group. For any large group, selective or private benefits provide more of an incentive for participation than do collective goods, whose fruits are also enjoyed by non-participants (Olson 1965). If we apply this to business interests and public policy, then we should expect trade associations to pursue narrow selective benefits for their particular industry or segment, rather than broad issues that have a significance for business in general.

In a limited study of industry lobbying in the United States, Kenneth Godwin and Barry Seldon use this distinction between private and collective goods in examining the sorts of issues that trade associations pursue. They concluded that 'trade associations rarely lobbied on any issue that did not affect directly (and almost exclusively) their members. In other words, trade associations seldom lobbied for goods that were collective beyond their industry' (Godwin and Seldon 2002, 221). Given that policy analysis is ultimately directed towards policy influence, we might expect the same thing to apply to trade associations' analytical activities as well as lobbying. But is this true in Canada?

The data from this survey suggest a more qualified picture. Many issues mentioned by Canadian associations were clearly specific to a particular industry or sector. These included such things as insurance industry regulations, food labelling, shipbuilding policy, dairy pricing, building code regulations, and broadcasting policy. Other issues such as license fees, government price controls and subsidies for research and development had a more generic appearance. However, when cross-checked with other sources such as association websites, it became evident that the relevant associations were often not interested in fees, price controls and subsidies in general, but in their specific application to that industry. In total, 62 per cent of the issues mentioned could be classified as specific to an association's line of business. Of the remaining 38 per cent, there were undoubtedly some issues where the generic-sounding response, for example, 'tax issues' or 'trade policy,' masked a more specific focus, but where this could not definitely be determined. Alongside these were issues that had a more general impact on business, such as the Kyoto Accord/climate change, payroll taxes, and privacy legislation. These policies cover a broad range of industries and suggest that trade associations in Canada are not exclusively motivated by narrow selective benefits for their own industry but, from time to time, are also involved in pursuing more general collective goods for business.

Several of the industry-specific issues mentioned were fairly narrow and technical, such as fuel cell commercialization, office products tendering processes, sleepware flammability rules, and natural health product regulations. These sorts of issues are important to the industries concerned but they do not normally generate much public interest or media attention. Analysis by the relevant trade associations in these areas is likely to have an advantage in the advocacy process due to the relative paucity of competing perspectives to challenge this specialized expertise. Policy relations with government agencies on these sorts of issues are more likely to be characterized by bureaucratic patron-client linkages than by intense pluralistic competition.

Besides looking at the level of issue generality, the survey also permitted an examination of the substantive policy areas that business associations considered to be most important. As can be seen in table 18.5 below, taxation led the list, with 34.3 per cent of groups reporting that tax issues were at least one of the three most important issues over the last few years. This is not too startling given the perennial concern that the business community has with the fiscal burden placed on the private sector by all levels of government. Nor is it surprising to find

Table 18.5. Top Issue Areas for Groups Doing Policy Analysis

	Groups Mentioning Issue (%)
Taxes	34.3
Environment	27.1
International trade	25.7
Subsidies	15.7
Health and social policy	15.7
Privacy	10.0

the high degree of importance attached to environmental issues, as business has faced widespread challenges in this area from environmental groups and governments. Concerning the environment, there are at least two significant issues that have constituted a focus for the attention of business associations over recent years. One is the Kyoto Accord on climate change and greenhouse gases, which Canada has ratified and, if enforced, will impose restrictions on many industries. The other is the review of the Transportation of Dangerous Goods Act, initiated in 2002, on which industry associations were invited to make submissions. Both these initiatives can be credited with encouraging a high level of business analysis on the environment.

International trade was another expected priority area for business associations, given Canada's extensive trade dependency and the significance of NAFTA and WTO rules for Canadian industry. Bilateral trade issues have become additionally important since 9/11, with concerns about tightening access at the U.S. border, and this was reflected in some of the recent analysis done by Canadian business groups. An unforeseen issue that did make it onto the list was that of privacy. A central reason for this is the Personal Information Protection and Electronic Documents Act (PIPEDA), which came into effect in 2001, and which imposes a variety of regulations and requirements on commercial enterprises concerning the collection, use and disclosure of information about individuals. Originally, this Act applied only to federally regulated industries such as banking, broadcasting, airlines, etc., but from January 2004 it was extended to cover all businesses. The potential costs imposed by PIPEDA across the spectrum of business activity provided a strong incentive for analyzing the implications of this Act.

One issue area where policy analysis by business associations appears to have had a significant impact is in regard to border-crossing procedures in the wake of 9/11. In October 2001, a coalition of over 45 business groups and individual companies was formed, known as the Coalition for Secure and Trade-Efficient Borders, which included Canadian Manufacturers and Exporters, the Canadian Federation of Independent Business, the Canadian Chamber of Commerce, the Tourism Industry Association of Canada, and several other groups. This coalition analysed the problems of border access and security and issued three reports recommending policy improvements.

The coalition's goals have been to make it easier for low-risk goods and individuals to cross the border, as well as strengthening Canadian border management and improving co-operation with the United States against the entry of terrorists, illegal immigrants, contraband, etc. The efforts of this broad business coalition have been instrumental in reinstating and expanding the NEXUS program of preclearance for frequent, low-risk travellers, as well as implementing the FAST system for moving pre-approved goods quickly across the Canada-U.S. border. It is an example of concerted business action across a variety of sectors that goes against the more customary picture of disaggregated activity amongst Canadian business associations and a lack of unity amongst Canada's business elites.

This coalition is also noteworthy for including individual companies – such as General Motors of Canada, Pratt & Whitney Canada, and Canadian Pacific, along with trade associations – in a collective research and advocacy effort. Another example of such co-operation is in the banking sector, where RBC Financial Group has conducted two studies of small business growth in Canada in conjunction with the Canadian Manufacturers and Exporters, the Canadian Federation of Independent Business, and Queen's University Business School. These focused on barriers to growth and made recommendations for changes to tax and regulatory policies. Although they are beyond the scope of this study, large corporations in Canada have the capacity for their own policy analysis, and can be useful partners in collaborative analytical activity with other business organizations. However, an earlier study suggests that this capability is only fulfilled by a minority of top Canadian companies, and that only 34 per cent of *Financial Post 500* corporations have their own government relations unit (Taylor, Warrack, and Baetz 1999, 182).

Small businesses generally have little option but to use business associations if they want to participate in the policy process, but even for large corporations these groups have a number of advantages. In addition to pooling the financial costs of political action, business associations can also relieve corporate executives of some of the demands on their time from dealing with political issues. Isaiah Litvak maintains that CEOs of large corporations in Canada commonly spend up to half their time on public affairs issues (1994, 132). If this is true, then the use of business associations may help to prevent executives from being even more inundated with political concerns. Business associations also have an advantage in gaining access to policy makers. This is partly because it is more efficient for officials to deal with a single set of aggregated interests than with a variety of possibly dissonant corporations, and partly because the legitimacy of corporate lobbying is enhanced, even in oligopolistic industries, by wrapping narrow interests in 'the collective drapes of an association' (Coleman 1988, 12–13).

Yet, the use of business associations also has some shortcomings for large corporations. For conglomerates, no single industry association will adequately cover all the corporation's interests and, as mentioned earlier, the risk of internal conflict in broad-based groups means that the message is often diluted. Also, some corporations have fairly specific political interests, for example, a particular contract, or tax break or trade barrier, and a lot of association activity may not be relevant to their concerns. In such circumstances, corporations may find it more useful to participate in ad hoc business coalitions than become involved as full-time members of a permanent association.

Dissemination of Results

For business associations, policy analysis has little use unless it is communicated to actors who have a direct or indirect impact on the course of public policy. Even if it is just a matter of the association's officers referring to the results in meetings with government officials, the message has to get out in some form to policy-relevant constituencies. Consequently, associations were asked whether they circulated the results of their analyses to various groups or organizations, and the responses are shown in table 18.6. Trade associations exist to serve their members and so it is only to be expected that a given group's officers would keep the 'rank-and-file' informed about analysis that was being conducted on their behalf. So the 90 per cent figure in this category is no surprise. For outside groups, however, the findings are less clear-cut. Over half the associations disseminate their analyses directly to government officials as a matter of course, but for a substantial minority this is not automatic. Results of policy analyses do not always come out as expected, and it makes no sense for business groups to supply govern-

Table 18.6 Dissemination of Analyses to Various Constituencies

	(% of groups) Yes	Sometimes	No
Association members	90.0	0	10.0
Government officials	52.8	42.9	4.3
General public	8.7	56.5	34.8
Political parties	20.0	54.3	25.7
Other business associations	30.0	64.3	5.7

ment officials with information that is incongruent with their members' interests. The same logic applies for the dissemination of analyses to other outside constituencies and there was a high percentage of qualified responses for all of these.

For the general public and political parties, there was also a relatively high percentage of associations that declined to make their analyses available at all. Parties may be central institutions of democracy but, as William Cross points out, between elections party organizations do not play a significant role in policy development (2004, 1) Given this deficiency, it is understandable that business groups would generally give a fairly low priority to these institutions. The fact that many groups still do send the results of their analyses to political parties, at least some of the time, is probably explained by the natural inclination to disseminate favourable results as widely as possible in the hope of having some impact on agenda setting for the future. Once the analysis has been completed, the additional costs of including parties as recipients would be minimal.

As for the public, business analysis can have an effect on policy development by influencing popular opinion, and business groups are generally concerned about managing issues in the public realm. Yet there are several disadvantages here: (1) the impact of public opinion is only indirect; (2) many issues mentioned by business groups are too specialized or technical to generate much public attention – for example, federal capital cost allowances or Canadian pilotage policies for shipping; (3) the costs of reaching a mass audience are more substantial; and (4) there is always a risk of mobilizing opposition. However, when business associations do disseminate their research publicly they tend to do so across a broad front, employing a plurality of media, with the most popular medium being the Internet website. When groups go public with their analyses, 92 per cent use websites.

A final noteworthy finding about the dissemination of results is that over 94 per cent of Canadian business groups share their analyses with other business associations, at least some of the time. This reinforces an earlier point that informal mechanisms of integration may help to compensate for the structural fragmentation of business groups in Canada. Linkages between groups in both the conduct and dissemination of policy analysis, as well as other areas of informal co-operation, can serve to moderate the general picture of business disunity.

Conclusions

This survey has tried to provide some basic information about the extent, means, focus and dissemination of policy analysis by Canadian national business associations, about which very little was previously known. The findings here must be taken with a degree of caution, given the limited numbers of national trade associations, particularly when responses are broken down by sector. It would also be useful to have more qualitative information about the analytical activities of business groups to supplement the quantitative data. With these caveats in mind, a number of conclusions can be highlighted.

There was, first of all, a considerable variation in the extent to which groups engaged in policy analysis. While over 60 per cent conduct policy analysis frequently or continuously, a significant minority of 23 per cent never do any, and even amongst the analytically active groups there is a wide disparity in the intensity of analysis. A picture emerges of a class-structure within the universe of Canadian business associations. Of the analytically active groups, a large proportion devote few human resources to this function, while at the top end of the scale there is an elite group of 'super-analysts,' comprising about 16 per cent of the total, with high levels of activity and resources. These groups did more analysis, more often, and were more likely to employ formal quantitative techniques such as cost-benefit analysis. Trade associations representing larger companies were strongly represented in this category. However, for all classes of active groups, policy analysis has become more extensive over the last five years, with an aggregate figure of 70 per cent reporting an increase. At the same time, policy analysis in the public sector is under pressure from budgetary restrictions, and the net effect is a shift towards greater privatization of policy analysis in Canada. The danger here is that public policy will become increasingly shaped by the self-interested analysis of private-sector groups.

Besides relying on their own internal resources, many groups also use external agencies for policy research, including consultancy firms, law firms, polling firms, other business associations, research councils, and universities. Consultancy firms were the most important external resource, offering several advantages for business associations, but law firms, research councils, and other business associations were all prominent. In particular, the use of other business associations for policy analysis suggests that informal linkages between groups may help to offset the overt structural fragmentation of Canadian trade associations. This was reinforced by similarly close links between groups in the dissemination of policy research.

The analytical focus of business groups was also examined, with attention being paid to the relative importance of different levels of government, as well as the sorts of issues analysed. In addition to their focus at the federal level, national business associations also give considerable attention to policy at the provincial level. This accommodates the realities of divided policy authority within Canadian federalism and constitutes a priority that is not always reflected in the academic policy literature. Nor was the international level overlooked, and a sizeable minority of associations gave high priority to analyzing policies of foreign governments and international organizations, despite the additional problems involved. Business groups thus adapted themselves to the reality of a Canadian policy regime that is pulled simultaneously by strong subnational and supranational forces.

International concerns were also apparent in the issues chosen for analysis, with trade and the environment being the two most important areas after taxation. Under the environmental heading, the principal concern was with the Kyoto Accord and measures to combat global warming. However, in general, Canadian business associations analysed a broad array of issues, sometimes reflecting narrow sectoral interests and at other times addressing topics that had a wider impact over a range of different industries. In so doing, they dealt with issues that could be defined as collective goods for broad sections of the business community, as well as with more narrowly focused private goods.

Finally, the survey examined questions about the dissemination of policy analysis. For business associations policy analysis is intrinsically linked to advocacy, and the dissemination of results is directed towards this end. Other than informing their own members, business groups gave highest priority to circulating results to government officials or legislators where their efforts were more likely to have a direct impact on policy. A lower level of importance was attached to the general public and political parties, but when groups did go public with their analyses, they generally employed a range of different media, of which the most widely used were Internet websites.

This survey has provided a variety of information about policy analysis conducted by Canadian business associations, an expanding area of activity over the last five years and one that is largely ignored in the policy studies literature. The study answers some questions and suggests directions for further research. In particular, future survey data would allow us to get a better sense of how the patterns identified here are evolving, and it would also be useful to examine the policy analysis functions of individual corporations and how these mesh (or not) with the activities of associations. In addition, there is plenty of scope for more qualitative research on policy analysis by both corporations and business groups.

Appendix: Policy analysis questionnaire

Canadian Business Associations – Policy Analysis Survey

This survey is part of a broader academic research study on the extent and character of policy analysis throughout Canadian government and society. Please see the covering letter for further information.

We are interested in the functions of Canadian national business associations in analyzing the content and impact of government policies, whether this involves analysis conducted in-house by the association's own staff or analysis that is contracted-out to external bodies.

Q 1. How often does your association conduct analyses of public policies, either using in-house resources or external agencies?

○ Never
○ Occasionally
○ Frequently
○ Continuously

If your association never conducts any sort of policy analysis please return the questionnaire at this point using the stamped-addressed envelope. This will be useful in helping us to assess the extent of policy analysis amongst Canadian business associations. If there are any additional comments you would like to make we invite you to do so in the space at the end of the questionnaire. Thank you for your participation.

Q 2. Is this function generally performed in-house by the association's own staff, or do you use external agencies, or both?

○ In-house (Skip Q5)
○ External agencies (Skip Q3 & Q4)
○ Both

Q 3. If some policy analysis is done in-house, how many analysts do you normally have?

○ One person who also has other responsibilities
○ One person, full-time (or equivalent)
○ 2–3 full-time personnel (or equivalent)
○ 4–5 full-time personnel (or equivalent)
○ More than 5 full-time personnel (or equivalent)

Q 4. Over the last 2 or 3 years has your in-house policy analysis ever included formal quantitative techniques of program evaluation, such as cost-benefit analysis or cost-effectiveness analysis?

○ Yes
○ No

Q 5. If you use external resources for some of your policy analysis, how important are the following bodies? (Please circle the appropriate number.)

	Not very important			Very important	
Consultancy firms	1	2	3	4	5
Polling organizations	1	2	3	4	5
Law firms	1	2	3	4	5
Other business associations	1	2	3	4	5
Research institutes or councils	1	2	3	4	5
Universities	1	2	3	4	5

Q 6. Over the last five years would you say that the policy analysis function of your association has become more extensive, less extensive, or stayed about the same?

○ More extensive
○ Less extensive
○ About the same

Q 7. How important are the following levels of government as a focus for your policy analysis? (Please circle the appropriate number.)

	Not very important				Very important
Canadian federal government...	1	2	3	4	5
Provincial government	1	2	3	4	5
Municipal government	1	2	3	4	5
Foreign governments	1	2	3	4	5
International organizations	1	2	3	4	5

Q 8. How important are the following areas of activity as a focus for your policy analysis? (Please circle the appropriate number.)

	Not very important				Very important
Legislation or legislative proposals	1	2	3	4	5
Government regulations/ orders in-council	1	2	3	4	5
Departmental reports or reviews	1	2	3	4	5
Parliamentary committee reports	1	2	3	4	5
Judicial decisions...	1	2	3	4	5
Commissions of inquiry or task forces	1	2	3	4	5
Policies of non-governmental groups	1	2	3	4	5

Q 9. Please list the 3 most important issues over the last few years on which your association has conducted policy analysis, either in-house or using external resources.

1. _____

2. _____

3. _____

Q 10. On which issue has policy analysis yielded the most satisfactory results for your association?

Additional comments (if any):

Q 11. We are also interested in how the results of your policy analyses are disseminated. In general, are the results of your analyses circulated to the following groups, or does it depend on the issue?

	Yes	No	Depends
Directly to the association's members	O	O	O
Government officials or legislators	O	O	O
The general public	O	O	O
Political parties	O	O	O
Other associations	O	O	O

Additional comments (if any)

Q 12. If the results are made available to the general public, which of the following media are used?

	Yes	No
Publications	O	O
Press releases	O	O
Speeches by association officers	O	O
Internet website	O	O

O Other (please specify):_____

Q 13. In general, which of the following categories best describes the business members of your association?

O Mostly small independent businesses
O Small and medium-sized enterprises
O Medium-sized/large companies

    ○ Large national or multinational corporations
    ○ Businesses of all sizes
    ○ Other (please specify):_____

Additional Comments (if any):

Thank you very much for taking the trouble to fill out this questionnaire. Your participation is much appreciated. Please return the questionnaire in the stamped-addressed envelope provided.

NOTES

1 A study by Mark A. Smith (2000, 8) challenges this contention, arguing that issues where business is united are those where government decisions are most responsive to electoral outcomes and preferences of constituents. However, his study puts an inordinate amount of faith in both the integrity of the American electoral process and the saliency of issue voting amongst the American electorate.
2 The survey was mailed to 180 business associations in Canada whose activities and organization transcended a single province or region, and whose members were mainly private-sector companies rather than individuals. The latter was to distinguish between trade associations and professional groups. Also excluded were international or U.S. associations that included Canadian members, as well as various ad hoc business coalitions that are set up from time to time for specific purposes. 'Super-associations' such as the Formulated Products Industry Coalition, which is an association made up of other trade associations, were similarly excluded. The survey was conducted during the spring of 2004 and the response rate was just over 50 per cent. There were few outstanding variations in response rate by sector, with business services being the lowest at 25 per cent and communications being the highest at 73 per cent. However, 70 per cent of sectors were within one standard deviation of the mean.
3 The 'Low' category consisted of those groups that employed only one analyst either part-time or on a less than continuous basis. The 'High' category consisted of those groups that employed four or more full-time analysts on a continuous basis, and the 'Moderate' category consisted of those groups in between.

4 Sectors were based on a slightly modified version of Statistics Canada's former Standard Industrial Classification. This corresponded more readily with the division of labour amongst Canadian trade associations than did the more recent North American Industry Classification System.

REFERENCES

Abelson, Donald E. 2007. 'Any Ideas? Think Tanks and Policy Analysis in Canada.' This volume.
Abonyi, Arpad, and Michael Atkinson. 1983. 'Technological Innovation and Industrial Policy: Canada in an International Context.' In Michael M. Atkinson and Marsha A. Chandler, eds., *The Politics of Canadian Public Policy*, 93–126. Toronto: University of Toronto Press.
Atkinson, Michael M., and William D. Coleman. 1989. *The State, Business, and Industrial Change in Canada*. Toronto: University of Toronto Press.
– 1996. 'Policy Networks, Policy Communities, and the Problems of Governance.' In L. Dobuzinskis, M. Howlett, and D. Laycock, eds., *Policy Studies in Canada: The State of the Art*, 193–218. Toronto: University of Toronto Press.
Brooks, Stephen, and Andrew Stritch. 1991. *Business and Government in Canada*. Scarborough, ON: Prentice-Hall.
Brownlee, Jamie. 2005. *Ruling Canada: Corporate Cohesion and Democracy*. Halifax: Fernwood Publishing.
Brym, Robert J, ed. 1985. *The Structure of the Canadian Capitalist Class*. Toronto: Garamond Press.
Bucovetsky, Meyer. 1975. 'The Mining Industry and the Great Tax Reform Debate.' In A. Paul Pross, ed., *Pressure Group Behaviour in Canadian Politics*, 89–114. Scarborough, ON: McGraw-Hill Ryerson.
Carroll, William. 1986. *Corporate Power and Canadian Capitalism*. Vancouver: University of British Columbia Press.
– 2004. *Corporate Power in a Globalizing World: A Study in Elite Social Organization*. Toronto: Oxford University Press.
Clancy, Peter. 2004. *Micropolitics and Canadian Business: Paper, Steel and the Airlines*. Peterborough, ON: Broadview Press.
Clement, Wallace. 1975. *The Canadian Corporate Elite*. Toronto: McClelland and Stewart.
Coleman, William D. 1988. *Business and Politics: A Study of Collective Action*. Kingston and Montreal: McGill-Queen's University Press.
Coleman, William D., and Henry J. Jacek, 1983. 'The Roles and Activities of

Business Interest Associations in Canada.' *Canadian Journal of Political Science* 16(2), 257–80.

Coleman, William, and Grace Skogstad, eds. 1990. *Policy Communities and Public Policy in Canada: A Structural Approach*. Mississauga, ON: Copp Clark Pitman.

Cross, William. 2004. 'Political Parties Capacity for Policy Study and Development.' Paper presented at the Canadian Political Science Association annual conference, Winnipeg, 3 June 2004.

Dodd, L.C., and R.L. Schott. 1979. *Congress and the Administrative State*. New York: John Wiley and Sons.

Godwin, R. Kenneth, and Barry J. Seldon. 2002. 'What Corporations Really Want from Government: The Public Provision of Private Goods.' In A.J. Cigler and B.A. Loomis, eds., *Interest Group Politics*, 6th ed., 205–24. Washington, DC: CQ Press.

Greenwald, Carol S. 1977. *Group Power: Interest Groups, Lobbying and Public Policy*. New York: Praeger.

Heclo, Hugh. 1978. 'Issue Networks and the Executive Establishment.' In A. King, ed., *The New American Political System*, 87–124. Washington, DC: American Enterprise Institute.

Heineman, Robert A., et al. 2002. *The World of the Policy Analyst: Rationality, Values and Politics*. 3rd ed. New York: Chatham House.

Irwin, Lewis G. 2003. *The Policy Analyst's Handbook: Rational Problem Solving in a Political World*. Armonk, NY: M.E. Sharpe.

Jacek, Henry J. 1986. 'Pluralist and Corporatist Intermediation, Activities of Business Interest Associations, and Corporate Profits: Some Evidence from Canada.' *Comparative Politics* 18(4), 419–37.

Langille, David. 1987. 'The Business Council on National Issues and the Canadian State.' *Studies in Political Economy* 24, 41–85.

La Palombara, Joseph. 1964. *Interest Groups in Italian Politics*. Princeton, NJ: Princeton University Press.

Lindquist, Evert A. 1996. 'New Agendas for Research on Policy Communities: Policy Analysis, Administration and Governance.' In L. Dobuzinskis, M. Howlett, and D. Laycock, eds., *Policy Studies in Canada: The State of the Art*, 219–41. Toronto: University of Toronto Press.

Litvak, Isaiah. 1994. 'Government Intervention and Corporate Government Relations.' *Business Quarterly* 58(4), 130–7.

Mahon, Rianne. 1984. *The Politics of Industrial Restructuring: Canadian Textiles*. Toronto: University of Toronto Press.

McArthur, Doug. 2007. 'Policy Analysis in Provincial Governments in Canada: From PPBS to Network Management.' This volume.

McBride, Stephen, and John Shields. 1997. *Dismantling a Nation: The Transition to Corporate Rule in Canada.* 2nd ed. Halifax: Fernwood Publishing.

McConnell, Grant. 1966. *Private Power and American Democracy.* New York: Alfred A. Knopf.

Mizruchi, Mark S. 1992. *The Structure of Corporate Political Action: Interfirm Relations and Their Consequences.* Cambridge, MA: Harvard University Press.

Munger, Michael C. 2000. *Analyzing Policy: Choices, Conflicts and Practices.* New York: W.W. Norton.

Olson, Mancur. 1965. *The Logic of Collective Action.* Cambridge, MA: Harvard University Press.

Panitch, Leo, ed. 1977. *The Canadian State: Political Economy and Political Power.* Toronto: University of Toronto Press.

Prince, Michael J. 2007. 'Soft Craft, Hard Choices, Altered Context: Reflections on Twenty-Five Years of Policy Advice in Canada.' This volume.

Richardson, J.J., and A.G. Jordan. 1985. *Governing Under Pressure.* New York: Basil Blackwell.

Ripley, R.B., and G.A. Franklin. 1984. *Congress, the Bureaucracy and Public Policy.* 3rd ed. Homewood, IL: Dorsey Press.

Schmitter, Phillipe C., and Wolfgang Streeck. 1981. *A Research Design to Study the Associative Action of Business in the Advanced Industrial Societies of Western Europe.* Berlin: International Institute of Management.

Schultz, Richard. 1980. *Federalism, Bureaucracy and Public Policy.* Kingston and Montreal: McGill-Queen's University Press.

Smith, Mark A. 2000. *American Business and Political Power: Public Opinion, Elections and Democracy.* Chicago: University of Chicago Press.

Speers, Kimberley. 2007. 'The Invisible Private Service: Consultants and Public Policy in Canada.' This volume.

Stanbury, W.T. 1986. *Business-Government Relations in Canada.* Toronto: Methuen.

Taylor, D. Wayne, Allan A. Warrack, and Mark C. Baetz. 1999. *Business and Government in Canada: Partners for the Future.* Scarborough, ON: Prentice-Hall.

Useem, Michael. 1984. *The Inner Circle: Large Corporations and the Rise of Business Political Activity in the US and UK.* New York: Oxford University Press.

Veltmeyer, Henry. 1987. *Canadian Corporate Power.* Toronto: Garamond Press.

Vining, Aidan R., and Anthony E. Boardman. 2007. 'The Choice of Formal Policy Analysis Methods in Canada.' This volume.

Vogel, David. 1989. *Fluctuating Fortunes: The Political Power of Business in America.* New York: Basic Books.

19 Policy Analysis by the Labour Movement in a Hostile Environment

ANDREW JACKSON AND BOB BALDWIN

Introduction: From Junior Insiders to Outsiders

Canadian unions have been, and perceive themselves to be, very much on the defensive, facing major challenges to their legitimacy, role and effectiveness within the workplace, and relatively marginalized from the policy process. The latter role of unions has been little studied compared to extensive research on union impacts on the economy and the workplace, and on union involvement in party politics. This paper explores policy analysis by Canadian labour against the background of a changing relationship to the policy process.

Canadian unions are a significant economic and social force. One in three employees belongs to a trade union, with membership now divided equally between women and men. The unionization rate has slipped from 36 to 30 per cent since the mid-1980s, and private-sector density has fallen from 26 to 18 per cent over this period (Akyeampong 2004). By most accounts, union bargaining power, the ability to organize new members and political influence have eroded over the past two decades (Rose and Chaison 2001). Nonetheless, the Canadian labour movement is also widely judged to have been relatively successful in adjusting to the major economic and social changes that have affected organized labour in all advanced industrial countries. Canadian unions remain a significant force in the workplace, and have been engaged in an ongoing process of renewal and internal change to retain relevancy (Kumar and Murray 2003).

This section provides a broad historical overview of labour's role within, and growing marginalization from, the policy process, with some comments regarding the historical evolution of the policy analysis function within the labour movement. Section 2 reports on labour's relationship to the policy process, and specific policy analysis activities over the past decade or so. Section 3 details attempts by labour to shift the terms of public debate over policy, and section 4 provides some concluding observations.

Given the paucity of published research, this chapter is based mainly on the personal knowledge of the authors. Due to space limitations, only a few comments are made on policy analysis at the provincial level, and the paper does not cover the activities of unions that are not affiliated to the Canadian Labour Congress.

In the so-called Golden Age of the postwar period through to the mid-1970s, Canadian labour grew in numbers (mainly because of the strong growth of public services unions in the 1960s), successfully translated rising productivity into real wage gains for members, greatly expanded workplace pension and other benefits, and was a significant political force behind the expansion of social programs and public and social services (Morton 1998; Heron 1996). Organized labour played a major role in winning key social gains of the 1960s and early 1970s, such as the Canada/Quebec Pension Plan, the Canada Assistance Plan, medicare, and an expanded unemployment insurance system. The extent of incorporation of labour into the 'Fordist' Canadian economic and social order was limited, reflected in very high levels of industrial conflict compared to many other countries, but the legitimacy of collective bargaining in larger private-sector workplaces and, later, in public and social services, was generally accepted. In this context of relative acceptance, labour played what could be described as a junior insider role in the policy process.

Indicative of this junior insider role, from 1956 (when the Canadian Labour Congress or CLC was formed from a merger of two earlier labour central bodies), the CLC presented a lengthy annual policy memoranda (the so-called 'cap-in-hand brief') to an annual meeting of labour leaders with the prime minister and senior ministers covering the major economic and social policy issues of the day. Ministers of Labour, usually senior cabinet ministers with recognized responsibility for co-operatively managing the government's political and policy relationship with labour, ensured ongoing labour contact with other ministers. They were even invited to address labour conventions. The CLC nominated representatives to a wide range of advisory boards and commissions, notably (to take 1974 as an example) the Economic Council of Canada, the Unemployment Insurance Advisory Committee, the

Canadian Manpower and Immigration Council, the Canada Pension Plan Advisory Committee, and various advisory boards on training and adjustment, and also had a say in some government appointments (Forsey 1990, 88). The legitimacy of formal labour input, especially on labour market and workplace issues, was recognized, though advisory bodies operated at some distance from the policy process. For example, the mandate of the Economic Council of Canada was to study medium- to long-term issues, and it operated more in a research than consensus-building capacity in its later years. Labour representatives also participated as junior partners of business in policy forums such as the C.D. Howe Institute and the British North American Committee.[1]

The policy analysis role of labour in this period was modest, confined to a handful of staff in the CLC research and legislation department in Ottawa and research departments in the larger unions. Some linkages were maintained with labour-friendly economists, such as Jack Weldon at McGill. The recollections of long-time CLC research director, Eugene Forsey, and former CUPE research director, Gil Levine, suggest that only a few research staff with advanced educational qualifications were in place before the 1970s, when labour leaders gradually began to see the need for more than purely technical support (Levine 1997; Forsey 1990). Until at least the mid-1970s, the main focus of union research was on collective bargaining rather than public policy issues, and even CLC staff spent a lot of time on bargaining as opposed to policy issues. Labour staff did, however, prepare respected analyses and prescriptions on economic and social issues. One notable example is the lengthy CLC brief to the Gordon Commission on Canada's Economic Prospects. Levine notes that co-ordination of research between the CLC and researchers in unions was limited and exceptional.

Labour's linkages to formal processes were influenced by ties with the NDP. These were closest for the former CIO industrial unions, which tended to the view that policy issues could safely be left to the party. However, labour never put all of its political eggs in a single basket, and maintained close contacts with Liberal governments until the major parting of the ways over wage and price controls in 1976. This involved labour withdrawal from the annual meetings with the prime minister and from many consultative boards and processes, including the Economic Council of Canada. However, some notable attempts to renew the relationship were made through consultative processes during, and in the aftermath of, controls. Despite a major shift in macroeconomic and social policy, the Trudeau government continued to be interested in microeconomic planning, and labour's ties to the NDP had been loosened by its position on wage controls.

Several rounds of tripartite (government/business/labour) discussions closely involving the CLC officers and research staff were held to discuss alternatives to, and ways out of, controls, and some direct discussions were also held with business. The CLC briefly flirted with the concept of a continental, European-style, formalized tripartist approach to economic and social policy making, advanced most coherently in the 1976 CLC document 'Labour's Manifesto for Canada,' drafted by CLC research director Ron Lang (Morton 1998, chapter 26; Waldie 1986). Such proposals were deeply controversial within the labour movement and did not move beyond the discussion stage with ministers. However, in the late 1970s, the CLC and its affiliates were consulted quite closely on labour market policies, and played a major role on bipartite (business/labour) task forces dealing with a wide range of economic issues. Labour economists played a major role in the drafting of the so-called Tier II report on industrial and labour market strategies and the Report of the Major Projects Task Force. These set a model for consultative processes in which labour nominated a co-chair and had its own staff, and the close involvement of expert labour staff in these processes was seen by unions as key to their success (Waldie 1986).

The bipartite Canadian Labour Market and Productivity Centre was set up with a major endowment of government funds in 1984 to provide joint policy advice on productivity and labour market issues to the federal government. It was partly the result of government interest in a productivity institute, and partly the result of labour advocacy for a labour market planning board on the Swedish model. One notable feature of the CLMPC staff reorganization of 1987 was the establishment of a separate, small research staff to serve each of the labour and business sides. From 1988 through 1991, the CLMPC labour branch not only supported labour members on bipartite CLMPC taskforces on training and other issues, but also published a series of policy-related research studies and bulletins.

Formal policy consultations and the modest expansion of the policy analysis function ran out of steam by the early 1980s as the shift to restrictive macroeconomic policies generated very high unemployment, and as labour involvement in such processes became more controversial within the movement. However, labour continued to be represented on the Canadian Employment and Immigration Advisory Council through the 1980s, until it was abolished in 1992. This was an advisory council to the minister with several labour and business members, which met about six times a year and issued major reports on such issues as labour adjustment policies for older workers. One CLC staff person sat on the committee and spent much of his time in the development of labour recommendations and the drafting of council reports.

In the 1980s, unions also engaged in policy analysis through the then popular medium of royal commissions. Labour was (not without internal controversy) represented on the Macdonald Royal Commission on the Economic Union and Development Prospects for Canada of 1982–1985 in the person of Gerard Docquier, president of the Steelworkers Union. He obtained only limited labour-staff support. Docquier's dissenting comments in the final report highlighted the gulf between the research program of the commission, which was heavily influenced by mainstream academic economists advocating free trade, deregulation, privatization, and labour market deregulation, and what commissioners heard from a wide range of unions and non-governmental organizations. The critical research capacity of the labour movement was shown in *The Other Macdonald Report* (Drache and Cameron 1985), a book of against-the-trend submissions to the commission, which included major critiques of the prevailing drift of economic and social policy by the UAW and CUPE, among other unions and organizations. This book marked the start of the great ideological cleavage over free trade between labour, on the one hand, and governments and business on the other, adding to the growing gulf over macroeconomic and social issues.

Labour also played a notable role on the Forget Commission of Inquiry into Unemployment Insurance (1986) and, indeed, all but hijacked its work. Labour staff were very closely involved in the research work of the commission, and ultimately the two labour commissioners produced a book-length minority report of detailed program analysis and recommendations that was the product of close labour staff involvement. Surprisingly, the labour minority report was broadly endorsed by the Conservative majority on the relevant House of Commons committee, and was closely heeded by the opposition parties. While the UI program was trimmed in 1989, major cuts were not implemented until the mid-1990s.

While labour was involved in a number of consultative activities through the 1980s that involved policy research and analysis, these must be seen against the backdrop of government rejection of most policy advice from labour. From a labour perspective, the years from the mid-1970s to today have been marked by a series of losses. The limited postwar consensus on economic and social policy was torn apart. Unemployment was deliberately tolerated and increased through tough monetary policies in order to contain wages. Unions and labour market regulation measures, such as the minimum wage and employment standards, came to be constructed as barriers to job creation and sources of economic inefficiency. The ability of unions to organize and strike was increasingly constrained through legislation. Social programs (particularly income supports for unemployed workers) were trimmed and then slashed. Previously regulated industries, such as transportation and communications, were deregulated. Public enterprises were privatized. Activist and nationalist economic development policies were abandoned in favour of the free market and free trade. The squeeze on public finances arising from slower economic growth and the drive to balance budgets brought governments into particularly sharp conflict with public-sector unions, while the great national debate over the Canada-U.S. Free Trade Agreement marked a very fundamental cleavage of views between the labour movement and business.

In this context of fundamental disagreement, continued participation in consultative and formal policy processes became highly problematic within the labour movement. The explicitly anti-union content of economic orthodoxy and its rejection of most of organized labour's policy agenda for labour market regulation and income security made critical distance all but inevitable (on the centrality of labour market deregulation to current economic orthodoxy, see Baker et al. 2002). There has been ongoing tension between engaging in policy analysis to change the details of policy and challenging the fundamental assumptions on which policy has been based. While this tension has never been resolved definitively, more attention came to be focused on the development of labour's broad policy alternatives. Public policy statements at CLC and union conventions denounced the shift away from centrist and social democratic policies to the nostrums of the new right, the increased dominance of business in economic and social policy making, and the perceived exclusion of labour from participation and influence in the policy process. Leaving aside some brief periods of harmony with relatively labour-friendly provincial governments, organized labour has been, and has seen itself to be, an outsider in the policy process for a generation and more. This has clearly shaped the policy analysis activity of the movement.

The Contemporary Labour Movement and the Policy Process: Structure and Policy-Related Activities of Unions and the Canadian Labour Congress

Following a series of mergers and new organizing in non-traditional sectors, most unions are very large and diverse. Industrial unions, such as the auto workers (CAW) and steelworkers (USWA), have organized workers far outside their traditional areas of jurisdiction, and boundaries between the private and public sectors have become blurred as public sector unions like the Canadian Union of Public Employees (CUPE) have organized in the non-governmental social services sector. Two-thirds of CLC members now belong to the eight largest unions, each of which has more than 100,000 members. CUPE alone has more than 500,000 members (Workplace Information Directorate 2003). The dominant activities of these unions are, naturally, collective bargaining, ongoing management of industrial relations, union education, and organizing new members, but policy-related work by professional research staff is significant. All large unions have become more important policy actors and sites of policy analysis than in the past. Public-sector unions have become major intervenors in policy debates over how such public and social services should be financed, organized, and delivered, partly because public policies impact very directly upon the employment and working conditions of members.

Most large unions have policy analysis capacity within their research departments and produce policy-related research on a regular basis. Visitors to their websites will find a considerable amount of policy-related research, with a tilt towards issues of greatest immediate interest to members. Unions have clearly recognized that public policies are of fundamental importance in shaping the evolution of sectors in which their members are employed, and put forward not just critiques, but also reasoned alternatives. There are many notable recent examples of sophisticated policy research analysis and prescription.

The CAW has undertaken detailed analytical work on shifts of investment and production in the North American automotive industry and advanced the case for a new automotive industry policy featuring targeted subsidies to new investment and support for a new generation of highly energy-efficient vehicles (Canadian Auto Workers 2002).

CUPE has undertaken extensive research on public finance and the changing contours of public service delivery at the local government and community social services level through privatization, municipal contracting, alternative service delivery, and public/private partnerships. It has also commissioned research on practical public finance alternatives, such as centralized municipal borrowing facilities and greater scope for pension-fund financing of local governments.[2]

The CEP has undertaken extensive work on forestry, climate change, and energy issues, linking environmental and employment issues. The CEP's energy policy is comprehensive, and a conscious attempt to articulate an alternative to current export and resource extraction intensive policies (see Canadian Energy and Communications Workers 2005). It proposes dealing with pressing environmental issues such as global warming and rapid conventional resource depletion through closer control of exports and greater investment in conservation and renewable sources of energy in such a way as to maintain high-quality employment in the energy-related sectors where the union has many members. This work, which emerged from close consultation with members, was important in building broad political support for Canadian implementation of the Kyoto Accord, and undercut the attempt by some parts of the energy industry to mobilize employee opposition to its provisions. Currently, the CEP and other unions are closely involved in the Kyoto implementation plan.

A particularly notable recent union intervention in public policy making came when the Canadian Federation of Nurses Unions advanced a detailed proposal and arguments for a national drug plan as one potential vehicle for renewed federal government involvement in health care (Canadian Federation of Nurses Unions 2004). This proposal directly influenced provincial premiers and briefly dominated the run-up to the federal/provincial health accord of 2004 (Campbell 2004).

Some three in four union members belong to unions affiliated to the Canadian Labour Congress (the major exceptions being the CSN and the CEQ in Quebec and some large teachers' unions). With a total annual budget from affiliation fees of some $15 million, and some 100 national and regional staff, the CLC has significant resources for a nongovernmental organization. The congress currently has almost no direct involvement in collective bargaining or union organizing, though many of its activities, such as union education, are internal to the labour movement. A major role of the CLC is to represent the labour movement in policy terms nationally and internationally. It is the single most important site of policy analysis work by labour, though policy analysis is only one small part of CLC activities, and member unions play a major role. The provincial federations of labour play a comparable role to the CLC at the provincial level, though rates of affiliation are often lower and staff resources are very limited. (The FTQ in Quebec has a formalized special status relationship with the national labour movement and much greater resources.) Well over one hundred local labour councils also exist across the country.

The CLC's elected officers have responsibility for directing and promoting the policy work of Canadian labour between policy-making conventions, with the advice and direction of the heads of affiliated unions and provincial federations who sit on the CLC Executive Council. This body meets at least three times per year and takes the lead role on social and economic policy and international issues. At the staff level, most policy analysis activity is undertaken by the Department of Social and Economic Policy. However, some related activity is also undertaken in the International Department and the departments of Women's and Human Rights, Anti-Racism and Human Rights, and Health, Safety and Environment. Currently, the Social and Economic Policy Department has five professional staff, down from a high of about eight in the mid-1980s. Some sense of current policy priorities can be gained from the rough division of labour among staff, with one person being primarily responsible for each of the following: pensions and retirement issues; economic policy, including macroeconomic policy and labour market analysis; social policy, health policy, and privatization; unemployment insurance and training; and international economic issues. The core focus on economic, pension, labour market, training, and income-support issues is long-standing, while that on international economic issues is more recent and has been one product of labour's engagement with trade issues and the new realities of 'globalization.'

In addition to providing technical material to support the work of the CLC officers, the Social and Economic Policy Department is primarily responsible for producing briefs and submissions to ministers, officials and parliamentary committees, and also produces research papers, labour position papers, and material for policy and political campaigns (much of the policy analysis material is posted at http://www.clc-ctc.ca/web/issues/policy/en_index.shtml).

The department has produced 30 research papers since 1995, produces some half-dozen briefs and submissions to government per year, and publishes regular research bulletins on economic, pension, and unemployment insurance issues. This material is extensively circulated within the labour movement, and to an external mailing list that includes the media, elected politicians, government officials, academics, researchers, and activists in other organizations. Some policy-related work has also been published in books and journals (e.g., Jackson 2005). Staff in the department maintain regular contact with research staff in unions through committees (e.g., on training and technology, and on pension issues) and through an annual meeting of labour researchers. There is some informal sharing and co-ordination of policy research between the CLC and affiliated unions.

Continuity and Change in Labour's Policy Goals

Economic and social policy statements passed at recent CLC conventions show a broad continuity in key priorities from at least the postwar period: a full employment objective in macroeconomic policy; a high level of public services, such as health and post-secondary education, delivered on a citizen entitlement basis through the public sector and supported by federal transfers with broad national standards; decent income support for the unemployed; good public pensions; support for policies of income security for all workers as well as redistributive social transfers funded from a progressive tax system; support for unions and legislated minimum labour standards; and advocacy of greater public and employer investment in training and labour adjustment policies. There have, however, been some changes dating back to at least the late 1980s.

First, labour has become more explicit about defining its own policy goals and objectives, as opposed to simply attempting to marshal electoral support for the NDP. 'Labour's Manifesto for Canada' of 1976, which called for a major labour role in economic policy, reflected some tension with the NDP role in the debate on wage and price controls. This turn was reinforced by the election of 1988, when the CLC rather than the NDP took the lead in forming a broad popular coalition in opposition to the Canada-U.S. Free Trade Agreement. Experiences with NDP governments and, most importantly, growing recognition that 'the corporate agenda' and ascendant 'neo-liberalism' had to be fought through a battle of ideas, have all reinforced the felt need to develop labour's own policy agenda. CLC conventions, which used to spend much of their policy time debating short resolutions, have been presented with increasingly lengthy and analytical policy statements, drafted mainly by union research staff over a series of meetings and approved for discussion by the CLC Executive Council.

Second, partly reflecting the stronger voice of union women and workers of colour, labour's policy goals have expanded to include more explicit support for human rights instruments (e.g., pay and employment equity legislation; support for expansive interpretations of the Charter; measures to accommodate persons with disabilities in the workplace and in the community) and closer attention to issues facing working women and families, such as access to quality child and elder care, and hours of work (see recent CLC convention policy statements and prebudget briefs to the House of Commons Finance Committee, available fromm http://www.clc-ctc.ca). Legal action on human rights issues has become an increasingly common means to shape policy.

Third, much greater focus has been placed upon developing labour's alternatives to the current set of so-called free trade agreements and to specifying needed changes in global economic institutions. Indeed, arising from the experience of the new generation of trade agreements, which began with the Canada-U.S. Free Trade Agreement and NAFTA, the CLC has played something of a policy leadership role in international trade union organizations, such as the International Confederation of Free Trade Unions (ICFTU) and the Trade Union Advisory Committee (TUAC) to the OECD. The CLC has supported the ICFTU case for core labour rights to be entrenched in trade and investment agreements, but has successfully pushed for a wider critique of the way in which these agreements intrude upon national policy choices in such key areas as how to deliver public and social services. Through the ICFTU and TUAC, the CLC has been quite closely engaged in international policy debates, participating, for example, in fora with heads of state prior to G7 summits, OECD ministerial councils, and meetings with senior officials at the IMF and the World Bank.

Policy Analysis Related to Party Politics

Through the 1990s, the CLC and many of its affiliates spent a great deal of staff time and funds on political action, usually meaning attempts to directly and indirectly mobilize electoral support for the NDP. However, changes to federal party financing legislation, which labour supported, will force a turn to campaigns around issues rather than partisan activity. There has long been ongoing, informal contact between labour researchers and the research staff of the federal NDP and formal involvement in the policy development processes of the party. Research staff from the CLC and some major affiliates, notably the steelworkers, have been very closely involved in the development of the federal NDP election platforms since the party lost much of its research capacity following the electoral setbacks of the 1990s. This has been particularly the case with respect to technical details and costing.

Engagement in the Formal Policy Process

As noted, labour today tends to intervene in the policy process at a general and political rather than bureaucratic and specific level, and conducts its policy analysis activities accordingly. Between elections, the CLC is fairly closely engaged with the parliamentary process, producing an annual pre-budget brief to the Standing Committee on Finance and frequently appearing before parliamentary committees considering legislation or holding general policy reviews. Some affiliates also participate in these processes. Engagement with ministers and public servants is less frequent, but not uncommon. The CLC usually has ongoing contact with the ministers of Labour and of Human Resources Development (now Human Resources and Skills Development) with regard to issues of worker training, workplace issues (including labour issues in the federal jurisdiction), and unemployment insurance, though these relations tend to wax and wane depending upon personal relationships between ministers and the labour leadership. On occasion, the depth of engagement has been considerable, and this has been particularly true with respect to training issues.

The CLC and labour leaders, closely supported by union research staff, played a major role in the taskforces on training and labour adjustment called for and funded by the Mulroney government in 1988. The task forces were conducted under the auspices of the bipartite (labour/business) Canadian Labour Market and Productivity Centre, and their reports (CLMPC 1990) directly led to the creation of the Canadian Labour Force Development Board in 1990 as a formal advisory body to the federal government (Haddow 1995; the board was abolished in 1998). A somewhat parallel process of extensive engagement by labour leaders and staff in tripartite consultative processes led to the establishment of provincial training boards and some bipartite sectoral training initiatives in the 1990s, notably in Ontario (Gunderson and Sharpe 1998; Sharpe and Haddow 1997). In a handful of industries, notably steel and electronic products manufacturing, rather extensive training and adjustment programs were developed and delivered jointly by unions and employers in the early 1990s with government financial support. Despite the general demise of training boards, broad planning for labour needs continues to take place today through bipartite national sector councils.

It could be argued that the rather pronounced shift to bipartite policy input and design of government-funded training and labour market planning at the national, provincial and sectoral level in the early 1990s partly reflected policy analysis and innovation by the labour movement. Labour thinking was influenced in some significant ways by a major policy paper issued by the Canadian steelworkers in 1988, 'Empowering Workers in the New Global Economy,' which called for expanding labour's role from collective bargaining and political action to taking an independent advocacy role in industrial restructuring and training through social bargaining with employer associations and governments. A labour paper, 'A Labour Perspective on Training,' was issued as part of the CLMPC reports, and major position papers on training and workplace change were issued by a number of unions in the early to mid-1990s. Labour leaders and research staff were intimately involved in the policy processes leading to the creation of the Ontario Training and Adjustment Board and in the experiments in sectoral industrial policies under the Rae government, which have been described as near-corporatist in terms of devolving policy responsibility from government to business and labour (Atkinson and Pervin 1998; Bradford 1998). However, there were significant divisions of opinion within labour over how deeply to embrace what critics denounced as the politics of 'progressive competitiveness' (Bradford 1998; on the internal labour debate, see the contributions by Hugh Mackenzie, and Sam Gindin and David Robertson in Drache 1992).

These attempts to devolve some responsibility for training and labour market policies to boards including labour, let alone embrace union-initiated sectoral strategies, ultimately foundered in the face of difficulties in forging an employer/labour consensus, and the reluctance of the federal government in particular to genuinely cede authority to an arm's length body (Sharpe and Haddow 1997). Ultimately, labour engagement in social bargaining with employers and governments depends on the willingness of governments to promote such arrangements in the face of employer indifference or hostility, and this has only rarely been forthcoming.

Labour appointees and staff also played a major role in developing and drafting the analysis and policy recommendations of the Donner Task Force (the Report of the Advisory Group on Working Time and the

Distribution of Work, 1995) and the Collective Reflection on the Changing Workplace (1997), though advocacy of changes to employment standards in both reports fell on deaf ears. Consultative processes involving labour in discussion of labour law, employment standards, and workplace issues generally have been very difficult due to fundamental differences of view with employers, and government's unwillingness to act on labour proposals in the absence of bipartite consensus. While the federal government abandoned formal consultative structures on unemployment insurance with the abolition of the Canadian Employment and Insurance Advisory Committee, there is still some scope for continuing input into the EI policy process through the office of the workers' commissioner and ad-hoc meetings with public servants. Labour also has some continuing input into the detailed shaping of policies with respect to public and private pensions, which have been the subject of numerous CLC briefs and several research papers.

Neither has labour been entirely absent from discussions of economic policy. Even in the immediate wake of the Free Trade Agreement, CLC and other labour representatives participated in the International Trade Advisory Committee and the Sectoral Advisory Groups on International Trade. With respect to macroeconomic policy, meetings of CLC officers take place with the minister of finance and the governor of the Bank of Canada, and trade union economists currently meet annually with Department of Finance and Bank of Canada officials.

In summary, labour had some very modest, continuing input to the federal government's policy process through the 1990s, especially in areas such as training, where unions are perceived to have some expertise and play an independent role in the workplace that policy makers have to take into account in order to achieve their objectives. Somewhat surprisingly, links through consultations were arguably somewhat closer under the Mulroney government, despite the free trade schism, than proved to be the case under the Chrétien government until very late in its mandate, when the focus began to shift from deficit reduction and tax cuts back to social investment. Labour's relations with the federal government have become somewhat closer in the recent period of social reinvestment, marked by recent rounds of meetings with ministers by the CLC Executive Council, and a meeting of the labour leadership and the prime minister in November 2004. As of late 2004, the labour movement was quite actively engaged with the newly re-elected Martin government on a few priority issues: health, child care, employment insurance reform, training, pensions, and bankruptcy legislation.

Detailed policy analysis work at the CLC has been undertaken in support of all of these activities. Most notably, the CLC has conducted significant empirical research on the impacts of changes to the employment insurance program and has advanced specific program alternatives with respect to EI entitlements and access to training through EI.

Policy Analysis by Labour at the Provincial Level

Provincial labour organizations engage in a wide range of policy analytical activities. Into the 1990s, there have been some continued examples of sustained consultative processes that have deeply involved labour leaders and research staff, notably in Quebec under PQ governments, in Ontario through the Premiers Council in the early 1990s, and most recently in Newfoundland and Labrador. The Quebec situation is unique, given the strength of the labour movement, its capacity to be a policy innovator, and the close relations it has often enjoyed with the government of the day. In the rest of Canada, labour has been a weaker actor with less policy capacity, and significant influence and engagement in the policy process has usually depended upon the election of NDP governments. Relations of labour to such governments have been highly variable and always marked by tensions over funding of public services and public-sector labour relations. That said, many examples could be cited of labour's role as a policy innovator at the provincial level. In general terms, this capacity has usually been very modest, and often weakened by the movement of labour staff into government positions when NDP governments have been elected. Provincial governments have often engaged with individual unions rather than with provincial federations of labour.

Shifting the Contours of Public Policy 'Against the Prevailing Winds' CLC Research

As indicated, a major goal of policy analysis by the labour movement has been to shift the broad contours of public and policy debate away from current neoliberal orthodoxy. One way of doing so has been to conduct detailed empirical research on the wages and living standards of Canadian workers, highlighting the trends evident through much of the 1990s: stagnation of real wages, declining employment security, increasing family income inequality, cuts to social transfers, and deteriorating conditions in workplaces. (Some of these dismal trends have started to reverse to some degree in more recent years.) Currently, such analytical material is published in the quarterly CLC publication, *Economy*, and in an annual report on the state of the labour market, titled 'Is Work Working for You?' In 2000, the Canadian Centre for Policy Alternatives published mainly CLC research on labour market, workplace and income issues in 'Falling Behind: The State of Working Canada 2000,' and similar material was published as *Work and Labour in Canada: Critical Issues* (Jackson 2005). CLC research has closely tracked income trends among the elderly, changing patterns of retirement, and the impact of public and private pension policies on income security in retirement (Baldwin and Laliberté 1999; Baldwin 2004).

This analytical work has sought to draw some links from major changes in macroeconomic, trade, and social policies to working and living conditions, and has been policy prescriptive to a limited degree in highlighting the positive economic and social impacts of trade unions, labour market regulation and social programs. For example, CLC pension work has detailed the success of the public and private pension arrangements put in place by the mid-1970s in terms of achieving income security and rising incomes in retirement. CLC research papers have also developed detailed critiques of the orthodox prescription for labour market deregulation as the key to job creation in an attempt to influence policy. To give one example, a CLC research paper on the negative impacts of the theory of a NAIRU (or 'non-accelerating inflation rate of unemployment')-driven monetary policy on employment in Canada was presented to an OECD seminar, circulated to Department of Finance and Bank of Canada officials, presented to the annual meetings of the Canadian Economics Association, and published in Canadian Business Economics (Jackson 2000). In sum, the CLC has sought to develop some credibility and technical expertise in labour market and income security issues in order to influence the general tenor of public debate over the relative success or failure of current policies. Trade union economists and researchers have also published books, articles, and technical papers on social and economic policy issues (e.g., Stanford 1999; contributions to Scarth 2004).

Labour Policy Analysis in Relation to Nongovernmental Organizations and Think Tanks

Labour has also intervened in the policy debate by supporting and actively participating in the work of non-governmental organizations and policy research institutes. The CLC and individual unions are quite closely engaged in the activities of a number of umbrella policy advocacy groups, including the Canadian Health Coalition, the major lobby organization for a public health care system; the Child Care Advocacy Association of Canada; Campaign 2000, the national coalition dealing with child poverty issues; and the Canadian Council on International Co-operation. In recent years, labour researchers have participated in the policy analysis and development activities of each of these organizations. Partly as a result, elements of labour's policy agenda have been included in the policy positions of advocacy coalitions. For example, the 2004 Report of Campaign 2000 stressed the importance of raising the wages of the working poor through labour market regulation as part of any solution to child poverty, and the Canadian Council on International Co-operation has supported and promoted the importance to international development of trade union rights as defined in the conventions of the International Labour Organization. At the same time, the CLC and unions have incorporated the policy work of these organizations into their own positions and work. For example, the CLC budget brief of 2004 spoke to the importance of the detailed positions being advocated by the Child Care Advocacy Association and the Canadian Council on International Co-operation.

In terms of linkages to policy think tanks, the closest ties have been to the Canadian Centre for Policy Alternatives (CCPA). However, labour representatives have also been involved in an expert advisory capacity with the research work conducted by the Work Network of the Canadian Policy Research Networks, with the work on social policy of the Canadian Council on Social Development, and some labour research has been published and circulated by the Caledon Institute of Social Policy. Labour links to the CCPA are very close, and this institution was launched in the early 1980s with labour support explicitly in order to counter the increasingly influential policy interventions of the business-supported think tanks, notably the Fraser Institute and the C.D. Howe Institute. The CCPA is still partly labour financed, and a number of labour movement policy analysts are intimately involved in its activities, along with independent researchers and academics. Provincial CCPA offices have now been established in British Columbia, Saskatchewan, Manitoba, and Nova Scotia, and in Ontario, specific studies have been undertaken (see www.policyalternatives.ca).

Two streams of CCPA work over recent years are examples of 'best practice' labour policy analysis. First, the CCPA's trade and investment

research project, funded from labour contributions, has been responsible for several monographs and books on the policy impacts of trade
and investment agreements such as the NAFTA and the General Agreement on Trade in Services. These have highlighted the shrinking policy
space open to Canadian governments in a range of domains, a result of
obligations entered into through trade and investment agreements.
Labour researchers, notably from the CLC, CUPE, the CAW, and the
Canadian Union of Postal Workers (CUPW), have been closely involved in initiating subjects for research and have provided continuing
input to the research program. Perhaps the most notable result of this
work was the CCPA research program on globalization and health,
which was commissioned by the Romanow Commission on health care.
This research suggested that trade and investment agreements (particularly provisions for investor compensation in the NAFTA and GATS
provisions still under discussion) could potentially undercut the ability
of Canadian governments to continue to mainly deliver health services
through public and not-for-profit institutions and agencies, as opposed
to for-profit, commercial delivery. The central argument was that experimentation with privatized delivery had the potential to turn into a
one-way street due to trade obligations. The CCPA research (Canadian
Centre for Policy Alternatives 2002) and the Romanow report made some
recommendations for how to avoid these constraints through changes in
both trade and health delivery policies. In short, labour has been increasingly engaged in sophisticated analyses of the implications of complex
provisions of trade agreements and in the specification of clear alternatives that would retain policy space for Canadian governments. These
recommendations are being increasingly heeded by policy makers.

A second major ongoing area of CCPA activity has been the annual
preparation of alternative federal budgets (AFB). (These have now also
been produced for several provinces, including British Columbia,
Saskatchewan, Manitoba, Ontario, and Nova Scotia.) The first federal
AFB was produced in 1995 as a joint project of the CCPA and a Manitoba
organization, Choices, and the project continues into 2007 in somewhat
changed form (on the history and impact of the AFB, see Loxley 2003,
and contributions to Akram-Lodhi et al. 2004).

From its inception, the AFB has closely involved labour movement
policy analysts from the CLC and almost all of the larger CLC-affiliated
unions, as well as staff from various popular sector organizations concerned with social policy, international development and environmental issues, and CCPA staff, and a few academics. While the AFB project

is collaborative and has involved many people, it is relevant here to note that much of the analytical work on macroeconomic policy in the first few AFBs was undertaken by Jim Stanford of the CAW, that Hugh Mackenzie of the USWA took the lead on tax issues, and that staff from the CLC Social and Economic Policy Department have taken the lead in a number of specific issue areas such as health care, EI, training, and employment issues.

In the period before 1997, the major focus of the AFB and its associated technical papers was upon demonstrating how alternative macroeconomic policies could reduce and eliminate the federal deficit and the debt without reducing levels of spending on social programs and public services. Since 1997, the focus has shifted to showing that more ambitious social investment programs than those introduced by the Liberals were fiscally feasible, and to arguing the economic and social case for public investment as opposed to tax cuts and debt repayment. The AFB has advanced numerous specific expenditure proposals, such as a national childcare and early childhood development program and expanded child benefits, a comprehensive tax reform agenda, proposals for a fundamental restructuring of federal-provincial fiscal arrangements, and a detailed environmental and international development agenda. In sum, the AFB – particularly the book-length versions published as the alternative federal budget papers in 1997 and 1998 – has amounted to a broad, multi-year, costed, internally consistent alternative legislative and budgetary program for the federal government. This program is seen as technically feasible, and it has been explicitly endorsed at CLC conventions as a concrete translation of labour's policy goals into a detailed agenda.

The AFB has had several notable impacts. It has promoted collaborative policy-related work among labour researchers to a greater degree than used to be the case, and has also fostered closer links with policy researchers from non-labour organizations. Many non-governmental organizations – from child care and anti-poverty advocates to environment groups – have helped shape AFB spending proposals, and have used it as an analytical framework within which to advance their own proposals. To some degree, then, the AFB has promoted unity of policy analysis and proposals among groups which used to compete for attention in the policy process. The AFB has advanced the credibility of labour and popular sector organizations on fiscal, economic, and social policy issues, and has played an important role in terms of labour's internal education programs.

In essence, the AFB has come to be regarded as holding up one side of the national debate on broad budgetary priorities. Arguably, it had some impact upon the slow shift back towards social investment in federal program spending from around the year 2000. The AFB also helped promote greater labour and popular sector participation in the policy process. As minister of finance, Paul Martin engaged in lengthy annual meetings with lead project participants on the AFB and encouraged some follow-up with government officials in specific areas (while also making very clear his substantive disagreements). Overall, the AFB can be judged as a success in terms of deepening policy analysis within the labour movement and advancing labour's policy agenda.

Labour Collaboration with Academic Researchers

In the past, labour researchers have rather episodically collaborated with academic researchers, for example, in studies of workplace conditions and the restructuring of work. Formalized links and contacts between academics and trade unions have been established through university research centres, most notably the Centre for Research on Work and Society (CRWS) at York University, which has organized numerous conferences and publishes research papers. As well, an electronic annual journal, *Just Labour*, publishes some policy-relevant work by both academic and labour researchers. More recently, funding for academic research programs closely involving labour researchers has been facilitated though the Community-University Research Alliance and other programs of the Social Sciences and Humanities Research Council (SSHRC).

As of 2004, there are several major academic research programs underway which bring academic and trade union researchers together in policy-relevant work. For example, the 'Restructuring Work and Labour in the New Economy' project, coordinated by the CRWS, brings together researchers from 10 universities and eight unions, and specific projects are examining the role and impact of labour standards on quality of work and the role of unions in training and skills recognition. A project based at the University of Montreal is undertaking policy-relevant work on labour market regulation in the new economy (CRIMT: 'Rethinking Institutions for Work and Employment in a Global Era') and joint projects are underway on pensions, workforce aging, and training for the new economy. Union researcher involvement goes beyond participation in conferences and advisory groups to include partnerships on specific research projects. While these projects are still in their early stages, new funding mechanisms and the growing interest of academics in working with union researchers is likely to lead to a major increase in sophisticated, policy-relevant research by the labour movement. Unions also often engage academics in their own research activities, and sometimes support academic research and conferences on issues that mesh with labour's policy agenda.

Concluding Thoughts

Policy analysis by the labour movement has been neglected as an area of study, but is nonetheless significant. The CLC and member unions employ a modest number of professional staff who are engaged in serious research, and this function has become more, rather than less, important in recent years. Labour has been relatively marginalized from the national policy process for more than a generation, and this has shaped the policy analysis activities of the CLC and member unions. On the one hand, continuing efforts are still made to shape the details of public policy through formal and informal consultations. Government demand for policy advice from labour has usually been confined to workplace and labour market issues where unions are still important actors. Even here, labour advice has tended to be heeded only when it has been part of bipartite processes, which have receded greatly in importance since the early 1990s. Labour's role as a critic of the general drift of policy and as an advocate for fundamental change has, however, increased greatly, and become more sophisticated. Notable examples exist of labour policy research undertaken independently or in collaboration with other popular sector organizations and with labour-friendly academics. Both of these poles of activity will likely continue, while the balance will shift with changes in the overall policy climate.

NOTES

1 Details of CLC policy-related activities are reported in the reports of the Executive Council to CLC Conventions, available in the CLC Library. See also http://canadianlabour.ca/index_php/economic_issues.
2 For a list of CUPE publications on privatization of public services, see http://www.cupe.ca/www/privatization.

REFERENCES

Akram-Lodhi, H., R. Chernomas, and A. Sepehri, eds. 2004. *Globalization, Neo-conservative Policies, and Democratic Alternatives. Essays in Honour of John Loxley.* Winnipeg: Arbeiter Ring Publishing.

Akyeampong, E. 2004. 'The Union Movement in Transition.' *Perspectives on Labour and Income* (August). Ottawa: Statistics Canada.

Atkinson, M.M., and C.W. Pervin. 1998. 'Sector Councils and Sectoral Corporatism: Viable? Desirable?' In Morley Gunderson and A. Sharpe, eds., *Forging Business-Labour Partnerships: The Emergence of Sector Councils in Canada.* Toronto: University of Toronto Press.

Baker, D., A. Glyn, D. Howell, and J. Schmitt. 2002. *Labour Market Institutions and Unemployment: A Critical Assessment of the Cross-Country Evidence.* Centre for Economic Policy Analysis Working Paper 2002–17. http://www.newschool.edu/cepa.

Baldwin, B. 2004. *Trade Unions, Older Workers and the Age of Retirement.* CLC Research Paper no. 29. Ottawa: Canadian Labour Congress.

Baldwin, B., and P. Laliberté. 1999. *Incomes of Older Canadians: Amounts and Sources, 1973–1996.* CLC Research Paper no. 15. Ottawa: Canadian Labour Congress.

Bradford, N. 1998. 'Ontario's Experiment with Sectoral Initiatives: Labour Market and Industrial Policy, 1995–1996.' In Morley Gunderson and A. Sharpe, eds., *Forging Business-Labour Partnerships: The Emergence of Sector Councils in Canada.* Toronto: University of Toronto Press.

Campbell, M. 2004. 'How the Door to National Pharmacare Swung Open.' *Globe and Mail,* 31 July.

Canadian Auto Workers. 2002. 'Getting Back in Gear: A New Policy Vision for Canada's Auto Industry.' Ottawa: CAW. http://www.caw.ca/campaigns&issues/ongoingcampaigns/autopolicy/index.asp

Canadian Centre for Policy Alternatives. 2002. *Globalization and Health: Implications and Options for Health Care Reform.* Ottawa: CCPA.

Canadian Energy and Communications Workers. 2005. *CEP Energy Policy, Policy 917.* Ottawa: CEP. http://www.cep.ca/policies/policy_917_e.pdf.

Canadian Federation of Nurses Unions. 2004. *Can We Afford to Sustain Medicare? A Strong Role for Federal Governments.* Ottawa: CFNU. http://www.nursesunions.ca/docs/Sustainability-Report-2004–07–29-en.pdf.

Canadian Labour Market and Productivity Centre. 1990. *Report of the CLMPC Task Forces on the Labour Force Development Strategy.* Ottawa: CLMPC.

Drache, D., ed. 1992. *Getting on Track: Social Democratic Strategies for Ontario.* Toronto: CCPA and McGill-Queen's University Press.

Drache, D., and D. Cameron, eds. 1985. *The Other Macdonald Report.* Toronto: James Lorimer.

Forsey, E. 1990. *Life on the Fringe: Memoirs of Eugene Forsey.* Toronto: Oxford University Press.

Gunderson, M., and A. Sharpe, eds. 1998. *Forging Business-Labour Partnerships: The Emergence of Sector Councils in Canada.* Toronto: University of Toronto Press.

Haddow, R. 1995. 'Canada's Experiment with Labour Market Corporatism.' In K.G. Banting and C.M. Beach, eds., *Labour Market Polarization and Social Policy Reform.* Kingston: School of Policy Studies, Queen's University.

Heron, C. 1996. *The Canadian Labour Movement: A Brief History.* Toronto: James Lorimer.

Jackson, A. 1998. *The NAIRU and Macroeconomic Policy in Canada.* CLC Research Paper no. 12; reprinted *Canadian Business Economics* 8(2) (July 2000), 66–82.

– 2005. *Work and Labour in Canada: Critical Issues.* Toronto: Canadian Scholars Press.

Kumar, P., and G. Murray. 2003. 'Strategic Dilemma: The State of Union Renewal in Canada.' In P. Fairbrother and C. Yates, eds., *Trade Unions in Renewal: A Comparative Study.* London and New York: Continuum.

Levine, G. 1997. 'Economic Research in Labour Unions.' *Canadian Business Economics* 5(2–3), 69–78.

Loxley, J. 2003. *Budgeting as if People Mattered.* Halifax: Fernwood Books.

Morton, D. 1998. *Working People: An Illustrated History of the Canadian Labour Movement.* 4th ed. Montreal and Kingston: McGill-Queen's University Press.

Rose, J., and G. Chaison. 2001. 'Unionism in Canada and the United States in the 21st Century: Prospects for Revival.' *Industrial Relations/Relations Industrielles* 56(1), 34–62.

Scarth, T., ed. 2000. *Hell and High Water: An Assessment of Paul Martin's Record.* Ottawa: Canadian Centre for Policy Alternatives.

Sharpe, A., and R. Haddow, eds. 1997. *Social Partnerships for Training.* Ottawa: Caledon Institute of Social Policy, and Centre for the Study of Living Standards.

Stanford, J. 1999. *Paper Boom.* Ottawa and Toronto: Canadian Centre for Policy Alternatives and James Lorimer.

Waldie, K. 1986. 'The Evolution of Labour-Government Consultation on

Economic Policy.' In W.C. Riddell, ed., *Labour-Management Co-operation in Canada.* Vol. 15 of Research Papers for the Royal Commission on the Economic Union and Development Prospects for Canada. Toronto: University of Toronto Press.

Workplace Information Directorate, Labour Program Human Resources and Skills Development Canada. 2003. *Union Membership in Canada.* Ottawa: HRSDC.

20 Policy Analysis and the Voluntary Sector: Evolving Policy Styles

SUSAN D. PHILLIPS

It is widely accepted that the policy process has become porous, open at many points to influence from the outside, with such influence being broadly divided and dispersed across multiple actors. The shift to a new model of 'governance' that emphasizes governing through collaboration, networks and horizontal management and that makes use of a varied array of policy instruments has done more than open wider cracks in policy making through which the influence of interest groups and other non-governmental actors can seep in. The new governance has systematized and institutionalized their involvement (Salamon 2001; Prince 2007). That's the story, anyway.

In fact, given the limited study of interest groups and the voluntary/ nonprofit sector in Canadian policy studies, we know relatively little about how and to what extent such groups conduct policy analysis in the current context, how they use it to exert policy influence, and to what end. Have civil society organizations adopted policy styles that are compatible with a supposedly more open, inclusive, and participatory system of governance? Are they effective participants in policy networks and in shaping Canadian public policy? If not, why not? Are policy processes in Canada actually as open and as participatory as this model of 'governance' suggests? This chapter examines both the contributions of Canada's voluntary sector to policy development and the challenges it faces in conducting policy analysis and participating effectively.

As Howlett and Lindquist note in their chapter, how policy analysis is conducted and how policy influence is exerted differs according to governance contexts and analytical cultures. The policy styles adopted by nongovernmental organizations are affected not only by the political opportunities afforded by the governance context, but by their capacities and decisions to take up these opportunities. The purpose of this chapter is to explore how political opportunities, capacities and strategies are shaping the policy analytical styles and the participation of the voluntary sector in the current environment. It argues that while policy participation may be diffused in some ways by the fact that there are more actors, it is also constrained and concentrated for a variety of reasons. The funding cutbacks and the offloading and co-production of services that occurred in the 1990s has forced voluntary organizations to rely on project-based funding and to adopt a more complex duality of their roles as advocates and as service providers. Consequently, few voluntary sector organizations, including the national infrastructure and peak associations, have the policy capacity to participate effectively, nor have they been able to build ongoing, institutionalized connections with government departments, as the paradigm of governance presupposes. In addition, the regulatory regime governing the large part of the voluntary sector that has legal status as registered charities imposes further restrictions on undertaking active advocacy and, in combination with the instability of the funding regime, contributes to a generalized 'advocacy chill' (Scott 2003). While governments have created more opportunities for public consultation, these spaces are paradoxically less available to organized interests because the usual intent is to involve citizens representing themselves. We begin by defining and delimiting the boundaries of the concept of the 'voluntary sector.'

The Voluntary Sector Defined

Traditionally, the policy literature has referred to citizen-based nongovernmental organizations as 'public interest groups' (Pross 1986; Pal 1993).[1] This chapter adopts a broader and more inclusive concept of the voluntary and nonprofit sector which can be defined as the aggregation of organizations that: 'exist to serve a public benefit, are self-governing, do not distribute any profits to members, and depend to a meaningful degree on volunteers. Membership or involvement in these organizations is not compulsory, and they are independent of, and institutionally distinct from the formal structures of government and the private sector. Although many voluntary sector organizations rely on paid staff to carry out their work, all depend on volunteers, at least on their boards of directors' (Government of Canada/Voluntary Sector 2001, 3).

The advantages of this broader concept are threefold. First, it respects self-naming. As Jenson (1995, 114) argues, the self names chosen by political actors matter because they reflect identities and because they signal the opportunities that these actors will choose to take up or attempt to configure. During the backlash against organized interests that occurred in the late 1980s and 1990s as part of neoliberalism and the populism of the Canadian right, the credibility of most public interest groups came under attack, and they were often assigned the somewhat derogatory label, 'special interest groups.' As a result, few of the organizations that policy analysts would normally describe as public interest groups (e.g., the Canadian Consumers' Association, the Sierra Club, the Canadian Mental Health Association, the Canadian Council on Social Development) call themselves interest groups. Rather, the terms voluntary, nonprofit, nongovernmental, or charitable organization are the preferred self names.

Second, the more inclusive concept of voluntary organization signals that, just as the policy process has become more complex in recent years, so too have the roles of nongovernmental actors. To be sure, some voluntary organizations exist solely for purposes of influencing policy and exerting pressure. As governments offloaded a wide variety of services over the past two decades, many groups which had been policy oriented, by necessity, became much more heavily invested in service delivery and contracting as a means of revenue generation (Laforest 2001). Charities and other organizations that were created primarily to provide services increasingly found they needed to have a policy voice because they knew, often better than governments, what was really working and what was not, based on their firsthand experience with programming. Third, the notion of a voluntary *sector* is a reminder that the sector itself has a structure involving both horizontal connections among groups from different policy fields and vertical integration through infrastructure organizations, umbrella groups, or federations that connect the local to the regional to the national levels.[2] And, as we will see, the preliminary challenge – and indeed the major success – of voluntary organizations in recent years has been to get the notion of a voluntary *sector* on governmental agendas and to encourage more critical thinking about public policies affecting the sector as a whole.

While it is relatively easy to delineate a (large) central core of organizations that constitute the voluntary/nonprofit sector, there are numerous grey zones around the definitional edges. The core is estimated to constitute over 160,000 organizations, of which approximately 80,000 are charities registered with the Canada Revenue Agency (CRA), which enables them to issue tax receipts for donations and makes them subject to federal regulations. These organizations work in a wide array of policy fields, often classified as (in descending order of numbers of organizations) sports and recreation; religion; social services; grant making, fundraising, and volunteerism promotion; arts and culture; housing and development; education and research; health; environment; law, advocacy, and politics; international development; hospitals; universities and colleges; and other (Statistics Canada et al. 2004, 13).

While impressive in the aggregate, there is an enormous bifurcation within the sector between a very small slice of large organizations and a multitude of very small ones. The one per cent of charitable and nonprofit organizations with over $10 million in annual revenues account for over 60 per cent of the entire revenues of the sector, half the staff, and a fifth of the volunteers.[3] By contrast, two-thirds of voluntary organizations have annual revenues of under $100,000 and half are operated solely by volunteers. Many of these have little or no interest in participating in public policy at all, and are not of direct relevance to this discussion.

In a sector this large and diverse, there are naturally many hybrid organizations that have characteristics of public or private as well as voluntary sector bodies. For instance, cooperatives often pursue a public benefit but distribute profits to their members. Should they be considered part of the voluntary sector? Where do business or professional associations whose members are for-profit entities but which are themselves nonprofit fit?[4] For the purposes of this chapter, which will necessarily entail considerable generalizations given the differences within even the core parts of this sector, we do not need to be unduly precise about the nuances of the definition. We will focus on the core of the sector that involves public benefit, nonprofit organizations, and will leave the discussion of business associations and labour unions to the chapters by Stritch and by Jackson and Baldwin respectively.

The Governance Context: New Opportunities

The presence and impact of nongovernmental actors in policy development depends, in part, on the opportunity structure and, in part, on the capacities, styles and strategies of these actors. Some policy styles are better suited to and more likely to succeed in particular institutional contexts than others, and institutions may be more or less open to different styles and more or less subject to change over time. This section argues that certain policy styles are indeed being privileged by a 'governance' model and that policy advocacy by the voluntary sector is being shaped not only by pressure for adaptation in policy styles, but by direct regulation.

Elements of a Policy Style for the New Governance

The notion of policy styles is rooted in institutionalism, which takes as a starting point the position that institutions – and the rules, norms, processes, and cultures associated with them – affect actors by shaping their understanding of policy problems, analytical approaches to grappling with them, perceived solutions, and preferred courses of action (see Howlett 2004). There is a degree of path dependency as the institutional contexts reward certain styles by taking the political actors and their positions more seriously and by granting greater access to the policy process and more influence over policy outcomes. The impact of the institutional context is not unidirectional, however. Agents actively construct their institutional contexts to some extent by taking up certain opportunities and eschewing others and by adapting to or resisting change (see Dobrolowsky and Saint-Martin 2005; Thelen 2003). Through the influence of both institutional contexts and actors' choices, successful policy styles become channellized over time, forming grooved patterns that are copied to the extent possible by other political actors. While it may be possible to articulate broad policy analytical styles that characterize different nations (Richardson, Gustafsson, and Jordan 1982) or time periods, it is also important to note that policy styles may vary by policy field and that they evolve, sometimes quite quickly, as governing contexts, prevailing policy ideas, strategies, or other factors change (see Howlett and Lindquist 2007; Richardson 2000).

Canada's voluntary sector is arguably in a period of significant transition in policy styles. A key factor in this transition has been the move away from neoliberalism and a governing philosophy of New Public Management (NPM) that relied heavily on contracting-out and market-based policy tools. The model of horizontal 'governance' that appears to be replacing NPM emphasizes collaboration with non-governmental actors and participation by citizens, involvement and coordination through networks rather than hierarchies, negotiated self-governance with communities, cities, and industries, the blurring of boundaries between economic and social issues, the use of reflexive and responsive policy tools, and management styles that enable rather than control (Newman 2001, 24; Salamon 2001). For the voluntary sector, this reconfiguration of the governing context favours the development of policy styles that are characterized by three main features.

First, both governments and those who seek a role in influencing public policy are under pressure to produce research and analysis that is evidence-based (Laforest and Orsini 2004; Newman 2001, 69). The interest in evidence-based research is not simply a resurrection of a rational model of policy, but is driven largely by political imperatives (Newman 2003, 70–71). In a post-neoliberal era, politics tends to be more pragmatically oriented rather than ideologically driven. Combined with a well-informed public that has widespread access to information technologies, less deference to authorities, and reduced trust in government, expectations rise that governments will do what works and will demonstrate results. This has taken on particular saliency in Canada as a result of the development of a mode of 'instrumental federalism' in the late 1990s (Phillips 2003) in which accountability for federal transfers is secured by requiring public reporting on policy outcomes and in which the public and voluntary associations are expected to serve as watchdogs in identifying, comparing, analysing, and using this hard evidence to agitate for policy reform.

The second dimension of a new policy style derives from the importance of networks as the central institutional form in the new governance. Networks can be seen as institutions in their own right that determine the nature of interactions and rules of conduct among members and potential members (Rhodes 1996; Klijn and Koppenjan 2004). One implication is that trust and trustworthiness as a basis for relationship building matter more than ever. Who you know, and perhaps more importantly who knows you – and whether they trust you – determines one's position within various networks and facilitates ongoing involvement in them. Because trustworthiness is enhanced through repeated positive interactions, voluntary organizations come under pressure to be consistently professional in their interactions. In addition, the expansion of opportunities for participation through a variety of means (such as public consultations, partnerships, co-production) makes the ability to broker knowledge – about communities, other players, and policy issues – a highly valued asset.

With attempts to manage policy processes in a more horizontal fashion involving greater coordination among relevant government departments and with increased complexities in the intergovernmental environment, stemming in part from the rise of urban governments, a third aspect is the ability to function in a multi-scalar, multi-level way. Horizontality implies a need to be able to frame and reframe policy so as to be relevant to the interests of a number of departments. It necessitates a good working knowledge about the processes of governing so as to figure out what various departments are doing and to understand the coordination mechanisms (such as interdepartmental or intergovernmental committees) that often work in quite invisible ways. More multi-layered governance also entails having a presence at several scales of operation – local/regional, provincial, national, and international – and an ability to shift attention and action among them as necessary.

In short, the context of governance entails a more complex mix of expertise in both policy and process. A nongovernmental actor seeking to influence policy has to be not only a specialist in a policy field, but a sufficient generalist to know how to make connections with those in different policy fields. But policy substance is not enough. As a recent, rather cheeky and somewhat cynical account of lobbying in Ottawa stated, 'Showing up on Parliament Hill and briefing a Member of Parliament is just one leg in a long and tortuous journey that can lead to nowhere unless you understand government or have retained the services of someone who does' (Donovan 2005, 23). Understanding of process is as important as policy substance in enabling a nonprofit to navigate through interconnected and multi-level governmental channels.

Regulating Policy Participation

In some respects, the governing context may shape the development of policy styles in quite subtle ways through a learning process that sees certain types of behaviours rewarded over others. In other respects, policy styles are shaped in more direct and overt ways. For a large part of the voluntary sector, those organizations with charitable status, the federal regulatory regime is a major determinant of how, and how much, they engage in public policy advocacy, because it directly limits policy-related activities in two ways. The first is the means for determining which kinds of organizations qualify to be registered as charities, thereby enabling them to issue tax receipts that provide incentives for donations and, perhaps even more importantly, conferring legitimacy and facilitating funding from provincial lottery agencies, corporate sponsorships, and philanthropic foundations. In Canada, such eligibility is determined under the common law rather than by legislation. Canada has been conservative compared to other countries in reviewing and modernizing the common law view of charitable purposes, benchmarked by a British court case in the late 1800s, in order to make it congruent with the realities of contemporary society (Broder 2002; Drache with Boyle 1998; VSI Joint Regulatory Table 2003). The primary means for keeping the common law fresh and responsive to changing conditions is to ensure it is subject to regular judicial review or, alternatively, to codify acceptable purposes or a public benefit test in legislation. Canada's conservatism arises in large part from the fact that the designated court of first instance, the Federal Court of Appeal, is a very expensive route for voluntary organizations to take in order to challenge a denial by the CRA of their applications for charitable status. As a result of limited judicial review, the types of voluntary organizations that do not qualify for access to the tax system and its associated legitimacy are much broader in Canada than in the UK, the United States, or many other democratic nations (Broder 2002).

Once registered, charities are limited in the type and amount of political activities they can undertake. No partisan political activity is permitted, although this has not been seen as restrictive because voluntary organizations are rarely allied with political parties, nor do they see any benefit to being partisan or expect the public to support such activity with the use of tax expenditures.[5] This has begun to change to some extent in recent debates on policy issues that have a moral dimension, notably around abortion and same sex marriage, in which certain leaders of religious congregations have pushed the regulatory boundaries by their public comments.

At the other end of the spectrum, consultations invited by governments are unrestricted. There is a large swath of policy-related activity between these two extremes, however, that conceivably includes coalition building, conferences, advertising, meetings with public servants and other standard means of influencing public policy. The regulations require that such activity be ancillary to the charitable purposes of the organization, which is normally interpreted to mean that no more than 10 per cent annually (recently adjusted upward to 20 per cent for small organizations) of all of the financial, human, and physical resources of a registered charity be devoted to such activities. Although the CRA has recently tried to clarify what ancillary political activity means, there is still considerable latitude for interpretation by government as to what is allowed under the '10 per cent rule' and discretion over who gets called for overstepping the limit. Given that the sanction is severe, potential loss of charitable status, the effect of the regulation is to promote self-censorship. In a longitudinal study of 20 'public interest groups' (mainly national organizations involved in the health, 'good government' or the social justice fields), Pross and Webb (2003) were struck by the number of times these groups said they restricted participation in public policy advocacy for fear of jeopardizing their status as registered charities. No such restrictions are in place for business associations or corporations and in fact, many of the costs of policy advocacy can be deducted by for-profits as business expenses, thereby reducing taxes payable and providing a form of indirect subsidy. From the perspective of voluntary organizations, this creates an unfair disadvantage in policy participation from the start, one that is further exacerbated by differentials in policy capacity.

Capacities for Policy Participation

An understanding of policy styles needs to account for both the constraints and opportunities afforded by governing contexts *and* the capacities and strategies of different sets of policy actors. In his chapter for this volume, Prince articulates the importance of capacity in understanding who participates and how they participate in policy making. Capacity refers to tangible resources and assets – the 'human and financial resources, technology, skills, knowledge and understanding required to permit organizations to do their work and fulfill what is expected of them by stakeholders' (PAGVS 1999, 18). It also involves less tangible elements, such as the trust relationships and the 'negotiated practices' that, in Prince's words, support the craft as well as the art of policy. The notion of capacity embodies more than the level or mix of resources, however; it also entails the ability and choices to convert these resources into action. In effect, it reflects an investment in strategy: 'The relationship with government is not so much a function of a nonprofit's resources as it is what it does with those resources ... Rather than thinking of a nonprofit as a political group using its resources to push arguments forward, envisage an organization making hard decisions on how to allocate scarce resources: Those decisions determine the capacity of an organization to achieve its goals' (Berry with Arons 2003, 125).

The tough decisions and tradeoffs that voluntary organizations make generally relate to three key areas:

1 *Policy capacity:* the ability to provide policy analysis and advice, participate effectively, and exert influence in policy development.

2 *Network capacity:* the resources and practices for building and sustaining partnerships, trust coalitions, and good working relationships with members, users, and other nongovernmental organizations as well as with governments, the media, corporations, and the public (Canadian Center for Philanthropy et al. 2003, 6).
3 *Project or program capacity:* the production of services, programs, or projects that support an organization's mission and its sustainability.

In the space of this chapter, a full assessment of the capacities of Canada's voluntary sector is impossible due, among other things, to the considerable differences across policy fields. Nevertheless, recent surveys of the voluntary sector point to one overarching trend that affects virtually all types of voluntary organizations: the instability of financial support inherent in project-based funding regimes. Over the past two decades, there has been a significant reduction in government funding for voluntary organizations that has resulted in greater competition for other sources of funding. As significant as the overall level of support is the replacement of core with project or contract funding (Scott 2003). Because project funding has short-term horizons, it produces enormous instability and vulnerability. In particular, it makes long-term strategic planning and the ability to retain qualified staff whose salaries are project-dependent very difficult and it usually covers very limited, if any, expenses for policy development. In looking at explanations for the capacities for policy, networking, or programming, one does not need to scratch very deeply to see the effects of unstable funding.

Policy Capacity

In a recent empirical study of the policy capacity of American nonprofits, Berry and Arons (2003, 144–5) argue that the two most significant factors in determining political effectiveness are, first, whether an organization has made government relations someone's job and, second, the nonprofit's facility with research. Once policy analysis and government relations becomes the explicit responsibility of someone, whether a designated government relations/public affairs officer, the executive director, or a volunteer member of the board, that person can make claims on other organizational resources. Because many voluntary organizations, and particularly those registered as charities, start out with a primary mission to provide services rather than participate in public policy, the position of government relations officer is usually an afterthought, if such a position exists at all. A recent survey of Canadian voluntary organizations working in health, which include some of the better-resourced and most policy-conscious organizations in the sector, attests to the limited human resources dedicated to policy work (Voice in Health Policy 2004). Only 16 per cent of provincial and national health organizations had paid staff devoted to policy development or government relations (see Stritch 2007).[6] This was supported by a very small and quick survey conducted for this chapter of other types of national voluntary organizations that would be expected to be policy leaders in their respective areas. Only two of seven indicated that they have paid staff whose primary job is to conduct policy research or to handle government relations and public affairs. What this suggests is that this responsibility is often tacked on to the role of the executive director or other senior management, although the time that they can set aside for policy is limited. As well, voluntary organizations often rely on volunteers from their boards of directors to take the lead on government relations. This may not be a viable long-term strategy, however, as organizations face serious problems in recruiting board members, in large part due to liability issues.

When dedicated policy positions have been established in voluntary organizations, they are seldom staffed with policy specialists. Instead, most voluntary organizations 'struggle to get by with staffs composed almost entirely of self taught generalists' (Canadian Centre for Philanthropy 2003, 33). Policy staff tend to have come up through the voluntary sector, moving from program delivery and administration to policy work, rather than coming to the sector with experience from government or the private sector. Unlike industry and business associations, government relations in voluntary organizations are not the next step for early retiring senior public servants or political refugees from ministerial offices following lost elections. This means that those responsible for government relations in the voluntary sector may have strong abilities to establish networks within the sector, as they know the other players and the issues, but they are less likely to know the people or the processes of government well, both of which are increasingly important in the current opportunity structure. One small signal of change is that in hiring its first ever vice-president of 'public policy and government relations' in late 2004, the primary infrastructure organization engaged in public policy, Imagine Canada (created from a merger of the Canadian Centre for Philanthropy and the Coalition of National Voluntary Organizations), chose an individual with experience as a policy advisor in both a federal government department and the Prime Minister's Office.

While the craft of policy analysis may be changing for voluntary organizations so, too, is the art and the science. As noted above, one of the shifts in the political opportunity structure in recent years has been toward the production of evidence-based research. The need to make a policy case based on 'objective' evidence rather than on opinion is not new for Canadian voluntary organizations which are registered as charities, because regulations have always required that in order to be eligible for such status, the education or information that they produce has to be grounded in fact, not opinion, and it has to be balanced. What is new is the sophistication and the amount of evidence required. With more research being contracted out by governments and project funding, whether from governments or foundations, more likely to fund short-term research projects than core operations, voluntary organizations seem to be undertaking more research, and sometimes displacing more action-oriented advocacy in the process (Laforest 2001). While voluntary organizations may also be taking advantage of the research produced by various think tanks to make their case, their need to secure project funding, and the fact that such funding can often be directed only to research, means that they are also generating more research activity of their own. An increase in the production of evidence-based research has two main effects on voluntary organizations (Laforest and Orsini 2004). First, it enhances their professionalism as they develop new analytical skill sets through training or by hiring researchers with these skills. And, as expertise replaces experiential knowledge, it often effects a culture change that is more top-down and less directed by members. Second, the claims made and action repertoires are affected. Ideas become more mainstream, claims increasingly cautious, and political tactics more conventional. As Laforest and Orisini found with family and social service organizations, 'claims that cannot be supported by legitimate forms of research tend to be watered down or abandoned altogether in favour of claims that are achievable' (2004, 490–1).

Even when voluntary organizations have produced solid research – or perhaps *because* they have produced such research – they may not choose to be active advocates for policy change. Indeed, the distinct advocacy chill that hangs over the sector as a result of the funding and regulatory regimes is producing significant self-restraint on the part of many organizations (Scott 2003). Policy advocacy is rarely supported

by project funding from governments or foundations and is often specifically prohibited (Pross and Webb 2003, 89). More importantly, many
voluntary organizations remember well the lessons of the 1990s, when
the funding of advocacy organizations was cut suddenly and dramatically, and are fearful of putting their funding at risk by being critical of
governments. So they keep their heads down. As Pross and Webb
emphatically conclude: 'government funding moderates public interest
advocacy' (2003, 82; see also Berry 2003). Even when government is not
funding their work, voluntary organizations may restrain how vocally
and visibly they pursue certain causes if this entails criticism of governments, if it makes conservative donors nervous, or if it puts their charitable status at risk. As a 2003 study of funding practices reported,
'When organizations must cobble together projects and partners to
survive, being seen as an outspoken advocate on behalf of one's client
group can be regarded as too risky, despite the justice of the cause. You
do not want to have your name in the media when your next funding
submission comes up for approval' (Scott 2003, 17).

Obviously, some groups do retain a strong political voice and seek
media attention to advance their cause. If the self-reports from the
sector are correct, however, it suggests a growing divide between a
small number of politically active groups and the rest. New battle lines
have been drawn, suggest Laforest and Orsini, 'creating one group of
privileged organizations, which enjoy access and influence and have
the necessary resources to influence policy, and another group of organizations, which has been frozen out of the policy process for reasons of
ideological opposition, lack of technical skills/capacity, or both' (2004,
492).

Network Capacity

By all accounts, there is a growing emphasis on network building in
both policy development and service delivery. Congruent with this,
networking is seen by voluntary organizations to be one of their distinctive strengths. According to the recent National Survey of Nonprofit
and Voluntary Organizations (NSNVO), only 24 per cent of voluntary
organizations indicated that they had difficulty in collaborating with
other organizations and for only 2 per cent of them was this a serious
problem. Indeed, it was through effective networking that the voluntary sector managed to get itself on the federal government's political
radar in the late 1990s. Until that point, neither government nor the

organizations themselves would have recognized them as a distinct 'sector.'

After the dramatic cutbacks to voluntary organizations, particularly those engaged in advocacy that had begun in the late 1980s and were accelerated during federal Program Review in the mid-1990s, the sector was badly in need of policy leadership at the national level. None of the national umbrella or infrastructure organizations had the capacity or the credibility to step up to this task, however. In 1995, 12 national organizations and coalitions from diverse parts of the sector formed a very minimalist, unincorporated, and intentionally short-lived body, known as the Voluntary Sector Roundtable (VSR). Its purpose was to strengthen the voice of Canada's charitable, voluntary sector, and begin a dialogue with the federal government around cross-cutting policy matters affecting the sector as a whole. Recognizing that its credibility to make claims about the sector's own governance and about reforming relationships with governments would be enhanced by expert, independent advice, it commissioned the Panel on Governance and Accountability in 1997. This was the first-ever step by the sector to commission research and advice in such a visible manner and in a way intended to speak to the sector as a whole. Chaired by Ed Broadbent (former leader of the federal NDP), the panel consisted of six experts, all of whom served as volunteers, and a faculty member (this author) as a part-time research director who, with a research consultant, prepared background briefing papers for use by panel members. The process and the report, released in February 1999, were milestones for the voluntary sector because they set out an agenda for action, helped voluntary organizations begin to coalesce as a sector, and gained the VSR and the sector considerable respect within government.

The federal government had been working independently, first through an interdepartmental committee and, when that did not make much progress, through a task force housed at the Privy Council Office, to develop a strategy for implementing the 1997 election promises to enhance capacity and engage the sector. Soon recognizing that it would need to work collaboratively with the voluntary sector to move the file forward, the federal government established three 'joint tables,' consisting of equal numbers of senior public servants and leaders from the sector. Over a three-month period in 1999, these joint tables successfully developed an extensive set of recommendations that fairly closely resembled those of the Broadbent Panel. In June 2000, the Government of Canada established the five-year, $95-million Voluntary Sector Initiative (VSI) to carry forward these proposals, the first two years of which were to be conducted mainly through a second, more elaborate set of joint tables.

The VSI is widely regarded to have gone a long way in developing a deeper mutual understanding and trust among the more than 130 public servants and sector representatives who participated (Social Development Canada 2004a). As a means of developing and institutionalizing *organizational* linkages between voluntary organizations and government departments, however, the VSI was limited in three respects (Phillips 2004). First, while an explicit choice was made to promote involvement by a broad cross-section of the voluntary sector, the participants were chosen as individuals, rather than as representatives of national or regional organizations. Consequently, a number of the participants who worked in very small organizations had little experience in policy work and not much contact with the federal government, and could not contribute fully to the policy discussions or take the policy work back to their constituencies. A second factor was the lack of consistency in participation, particularly on the government's side. Over the course of the 18 months of the active joint work of the VSI, the membership in the joint tables saw a 30 per cent turnover rate: 10 per cent for the voluntary sector and 50 per cent for government (Social Development Canada 2004a). A third concern arose as a paradox of partnership. From the sector's perspective, the initial mandate of the VSI did not include considerations of its top policy issues; during the course of the VSI, many sector representatives felt that they lost their policy voice. They found it difficult to step outside the collaboration to go to the ministerial level on outstanding matters. This occurred partly because they were consumed with the enormous operational details of the VSI, which left little time to deal with policy, and because they were discouraged from going a more political route until some of the contentious issues had been resolved *within* the VSI. As these were never resolved, the political routes were not readily accessible.

The VSI was also intended to build stronger relationships at a bilateral level, between departments and their constituencies. The largest program of the initiative, known as Sector Involvement in Departmental Program Development (SIDPD), set aside $30 million as project funding to go to departments and voluntary organizations that wished to develop new, innovative ways for working together. Over two rounds of funding, 67 SIDPD projects were undertaken involving a wide range of departments and voluntary organizations. These projects enabled voluntary organizations to have greater input into policy, but did not enhance their impact on policy (Social Development Canada 2004b). Moreover, many participating organizations felt that departments continued to treat their involvement in the same manner as traditional one-shot consultations, rather than as ongoing collaborations. Many departments 'held the view that it was a process that relies on the status quo whereby the federal departments define and develop the policy issues of concern, and then invite voluntary sector representatives to comment' (Social Development Canada 2004b, 51). Even when more collaborative relationships had developed, the mobility of public servants and the end of the SIDPD project funding put their sustainability at risk.

The high level of mobility in most Canadian governments due to retirements and the flat demographic profile is a serious challenge to network building, one for which there is no easy solution. On average, senior federal public servants remain in their positions for less than two years. Such mobility is rendering policy networks of all sorts highly unstable: no sooner do voluntary organizations begin to foster good working relationships and understanding with the key public servant responsible for policy in their area, which probably takes at least a year, than the official moves on. A related problem is that with the highly stringent accountability regime over grants and contributions that was imposed in 2000, the role of the program or project officer (the public servant who is responsible for both internal and external contact regarding grants, contribution agreements, or programs) has been recast from a role of facilitator to one of auditor (Good 2003; Phillips and Levasseur 2004). This is important because the project officer is often the primary point of ongoing contact for voluntary organizations outside of the policy process. When these organizations have a good working relationship with 'their' program officer, they generally feel that they have a good relationship with government as a whole. When the program officer is primarily an auditor and policer, however, there is little basis for developing a trusting relationship.

The challenges in building network capacity cannot all be attributed to the political opportunity structure. One of the key challenges for the voluntary sector is the relatively underdeveloped capacity of its infrastructure organizations, those whose primary function is to serve the rest of the sector through research, advice, standard setting and policy leadership (Abramson and McCarthy 2002). A comparison with the resources of the main infrastructure organizations in the UK, which are more modest than those in the United States, is telling. Take as an example Imagine Canada. While it has substantial research resources, supported mainly by federal project money, it has only one full-time public affairs specialist. With significant core funding from government, its counterpart in England, the National Council of Voluntary Organizations, has three teams focused on policy-related initiatives and devotes 10 per cent of its £490,000 annual budget to providing policy leadership to the voluntary sector on new issues alone.

Canada's underdeveloped sectoral infrastructure is largely a result of the peculiarly low value that policy makers, and parts of the voluntary sector, place on infrastructure organizations. In this, scholarship is partly to blame. The Canadian policy literature pays very little attention to the voluntary sector and even less to the study of intermediary, infrastructure and umbrella organizations. Consequently, such organizations are poorly understood and grossly undervalued (Pratt 2003).

Project and Program Capacity

Although the focus of this chapter is on policy capacity, the spillover effects of the service and program responsibilities of voluntary organizations cannot be overlooked. On the service delivery side, the overwhelming challenge is the lack of financial resources, as it is for policy capacity, but it is probably felt even more acutely in services. The triple whammy of the cutbacks in the public sector during the 1990s was not simply that government funding was cut and competition for other sources of funding grew, but that demands for services increased as well. There is no shortage of stories from voluntary organizations to this effect. As the representative of an organization from Regina recalled in the focus groups done for the NSNVO, 'from 12 years ago until now we've had an 80 per cent increase in the demand for our services, but no additional funding for staff to provide services' (Canadian Centre for Philanthropy 2003, 22).

The fact that people rely on these programs and services creates an immediacy for this type of capacity. With limited resources and time, it is more likely that policy work will get put aside than that users of services will be turned away. In a sense, then, policy capacity becomes the residual of project capacity, seldom to its advantage. Given that there is little reason to believe that funding for the services provided by voluntary organizations will increase significantly or that demand will decrease, it would appear that the policy role is likely to continue to be short-changed. Is there any way out of this dilemma without a massive injection of funding? One route for enhancing policy capacity within the sector as a whole without taking resources away from service delivery is to increase the capacity of infrastructure organizations.

Matching Opportunity and Capacities: The Policy Presence of the Voluntary Sector

In this section, we examine the policy presence of the voluntary sector: Where do they show up in policy development and how do they think they are doing in affecting public policy in Canada? One way to conceive of the optimum relationship of a policy actor with government in the context of the 'new governance' is that they jointly produce public policy (Berry and Arons 2003, 130). This does not imply that there will always be agreement among these co-producers, nor that the voluntary sector organizations will be equal partners with government. Rather, it indicates that there are sufficient incentives on both sides to partner and that the voluntary organizations can maintain a presence in the policy process.

The evidence suggests that voluntary organizations in most fields are far from being able to jointly produce policy. In the NSNVO, almost 40 per cent of voluntary organizations reported that participation in public policy is a problem for them (Statistics Canada et al. 2004). This is related to, but is not simply a matter of capacity. In fact, the perceived difficulty of involvement in public policy increases according to the financial resources of the organization, such that 58 per cent of voluntary organizations with annual revenues of $1 million to $9 million report a problem. Involvement in policy is particularly difficult for voluntary organizations whose main source of income is government funding. Nor can the difficulty be explained by a lack of interest, i.e., that only groups for which public policy is not particularly important report difficulties. The problem of participation is even more pronounced for the very types of organizations that have an active, ongoing interest in public policy: 65 per cent of universities and colleges; 64 per cent of health organizations; 57 per cent of 'law, advocacy, and politics' groups; and 56 per cent of environment and of social services organizations reported difficulties in involvement in public policy. While the NSNVO does not speculate on why policy participation is seen to be so difficult, one factor may be where and when voluntary organizations access the process.

Table 20.1 Presentation of Briefs to the House of Commons Health and Human Resources Parliamentary Committees, 2001–2004*

Committee	Voluntary sector	Industry/ professional Assocs/Unions	Think tanks/ academics	Corporations/ other
Health	75	62	44	9
Human Resources	199	87	102	43

* These figures are rough estimates, as the boundaries are sometimes unclear between categories; representatives of governments are not included. Source: List of witnesses before the HEAL and HUMA committees from the Parliament of Canada Web site, http://www.parl.gc.ca/committee.

In the most visible part of the policy process, participation in parliamentary committees, voluntary organizations have a relatively strong presence, although this varies substantially by issue and by committee. In the Human Resources Development and Status of Persons with Disability and the Health Committees, for example, more briefs were presented by representatives of voluntary organizations than by industry associations, unions, or think tanks during the course of the 37th Parliament (from January 2001 to February 2004). If this were the sole access point for voluntary organizations, however, they could probably count on having minimal real influence, because review by parliamentary committees comes so late in the policy process that there is usually scope for only relatively minor change. Although we only have a sketchy picture of the other ways in which voluntary organizations participate in policy, they do not appear to have extensive inroads into earlier points in the policy process. The survey of health organizations indicated that most (60 per cent) do the requisite preparatory work, such as environmental scanning, data collection, and analysis, and they make extensive efforts to collaborate with other health organizations, consult with stakeholders, communicate with the media, and work with politicians (Voice in Health Policy 2004). Their least common policy activity is working with Health Canada. Indeed, only a quarter of these organizations felt that they had an influence with the department (Voice in Health Policy 2004). Are they shut out by the department or do they not know the way in? The answer is probably a bit of both. On the one hand, less than a third of the health organizations felt that they were offered adequate participation by the department. On the other hand, only a third said that they understood the policy process or the best ways to be involved. In addition, the '10 per cent rule' on advocacy is seen to be a constraining factor, as organizations are uncertain as to whether participating in policy discussions would be considered part of their allowable limit. If this relatively sophisticated segment of the voluntary sector does not understand the policy process and is not able to build strong relationships with the public service, it is unlikely that the rest of the sector has been able to do so.

This contradicts the impression that the policy process has become more permeable and that increased citizen engagement has been effective in making policy development more inclusive. In reality, the interest in citizen engagement has created a paradox for voluntary organizations so that there is both more and less consultation. While there may be more active consultation by governments, the basis of this engagement has shifted. Beginning in the 1990s, there has been an interest both in a variety of new deliberative processes (such as citizen juries, panels, and assemblies) and in involving 'ordinary citizens' – individuals who represent themselves rather than organized interests. In many instances, organizations are intentionally shut out of these dialogues and the emphasis is often more on the process than it is on ensuring that such engagement informs policy decisions in any real way (Laforest and Phillips 2007).

When government departments do consult with organized interests, voluntary organizations perceive that their influence is diminishing. There are widespread reports of consultation 'fatigue,' but this is not produced so much by the sheer numbers of consultations in which they are expected to participate, although the number has increased to be sure, but by a degree of scepticism as to whether governments actually value or use their input (Canadian Centre for Philanthropy 2003, 43; Scott 2003). Indeed, the picture drawn by Pross and Webb of the consequences for a vibrant policy process is really quite bleak: 'There is a sense that governments are abandoning a tradition of tolerance for diverse views and a commitment to ensure that such views are heard. "We are moving to a place of having to be more constrained. It hasn't always been that way. In the past there has been a view that government has a responsibility to ensure that multiple voices are heard." Or in the words of another group leader, "there has been an increasing emphasis on the provision of services and a decline of a community-based voice"' (2003, 110).

In short, while there appear to be more doors opening in the area of policy processes, many of these either are not opening for much of the voluntary sector, or organizations are unable to go through them.

Conclusion: Implications for Policy Studies

This chapter has argued that shifts in the approaches to governing are forging new policy analytic styles. As we evolve toward a new model of 'governance,' in which relationships are the key dimensions of institutions and in which nongovernmental actors play increasingly significant roles, greater attention will need to be paid to the capacity of these nongovernmental actors to be effective policy participants and governance partners. Governance creates demands for policy analytical styles that feature quality, evidence-based research, an ability to connect across networks and knowledge of how to navigate through the various channels, islands and scales of government. To be effective in this governance context entails a good knowledge of both policy substance and process. Such a policy style does not seem particularly well suited to most voluntary organizations, however.

While voluntary organizations are highly adept at collaborating and communicating within their own networks and with their users and stakeholders, they face a serious lack of policy capacity. A funding environment that is based largely on short-term project funding produces enormous instability, reducing the ability to plan strategically over the longer term and to dedicate adequate resources to policy development. There is clear evidence that this funding environment, coupled with very conservative regulations on advocacy by registered charities, has produced a distinct advocacy chill. Preoccupied by service delivery and the search for revenues *and* concerned about alienating funders or risking their charitable status, voluntary organizations restrain their policy activities. Even relatively few policy-oriented organizations have personnel dedicated to public affairs and governmental relations. Moreover, voluntary organizations cannot always rely on their infrastructure or peak associations to carry the policy analysis and advocacy ball on their behalf, because these organizations, too, survive mainly on project funding. Indeed, Canada is one of the few democratic countries in which the peak infrastructure organizations that represent cross-sectoral interests do not receive substantial core funding from either governments or foundations.

One clear path to enhancing the policy capacity of the sector as a whole is to better support the work of infrastructure organizations. A second is to bring greater policy expertise, particularly knowledge of the policy process, into the voluntary sector. This entails more policy training, greater information by government departments about how policy works, more exchanges and career movement between government and the sector, and adjustments to project funding to support policy work and policy staff.

There is a considerable role in this for schools and programs in public policy and administration. One thing that should be evident from this chapter is that we have significant knowledge gaps related to the voluntary sector in Canada. In one respect, research on the sector has burgeoned in recent years. Most of this work has been conducted by the sector and funded or commissioned by the federal government. Research on the sector in the academy is still very limited, however, and the expanded 'grey literature,' as it is sometimes disparagingly called, does not have much take-up by academics. An important first step is to expand and enrich our scholarship. Equally important is to integrate this knowledge into curricula. If schools and programs in the field of public administration are to prepare students well for careers in a governance environment in which the public sector is truly collaborative and networked, we will need to incorporate content into the curricula that gives students a better understanding of the voluntary sector as governance partners and as part of an expanded public sector.

NOTES

The research assistance of Elaina Mack and Brian Desroiries Tam and the constructive advice provided by the editors are appreciated. Research for this chapter was supported by a strategic grant from the nonprofit granting stream of the Social Sciences and Humanities Research Council.

1 Interest (or pressure) groups are commonly defined as 'organizations whose members act together to influence public policy in order to promote their common interest' (Pross 1986, 13).
2 Whether there is sufficient cohesion for Canadian voluntary associations to be called a sector at all is contested, as is the choice of an appropriate name. There are national differences in naming this sector: in the United States, 'nonprofit' is the most common label; in the UK, 'voluntary and community' is widely used; and in Canada, 'voluntary' or 'voluntary and nonprofit' has become popular. The term 'third sector' is used more commonly in the academic literature than it is among organizations in this sector.
3 One reason for a bifurcation is that universities, colleges, and hospitals, which are registered charities, are included in the NSNVO, and they skew indicators of size and revenues to the high end.

4 The NSNVO includes professional and business associations and unions, which collectively constitute 5.3 per cent of the voluntary and nonprofit sector (Statistics Canada et al. 2004, 18).

5 Federal regulations also severely limit the ability of third parties, including voluntary and business associations and corporations, to advocate policy positions during electoral campaigns by purchasing advertising, a limit that was recently upheld by the Supreme Court. For a discussion of this aspect of regulation see Pross and Webb (2003, 104).

6 As Stritch notes in the following chapter, business associations also have fewer staff doing policy work than the popular image of powerful business lobbies might suggest. Nevertheless, the comparison is stark: whereas 63 per cent of business associations have one person or fewer in policy positions, 84 per cent of voluntary organizations (extrapolating from the study of health organizations) have no policy staff at all.

REFERENCES

Abramson, Alan J., and Rachel McCarthy. 2002. 'Infrastructure Organizations.' In Lester M. Salamon, ed., *The State of Nonprofit America*, 331–54. Washington, DC: Brookings Institution.

Berry, Jeffrey M., with David F. Arons. 2003. *A Voice for Nonprofits*. Washington, DC: Brookings Institution.

Broder, Peter. 2002. 'The Legal Definition of Charity and Canada Customs and Revenue Agency's Charitable Registration Process.' *The Philanthropist* 17(3), 3–56.

Canadian Centre for Philanthropy et al. 2003. *The Capacity to Serve: A Qualitative Study of the Challenges Facing Canada's Nonprofit and Voluntary Organizations*. Toronto: Canadian Centre for Philanthropy.

Dobrowolsky, Alexandra, and Denis Saint-Martin. 2005. 'Agency, Actors and Change in a Child-Focused Future: Path Dependency Problematized.' *Commonwealth and Comparative Politics* 43(1) (March), 1–33.

Donovan, Dan. 2005. 'Advocacy and Lobbying: Who's Winning, Who's Losing.' *Ottawa Life* (January), 23–5.

Drache, Arthur B.C., and F.K. Boyle. 1998. *Charities, Public Benefit and the Canadian Income Tax System: A Proposal for Reform*. Toronto: Kahanoff Nonprofit Sector Research Initiative.

Good, David A. 2003. *The Politics of Public Management*, Toronto: IPAC.

Government of Canada/Voluntary Sector. 2001. *An Accord between the Government of Canada and the Voluntary Sector*. Ottawa: Voluntary Sector Initiative Secretariat.

Howlett, Michael. 2002. 'Administrative Styles and Regulatory Reform: Institutional Arrangements and Their Effects on Administrative Behavior.' *International Management Review* 5(2), 13–35.

Jenson, Jane. 1995. 'What's in a Name? Nationalist Movements and Public Discourse.' In Hank Johnston and Bert Klandermans, eds., *Social Movements and Culture*, 107–26. London: UCL Press.

Klijn, Erik-Hans, and Joop Koppenjan. 2004. *Managing Uncertainties in Networks: A Network Approach to Problem Solving and Decision Making*. London: Routledge.

Laforest, Rachel. 2002. 'Rethinking the Contours of Advocacy.' Paper presented to the 74th Annual Meeting of the Canadian Political Science Association, Toronto, 2 June.

Laforest, Rachel, and Michael Orsini. 2005. 'Evidence-Based Engagement in the Voluntary Sector: Lessons from Canada.' *Social Policy and Administration* 39(5) (October), 481–97.

Laforest, Rachel, and Susan D. Phillips. 2007. 'Citizen Engagement: Rewiring the Policy Process.' In Michael Orsini and Miriam Smith, eds., *Critical Policy Studies*. Vancouver: UBC Press.

Larner, Wendy. 2004. *Neoliberalism in (Regional) Theory and Practice: The Stronger Communities Action Fund*. Research Paper 14, Local Partnerships and Governance, University of Auckland.

Newman, Janet. 2001. *Modernising Governance: New Labour, Policy and Society*. London: Sage Publications.

Pal, Leslie A. 1993. *Interests of State: The Politics of Language, Multiculturalism, and Feminism in Canada*. Montreal and Kingston: McGill-Queen's University Press.

Panel on Accountability and Governance in the Voluntary Sector (PAGVS). 1999. *Building on Strength: Improving Governance and Accountability in Canada's Voluntary Sector*. Ottawa: Voluntary Sector Roundtable.

Phillips, Susan D. 2003. 'SUFA and Citizen Engagement: Fake or Genuine Masterpiece.' In Sarah Fortin, Alain Noël, and France St-Hilaire, eds., *Forging the Canadian Social Union*, 93–124. Montreal: IRPP.

– 2004. 'The Limits of Horizontal Governance: Voluntary Sector-Government Collaboration in Canada.' *Society and Economy* 26(2–3), 393–415.

Phillips, Susan D., and Karine Levasseur. 2004. 'The Snakes and Ladders of Accountability: Contradictions in Contracting and Collaboration for Canada's Voluntary Sector.' *Canadian Public Administration* 27(4), 451–74.

Pierson, Paul. 2000. 'Increasing Returns, Path Dependence, and the Study of Politics.' *American Political Science Review* 94(2), 251–67.

Pratt, Jon. 2004. 'The Future of the Infrastructure.' *The Nonprofit Quarterly* 12(4), 16–21.

Pross, A. Paul. 1986. *Group Politics and Public Policy.* Toronto: Oxford University Press.

Pross, A. Paul, and Kernaghan R. Webb. 2003. 'Embedded Regulation: Advocacy and the Federal Regulation of Public Interest Groups.' In Kathy L. Brock, ed., *Delicate Dances: Public Policy and the Nonprofit Sector,* 63–121. Montreal and Kingston: McGill-Queen's University Press.

Rhodes, R.A.W. 1996. 'The New Governance: Governing without Government.' *Political Studies* 44(4), 652–67.

Richardson, Jeremy. 2000. 'Government, Interest Groups and Policy Change.' *Political Studies* 48, 1006–25.

Richardson, Jeremy, Gunnel Gustafsson, and Grant Jordan. 1982. 'The Concept of Policy Style.' In J.J. Richardson, ed., *Policy Styles in Western Europe,* 1–16. London: George Allen and Unwin.

Salamon, Lester M. 2002. 'The New Governance and the Tools of Public Action: An Introduction.' In Lester M. Salamon, ed., *The Tools of Governance: A Guide to the New Governance,* 1–47. Oxford: Oxford University Press.

Scott, Katherine. 2003. *Funding Matters: The Impact of Canada's New Funding Regime on Nonprofit and Voluntary Organizations.* Ottawa: Canadian Council on Social Development.

Social Development Canada. 2004a. *Process Evaluation of the Voluntary Sector Initiative.* Ottawa: Social Development Canada. http://www.vsi-isbc.ca.

– 2004b. *An Evaluation of the Sectoral Involvement in Departmental Policy Development (SIDPD).* Ottawa: Social Development Canada. http://www.vsi-isbc.ca.

Statistics Canada et al. 2004. *Cornerstones of Community: Highlights of the National Survey of Nonprofit and Voluntary Organizations.* Ottawa: Minister of Industry.

Thelen, Kathleen. 2003. 'How Institutions Evolve: Insights from Comparative Historical Analysis.' In J. Mahoney and D. Rueschemeyer, eds., *Comparative Historical Analysis in the Social Sciences,* 208–40. Cambridge: Cambridge University Press.

Voice in Health Policy. 2004. 'Participation in Health Policy.' Ottawa: Voluntary Sector Inititative. http://www.projectvoice.ca.

Voluntary Sector Initiative, Joint Regulatory Table. 2003. *Strengthening Canada's Charitable Sector: Regulatory Reform.* Ottawa: Voluntary Sector Initiative.

PART VI

Academic and Advocacy-Based Policy Analysis

This final section of the book investigates the contexts of and orientations to policy analysis undertaken by several key players in the broad policy community: the media, think tanks, and academics. Each of the authors notes that the general shape and impact of policy analysis conducted by these players is ambiguous because it is less than fully public, less than systematically rigorous and/or internally quite heterogeneous. Yet between them the media, think tank employees or associates, and academics contribute a huge amount to policy debate and arguably to both the broad outlines and specific elements of public policy. So if their efforts to shape debates on public policy and its implementation are backed by unsystematic, biased, politically naive, or otherwise suspect policy analysis, it is important for us to know why this is the case.

Catherine Murray shows that we know remarkably little about the training, policy analytic orientations, or actual policy roles of journalists and the media who employ them. She sheds light on the shared professional norms, corporate media operating principles, and obstacles to journalists' access to state-generated information that constrain even innovative and analytically ambitious journalists. Chapter 21 emphasizes the importance of institutional improvements to the *Freedom of Information Act* and whistle-blowing legislation as aids to journalists wishing to contribute key information to public debate and sound policy analysis.

In chapter 22, Donald Abelson offers an overview of Canadian think tanks: the types, and their objectives and broad policy foci. He points out that there are far fewer access points in the Canadian political system than the American system, due to our party discipline and concentration of legislative and executive power. He shows that think tank efforts to influence public policy are on the increase, though it is difficult to measure how much this results in actual policy influence. Think tank resources are committed to a combination of policy analysis and advocacy, so it is hard to identify the proportion of these resources allocated to the former. Abelson also notes the varied patterns of think tank connections to government agencies and policy agendas, and the range of connections think tanks have to universities, the business community, trade unions, and the policy communities they inhabit. Along with this variety comes a diversity of approaches to policy analysis undertaken by think tank employees and associates.

In the volume's last chapter, Daniel Cohn sets the policy analytical efforts made by academics in the service of broadening the range of policy choices in two contexts: a stylized classification of academic policy interventions, and the broader political dynamics of policy development and choice by state actors. He argues that academics are often unaware of unintended negative consequences that may follow from the adoption of parts of their wider policy proposals, and of the need to assess and then engage the array of political actors working within and alongside 'advocacy coalitions.' As difficult – and for many academics, out of character – as the latter task is, Cohn suggests that if academics wish to have the kinds of impact on policy development and choice that often motivates their policy analysis in the first place, they must not remain disengaged from the complex, often less than transparent, and certainly time-consuming political processes that condition opportunities to 'speak truth to power.'

21 The Media

CATHERINE MURRAY

Introduction

With their resources, reach, and potential leverage of elite and public opinion, the Canadian news media play an important part in Canadian policy networks. But as institutions and actors at the meso- and micro-levels of the policy system, the media are apparently disaggregated and uncoordinated, negotiating highly differential access to the policy sphere depending on personal political capital, economic constraints of ownership, and the news culture within each organization. It is thus not surprising that little is systematically known about the media's role in reporting, interrogating, investigating, or interpreting public policy in Canada. Early public policy texts rarely included them in the policy analysis dance (Pal 2001). Others conceded them a limited or sporadic role in the theory of policy analysis but still considered them an undifferentiated policy actor (Howlett and Ramesh 1995; Johnson 2002). A systemic blindspot about the media's role in public policy continues to be widespread in the craft of policy case studies.[1]

Often considered 'outside' of the policy process by virtue of the convention of journalistic autonomy, journalists are expected at best to be brokers, not generators, of policy knowledge, unlikely to have a direct interest-based stake in policy intervention. There is therefore little critical analysis of media effects on policy. Instead, the media are assumed to have a 'limited effect,' exerting little influence as an independent variable in policy formation. In this view, media attention and public reaction are not usually sufficient to initiate, create, or veto a new policy, but may cause adjustments or tweaking (Fletcher and Sottile 1997). While agenda-setting theories are beginning to involve the media more fully in models of deliberative politics – framing issues, prompting action, and mobilizing consent in policy communities (Soroka 2003) – they rarely control for anything other than reportage or idea brokerage in the press cycle. Others (Good 2003; Spizer 1993) argue that the media have a very significant direct – and insider – influence on the policy process through investigative journalism, editorials, and commentaries, although views differ sharply on whether it is positive or negative.

This chapter contends that contemporary policy analysis must explore how the media report and interpret policy, facilitate, or obstruct it, since their direct and indirect roles in modern governance are growing. Media attention is increasingly important to other policy players, from policy institutes and academics to civil society organizations, in accumulating political capital in the marketplace of ideas. No other set of so-called 'third sector' policy players is as often assumed to be adversarial, or as formidable, and yet no other is as interdependent.

The Media as Policy Player

Policy-relevant media refer to the conventional news media, that is, the genre of reporting on TV or in print about the everyday activities of government which are widely accessible to citizens. Neo-institutional definitions of policy actors start with a clear identification of rational self-interest and intent, neither of which easily applies to the conventional media. As actors, the media function as a complex, plural constellation. Journalists have a certain licensed autonomy within their organizations, and news organizations typically rely on a range of commentators covering the political spectrum. Only the convention of the editorial in newspapers, a small fraction of total annual content, expresses a paper's unitary position on a public issue. Certain news outlets tend to be associated with certain political parties or tendencies, but they do not pursue their self-interest in typical ways. Unlike public interest groups, business associations, or think tanks, journalists and their media organizations do not directly intervene with formal legal or representative standing to advance a policy interest or champion specific policy options, although they may be called to provide evidence in criminal or civil inquiries.

No other independent institution in Canada's policy networks reaches as many citizens daily. Few are as apparently competitive: there are several hundred daily newspapers, several thousand community papers and radio stations, three national conventional TV news services, and a growing number of mostly commercial specialty 24-hour national and international news channels. This ubiquity explains why the most direct potential interest in policy is economic: the media easily outspend think tanks or interest groups on news and policy monitoring.[2] Among policy players, then, the media are *potentially* the best resourced, should they devote even a small proportion of these expenditures to original policy analysis. They would also seem to have the most stable financial capacity: media return on investment outperforms that of many other sectors.

The political media cycle is typically understood to include four stages that intersect with public policy in different ways: factual reportage, interrogation, investigation and interpretation (McNair 2000). Each stage requires greater financial and editorial resources, different forms of policy analysis, and successive refinement of policy positions, in some cases involving disclosure of preferred policy stances. They may be conceived of as moving from relatively passive to more active policy orientation, and from the outer boundaries of the policy community to the inner network. Reportage and interrogation conform to the media's conventional brokerage role in policy analysis. Investigation and interpretation assert a policy analysis role, with ambit for individual initiation, policy advocacy, and knowledge creation. Stories move in and out of these stages; a single story may not move in a linear fashion all four. Very few stories are sustained in all four phases of the media attention cycle through time. The purpose of this chapter is to map each phase of the press cycle, bringing into finer focus the way the media may contribute to policy analysis, and the constraints upon them.

Reporting and Framing Policy

By informing Canadians about the policy research that affects them, the media play an essential role in the policy development process. Media selectively report on government press releases, policy statements, reports, memoranda, what they hear from MPs and opposition critics, the prime minister and the PMO, ministers and their staffs, as well as what interested parties outside of government say. There is a continuum to reportage, ranging from typical or objective coverage of the facts to more specialized reporting that aims to explain programs and issues by presenting rationales through longer series and op-ed content.

Most reporting is built around Question Period in the House and daily scrums, with a series of formal and informal press conferences on important events in the parliamentary cycle (Throne Speech, budget, and so on) that are the routine stuff of the political news cycle. Traditions of cabinet solidarity and centralization of power in the Prime Minister's Office, offset only recently by empowerment of backbench MPs in parliamentary committees, have restricted media access to the parliamentary process. Few journalists cover the activities of parliamentary committees due to their low news value in the current system, and even fewer cover discussions of parliamentary or public service reform.

It is often speculated that the culture of political journalism in Canada, like the lobby culture, is not as tight as it is in the United States, with less frequent off-the-record social contacts and mutual information exchanges between political or public service elites. Journalism in Canada is sharply localized, looser, and less socially stratified, mainly because journalism schools are not attached to Canadian Ivy League institutions, where leading law or business or public policy students are recruited to political careers. If the central nervous system of the political media is the parliamentary press gallery, fewer and fewer journalists register, and only 40 per cent last more than one election. Gallery turnover increased during the 1990s, while turnover of MPs stabilized (Malloy 2003). Turnover is significantly higher in provincial press galleries. The journalist-politician link or journalist-public servant link in Canadian policy networks is thus a weak, contingent one, under constant negotiation. Nonetheless, reporters, politicians, and staff are part of a policy network of carefully cultivated relationships on three levels: between competitors in the press gallery hub of political news coverage on Parliament Hill; between a party and a news organization; and between government members and reporters (Fletcher and Sottile 1997). Cabinet ministers, political leaders, and senior public servants meet informally with editorial boards and participate in annual press gallery social functions, but these are low-stakes involvements. On-line media extensions, which offer opportunities for posted comment or 'talk back,' in theory allow media-policy networks to broaden, but their impact is not yet known. To prevent perceptions of conflict of interest by accepting undue benefit, codes of journalistic ethics police the boundaries of this licensed autonomy or arm's-length relationship between journalists and policy makers or other policy actors. Formal insulation from government policy networks is not uncommon, although norms may be relaxing. In the 'Relève' exercises for the federal civil service, for example, journalists were rarely invited to policy roundtables or published in *Horizon*, and they did not find this unusual. The pattern is more relaxed at the local level, when informal policy roundtables may well include invited journalists. Since straight news reportage makes frequent recourse to outside experts in order to balance points of view, participation in such roundtables as independent experts is important to journalists, diversifying access to a pool of researchers in independent think tanks, universities and civil society organizations.

The chief assets of the media's power in policy networks are their access to the public and their public reputation. A key determinant of political capital in policy circles is the existence of transparent, well-reasoned professional news standards, which are administered by press or broadcast standards councils, are consistent with the Charter on freedom of expression, and develop informal organic law or jurisprudence on complaints. In this regard, the Canadian press is advanced over many of its counterparts. However, press councils are often criticized for their relative obscurity and inability to promulgate precedent-built or organic rulings, and calls to improve the ombudsman process have escalated. Nor have editors accepted that the model of the press ombudsman may influence the way reporters and editors work, or assist in providing critical assessments of their news product. Policy practitioners like David Good, a senior deputy minister involved in an epic struggle to frame a policy issue with the press that will be discussed later, have called for clear codes of conduct to guide accuracy and fairness of journalistic coverage and comment, consistent with a concern about distortion. There have been no studies of factual accuracy in Canadian papers, but surveys of American media find one in two newspaper articles have at least one error – a disturbing finding. Reformers question the system of professional self-regulation, which retains an outmoded structural separation between press and broadcast standards councils in an era of cross-media ownership, and call for a 1–800 complaint line and more public awareness campaigns; wider appointments to deliberative juries; and more transparency in reasons for judgments.

The related variable affecting the public reputation of the media in policy analysis is whether there are independent think tanks or institutes that regularly monitor and comment on the quality of journalism and its interventions in public policy arenas. In this, Canada is far behind the United States, which has institutes on both the left and the right (FAIR or Fairness and Integrity in Reporting, and Accuracy in the

Media or AIM) and prestigious independent foundations (Pew Research Center for People and the Press) and university monitoring centres (Annenberg School and Columbia Journalism School).[3] However, the Canadian media-politics monitoring scene has two important recent additions.[4] To enable these new media monitoring agencies in the policy networks, substantial investment must be made in developing better software programs to search and analyze digital audiovisual as well as print media databases.

If balance is defined as avoidance of objective errors of fact, subjective errors such as over-emphasis or under-emphasis, or omissions (CMRC 2004), 37 per cent of Canadians consider the news they see and read to be often fair and balanced, with 42 per cent saying it is sometimes balanced. This indicates a fairly good reputation for reportage, better than ratings of U.S. media. Yet most news stories are derived from situations over which politicians have complete control and are thus rarely checked. A recent study (Richards and Rehberg-Sedo 2004) suggests that 'routine' official channels account for 72 per cent of stories in the *National Post* and 65 per cent in the *Globe and Mail*, based on a random sample of front pages between 1998 and 2003. Use of wire service stories is on the increase, filling one-third to one-half of the Canadian daily newspaper, inversely related to size of organization, which suggests a trend to delegated news discretion.

A great deal of press reputation resides in the media's perceived independence from other powerful interests in society, and relative influence, but that reputation is failing. Indeed, Canadians consider the media and business leaders to have too much influence on political affairs.[5] Perceptions of a disproportionate share of policy voice are directly derived from conventions of attribution. Who the media include as legitimate sources for commentary, analysis or deliberation on a policy issue is of prime importance. There is often an implied hierarchy, selected with an eye to accuracy and needs for balance in a story. Top of the list are other governments, within or outside Canada. In health issues, for example, journalists tend to foreground premiers, rather than health institutes, as adversaries to federal health plans. Second are independent research groups, institutes, and foundations. Third are independent academics, and fourth are public or special interest groups or civil society organizations (CSOs).

Institutes, academics and interest groups must possess fairly respectable political resources to gain media coverage: notable persons associated with boards; consistent, well-researched, and accessible policy positions; targeted media liaisons; and the capacity to follow up on a story. Business groups tend to be better financed and more consistent in their press relations than public interest groups, though Andrew Stritch (chapter 18, this volume) has found their policy research capacity is more restricted than supposed. Occasionally, the normal hierarchy of sources is circumvented. CSOs that offer novelty, identity politics, and new coalitions may break through the news screen. Two recent policy cases explore how disability interest groups made an impact on Ottawa (Prince 2001) and how a new coalition of energy companies and environmental groups lobbied on Kyoto to expand renewable energy policy options (Vannijnatten and MacDonald 2003). But interest groups rarely believe they are maximizing their media coverage in the way they would like, and few have the resources to mount an effective, long-term press relations strategy. Independent policy actors rarely have the training to understand the demands of journalism, and what sets the news agenda. As Cobb and Ross (1997) indicate, media agenda setting is closely attuned to picking a story based on the scope of conflict, anticipating if and when it will expand, how intense it is, how committed the players are and how visible it may be. Stories are chosen for their relative level of conflict, relevance, timeliness, unexpectedness, simplicity, personalization, cultural salience, reference to elites; or negativity (Good 2003; Allan 1999). Wise press officers learn to work within this culture.

A final indicator of media insinuation in the policy process, then, is whether the advocacy programs of interest groups or think tanks increasingly rely on professional media relations experts or media monitoring to improve their access to the media. The only organization serving a similar function to the conservative AIM in the United States is the Fraser Institute, which regularly releases ideological commentary on media coverage. Most interest groups do not have sufficient resources for regular media monitoring, much less media relations experts to get their message out. The pressure of news deadlines frequently tends to make journalists' consultations with independent policy experts instrumental and extractive, and a standard defence in executive training in external policy networks is to learn how to fight the tendency to let the quotation be taken out of context, how to stay on message or, conversely, how to just plain avoid the reporter's unexpected call. On the other hand, the media are constantly searching for knowledge aggregators who can be effective in translating policy into plain language and transparent interest. In Canada, as in the United

States, the right-wing policy actors are marginally ahead. The Fraser Institute has launched CANSTATS, a project to help the media communicate complex data to the public. It focuses on public health data, crime trends and legal issues (www.canstats.org). The left-leaning Centre for Policy Alternatives has no such resources available to journalists, but the Canadian Association of Journalists (CAJ) is helping to develop some after a study discovered conservative think tank references outnumber the opposite three to one in press reports.

As a tactic to gain policy advantage, media report cards by CSOs are here to stay. A recent study by the Canadian Centre for Policy Alternatives, for example, found that five new drugs have been released since 2000. Most (68 per cent) media articles reported the new drug benefits without mentioning risk and 26 per cent were wrong or misleading (Cassels et al. 2003). Such monitoring projects uncovering problems in factual interpretation or witting/unwitting bias are widely called for by civil society movements to improve the quality of policy reporting in the media, and to foster more involvement by academics, institutes, and CSOs in project design and public dissemination.

Interrogation and Whistle-blowing

Historical swings between attack and collaboration, scandal mongering, and a constructive policy focus are no less characteristic of Canadian journalism than British (Taras 1990). Liberal democratic theory about the watchdog role places interrogation at the centre of the democratic purpose of the press, in order to expose and prevent abuse of power. Survey evidence is emerging on both professional and popular Canadian public opinion about media ideology. Consistent with classical libertarian views, a watchdog model conceives of the media's role in the policy process as adversarial and outsider only. This philosophy, which has a contemporary strain associated with the Fraser Institute or Alliance fragment of the Conservative Party and the first epoch of the *National Post*, continues to be influential but not dominant in Canadian political culture.

Such rhetoric should not obscure the continuum of interrogation in the press's power. Interrogation in its classic sense merely means asking questions. It may be soft or patently participatory and pluralist or it may be hard, that is, partisan with a direct policy interest or intent. It may be direct, of course, but it is also indirect, since the media often provide Opposition MPs with ammunition for Question Period. A soft version of direct interrogation simulates Question Period off the Hill, involving ministers or officially designated spokespersons on talk shows or Town Halls, where citizens selected to represent different constituencies or sectors of opinion, or leaders of relevant community groups, can directly question their leaders about policy. Consistent with its mandate, the Canadian Broadcasting Corporation's news coverage has taken this art form the furthest, and it is important in the media's overall maintenance of the perceived legitimacy of the democratic process. Interrogation may also involve harder-edged questions by journalists in scrums or press conferences, but these are often one-off, and not consistent enough over time. Given that reporters remain seriously outnumbered and out-resourced by government communication strategists, most systematic interrogation depends on the journalist's access to good sources – say, a policy analyst acting within government. Interrogation in this hardest sense involves journalists recruiting whistle-blowers from inside the public service. Public servants may be expected to blow the whistle if the information serves a significant public interest, such as exposing a breach of statute, danger to public health and safety, or significant danger to the environment. The information is generally accepted not to be frivolous, and the whistle-blowing action must serve some higher purpose, such as to expose crime or serious negligence or to fairly debate important matters of general public concern. But leaking wrongdoing – even if anonymously – may risk reprisals if it is not major enough, exposing whistle-blowers to retaliatory investigations, harassment, intimidation, demotion, or dismissal and blacklisting by employers.

Whistle-blowing has been an important theme in recent Canadian journalism history. Major stories about politicians' conflict of interest (Shawinigan-gate), secrecy (patronage scandal) and corruption (Radwanski and the Office of the Privacy Commissioner) or colossal incompetence (fast ferry fiasco of BC's NDP government) have involved an anonymous public servant whistle-blower who had the courage to tip off a House of Commons committee, prompt MPs to use their investigative powers, fuel Opposition questions in Question Period or choreograph a leak to the media. Not all whistle-blowers are heeded. Despite intimations of a cover-up, newspapers took several years to develop the tainted blood story (Miller 1995). In perhaps understandable reaction, there were suggestions that the federal Liberal government became a chilly environment for whistle-blowers in routine day-to-day government communication. On 17 February 2004, the Standing Committee on Public Accounts unanimously adopted a motion urging the government to introduce effective whistle-blowing legislation at the earliest opportunity. Although the fall 2004 Throne Speech affirmed this intention, the minority Parliament did not pursue the promise before proroguing.[6] Protection of sources in a case of whistle blowing is important to the integrity of journalism, but there is little defence for journalists involved in criminal, civil, or national security cases (as revealed by the 2005 Ontario Superior Court ruling fining reporter Ken Peters for failing to disclose his source).

The rise in political significance of the Office of the Auditor General goes a long way to set the political news agenda for interrogation, leading to an increase in this journalistic mode of address. But it is still not part of the majority of stories. Only 30 per cent of Access to Information requests filed by the media over ten years look for wastage in government spending or other abuses that point to a classic scandal hunt (Attallah and Pyman 2002).

One of the few insider perspectives is David A. Good's account (2003) of a routine release of Human Resource Development Canada's audit of grants and contributions on a slow news day in January 2000. The HRDC story is a textbook case of a media crisis from a senior deputy's optic: how a news 'crisis' took shape, was refuelled, and almost spun out of government control over ten months.[7] Senior politicians and policy insiders attribute the length of the media attention cycle to the arrival of the *National Post* under Conrad Black, which escalated competition among national news media and provoked a string of scandal-mongering. Good outlines how the media developed a tightly scripted storyline that the grants were used for political purposes and corruption. The Reform Party kept up the heat in the House, using *Post* stories and fuelling the fire on a storyline of '$1 billion lost' – a 'stunning' revelation about government mismanagement on a monumental scale. A subsequent inquiry found overpayments were less than $100,000 – an error of such magnitude that Good attributes it to a 'distorted mirror' theory at work. He argues that the media had a vested interest in *not* modifying or adjusting the 'truth' of the initial story since it was the basis for generating new developments and reactions on which they were busy reporting. Reporters made little effort to seek out and report views other than the Opposition's, or delve below the department's own remedial audit plan, which Good says they saw as complicated, routine, impersonal, and bureaucratic (2003, 210–220). Bluntly put, bad news trumped good news. The HRDC case has a number of lessons for policy makers. Media scripts, if well crafted, lead to additional substories and become more entrenched over time, confirming Stewart Soroka's thesis (2002) that heightened issue salience creates such a herd mentality that it will flatten variation by regional or ownership group or ideological orientation of the outlet. Second, the entire concept of public service reform, improved administrative accountability and performance management is of little interest to journalists, who remain skeptical about its intent but determined to extract greater clarity and transparency (English and Lindquist 1998). Third, the belief that all journalists are out to attack is part of a politicization of the senior civil service, and has led to centralization of government communications and more adversarial press relations. Finally, the historical context of the HRDC audit started the string of scandals that rocked both the federal government and the federal Liberal Party over the next five years. Scandal-mongering is the classic stuff of telling truth to power, an adage which is as much one of the professional passports of political journalists as it is of professional civil servants. However, it is no substitute for independent policy investigation (Fletcher and Sottile 1997).

Investigation and Policy Analysis

The most direct overlap between the media press cycle and the government policy cycle is in the investigative phase. Newpapers may commission traditional investigative reports on new topics, raise important political agenda items or controversial issues, or use professional networks to provide forums for policy makers to come together to discuss issues (Hawthorne 2003). Surveys of Canadians suggest a social responsibility view of the media is widespread, where the Charter right of free speech/media is balanced with the media's responsibility to provide citizens with sufficient quality and scope of information to exercise their democratic rights. In this normative theory, a range of types of media-policy entrepreneurial styles may be possible: the honest broker, the educator, the mirror of social change, the policy advocate, the political entrepreneur (Fletcher and Stahlbrand 1992) – a menu of potential roles most often associated with the social crusades of the *Toronto Star*. Yet most papers are uneasily typed into any one category. Instead, journalists today operate under contradictory rules and market imperatives: to be neutral yet investigate, to be fair-minded yet have edge, to be disengaged from politics yet have impact (Jamieson and Waldman 2003).

The litmus test of how seriously a news organization takes its obligations to inform the public on important policy issues is its investment in independently generated investigative journalism. Investigation involves Access to Information requests, commissioning of polls or other comparative policy research or even, although rarely, policy initiation. This stage of the cycle may best conform to the outside policy initiative model, which has the press articulating a grievance, expanding interest, endorsing a solution, and then creating sufficient pressure for governments to act. The pattern of effective mobilization is not dissimilar to other outside policy actors, depending on how well journalists can frame or present issues in new ways, seek the most favourable arenas to fight their battles, and broaden the policy network's scope and density to maximize access to necessary information (Keck and Sikkink 1998).

Successful investigative reporting requires a supportive organizational atmosphere. News executives must encourage it and be prepared to undertake the risks. Legal protections must be reliable and strong. Interested news consumers must read and respond, and subjects or targets must review the investigative series and take action (Greenwald and Bernt 1998). Canadian journalists' memoirs abound with anecdotal evidence of investigative news impact on policy (Frederick J. Fletcher [1997] argues that the rent control policy in Ontario's 1975 campaign was due to a *Toronto Star* crusade). Yet such stories are rare and memories often faulty. Journalists seem a self-effacing lot. Surveys of them find they are not often able to point to examples of their influence, possibly because this phase of the media cycle occupies so little of their time. If 'original' investigative reporting may be defined to include independent research, interviews at a reporter's initiative or the reporter's own analysis provide just 12 per cent of front-page content (Richards and Rehberg-Sedo 2004).

The costliest element of mediated policy making, this phase of the press cycle also faces the largest economic and legal constraints. The first limit on journalistic investigation is the ownership structure, which provides loose coordination of news services, available on-line research resources, professional training, and access to legal services. The past decade has seen a remarkable concentration of cross-media ownership in Canada (Interim Senate Report 2004). There is a hypothesis that such concentration affects the operational culture for journalists and the diversity and quality of media content. There are allegations of reduced editorial staff, increased outsourcing to freelance journalists, and sharp cuts in editorial spending to alleviate the debt accrued from acquisition.

The principal media players to watch in policy investigation and independent analysis tend to be journalists from the larger companies that can invest resources and strategic planning in policy inquiries, as Andrew Stritch's (chapter 18, this volume) survey of business organizations has also found. But more than just scale of enterprise is at work. The biggest predictor of editorial news culture is if ownership is widely held (Bell Canada Enterprises, BCE) or narrowly held (CanWest Global, Hollinger). Charismatic entrepreneurial publishers (with sharply preferential share systems) like Conrad Black or Israel Asper have made controversial imprints on policy news. Managerial media styles have long vacillated between the autocratic and authoritarian or decentralized and autonomous in Canadian news history (Hebert et al. 1981).

When it comes to generating their own policy intelligence (as we will see below), the political press owners do *not* support their own policy research institutes or foundations that act in policy research, or regular partnerships with independent institutes. The exception is the Atkinson Foundation, which, while not commissioning policy research, does fund an annual policy research fellowship on the academic sabbatical model. The commercial setting for most news research in Canada significantly constrains the media's capacity for policy analysis; cuts in public spending on the Canadian Broadcasting Corporation have had similar effect.

The capacity to undertake investigative journalism or policy analysis varies sharply among Canadian news organizations and journalists. Journalists' education level is increasing; they are twice as likely as the general public to have a post-secondary degree, often in the social sciences (Miljan and Cooper 2003), but it is not often specialized in a particular policy field or, indeed, a professional policy degree. A recent Senate inquiry into the state of journalism identified gaps in professional training and a need for alternative models of specialization and for regional centres of excellence. Little is known about the resources individual journalists bring to their craft, or their capacity to conduct policy analysis. The contemporary newsroom has a loose beat system, usually defined by jurisdiction, not substantive policy area. In most cases, journalists would not work as practitioners of advanced policy analysis. Indeed, the career path between journalism and the public sector does not seem to have broken out of the narrow public relations paradigm for communications specialists. Few journalists go on to work in a specialist position in a policy field, and many become political staff in the public service hierarchy, not policy advisors.

What tools of policy analysis would journalists use? The type of analysis the media may conduct is less often full formal policy analysis – using statistical social or econometric techniques on original data – and more likely to be discursive, historical, comparative, and political. This is consistent with a self-acknowledged knowledge broker role, increasingly happening online. But journalists' key methodological approach is telling the story using typical reporting conventions: the sources of the problem, the issues, the interests, and policy alternatives available. Limitations to discursive techniques are well-known. In a history of reporting trends in environmental policy, Fletcher and Stahlbrand (1992) found that editors rarely understood issues well enough to identify and support a journalist's call for editorial assistance, and that lack of expertise left journalists at the mercy of experts, unable to assess claims. Nonetheless, new techniques of secondary data analysis, cost-benefit, and other methods in the policy toolkit are increasingly used by the news media. In a six-week series published in 2004, the *Independent*, a small weekly from Newfoundland and Labrador, presented a cost-benefit analysis of the province in Confederation, which suggested that the rest of Canada benefited more. Provoking heated commentary and rebuttal, the newspaper's work was found worthy of a citation of merit for making a significant contribution to debate about equalization and the province's role in Canada.

Cost-effective online databases and new software programs useful in policy analysis are shifting the balance in favour of more sophisticated investigative reporting and independent policy analysis. Barring a large-scale survey of journalists or annual production of investigative news, a good indicator of press investigative intensity may be found in the archives of one of the most prestigious and longest-running press awards (bestowed by the governor general since 1970 but little known among public servants). The Michener Award recognizes news organizations for reports that have an outstanding impact on the public good: *La Presse*, the *Toronto Star*, the *Kitchener-Waterloo Record*, and the CBC in the last five years for series on home care, financial mismanagement at the municipal level, two crime cases, and illegal provincial election actions. The 2004 Michener Award went to the *Globe and Mail* for its four-year series on the federal sponsorship scandal, which began with reporter Daniel Leblanc's access to information request. The *Globe* also received five honourable mentions, indicating a high degree (and high quality) of annual investigative activity. The *Toronto Star* and *Winnipeg Free Press* each received three, the *Ottawa Citizen* and CBC News (the *Fifth Estate* and *Saskatchewan News*) two each. Since the largest single supplier of government news wire content is the Canadian Press, it is hardly confidence-inducing to discover it and nine newspapers received only one honourable mention each in five years; the surprise is that the *National Post* received only one despite its carefully manicured reputation for activist journalism. Comparing these results to the number of daily news organizations, the overall incidence of investigative activity appears low: not more than 10 per cent of papers and just over a dozen journalists have been found to be actively using the full powers of access legislation to aid their work (Roberts 2004).

In one of the best-known recent cases, the *Toronto Star* spent two years on an investigative series that was published in October and November of 2002. The newspaper asked the Toronto Police Services for information contained in the Criminal Information Processing System (CIPS), and was denied access. Data were released after an Ontario Privacy Commissioner ruling, and the newspaper employed a consulting academic to do the statistical work. The *Star* analysis showed that Toronto police treated blacks differently than whites in one of the world's most ethnically diverse cities, sparking national debate. Black activists called for immediate action; Toronto's police chief and chiefs in other jurisdictions had to handle a crisis; and the police officers' union sued the *Star* for libel. Responding to public outrage, the Ontario Human Rights Commission announced an inquiry into racial profiling, and former Lieutenant Governor Lincoln Alexander convened a summit of community leaders, creating sufficient pressure that the solicitor general also announced a review. The Toronto police began a race relations outreach program. This multiple-award-winning *Star* series represents a textbook example of policy entrepreneurship.[8] It relied extensively on a coalition of actors in the policy network – ethnocultural groups, academics, and other civil society actors – in order to effect change at a highly charged time in public discourse about racial profiling and the Anti-Terrorism Act.

Other high-profile investigative cases take the precedent a step further by paying for access to information when necessary, and publishing the data for other policy analysts to use. A 2004 CBC series, *Faint Warning*, about underreporting of adverse drug reactions in Canada, involved a multi-year battle for access to information from Health Canada, advanced secondary data analysis, and then a public posting of the database; it won an award from the Online Journalism Association and a citation of merit. The *Hamilton Spectator* accessed Ontario data on vehicle emission testing to challenge the efficacy of compulsory testing.

As Don Abelson (this volume) concludes in his study of the policy analysis activity of think tanks, it is difficult to determine coherent policy patterns – or cumulative policy intelligence – in these much-recognized investigative series. Analysis shows that most series explore social policy, followed by health, broadening out from the old staple of crime. Over the years, there are fewer Michener nominations for very long series (10 parts or more) or multi-year investigations, suggesting less editorial spending in this area. This is at odds with the hypoth-esized increase in investigative activity due to the advent of national newspaper competition. However, editors and journalists argue that award competitions and jury evaluations uncover only the tip of the iceberg of their investigative activity. Policy analysts counter that such awards are the product of rather unrepresentative deliberative juries, and an unreliable barometer of value, much less true policy impact.

The promotional skew to much evaluation of the policy contribution made by investigative journalism obscures a growing chill in Canada's investigative climate. The conundrum is that policy research and advo-cacy are now effectively fused in political journalism, as Don Abelson has found for think tanks. Such developments reflect what British po-litical communication scholar Brian McNair (2003) has aptly called a trend to media-ocracy or *mediatized* policy making. A public relations 'spin' mindset is pervasive in new journalism, new public management theory, contemporary political marketing, and, by extension, contem-porary policy analysis. Reflecting a broader trend in public discourse, this focus on 'spin' sets a trap that constrains the media's access to information, types them as high risk in adversarial politics and rein-forces a gap between communications professionals and policy analysts in the public service. The cynical public relations mindset also has a chilling effect on media policy activism as it works out in the culture on Access to Information and, by extension, the policy analyst's inclusion of the media in policy networks.

How chilly is the investigative climate? Previous Federal Access to Information commissioners have failed several federal departments for lack of compliance with the legislation, and Gilles Paquet has found that as many as 40 per cent of requests are now vetted at the assistant deputy level or higher, reflecting what he calls a growing public rela-tions spin paranoia (Juillet and Paquet 2003), however justified, as David Good argues (2003). Reporter Ann Rees, whose research was funded on an Atkinson Public Policy Fellowship, has discovered a growing practice of risk management. Regimes at both levels in Canada appear to disadvantage press queries, treating them as equivalent to an Opposition request and adding a delay in processing (Rees 2004; Roberts 2004). Media requests are often reviewed by the minister's political staff, and advance communication releases prepared in anticipation of any controversy that may arise. Indeed, federal officials from the Privy Council Office can regularly access a central database on all Access to Information requests (the CAIRS system). Breach of a reporter's privacy in filing such requests has been alleged. A searchable database of access requests (http://track.foi.net) is maintained by Alasdair Roberts, a noted Freedom of Information researcher at the Campbell Public Affairs Institute in Syracuse University. The monthly 'amberlist' report is a 'must read' for policy analysts who want an insight into press investigative activity.[9] While it is difficult to see a pattern to the requests in a sample month (journalists try to minimize their risk rating or avoid alerting the competition), the surprises are the level of detail – which implies a good level of basic policy sophistication – the incidence of health policy queries, and the paucity of questions for finance, security readiness, and defence.

Journalism schools now offer training in investigative techniques, including how to use Access to Information legislation, but these skills are often not used. Professional associations are targeting training in computer-assisted reporting services (CARS) to improve the quality of investigative reporting, and online networks of investigative journalists are widening, improving the potential for information swapping and more timely response to research queries. Such specialized development of online research tools may hold at least a modicum of hope for improvement in the quality of investigative journalism, but without reform to the Access legislation, a more open managerial culture of access to information and support from the commercial newsroom culture, the prognosis is not good.

Interpretation, Policy Evaluation and Advocacy

UK scholar Brian McNair (2000) notes more popular media output in the public sphere, in which evaluation of and opinion about the substance, style, policy content or process of political affairs are replacing straight reportage. Speculation and conjecture outweigh facts. It is in this area of popular policy interpretation that charges of 'tabloidization' and 'hyperadversarialism' are most often levied. The media are often blamed as the messenger in contemporary speculation about declining political literacy, falling rates of civic engagement, or the democratic deficit in mobilizing elites around anything other than special interests. Conversely, they are criticized for their focus on celebrity, for creating passive spectators of political events by weaving political morality tales, for sensationalizing or personalizing the news, or for sliding democratic discourse down the slippery slope of infotainment. They may also be blamed for anti-government nuisance or obstruction (Good 2003; Taras 1990). A new ideologically veiled criticism calls journalists to account for their low level of policy literacy by providing regular 'correct' newsfeeds (see www.fraserinstitute.ca/about RSS.asp). Normative in focus, proponents of these diatribes masked as theories rarely seek empirical proof, and they are thus of little use in understanding the interpretation phase of the press cycle and how it intersects with policy analysis.

Interpretation involves commentary, editorials, documentary or point-of-view public affairs shows such as *The Fifth Estate* and *W-5*, op-ed pages, and call-in shows, which provide a clear evaluative position. Such political talk represents a challenge to the positivist conception of news objectivity. Les Pal (2001) introduces the idea of a discourse coalition defined as a range of policy actors united by broad ideas about the policy field, and argues that such discourse coalitions are useful analytic concepts in postpositive policy studies. Columnists and editorial writers can be direct actors in such coalitions, although paradoxically they will most often hold themselves at arm's length. Good interpretation takes time, and time is not the stock of the ordinary journalist. That is why sabbatical programs or honorary fellowships to renew the research edge of professional journalists are becoming increasingly important. Those who produce books tend to increase their political capital and become more frequently cited as policy experts in other media coverage.

The interpretative moment in the press cycle causes particular problems for policy analysis, since it requires explicitly value-based and qualitative approaches to the study of public discourse. When does interpretative journalism take the partisan or polemical voice and when the analytical, advisory or satirical tone as its mode of address? What do we know about the relative impacts of each? Media interpretation all too soon can become punditry, according to most policy analysts who understandably want a monopoly on telling the tale. The history of the political columnist is tied to the twentieth-century tendency to brand and commodify news output, but risks turning into an overly ritualized, fetishistic commentary. With convergence of Canadian media ownership, print journalists are increasingly appearing as pundits on television, and vice versa, most often within their own ownership group. The rationalization of the media industry, together with fragmentation of political news sources, has meant it is harder for trusted, credible national columnists to emerge, and many speak of a shrinking cadre of political reporters who build up political capital over long careers. As a consequence, there are few policy stars in the firmament of English Canadian journalism, unlike Quebec or the UK and the United States, where journalists have more social status.

Unlike the area of investigative journalism, where at least some attention to new performance standards of the effectiveness of news coverage is emerging, debate over standards of policy interpretation is not well advanced in Canada. Editorials, year-end reviews of political events, or efforts to review the record of parliaments all contribute to this form of journalism, but there are few awards for such commentary, and even fewer distinguished policy interpretations over time. Nonetheless, senior public servants frequently follow such distinguished columnists – at the peak of their professional prestige – as opinion bellwethers. Some noted columnists are known to be more open to policy deliberation and debate than others, in joint ventures with the academy and key institutes or as sources of information for public interest groups. It is perhaps easier to sustain a hypothesis about selective impact of media interpretation on others in policy learning, rather than policy analysis. Anecdotal case studies of influential commentary are infrequent in policy analysis, but it would be interesting to mine political memoirs to determine the influence of noted political journalists on civil servants or the politicians of the day. Canadian experience suggests that commentary can be more influential when it amplifies the work of others. Robert Campbell (1999) has found the media intervened in a policy vacuum to assist in priority setting after federal budget surpluses were announced in competition with, or triggered by, a C.D. Howe report. Conversely, the sometimes lonely crusade of Jeffrey Simpson in challenging conventional wisdom in the universal health care debate well before the Kirby or Romanow reports, and indeed the Supreme Court ruling, is well-known even if unevenly endorsed in policy circles.

The real work in decoding interpretation is of course discursive. However, it is not easy. Many reporters of a certain age are loath to surrender a traditional positivist or objective professional ideology, believing they should present all legitimate sides of a controversy to allow citizens to make up their own minds. Such a liberal stance can absolve the journalist of critical self-awareness of the media's role in the reproduction of ideology. News organizations and their workers share a world-view, essentially pluralist, that they disseminate effectively (but mostly unconsciously) to the general public and to policy makers. This world-view – capitalist, consumption-oriented, cynical about government and politics, etc. – shapes the context in which problems are identified and framed at the regime level. For example, social theorists have often criticized the narrow definition of politics in much news coverage, one that excludes social movements or trivializes, polarizes, disparages, or emphasizes internal dissension in reporting alternative politics. The media regime polices the boundaries of elite and public discourse, making some policies appear legitimate and others illegitimate and thus beyond consideration (Hackett and Zhao 1998). As a result, we have seen a low level of media resistance to deficit reduction in Canada (Fletcher 1999); editorials on the orthodoxy of the new economy that outweigh editorial attention to poverty in Canada (Rice 2002); and reportage that mostly tends to support the status quo on equalization payments (Prince 2002).

Framing provides a useful concept in the analysis of policy reports in the news media. Narrative frames determine what is included and what is ignored, depending upon a shared repertoire of concepts, notions of what may be possible, what is good and bad, what is important, and what is related (Gitlin quoted in Hackett and Zhao 1998; Allan 1999). Critics routinely identify a relatively narrow range of news scripts in the cognitive repertoire of editors and journalists. The craft rarely makes explicit the assumptions of some of the policy terms in use. Case studies of the change in social policy language at the *Ottawa Citizen* – from talk about prioritizing the issues of Canada's neediest children to providing tax relief for low- and middle-income Canadians – show little responsibility in syntax. Indeed, the silence on social policy reform throughout the 1990s suggests reporters are often unaware when policy may be made by stealth at the regime level (Prince 1999). Finally, the dominant tendency in interpretation is to focus on strategy, and recent studies suggest that reporters are socialized to be much more comfortable making evaluative strategic statements than ones concerning policy (Fletcher 1997; Jamieson and Waldman 2003; McNair 2000). Part of the fault lies with inadequate training in policy analysis. There is also a bias inherent in the field against an ethical theory of policy making and an inability to interrogate experts on complex value trade-offs effectively in order to make judgments on policy risk, success, or failure.

Conclusion

The media represent arguably the best resourced and most widely heard potential actor in the so-called third sector of policy networks, but little is known about their role. This chapter contends that policy studies has to move beyond the liberal tendency to discount the media's contribution as just another knowledge aggregator in policy advocacy coalitions, used to advance the agendas of think tanks or CSOs, or the conservative tendency in much new public management theory to manipulate them as sultans of spin. To better understand the *mediated public policy process* in contemporary democracies, theory about the role of the media in the agenda-setting process needs to be adapted to account for the investigative and interpretive stages of the press cycle. Critical thought must be given to criteria for the evaluation of media impact on policy. As a proportion of the overall press cycle, investigative activity is infrequent, but it is now a part of a seamless and expanding web of press activity that cannot be ignored by students of policy networks, especially in health and social policy, the areas most often recognized for independent policy analysis in media awards.

There are several priorities in improving the capacity for policy analysis in the media. The first is to redress a large gap in original research into the sociology of the media and policy networks in Canada. How 'tight' are the links, how frequent the exchanges, and how do the networks actually work? There are sharp regional differences in policy competence and political capital at the operating level in journalistic networks that merit exploration. The second priority is to improve the content of journalists' training in policy analysis, but before this is feasible, public policy and journalism schools must realize that, in order to be widely adopted, the methods taught have to be more relevant to the press cycle, and the discursive, postpositive techniques most often used in the journalistic craft need to be critically evaluated. The third priority is related to infrastructure: meaningful incentives for policy research by commercial news organizations need to be developed, possibly enabling the development of policy research foundations as seen in the U.S. media, and the effect of the CBC on news cultures must also be further explored. More resources are needed to develop media relations services and coordination among civil society actors (think tanks, universities, and public interest groups) to improve the quality of public policy coverage. Finally, the appropriate models for self-regulation of standards of content must be re-examined in light of changing political values in modes of discourse, and they must be made more inclusive and more representative.

This chapter has argued that several serious institutional deficiencies in the accountability of media in independent policy analysis need correction. Strong cases can be made for improving whistle-blowing legislation, opening the culture of Access to Information and assessing its impact on the citizen's right to know. Despite the tendency of executives in the Privy Council and Prime Minister's Office in Ottawa (or the embattled HRDC) to write off the press as adversarial special interests, the story is more complex. The Canadian media can still occasionally act in the public interest, and contribute to good mediated policy analysis. How they do so and under what conditions needs to be explored through systematic theory building. This will highlight the difference between *mediated* and *mediatized* policy: the former is a democratic investment, the latter a tabloidization of contemporary governance.

NOTES

1 A survey of the past four years of *How Ottawa Spends* reveals 14 of 45 articles make ancillary reference to the media, with only two ascribing an influential role. Media sources apparently are not monitored, not considered useful, or not acceptable for citation in academic policy analysis.
2 In terms of resources invested, the media surpass all but the university sector. The regulated sector of news media must report expenditures on programming to their regulatory agency. In 2002, private commercial TV broadcasters spent $288 million on news in English, closely followed by $230 million spent by the CBC. Total spending combined in Quebec was $135 million, for a Canadian total of $654.18 million (*Interim Senate Report*, 25). On a per-capita basis, this represents about $21 per annum to reach citizens. Numbers on print newsroom budgets are not available, but are expected to be about twice that.
3 In the United States, Pew and Columbia University now jointly produce an annual report on the state of the media that offers a useful compendium of content analyses, overview of trends, and surveys of editors and journalists to speak to the political climate. See http://www.stateofthemedia.org/narrative_newspapers_contentanalysis.asp?cat=2&media=2.
4 The first is the McGill Observatory on the Media and Public Policy, which, together with the Institute of Research on Public Policy, mounted an elec-

tion coverage monitoring project (www.ompp.mcgill.ca/). The second is the industry-financed Canadian Media Research Consortium, which has produced the first report card on the Canadian media. See www.cmrccrm.ca/english/reportcard2004/01.html.

5 When Canadians are asked to rate how much influence each actor actually has on decisions concerning major public issues and how much each should have, the media experience an 'influence gap,' with 79 per cent saying they have moderate to great influence (5 to 7 on a 7-point scale), while just 34 per cent approve of this influence. Frank Graves (1999, 37–75) argues that the media and big business are the two main policy actors whose power Canadians would like to see reduced.

6 See Tuck 2004. Public servants with complaints of wrongdoing will be able to go directly to the president of the Public Service Commission as a neutral third-party refuge, but some argue this function should be filled by the Auditor General's Office.

7 It is important to realize two facts: the audit was not produced by Access to Information requests by the press or Opposition (although it followed on some by the *National Post* about job creation in the prime minister's riding) and it did not subsequently become an election issue, suggesting spinout was not complete. But in light of the subsequent reorganization of HRDC, the issue clearly gained media traction.

8 It won the CAJ (Canadian Association of Journalists), CAN (Canadian Association of Newspapers), Justicia, and Michener Awards.

9 It provides important insight into developing agenda stories and continuing ones still meriting press attention. In June 2004, immediately after the federal election, 109 media requests were logged, and 32 Opposition parliamentary requests. The bulk of requests were around briefing notes to new ministers, but others covered health issues to do with adverse drug reaction information, risks of avian flu, or mad-cow disease, and data on the extent of the drug trade in the Internet pharmacy sector. Two actually probed government responses to media investigations: to a CTV and *Globe* investigative report on pharmaceutical products in the water, and CBC's *Faint Warning* series on new drug side effects that aired 16 February 2004.

REFERENCES

Attalah, Paul, and Heather Pyman. 2002. *How Journalists Use the Federal Access to Information Act.* Report 8 of the Government of Canada, Access to Information Review Task Force. www.atirtf-geai.gc.ca/paper-journalist1-e.html.

Allan, Stuart. 1999. *News Culture*. Buckingham, UK: Open University Press.

Campbell, Robert M. 1999. 'The Fourth Fiscal Era: Can There Be a 'Post-Neo-Conservative Fiscal Policy?' In Leslie A. Pal, ed., *How Ottawa Spends 1999–2000. Shape Shifting: Canadian Governance Toward the 21st Century*, 113–50. Don Mills, ON: Oxford University Press.

Canadian Association of Journalists. 2004. 'Special Issue. Handcuffed: Investigative Journalists in Canada Fight to Remain Free of Interference from Politicians, Police and Courts.' *Media* 10(3), 5–9.

Canadian Centre for Management Development. 2004. *Report on the Future of Government Communications*. Action-Research Roundtable on Managing Communications and Public Involvement. Ottawa, 23 March.

Canadian Media Research Consortium. 2004. *Report Card on Canadian News Media*. www.cmrcccrm.ca/English/reportcard2004/01.html.

Cobb, Roger W., and Howard Ross, eds. 1997. *Cultural Strategies of Agenda Denial: Avoidance, Attack and Redefinition*. Lawrence: University Press of Kansas.

Edwards, Meredith. 2001. *Social Policy, Public Policy: From Problem to Practice*. Crowsnest, NSW: Allen and Unwin.

English, John, and Evert Lindquist. 1998. *Performance Management: Linking Results to Public Debate*. Toronto: Institute of Public Administration in Canada.

Fletcher, Frederick J., and Rose Sottile. 1997. 'Spinning Tales: Politics and News in Ontario.' In Graham White, ed., *The Government and Politics of Ontario*, 5th ed. Toronto: University of Toronto Press.

Fletcher, Frederick J., and Lori Stahlbrand. 1992. 'Mirror or Participant? The News Media and Environmental Policy.' In Robert Boardman, ed., *Canadian Environmental Policy: Ecosystems, Politics, and Process*, 79–102. Toronto: Oxford University Press.

Good, David A. 2003. *The Politics of Public Management: The HRDC Audit of Grants and Contributions*. Toronto: The Institute of Public Administration in Canada and University of Toronto Press.

Hackett, Robert A., and Yeshiva Zhao. 1998. *Sustaining Democracy: Journalism and the Politics of Objectivity*. Toronto: Garamond.

Hawthorne, Michael R. 2003. 'The Media, Economic Development and Agenda Setting.' In Robert J. Spitzer, ed., *Media and Public Policy*, 81–99. Westport, CT: Praeger.

Howlett, Michael, and M. Ramesh. 1995. *Studying Public Policy: Policy Cycles and Policy Subsystems*. Toronto: Oxford University Press.

Jamieson, Kathleen Hall, and Paul Waldman. 2003. *The Press Effect: Politicians,*

Journalists and the Stories that Shape the Political World. New York: Oxford University Press.

Johnson, David. 2002. *Thinking Government: Public Sector Management in Canada.* Toronto: Broadview.

Juillet, Luc, and Giles Paquet. 2003. 'The Neurotic State.' In G. Bruce Doern, ed., *How Ottawa Spends 2002–2003: The Security Aftermath and National Priorities,* 69–87. Don Mills, ON: Oxford University Press.

Malloy, Jonathan. 2003. 'The House of Commons under the Chretien Government.' In G. Bruce Doern, ed., *How Ottawa Spends 2003–2004: Regime Change and Policy Shift,* 59–71. Don Mills, ON: Oxford University Press.

McNair, Brian. 2000. *Journalism and Democracy: An Evaluation of the Political Public Sphere.* London: Routledge.

Miljan, Lydia, and Barry Cooper. 2003. *Hidden Agendas.* Vancouver: UBC Press.

Miller, John. 1998. *Yesterday's News: Why Canada's Daily Newspapers Are Failing Us.* Toronto: Fernwood.

Pal, Leslie A. 1992. *Policy Analysis: An Introduction.* 2nd ed. Toronto: Nelson.

– 2001. *Beyond Policy Analysis: Public Issue Management in Turbulent Times.* Toronto: Nelson.

Paquet, Gilles. 2004. *Access to Information: Making it Work for Canadians.* Report to the Federal Access to Information Review Task Force. http://www.atirtf-geai.gc.ca/accessReport-e.pdf.

Prince, Michael. 1999. 'From Health and Welfare to Stealth and Farewell: Federal Social Policy 1980–2000.' In Leslie A. Pal, ed., *How Ottawa Spends. 1999–2000: Shape Shifting: Canadian Governance Toward the 21st Century,* 151–96. Don Mills, ON: Oxford University Press.

Rees, Ann. 2003. 'The Right to Know.' http://www.atkinsonfoundation.ca/publications/Atkinson1_Ann_Rees.pdf.

Rice, James J. 2002. 'Being Poor in the Best of Times.' In G. Bruce Doern, ed., *How Ottawa Spends 2002–2003: The Security Aftermath and National Priorities,* 102–21. Don Mills, ON: Oxford University Press.

Richards, Trudie, and DeNel Rehberg-Sedo. 2004. 'Journalists Rely Too Heavily on Spinmeisters.' *Media* 18(2) (fall), 3–5.

Roberts, Alasdair. 2004. 'Singled Out for Special Treatment.' *Media* 18(2) (fall) 16–17.

Senate of Canada. 2004. *Interim Report on the Canadian News Media.* Standing Senate Committee on Transport and Communications. April.

Soroka, Stuart N. 2002. *Agenda-Setting Dynamics in Canada.* Vancouver: UBC Press.

Spitzer, Robert J. 1993. *Media and Public Policy.* Westport, CT: Praeger.

Taras, David. 1990. *The Newsmakers: The Media's Influence on Canadian Politics.* Toronto: Nelson.

Vannijnatten, Debra L., and Douglas MacDonald. 2003. 'Reconciling Energy and Climate Change Policies.' In G. Bruce Doern, ed., *How Ottawa Spends, 2003–2004: Regime Change and Policy Shift,* 72–89. Don Mills, ON: Oxford University Press.

22 Any Ideas? Think Tanks and Policy Analysis in Canada

DONALD E. ABELSON

Introduction

At different times and in different contexts, they have been described as brain trusts, idea brokers, laboratories for ideas, public policy research institutes, policy clubs, and policy planning organizations. In the mainstream media and in the academic literature, they are best known as think tanks. Although the vast majority of the world's 5,000 or more think tanks are located in the United States, most advanced and developing countries count think tanks among the many types of non-governmental organizations that engage in research and analysis. Along with interest groups, trade associations, human rights organizations, advocacy networks, and a handful of other bodies, think tanks rely on their expertise and knowledge to influence public opinion and public policy. What has distinguished think tanks in the past from the other organizations mentioned above is their reputation for being objective, scientific, and non-partisan. However, in recent years, as think tanks have become more invested in the outcome of key policy debates, their image as scholarly and policy neutral organizations has been called into question. Indeed, by combining policy research with political advocacy, it has become increasingly difficult to differentiate between think tanks, lobbyists, consultants, and interest groups.

As think tanks have come to occupy a stronger presence in the policy-making community, academic interest in their role and function has intensified. While some scholars (Rich 2004; Abelson 1996, 2006; Stone 1996; McGann 1995; Ricci 1993; Smith 1991; Weaver 1989) have been preoccupied with how and to what extent think tanks have been able to access the highest levels of the American government, others have paid close attention to how think tanks have tried to make an impact in Westminister parliamentary democracies such as Canada and Great Britain (Savoie 2003; Baier and Bakvis 2001; Lindquist 1998; Dobuzinskis 1996). This research has led to several comparative studies in the field (Stone et al. 2004, 1998; McGann and Weaver 2000), which have focused on, among other things, the extent to which different political systems facilitate or frustrate the efforts of think tanks to participate in the policy-making process. For example, there have been several recent studies (Abelson 2002; Abelson and Carberry 1998) that have tried to explain why American think tanks enjoy far more visibility and prominence than their Canadian counterparts. I have argued elsewhere (Abelson 2002, 2006) that in a country like the United States, where political parties are weak, where political power is shared among different branches, and where there is a revolving door between the upper echelons of the bureaucracy and the policy research community, think tanks have multiple opportunities to convey their ideas. Conversely, in Canada, where political power is concentrated in the hands of the executive and where strict party discipline is enforced, think tanks have far fewer access points.

Throughout the chapter, some similarities and differences between Canadian and American think tanks will be highlighted, but this will not be the focus of the study. Rather, the purpose here is two-fold: to examine the diversity of Canadian think tanks and their efforts to inject ideas into the body politic, and to discuss how scholars can offer more informed insights about the nature and impact of think tank influence. In providing an overview of Canada's think tank community, particular emphasis will be placed on the types of policy research and analysis these organizations produce and some of the many projects in which they are engaged. What we will discover is that think tanks in Canada examine a wide range of issues and elect to showcase their findings in different ways. Some think tanks, including the C.D. Howe Institute, place considerable emphasis on hiring academics from universities to write peer reviewed studies. Although many of their publications are produced in-house, the vast majority are contracted out. By contrast, think tanks such as the Caledon Institute (Battle 2004) rely on their small staff to conduct research and analysis on social policy issues, ranging from how to build vibrant communities to the various ways of reducing poverty. And ironically, there are some think tanks that, until recently, have produced very little research. Instead of devoting their time and energy to preparing studies, think tanks such as Ottawa's

Public Policy Forum (PPF), prefer building networks between government and the private and nonprofit sectors. In short, think tanks do not place the same priority on providing rigorous policy analysis, nor do they necessarily measure their success by the number of publications they produce. As will be discussed, both think tanks and the scholars that study them have very different notions of what constitutes influence and how it should be assessed. However, if scholars are to make further inroads into this field of inquiry, they can no longer afford to make sweeping and unsubstantiated assertions about how much or little influence think tanks wield in Canada.

Influence, as will be discussed, is not simply about an individual or organization convincing a policy maker or a group of policy makers to enact legislation compatible with their interests, nor is it about discouraging elected officials from imposing a policy that may have a detrimental impact (Pal and Weaver 2003). If it were, very few think tanks, or other nongovernmental organizations for that matter, could claim sole responsibility for having swayed key policy decisions. Scholars who have written detailed case studies of Canadian think tanks (Abelson 2002; Tupper 1993; Lindquist 1989) have concluded that claims of think tank influence have been greatly exaggerated. In virtually every policy field and in every policy debate, there are dozens of individuals and organizations that try to leave an indelible mark on the decision-making process. Still, determining which of these actors played a pivotal role in influencing a final decision often proves futile. Recognizing the complex nature of the policy-making process and the many different roles played by think tanks, it is critical to develop a more sophisticated and nuanced understanding of how these organizations achieve policy influence. By acknowledging that influence is not always tied directly to policy outcomes, but can be exercised at other stages of the policy cycle, it will become evident that think tanks in Canada can and have contributed to important policy debates. Think tanks represent but one set of actors competing for power and prestige in an increasingly congested marketplace of ideas, but their unique role often allows them to stand out.

In the first section of this chapter, the various types of think tanks that have emerged on the Canadian political landscape will be discussed. Four waves or periods of think tank growth will be identified: 1900–45, 1946–70, 1971–89, 1990–2004. Since there is no consensus on what constitutes a think tank, a term coined in the United States during World War II to describe a secure room where policy makers and defence planners could meet, several scholars (Abelson 2002, 2006; Stone 1996; McGann 1995; Lindquist 1989; Weaver 1989) have constructed various typologies to identify the organizations that have taken root in the policy research community. To date, most of these typologies have been designed to identify American think tanks. While useful, they have to be modified to better suit the Canadian think tank experience. In this chapter, a modified version of Weaver's think tank typology will be employed to better understand the nature and diversity of Canadian think tanks. Once the growth of Canadian think tanks has been chronicled, attention will shift to the types of policy analysis conducted at think tanks and the various strategies they employ to share their findings with appropriate stakeholders and target audiences. In the final section, some suggestions on how to measure or assess the impact of think tanks during different stages of the policy-making process will be offered.

Classifying Think tanks

In his study, Weaver (1989) identified three types of American think tanks, which he labelled universities without students, government contractors, and advocacy think tanks. Table 21.1 highlights the distinguishing characteristics of these types of think tanks. With some modifications, Weaver's typology can also be useful in studying the Canadian think tank community. As will be discussed, although Canada is not home to such prominent policy research institutions as Brookings or the Hoover Institution, it has several organizations that resemble those found in the United States.

By identifying the different types of think tanks that exist in the United States and in Canada, it is possible for scholars to better understand why some institutions are better positioned and equipped to engage in short-, medium- or long-term policy analysis. In other words, the mandate and resources of think tanks, not to mention the priority they assign to policy research and political advocacy, influence significantly both the direction and substance of their research. For example, advocacy think tanks should not be expected to produce highly detailed and technical research when one of their primary goals is to gain access to policy makers and the media. Since journalists and policy makers rarely have the time or the inclination to sift through studies that run to several hundred pages, staff at advocacy think tanks provide their major target audiences with short and timely policy briefs. By

Table 22.1 Classifying Think Tanks

Category	Nature of Policy Analysis	Personnel	Research Products	Funding
Universities without students	Medium- and long-term research and analysis.	Majority of policy experts hold PhDs or other advanced degrees. Most have had government experience.	Focus on book-length studies, academic journals, and occasional papers.	Rely on funding from government, philanthropic foundations, corporations, and individual donors.
Government contractors	Short- and medium-term research and analysis.	Majority of policy experts hold PhDs and other advanced degrees. Many have had government and private sector experience.	Technical reports and studies for government departments and agencies, conference papers, etc.	Funding comes primarily from government and private sector.
Advocacy think tanks	Short- and medium-term research. Emphasis on 'quick response' policy research. Emphasis on marketing ideas, not developing them.	Some policy experts hold PhDs and other advanced degrees. Tend to recruit younger personnel directly out of university.	Mixture of books, articles, opinion magazines. Emphasis on brief reports and memos circulated to policy makers and the media.	Little or no funding from government. Funds raised from philanthropic foundations, corporations, and individual donors.
Policy clubs	Little emphasis on policy research and analysis. Interested in providing a forum for policy discussions.	Few PhDs. Some staff with graduate degrees and previous government experience.	Academic journals, conference papers.	Funding from private sector, government, and corporate and individual donors.
Government councils	Medium- and long-term research and analysis.	Most staff hold advanced degrees.	Technical papers, reports, studies.	Funding from government.

contrast, think tanks that are more interested in stimulating debate within the academic community and in the senior levels of the bureaucracy tend to invest far more resources in hiring experts who are capable of producing the type of sophisticated policy analysis that key stakeholders require. Put simply, think tanks must draw on the resources they require to respond to the needs of those they are trying to reach, a subject that we will return to shortly.

In the following section, a brief overview of the types of think tanks that have emerged in Canada since the early 1900s will be provided. Although this section provides little more than a snapshot of Canada's think tank community, it does allow scholars to better acquaint themselves with the diversity and expertise available at some of the nation's leading policy research institutions. This section will also help to explain why we cannot assume or expect that all think tanks will engage in rigorous policy analysis.

The Canadian Think Tank Experience

The First Wave, 1900–45

Despite the emergence of several prominent American research institutions in the early 1900s, including the Carnegie Endowment for International Peace (1910), the Institute for Government Research (1916, which merged with two other organizations to form the Brookings Institution in 1927), the Hoover Institution (1919), and the Council on Foreign Relations (1921), think tanks were noticeably absent in Canada during this period. There were a handful of relatively small organizations concerned about Canadian foreign policy, including the Canadian Institute of International Affairs (CIIA), established in 1928 as the first offshoot of the British Institute of International Affairs (BIIA, later the Royal Institute of International Affairs, RIIA), but even the CIIA was created more as an influential group of Canadians interested in the study of international affairs and Canada's role in it, than as a policy research institution dedicated to the study of world affairs. There were also some organizations committed to the study of domestic policy, including the National Council on Child and Family Welfare. This organization led to the creation in 1920 of the Canadian Council on Social Development. Still, with few exceptions, the think tank landscape in Canada remained relatively barren until the postwar period (Abelson 2002, 24–5).

Table 22.2 A Selected Profile of Canadian Think Tanks in Chronological Order

Institution	Location	Date Founded	Staff	Budget Category (2003–04) $Millions
Canadian Council on Social Development	Ottawa	1920	24	1.5–3
Canadian Institute of International Affairs	Toronto	1928	9	0.5–1.5
Canadian Tax Foundation	Toronto	1945	27	3–5
Conference Board of Canada	Ottawa	1954	200	>30
Science Council of Canada (defunct, figures for 1992)	Ottawa	1963	29	2–5
Economic Council of Canada (defunct, figures for 1992)	Ottawa	1963	118	> 10
Vanier Institute of the Family	Ottawa	1965	9	1
National Council of Welfare	Ottawa	1968	5	< 1
Parliamentary Centre	Ottawa	1968	24	1–2
Canada West Foundation	Calgary	1971	13	1.5
Institute for Research on Public Policy	Montreal	1972	19	2–3
C.D. Howe Institute	Toronto	1973	13	1.5–3
The Fraser Institute	Vancouver	1974	48	6–7
Canadian Institute of Strategic Studies	Toronto	1976	3	< 1
The North-South Institute	Ottawa	1976	20	1.5–3
Canadian Centre for Policy Alternatives	Ottawa	1980	20	.5–1.5
Canadian Institute for International Peace and Security (Defunct) (figures for 1992)	Ottawa	1984	12	5–10
Mackenzie Institute	Toronto	1986	3	< 1
Public Policy Forum	Ottawa	1986	26	3–4
Institute on Governance	Ottawa	1990	15	1.5–3
Caledon Institute for Social Policy	Ottawa	1992	5	1–2
Pearson-Shoyama Institute	Ottawa	1993	2	< 1
Canadian Policy Research Networks	Ottawa	1994	29	4–5
Atlantic Institute for Market Studies	Halifax	1994	8	<1
Canadian Council for International Peace and Security (formerly Canadian Centre for Global Security and Canadian Centre for Arms Control and Disarmament)	Ottawa	1995	3	< 1
Canadian Centre for Foreign Policy Development	Ottawa	1996	6	2–5

These data have been obtained from various think tank websites and correspondence with their staff.

The Second Wave, 1946–70

Several think tanks emerged in Canada in the decades following World War II, including the Toronto-based Canadian Tax Foundation (CTF), founded in 1946 by representatives of the national law and accounting societies to conduct and sponsor research on taxation. Eight years later, a branch office of the New York-based Conference Board was established in Montreal to serve its Canadian members. The Conference Board of Canada has since evolved into Canada's largest policy institute, with over two hundred staff and a budget exceeding $30 million. In 1954, the Atlantic Provinces Economic Council (APEC) was formed to promote economic development in the Atlantic region. And in 1958, the Private Planning Association of Canada (PPAC) was founded as a counterpart to the National Planning Association (NPA) in the United States. PPAC was created by 'business and labour leaders to undertake research and educational activities on economic policy issues.'

The growth of think tanks in postwar Canada did not end there. The Vanier Institute of the Family was established in 1965 by Governor-General Georges Vanier and Madame Pauline Vanier to study 'the demographic, economic, social and health influences on contemporary family life' (Abelson 2000, 30). And in 1968 the Parliamentary Centre for Foreign Affairs was created to provide research support to parliamentary committees and government departments examining various foreign policy issues.

By the early 1960s, the Canadian government also began to demonstrate interest in creating several research institutes. During this period, as Laurent Dobuzinskis points out in his chapter in this volume, several government councils were formed, including the Economic Council of Canada (1963), the Science Council of Canada (1966), the National Council of Welfare (1968), and the Law Reform Commission of Canada (1970). Despite operating at arm's length to its employer, tensions between the councils and various governments eventually began to surface. The system of parliamentary and responsible government was simply not conducive to allowing organs of the state, no matter how independent, to express views on public policy that were at variance with government priorities and policies. In 1992, the federal government took drastic measures to sever its institutional ties with the various councils. In that year's budget, the Mulroney government disbanded close to two dozen policy institutes, including the Economic Council of Canada, the Science Council of Canada, the Law Reform Commission, and the Canadian Institute for International Peace and Security.

The Third Wave 1971–1989

Three distinct waves of think tank development were beginning to emerge in Canada during this period. First, by the late 1960s, the federal government came to realize the potential benefits of having a large independent research institute in Canada, similar to the Brookings Institution. In 1968, Prime Minister Trudeau commissioned Ronald Ritchie to consider the feasibility of creating such an independent interdisciplinary policy institute. The report, submitted the following year, led to the creation of the Institute for Research on Public Policy in 1972 (now based in Montreal), with endowment funding from the federal government and plans to receive additional support from the private sector and provincial governments.

Second, four established organizations underwent significant transitions into modern think tanks during this period and several new ones were created: the Canadian Welfare Council, established in 1920, was transformed into a social policy institute called the Canadian Council on Social Development (CCSD); the small Montreal office of the New York-based Conference Board relocated to Ottawa, which contributed to its growing expertise in developing economic forecasting models for both the public and private sectors; and the C.D. Howe Research Institute was formed in 1973 following a merger of the Private Planning Association of Canada (PPAC) and the C.D. Howe Memorial Foundation, and has become a centre for short-term economic policy analysis. Finally, the profile of the Canadian Tax Foundation increased significantly during the early 1970s due to a national debate stimulated by the Royal Commission on Taxation (Abelson 2000, 32).

Several new think tanks in Canada were established as well. In the area of foreign policy, two opened their doors in 1976: the Ottawa-based North-South Institute which currently receives the bulk of its funding from the Canadian International Development Agency (CIDA) to examine development issues, and the Canadian Institute of Strategic Studies in Toronto. In addition, the Canadian Centre for Philanthropy was formed in 1981 to advance 'the role and interests of the charitable sector for the benefit of Canadian communities' (Abelson 2000, 33). Moreover, following Prime Minister Trudeau's 'north-south' initiative, the federal government agreed to establish and fund the Canadian Institute for International Peace and Security (CIIPS) in 1984. CIIPS was neither a government council nor, as it discovered in 1992, as independent as the Institute for Research on Public Policy. The Mackenzie Institute, known for its work on terrorism and extremist political movements, became part of Canada's think tank landscape in 1986, and in 1987 the Public Policy Forum was established to improve public policy making by providing a forum for representatives from the public, private, and nonprofit sectors to consider a wide range of policy initiatives. Three years later, the Institute on Governance was formed to promote effective governance. Among other things, it advises the Canadian government and those of developing nations about how to better manage public services. It also serves as a broker for Canadian agencies seeking to assist governments in the developing world.

Third, several institutions devoted to the advocacy of particular points of view, reflecting the most significant 'wave' of U.S. think tank growth, also made their presence felt in this period. The Canada West Foundation was established in Calgary in 1971 to inject Western perspectives on national policy debates. The Fraser Institute was created in 1974 to promote the virtues of free-market economics. And in 1979, the Canadian Institute for Economic Policy was formed by Walter Gordon, a former Liberal finance minister, to sponsor a five-year research program revolving around the themes of economic nationalism. The following year, the Canadian Centre for Policy Alternatives (CCPA) was established by supporters of social democratic principles to counter the influence of the Fraser Institute. The CCPA has worked closely with the leadership of the New Democratic Party and several public advocacy coalitions, including the Council of Canadians, to convey its concerns on issues ranging from the North American Free Trade Agreement to the latest round of WTO negotiations. The trend toward more advocacy-driven think tanks also appealed to the Progressive Conservative Party. Following their defeat in 1980, several party members supported the creation of a think tank on economic, social, and international issues, but the initiative foundered when the party chose a new leader (Abelson 2000, 34).

The Fourth Wave? 1990–2004

Legacy-based think tanks represent the latest type of think tank to emerge in the United States and include among their ranks the (Jimmy) Carter Center at Emory University (1982) and the Washington-based (Richard) Nixon Center for Peace and Freedom (1994). As the latter name suggests, they have developed a wide range of research programs to help advance the legacies of their founders. Vanity think tanks, by contrast, appear more concerned with engaging in political advocacy

and are particularly interested in generating or at the very least repackaging ideas that will help lend intellectual credibility to the political
platforms of politicians, a function no longer performed adequately by
mainstream political parties (Baier and Bakvis 2001).

In theory, there are few barriers to creating vanity- or legacy-based
think tanks in Canada. However, with the possible exceptions of the
C.D. Howe Institute, named after its founder, a former Liberal cabinet
minister, and the Pearson-Shoyama Institute (created in Ottawa in 1993
to examine issues related to citizenship and multiculturalism and named
after former prime minister Lester Pearson and former federal deputy
finance minister Thomas Shoyama), such institutes have not yet emerged
in significant numbers. In an odd sort of way, the closest examples of
legacy think tanks are the Canadian Institute for Economic Policy,
formed, as noted, by a former finance minister to further his ideas on
economic nationalism, and the Canadian Institute for International Peace
and Security, whose creation was largely inspired by Prime Minister
Trudeau's 1984 north-south initiative. Nevertheless, none of these think
tanks can be construed as committed to promoting the legacy of their
namesakes.

A more significant trend in Canada in the past decade has been the
privatization of existing government research capacity. In 1992, the
Caledon Institute of Social Policy was created in Ottawa with support
from the Maytree Foundation to enable Ken Battle, a former executive
director of the National Council of Welfare, to develop a research agenda
without the constraints of serving a government council. Furthermore,
in 1994, the Canadian Policy Research Networks Inc. was created by
Judith Maxwell, the former head of the Economic Council of Canada, to
sponsor longer-term, interdisciplinary policy research programs on social and economic policy issues, and to lever research capabilities from
across Canada. In addition to these think tanks, four other institutes
were recently created: the Atlantic Institute for Market Studies (1994),
the Canadian Council for International Peace and Security (1995), which
evolved from the Canadian Centre for Arms Control and Development
and the Canadian Centre for Global Security, the Centre for the Study of
Living Standards (1995), and the Canadian Centre for Foreign Policy
Development (1996), currently housed in the Department of Foreign
Affairs and International Trade (DFAIT).

The emergence of several aforementioned think tanks was influenced
by important and telling developments in public-sector think tanks. As
noted, the federal government, as part of the first wave of serious

budget cutting in 1992, eliminated the Economic Council of Canada, the Science Council of Canada, the Law Reform Commission of Canada, and the Canadian Institute for International Peace and Security – only the tiny National Council of Welfare was left untouched. The creation of the Caledon Institute and the Canadian Policy Research Networks were direct reactions to these developments. The irony was that the government justified its decision not simply in terms of savings, but also because of the great number of nonprofit think tanks that had emerged in Canada since the 1960s. Among other things, Prime Minister Mulroney and his colleagues argued that in the 1990s, there was sufficient policy capacity located outside government to supplement the research needs of federal departments and agencies, a claim widely disputed in the media and in some academic circles (Abelson and Lindquist 1998).

In reviewing these periods of think tank growth, it is important to keep in mind that each new wave of think tanks has not supplanted those institutions that preceded it, but rather added new patches to an already complex and colourful tapestry. At the same time, however, a more crowded marketplace of ideas has increased competition for funding and modified the practices of the older institutions, creating a greater awareness of the need to make findings accessible to and easily digestible by policy makers. In short, the institutes that comprise the think tank community in Canada may have been created at different times and with different goals in mind, but they recognize the importance of adopting the most effective strategies to convey their ideas.

Determining how to properly market ideas is a task normally assigned to think tank directors. Scholars working at think tanks are expected to conduct research on various topics and to make policy recommendations. But in the final analysis, it is the role of senior administrators to determine how best to convert their institute's products into policy influence. Before delving into some of the many strategies that Canadian think tanks employ to promote their ideas, it is important to focus more closely on the type of policy analysis conducted at think tanks and the nature of the publications they produce. This will serve to better illustrate the enormous diversity of Canada's think tank community.

Think Tanks at Work

As mentioned, think tanks in Canada differ enormously in terms of staff size, budget, areas of research, ideological orientation, funding models, and publication programs. While think tanks share a common desire to influence public opinion and public policy, how and to what extent they become involved at different stages of the policy cycle is profoundly influenced by their mandate, resources, and priorities. Although it is generally assumed that research and analysis are their hallmarks, we cannot expect all institutes to assign the highest priority to these functions. This may in part explain why some think tanks in Canada have very few, if any, PhDs among their ranks. While a doctorate is the minimum requirement for admission to America's premier research institutions, including Brookings and Rand, at most Canadian think tanks it is the exception rather than the rule. Several factors, including low salaries and the high demand for freshly minted PhDs at Canadian universities, may account for this, but the final result is the same. The majority of think tanks in Canada do not have policy experts who have been trained to produce rigorous academic research. Moreover, as noted in the introduction to this volume, even if they had a surplus of staff with advanced degrees, we cannot assume that all organizations would be committed to undertaking sophisticated research and analysis. How much emphasis think tanks place on research and analysis may be a reflection of the type of staff they have assembled, but it depends ultimately on how they see their role in the policy-making community. In short, those that are more advocacy oriented have few incentives to engage in rigorous academic research. The same cannot be said for more research-driven think tanks, whose credibility rests on the quality of their studies. Even if we assume that all think tanks assign the highest priority to producing academic research, we cannot take for granted that they all have the resources to mount an extensive research program. Unlike in the United States, where think tanks such as the Brookings Institution, the Hoover Institution, and Rand can draw on multimillion-dollar budgets to sustain multiple research projects, in Canada there are few think tanks that are in a position to support a high-profile research program. Limited resources place enormous constraints on what think tanks in this country can provide.

Documenting the type of research and analysis in which think tanks are involved requires little effort. We need simply to access their websites and compile a list of ongoing projects. For example, the Canadian Council on Social Development has focused recently on the well-being of Canadian children and families. By contrast, the Canadian Institute of International Affairs is concerned about several foreign policy issues, including rebuilding societies in crisis, and the Canadian Tax Foundation is preoccupied with figuring out new finance options for local governments. The considerable range of topics being explored confirms that think tanks are trying to carve out their own niche. It also confirms that there is no identifiable trend in terms of research being conducted. Although the type of funding think tanks receive may influence the direction of their research, in the final analysis, the organizations must set their own research agenda. For some, including the Canada West Foundation and the Atlantic Provinces Economic Council, this has meant concentrating on regional political and economic issues. Yet, for others such as the C.D. Howe, the Fraser Institute, and the IRPP, this has meant trying to identify emerging national issues, including reforming the constitution and the health-care system. Some think tanks list a handful of projects while others indicate that they have over 200 on the go. Moreover, while some of the analysis undertaken at think tanks is highly technical, particularly the long-range economic forecasting models developed at the Conference Board of Canada, much of it is of a more general nature, such as the Canadian Centre for Policy Alternative's work on the environmental and social implications of free trade.

In this volume, several authors have discussed the types of analytical approaches and models that are employed by staff at various federal and provincial government agencies and departments and at a host of nongovernmental organizations. What Vining, Boardman, Stritch, and others discovered is that there is little consistency in how public policy issues are studied and analysed (see chapters 3, 8, 9, and 18 in this volume). The same can be said for how research and analysis is conducted at Canada's think tanks. Some, including the C.D. Howe Institute, rely heavily on quantitative approaches to the study of policy analysis, whereas others, such as the Caledon Institute and the Canadian Institute of Strategic Studies, draw more heavily on qualitative methods. Moreover, unlike some political science departments that have developed a reputation for expertise in critical theory or in game theory, few think tanks in Canada are known for embracing a particular methodological approach to study public policy. Indeed, as noted, the range of research products generated at think tanks is as diverse as the think tank community itself.

Unfortunately, tracking the types of projects being conducted tells us little about how many resources are devoted to each initiative and what form the final product will take. For this information, it is generally helpful to study the annual reports of think tanks to ascertain what percentage of their budget is allocated for research and publications, a clear indication of an institute's priorities. This can also provide some insight into the nature of these organizations. In recent years, the trend has been to move away from book-length studies to shorter analyses, a recognition in part that policy makers, opinion leaders, and journalists much prefer to skim through brief reports than highly technical and lengthy studies on various policy issues (Laskin and Plumptre 2001). In this sense, many Canadian think tanks have followed the lead of their American counterparts by becoming more advocacy oriented. As the Heritage Foundation has demonstrated, providing brief reports to policy makers and journalists can have a much greater impact in shaping public opinion and public policy than producing weighty volumes that gather dust on bookshelves. The obvious advantage for think tanks is that it allows them to comment on important issues in a timely fashion, a quality that makes them attractive to the 24-hour news media. The media, as Catherine Murray points out in chapter 21 above, rely on various external sources of policy expertise to produce their own policy analysis. The downside for think tanks courting the media is that by following the most trendy political issues, they have less time to focus on the long-term interests of the nation. The consequences of making an institutional shift from policy research to political advocacy cannot be ignored.

In theory, policy makers in Canada turn to think tanks for advice and expertise because few bureaucratic departments and agencies have the luxury of engaging in long-term strategic analysis. They certainly do not rely on think tanks because of their financial and staff resources – after all, most have approximately a dozen staff and a budget hovering around $1 million, hardly competition for the well-heeled bureaucracy. What many bureaucratic departments lack, however, is the opportunity to think about how policy issues might play out over several years. In short, what think tanks can offer is the time to reflect and to think critically about important policy matters. Yet, as think tanks have become more concerned about responding to the short-term needs of policy makers and journalists, they have sacrificed their strategic advantage. By focusing on quick-response policy research, think tanks have in effect given up what they could do best – providing an independent and informed perspective on a wide range of issues. The result is that much of the analysis they produce reflects the immediate concerns of policy makers and opinion leaders, not the long-term needs of the country.

Having said this, it is not at all clear that policy makers are overly concerned about the direction think tanks have taken. While elected officials and career civil servants might not be able to draw as much on think tanks for their long-term expertise, they can and do rely on them for other purposes. As Abelson (2000, 144–61) and Lindquist (1989, 227) discovered in their research on the involvement of think tanks in various public policy debates, policy makers can benefit by aligning themselves with think tanks because they are seen as operating at arm's length from government. In doing so, they can serve the needs of government, but not in the way one might imagine. Despite the preoccupation of think tanks in providing timely advice, many continue to produce a variety of publications. Think tanks publish books (usually edited collections), conference papers, opinion magazines, newsletters, occasional papers, and on-line reports. In fact, many think tanks prefer to post their publications on-line rather than incurring the expense of printing hundreds of documents. Allowing readers to download publications also provides think tanks with an indication of which projects are in greatest demand.

The sheer number of publications distributed by think tanks may tell us which organizations are the most productive, but it says little about the quality of their work and the contribution made to important policy debates. Publishing dozens of studies each year might look impressive in an annual report, but if journalists, academics, and policy makers are not reading and commenting on them, think tanks cannot in good conscience claim to have had an impact. That is why scholars must pay close attention to how institutes involved in particular policy debates have sought to convey their ideas and whether their views have indeed found a welcome audience.

As the number of think tanks in Canada has grown since the early 1970s, many journalists and political pundits have assumed that their influence is on the rise. Indeed, given the frequency with which their staff are quoted by the print and broadcast media, we are often left with the impression that these organizations are largely responsible for shaping Canada's political and economic agenda. Although it is difficult to assess how much or little influence think tanks wield in the policy-making process, it is nonetheless possible to make informed judgments about the nature of their influence.

Of all the public uses of think tank influence, none is more visible than the efforts to secure access to the media. As will be discussed in more detail later in this chapter, since directors of think tanks often equate media exposure with policy influence, many devote considerable resources to enhancing their public profile. However, as we will discover below, while it is important for think tanks to communicate their views to the public on television broadcasts or on the op-ed pages of Canadian newspapers, media exposure does not necessarily translate into policy influence. Generating media attention may enable some think tanks to share their research findings with the public and with policy makers, but it does not necessarily guarantee that their views will have a lasting impact on important policy debates.

Competing in the Marketplace of Ideas

Testifying before a high-profile parliamentary committee or publishing a study on a controversial domestic or foreign policy issue may attract attention in some policy-making circles, but it is unlikely to generate the amount of exposure an appearance on the CBC or CTV evening news or an op-ed article (opposite the editorial page) in the *National Post* or the *Globe and Mail* would. This may explain why some Canadian think tanks assign a higher priority to their media profile than to their research output. It might also explain why the competition for media exposure is so intense. As Patricia Linden notes, for think tanks to compete, 'their ideas must be communicated; otherwise the oracles of tankdom wind up talking to themselves. The upshot is an endless forest of communiqués, reports, journals, newsletters, Op-Ed articles, press releases, books, and educational materials. The rivalry for attention is fierce; so much so that the analysts have come out of their think tanks to express opinions on lecture and TV circuits, at seminars and conferences, and press briefings' (1987, 100).

Securing access to the media on a regular basis provides think tanks with a valuable opportunity to help shape public opinion and public policy. At the very least, media exposure allows think tanks to plant seeds in the mind of the electorate that over time may develop into a full-scale public policy debate. For instance, by discussing her institute's study on the problems confronting day care centres in Canada on the CBC and CTV evening news, Judith Maxwell reminded policy makers and the public of the need to provide better funding for and more spaces in day care facilities. Although Maxwell's institute, the CPRN, is not the first organization to raise this issue, its well-publicized study sparked further policy discussions. In doing so, it accomplished some of its goals.

In addition to contributing to the public dialogue, think tanks understand that media exposure helps foster the illusion of policy influence, a currency they have a vested interest in accumulating. The Fraser Institute is just one of many think tanks that equates media exposure with policy influence. Although the institute's former chairman Alan F. Campney acknowledged in the institute's 1976 annual report that it 'is almost as difficult to measure the effects of the Institute's work as it is to ascertain what Canada's economic problems are' (Abelson 2002, 83), the Fraser Institute has consistently relied on media coverage to assess its impact. According to its 25-year retrospective, 'One of the indicators the Institute has used from its inception [to measure performance] is media coverage. How many mentions does an Institute book receive in daily newspapers? How many minutes of airtime do Institute authors and researchers receive during interviews?' (Abelson 2002, 83).

The potential benefits of being a guest commentator on a national newscast or radio program or publishing op-ed articles on a regular basis are vast. Not only does it bode well for think tank scholars looking for a broader audience to convey their ideas, but it can also help promote the goals of the institutions they represent. It is not difficult to understand why think tanks covet media attention.

Thus far, we have provided an overview of the think tank community in Canada and the importance they assign to marketing their ideas. In the final section, we will shift the focus of our discussion to some of the many difficulties scholars experience in assessing their impact. By doing so, we can begin to lay the groundwork for how to better understand what think tanks do and how best to evaluate their performance.

Think Tanks and Policy Influence

Think tanks in Canada may have modest resources, particularly when compared to their American counterparts, but they are rarely bashful when it comes to talking about their influence. On its website, the Institute for Research on Public Policy flashes a June 1992 quote from *Maclean's* claiming that it is 'the country's most influential think tank.' This news must have come as a shock to Michael Walker of the Fraser Institute, who remarked around the same time that 'the Fraser Institute has played a central role in most policy developments during the last decade' (Abelson 2002, 86). And when he was opposition leader, Stephen Harper commented (AIMS 2004) that, 'dollar for dollar, AIMS (The

Atlantic Institute of Market Studies) is the best think tank in Canada.' Interestingly enough, in making these bold claims, no one bothered to explain what criteria they or others used to evaluate the influence of their favourite think tank.

To a large extent, evaluating think tank influence is notoriously difficult because directors of policy institutes, not to mention the scholars and journalists who write about them, have different perceptions of what constitutes influence and how it can best be obtained. As noted, for some directors, the amount of media exposure their institute generates, the number of publications they produce, or the frequency of downloads from their Web site are all indicative of how much influence they wield. Conversely, some think tank administrators rely on other performance indicators, such as the size of their budget, or the number of studies they publish to assess their impact. What makes evaluating think tank influence even more difficult is that the policy makers, academics, and journalists who subscribe to think tank publications or attend the conferences they sponsor invariably have different impressions of the usefulness or relevance of their work. As a result, scholars cannot assume that think tanks measure influence in the same way, nor can they assume that policy makers and other consumers of their products use similar criteria to evaluate their products.

Even if think tanks used the same performance indicators and assigned the same priority to becoming involved at each stage of the policy-making process, scholars would still have to overcome numerous methodological obstacles to accurately measure their influence in public policy. Since dozens of individuals and organizations seek to influence policy debates through various channels, tracing the origin of a policy idea becomes problematic. In an increasingly crowded political arena, it is often difficult to isolate the voice or voices that made a difference. Moreover, it can take months, if not years, before an idea proposed by a think tank, or any other non-governmental organization for that matter, has any discernible impact on policy makers. Indeed, by the time a policy initiative is introduced, it may not even resemble a think tank's initial proposal.

Directors of think tanks can and often do provide anecdotal evidence to flaunt how much influence their institutes wield, but such pronouncements offer little insight into their relevance in the policy-making process. Claiming to have influence is far simpler than documenting how it was achieved. Rather than assuming that in general think tanks have influence or that some think tanks have more influence than others, we should evaluate which think tanks in Canada appear to be involved most actively at key stages of the policy-making process. Before doing this, it is important to keep a few things in mind.

First, as this chapter has demonstrated, no two think tanks in Canada are exactly alike. They have different mandates, resources, and most importantly, different priorities. While helping to frame the parameters of key policy debates is a priority for some, including the Fraser Institute, other think tanks, such as the Caledon Institute and the Canadian Policy Research Networks, may place a higher priority on working with senior officials in the bureaucracy. And still other think tanks, including the C.D. Howe Institute and the Institute for Research on Public Policy, may prefer to work closely with the academic community to help draw attention to a particular issue. If we acknowledge that think tanks do indeed have different priorities and seek to become involved in the policy-making process in different ways, we can then begin to understand how to assess their influence. For example, if some think tanks admit that attracting national media exposure is the most important priority, we can use various databases to determine which organizations generated the lion's share of attention. Alternatively, if those same think tanks acknowledge that publishing their findings is the highest priority, we can use a different set of indicators to evaluate their output. In short, identifying a think tank's priorities allows scholars to employ useful and appropriate methods to evaluate its performance.

Such an approach would be useful in assessing how much visibility think tanks enjoy in the public sphere and in the academic and policy communities. However, to acquire a more thorough understanding of how they interact with policy makers, scholars would have to draw on various conceptual models and frameworks commonly employed in the field of public policy and public administration. A policy community framework, for example, would help scholars to identify the various nongovernmental organizations (including think tanks) and governmental bodies that have coalesced around a particular policy issue. Moreover, Kingdon's work on agenda setting (1984) would go a long way in assisting scholars to isolate where in the policy cycle think tanks have had the greatest impact. These approaches could also be supplemented with interviews and questionnaires distributed to key stakeholders who are in a position to evaluate the contribution of think tanks to different policy issues.

Understanding the nature of think tank influence is not a simple endeavour, but it is one that needs to be undertaken. The alternative – the assumption that think tanks have influence by virtue of their size and/or media profile – does little to advance our knowledge in the field. If we are prepared to acknowledge that the policy-making process is complex, then we must also be prepared to accept that the organizations that seek to shape it must navigate their way through a complicated and crowded environment. It is this ongoing struggle to convey ideas to policy makers and to the public that makes think tanks so interesting to study.

Conclusion

Policy influence, as noted, is not simply about achieving desirable outcomes. It is a process that allows various individuals and organizations to exchange ideas with journalists, academics, members of the attentive public, and policy-makers throughout government. It is important, however, to remember that this process does not occur overnight, but may take months and years to unfold. If seen in this light, it would be difficult to ignore the contribution think tanks in Canada have made to shaping public policy and public opinion. Through their publications, testimony before parliamentary committees, workshops and conferences, and discussions in the media, think tanks have shared their ideas, both good and bad, with different audiences. On the other hand, if scholars continue to adhere to a rigid definition of influence, whereby only those organizations and individuals who can legitimately take credit for altering a policy decision are considered important, then few think tanks would receive a passing grade.

In recent years, think tanks have become more preoccupied with political advocacy. However, they cannot afford to relinquish their commitment to policy analysis. After all, it is their ability to think about policy issues in novel ways that makes them unique. In Canada, as Susan Phillips and Kimberly Speers explore in their respective chapters in this book, there is an abundant supply of interest groups, advocacy coalitions, lobbyists, consultants, and other groups intent on imposing their will on the electorate. Policy makers do not need more organizations that are motivated to advance their own interests. They require organizations, including think tanks, that can better serve the public interest.

REFERENCES

Abelson, Donald E. 1996. *American Think Tanks and their Role in U.S. Foreign Policy*. London and New York: Macmillan and St. Martin's Press.
– 2002. *Do Think Tanks Matter? Assessing the Impact of Public Policy Institutes.* Montreal and Kingston: McGill-Queen's University Press.
– 2006. *A Capital Idea: Think Tanks and US Foreign Policy*. Montreal and Kingston: McGill-Queen's University Press.
Abelson, Donald E., and Christine M. Carberry. 1998. 'Following Suit or Falling Behind? A Comparative Analysis of Think Tanks in Canada and the United States.' *Canadian Journal of Political Science* 31(3), 525–55.
Abelson, Donald E., and Evert A. Lindquist. 1998. 'Who's Thinking About International Affairs? The Evolution and Funding of Canada's Foreign and Defence Policy Think Tanks.' Paper presented at the Annual Meetings of the Canadian Political Science Association, Ottawa, Canada.
– 2000. 'Think Tanks in North America.' In R. Kent Weaver and James G. McGann, eds., *Think Tanks and Civil Societies: Catalyst for Ideas and Action*, 37–66. Piscataway, NJ: Transaction.
Atlantic Institute for Market Studies. 2004. 'AIMS National and International Profile Continues to Build.' AIMS Media Release, 24 February.
Baier, Gerald, and Herman Bakvis. 2001. 'Think Tanks and Political Parties: Competitors or Collaborators?' *ISUMA* 2(1), 107–13.
Battle, Ken. 2004. 'The Role of a Think Tank in Public Policy Development.' *Policy Research Initiative* 6(1), 11–15.
Dobuzinskis, Laurent. 1996. 'Trends and Fashions in the Marketplace of Ideas.' In Laurent Dobuzinskis, Michael Howlett, and David Laycock, eds., *Policy Studies in Canada: The State of the Art*, 91–124. Toronto: University of Toronto Press.
Graves, Frank. 1999. 'Rethinking Government As If People Mattered: From "Reaganomics" to "Humanomics."' In Leslie A. Pal, ed., *How Ottawa Spends 1999–2000*, 37–75. Don Mills, ON: Oxford University Press.
Kingdon, John W. 1984. *Agendas, Alternatives and Public Policies*. New York: Harper Collins.
Laskin, Barbara, and Tim Plumptre. 2001. 'Think Tanks and Policy Institutes: An Overview of Issues, Challenges and Successes in Canada and Other Jurisdictions.' Ottawa: Institute on Governance.
Linden, Patricia. 1987. 'Powerhouses of Policy: A Guide to America's Think Tanks.' *Town and Country*, January.
Lindquist, Evert A. 1989. 'Behind the Myth of Think Tanks: The Organization and Relevance of Canadian Policy Institutes.' PhD dissertation, University of California, Berkeley.

– 1998. 'A Quarter-Century of Think Tanks in Canada.' In Diane Stone et al., eds., *Think Tanks Across Nations: A Comparative Approach*, 127–44. Manchester: Manchester University Press.

McGann, James G. 1992. 'Academics to Ideologues: A Brief History of the Public Policy Research Industry.' *PS: Political Science and Politics*. 24(4), 739–40.

– 1995. *The Competition for Dollars, Scholars and Influence in the Public Policy Research Industry*. Lanham, MD: University Press of America.

McGann, James G., and R. Kent Weaver. 2000. *Think Tanks and Civil Societies: Catalysts for Ideas and Action*. Piscataway, NJ: Transaction.

Pal, Leslie A., and R. Kent Weaver, eds. 2003. *The Government Taketh Away: The Politics of Pain in the United States and Canada*. Washington, DC: Georgetown University Press.

Ricci, David M. 1993. *The Transformation of American Politics: The New Washington and the Rise of Think Tanks*. New Haven, CT: Yale University Press.

Rich, Andrew. 2004. *Think Tanks, Public Policy, and the Politics of Expertise*. Cambridge: Cambridge University Press.

Savoie, Donald J. 2003. *Breaking the Bargain: Public Servants, Ministers, and Parliament*. Toronto: University of Toronto Press.

Smith, James A. 1991. *The Idea Brokers: Think Tanks and the Rise of the New Policy Elite*. New York: The Free Press.

Stone, Diane. 1996. *Capturing the Political Imagination: Think-Tanks and the Policy Process*. London: Frank Cass.

Stone, Diane, Andrew Denham, and Mark Garnett, eds. 1998. *Think Tanks Across Nations: A Comparative Approach*. Manchester: Manchester University Press.

Stone, Diane, and Andrew Denham, eds. 2004. *Think Tank Traditions: Policy Research and the Politics of Ideas*. Manchester: Manchester University Press.

Tuck, Simon. 2004. 'Liberals Unveil New Whistle Blower Legislation.' *Globe and Mail*, 9 October, A1.

Tupper, Allan. 1993. 'Think Tanks, Public Debt, and the Politics of Expertise in Canada.' *Canadian Public Administration* 36(4), 530–46.

Weaver, R. Kent. 1989. 'The Changing World of Think Tanks.' *PS: Political Science and Politics* 22(2), 563–78.

23 Academics and Public Policy: Informing Policy Analysis and Policy Making

DANIEL COHN

Introduction

Academics – those who hold permanent faculty positions at universities and colleges – have a somewhat privileged position when it comes to public policy making and analysis in liberal democracies such as Canada. Unlike bureaucrats, they are not burdened by the responsibility to represent an official position they might not agree with. Unlike politicians and corporate actors, they are free from the need to produce immediate results. These and other freedoms also impose a heavier responsibility on academic experts to advocate for good policy that is the result of careful analysis, that goes beyond simple technical advice and which is developed in the service of norms (Cairns 1995, 288–9; Lasswell 1951, 9–10). It is sometimes suggested that this creates two separate and distinct worlds of policy research (see, for example, Caplan 1979). In one, academics sit comfortably in their ivory towers attempting to generate knowledge aimed at creating a perfect world. In the other, public servants sweat away in the trenches of government searching for information that can be employed to analyse situations and develop workable policies that will meet the needs of less than perfect people and that will, hopefully, make the world a little less imperfect.

In this chapter we will see that there is indeed some truth behind this view. However, it is also substantially false. As has been discussed in the introductory chapter to this volume, the two communities argument is itself problematic, as it ignores the large number of individuals and organizations that constitute a third community interested in policy inquiry, the knowledge brokers. These individuals are neither disinterested academics, nor are they the ultimate public policy decision makers, such as senior public servants and political leaders (Lindquist 1990). As McNutt notes (2005, 35), it is impossible to understand how knowledge is utilized without adequately taking account of this large group of actors. So as to avoid confusion, this chapter will reserve the title of decision makers for senior officials and politicians. Other public servants, those described in the introductory chapter as being 'proximate' to power, but not the final decision makers, such as policy analysts, research staffers, and members of advisory commissions and councils, will be referred to as policy advisers. When reference is made to both decision makers and policy advisers together, the term policy makers will be used.

Knowledge brokers, as the title suggests, have one foot in the academic camp, where science is used in an effort to generate knowledge and information, and one foot in the policy-making camp, where knowledge and information are acted upon. Knowledge brokers are found both in the state and in the myriad of organizations that try to influence the state. There is considerable overlap among the individuals who constitute the three communities and a continuing dialogue between the members of the three communities. As will be seen, many public policy advisers try to stay abreast of the knowledge and information produced by academic researchers and often incorporate the findings of academic research into the work they conduct on behalf of decision makers. Similarly, many academics understand that there is a difference between the ideal world of theoretical studies and the needs of policy advisers and decision makers. They frequently redraft their scholarly works so as to more clearly convey the lessons that they hold for policy makers facing specific situations, and disseminate their research findings in ways that make them more accessible (Landry et al. 2003; Landry et al. 2001). One reason that this dialogue is often overlooked is because those searching for evidence of its existence sometimes fail to discover the places where it can be found (Lavis et al. 2002, 147).

The chapter also looks at the ways in which the hypothesized gap between academic researchers and policy makers can become an issue for concern. This gap can result in meaningful harm if the causes for it are not properly understood by academic experts attempting to create knowledge and information. Academics have to accept that the scientific knowledge that they seek to create is only one of many different types of evidence that policy advisers have to take account of when they conduct policy analyses. Most notably, policy advisers and the decision makers whom they serve must consider the fit between any proposed policy and the context in which it is being proposed. This is sometimes set up as a battle between truth (as revealed by impartial academic research) and ignorance (as revealed by political activity). However, democratic political processes are in fact a mechanism for reconciling, or at least selecting among, multiple truths. The policy recommendations generated by academic researchers are only one of these many competing truths (Albaek 1995).

Knowledge Users, Generators, and Brokers

As stated above, the division between decision makers (the first community) and academics engaged in the creation of knowledge and information (the second community) is not as great as it first appears. This is because the divide is bridged to a considerable degree by a third community, the knowledge brokers. Lindquist argues that the third community is comprised of: 'Individuals and organizations that do not have the power to make policy decisions, but, unlike the academic community, they do possess a clear aspiration of policy relevance in the work they undertake. This work – called policy inquiry ... consists of publication and convocation activities as well as the generation of information' (1990, 31).

In simple terms, these actors use knowledge and information to produce products such as analyses that are useful to decision makers and then disseminate these products so as to influence or advise decision makers. In Lindquist's understanding, members of this third community can be divided into four groups depending on whether they work inside the state or in the private sector (including both market organizations and civil society groups) and by whether or not their work is designed primarily for public consumption or the proprietary use of their organization (1990, 37). Those we are calling policy advisers work inside the state and their work is primarily for the proprietary use of the state.

This third community helps us understand how the gap between academics and decision makers is bridged when it is realized how pervasive this third community is and how much overlap there is between it and academics. The research staffs (both permanent employees and contractors) for government ministries, cabinet committees, central agencies, and taskforces are all part of the third community, as are investigatory commissions, public inquiries, and research councils.

In the private sector there are consultants, research staffers in political parties, interest groups of every sort, and research centres (sometimes called think tanks). Many of the chapters in this book are devoted to organizations and individuals who comprise this third public policy community (see for example the contributions by Abelson, Jackson and Baldwin, Phillips, Speers, and Stritch).

The Canadian federal and provincial states have invested considerable time and effort in facilitating dialogue among third community actors as well as between them and actors from the other two communities in the hope of improving public policy. Examples include the recently created Policy Research Initiative, or PRI, and the more narrowly focused and now defunct Economic Council of Canada (Dobuzinskis 2007; Voyer 2007). Royal commissions also often 'sponsor extensive research programs in the course of their work, which serve a similar purpose of bringing together all three communities in a given field. As Salter notes (2007), even if a given commission's findings are not adopted, its research program can have a substantial long-term impact. However, the Canadian federal state's investments in policy research and analysis have been somewhat erratic. Many of the major institutions that once provided the Canadian federal state with internal policy analysis and policy-making capacity, and which were built up over the years, such as the above-mentioned Economic Council of Canada, were swept away in the cost-cutting of the 1980s and 1990s. The government found itself increasingly deficient in analytical and policy-making capacity in the late 1990s. Initiatives such as the PRI were intended to create an inter-departmental cohort of policy analysts to address medium to long-term research questions. Importantly, the PRI also aims to build bridges to external members of the third community in academia and the private sector (Voyer 2007).

Academics who have become active in shaping policy play important roles in most forms of third community organizations. It should be acknowledged that the involvement of English-Canadian academics in private-sector third community organizations has historically been regarded as low when measured by the standards of Quebec or the behaviour of academics in other countries. It has been argued that English-Canadian academics are instead more likely to participate in third community activities by serving as short-term (or contract) policy-advisors to the state or by assuming more permanent roles either as policy advisors or decision makers (Brooks and Gagnon 1988). How-

ever, this view might be outdated (Bradford 1998, 108), especially with
the widespread growth of what Lindquist (1993, 576) calls 'policy club'-
style research centres in Canada. Abelson (2002, 20–1) specifically describes these organizations as seeking to bring together academic
researchers and policy makers with similar interests. In fact, most of the
contributors to this volume, including the author of this chapter, have
one foot in the academic community and one foot (or at least a couple of
toes) in the third community; some have also had careers in the decision-making community.[1]

With this in mind, it should not be surprising that when Landry et al.
surveyed Canadian social scientists, nearly 50 per cent reported that
they always or usually make an effort to transmit the results of their
research to those with the ability to shape public policy. On the other
hand, only 12 per cent felt that their research findings led to applications, and only 3 per cent were willing to say that their research always
led to policy applications (2001, 339–40). On the surface, this result
would seem quite depressing. However, these descriptive statistics are
only part of the story. As I will show, academic researchers are often more
influential than they may appear. Furthermore, I also argue that whether
or not academic researchers engage in third community activities is an
important predictor of how much of an impact their research will have.

Academic Research and Public Policy: Decisions and Analysis

Before dealing with the literature on how academic research is used in
policy analysis and policy making, we must first pause and consider
how policy advisors make decisions as to how to go about their jobs. Do
they carefully analyse situations to the smallest detail, weigh up the
costs and benefits associated with each and every potential option, and
then recommend the best solution? Or, do they seek to take some short
cuts? This is essentially the debate between those who see public policy
analysis and policy making as rational processes and those who see
them as more sufficing activities. Those who describe policy analysis
and policy making as sufficing activities, argue that policy advisers and
the decision makers whom they serve are not so much looking for an
ideal solution as one that works reasonably well. Authors have proposed different theories that seek to explain how policy advisers and
decision makers take short cuts, limiting the range of potential solutions that they consider when making decisions. One of the most promi-

nent and earliest of these was Charles E. Lindblom (1959), who suggested that those engaged in policy making in democratic states act 'incrementally.' In other words, in most cases policy advisers start their search for solutions with the status quo. Those solutions closest to the status quo are canvassed first, those furthest away last. When choosing between alternatives, decision makers will prefer solutions found in a range bounded by the minimum change that is necessary to more or less accomplish the new goals of public policy and the maximum change that is possible without incurring undue political resistance. Sometimes policy advisers cannot find recommendations that fall into that ideal space, and the decision makers whom they serve have to settle for either a policy that even more imperfectly meets their goals but can be more easily adopted or a policy that meets their goals but is likely to create substantial political resistance.

Others since Lindblom have created models that seek to detail when decision makers can be expected to act incrementally and when they might feel free to accept advice to act more radically. These opportunities are described as policy windows and are said to come about when society deems the current state of affairs in some area of policy as a problem, potential solutions become known, and the political will to act also simultaneously materializes (Kingdon 1984). Some windows are narrower and only provide the opportunity for incremental policy changes, while others are larger and allow for more radical changes in public policy. Other authors have developed more sophisticated models that describe forms of decision making other than rationality and incrementalism. Howlett and Ramesh (2003, 162–84) provide a summary of these more advanced attempts to model public policy making. Perhaps the simplest way to think about these various styles of policy making is as a continuum. At one pole are rationalist approaches, where it is predicted that decision makers and the policy advisers that assist them are searching for the best solution to a problem, regardless of the difficulties or complications that this ideal solution might present, and the time it takes to find the best solution. At the other pole are the sufficing styles epitomized by the incrementalist approach, where it is predicted that decision makers and the policy advisers are searching for the solution that is quickest to find and which presents the least difficulties and complications, even if this is not perfect for the policy problem under consideration. It is equally important to remember, as the concept of policy windows suggests, that under different circumstances the same actors might be more rational or sufficing. Therefore, one must also take account of context.

As Howlett and Lindquist argue (2007), different decision-making strategies and contexts ought to be reflected to some degree in the decisions made by policy advisers to use different policy analysis techniques. Vining and Boardman (2007) group these techniques into four large families depending on whether or not the impacts to be considered are restricted to those that can be fully monetized (in other words, whether or not all the costs and benefits can be expressed in dollar terms) and whether or not efficiency is the sole goal that is to be maximized, or whether one must also consider other goals, such as equity, the impact of the policy on governmental revenue, ethics, and political feasibility. If one were engaged in a more sufficing style of decision making, it might be conceived as leading to an analytic process that reduces consideration of such impacts and goals that confound ease of analysis or political feasibility.

With this in mind, it is easy to see why academic researchers and policy makers can sometimes be uneasy partners. While academic researchers are trained to rationally search for *the* right answer, this answer might not fit the context within which public policy advisers feel compelled to operate on a given issue at a given time, due to the concerns that decision makers are known to have. It also might take so long to find the right answer that its proponents miss the proverbial boat, with the policy window narrowing appreciably during the time that a highly rational search takes. In this sense, there is sometimes too much expected of academic research (Albaek 1995, 79–80). The idea that any one article or book is going to produce a specific, relatively immediate, and predictable change in the course of public policy, regardless of the context within which policy makers are acting, is somewhat unrealistic and likely to lead to disappointment (Landry et al. 2003, 193). However, on occasion, such 'instrumental' utilizations of knowledge do happen (Gerson 1996, 5–6; Borins 2003, 248–50).

The impact of academic research on public policy is perhaps more realistically captured by envisioning the research as 'informing' policy making and analysis, rather than searching for concrete examples showing that a specific piece of research caused a specific policy decision (Lavis et al. 2002, 140). This approach to knowledge utilization sees the impact of academic research on public policy as occurring when policy makers become aware of a school of thought regarding an issue that has come to prominence within some academic field. They will adopt the general findings of this approach into their work if and when they encounter a problem for which it proves useful. In this sense, it is not possible to understand the impact of academic research outside of the context within which it is used. Second, it is not so much the individual works of academics that are influencing policy makers but the schools of thought towards given issues, sometimes called policy paradigms, that these specific works represent and collectively compose (Landry et al. 2003, 193). Hall describes a policy paradigm as defining 'the broad goals behind policy, the related problems or puzzles that policy-makers have to solve to get there, and, in large measure the kind of instruments that can be used to attain these goals' (1990, 59). In other words, policy paradigms, when adopted from academic work into policy making and accepted by decision makers, can help policy advisers take shortcuts in their analyses. More will be said about policy paradigms below. Before proceeding, however, it is important to note that this approach to understanding how academic work influences policy does not see knowledge utilization as a single act, but rather a multiple stage process by which ideas are converted into actions.

When Landry et al. (2003) investigated the utilization of university research in Canadian public policy, they employed a modified version of the Knott and Wildavsky multi-stage model of knowledge utilization (1980), which breaks down utilization into the following categories:

1 Reception: policy makers receive academic research relevant to their work.
2 Cognition: policy makers read and understand the academic work they have received.
3 Discussion: policy makers engage in meetings, conferences or workshops to discuss the findings of the academic work.
4 Reference: policy makers cite the work and its findings in their own reports or documents.
5 Adoption: policy makers encourage the adoption of the results reported in the work as official policy.
6 Influence: the findings of the work in question influence decisions in the policy makers' administrative unit.

Landry et al. (2003) surveyed 833 policy makers and found that when expectations for individual academic works are reduced to a more realistic level, and instead, an assessment is made of the impact of academic research as a whole, rather than the impact of any one researcher on a specific policy outcome, the output of academia appears influential in most public policy fields. However, there is no denying that the stages of knowledge utilization laid out above form something of an inverted pyramid or a funnel, with fewer and fewer ideas being utilized by policy makers at latter stages of the process.

One limit to using the evidence from Landry et al.'s study in this chapter is that they do not differentiate between those public or official policy advisors we have described here as third community actors (knowledge brokers engaged in policy inquiry), and first community actors (those engaged in decision making). Based on Landry et al.'s discussion of how they went about collecting their sample (2003, 196–7), it is likely that many of those they surveyed are indeed third community actors rather than those that have been described here as public policy decision makers. On the other hand, their adaptation of Knott and Wildavsky's multi-stage approach to decision making is instructive to think about in three community terms. It could be argued that as one progresses from the earlier to the later stages of the process, interaction shifts from that between the second (or academic) community and the third community (of knowledge brokers and policy inquiry) to that between the third community and the first (public policy decision-makers). It is in the third community that knowledge and information generated by academic research is put to use in policy analysis and the development of potential policy solutions for the phenomena defined as problems. Therefore, the work of such actors is as important to the development of policy paradigms as are the academics of the second community.

Landry et al. (2001 and 2003) also explored what makes some academic research findings more influential than others. What they found is that the adoption of research findings into the policy-making process is primarily an interactive affair. One of the most important predictors of the influence of academic research proved to be 'user context.' This means tailoring academic work to the expected needs of policy makers would be next to impossible outside of the very immediate short term, because such tailoring would require academics to predict the future. Not just future developments in their own fields of research, but the entire context in which decision makers and policy practitioners will need knowledge and information from their fields. What is possible is to establish academics as a reliable source of usable knowledge and information. Therefore, it is not enough for academic researchers simply to produce publications, they must also advocate for their work.

They must make an effort to put their work in front of policy makers in a format that highlights the policy implications, so that when a relevant policy window opens, the information is there. This is best done through forging linkages between academia and public policy makers at a more general level; by organizing events and forums that bring academics and policy makers together, such as the events and collaborative research sponsored by programs such as the PRI (Voyer 2007) and by opening up avenues for academics to spend time within the public sector, and for policy makers to spend time within academia (Borins 2003, 250). 'Knowledge utilization depends on disorderly interactions between researchers and users, rather than on linear sequences beginning with the needs of researchers or the needs of users ... The more sustained and intense the interaction between researchers and users, the more likely utilization will occur' (Landry et al. 2003, 195).

In other words, academics must engage in the activities of the third community in order to improve the likelihood that their work will have an impact on public policy. This finding has been generally confirmed in other research, for example, Lavis et al.'s (2002) exploratory study of the utilization of health services research in Canadian provinces. Lavis et al. drive the point home in their recommendation that researchers and those who fund research should consider activities of the sort noted above to be part of the '"real" work of research, not a superfluous add-on' (2002, 146).

Activated Academics in Action: Economic Reform

One of the best examples of a group of academic researchers successfully following the approach described above are the economists and others who advocated for a change in Canada's macroeconomic policies away from state intervention during the late 1970s. Working in conjunction with business spokespeople and interest groups, they developed a coherent argument that Canada's overall economic policies, developed since the end of the Second World War, had reached a dead end. According to this position, the economic crises of the 1970s were as much the result of public policy miscues brought on by the Keynesian economic policy paradigm as economic conditions.

Keynesianism takes its name from the British economist John Maynard Keynes, who was a critic of the economic orthodoxy prevailing during the economic depression of the 1930s.[2] The basic problem identified by Keynesianism was the propensity of capitalist economies to fall into situations of either extreme unemployment or extreme price inflation that could become persistent enough to disrupt the viability of democratic societies and which cannot be corrected by market forces alone. The paradigm holds that it is a key responsibility of the state to intervene in the economy by acting 'counter-cyclically' to manage demand (the ability of people to purchase things) so as to moderate these extreme variations in the business cycle. Keynesians argued that the best way to do this was through policies that supplement the incomes of ordinary families in times of low economic demand so as to boost economic activity, and that withdraw such state aid or even tax it back in times of high demand so as to slow the economy. Income support programs (such as social assistance, unemployment insurance, pension plans, and price supports for farmers), and 'make-work schemes' that provide jobs in poor economic times were all supported by Keynesians as mechanisms for stabilizing the economy. Therefore, this policy paradigm is also associated with the development of modern welfare states. In Keynesian terms, debt and deficit levels as well as tax rates are not seen as goals a government ought to meet but as tools for managing the economy. Gradually, Keynesian economists came to believe that they could not only use these techniques to stave off major catastrophes but also to fine-tune the economy so as to produce ever more consistent economic performance. The aim of Keynesian economists shifted from preventing the sort of mass unemployment seen in the Depression to ensuring full employment (Leeson 1999 and 1997).

It should be noted that for many years there was a strong public consensus in favour of the Keynesian policy paradigm. Moderating the swings of the business cycle benefited not only workers but corporations as well. In fact, in both the United States and Canada, prominent business leaders were at the forefront of coalitions that pressured the governments to adopt the Keynesian policy paradigm (Ferguson 1995, 79–98; Finkle 1977, 356–7). However, in the 1970s something unexpected occurred. Canada and the other Western industrialized democracies entered a period of severe economic crisis as technological developments, changing trade patterns, and rising oil prices hit the global economy almost simultaneously (Cox 1987, 273–84). As the decade progressed, things got worse as so-called 'stagflation' set in, characterized by persistent and simultaneously high unemployment and inflation (Tobin 1982, 518). For policy advisers trained in Keynesian analysis, this posed a dilemma, forcing them to choose between stimulating employment but risking more inflation, or fighting inflation but risking more unemployment (Boothe and Purvis 1997, 210). In the meantime, academic economists and a small but growing body of analysts in both the public and private third community began to ask decision makers to consider two interesting questions: Why was it that countries such as Canada had such difficulty in adjusting to changing circumstances? Was it possible that attempts to stabilize the economy, maintain employment in spite of crises, and generally protect Canadians from risks and change were in fact compounding the problems faced by the country (see for example Walker 1977; Courchene 1980 and 1984; Grubel 1984; Lipsey 1984)?

Two ideas emerging from academic economics were of particular concern in Canada and other industrialized democracies: the natural rate of unemployment and the rational expectation theories. The natural rate of unemployment theory holds that in every country there is a rate of unemployment which is inevitable due to the structure of the economy and the public policies that govern it. According to this theory, efforts to force unemployment lower than this structural level tend to create inflation in the short term (Friedman 1968). Therefore, longer-term measures (such as policies to improve educational levels and promote new investments) that change the structure of the economy are seen as more desirable than the short-term measures favoured by Keynesians, which fight unemployment by encouraging demand.

Meanwhile, the rational expectations theory argued that Keynesianism might actually raise this natural rate of unemployment in the long term. Based on the work of Robert E. Lucas and Thomas J. Sargent (see for example 1976), rational expectations theory argues that investors are forward looking and base a substantial part of their predictions about the economy on what government does and says today. If investors expect government to allow the inflation rate to increase in the future by stimulating employment today, they will demand a higher interest rate. This will make it more expensive to borrow, dampen demand, and cancel out the unemployment-fighting impact of the stimulus, unless the government surprises lenders and stimulates the economy to a greater amount than anticipated. Recognizing their mistake, investors will build a greater inflation risk premium into future transactions. This will tend to raise the natural rate of unemployment. As a result, each time the government tries to stimulate the economy it must spend more money to get the same boost in employment while risking greater debts and inflation. Consequently, rational expectations economists argued that governments could not fight unemployment in the long term because ordinary investors, in pursuing their own self-interests, would behave in ways that subvert this policy or any other that distorts economic equilibrium (Thurow 1983, 143–4 and 155–9).

In other words, proponents of the natural rate of unemployment and the rational expectations theories claimed that they could settle the debate puzzling policy advisors as to whether it was better to fight unemployment or inflation in the late 1970s and early 1980s. They believed that they could demonstrate that there was nothing that could be done about unemployment in the short term (or provide any other short-term economic security against changing circumstances) and if governments would only stop trying to fight unemployment, inflation would take care of itself. Furthermore, doing this would solve the flexibility problem, as without government protection, both investors and workers would have to adapt more quickly to changing circumstances. While little could be done in the short term, they argued that in the long term this would lower the natural rate of unemployment. The identification of this problem of flexibility and the argument that Canada's lack of flexibility was a product of its previous economic policies formed the central core of a new post-Keynesian economic paradigm sometimes called neoclassicalism or neoliberalism.

Brooks (1990, 89–0) observes that while it is common to argue that neoliberalism is a pro-business economic policy paradigm, business was in fact the late-comer to the party. The ideas that form the core of neoliberalism were in development among academics and the third community organizations they created to promote them long before mainstream business leaders began to seriously advocate for them in the late 1970s and early 1980s (Kelley 1997; Harris 2005). This is because, as noted above, business did well for many years under the previous paradigm. Government efforts to mitigate swings in the business cycle had obvious value. However, the events of the 1970s showed business leaders that these efforts could fail spectacularly. An alternative avenue for ensuring profitability was to be as flexible as possible, adapting rapidly to the market rather than expecting government action to adapt the market to the dictates of mass production (Piore and Sabel 1984, 205–20). It was with this in mind that Canada's business leaders formed the Business Council on National Issues (now renamed the Canadian Council of Chief Executives) to lobby for an economic policy paradigm that emphasized the need for flexibility and a reduced role for state intervention (Bradford 1998, 106).

Neoliberals urged governments to encourage both as much economic competition as possible and policies that promote flexibility in adjusting to these forces among Canadian families and businesses. A key ingredient in doing this would be to negotiate trade and investment liberalization agreements with the United States and if possible other countries as well. In the words of Grinspun and Kreklewich (1994), who are critics of this coalition, such agreements act as a 'conditioning framework' that rewards societies promoting flexibility and competition, and punish those that seek to protect citizens from economic forces.

This coalition of academic researchers and business advocates developed a network of third community institutions and venues through which they could interact with public-sector policy advisers. As well, they also used the network to educate and lobby both public decision makers and those who help to shape public opinion. In sum, it served to coordinate their actions, to expand the circle of people concerned about public policy who understood their ideas, and as a means to develop their arguments into a properly articulated policy paradigm (Ernst 1992; Langille 1987; Carroll and Murray 2001). The policy window that they needed came in 1982 when the Liberal government of Pierre Trudeau appointed a royal commission to study the Canadian economy. The appointment of the Macdonald Commission was a tacit acknowledgment that the status quo in terms of economic policy was failing. The commission broadly endorsed the line of thought advanced by the neoliberals (Bradford 1998, 115) and, as is well-known, the Mulroney government followed up on the Macdonald Commission's recommendations by signing first the Canada-U.S. Free Trade Agreement and the subsequent North American Free Trade Agreement (Doern and Tomlin 1991; Cameron and Tomlin 2000).

Sabatier (1987) uses the term advocacy coalition to describe partnerships such as the one that emerged between neoliberal academic economists, business, policy advisers, and the decision makers who eventually implemented the Macdonald Commission's recommendations. This is a collection of individuals who share normative and empirical beliefs and seek to work in concert with one another. He also argues that to be a genuine advocacy coalition, the partnership must be relatively stable and last for a considerable amount of time, a decade or two rather than months. The forming of an advocacy coalition represents a substantial realignment of political forces and in the case described here, this realignment eventually produced a change in the policy paradigm within which economic policy is made in Canada.

Thomas J. Courchene, professor of economics and public policy at Queen's University, was a central actor in this coalition. Addressing those who might be interested in promoting further economic liberalization, he had the following advice: 'It is instructive to recall the free trade issue. Here, we economists had done our homework well, so that when the window of opportunity arose, we were well prepared' (1999, 313–14). As we have seen, context is an important variable. It determines the scope that policy advisors have to search for solutions to the problems that they are dealing with and the range of goals and impacts that they can include in their analyses, as well as the sorts of answers sought by the decision makers whom they advise.

Academics and Policy Making: Taking Account of Context

To summarize the argument made so far, it can be noted that academics generally do not influence policy directly. They can have a greater impact by engaging in third community activities and by building alliances with other third community actors (both in the public and private sector), and ideally also with public decision makers. These alliances sometimes coalesce into advocacy coalitions. Second, the glue which often unites an advocacy coalition is a policy paradigm. These are comprised of definitions of problems, understandings of the processes that create these problems and views as to which policies are best suited for dealing with them. Over the long term, these policy paradigms steer analysis by indicating which goals ought to be prioritized and which impacts should be evaluated or ignored. Third, context is crucial for understanding how and when these coalitions can succeed and also for understanding the degree to which such success is likely to occur. Figure 23.1 depicts the relationship between these ideas as they impact on policy making.

This figure represents the likely range of movement in four major areas of welfare state policy. Following Kingdon (1984), we can call these policy windows. These windows are produced by a hypothetical context as seen from the perspective of those academic researchers who are members of an advocacy coalition promoting policies based in an equally hypothetical policy paradigm. Note that policies have a current position on a continuum ranging from poor to good. This is based on the opinions of the advocacy coalition members, whose work is informed by this particular policy paradigm. Also note that the range of movement that is likely, whether positively, or negatively, in each of the

Figure 23.1 Policy Paradigms and Policy Windows

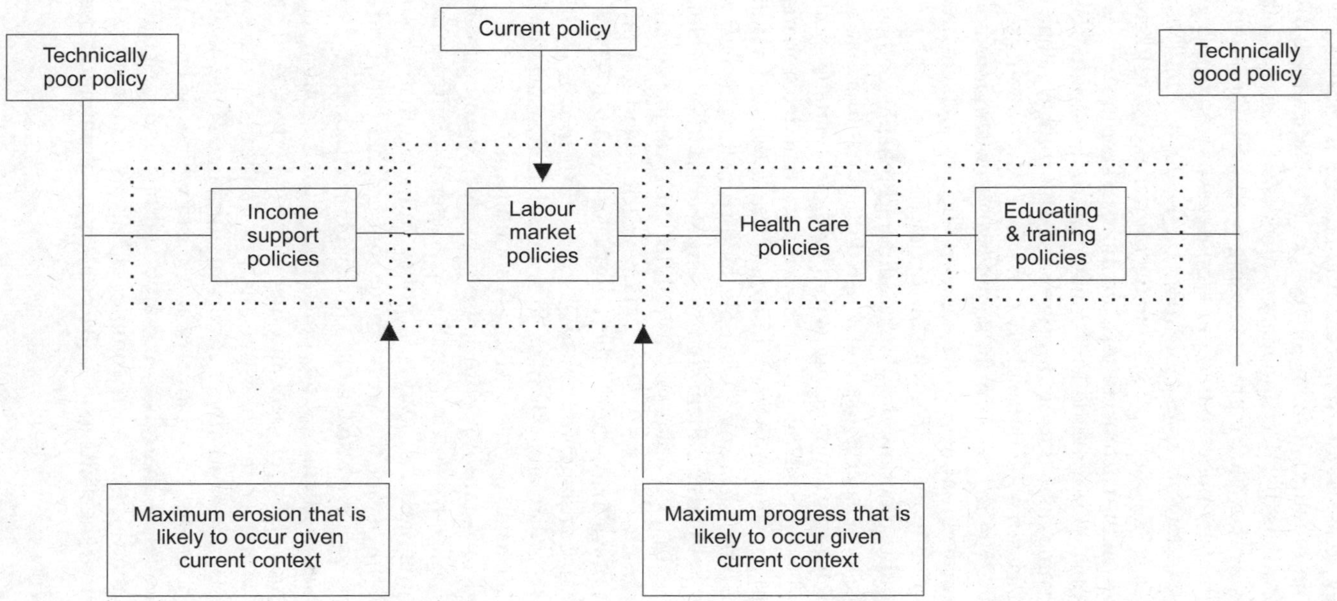

four policy areas, is not evenly distributed. In some cases the window provides more room on the positive side. This indicates that the range of policy options that decision makers are likely to see as feasible, given the current context, are more in keeping with what those who support this hypothetical policy paradigm would see as good policy. In other cases the window provides more room on the downside. This indicates that the range of policy options that decision makers are likely to see as feasible, given the current context, are more in keeping with what those who support this hypothetical policy paradigm would see as poor policy. In some cases the window is wider. This indicates that, given the context, decision makers are likely to have more autonomy to deal with the policy issue in question. In some cases this window is narrower, which indicates that, given the context, decision makers are likely to have less autonomy to deal with the policy issue.

If we could somehow develop a valid and reliable methodology for measuring these spaces, we could use these ideas to assist academics, private-sector third community actors, and most notably policy advisers, to predict both the range of policy options that decision makers will feel free to consider in terms of distance from the status quo and the direction of change at any given time. Unfortunately, the best we can do at present is to advise them that certain events, when combined with other contextual variables such as political institutions, social, political, and economic forces, as well as policy legacies, tend to lead to bigger policy windows than would otherwise occur (Keeler 1993; Pierson and Smith 1993). Consequently, those seeking to incorporate political feasibility into a policy analysis have to accept that measures of feasibility will have a certain degree of softness about them.

These ideas regarding context also provide a warning for those who produce knowledge and information in academia. Failure to take proper account of context can lead to a policy initiative that goes nowhere. However, this is not the worst thing that can happen. Under certain circumstances it can also lead to a policy intervention that, while begun with the best of intentions, has potentially harmful consequences. Academics thinking about ideal and theoretically perfect solutions have a tendency to engage in exhaustive analysis that leads to complex policy recommendations and advice involving numerous inter-related policy recommendations, the removal of any one of which can erase the anticipated benefits of the other recommendations and potentially cause harm. In many cases, such complex advice is tantamount to recommending that the state change the policy paradigm that it uses to deal with a given policy area. As was also noted, at some point information derived from sources other than academic research will also have to be considered. As a result, it can be assumed that the ideas and concerns of others will be raised and have to be given consideration by policy advisors when they analyse the problem and by the decision makers whom they advise (Gagnon 1989, 564).

Without a very strong advocacy coalition comprising partners from all three communities (academics, knowledge brokers, and decision makers), as well as a coherent argument as to why the previous policy paradigm is flawed (rather than just a consensus that current policy is flawed), it is unlikely that a policy paradigm shift will occur along the lines favoured by academic researchers or even that a complex policy will be adopted in anything close to its entirety. Such an outcome should not be seen as surprising, or as necessarily bad. Rather, it should be understood as the result of the compromise and bartering that are the daily chores of politicians and their advisers who seek to steer policy through democratic institutions. Cohn (2004) documents two cases where academics failed to take proper account of context when advising the state to undertake complex policy reform (Canadian Medical Human Resources Policy and American Social Assistance Reform). In both cases the recommendations formulated by the academics were only adopted to the extent that they fit the needs of advocacy coalitions and policy paradigms that the academics did not subscribe to. The resulting policies were seen as potentially harmful for society by the academics involved (Ellwood 1996a and 1996b; Barer and Stoddart 1999, 40; Stoddart and Barer 1999).

Academic experts who wish to participate in third community activities would be well advised to think carefully about the task they are about to embark on. What is the relationship between what they wish to propose and the paradigm presently shaping public policy? Who will support their views, and who will oppose them? Is there a coherent policy paradigm that unites them or are they partners of convenience? In other words, is there an advocacy coalition that they can participate in and rely on for support?

Is there anything that can be done to either reduce the chances of ending up with a poor policy or to improve the chances of ending up with a good one? Three strategies seem to stand out. The first is to accept the limits imposed by the context and not make proposals that go outside of its anticipated limits. Following Lindblom (1959), this can be described as adopting an incremental approach. The second strategy that academic policy experts can employ is to provide a set of recommendations that will each have a positive impact but do not have to be adopted in total to produce some benefit. The final option is much tougher, and time consuming. Rather than immediately engaging in trying to shape policy, the experts can undertake political activity to shift the context within which policy is made by working with other like-minded individuals in both the third and first community to create an effective advocacy coalition and a coherent policy paradigm to rival the one presently guiding state decisions. As Landry et al. (2003; 2001) note, those who choose this path must develop mechanisms for engaging decision makers, venues where they can discuss their ideas with them and publications geared to their needs. It is only with such support that a complex policy is likely to move through the political process as a whole piece.

Here, the example of Canada's neoliberal academics and the business advocacy coalition is instructive. One of the reasons given by the Mulroney government for discontinuing the Economic Council of Canada was that it represented an increasingly unnecessary expense, given the reliance policy makers were placing on advice from external third community sources such as academics and private-sector research centres (Dobuzinskis 2007). In other words, the neoliberal academics had moved from their self-perceived status as outsiders to that of insiders, capable of trumping and even displacing major bureaucratic institutions. In the shape of Canadian business, they had won over a powerful interest to their viewpoint and, within the state, a cadre of policy advisers and decision makers as well. This advocacy coalition succeeded not only in shifting policy, but the whole policy paradigm within which economic issues are analysed and policy is made. As a result, they also improved the chances that their views would dominate public policy making over the long term. Few academic researchers and social groups have goals that lofty; however, the general approach is still sound, even for those with more modest ambitions.

NOTES

The author's interest and concern with the issues covered in this chapter grew from his reading of Alain C. Cairns's 'Citizens, Scholars and the Constitution' (1995). It further develops ideas first presented in a paper written for a conference honouring the career of Professor Cairns, which was titled 'Rethinking Citizenship in the Canadian Federation.'

1 Alongside of his purely academic work, the author is (or has been) a member of the Executive Board of the Institute of Public Administration of Canada's Vancouver Regional Chapter, an associate member of two university-based public policy research centres, as well as a research associate with a private-sector research centre. On occasion, he has also served as a contract researcher to government agencies, appeared as a witness before legislative committees, and been a participant in 'stake-holder consultations' convened by governmental agencies.

2 Keynes, in his book *The General Theory of Employment, Interest and Money* (1936) is credited with theoretically demonstrating why labour markets do not necessarily reach a balance of supply and demand no matter how far wages fall. In doing this, Keynes himself was giving voice to a growing school of thought within economics that the interventionist policies already adopted by several governments throughout the Western world to combat the Depression of the 1930s, were not simply expedient measures, but theoretically sound policies that ought to be continued after the crisis had abated.

REFERENCES

Abelson, Donald E. 2002. *Do Think Tanks Matter? Assessing the Impact of Public Policy Institutions.* Kingston and Montreal: McGill-Queen's University Press.
– 2007. 'Any Ideas? Think Tanks and Policy Analysis in Canada.' This volume.
Albaek, Erik. 1995. 'Between Knowledge and Power: Utilization of Social Science in Public Policy-making.' *Policy Sciences* 28(1), 79–100.
Barer, Morris L., and Greg L. Stoddart. 1999. *Improving Access to Needed Medical Services in Rural and Remote Canadian Communities: Recruitment and Retention Revisited.* Ottawa: Federal-Provincial-Territorial Advisory Committee on Health Human Resources.
Boothe, Paul, and Douglas Purvis. 1997. 'Macroeconomic Policy in Canada and the United States: Independence, Transmission, and Effectiveness.' In Keith Banting, George Hoberg, and Richard Simeon, eds., *Degrees of Freedom: Canada and the United States in a Changing World,* 189–230. Kingston and Montreal: McGill-Queen's University Press.
Borins, Sandford. 2003. 'From Research to Practice: A Survey of Public Administration Scholars in Canada. *Canadian Public Administration* 46(2), 243–56.
Bradford, Neil. 1998. *Commissioning Ideas: Canadian National Policy Innovation*

in Comparative Perspective. Toronto: Oxford University Press.

Brooks, Stephen. 1990. 'The Market for Social Scientific Knowledge: The Case of Free Trade in Canada.' In Stephen Brooks and Alain-G. Gagnon, eds., *Social Scientists, Policy and the State,* 79–94. New York: Praeger.

Brooks, Stephen, and Alain-G. Gagnon. 1998. *Social Scientists and Politics in Canada: Between Clerisy and Vanguard.* Kingston and Montreal: McGill-Queen's University Press.

Cairns, Alan C. 1995. 'Citizens, Scholars and the Canadian Constitution.' *International Journal of Canadian Studies* 12, 285–9.

Cameron, Maxwell A., and Brian W. Tomlin. 2000. *The Making of NAFTA: How the Deal was Done.* Ithaca, NY: Cornell University Press.

Caplan, Nathan. 1979. 'The Two Communities Theory and Knowledge Utilization.' *American Behavioral Scientist* 22(3), 459–70.

Carroll, William K., and Shawn Murray. 2001. 'Consolidating a Neoliberal Policy Block in Canada 1976–1996.' *Canadian Public Policy* 27(2), 195–217.

Cohn, Daniel. 2004. 'The Best of Intentions, Potentially Harmful Policies: A Comparative Study of Scholarly Complexity and Failure.' *Journal of Comparative Policy Analysis. Research and Practice* 6(1), 39–56.

Courchene, Thomas J. 1980. 'Towards a Protected Society: The Politicization of Economic Life.' *Canadian Journal of Economics* 13(4), 556–77.

– 1984. 'The Citizen and the State: A Market Perspective.' In George Lermer, ed., *Probing Leviathan: An Investigation of Government in the Economy,* 39–56. Vancouver: Fraser Institute.

– 1999. 'Alternative North American Currency Arrangements: A Research Agenda.' *Canadian Public Policy* 25(3), 308–14.

Cox, Robert W. 1987. *Production, Power and World Order: Social Forces in the Making of History.* New York: Columbia University Press.

Dobuzinskis, Laurent. 2007. 'Back to the Future? Is There a Case for Re-establishing the Economic Council and/or the Science Souncil?' This volume.

Doern, G. Bruce, and Brian W. Tomlin. 1991. *Faith and Fear: The Free Trade Story.* Toronto: Stoddart.

Ellwood, David T. 1996a. 'Welfare Reform as I Knew It: When Bad Things Happen to Good Policies.' *American Prospect* (May), 22–9.

– 1996b. 'Welfare Reform in Name Only.' *New York Times,* 22 July, A19.

Ernst, Alan. 1992. 'From Liberal Continentalism to Neoconservatism: North American Free Trade and the Politics of the C.D. Howe Institute.' *Studies in Political Economy* 39, 109–40.

Ferguson, Thomas. 1995. *Golden Rule: The Investment Theory of Party Competition and the Logic of Money Driven Political Systems.* Chicago: Chicago University Press.

Finkle, Alvin. 1977. 'Origins of the Welfare State in Canada.' In Leo Panitch,
   ed., *The Canadian State: Political Economy and Political Power*, 344–72. Toronto:
   University of Toronto Press.
Friedman, Milton. 1968. 'The Role of Monetary Policy.' *American Economic
   Review* 58(1), 1–17.
Gagnon, Alain-G. 1989. 'Social Science and Public Policies.' *International Social
   Science Journal* 41(4), 555–66.
Gerson, Mark. 1996. *The Neoconservative Vision: From Cold War to Culture Wars.*
   Lanham, MD: Madison Books.
Grinspun, Ricardo, and Robert Krelowich. 1994. 'Consolidating Neoliberal
   Reforms: Free Trade as a Conditioning Framework.' *Studies in Political
   Economy* 43, 33–61.
Grubel, Herbert. 1984. 'The Costs of Canada's Social Insurance Programs.' In
   George Lermer, ed., *Probing Leviathan: An Investigation of Government in the
   Economy*, 59–86. Vancouver: Fraser Institute.
Hall, Peter A. 1990. 'Policy Paradigms, Experts, and the State: The Case of
   Macroeconomic Policy-Making in Britain.' In Stephen Brooks and Alain-G.
   Gagnon, eds., *Social Scientists, Policy and the State*, 53–78. New York: Praeger.
Harris, Ralph. 2005. 'Behind Enemy Lines.' In Philip Booth, ed., *Towards a
   Liberal Utopia?*, 281–93. London: Institute of Economic Affairs/Hobart
   Paperback.
Howlett, Michael, and Evert Lindquist. 2007. 'Beyond Formal Policy Analysis:
   Governance Context, Analytic Styles, and the Policy Analysis Movement in
   Canada.' This volume.
Howlett, Michael, and M. Ramesh. 2003. *Studying Public Policy: Policy Cycles
   and Policy Subsystems*. 2nd ed. Toronto: Oxford University Press.
Jackson, Andrew, and Bob Baldwin. 2007. 'Policy Analysis by the Labour
   Movement in a Hostile Environment.' This volume.
Keeler, John T.S. 1993. 'Opening the Window for Reform.' *Comparative Political
   Studies* 25(4), 433–86.
Kelley, John L. 1997. *Bringing the Market Back In: The Political Revitalization of
   Market Liberalism*. New York: New York University Press.
Keynes, John Maynard. 1936. *The General Theory of Employment, Interest and
   Money*. London: Macmillan.
Kingdon, John W. 1984. *Agendas, Alternatives and Public Policies*. Boston: Little,
   Brown.
Landry, Réjean, Nabil Amara, and Moktar Lamari. 2001. 'Utilization of Social
   Science Research Knowledge in Canada.' *Research Policy* 30(2), 333–49.
Landry, Réjean, Moktar Lamari, and Nabil Amara. 2003. 'The Extent and
   Determinants of Utilization of University Research in Government Agen-

cies.' *Public Administration Review* 63(2), 192–205.

Langille, David. 1987. 'The BCNI and the Canadian State.' *Studies in Political Economy* 24, 41–85.

Lasswell, Harold D. 1951. 'The Policy Orientation.' In Daniel Lerner and Harold D. Lasswell, eds., *The Policy Sciences*. Stanford, CA: Stanford University Press.

Lavis, John N., Suzanne E. Ross, Jeremiah E. Hurley, Joanne M. Hohenadel, Gregory L. Stoddard, Christel A. Woodward, and Julia Abelson. 2002. 'Examining the Role of Health Services Research in Public Policymaking.' *Milbank Quarterly* 80(1), 125–54.

Leeson, Robert. 1997. 'The Political Economy of the Inflation-Unemployment Trade Off.' *History of Political Economy* 29(1), 117–56.

– 1999. 'Keynes and the "Keynesian" Phillips Curve.' *History of Political Economy* 31(3), 493–509.

Lindblom, Charles, E. 1959. 'The Science of Muddling Through.' *Public Administration Review* 19(2), 79–88.

Lindquist, Evert. A. 1990. 'The Third Community, Policy Inquiry, and Social Scientists.' In Stephen Brooks and Alain-G. Gagnon, eds., *Social Scientists, Policy and the State*, 21–51. New York: Praeger.

– 1993. 'Think Tanks or Clubs? Assessing the Influence and Roles of Canadian Policy Institutes.' *Canadian Public Administration* 36(4), 547–79.

Lipsey, Richard G. 1984. 'Can the Market Economy Survive?' In George Lermer, ed., *Probing Leviathan: An Investigation of Government in the Economy*, 33–8. Vancouver: Fraser Institute.

Lucas, Robert E. Jr., and Thomas J. Sargent. 1979. 'After Keynesian Macroeconometrics.' *Federal Reserve Bank of Minneapolis Quarterly Review* 3(2), 1–6. Reprinted in Robert E. Lucas Jr. and Thomas J. Sargent, eds. 1981. *Rational Expectations and Econometric Practice*, 295–319. Minneapolis: University of Minnesota Press.

McNutt, Kathleen. 2005. *Navigating Small Worlds: A Research Proposal.* Burnaby, BC: Simon Fraser University Department of Political Science (unpublished).

Phillips, Susan D. 2007. 'Policy Analysis and the Voluntary Sector: Evolving Policy Styles.' This volume.

Pierson, Paul, and Miriam Smith. 1993. 'Bourgeois Revolutions? The Policy Consequences of Resurgent Conservatism.' *Comparative Political Studies* 25(4), 487–520.

Piore, M.J., and C.F. Sabel. 1984. *The Second Industrial Divide: Possibilities for Prosperity.* New York: Basic Books.

Sabatier, Paul A. 1987. 'Knowledge, Policy-Oriented Learning, and Policy Change: An Advocacy Coalition Framework.' *Knowledge: Creation, Diffusion,*

Utilization 8(4), 649–92.

Salter, Liora. 2007. 'The Public of Public Inquiries.' This volume.

Speers, Kimberley. 2007. 'The Invisible Private Service: Consultants and Public Policy in Canada.' This volume.

Stoddart, Greg L., and Morris L. Barer. 1999. 'Will Increasing Medical School Enrolment Solve Canada's Physician Supply Problems?' *Canadian Medical Association Journal* 161 (19 October), 983–4.

Stritch, Andrew. 2007. 'Business Associations and Policy Analysis in Canada.' This volume.

Thurow, Lester C. 1983. *Dangerous Currents: The State of Economics.* New York: Random House.

Tobin, James. 1982. 'Inflation.' In Douglas Greenwald, ed., *Encyclopedia of Economics*, 510–23. New York: McGraw-Hill.

Vining, Aidan R. and Anthony E. Boardman. 2007. 'The Choice of Formal Policy Analysis Methods in Canada.' This volume.

Voyer, Jean-Pierre. 2007. 'Policy Analysis in the Federal Government: Building the Forward Looking Policy Research Capacity.' This volume.

Walker, Michael, ed. 1977. *Which Way Ahead? Canada after Wage and Price Control.* Vancouver: Fraser Institute.

Contributors

Donald E. Abelson is the leading scholar of Canadian public policy think tanks and has published extensively on the subject. He is author of *Do Think Tanks Matter? Assessing the Impact of Public Policy Institutes* and of other publications on policy institutes. He is the co-director of the Centre for American Studies and the chair of the Department of Political Science at the University of Western Ontario.

Bob Baldwin is an Ottawa based consultant who specializes in pensions, aging society, and labour market issues. He is a senior associate with Informetrica Ltd and an adjunct research professor in the School of Public Policy and Administration at Carleton University. Mr Baldwin was director of social and economic policy at the Canadian Labour Congress from 1995 to 2005 and was the CLC's pension specialist from 1977 to 2005.

Stephen Brooks is the author of *Canadian Democracy: An Introduction* and *Public Policy in Canada: An Introduction*, and has written extensively on policy research and the development of the policy analysis profession in Canada. He teaches political science at the University of Windsor.

Anthony E. Boardman is the Van Dusen Professor of Business Administration in the Strategy and Business Economics Division at the University of British Columbia. He has published articles on policy analysis in many journals, including texts on analytical techniques such as cost-benefit analysis.

Daniel Cohn has taught political science at Simon Fraser University and now teaches public policy at York University. His research interests include health policy and Canadian federalism. He has published several works on the role academics play in the policy process in Canada.

William Cross is a leading student of Canadian political party behaviour. He is the author of *Political Parties* and several other publications on Canadian politics. He teaches political science at Carleton University.

James Desveaux is Director of the UCLA Washington Center, Washington, DC. He has wriiten several books on policy-making, including studies of the energy sector in Canada. He is the author of *Designing Bureaucracies: Institutional Capacity and Large-Scale Problem Solving*.

Laurent Dobuzinskis is co-editor of *Turbulence and New Directions in Global Political Economy*, *Global Instability*, and *Policy Studies in Canada: The State of the Art* and has written on policy-making, political theory, and political economy. He teaches political science at Simon Fraser University.

Jonathan Fershau is a committee research analyst with the Legislative Assembly of British Columbia in Victoria BC. He served as a legislative intern in Victoria before accepting his present position. He is a graduate in political science from SFU and holds an MA degree in that subject. He has published on committee issues in *Canadian Parliamentary Review* and elsewhere.

Iris Geva-May teaches in the Faculty of Education at Simon Fraser University. She holds a number of awards, has written extensively on comparative public policy, and is the founder and editor-in-chief of the international *Journal of Comparative Policy Analysis: Research and Practice*.

Michael Howlett is co-author of *Studying Public Policy*, *In Search of Sustainability*, *The Political Economy of Canada*, and *Canadian Natural Resource and Environmental Policy*. He edited *Canadian Forest Policy* and co-edited *Executive Styles in Canada*, *Designing Government*, *The Real Worlds of Canadian Politics*, *The Provincial State in Canada*, *Innovation Systems in a Global Context*, *Policy Studies in Canada*, and *The Puzzles of Power*. His articles have been published in numerous professional journals. He is the Burnaby Mountain Professor in the Department of Political Science, Simon Fraser University.

Andrew Jackson has been senior economist with the Canadian Labour Congress since 1989. He is also a research professor in the Institute of Political Economy at Carleton University, and a research associate with the Canadian Centre for Policy Alternatives. During a leave of absence from the CLC in 2000-02, he was director of research with the Canadian Council on Social Development. Mr Jackson studied at the London School of Economics and Political Science and at the University of British Columbia. At the CLC, he was responsible for research on issues of employment, fiscal and monetary policies, taxation and international economics. He is the co-author of several books, including *Falling Behind: The State of Working Canada 2000*, has also published numerous papers in academic journals and books, and has been a frequent speaker at policy conferences and before Parliamentary Committees.

Evert Lindquist is director of the School of Public Administration at the University of Victoria, and is a member of the Academic Advisory Panel of the Secretary to the Treasury Board of Canada and the External Advisory Panel for the Treasury Board of Canada's annual report on Canada's Performance. He has published on governance and public policy in several journals.

Allan M. Maslove is dean of the Faculty of Public Affairs and Management and professor in the School of Public Policy and Administration at Carleton University. His research interests include public policy and finance, federal-provincial relations, taxation, aboriginal financial policy and health policy, and health care finance.

Doug McArthur teaches in the Master of Public Policy program at Simon Fraser University, Harbour Centre. At various times he was deputy minister to the Premier and cabinet secretary and deputy minister of Aboriginal Affairs in British Columbia, chief land claims negotiator in the Yukon, and deputy minister of Agriculture and deputy minister of Northern Saskatchewan in Saskatchewan. He was minister of Education in Saskatchewan from 1978 to 1982 and is currently an advisor to the federal government on the HRDC social policy review and on fiscal federalism. He also advises the Tsawwassen First Nation on treaty negotiations and on development issues.

Michael Mintrom is the author of many works on policy analysis including *Policy Entrepreneurs and School Choice* and *People Skills for*

Policy Analysts, and has served as the president of the organized section on public policy of the American Political Science Association. He teaches in the Department of Political Studies at the University of Auckland, New Zealand.

Catherine Murray teaches in the School of Communication at Simon Fraser University where she specializes in media studies. She is co-author of *Researching Communication* and several other publications on this subject and has served on national-level inquiries into broadcasting policy in Canada.

François Pétry teaches political science at Université Laval where he is a long-time member of the Group for Public Policy Research. He has written extensively on public opinion and elections, provincial politics, and many other subjects.

Susan D. Phillips is the director of the School of Public Policy and Administration at Carleton University. She is one of Canada's leading experts on 'third' and 'fourth' sector organizations and has published extensively on these subjects. She is co-author of *Urban Governance in Canada* and co-editor of *Urban Affairs Back on the Policy Agenda*.

Michael Prince is the Lansdowne Professor of Social Policy in the Faculty of Human and Social Development at the University of Victoria. He is author of many articles and books on policy analysis in Canada, as well as co-author of *Changing Politics of Canadian Social Policy*.

Liora Salter teaches at Osgoode Hall Law School and in the Faculty of Environmental Studies, York University. She has written extensively on communication and science policy and is Canada's leading expert on royal commissions, task forces, and other forms of public inquiries.

Josie Schofield is research analyst, Office of the Clerk of Committees, Legislative Assembly of British Columbia. She holds a PhD from the University of British Columbia and taught for many years in the Department of Political Science at the University of Victoria before moving to the provincial legislature.

Patrick J. Smith teaches political science at Simon Fraser University and is a member of that institution's Urban Studies Program. He has authored books and articles on Canadian political parties, elections, local/urban/regional and metropolitan governance, provincial-municipal relations, aboriginal issues, affirmative action, labour market policy, democratic socialism, public sector ethics, international cities, planning, and community economic development.

Kimberly Speers teaches in the Department of Political Science at the University of Manitoba. She is a PhD candidate in political science at the University of Alberta with extensive experience working as a consultant for the Government of Alberta and major multinational public affairs corporations.

Kennedy Stewart teaches in the Master of Public Policy program, Simon Fraser University, Harbour Centre. His research interests include democratic theory, electoral and non-electoral public participation, electoral systems, urban governance, and world cities.

Andrew Stritch teaches political science at Bishop's University and is a leading student of business-government relations in Canada, having written several well-known texts in these areas. His research interests revolve around American and Canadian public policy, workers' compensation policy, and business-government relations. He has written several books and articles in these areas.

Aidan R. Vining is the CNABS Professor of Business and Government Relations in the Business Executive MBA Program at Simon Fraser University. He is co-author with David Weimer of the multi-edition *Policy Analysis: Concepts and Practice* and many other publications on policy analysis in Canada and the United States.

Jean-Pierre Voyer, an economist by training, was head of the Policy Research Initiative of the Government of Canada at the time his chapter was written; he is currently the executive director of the Social Research and Demonstration Corporation.

The Institute of Public Administration of Canada Series in
Public Management and Governance